CROSSWORD PUZZLE DICTIONARY

TABLE OF CONTENTS

a *(SYN.)* any, one.

abandon *(SYN.)* relinquish, resign, surrender, leave, give up, cease, forsake, waive, evacuate, withdraw.
(ANT.) support, keep, fulfill, engage, unite, retain.

abandoned *(SYN.)* depraved, deserted, desolate, forsaken, rejected, cast off.
(ANT.) befriended, cherished, chaste, moral, respectable.

abase *(SYN.)* make humble, reduce, despise, humiliate.
(ANT.) exalt, cherish, elevate, uplift, respect, dignify.

abash *(SYN.)* disconcert, bewilder, confuse, put off, discompose, nonplus.
(ANT.) comfort, relax, hearten, nerve.

abashed *(SYN.)* confused, ashamed, embarrassed.

abate *(SYN.)* lessen, curtail, reduce, decrease, restrain.
(ANT.) grow, prolong, increase, extend, intensify, enhance, accelerate.

abbey *(SYN.)* nunnery, convent, cloisters, monastery.

abbot *(SYN.)* friar, monk.

abbreviate *(SYN.)* shorten, lessen, abridge, condense, curtail, reduce, cut.
(ANT.) lengthen, increase, expand, extend, prolong.

abbreviation *(SYN.)* abridgment, reduction, shortening, condensation.
(ANT.) expansion, extension, amplification, lengthening.

abdicate *(SYN.)* relinquish, renounce, vacate, waive.
(ANT.) maintain, defend, stay, retain, uphold.

abdomen *(SYN.)* paunch, belly, stomach.

aberrant *(SYN.)* capricious, devious, irregular, unnatural, abnormal, unusual.
(ANT.) methodical, regular, usual, fixed, ordinary.

aberration *(SYN.)* oddity, abnormality, irregularity, deviation, monster, abortion.
(ANT.) norm, conformity, standard, normality.

abet *(SYN.)* support, connive, encourage, conspire, help.
(ANT.) deter, check, hinder, frustrate, oppose, discourage.

abettor *SYN.)* accomplice, ally, confederate, accessory.
(ANT.) opponent, rival, enemy.

abeyance *(SYN.)* inaction, cessation, inactivity, rest.
(ANT.) ceaselessness, continuation, continuity.

abhor *(SYN.)* dislike, hate, loathe, execrate, avoid, scorn, detest, despise.

abhorrent *(SYN.)* loathsome, horrible, detestable, nauseating, terrible, revolting.

abide *(SYN.)* obey, accept, tolerate, endure, dwell, reside.

ability *(SYN.)* aptness, capability, skill, dexterity, faculty, power, talent, aptitude, efficiency, capacity.
(ANT.) incapacity, incompetency, weakness, ineptitude, inability, disability.

abject *(SYN.)* sordid, infamous, mean, miserable.

abjure *(SYN.)* relinquish, renounce, vacate, waive, desert, quit, leave, forsake, abdicate, resign, surrender.
(ANT.) cling to, maintain, uphold, stay.

able *(SYN.)* qualified, competent, fit, capable, skilled, efficient, clever, talented.
(ANT.) inadequate, trained, efficient, incapable, weak.

abnegation *(SYN.)* rejection, renunciation, self-denial, refusal, relinquishment.

abnormal *(SYN.)* unnatural, odd, irregular, monstrous, eccentric, weird, strange.
(ANT.) standard, natural, usual, normal, average.

abode *(SYN.)* dwelling, habitat, residence, quarters, lodging.

abolish *(SYN.)* end, eradicate, annul, cancel, revoke, invalidate, overthrow, obliterate, abrogate, erase.
(ANT.) promote, restore, continue, establish, sustain.

abominable *(SYN.)* foul, dreadful, hateful, revolting, vile, odious, loathsome, detestable, bad, horrible.
(ANT.) delightful, pleasant, agreeable, commendable, admirable, noble, fine.

abominate *(SYN.)* despise, detest, hate, dislike, abhor.
(ANT.) love, like, cherish, approve, ad-

mire.

abomination *(SYN.)* detestation, hatred, disgust, loathing, revulsion, antipathy.

abort *(SYN.)* flop, fizzle, miscarry, abandon, cancel.

abortion *(SYN.)* fiasco, disaster, failure, defeat.

abortive *(SYN.)* unproductive, vain, unsuccessful, useless, failed, futile.
(ANT.) rewarding, effective, profitable, successful.

abound *(SYN.)* swarm, plentiful, filled, overflow, teem.
(ANT.) scarce, lack.

about *(SYN.)* relating to, involving, concerning, near, around, upon, almost.

about-face *(SYN.)* reversal, backing out, shift, switch.

above *(SYN.)* higher than, overhead, on, upon,'over, superior to.
(ANT.) under, beneath, below.

aboveboard *(SYN.)* forthright, open, frank, honest, overt, straightforward, guileless.
(ANT.) underhand, ambiguous, sneaky, wily.

abracadabra *(SYN.)* voodoo, magic, charm, spell.

abrasion *(SYN.)* rubbing, roughness, chafe, scratching, scraping, friction, chap.

abrasive *(SYN.)* hurtful, sharp, galling, annoying, grating, irritating, caustic.
(ANT.) pleasant, soothing, comforting, agreeable.

abreast *(SYN.)* beside, side by side, alongside.

abridge *(SYN.)* condense, cut, abbreviate, shorten, reduce, summarize, curtail.
(ANT.) increase, lengthen, expand, extend.

abridgment *(SYN.)* digest, condensation, summary.
(ANT.) lengthening, expansion, enlargement.

abroad *(SYN.)* away, overseas, broadly, widely.
(ANT.) at home, privately, secretly.

abrogate *(SYN.)* rescind, with-draw, revoke, annul, cancel, abolish, repeal.

abrupt *(SYN.)* sudden, unexpected, blunt, curt, craggy, precipitous, sharp, hasty.

(ANT.) foreseen, smooth, courteous, gradual, smooth.

abscess *(SYN.)* pustule, sore, wound, inflammation.

absence *(SYN.)* nonexistence, deficiency, lack.
(ANT.) attendance, completeness, existence, presence.

absent *(SYN.)* away, truant, departed, inattentive, lacking, not present, out, off.
(ANT.) attending, attentive watchful, present.

absent-minded *(SYN.)* inattentive, daydreaming, preoccupied, absorbed, distrait.
(ANT.) observant, attentive.

absolute *(SYN.)* unconditional, entire, actual, complete, thorough, total, perfect.
(ANT.) partial, conditional, dependent accountable.

absolutely *(SYN.)* positively, really, doubtlessly.
(ANT.) doubtfully, uncertainly.

absolution *(SYN.)* pardon, forgiveness, acquittal, mercy.

absolutism *(SYN.)* autarchy, dictatorship.

absolve *(SYN.)* exonerate, discharge, acquit, pardon, forgive, clear, excuse.
(ANT.) blame, convict, charge, accuse.

absorb *(SYN.)* consume, swallow up, engulf, assimilate, imbibe, engage, engross.
(ANT.) discharge, dispense, emit, exude, leak, eliminate, bore, tire, weary, drain.

absorbent *(SYN.)* permeable, spongy, pervious, porous.
(ANT.) moisture-proof, water-proof, impervious.

absorbing *(SYN.)* engaging, exciting, engaging, engrossing, entertaining, thrilling.
(ANT.) dull, boring, tedious, tiresome.

abstain *(SYN.)* forbear, forego, decline, resist.
(ANT.) pursue.

abstemious *(SYN.)* abstinent, sparing, cautious, temperate, ascetic, self-disciplined.
(ANT.) uncontrolled, indulgent, abandoned, excessive.

abstinence *(SYN.)* fasting, self-denial, continence, sobriety, refrain, abstention.

(ANT.) gluttony, greed, excess, self-indulgence, pursue.

abstract *(SYN.)* part, appropriate, steal, remove, draw from, separate, purloin.

(ANT.) return, concrete, unite, add, replace, specific, clear.

abstruse *(SYN.)* arcane, obscure, complicated, abstract, refined, mandarin.

(ANT.) uncomplicated, direct, obvious, simple.

absurd *(SYN.)* ridiculous, silly, unreasonable, foolish, irrational, nonsensical.

(ANT.) rational, sensible, sound, meaningful.

absurdity *(SYN.)* foolishness, nonsense, farce, drivel, joke, paradox, babble.

abundance *(SYN.)* ampleness, profusion, large amount, copiousness, plenty.

(ANT.) insufficiency, want, absence, dearth, scarcity.

abundant *(SYN.)* ample, overflowing, plentiful, teeming, profuse, abounding.

(ANT.) insufficient, scant, not enough, scarce, deficient, rare, uncommon, absent.

abuse *(SYN.)* maltreatment, misuse, reproach, defamation, mistreat, damage, ill-use, reviling, aspersion.

(ANT.) plaudit, respect, appreciate, commendation.

abusive *(SYN.)* harmful, insulting, libelous, hurtful, slanderous, defamatory.

(ANT.) supportive, helpful, laudatory, complimentary.

abut *(SYN.)* touch, border, meet, join, connect with.

academic *(SYN.)* learned, scholarly, theoretical, erudite, formal, pedantic.

(ANT.) ignorant, practical, simple, uneducated.

accede *(SYN.)* grant, agree, comply, consent, yield, endorse, accept, admit.

(ANT.) dissent, disagree, differ, oppose.

accelerate *(SYN.)* quicken, dispatch, facilitate, hurry, rush, forward, hasten, expedite.

(ANT.) hinder, retard, slow, delay, quicken.

accent *(SYN.)* tone, emphasis, inflection,

stress, consent.

accept *(SYN.)* take, approve, receive, allow, consent to, believe, adopt, admit.

(ANT.) ignore, reject, refuse.

access *(SYN.)* entrance, approach, gateway, door.

accessory *(SYN.)* extra, addition, assistant, supplement, contributory, accomplice.

accident *(SYN.)* casualty, disaster, misfortune, mishap.

(ANT.) purpose, intention, calculation.

accidental *(SYN.)* unintended, fortuitous, unplanned, unexpected, unforeseen.

(ANT.) calculated, planned, willed, intended, intentional, on purpose, deliberate.

acclaim *(SYN.)* eminence, fame, glory, honor, reputation, credit, applaud.

(ANT.) infamy, obscurity, disapprove, reject, disrepute.

acclimated *(SYN.)* adapted, habituated, acclimatized, accommodated, reconciled.

accommodate *(SYN.)* help, assist, aid, provide for, serve, oblige, hold, house.

(ANT.) inconvenience.

accommodation *(SYN.)* alteration change, adaptation, acclimatization, aid, help, kindness, service, courtesy.

(ANT.) inflexibility, rigidity, disservice, stubbornness.

accompany *(SYN.)* chaperon, consort with, escort, go with, associate with, attend.

(ANT.) abandon, quit, leave, desert, avoid, forsake.

accomplice *(SYN.* accessory, ally, associate, assistant, sidekick, confederate.

(ANT.) opponent, rival, enemy, adversary.

accomplish *(SYN.)* attain, consummate, achieve, do, execute, fulfill, complete.

(ANT.) fail, frustrate, spoil, neglect, defeat.

accomplished *(SYN.)* proficient, skilled, finished, well-trained, gifted, masterly.

(ANT.) unskilled, amateurish, crude.

accomplishment *(SYN.)* deed, feat, statute, operation, performance, action.

(ANT.) cessation, inhibition, intention, deliberation.

accord *(SYN.)* concur, agree, award, harmony, conformity, agreement, give, tale. *(ANT.)* difference, quarrel, disagreement.

accordingly *(SYN.)* consequently, therefore.

accost *(SYN.)* approach, greet, speak to, address. *(ANT.)* avoid, shun.

account *(SYN.)* description, chronicle, history, narration, reckoning, rate, computation, detail, narrative. *(ANT.)* confusion, misrepresentation, distortion.

accredited *(SYN.)* qualified, licensed, certified, commissioned, empowered. *(ANT.)* illicit, unofficial, unauthorized.

accrue *(SYN.)* amass, collect, heap, increase, accumulate. *(ANT.)* disperse, dissipate, waste, diminish.

accrued *(SYN.)* accumulated, totaled, increased, added, amassed, expanded.

accumulate *(SYN.)* gather, collect, increase, accrue. *(ANT.)* spend, give away, diminish, dissipate.

accurate *(SYN.)* perfect, just, truthful, unerring, meticulous, correct, all right. *(ANT.)* incorrect, mistaken, false, wrong.

accursed *(SYN.)* ill-fated, cursed, doomed, condemned, bedeviled, ruined. *(ANT.)* fortunate, hopeful.

accusation *(SYN.)* charge, incrimination, indictment. *(ANT.)* pardon, exoneration, absolve.

accuse *(SYN.)* incriminate, indict, censure, denounce, charge, arraign, blame. *(ANT.)* release, vindicate, exonerate, acquit, absolve.

accustom *(SYN.)* addict, familiarize, condition.

accustomed *(SYN.)* familiar with, comfortable with. *(ANT.)* strange, unusual, rare, unfamiliar.

ace *(SYN.)* champion, star, king, queen, winner, head.

acerbity *(SYN.)* bitterness, harshness, acidity unkindness, sourness. *(ANT.)* sweetness, gentleness, kindness, tenderness.

ache *(SYN.)* hurt, pain, throb.

achieve *(SYN.)* do, execute, gain, obtain, acquire, accomplish, perform. *(ANT.)* fail, lose, fall short.

achievement *(SYN.)* feat, accomplishment, attainment, exploit, realization. *(ANT.)* botch, dud, mess, omission, defeat, failure.

acid *(SYN.)* tart, sour, bitter, mordant, biting, biting. *(ANT.)* pleasant, friendly, bland, mild, sweet.

acknowledge *(SYN.)* allow, admit, concede, recognize, answer, accept, receive. *(ANT.)* reject, refuse, disavow, refute, deny.

acme *(SYN.)* summit, top, zenith, peak, crown. *(ANT.)* bottom.

acquaint *(SYN.)* inform, teach, enlighten, notify, tell.

acquiesce *(SYN.)* submit, comply, consent, succomb. *(ANT.)* refuse, disagree, rebel, argue.

acquire *(SYN.)* attain, earn, get, procure, assimilate, obtain, secure, gain. *(ANT.)* miss, surrender, lose, forego, forfeit.

aquirement *(SYN.)* training, skill, learning, achievement, attainment, education.

aquisition *(SYN.)* procurement, gain, gift, purchase, proceeds, possession, grant.

aquisitive *(SYN.)* greedy, avid, hoarding, covetous.

acquit *(SYN.)* forgive, exonerate, absolve, cleanse, pardon, found not guilty. *(ANT.)* doom, saddle, sentence, condemn.

acrid *(SYN.)* bitter, sharp, nasty, stinging, harsh. *(ANT.)* pleasant, sweet.

acrimonious *(SYN.)* sharp, sarcastic, acerb, waspish, cutting, stinging, testy. *(ANT.)* soft, kind, sweet, pleasant, soothing.

act *(SYN.)* deed, doing, feat, execution, accomplishment, performance, action, operation, transaction, decree, exploit, pretense. *(ANT.)* inactivity, deliberation, intention, cessation.

action *(SYN.)* deed, achievement, feat, activity, exploit, behavior, battle, performance, exercise.

(ANT.) idleness, inertia, repose, inactivity, rest.

activate *(SYN.)* mobilize, energize, start, propel.

(ANT.) paralyze, immobilize, stop, deaden.

active *(SYN.)* working, operative, alert, agile, nimble, sprightly, busy, brisk, lively

(ANT.) passive, inactive, idle, dormant, lazy, lethargic.

activist *(SYN.)* militant, doer, enthusiast.

activity *(SYN.)* action, liveliness, motion, vigor, agility, movement, briskness.

(ANT.) idleness, inactivity, dullness, sloth.

actor *(SYN.)* performer, trouper, entertainer.

actual *(SYN.)* true, genuine, certain, factual, authentic, concrete, real.

(ANT.) unreal, fake, bogus, nonexistent, false.

actuality *(SYN.)* reality, truth, occurrence, fact, certainty.

(ANT.) theory, fiction, falsehood, supposition.

acute *(SYN.)* piercing, severe, sudden, keen,sharp, perceptive, discerning, shrewd, astute, smart, intelligent.

(ANT.) bland, mild, dull, obtuse, insensitive.

adamant *(SYN.)* unyielding, firm, obstinate.

(ANT.) yielding.

adapt *(SYN.)* adjust, conform, accommodate, change, fit, alter, vary, modify.

(ANT.) misapply, disturb.

add *(SYN.)* attach, increase, total, append, sum, affix, unite, supplement.

(ANT.) remove, reduce, deduct, subtract, detach.

address *(SYN.)* greet, hail, accost, speak to, location, oration, presentation.

(ANT.) avoid, pass by.

adept *(SYN.)* expert, skillful, proficient.

(ANT.) unskillful.

adequate *(SYN.)* capable, commensurate, fitting, satisfactory, sufficient, enough, ample, suitable, plenty, fit.

(ANT.) lacking, scant, insufficient, inadequate.

adhere *(SYN.)* stick fast, grasp, hold,

keep, retain, cling, stick to, keep, cleave.

(ANT.) surrender, abandon, release, separate, loosen.

adjacent *(SYN.)* next to, near, bordering, touching adjoining, neighboring.

(ANT.) separate, distant, apart.

adjoin *(SYN.)* connect, be close to, affix, attach.

(ANT.) detach, remove,

adjourn *(SYN.)* postpone, defer, delay, suspend, discontinue, put off.

(ANT.) begin, convene, assemble.

adjust *(SYN.)* repair, fix, change, set, regulate, settle, arrange, adapt, suit, accommodate, modify, alter.

administration *(SYN.)* conduct, direction, management, supervision.

admirable *(SYN.)* worthy, fine, praise, deserving, commendable, excellent.

admire *(SYN.)* approve, venerate, appreciate, respect, revere. esteem, like.

(ANT.) abhor, dislike, despise, loathe, detest, hate.

admissible *(SYN.)* fair, justifiable, tolerable, allowable.

(ANT.) unsuitable, unfair, inadmissible.

admission *(SYN.)* access, entrance, pass, ticket.

admit *(SYN.)* allow, assent, permit, acknowledge, welcome, concede, agree.

(ANT.) deny, reject, dismiss, shun, obstruct.

admittance *(SYN.)* access, entry, entrance.

admonish *(SYN.)* caution, advise against, warn, rebuke, reprove, censure.

(ANT.) glorify, praise.

admonition *(SYN.)* advice, warning, caution, reminder.

ado *(SYN.)* trouble, other, fuss, bustle, activity, excitement, commotion, hubbub.

(ANT.) tranquillity, quietude.

adolescent *(SYN.)* young, immature, teenage.

(ANT.) grown, mature, adult.

adoration *(SYN.)* veneration, reverence, glorification.

adore *(SYN.)* revere, venerate, idolize, respect, love, cherish, esteem, honor.

(ANT.) loathe, hate, despise.

adorn *(SYN.)* trim, bedeck, decorate, ornament, beautify, embellish, glamorize. *(ANT.) mar, spoil, deform, deface, strip, bare.*

adrift *(SYN.)* floating, afloat, drifting, aimless, purposeless, unsettled. *(ANT.) purposeful, stable, secure, well organized.*

adroit *(SYN.)* adept, apt, dexterous, skillful, clever, ingenious, expert. *(ANT.) awkward, clumsy, graceless, unskillful, oafish.*

advance *(SYN.)* further, promote, bring forward, adduce, progress, advancement, allege, improvement, promotion, upgrade. *(ANT.) retard, retreat, oppose, hinder, revert, withdraw, flee.*

advantage *(SYN.)* edge, profit, superiority, benefit, mastery, leverage, favor. *(ANT.) handicap, impediment, obstruction, disadvantage, detriment, hindrance.*

adventure *(SYN.)* undertaking, occurrence, enterprise, happening, event, project.

adventurous *(SYN.)* daring, enterprising, rash, bold. *(ANT.) cautious, timid, hesitating.*

adversary *(SYN.)* foe, enemy, contestant, opponent. . *(ANT.) ally, friend.*

adverse *(SYN.)* hostile, counteractive, unfavorable, opposed, disastrous, contrary. *(ANT.) favorable, propitious, fortunate, friendly, beneficial.*

adversity *(SYN.)* misfortune, trouble, calamity, distress, hardship, disaster. *(ANT.) benefit, happiness.*

advertise *(SYN.)* promote, publicize, make known, announce, promulgate.

advertisement *(SYN.)* commercial, billboard, want ad, handbill, flyer, poster.

advice *(SYN.)* counsel, instruction, suggestion, warning, information, caution, exhortation, admonition.

advise *(SYN.)* recommend, suggest, counsel, caution, warn, admonish.

adviser *(SYN.)* coach, guide, mentor, counselor.

aesthetic *(SYN.)* literary, artistic, sensitive, tasteful. *(ANT.) tasteless.*

affable *(SYN.)* pleasant, courteous, sociable, friendly, amiable, gracious. *(ANT.) unfriendly, unsociable.*

affair *(SYN.)* event, occasion, happening, party, occurrence, matter, festivity, business, concern.

affect *(SYN.)* alter, modify, concern, regard, touch, feign, pretend, influence, sway, transform, change.

affected *(SYN.)* pretended, fake, sham, false.

affection *(SYN.)* fondness, kindness, emotion, love, feeling, tenderness, attachment, disposition, endearment, liking, friendly, friendliness, warmth. *(ANT.) aversion, indifference, repulsion, hatred, repugnance, dislike, antipathy.*

affectionate *(SYN.)* warm, loving, tender, fond, attached. *(ANT.) distant, unfeeling, cold.*

affirm *(SYN.)* aver, declare, swear, maintain, endorse, certify, state, assert, ratify, say, confirm, establish. *(ANT.) deny, dispute, oppose, contradict, demur, disclaim.*

afflict *(SYN.)* trouble, disturb, bother, agitate, perturb. *(ANT.) soothe.*

affliction *(SYN.)* distress, grief, misfortune, trouble. *(ANT.) relief, benefit, easement.*

affluent *(SYN.)* wealthy, prosperous, rich, abundant, ample, plentiful, well-off, bountiful, well-to-do. *(ANT.) poor.*

afford *(SYN.)* supply, yield, furnish.

affront *(SYN.)* offense, slur, slight, provocation, insult.

afraid *(SYN.)* faint-hearted, frightened, scared, timid, fearful, apprehensive, cowardly, terrified. *(ANT.) assured, composed, courageous, bold, confident.*

after *(SYN.)* following, subsequently, behind, next. *(ANT.) before.*

again *(SYN.)* anew, repeatedly, afresh.

against *(SYN.)* versus, hostile to, opposed to, in disagreement. *(ANT.) with, for, in favor of.*

age *(SYN.)* antiquity, date, period, generation, time, senility, grow old, senescence, mature, epoch.

(ANT.) youth, childhood.

aged (SYN.) ancient, elderly, old.

(ANT.) youthful, young.

agency (SYN.) office, operation.

agent (SYN.) performer, doer, worker, actor, operator.

aggravate (SYN.) intensify, magnify, annoy, irritate, increase, heighten, nettle, make worse, irk, vex, provoke, embitter, worsen.

(ANT.) soften, soothe, appease, pacify, mitigate, ease, relieve.

aggregate (SYN.) collection, entirety, accumulate, total, compile, conglomeration.

(ANT.) part, unit, ingredient, element.

aggression (SYN.) assault, attack, invasion, offense.

(ANT.) defense.

aggressive (SYN.) offensive, belligerent, hostile, attacking, militant, pugnacious.

(ANT.) timid, withdrawn, passive, peaceful, shy.

aghast (SYN.) surprised, astonished, astounded, awed, thunderstruck, flabbergasted, bewildered.

agile (SYN.) nimble, graceful, lively, active, alert, fast, quick, athletic, spry.

(ANT.) inept, awkward, clumsy.

agility (ANT.) quickness, vigor, energy, activity, motion.

(ANT.) dullness, inertia, idleness, inactivity.

agitate (SYN.) disturb, excite, perturb, rouse, shake, arouse, disconcert, instigate, inflame, provoke, jar, incite, stir up, toss.

(ANT.) calm, placate, quiet, ease, soothe.

agitated (SYN.) jumpy, jittery, nervous, restless, restive, upset, disturbed, ruffled.

agony (SYN.) anguish, misery, pain, suffering, torture, ache, distress, throe, woe, torment, grief.

(ANT.) relief, ease, comfort.

agree (SYN.) comply, coincide, conform, concur, assent, accede, tally, settle, harmonize, unite, consent.

(ANT.) differ, disagree, protest, contradict, argue, refuse.

agreeable (SYN.) amiable, charming, able,

gratifying, pleasant, suitable, pleasure, welcome, pleasing, acceptable, friendly, cooperative.

(ANT.) obnoxious, offensive, unpleasant, disagreeable, quarrelsome, contentious, touchy.

agreement (SYN.) harmony, understanding, unison, contract, pact, stipulation, alliance, deal, bargain, treaty, contract, arrangement, settlement, accord, concord.

(ANT.) variance, dissension, discord, disagreement, difference, misunderstanding.

agriculture (SYN.) farming, gardening, tillage, husbandry, agronomy, cultivation.

ahead (SYN.) before, leading, forward, winning, inadvance.

(ANT.) behind.

aid (SYN.) remedy, assist, helper, service, support, assistant, relief, help.

(ANT.) obstruct, hinder, obstacle, impede, hindrance.

ail (SYN.) bother, trouble, perturb, suffer, feel sick.

ailing (SYN.) sick, ill.

(ANT.) hearty, hale, well.

ailment (SYN.) illness, disease, affliction, sickness.

aim (SYN.) direction, point, goal, object, target, direct, try, intend, intention, end, objective.

aimless (SYN.) directionless, adrift, purposeless.

air (SYN.) atmosphere, display, reveal, expose, publicize.

(ANT.) conceal, hide.

airy (SYN.) breezy, gay, light-hearted, graceful, fanciful.

aisle (SYN.) corridor, passageway, lane, alley, opening, artery.

ajar (SYN.) gaping, open.

akin (SYN.) alike, related, connected, similar, affiliated, allied.

alarm (SYN.) dismay, fright, signal, warning, terror, apprehension, affright, consternation, fear, siren, arouse, startle, bell.

(ANT.) tranquillity, composure, security, quiet, calm, soothe, comfort.

alarming (SYN.) appalling, daunting, shocking.

(ANT.) comforting, calming, soothing.

alcoholic *(SYN.)* sot, drunkard, tippler, inebriate.

alert *(SYN.)* attentive, keen, ready, nimble, vigilant, watchful, observant.
(ANT.) logy, sluggish, dulled, listless.

alias *(SYN.)* anonym, assumed name.

alibi *(SYN.)* story, excuse.

alien *(SYN.)* adverse, foreigner, strange, remote, stranger, different, extraneous.
(ANT.) germane, kindred, relevant, akin, familiar, accustomed.

alight *(SYN.)* debark, deplane, detrain, disembark.
(ANT.) embark, board.

alive *(SYN.)* existing, breathing, living, live, lively, vivacious, animated.
(ANT.) inactive, dead, moribund.

allay *(SYN.)* soothe, check, lessen, calm, lighten, relieve, soften, moderate, quite.
(ANT.) excite, intensify, worsen, arouse.

allege *(SYN.)* affirm, cite, claim, declare, maintain, state, assert.
(ANT.) deny, disprove, refute, contradict, gainsay.

allegiance *(SYN.)* faithfulness, duty, devotion, loyalty, fidelity, obligation.
(ANT.) treachery, disloyalty.

allegory *(SYN.)* fable, fiction, myth, saga, parable, legend.
(ANT.) history, fact.

alleviate *(SYN.)* diminish, soothe, solace, abate, assuage, allay, soften, mitigate, extenuate, relieve, ease, slacken, relax, weaken.
(ANT.) increase, aggravate, augment, irritate.

alley *(SYN.)* footway, byway, path, passageway, aisle, corridor, opening, lane.

alliance *(SYN.)* combination, partnership, union, treaty, coalition, association, confederacy, marriage, pact, agreement, relation, interrelation, understanding.
(ANT.) separation, divorce, schism.

allot *(SYN.)* divide, mete, assign, give, measure, distribute, allocate, share, dispense, deal, apportion.
(ANT.) withhold, retain, keep, confiscate, refuse.

allow *(SYN.)* authorize, grant, acknowledge, admit, let, permit, sanction, consent, concede, mete, allocate.

(ANT.) protest, resist, refuse, forbid, object, prohibit.

allowance *(SYN.)* grant, fee, portion, ration, allotment.

allude *(SYN.)* intimate, refer, insinuate, hint, advert, suggest, imply, mention.
(ANT.) demonstrate, specify, state, declare.

allure *(SYN.)* attract, fascinate, tempt, charm, infatuate, captivate.

ally *(SYN.)* accomplice, associate, confederate, assistant, friend, partner.
(ANT.) rival, enemy, opponent, foe, adversary.

almighty *(SYN.)* omnipotent, powerful.

almost *(SYN.)* somewhat, nearly.
(ANT.) completely, absolutely.

alms *(SYN.)* dole, charity, donation, contribution.

aloft *(SYN.)* overhead.

alone *(SYN.)* desolate, unaided, only, isolated, unaided, lone, secluded, lonely, deserted, solitary, single, apart, solo, separate.
(ANT.) surrounded, attended, accompanied, together.

aloof *(SYN.)* uninterested, uninvolved, apart, remote, unsociable, standoffish, separate, disdainful, distant.
(ANT.) warm, outgoing, friendly, cordial.

also *(SYN.)* in addition, likewise, too, besides, furthermore, moreover, further.

alter *(SYN.)* adjust, vary, deviate, modify, reserved, change.
(ANT.) maintain, preserve, keep.

alteration *(SYN.)* difference, adjustment, change, modification.
(ANT.) maintenance, preservation.

altercation *(SYN.)* controversy, dispute, argument, quarrel.

alternate *(SYN.)* rotate, switch, spell, interchange.
(ANT.) fix.

alternative *(SYN.)* substitute, selection, option, choice, replacement, possibility.

although *(SYN.)* though, even if, even though, despite, notwithstanding.

altitude *(SYN.)* elevation, height.
(ANT.) depth.

altogether *(SYN.)* totally, wholly, quite.
(ANT.) partly.

altruism *(SYN.)* kindness, generosity,

charity, benevolence, liberality.
(ANT.) selfishness, unkindness, cruelty, inhumanity.

always *(SYN.)* evermore, forever, perpetually, ever, unceasingly, continually, constantly, eternally.
(ANT.) never, rarely, sometimes, occasionally.

amalgamate *(SYN.)* fuse, unify, commingle, merge, combine, consolidate.
(ANT.) decompose, disintegrate, separate.

amass *(SYN.)* collect, accumulate, heap up, gather, increase, compile, assemble, store up.
(ANT.) disperse, dissipate, spend.

amateur *(SYN.)* beginner, dilettante, learner, dabbler, neophyte, apprentice, novice, nonprofessional, tyro.
(ANT.) expert, master, adept, professional, authority.

amaze *(SYN.)* surprise, flabbergast, stun, dumbfound, astound, bewilder, aghast, thunderstruck, astonish.
(ANT.) bore, disinterest, tire.

ambiguous *(SYN.)* uncertain, vague, obscure, dubious, equivocal, deceptive.
(ANT.) plain, clear, explicit, obvious, unequivocal, unmistakable, certain.

ambition *(SYN.)* eagerness, goal, incentive, aspiration, yearning, longing, desire.
(ANT.) indifference, satisfaction, indolence, resignation.

ambitious *(SYN.)* aspiring, intent upon.
(ANT.) indifferent.

amble *(SYN.)* saunter, stroll.

ambush *(SYN.)* trap, hiding place.

amend *(SYN.)* change, mend, better, correct, improve.
(ANT.) worsen.

amends *(SYN.)* compensation, restitution, payment, reparation, remedy, redress.

amiable *(SYN.)* friendly, good natured, gracious, pleasing, agreeable, outgoing, kind-hearted, kind, pleasant.
(ANT.) surly, hateful, churlish, disagreeable, ill-natured, cross, captious, touchy.

amid *(SYN.)* among, amidst, surrounded by.

amiss *(SYN.)* wrongly, improperly, astray,

awry.
(ANT.) properly, rightly, right, correctly, correct.

ammunition *(SYN.)* shot, powder, shells, bullets.

among *(SYN.)* amid, between, mingled, mixed, amidst, betwixt, surrounded by.
(ANT.) separate, apart.

amorous *(SYN.)* amatory, affectionate, loving.

amount *(SYN.)* sum, total, quantity, number, price, value, measure.

ample *(SYN.)* broad, large, profuse, spacious, copious, liberal, plentiful, full, bountiful, abundant, great, extensive, generous, enough, sufficient, roomy.
(ANT.) limited, insufficient, meager, lacking, cramped, small, confined, inadequate.

amplification *(SYN.)* magnification, growth, waxing, accrual, enhancement, enlargement, increase.
(ANT.) decrease, diminishing, reduction, contraction.

amplify *(SYN.)* broaden, expand, enlarge, extend.
(ANT.) confine, restrict, abridge, narrow.

amuse *(SYN.)* divert, please, delight, entertain, charm.
(ANT.) tire, bore.

amusement *(SYN.)* diversion, entertainment, enjoyment, pleasure, recreation.
(ANT.) tedium, boredom.

amusing *(SYN.)* pleasant, funny, pleasing, entertaining, comical.
(ANT.) tiring, tedious, boring.

analogous *(SYN.)* comparable, like, similar, correspondent, alike, correlative, parallel, allied, akin.
(ANT.) different, opposed, incongruous, divergent.

analysis *(SYN.)* separation, investigation, examination.

analyze *(SYN.)* explain, investigate, examine, separate.

ancestral *(SYN.)* hereditary, inherited.

ancestry *(SYN.)* family, line, descent, lineage.
(ANT.) posterity.

anchor *(SYN.)* fix, attach, secure, fasten.
(ANT.) detach, free, loosen.

ancient *(SYN.)* aged, old-fashioned, ar-

chaic, elderly, antique, old, primitive.
(ANT.) new, recent, current, fresh.

anecdote *(SYN.)* account, narrative, story, tale.

anesthetic *(SYN.)* opiate, narcotic, sedative, painkiller, analgesic.

angel *(SYN.)* cherub, archangel, seraph.
(ANT.) demon, devil.

angelic *(SYN.)* pure, lovely, heavenly, good, virtuous, innocent, godly, saintly.
(ANT.) devilish.

anger *(SYN.)* exasperation, fury, ire, passion, rage, resentment, temper, indignation, animosity, irritation, wrath, displeasure, infuriate, arouse, nettle, annoyance, exasperate.
(ANT.) forbearance, patience, peace, self-control.

angry *(SYN.)* provoked, wrathful, furious, enraged, incensed, exasperated, maddened, indignant, irate, mad, inflamed.
(ANT.) happy, pleased, calm, satisfied, content, tranquil.

anguish *(SYN.)* suffering, torment, torture, distress, pain, heartache, agony, misery.
(ANT.) solace, relief, joy, comfort, peace, ecstasy, pleasure.

animal *(SYN.)* beast, creature.

animate *(SYN.)* vitalize, invigorate, stimulate, enliven, alive, vital, vigorous.
(ANT.) dead, inanimate.

animated *(SYN.)* gay, lively, spry, vivacious, active, vigorous, chipper, snappy.
(ANT.) inactive.

animosity *(SYN.)* grudge, hatred, rancor, spite, bitterness, enmity, opposition, dislike, hostility, antipathy.
(ANT.) good will, love, friendliness, kindliness.

annex *(SYN.)* join, attach, add, addition, wing, append.

annihilate *(SYN.)* destroy, demolish, wreck, abolish.

announce *(SYN.)* proclaim, give out, make known, notify, publish, report, herald, promulgate, tell, advertise, broadcast, state, publicize.
(ANT.) conceal, withhold, suppress, bury, stifle.

announcement *(SYN.)* notification, report, declaration, bulletin, advertise-

ment, broadcast, promulgation, notice, message.
(ANT.) silence, hush, muteness, speechlessness.

annoy *(SYN.)* bother, irk, pester, tease, trouble, vex, disturb, molest, inconvenience, irritate, harass.
(ANT.) console, gratify, soothe, accommodate, please, calm, comfort.

annually *(SYN.)* once a year.

anoint *(SYN.)* grease, oil.

answer *(SYN.)* reply, rejoinder, response, retort, rebuttal, respond.
(ANT.) summoning, argument, questioning, inquiry, query, ask, inquire.

antagonism *(SYN.)* opposition, conflict, enmity, hostility, animosity.
(ANT.) geniality, cordiality, friendliness.

antagonist *(SYN.)* adversary, rival, enemy, foe, opponent.
(ANT.) ally, friend.

antagonize *(SYN.)* against, provoke, oppose, embitter.
(ANT.) soothe.

anthology *(SYN.)* garland, treasury, collection.

anticipate *(SYN.)* await, foresee, forecast, hope for, expect.

anticipated *(SYN.)* expected, foresight, preconceived.
(ANT.) dreaded, reared, worried, doubted.

antics *(SYN.)* horseplay, fun, merrymaking, pranks, capers, tricks, clowning.

antipathy *(SYN.)* hatred.

antiquated *(SYN.)* old, out-of-date, outdated, old-fashion.

antique *(SYN.)* rarity, curio, old, ancient, old-fashioned, archaic, out-of-date.
(ANT.) new, recent, fresh.

anxiety *(SYN.)* care, disquiet, fear, concern, solicitude, trouble, worry, apprehension, uneasiness, distress.
(ANT.) nonchalance, assurance, confidence, contentment, peacefulness, placidity, tranquillity.

anxious *(SYN.)* troubled, uneasy, perturbed, apprehensive, worried, concerned, desirous, bothered, agitated, eager, fearful.
(ANT.) tranquil, calm, peaceful.

anyway *(SYN.)* nevertheless, anyhow.

apartment *(SYN.)* suite, flat, dormitory.

apathy *(SYN.)* unconcern, indifference, lethargy.
(ANT.) interest, feeling.

aperture *(SYN.)* gap, pore, opening, cavity, chasm, abyss, hole, void.
(ANT.) connection, bridge, link.

apex *(SYN.)* acme, tip, summit, crown, top.

apologize *(SYN.)* ask forgiveness.

apology *(SYN.)* defense, excuse, confession, justification, alibi, explanation, plea.
(ANT.) denial, complaint, dissimulation, accusation.

apostate *(SYN.)* nonconformist, unbeliever, dissenter, heretic, schismatic.
(ANT.) saint, conformist, believer.

appall *(SYN.)* shock, stun, dismay, frighten, terrify, horrify.
(ANT.) edify, please.

appalling *(SYN.)* fearful, frightful, ghastly, horrid, repulsive, terrible, awful.
(ANT.) fascinating, beautiful, enchanting, enjoyable.

apparatus *(SYN.)* rig, equipment, furnishings, gear.

apparel *(SYN.)* clothes, attire, garb, clothing, garments, dress, robes.

apparent *(SYN.)* obvious, plain, self-evident, clear, manifest, transparent, unmistakable, palpable, unambiguous, ostensible, illusory, visible, evident.
(ANT.) uncertain, indistinct, dubious, hidden, mysterious.

apparition *(SYN.)* illusion, ghost, phantom, vision, fantasy, dream.

appeal *(SYN.)* plea, petition, request, entreaty, request, plead, petition, beseech, beg, entreat, attract.
(ANT.) repulse, repel.

appear *(SYN.)* look, arrive, emanate, emerge, arise, seem, turn up.
(ANT.) vanish, withdraw, exist, disappear, evaporate.

appearance *(SYN.)* advent, arrival, aspect, demeanor, fashion, guise, apparition, mien, look, presence.
(ANT.) disappearance, reality, departure, vanishing.

appease *(SYN.)* calm, compose, lull, quiet, relieve, assuage, pacify, satisfy, restraint, lesson, soothe, check, ease, alleviate, still, allay, tranquilize.
(ANT.) excite, arouse, incense, irritate, inflame.

append *(SYN.)* supplement, attach, add.

appendage *(SYN.)* addition, tail, supplement.

appetite *(SYN.)* zest, craving, desire, liking, longing, stomach, inclination, hunger, thirst, relish, passion.
(ANT.) satiety, disgust, distaste, repugnance.

appetizer *(SYN.)* hors d'oeuvre.

applaud *(SYN.)* cheer, clap, hail, approve, praise, acclaim.
(ANT.) disapprove, denounce, reject, criticize, condemn.

appliance *(SYN.)* machine, tool, instrument, device, utensil, implement.

applicable *(SYN.)* fitting, suitable, proper, fit, usable, appropriate, suited.
(ANT.) inappropriate, inapplicable.

apply *(SYN.)* affix, allot, appropriate, use, employ, petition, request, devote, avail, pertain, attach, ask, administer, petition, assign, relate, utilize.
(ANT.) give away, demand, detach, neglect, ignore.

appoint *(SYN.)* name, choose, nominate, designate, elect, establish, assign, place.
(ANT.) discharge, fire, dismiss.

appointment *(SYN.)* rendezvous, meeting, designation, position, engagement, assignment.
(ANT.) discharge, dismissal.

appraise *(SYN.)* value, evaluate, place a value on.

appreciate *(SYN.)* enjoy, regard, value, prize, cherish, admire, improve, rise, respect, esteem, appraise.
(ANT.) belittle, misunderstand, apprehend, degrade, scorn, depreciate, undervalue.

apprehend *(SYN.)* seize, capture, arrest, understand, dread, fear, grasp, perceive.
(ANT.) release, lose.

apprehension *(SYN.)* fear, misgiving, dread, uneasiness, worry, fearfulness, anticipation, capture, seizure.
(ANT.) confidence, composure, self-assuredness.

apprehensive *(SYN.)* worried, afraid, un-

easy, bothered, anxious, concerned, perturbed, troubled, fearful.
(ANT.) relaxed.
apprentice *(SYN.)* amateur, recruit, novice, beginner.
(ANT.) experienced, professional, master.
approach *(SYN.)* greet, inlet, come near, advance, access, passageway.
(ANT.) avoid, pass by, retreat.
appropriate *(SYN.)* apt, particular, proper, fitting, suitable, applicable, loot, pillage, purloin, rob, steal, embezzle, assign, becoming, apportion, authorize.
(ANT.) improper, contrary, inappropriate, buy, repay, restore, return, unfit, inapt.
approval *(SYN.)* commendation, consent, praise, approbation, sanction, assent, endorsement, support.
(ANT.) reproach, censure, reprimand, disapprove.
approve *(SYN.)* like, praise, authorize, confirm, endorse, appreciate, ratify, commend, sanction.
(ANT.) criticize, nullify, disparage, frown on, disapprove, deny.
approximate *(SYN.)* near, approach, roughly, close.
(ANT.) correct.
apt *(SYN.)* suitable, proper, appropriate, fit, suited, disposed, liable, inclined, prone, clever, bright, alert, intelligent, receptive.
(ANT.) ill-becoming, unsuitable, unlikely, slow, retarded, dense.
aptness *(SYN.)* capability, dexterity, power, qualification, skill, ability, aptitude.
(ANT.) incompetency, unreadiness, incapacity.
aptitude *(SYN.)* knack, talent, gift, ability.
aqueduct *(SYN.)* gully, pipe, canal, waterway, channel.
arbitrary *(SYN.)* unrestricted, absolute, despotic, willful, unreasonable, unconditional, authoritative.
(ANT.) contingent, qualified, fair, reasonable, dependent, accountable.
arbitrate *(SYN.)* referee, settle, mediate, umpire, negotiate.
architecture *(SYN.)* structure, building, construction.
ardent *(SYN.)* fervent, fiery, glowing, intense, keen, impassioned, fervid, hot, passionate, earnest, eager, zealous, enthusiastic.
(ANT.) cool, indifferent, nonchalant, apathetic.
ardor *(SYN.)* enthusiasm, rapture, spirit, zeal, fervent, eager, glowing, eagerness.
(ANT.) unconcern, apathy, disinterest, indifference.
arduous *(SYN.)* laborious, hard, difficult, burdensome, strenuous, strained.
(ANT.) easy.
area *(SYN.)* space, extent, region, zone, section, expanse, district, neighborhood, size.
argue *(SYN.)* plead, reason, wrangle, indicate, prove, show, dispute, denote, imply, object, bicker, discuss, debate, disagree.
(ANT.) reject, spurn, ignore, overlook, agree, concur.
argument *(SYN.)* debate, dispute, controversy.
(ANT.) harmony, accord, agreement.
arid *(SYN.)* waterless, dry, flat, dull, unimaginative, stuffy.
(ANT.) fertile, wet, colorful.
arise *(SYN.)* enter, institute, originate, start, open, commence, emerge, appear.
(ANT.) terminate, end, finish, complete, close.
aristocrat *(SYN.)* noble, gentleman, peer, nobleman.
(ANT.) peasant, commoner.
arm *(SYN.)* weapon, defend, equip, empower, fortify.
armistice *(SYN.)* truce, pact, deal, peace, treaty, contract, alliance, agreement.
army *(SYN.)* troops, legion, military, forces, militia.
aroma *(SYN.)* smell, odor, fragrance, perfume, scent.
arouse *(SYN.)* stir, animate, move, pique, provoke, kindle, disturb, excite, foment, stimulate, awaken.
(ANT.) settle, soothe, calm.
arraign *(SYN.)* charge, censure, incriminate, indict, accuse.
(ANT.) acquit, release, vindicate, exonerate, absolve.
arraignment *(SYN.)* imputation, charge, accusation, incrimination.

(ANT.) *pardon, exoneration, exculpation.*

arrange (SYN.) classify, assort, organize, place, plan, prepare, devise, adjust, dispose, regulate, order, group, adapt, catalog, systematize, distribute, prepare.
(ANT.) *jumble, scatter, disorder, confuse, disturb, disarrange.*

arrangement (SYN.) display, grouping, order, array.

array (SYN.) dress, adorn, attire, clothe, arrange, order, distribute, arrangement, display, exhibit.
(ANT.) *disorder, disorganization, disarray.*

arrest (SYN.) detain, hinder, restrain, seize, withhold, stop, check, obstruct, apprehend, catch, capture.
(ANT.) *free, release, discharge, liberate.*

arrival (SYN.) advent, coming.
(ANT.) *leaving, departure.*

arrive (SYN.) come, emerge, reach, visit, land, appear.
(ANT.) *exit, leave, depart, go.*

arrogance (SYN.) pride, insolence.
(ANT.) *humbleness, modesty, humility.*

arrogant (SYN.) insolent, prideful, scornful, haughty, cavalier, proud.
(ANT.) *modest, humble.*

art (SYN.) cunning, tact, artifice, skill, aptitude, adroitness, painting, drawing, design, craft, dexterity, composition, ingenuity.
(ANT.) *clumsiness, innocence, unskillfulness, honesty.*

artery (SYN.) aqueduct, pipe, channel.

artful (SYN.) clever, sly, skillful, knowing, deceitful, tricky, crafty, cunning.
(ANT.) *artless.*

article (SYN.) story, composition, treatise, essay, thing, report, object.

artifice (SYN.) trick, clever, scheme, device.

artificial (SYN.) bogus, fake, affected, feigned, phony, sham, unreal, synthetic, assumed, counterfeit, unnatural, manmade, unreal, manufactured, false, pretended, feigned.
(ANT.) *genuine, natural true, real, authentic.*

artisan (SYN.) worker, craftsman, mechanic.

artist (SYN.) actor, actress, painter, sculptor, singer, designer.

artless (SYN.) innocent, open, frank, simple, honest, candid, natural, unskilled, ignorant, truthful, sincere.
(ANT.) *artful.*

ascend (SYN.) rise, scale, tower, mount, go up, climb.
(ANT.) *fall, sink, descend, go down.*

ascertain (SYN.) solve, learn, clear up, answer.

ascribe (SYN.) attribute, assign.

ashamed (SYN.) shamefaced, humiliated, abashed, mortified, embarrassed.
(ANT.) *proud.*

ask (SYN.) invite, request, inquire, query, question, beg, solicit, demand, entreat, claim, interrogate, expect.
(ANT.) *order, reply, insist, answer.*

askance (SYN.) sideways.

askew (SYN.) disorderly, crooked, awry, twisted.
(ANT.) *straight.*

asleep (SYN.) inactive, sleeping, dormant.
(ANT.) *alert, awake.*

aspect (SYN.) appearance, look, view, outlook, attitude, viewpoint, phase, part, feature, side.

aspersion (SYN.) dishonor, insult, misuse, outrage, reproach, defamation, disparagement abuse.
(ANT.) *plaudit, respect, commendation, approval.*

asphyxiate (SYN.) suffocate, stifle, smother, choke, strangle, throttle.

aspiration (SYN.) craving, desire, hope, longing, objective, passion, ambition.

aspire (SYN.) seek, aim, wish for, strive, desire, yearn for.

ass (SYN.) mule, donkey, burro, silly, dunce, stubborn, stupid, fool.

assail (SYN.) assault, attack.

assassinate (SYN.) purge, kill, murder.

assault (SYN.) invade, strike, attack, assail, charge, bombard, onslaught.
(ANT.) *protect, defend.*

assemble (SYN.) collect, gather, meet, congregate, connect, manufacture.
(ANT.) *disperse, disassemble, scatter.*

assembly (SYN.) legislature, congress, council, parliament.

assent (SYN.) consent to, concede, agree, approval, accept, comply, permission.

(ANT.) deny, dissent, refusal, denial, refuse.

assert *(SYN.)* declare, maintain, state, claim, express, defend, support, aver, uphold, consent, accept, comply, allege, emphasize.
(ANT.) deny, refute, contradict, decline.

assertion *(SYN.)* statement, affirmation, declaration.
(ANT.) contradiction, denial.

assess *(SYN.)* calculate, compute, estimate, levy, reckon, tax, appraise.

asset *(SYN.)* property, wealth, capitol, resourses, goods.

assign *(SYN.)* apportion, ascribe, attribute, cast.
(ANT.) release, relieve, unburden, discharge.

assist *(SYN.)* help, promote, serve, support, sustain, abet.
(ANT.) prevent, impede, hinder, hamper.

assistance *(SYN.)* backing, help, patronage, relief.
(ANT.) hostility, resistance, antagonism, counteraction.

assistant *(SYN.)* accomplice, ally, associate, confederate.
(ANT.) rival, enemy.

associate *(SYN.)* affiliate, ally, join, connect, unite, combine, mingle, partner, mix.
(ANT.) separate, disconnect, divide, disrupt, estrange.

association *(SYN.)* organization, club, union, society, fraternity, sorority.

assorted *(SYN.)* varied, miscellaneous, classified, different, several, grouped.
(ANT.) alike, same.

assortment *(SYN.)* collection, variety, mixture.

assuage *(SYN.)* calm, quiet, lessen, relieve, ease, allay, moderate, alleviate.

assume *(SYN.)* arrogate, affect, suspect, believe, appropriate, pretend, usurp.
(ANT.) doff, demonstrate, prove, grant, concede.

assumption *(SYN.)* presumption, guess, theory, supposition, conjecture, postulate.

assurance *(SYN.)* confidence, conviction, self-reliance, surety, firmness, courage.
(ANT.) humility, shyness, suspicion, modesty.

assure *(SYN.)* promise, convince, warrant, guarantee.
(ANT.) equivocate, deny.

astonish *(SYN.)* astound, amaze, surprise, shock.
(ANT.) tire, bore.

astound *(SYN.)* shock, amaze, astonish, stun, surprise.

athletic *(SYN.)* strong, active, ablebodied, gymnastic.

atone *(SYN.)* repay, make up.

atrocious *(SYN.)* horrible, savage, brutal, ruthless, dreadful, awful, horrifying.
(ANT.) good, kind.

attach *(SYN.)* connect, adjoin, annex, join, append, stick.
(ANT.) unfasten, untie, detach, separate, disengage.

attachment *(SYN.)* friendship, liking, regard, adherence.
(ANT.) estrangement, opposition, alienation, aversion.

attack *(SYN.)* raid, assault, besiege, abuse, censure, offense, seige, denunciation.
(ANT.) surrender, defense, opposition, aid, defend, protect.

attain *(SYN.)* achieve, acquire, accomplish, gain, get, reach, win, complete, finish.
(ANT.) relinquish, discard, abandon, desert.

attainment *(SYN.)* exploit, feat, accomplishment, realization, performance.
(ANT.) omission, defeat, failure, neglect.

attempt *(SYN.)* essay, experiment, trial, try, undertaking, endeavor, effort.
(ANT.) laziness, neglect.

attend *(SYN.)* accompany, escort, watch, be serve, care for, follow, lackey, present.
(ANT.) desert, abandon.

attendant *(SYN.)* waiter, servant, valet.

attention *(SYN.)* consideration, heed, circumspection, notice, watchfulness.
(ANT.) negligence, indifference, omission, oversight.

attentive *(SYN.)* careful, awake, alive, considerate, mindful, wary, assiduous.
(ANT.) indifferent, unaware, oblivious, apathetic.

attest *(SYN.)* testify, swear, vouch, certify.

attitude *(SYN.)* standpoint, viewpoint, stand, pose, disposition, opinion.

attract *(SYN.)* enchant, interest, pull, fascinate, draw, lure, captivate, allure.
(ANT.) deter, repel, repulse, alienate.

attractive *(SYN.)* enchanting, winning, engaging, pleasant, seductive, magnetic, charming, inviting, alluring.
(ANT.) unattractive, obnoxious, repellent.

attribute *(SYN.)* give, apply, feature, nature, credit, quality, assign, ascribe.

audacious *(SYN.)* daring, bold, arrogant, foolhardy, cavalier, haughty, insolent.
(ANT.) humble, shy.

audacity *(SYN.)* effrontery, fearlessness, temerity.
(ANT.) humility, meekness, circumspection, fearfulness.

audible *(SYN.)* distinct, bearable, plain, clear.
(ANT.) inaudible.

augment *(SYN.)* enlarge, increase, raise, expand.

auspicious *(SYN.)* lucky, timely, favorable, promising, fortunate.
(ANT.) untimely, unfortunate.

austere *(SYN.)* stern, severe, harsh, strict.
(ANT.) lenient, soft.

authentic *(SYN.)* real, true, correct, verifiable, authoritative, trustworthy.
(ANT.) false, spurious, artificial, counterfeit, erroneous.

authenticate *(SYN.)* validate, warrant, guarantee, verify.

author *(SYN.)* father, inventor, originator, writer, composer

authoritative *(SYN.)* certain, secure, commanding, sure, tried, trustworthy, safe, influential, dependable.
(ANT.) uncertain, unreliable, dubious, fallible.

authority *(SYN.)* dominion, justification, power, permission, authorization.
(ANT.) incapacity, denial, prohibition, weakness.

authorize *(SYN.)* permit, sanction, legalize, assign, enable, approve, empower.
(ANT.) forbid, prohibit.

autocrat *(SYN.)* monarch, ruler, tyrant, dictator.

automatic *(SYN.)* self-acting, mechanical, spontaneous, self-working, self-moving.

(ANT.) hand-operated, intentional, deliberate, manual.

auxiliary *(SYN.)* assisting, helping, aiding.

avail *(SYN.)* help, profit, use, value, benefit, advantage.

available *(SYN.)* obtainable, accessible, prepared.
(ANT.) unavailable, out of reach, inaccessible.

average *(SYN.* moderate, ordinary, usual, passable, fair, middling, intermediate.
(ANT.) outstanding, exceptional, extraordinary.

averse *(SYN.)* unwilling, opposed, forced, against, involuntary.
(ANT.) willing.

aversion *(SYN.)* disgust, dislike, distaste, hatred, loathing, abhorrence, antipathy.
(ANT.) devotion, enthusiasm, affection.

avid *(SYN.)* greedy, eager.

avocation *(SYN.)* sideline, hobby.

avoid *(SYN.)* elude, forestall, evade, escape, dodge, avert, forbear, eschew, free shun.
(ANT.) oppose, meet, confront, encounter, seek.

award *(SYN.)* reward, prize, medal, gift, trophy.

aware *(SYN.)* mindful, perceptive, informed, apprised, realizing, conscious, observant, knowing, cognizant.
(ANT.) unaware, insensible, ignorant, oblivious.

away *(SYN.)* absent, departed, distracted, gone.
(ANT.) present, attentive.

awe *(SYN.)* surprise, respect, dread, astonishment, alarm.

awful *(SYN.)* frightful, horrible, aweinspiring, dire, terrible, unpleasant, imposing, appalling, cruel, wicked, brutal, savage, dreadful.
(ANT.) humble, lowly, commonplace.

awkward *(SYN,)* inept, unpolished, clumsy, rough, ungraceful, ungainly.
(ANT.) graceful, polished, skillful.

awry *(SYN.)* askew, wrong, twisted, twisted, crooked, disorderly.
(ANT.) straight, right.

axiom *(SYN.)* fundamental, maxim, principle, theorem, adage, byword.

babble *(SYN.)* twaddle, nonsense, gibberish, prattle, balderdash, rubbish.

baby *(SYN.)* newborn, infant, wee, little, undersized, midget, papoose, pamper.

babyish *(SYN.)* infantile, childish, baby, whiny, unreasonable, immature, puerile.
(ANT.) mature, adult, sensible, reasonable.

back *(SYN.)* help, assist, endorse, support, second, ratify, approve, stand by.
(ANT.) anterior, front, face, undercut, veto, undermine, accessible, near.

backbiting *(SYN.)* gossip, slander, abuse, malice, cattiness, aspersion, badmouthing.
(ANT.) compliments, praise, loyalty, approval.

backbone *(SYN.)* vertebrae, spine, pillar, support, staff, mainstay, character.
(ANT.) timidity, weakness, cowardice, spinelessness.

backbreaking *(SYN.)* exhausting, fatiguing, tough, tiring, demanding, wearing.
(ANT.) light, relaxing, undemanding, slight.

back down *(SYN.)* accede, concede, acquiesce, yield.
(ANT.) persevere, insist.

backer *(SYN.)* underwriter, benefactor, investor, patron.

backfire *(SYN.)* flop, boomerang, fail, disappoint.
(ANT.) succeed.

background *(SYN.)* training, practice, experience.

backing *(SYN.)* help, support, sympathy, endorsement.
(ANT.) criticism, detraction, faultfinding.

backlog *(SYN.)* inventory, reserve, hoard, amassment.

backslide *(SYN.)* relapse, revert, return, weaken, regress, renege.

backward *(SYN.)* dull, sluggish, stupid, loath, regressive, rearward, underdeveloped, slow, retarded.
(ANT.) progressive, precocious, civilized, advanced, forward.

bad *(SYN.)* unfavorable, wrong, evil, immoral, sinful, faulty, improper, unwholesome, wicked, corrupt, tainted, defective, poor, imperfect, inferior, sub-standard, contaminated, inappropriate, unsuited, rotten, unsuitable, sorry, upset, sick, suffering, unpleasant.
(ANT.) good, honorable, reputable, moral, excellent.

badger *(SYN.)* tease, question, annoy, pester, bother, taunt, bait, provoke.

baffle *(SYN.)* confound bewilder, perplex, puzzle, mystify, confuse, frustrate.
(ANT.) inform, enlighten.

bag *(SYN.)* catch, poke, sack.

bait *(SYN.)* enticement, captivate, ensnare, tease, torment, pester, worry, entrap, question, entice, lure, trap, harass, tempt, badger.

balance *(SYN.)* poise, stability, composure, remains, residue, equilibrium, compare.
(ANT.) unsteadiness, instability.

bald *(SYN.)* bare, hairless, nude, open, uncovered.
(ANT.) covered, hairy.

baleful *(SYN.)* evil, immoral sinful, destructive.
(ANT.) good, moral, reputable, excellent, harmless.

balk *(SYN.)* unwilling, obstinate, stubborn, stop.
(ANT.) willing.

ball *(SYN.)* cotillion, dance, globe, sphere, spheroid.

ballad *(SYN.)* song, ditty.

balloon *(SYN.)* puff up, enlarge, swell.
(ANT.) shrivel, shrink.

ballot *(SYN.)* vote, poll.

balmy *(SYN.)* soft, gentle, soothing, fragrant, mild.
(ANT.) tempestuous, stormy.

ban *(SYN.)* prohibit, outlaw, disallow, block, bar, exclude, obstruct, forbid.
(ANT.) allow, permit.

banal *(SYN.)* hackneyed, corny, vapid.
(ANT.) striking, original, fresh, stimulating, novel.

band *(SYN.)* company, association, crew, unite, gang.

bandit *(SYN.)* thief, robber, highwayman, marauder.

bang *(SYN.)* hit, strike, slam.

banish *(SYN.)* drive away, eject, exile, oust, deport.
(ANT.) receive, accept, shelter, admit,

harbor, welcome.

bank *(SYN.)* barrier, slope, storage, treasury, row.

banner *(SYN.)* colors, standard, pennant, flag.

banquet *(SYN.)* feast, celebration, festival, dinner, regalement, affair.

banter *(SYN.)* joke, tease, jest.

bar *(SYN.)* counter, impediment, saloon, exclude, obstacle, barricade, obstruct, shut out, hindrance, forbid, block, barrier, obstruction.
(ANT.) allow, permit, aid, encouragement.

barbarian *(SYN.)* brute, savage, boor, ruffian, rude, uncivilized, primitive, uncultured, barbaric, crude.
(ANT.) permit, allow, encouragement.

barbarous *(SYN.)* savage, remorseless, cruel, uncivilized, ruthless, inhuman.
(ANT.) kind, civilized, polite, humane, tasteful, cultivated.

barber *(SYN.)* coiffeur, hairdresser.

bare *(SYN.)* naked, nude, uncovered, undressed, unclothed, barren, empty, disclose, reveal, publicize, bald, expose, scarce, mere.
(ANT.) dressed, garbed, conceal, hide, disguise, clothed.

barefaced *(SYN.)* impudent, bold, insolent, brazen, shameless, rude.

barely *(SYN.)* hardly, scarcely.

bargain *(SYN.)* agreement, arrangement, deal, contract, arrange, sale.

baroque *(SYN.)* ornamented, elaborate, ornate.

barren *(SYN.)* unproductive, bare, unfruitful, infertile, sterile, childless.
(ANT.) productive, fruitful, fertile.

barricade *(SYN.)* fence, obstruction, shut in, fortification, barrier.
(ANT.) free, open, release.

barrier *(SYN.)* fence, wall, bar, railing, obstacle, hindrance, fortification, restraint.
(ANT.) assistance, aid, encouragement.

barter *(SYN.)* exchange, deal.

base *(SYN.)* bottom, rest, foundation, establish, found, immoral, evil, bad, poor, support, stand, low.
(ANT.) exalted, righteous, lofty, esteemed, noble, honored, refined, valuable.

bashful *(SYN.)* timorous, abashed, shy, coy, timid, diffident, modest, sheepish.
(ANT.) fearless, outgoing, adventurous, gregarious, aggressive, daring.

basic *(SYN.)* underlying, chief, essential, fundamental.
(ANT.) subsidiary, subordinate.

basis *(SYN.)* presumption, support, base, principle, groundwork, presupposition, foundation, postulate.
(ANT.) implication, trimming, derivative.

basket *(SYN.)* hamper, creel, dossier, bassinet.

bastion *(SYN.)* mainstay, support, staff, tower.

bat *(SYN.)* strike, hit, clout, stick, club, knock, crack.

batch *(SYN.)* group, set, collection, lot, cluster, bunch, mass, combination.

bath *(SYN.)* washing, shower, tub, wash, dip, soaping.

bathe *(SYN.)* launder, drench, swim, cover, medicate, immerse, wet, dip, soak.

bathing suit *(SYN.)* maillot, swimsuit, trunks.

bathos *(SYN.)* mawkishness, soppiness, sentimentality.

bathroom *(SYN.)* powder room, toilet, bath, lavatory.

baton *(SYN.)* mace, rod, staff, billy, crook, stick, fasces.

battalion *(SYN.)* mass, army, swarm, mob, drove, horde, gang, legion, regiment.

batten *(SYN.)* thrive, flourish, fatten, wax, expand, bloom.
(ANT.) decrease, weaken, fail.

batter *(SYN.)* pound, beat, hit, pommel, wallop, bash, smash, mixture, strike.

battery *(SYN.)* series, troop, force, rally, muster, set.

battle *(SYN.)* strife, fray, combat, struggle, contest, skirmish, conflict, fight, war, flight, warfare, action.
(ANT.) truce, concord, agreement, settlement, harmony, accept, concur, peace.

battlement *(SYN.)* parapet, crenellation, rampart, fort, bastion, escarpment.

bauble *(SYN.)* plaything, toy, trinket.

bawl *(SYN.)* sob, shout, wail, cry loudly,

bellow, weep, cry.

bay *(SYN.)* inlet, bayou, harbor, lagoon, sound, gulf.

bazaar *(SYN.)* fair, market, marketplace.

beach *(SYN.)* sands, seashore, waterfront, seaside, strand, coast, shore.

beacon *(SYN.)* light, signal, watchtower, guide, flare, warning, alarm.

bead *(SYN.)* globule, drop, pill, blob.

beak *(SYN.)* nose, bill.

beam *(SYN.)* gleam, ray, girder, cross-member, pencil, shine, glisten, glitter, gleam.

beaming *(SYN.)* joyful, bright, happy, radiant, grinning.
(ANT.) sullen, gloomy, threatening, scowling.

bear *(SYN.)* carry, support, take, uphold, suffer, convey, brook, transport, undergo, permit, abide, tolerate.
(ANT.) evade, shun, avoid, refuse, dodge.

bearable *(SYN.)* sufferable, supportable, manageable.
(ANT.) terrible, painful, unbearable, awful, intolerable.

bearing *(SYN.)* course, direction, position, posture, behavior, manner, carriage, relation, reference, air, way.

bearings *(SYN.)* orientation, whereabouts, location, direction, position, reading.

bear on *(SYN.)* affect.

bear out *(SYN.)* confirm, substantiate, justify, verify.

beast *(SYN.)* monster, savage, brute, creature, animal.

beastly *(SYN.)* detestable, mean, low, hateful, loath.
(ANT.) considerate, sympathetic, refined, humane, fine.

beat *(SYN.)* pulse, buffet, pound, defeat, palpitate, hit, rout, smite, throb, punch, conquer, batter, conquer.
(ANT.) stroke, fail, defend, surrender, shield.

beaten *(SYN.)* disheartened, dejected, licked, discouraged, hopeless.
(ANT.) eager, hopeful.

beatific *(SYN.)* uplifted, blissful, elated, happy, wonderful, joyful, divine.
(ANT.) awful, hellish, ill-fated, accursed.

beating *(SYN.)* whipping, drubbing, flog-ging, lashing, scourging, walloping.

beau *(SYN.)* lover, suitor, swain, admirer.

beautiful *(SYN.)* pretty, fair, lovely, charming, comely, handsome, attractive.
(ANT.) repulsive, hideous, unsightly, foul, homely, plainness, ugly, ugliness.

beauty *(SYN.)* handsomeness, fairness, charm, pulchritude, comeliness, grace.
(ANT.) ugliness, disfigurement, homeliness, plainness, deformity, eyesore.

becalm *(SYN.)* calm, quiet, smooth, still, hush, repose.

because *(SYN.)* inasmuch as, as, since, for.

because of *(SYN.)* as a result of, as a consequence of.

beckon *(SYN.)* call, signal, summon, motion, gesture.

becloud *(SYN.)* obfuscate, confuse, befog, confound.
(ANT.) illuminate, clarify.

become *(SYN.)* change, grow, suit, be appropriate, befit.

becoming *(SYN.)* suitable, meet, befitting, appropriate, attractive, pleasing, flatter.
(ANT.) unsuitable, inappropriate, incongruent, ugly, unattractive, improper.

bed *(SYN.)* layer, cot, vein, berth, stratum, couch, accumulation, bunk, deposit.

bedazzle *(SYN.)* glare, blind, dumbfound, flabbergast, bewilder, furbish, festoon.

bedeck *(SYN.)* deck, adorn, beautify, smarten, festoon.

bedlam *(SYN.)* tumult, uproar, madhouse.
(ANT.) calm, peace.

bedraggled *(SYN.)* shabby, muddy, sodden, messy.
(ANT.) dry, neat, clean, well-groomed.

bedrock *(SYN.)* basis, foundation, roots.
(ANT.) top, dome, apex, nonessentials.

beef *(SYN.)* brawn, strength, heft, gripe, sinew, fitness.

befall *(SYN.)* occur, come about, happen.

before *(SYN.)* prior, earlier, in advance, formerly.
(ANT.) behind, following, afterward, latterly, after.

befriend *(SYN.)* welcome, encourage, aid, stand by.

(ANT.) *dislike, shun, desert.*

befuddle (SYN.) stupefy, addle, confuse, rattle.

beg (SYN.) solicit, ask, implore, supplicate, entreat, request, importune, entreat.

(ANT.) *grant, cede, give, bestow, favor.*

beget (SYN.) sire, engender, produce, create, propagate, originate, procreate, father.

(ANT.) *murder, destroy, kill, abort, prevent, extinguish.*

beggar (SYN.) scrub, tatterdemalion, pauper, wretch.

begin (SYN.) open, enter, arise, initiate, commence, start, institute, create.

(ANT.) *terminate, complete, finish, close, end, stop.*

beginner (SYN.) nonprofessional, amateur, apprentice.

(ANT.) *veteran, professional.*

beginning (SYN.) outset, inception, origin, source, commencement.

(ANT.) *termination, completion, end, close, consummation, closing, ending, finish.*

begrime (SYN.) soil, dirty, smear, muddy, splotch.

(ANT.) *wash, clean, freshen, launder.*

begrudge (SYN.) resent, envy, stint, withhold, grudge.

begrudging (SYN.) hesitant, reluctant, resentful.

(ANT.) *willing, eager, quick, spontaneous.*

beguiling (SYN.) enchanting, interesting, delightful, intriguing, engaging, bewitching, enthralling, captivating.

(ANT.) *boring, dull, unattractive, tedious.*

behalf (SYN.) benefit, welfare, support, aid, part, interest.

behave (SYN.) deport, comport, manage, act, interact.

(ANT.) *rebel, misbehave.*

behavior (SYN.) manners, carriage, disposition, action, deed, conduct, demeanor.

(ANT.) *rebelliousness, misbehavior.*

behead (SYN.) decapitate, guillotine, decollate.

behest (SYN.) order, command, decree, mandate.

behind (SYN.) after, backward, at the back, in back of.

(ANT.) *frontward, ahead, before.*

behold (SYN.) look, see, view, notice, observe, perceive.

(ANT.) *overlook, ignore.*

being (SYN.) life, existing, existence, living, actuality, organism, individual.

(ANT.) *death, nonexistence, expiration.*

belabor (SYN.) repeat, reiterate, pound, explain.

belated (SYN.) late, delayed, overdue, tardy.

(ANT.) *well-timed, early.*

belch (SYN.) emit, erupt, gush, disgorge, bubble.

beleaguered (SYN.) bothered, beset, annoyed, beset, harassed, badgered, vexed.

belie (SYN.) distort, misrepresent, twist, disappoint.

belief (SYN.) trust, feeling, certitude, opinion, conviction, view, creed, assurance.

(ANT.) *heresy, denial, incredulity, distrust, skepticism.*

believe (SYN.) hold, apprehend, fancy, support.

(ANT.) *doubt, reject, distrust, disbelieve, question.*

believer (SYN.) adherent, follower, devotee, convert.

(ANT.) *doubter, critic, scoffer.*

belittle (SYN.) underrate, depreciate, minimize, decry, disparage, depreciate.

(ANT.) *esteem, admire, flatter, overrate, commend.*

bell (SYN.) pealing, ringing, signal, tolling, buzzer.

belligerent (SYN.) aggressive, warlike, hostile, offensive.

(ANT.) *easygoing, compromising, peaceful.*

bellow (SYN.) thunder, roar, scream, shout, yell, howl.

bellwether (SYN.) leader, pilot, guide, ringleader.

belly (SYN.) stomach, abdomen, paunch.

belonging (SYN.) loyalty, relationship, kinship, acceptance, rapport.

belongings (SYN.) property, effects, possessions.

beloved (SYN.) adored, sweet, loved,

cherished, prized.

below *(SYN.)* under, less, beneath, underneath, lower.

(ANT.) aloft, overhead, above, over.

belt *(SYN.)* girdle, sash, strap, cummerbund, band, waistband, punch.

bemoan *(SYN.)* mourn, lament, grieve, sorrow, regret.

bend *(SYN.)* turn, curve, incline, submit, bow, lean, crook, twist, yield, stoop,

(ANT.) resist, straighten, break, stiffen.

beneath *(SYN.)* under, below.

(ANT.) above, over.

benediction *(SYN.)* thanks, blessing, prayer.

beneficial *(SYN.)* salutary, good, wholesome, advantageous, useful, helpful.

(ANT.) harmful, destructive, injurious, disadvantageous, unwholesome, deleterious.

benefit *(SYN.)* support, help, gain, avail, profit, account, favor, aid, good, advantage, serve, interest, behalf.

(ANT.) handicap, calamity, trouble, disadvantage.

benevolence *(SYN.)* magnanimity, charity, tenderness, altruism, humanity, philanthropy, generosity, liberality, good will.

(ANT.) malevolence, unkindness, cruelty, selfishness.

benevolent *(SYN.)* kindhearted, tender, merciful, generous, altruistic, obliging, kind, good, well-wishing, philanthropy.

(ANT.) malevolent, greedy, wicked, harsh.

bent *(SYN.)* curved, crooked, resolved, determined, set, inclined, firm, decided.

(ANT.) straight.

berate *(SYN.)* scold.

beseech *(SYN.)* appeal, entreat, plead, ask, beg.

beset *(SYN.)* surround, attack.

besides *(SYN.)* moreover, further, except for, also, as well, furthermore.

besiege *(SYN.)* assault, attack, siege, bombard, raid.

bespeak *(SYN.)* engage, reserve, indicate, show.

best *(SYN.)* choice, prime, select.

(ANT.) worst.

bestial *(SYN.)* brutal, beastly, savage, cruel.

bestow *(SYN.)* confer, place, put, award, give, present.

(ANT.) withdraw, withhold.

bet *(SYN.)* gamble, give, stake, wager, pledge, ante.

betray *(SYN.)* reveal, deliver, expose, mislead, trick, deceive, exhibit, show.

(ANT.) shelter, protect, safeguard.

betrothal *(SYN.)* marriage, engagement, contract.

better *(SYN.)* superior, preferable, improve.

(ANT.) worsen.

beware *(SYN.)* take care, watch out, look sharp.

bewilder *(SYN.)* perplex, confuse, mystify, baffle, puzzle.

(ANT.) clarify, enlighten.

bewitch *(SYN.)* captivate, charm, delight, enchant.

beyond *(SYN.)* past, farther, exceeding.

bias *(SYN.)* slant, inclination, proneness, turn, bent, penchant, tendency, proclivity, prejudice, influence, warp.

(ANT.) fairness, justice, evenhandedness, equity.

bible *(SYN.)* guide, handbook, gospel, manual.

bibulous *(SYN.)* guzzling, intemperate, winebibbing, sottish, alcoholic.

(ANT.) sober, moderate.

bicker *(SYN.)* dispute, argue, wrangle, quarrel.

(ANT.) go along with, agree.

bid *(SYN.)* order, command, direct, wish, greet, say, offer, instruct, invite, purpose.

bidding *(SYN.)* behest, request, decree, call, charge, beck, summons, solicitation, invitation, instruction.

bide *(SYN.)* stay, tarry, delay, wait, remain.

big *(SYN.)* large, huge, bulky, immense, colossal, majestic, august, monstrous, hulking, enormous, tremendous.

(ANT.) small, little, tiny, immature, petite.

bighearted *(SYN.)* good-natured, liberal, generous, unselfish, openhanded, unstinting, charitable.

(ANT.) cold, selfish, mean, uncharitable.

bigoted (SYN.) intolerant, partial, prejudiced, biased.

bigotry (SYN.) bias, blindness, intolerance, unfairness, prejudice, ignorance, passion.

(ANT.) acceptance, open-mindedness.

bilk (SYN.) defraud, trick, cheat, hoodwink, deceive.

bill (SYN.) charge, invoice, account, statement.

billet (SYN.) housing, quarters, berth, shelter, barrack.

billow (SYN.) surge, swell, rise, rush, peaking.

(ANT.) lowering, decrease.

bin (SYN.) cubbyhole, box, container, chest, cubicle.

bind (SYN.) connect, restrain, band, fasten, oblige, obligate, engage, wrap, restrict.

(ANT.) unlace, loose, unfasten, untie, free.

binding (SYN.) compulsory, obligatory, mandatory, compelling, unalterable, imperative, indissoluble.

(ANT.) adjustable, flexible, elastic, changeable.

birth (SYN.) origin, beginning, infancy, inception.

(ANT.) finish, decline, death, disappearance, end.

bit (SYN.) fraction, portion, scrap, fragment, particle.

bite (SYN.) gnaw, chew, nip, sting, pierce, mouthful.

biting (SYN.) cutting, sharp, acid, sneering, sarcastic.

(ANT.) soothing, kind, gentle, agreeable.

bitter (SYN.) distasteful, sour, acrid, pungent, piercing, vicious, severe, biting, distressful, stinging.

(ANT.) sweet, mellow, pleasant, delicious.

bizarre (SYN.) peculiar, strange, odd, uncommon.

(ANT.) usual, everyday, ordinary, inconspicuous.

black (SYN.) sooty, dark, ebony, inky, swarthy, soiled, filthy, dirty, stained, somber, depressing, gloomy.

(ANT.) white, pure, cheerful, light-skinned, sunny, bright.

blackmail (SYN.) bribe, payment, bribery, extortion, shakedown, coercion.

blackout (SYN.) faint, coma, unconsciousness, oblivion.

bladder (SYN.) saccule, sac, vesicle, pouch, pod, cell.

blade (SYN.) cutter, lancet, knife, sword.

blame (SYN.) upbraid, criticize, fault, guilt, accuse, rebuke, charge, implicate, indict, responsibility.

(ANT.) exonerate, credit, honor, absolve.

blameless (SYN.) moral, innocent, worthy, faultless.

(ANT.) blameworthy, culpable, guilty.

blanch (SYN.) whiten, bleach, decolorize, peroxide, fade.

bland (SYN.) soft, smooth, gentle, agreeable, vapid.

(ANT.) harsh, outspoken, disagreeable.

blandish (SYN.) praise, compliment, overpraise, cajole, puff, adulate, salve, fawn, court, toady, please, jolly.

(ANT.) insult, deride, criticize, belittle.

blandisher (SYN.) adulator, booster, sycophant, eulogist, apple polisher, flunkey.

(ANT.) knocker, faultfinder, belittler.

blandishment (SYN.) applause, honey, adulation, fawning, compliments.

(ANT.) carping, belittling, criticism, deprecation.

blank (SYN.) unmarked, expressionless, uninterested, form, area, void, vacant.

(ANT.) marked, filled, alert, animated.

blanket (SYN.) quilt, coverlet, cover, comforter, robe, padding, carpet, wrapper, mantle, comprehensive, universal, panoramic, omnibus.

(ANT.) limited, detailed, restricted, precise.

blare (SYN.) roar, blast, resound, jar, scream, swell, clang, peal, trumpet, toot.

blasphemous (SYN.) profane, irreverent, impious, godless, sacrilegious, irreligious.

(ANT.) reverent, reverential, religious, pious.

blasphemy (SYN.) profanation, impiousness, cursing, irreverence, contempt.

(ANT.) respect, piety, reverence, devotion.

blast (SYN.) burst, explosion, discharge,

blowout.

blatant *(SYN.)* shameless, notorious, brazen, flagrant, glaring, bold, obvious. *(ANT.) deft, subtle, insidious.*

blaze *(SYN.)* inferno, shine, flare, marking, fire, outburst, holocaust, flame. *(ANT.) die, dwindle.*

bleach *(SYN.)* pale, whiten, blanch, whitener. *(ANT.) darken, blacken.*

bleak *(SYN.)* dreary, barren, cheerless, depressing, gloomy, bare, cold, dismal, desolate, raw, chilly. *(ANT.) lush, hopeful, promising, cheerful.*

bleary *(SYN.)* hazy, groggy, blurry, fuzzy, misty, clouded, overcast, dim, blear. *(ANT.) clear, vivid, precise.*

bleed *(syn.)* pity, lose blood, grieve, sorrow.

blemish *(SYN.)* injury, speck, flaw, scar, disgrace, imperfection, stain, fault, blot. *(ANT.) purity, embellishment, adornment, perfection.*

blend *(SYN.)* beat, intermingle, combine, fuse, unify, consolidate, amalgamate, conjoin, mix, coalesce, pound, combination, stir, mixture, commingle. *(ANT.) separate, decompose, analyze, disintegrate.*

bless *(SYN.)* thank, celebrate, extol, glorify, adore, delight, praise, gladden, exalt. *(ANT.) denounce, blaspheme, slander, curse.*

blessed *(SYN.)* sacred, holy, consecrated, dedicated, hallowed, sacrosanct, beatified. *(ANT.) miserable, sad, dispirited, cheerless.*

blessing *(SYN.)* benison, sanction, favor, grace, benediction, invocation, approbation, approval, compliment, bounty, windfall, gift, benefit, invocation. *(ANT.) disapproval, execration, curse, denunciation, malediction, rebuke, displeasure, condemnation.*

blight *(SYN.)* decay, disease, spoil, sickness, wither, ruin, damage, harm, decaying, epidemic, destroy.

blind *(SYN.)* sightless, unmindful, rash, visionless, ignorant, oblivious, purblind, unknowing, screen, unaware, thoughtless, shade, without thought, headlong. *(ANT.) discerning, sensible, calculated, perceiving, perceptive, aware.*

blink *(SYN.)* bat, glance, flicker, wink, twinkle.

bliss *(SYN.)* ecstasy, rapture, glee, elation, joy, blessedness, gladness, happiness, delight, felicity, blissfulness. *(ANT.) woe, sadness, sorrow, grief, unhappiness, torment, wretchedness, misery.*

blissful *(SYN.)* happy, elated, rapturous, esctatic, paradisiacal, joyous, enraptured.

blister *(SYN.)* bleb, swelling, welt, sore, blob, bubble, inflammation, boil, canker.

blithe *(SYN.)* breezy, merry, airy, lighthearted, light, gay, fanciful, graceful. *(ANT.) morose, grouchy, low-spirited, gloomy.*

blitz *(SYN.)* strike, onslaught, thrust, raid, lunge, drive, incursion, assault, sally.

blizzard *(SYN.)* storm, snowstorm, snowfall, gale, tempest, blast, blow, swirl.

bloat *(SYN.)* distend, puff up, inflate, swell. *(ANT.) deflate.*

blob *(SYN.)* bubble, blister, pellet, globule.

block *(SYN.)* clog, hinder, bar, impede, close, obstruct, barricade, blockade, check. *(ANT.) forward, promote, aid, clear, advance, advantage, assist, further, open.*

blockade *(SYN.)* barrier, fortification, obstruction.

blockhead *(SYN.)* dunce, dolt, fool, sap, idiot, simpleton, chump, booby, bonehead, woodenhead.

blood *(SYN.)* murder, gore, slaughter, bloodshed, ancestry, lineage, heritage.

bloodcurdling *(SYN.)* hair-raising, terrifying, alarming, chilling, stunning, scary.

bloodless *(SYN.)* dead, torpid, dull, drab, cold, colorless. *(ANT.) passionate, vital, ebullient, animated, vivacious.*

bloodshed *(SYN.)* murder, killing, slaying,

blood bath.

bloodthirsty *(SYN.)* murderous, cruel.

bloody *(SYN.)* cruel, pitiless, bloodthirsty, inhuman, ruthless, murderous.
(ANT.) kind, gentle.

bloom *(SYN.)* thrive, glow, flourish, blossom, flower.
(ANT.) wane, decay, dwindle, shrivel, wither.

blooming *(SYN.)* flush, green, vigorous, thriving, vital, abloom, healthy, fresh.
(ANT.) flagging, declining, whithering.

blooper *(SYN.)* muff, fluff, error, bungle, botch, blunder, fumble, howler.

blossom *(SYN.)* bloom, flower, flourish.
(ANT.) shrink, wither, dwindle, fade.

blot *(SYN.)* stain, inkblot, spot, inkstain, blemish, dishonor,obliterate, soil, dry.

blot out *(SYN.)* wipe out, destroy, obliterate, abolish, annihilate, cancel, expunge, strike out, shade, darken, shadow, cloud, eclipse.

blow *(SYN.)* hit, thump, slap, cuff, box, shock, move, drive, inflate, enlarge.

blowout *(SYN.)* blast, explosion, burst.

blue *(SYN.)* sapphire, azure, gloomy, sad, unhappy, depressed, dejected.
(ANT.) cheerful, optimistic, happy.

blueprint *(SYN.)* design, plan, scheme, chart, draft, prospectus, project, layout.

blues *(SYN.)* dumps, melancholy, depression, doldrums, moroseness.

blunder *(SYN.)* error, flounder, mistake, stumble.

blunt *(SYN.)* solid, abrupt, rough, dull, pointless, plain, bluff, edgeless.
(ANT.) tactful, polite, subtle, polished, suave, sharp, keen, pointed, diplomatic.

blur *(SYN.)* sully, dim, obscure, stain, dull, confuse.
(ANT.) clear, clarify.

blush *(SYN.)* redden.

board *(SYN.)* embark, committee, wood, mount, cabinet, food, get on, lumber.

boast *(SYN.)* vaunt, flaunt, brag, glory, crow.
(ANT.) humble, apologize, minimize, deprecate.

body *(SYN.)* remains, bulk, mass, carcass, form, company, cadaver, trunk.
(ANT.) spirit, intellect, soul.

bogus *(SYN.)* counterfeit, false,

pretend, fake, phony.
(ANT.) genuine.

boil *(SYN.)* seethe, bubble, fume, pimple, cook.

boisterous *(SYN.)* rough, violent, noisy, tumultuous.
(ANT.) serene.

bold *(SYN.)* daring, forward, adventurous, fearless, insolent, conspicuous, gallant.
(ANT.) modest, bashful, cowardly, timid, retiring.

bolt *(SYN.)* break away, fastener, flee, take flight, lock.

bombard *(SYN.)* shell, open fire, bomb, rake, assail.

bond *(SYN.)* fastener, rope, tie, cord, connection, attachment, link, promise.
(ANT.) sever, separate, untie, disconnect.

bondage *(SYN.)* slavery, thralldom, captivity, imprisonment, servitude.
(ANT.) liberation, emancipation, free, independence.

bonds *(SYN.)* chains, cuffs, fetters, shackles, irons.

bone up *(SYN.)* learn, master, study, relearn.

bonus *(SYN.)* more, extra, premium, gift, reward, bounty.

bony *(SYN.)* lean, lank, thin, lanky, rawboned, fleshless, skinny, gangling, weight.
(ANT.) plump, fleshy, stout.

book *(SYN.)* manual, textbook, work, booklet, mon, volume, paperback, text.

bookish *(SYN.)* formal, scholarly, theoretical.
(ANT.) simple, ignorant.

boom *(SYN.)* advance, grow, flourish, progress, gain, increase, roar, beam, rumble.
(ANT.) decline, fail, recession.

booming *(SYN.)* flourishing, blooming, thriving, vigorous, prospering, exuberant.
(ANT.) waning, dying, failing.

boon *(SYN.)* gift, jolly, blessing, pleasant, godsend.

boondocks *(SYN.)* sticks.

boor *(SYN.)* lout, clown, oaf, yokel, rustic, vulgarian.

boorish *(SYN.)* coarse, churlish, uncivil, ill-mannered, ill-bred, uncivilized, crude.
(ANT.) polite, cultivated, cultivated, well-mannered.

boost *(SYN.)* push, lift, help, hoist, shove.
(ANT.) depress, lower, belittle, submerge, disparage, decrease, decline, reduction.

booster *(SYN.)* supporter, fan, rooter, plugger, follower.

boot *(SYN.)* shoe, kick.

booth *(SYN.)* enclosure, cubicle, stand, compartment.

bootless *(SYN.)* purposeless, ineffective, profitless.
(ANT.) favorable, successful, useful.

bootlicker *(SYN.)* flunky, fawner, toady, sycophant.

booty *(SYN.)* prize, plunder, loot.

booze *(SYN.)* spirits, drink, liquor, alcohol.

border *(SYN.)* fringe, rim, verge, boundary, edge, termination, brink, limit, brim, outskirts, frontier, margin.
(ANT.) interior, center, mainland, core, middle.

borderline *(SYN.)* unclassifiable, indeterminate, halfway, indefinite, unclear.
(ANT.) precise, absolute, definite.

border on *(SYN.)* approximate, approach, resemble, echo, parallel, connect.

bore *(SYN.)* tire, weary, hole, perforate, pierce, drill.
(ANT.) arouse, captivate, excite, interest.

boredom *(SYN.)* ennui, doldrums, weariness, dullness.
(ANT.) stimulation, motive, activity, stimulus, excitement.

borrow *(SYN.)* copy, adopt, simulate, mirror, assume.
(ANT.) allow, advance, invent, originate, credit, lend.

bosom *(SYN.)* chest, breast, feelings, thoughts, mind.

boss *(SYN.)* director, employer, oversee, direct, foreman, supervisor, manager.
(ANT.) worker, employee, underling.

bossy *(SYN.)* overbearing, arrogant, domineering, highhanded, arbitrary, oppress.
(ANT.) flexible, easygoing.

botch *(SYN.)* blunder, bungle, fumble, goof, muff.

(ANT.) perform, realize.

bother *(SYN.)* haunt, molest, trouble, annoy, upset, fleeting, transient, harass.
(ANT.) prolonged, extended, long, protracted, lengthy.

bothersome *(SYN.)* irritating, vexatious, worrisome, annoying, distressing.

bottle *(SYN.)* container, flask, vessel, decanter, vial, ewer.

bottom *(SYN.)* basis, fundament, base, groundwork.
(ANT.) top, peak, apex, summit, topside.

bound *(SYN.)* spring, vault, bounce, skip, tied, shackled.
(ANT.) unfettered, free.

boundary *(SYN.)* bound, limit, border, margin, outline, division, frontier, edge.

boundless *(SYN.)* limitless, endless, inexhaustible, unlimited, eternal, infinite.
(ANT.) restricted, narrow, limited.

bounteous *(SYN.)* plentiful, generous, liberal, abundant.
(ANT.) scarce.

bountiful *(SYN.)* bounteous, fertile, plentiful, generous.
(ANT.) sparing, infertile, scarce.

bounty *(SYN.)* generosity, gift, award, bonus, reward.

bourgeois *(SYN.)* common, ordinary, commonplace.
(ANT.) upper-class, unconventional, loose, aristocratic.

bout *(SYN.)* round, contest, conflict, struggle, match.

bow *(SYN.)* bend, yield, kneel, submit, stoop.

bowl *(SYN.)* container, dish, pot, pottery, crock, jug, vase.

bow out *(SYN.)* give up, withdraw, retire, resign.

box *(SYN.)* hit, fight, crate, case, container.

boxer *(SYN.)* prizefighter.

boy *(SYN.)* male, youngster, lad, kid, fellow, buddy.
(ANT.) girl, man.

brace *(SYN.)* strengthen, tie, prop, support, tighten, stay, strut, bind, truss, crutch.

bracing *(SYN.)* stimulating, refreshing, restorative.

bracket *(SYN.)* join, couple, enclose, relate, brace.

brag *(SYN.)* boast, flaunt, vaunt, bluster, swagger.
(ANT.) demean, debase, denigrate, deprecate.

braid *(SYN.)* weave, twine, wreath, plait.

brain *(SYN.)* sense, intelligence, intellect, common sense, understanding.
(ANT.) stupid, stupidity.

brake *(SYN.)* decelerate, stop.
(ANT.) accelerate.

branch *(SYN.)* shoot, limb, bough, tributary, offshoot.

brand *(SYN.)* make, trademark, label, kind, burn.

brave *(SYN.)* bold, daring, gallant, valorous, adventurous, heroic, magnanimous.
(ANT.) weak, cringing, timid, cowardly, fearful, craven.

brawl *(SYN.)* racket, quarrel, fracas, riot, fight, melee.

brazen *(SYN.)* immodest, forward, shameless, bold.
(ANT.) retiring, modest, shy.

breach *(SYN.)* rupture, fracture, rift, break, crack, gap, opening, breaking, quarrel.
(ANT.) observation.

break *(SYN.)* demolish, pound, rack, smash, burst, rupture, opening, rupture.
(ANT.) restore, heal, join, renovate, mend, repair.

breed *(SYN.)* engender, bear, propagate, father, beget.
(ANT.) murder, abort, kill.

breeze *(SYN.)* air, wind, zephyr, breath.
(ANT.) calm.

breezy *(SYN.)* jolly, spry, active, brisk, energetic, lively.

brevity *(SYN.)* briefness, conciseness.
(ANT.) length.

brew *(SYN.)* plot, plan, cook, ferment, prepare, scheme.

bribe *(SYN.)* buy off.

bridle *(SYN.)* control, hold, restrain, harness, curb.
(ANT.) release, free, loose.

brief *(SYN.)* curt, short, fleeting, passing, compendious, terse, laconic, succinct.
(ANT.) long, extended, prolonged, lengthy, protracted, comprehensive, exten-

sive.

brigand *(SYN.)* bandit, robber, thief.

bright *(SYN.)* luminous, lucid, vivid, clear, smart, intelligent, lustrous, clever.
(ANT.) sullen, dull, murky, dark, gloomy, dim, lusterless, boring, backward, slow.

brilliant *(SYN.)* bright, clear, smart, intelligent, sparkling, shining, alert, vivid.
(ANT.) mediocre, dull, lusterless, second-rate.

brim *(SYN.)* border, margin, lip, rim, edge.
(ANT.) middle, center.

bring *(SYN.)* fetch, take, carry, raise, introduce, propose.
(ANT.) remove, withdraw.

brisk *(SYN.)* fresh, breezy, cool, lively, spry, refreshing, quick, active, animated.
(ANT.) musty, faded, stagnant, decayed, hackneyed, slow, lethargic, sluggish, still, dull, oppressive.

briskness *(SYN.)* energy, exercise, motion, rapidity.
(ANT.) inertia, idleness, sloth, inactivity.

brittle *(SYN.)* crumbling, frail, breakable, delicate, splintery, fragile, weak.
(ANT.) tough, enduring, unbreakable, thick, strong.

broach *(SYN.)* set afoot, introduce, inaugurate, start.

broad *(SYN.)* large, wide, tolerant, expanded, vast, liberal, sweeping, roomy.
(ANT.) restricted, slim, tight, limited, negligible.

broadcast *(SYN.)* distribute, announce, transmit, relay.

broaden *(SYN.)* spread, widen, amplify, enlarge, extend, increase, add to.
(ANT.) tighted, narrow, constrict, straiten.

broad-minded *(SYN.)* unprejudiced, liberal, unbigoted.
(ANT.) prejudiced, petty, narrow-minded.

brochure *(SYN.)* booklet, pamphlet, leaflet, mailing.

broken *(SYN.)* flattened, rent, shattered, wrecked, destroyed, reduced, smashed.
(ANT.) whole, integral, united, repaired.

brokenhearted *(SYN.)* disconsolate, forlorn, heartbroken.

bromide *(SYN.)* banality, platitude, stereotype, commonplace, slogan, proverb.

brook *(SYN.)* rivulet, run, branch, stream, creek.

brother *(SYN.)* comrade, man, kinsman, sibling.
(ANT.) sister.

brotherhood *(SYN.)* kinship, kindness, fraternity, fellowship, clan, society.
(ANT.) strife, discord, acrimony, opposition.

brotherly *(SYN.)* affectionate, fraternal, cordial, sympathetic, benevolent.

bruise *(SYN.)* hurt, injure, wound, damage, abrasion, damage, harm, wound.

brunt *(SYN.)* force, impact, shock, strain, oppression.

brush *(SYN.)* rub, wipe, clean, bushes, remove, shrubs, hairbrush, underbrush.

brush-off *(SYN.)* dismissal, snub, slight, rebuff.

brusque *(SYN.)* sudden, curt, hasty, blunt, rough, steep, precipitate, rugged, craggy, gruff, surly, abrupt, short.
(ANT.) smooth, anticipated, courteous, expected, gradual, personable.

brutal *(SYN.)* brute, cruel, gross, sensual, ferocious, brutish, coarse, remorseless, ruthless, mean, savage.
(ANT.) kind, courteous, humane, civilized, gentle, kindhearted, mild.

brute *(SYN.)* monster, barbarian, beast, animal, wild.

bubble *(SYN.)* boil, foam, seethe, froth.

buccaneer *(SYN.)* sea robber, privateer, pirate.

buck *(SYN.)* spring, jump, vault, leap.

bucket *(SYN.)* pot, pail, canister, can.

buckle *(SYN.)* hook, fastening, fastener, bend, wrinkle, clip, fasten, collapse, yield, warp.

bud *(SYN.)* develop, sprout.

buddy *(SYN.)* companion, comrade, friend, partner.

budge *(SYN.)* stir, move.

budget *(SYN.)* schedule, ration.

buff *(SYN.)* shine, polish, burnish, rub, wax.

buffet *(SYN.)* bat, strike, clout, blow,

knock, beat, crack, hit, slap, cabinet, counter.

buffoon *(SYN.)* jester, fool, clown, jokester, zany, comedian, chump, boor, dolt.

bug *(SYN.)* fault, hitch, defect, catch, snag, failing, rub, flaw, snarl, weakness, annoy, pester, hector, vex, nag.

bugbear *(SYN.)* bogy, specter, demon, devil, fiend.

build *(SYN.)* found, rear, establish, constructed, raise, set up, erect, assemble.
(ANT.) raze, destroy, overthrow, demolish, undermine.

building *(SYN.)* residence, structure, house, edifice.

buildup *(SYN.)* gain, enlargement, increase, praise, commendation, jump, expansion, uptrend, testimonial, plug, puff, blurb.
(ANT.) reduction, decrease, decline.

bulge *(SYN.)* lump, protuberance, bump, swelling, protrusion, extend.
(ANT.) hollow, shrink, contract, depression.

bulk *(SYN.)* lump, magnitude, volume, size, mass, most.

bulky *(SYN.)* great, big, huge, large, enormous, massive, immense, monstrous, clumsy, cumbersome, unwieldy.
(ANT.) tiny, little, small, petite, handy, delicate.

bull *(SYN.)* push, force, press, drive, thrust, bump.

bulldoze *(SYN.)* cow, bully, coerce, thrust, push.

bulletin *(SYN.)* news, flash, message, statement, newsletter, circular.

bullheaded *(SYN.)* dogged, stiff-necked, stubborn, mulish, rigid, pigheaded, willful, tenacious, unyielding.
(ANT.) flexible, submissive, compliant.

bully *(SYN.)* pester, tease, intimidate, harass, domineer.

bulwark *(SYN.)* wall, bastion, abutment, bank, dam, rampart, shoulder, parapet, backing, maintainer, embankment.

bum *(SYN.)* idler, loafer, drifter, hobo, wretch, dwadler, beggar, vagrant.

bumbling *(SYN.)* bungling, inept, blundering, clumsy, incompetent, awkward, maladroit, lumbering, ungainly.

(ANT.) facile, handy, dexterous.

bump *(SYN.)* shake, push, hit, shove, prod, collide.

bumpkin *(SYN.)* hick, yokel, rustic.

bumptious *(SYN.)* arrogant, self-assertive, conceited, forward, boastful. *(ANT.) sheepish, self-effacing, retiring, shrinking, unobtrusive, diffident.*

bumpy *(SYN.)* uneven, jolting, rough, jarring, rocky, coarse, craggy, irregular. *(ANT.) flat, smooth, flush, polished, level.*

bunch *(SYN.)* batch, bundle, cluster, company, collection, flock, group.

bundle *(SYN.)* package, mass, collection, batch, parcel, packet, box, carton.

bungalow *(SYN.)* ranch house, cabana, cabin, cottage, lodge, summer house.

bungle *(SYN.)* tumble, botch, foul up, boggle, mess up.

bunk *(SYN.)* berth, rubbish, nonsense, couch, bed, cot.

buoyant *(SYN.)* light, jolly, spirited, effervescent, blithe, sprightly, lively, resilient, vivacious, afloat, floating. *(ANT.) hopeless, dejected, sullen, depressed, heavy, despondent, sinking.*

burden *(SYN.)* oppress, afflict, trouble, encumber, tax, weight, load, worry, contents, trial, lade, overload. *(ANT.) lighten, alleviate, ease, mitigate, console, disburden.*

burdensome *(SYN.)* arduous, cumbersome, trying, hard, difficult.

bureau *(SYN.)* office, division, department, unit, commission, chest, dresser.

bureaucrat *(SYN.)* clerk, official, functionary, servant.

burglar *(SYN.)* thief, robber.

burial *(SYN.)* interment.

burly *(SYN.)* husky, beefy, heavyset, brawny, strapping. *(ANT.) skinny, scrawny.*

burn *(SYN.)* scorch, blaze, scald, sear, char, incinerate, fire, combust, flame. *(ANT.) quench, extinguish.*

burnish *(SYN.)* polish, shine, buff, rub.

burrow *(SYN.)* tunnel, search, seek, dig, excavate, hunt.

burst *(SYN.)* exploded, broken, erupt.

bury *(SYN.)* hide, inhume, conceal, immure, cover, inter, entomb, secrete. *(ANT.) reveal, display, open, raise.*

business *(SYN.)* employment, profession, trade, work, art, engagement, vocation, occupation, company, concern, firm. *(ANT.) hobby, avocation.*

bustle *(SYN.)* noise, flurry, action, trouble, fuss, ado, stir. *(ANT.) calmness, composure, serenity.*

bustling *(SYN.)* humming, busy, stirring, vibrant, bubbling, alive, active, moving, jumping, astir, zealous, enterprising.

busy *(SYN.)* careful, industrious, active, patient, assiduous, diligent, perseverant, hardworking. *(ANT.) unconcerned, indifferent, apathetic, lethargic, careless, inactive, unemployed, lazy, indolent.*

busybody *(SYN.)* gossip, tattletale, pry, meddler, snoop.

but *(SYN.)* nevertheless, yet, however, though, although.

butcher *(SYN.)* kill, murder, slaughter, assassinate, slay. *(ANT.) save, protect, vivify, animate.*

butt *(SYN.)* bump, ram, bunt, shove, jam, drive, punch, blow, push, thrust.

buttocks *(SYN.)* hind end, rump, posterior, backside, behind, bottom, rear.

button *(SYN.)* clasp, close, fasten, hook.

buttress *(SYN.)* support, brace, stay, frame, prop, reinforcement, bulwark, backing, encourage, sustain, reassure, boost, bolster.

buxom *(SYN.)* well-developed, chesty, ample, fleshy, full-figured, zaftig.

buy *(SYN.)* procure, get, purchase, acquire, obtain. *(ANT.) vend, sell.*

buzz *(SYN.)* whir, hum, thrum, burr.

by *(SYN.)* near, through, beside, with, from, at, close to.

bygone *(SYN.)* bypast, former, earlier, past, older. *(ANT.) immediate, present, modern.*

bypass *(SYN.)* deviate from, go around, detour around.

by-product *(SYN.)* offshoot, spin-off, effect, extra, outgrowth, bonus, side effecte issue, rider.

bystander *(SYN.)* onlooker, watcher, viewer, observer.

byway *(SYN.)* passage, detour.

byword *(SYN.)* adage, proverb, axiom.

cab *(SYN.)* coach, taxi, car, hack, taxicab, carriage.

cabin *(SYN.)* cottage, shack, shanty, hut, dwelling, house.

cad *(SYN.)* knave, rascal, scoundrel, rogue.

cafeteria *(SYN.)* cafe, diner, restaurant.

cagey *(SYN.)* cunning, wary, clever, tricky, cautious.
(ANT.) innocent, straight-foward, guileless, naive.

calamity *(SYN.)* ruin, disaster, casualty, distress, hardship, trouble, misfortune.
(ANT.) blessing, fortune.

calculate *(SYN.)* count, compute, figure, estimate, multiply, judge, reckon.
(ANT.) guess, miscalculate, assume, conjecture.

calculating *(SYN.)* crafty, shrewd, scheming, cunning.
(ANT.) simple, guileless, direct, ingenuous.

call *(SYN.)* designate, name, yell, cry, ask, shout, speak, phone, ring up, collect, waken, awaken, ring, wake.

calling *(SYN.)* occupation, profession, trade.

callous *(SYN.)* insensitive, impenitent, obdurate, unfeeling, insensible, heartless.
(ANT.) soft, compassionate, tender.

calm *(SYN.)* appease, lull, quiet, soothe, composed, tranquilize, dispassionate, pacify, alloy, assuage.
(ANT.) tempestuous, disturbed, emotional, turmoil, incite, inflame.

campaign *(SYN.)* movement, cause, crusade.

can *(SYN.)* tin, container.

canal *(SYN.)* gully, tube, duct, waterway.

cancel *(SYN.)* eliminate, obliterate, erase, delete, nullify, repeal, revoke, cross out, set aside, abolish.
(ANT.) perpetuate, confirm, ratify, enforce, enact.

candid *(SYN.)* free, blunt, frank, plain, open, sincere, honest, outspoken.
(ANT.) sly, contrived, wily.

candidate *(SYN.)* applicant, aspirant, nominee.

canine *(SYN.)* pooch, dog.

canny *(SYN.)* artful, skillful, shrewd, clever, cautious.

canopy *(SYN.)* awning, screen, shelter, cover.

cant *(SYN.)* dissimulation, patois, jargon, shoptalk, deceit, argot, pretense.
(ANT.) honesty, condor, frankness, truth.

cantankerous *(SYN.)* crabby, grouchy, irritable, surly, ill-natured, grumpy, irascible.

canyon *(SYN.)* gulch, gully, arroyo, ravine, gorge.

cap *(SYN.)* top, cover, crown, beat, lid, excel.

capability *(SYN.)* aptness, ability, capacity, aptitude, dexterity, power, efficiency.
(ANT.) incapacity, disability.

capable *(SYN.)* clever, qualified, able, efficient, competent, skilled, fit, skillful, accomplished, fitted.
(ANT.) unfitted, incapable, incompetent, unskilled, inept.

capacity *(SYN.)* capability, power, ability, talent, content, skill, volume, size.
(ANT.) inability, stupidity, incapacity, impotence.

cape *(SYN.)* pelisse, cloak, mantle, neck, point, headland, peninsula.

caper *(SYN.)* romp, frisk, cavort, frolic, gambol.

capital *(SYN.)* leading, chief, important, property, wealth, money, city, cash, assets, principal, resources, major, primary, first, funds.
(ANT.) unimportant, trivial.

capricious *(SYN.)* undependable, erratic, inconstant, fickle, changeable, irregular, inconsistent, unstable.

captain *(SYN.)* commander, authority, supervisor, leader, skipper, commander, master, officer.

caption *(SYN.)* heading, title.

captivate *(SYN.)* fascinate, charm, delight.

captive *(SYN.)* convict, prisoner, hostage.

captivity *(SYN.)* detention, imprisonment, custody, confinement, bondage, slavery.
(ANT.) liberty, freedom.

capture *(SYN.)* catch, grip, apprehend, clutch, arrest, snare, seize, nab, seizure.
(ANT.) set free, lose, liberate, throw, free, release.

car *(SYN.)* auto, automobile, motorcar, vehicle.

carcass *(SYN.)* remains, frame, corpse, form, bulk, mass, corpus, association. *(ANT.)* mind, spirit, intellect, soul.

cardinal *(SYN.)* chief, primary, important, prime, leading, major, essential. *(ANT.)* subordinate, secondary, auxiliary.

care *(SYN.)* concern, anxiety, worry, caution, solicitude, charge, ward, attention, regard, supervision, consider, consideration, keeping. *(ANT.)* neglect, disregard, indifference, unconcern.

career *(SYN.)* occupation, profession, job, calling, vocation, trade.

carefree *(SYN.)* lighthearted, happy, unconcerned, breezy, jolly, uneasy, nonchalant.

careful *(SYN.)* prudent, thoughtful, attentive, cautious, painstaking, scrupulous, heedful, circumspect, vigilant. *(ANT.)* heedless, messy, careless, accurate, incautious, sloppy, meticulous.

careless *(SYN.)* imprudent, heedless, unconcerned, inattentive, lax, indiscreet. *(ANT.)* careful, nice, cautious, painstaking, prudent.

caress *(SYN.)* hug, fondle, embrace, pet, pat, stroke, kiss. *(ANT.)* spurn, vex, buffet, annoy, tease.

cargo *(SYN.)* freight, load, freightload, shipment.

caricature *(SYN.)* exaggeration, parody, spoof, takeoff.

carnage *(SYN.)* massacre, liquidation, slaughter.

carnal *(SYN.)* base, corporeal, animal, lustful, worldly. *(ANT.)* intellectual, spiritual, exalted, temperate.

carnival *(SYN.)* fete, fair, jamboree, festival.

carol *(SYN.)* hymn, song.

carp *(SYN.)* pick, praise.

carpet *(SYN.)* mat, rug.

carping *(SYN.)* discerning, exact, captions, accurate, fastidious, important. *(ANT.)* superficial, cursory, approving, encouraging, unimportant, insignificant.

carriage *(SYN.)* bearing, conduct, action, deed, behavior, demeanor, disposition.

carry *(SYN.)* convey, transport, support, bring, sustain. *(ANT.)* drop, abandon.

carry off *(SYN.)* seize, abduct, capture, kidnap. *(ANT.)* set free, let go, liberate.

carry on *(SYN.)* go on, continue, proceed, misbehave. *(ANT.)* stop.

carry out *(SYN.)* succeed, complete, fulfill, win, accomplish, effect.

carve *(SYN.)* hew, shape, cut, whittle, chisel, sculpt.

case *(SYN.)* state, covering, receptacle, condition, instance, example, occurrence, happening, illustration, claim, lawsuit, crate.

cash *(SYN.)* currency, money.

casket *(SYN.)* coffin, box.

cast *(SYN.)* fling, toss, throw, pitch, form, company, shape, turn, actors, players.

caste *(SYN.)* class, grade, order, category, status, elegance, set, rank, station, social standing.

castle *(SYN.)* mansion, palace, chateau.

casual *(SYN.)* chance, unexpected, informal, accidental, incidental, offhand, unplanned, relaxed. *(ANT.)* planned, expected, calculated, formal, deliberate, dressy.

casualty *(SYN.)* calamity, fortuity, mishap, loss, injured, dead, wounded, accident, contingency, victim. *(ANT.)* design, purpose, intention, calculation.

catalog *(SYN.)* classify, roll, group, list, inventory, directory, index, record, file.

catastrophe *(SYN.)* mishap, calamity, disaster, adversity, accident, ruin. *(ANT.)* fortune, boon, triumph, blessing, advantage.

catch *(SYN.)* hook, snare, entrap, ensnare, capture, grip, apprehend, grasp, take, grab, nab, arrest, contract, snare, seize, apprehension, latch, bolt, pin. *(ANT.)* lose, free, liberate, throw, release.

catching *(SYN.)* contagious, pestilential, communicable, infectious, virulent. *(ANT.)* noncommunicable, healthful.

catchy *(SYN.)* tricky, misleading, attractive.

category *(SYN.)* class, caste, kind, order, genre, rank, classification, sort, elegance.

cater *(SYN.)* coddle, oblige, serve, humor, baby, mollycoddle, pamper, spoil.

cause *(SYN.)* effect, incite, create, induce, inducement, occasion, incentive, prompt, principle, determinant.

caustic *(SYN.)* bitter, disagreeable, distasteful, acrid, sour, spiteful, pungent, tart, painful, cruel, insulting.
(ANT.) mellow, sweet, delicious, pleasant.

caution *(SYN.)* heed, vigilance, care, prudence, counsel, warning, wariness, advice, warn, injunction.
(ANT.) carelessness, heedlessness, incaution, abandon.

cautious *(SYN.)* heedful, scrupulous, attentive, prudent, thoughtful, discreet.
(ANT.) improvident, headstrong, heedless, foolish.

cavalcade *(SYN.)* column, procession, parade.

cavalier *(SYN.)* contemptuous, insolent, haughty.

cave *(SYN.)* grotto, hole, shelter, lair, den, cavern.

cave in *(SYN.)* fall in, collapse.

cavity *(SYN.)* pit, hole, crater.

cavort *(SYN.)* caper, leap, frolic, hop, prance.

cease *(SYN.)* desist, stop, abandon, discontinue, relinquish, end, terminate, leave.
(ANT.) occupy, continue, persist, begin, endure, stay.

cede *(SYN.)* surrender, relinquish, yield.

celebrate *(SYN.)* honor, glorify, commemorate, keep.
(ANT.) decry, overlook, profane, disregard, disgrace.

celebrated *(SYN.)* eminent, glorious, distinguished, noted, illustrious, famed, well-known, popular.
(ANT.) obscure, hidden, anonymous, infamous.

celebrity *(SYN.)* somebody, personage, heroine, hero, dignitary, notable.

celestial *(SYN.)* godlike, holy, supernatural, divine, paradisiacal, utopian.
(ANT.) diabolical, profane, mundane, wicked.

cement *(SYN.)* solidify, weld, fasten, secure.

cemetery *(SYN.)* graveyard.

censure *(SYN.)* denounce, reproach, upbraid, blame, disapproval, reprehend.
(ANT.) commend, approval, forgive, approve, praise, applaud, condone.

center *(SYN.)* heart, core, midpoint, middle, nucleus, inside, hub, focus.
(ANT.) rim, boundary, edge, border, periphery, outskirts.

central *(SYN.)* chief, necessary, main, halfway, dominant, mid, middle, inner.
(ANT.) side, secondary, incidental, auxiliary.

ceremonious *(SYN.)* correct, exact, precise, stiff, outward, external, solemn, formal.
(ANT.) material, unconventional, easy, heartfelt.

ceremony *(SYN.)* observance, rite, parade, formality.
(ANT.) informality.

certain *(SYN.)* definite, assured, fixed, inevitable, sure, undeniable, positive.
(ANT.) probable, uncertain, doubtful, questionable.

certainly *(SYN.)* absolutely, surely, definitely.
(ANT.) dubiously, doubtfully, questionably.

certainty *(SYN.)* confidence, courage, security, assuredness, firmness, assertion.
(ANT.) humility, bashfulness, modest, shyness.

certificate *(SYN.)* affidavit, document.

certify *(SYN.)* validate, affirm, verify, confirm, authenticate, substantiate.

certitude *(SYN.)* confidence, belief, conviction, feeling, faith, persuasion, trust.
(ANT.) doubt, incredulity, denial, heresy.

cessation *(SYN.)* ending, finish, stoppage, termination, conclusion, end.

chain *(SYN.)* fasten, bind, shackle, restrain.

challenge *(SYN.)* question, dare, call, summon, threat, invite, threaten, demand.

chamber *(SYN.)* cell, salon.

champion *(SYN.)* victor, winner, choice,

best, conqueror, hero, support, select.

chance *(SYN.)* befall, accident, betide, disaster, opportunity, calamity, occur, possibility, prospect, happen.

(ANT.) design, purpose, inevitability, calculation, certainty, intention.

change *(SYN.)* modification, alternation, alteration, mutation, variety, exchange, shift, alter, transfigure, veer.

(ANT.) uniformity, monotony, settle, remain, endure, retain, preserve, immutability.

changeable *(SYN.)* fitful, fickle, inconstant, unstable.

(ANT.) stable, uniform, constant, unchanging.

channel *(SYN.)* strait, corridor, waterway, artery, duct, canal, way, trough.

chant *(SYN.)* singing, incantation, hymn, intone, sing, carol, psalm, song, ballad.

chaos *(SYN.)* confusion, jumble, turmoil, anarchy, disorder, muddle.

(ANT.) organization, order, tranquillity, tidiness, system.

chaotic *(SYN.)* confused, disorganized, disordered.

(ANT.) neat, ordered, systematic, organized.

chapter *(SYN.)* part, section.

char *(SYN.)* scorch, singe, burn, sear.

character *(SYN.)* description, class, kind, repute, mark, individuality, disposition, traits, personality.

charge *(SYN.)* arraignment, indictment, accusation, sell for, attack, assail, assault.

(ANT.) pardon, flee, exculpation, excuse, absolve, retreat, exoneration.

charity *(SYN.)* benevolence, kindness, magnanimity.

(ANT.) malevolence, cruelty, selfishness.

charm *(SYN.)* allure, spell.

chart *(SYN.)* design, plan, cabal, plot, sketch, stratagem, map, diagram, conspiracy, graph, intrigue.

charter *(SYN.)* lease, hire, rent, alliance.

chase *(SYN.)* hunt, run after, pursue, trail, follow, persist.

(ANT.) escape, flee, abandon, elude, evade.

chasm *(SYN.)* ravine, abyss, canyon, gorge.

(ANT.) crude, rude, impolite.

chivalry *(SYN.)* courtesy, nobility, gallantry.

choice *(SYN.)* delicate, elegant, fine, dainty, exquisite, pure, refined, subtle, splendid, handsome, option.

(ANT.) coarse, rough, thick, blunt, large.

choose *(SYN.)* elect, decide between, pick, select, cull.

(ANT.) reject, refuse.

chop *(SYN.)* hew, cut, fell.

chore *(SYN.)* routine, task, job, duty, work.

chronic *(SYN.)* persistent, constant, lingering, continuing, perennial, unending, sustained, permanent.

(ANT.) fleeting, acute.

chronicle *(SYN.)* detail, history, narrative, account, description, narration, recital.

(ANT.) misrepresentation, confusion, distortion.

circle *(SYN.)* disk, ring, set, group. class, club, surround.

circuit *(SYN.)* circle, course, journey, orbit, revolution.

circular *(SYN.)* chubby, complete, curved, bulbous.

(ANT.) straight.

circumference *(SYN.)* border, perimeter, periphery, edge.

circumspection *(SYN.)* care, worry, solicitude, anxiety.

(ANT.) neglect, negligence.

circumstance *(SYN.)* fact, event, incident, condition, happening, position, occurrence, situation.

cite *(SYN.)* affirm, assign, allege, advance, quote, mention, declare, claim.

(ANT.) refute, gainsay, deny.

citizen *(SYN.)* native, inhabitant, national, denizen, subject, dweller, resident.

civil *(SYN.)* courteous, cultivated, accomplished, public, municipal, respectful.

(ANT.) uncouth, uncivil, impertinent, impolite, boorish.

civilization *(SYN.)* cultivation, culture, education, breeding, enlightenment, society.

(ANT.) ignorance, vulgarity.

chaste *(SYN.)* clear, immaculate, innocent, sincere, bare.
(ANT.) polluted, tainted, foul, impure, sinful, worldly.

chat *(SYN.)* argue, jabber, blab, plead, consult, converse, lecture, discuss, talk.

chatter *(SYN.)* dialogue, lecture, speech, conference.
(ANT.) silence, correspondence, writing.

cheap *(SYN.)* poor, common, inexpensive, shabby, beggary.
(ANT.) honorable, dear, noble, expensive, costly.

cheat *(SYN.)* deceive, fool, bilk, outwit, victimize, dupe.

check *(SYN.)* dissect, interrogate, analyze, contemplate, inquire, question.
(ANT.) overlook, disregard, advance, foster, continue.

checkup *(SYN.)* medical examination, physical.

cheek *(SYN.)* nerve, effrontery, impudence, gall.

cheer *(SYN.)* console, gladden, comfort, encourage, applause, encouragement, joy, glee, gaiety, mirth.
(ANT.) depress, sadden, discourage, derision, dishearten.

cheerful *(SYN.)* glad, jolly, joyful, gay, happy, cherry.
(ANT.) mournful, sad, glum, depressed, gloomy, sullen.

cherish *(SYN.)* prize, treasure, appreciate, nurse, value.
(ANT.) disregard, neglect, deprecate, scorn, reject.

chest *(SYN.)* bosom, breast, coffer, box, case, trunk, casket, dresser, commode.

chew *(SYN.)* gnaw, munch, bite, nibble.

childish *(SYN.)* immature, childlike, infantile, babyish.
(ANT.) mature, adult, grown-up.

chill *(SYN.)* coolness, cold, cool, coldness, brisk, frosty.
(ANT.) hot, warm, heat, heated, warmth.

chilly *(SYN.)* cold, frigid, freezing, arctic, cool, icy, passionless, wintry.
(ANT.) fiery, heated, passionate, ardent.

chirp *(SYN.)* peep, cheep, twitter, tweet, chirrup.

chivalrous *(SYN.)* noble, brave, polite, valorous, gallant, gentlemanly.

civilize *(SYN.)* refine, tame, polish, cultivate, instruct.

claim *(SYN.)* aver, declare, allege, assert, affirm, express, state, demand, maintain.
(ANT.) refute, deny, contradict.

clamor *(SYN.)* cry, din, babel, noise, racket, outcry, row, sound tumult, shouting.
(ANT.) hush, serenity, silence, tranquility, stillness, quiet.

clan *(SYN.)* fellowship, kindness, solidarity, family.
(ANT.) discord, strife, opposition, acrimony.

clandestine *(SYN.)* covert, hidden, latent, private, concealed, secret, unknown.
(ANT.) exposed, known, conspicuous, obvious.

clarify *(SYN.)* educate, explain, expound, decipher, illustrate, clear, resolve, define, interpret, unfold.
(ANT.) darken, obscure, baffle, confuse.

clash *(SYN.)* clank, crash, clang, conflict, disagreement, opposition, collision, struggle, mismatch.
(ANT.) accord, agreement, harmony, blend, harmonize, match, agree.

clasp *(SYN.)* grip, hold, grasp, adhere, clutch, keep, have, maintain, possess, occupy.
(ANT.) relinquish, vacate, surrender, abandon.

class *(SYN.)* category, denomination, caste, kind, genre, grade, rank, order, elegance, classification.

classic *(SYN.)* masterpiece.

classification *(SYN.)* order, category, class, arrangement, ordering, grouping.

classify *(SYN.)* arrange, class, order, sort, grade, group.

clause *(SYN.)* condition, paragraph, limitation, article.

claw *(SYN.)* hook, talon, nail.

clean *(SYN.)* mop, tidy, neat, dustless, clear, unsoiled, immaculate, unstained, untainted, pure, dust, vacuum.
(ANT.) stain, soil, pollute, soiled, impure, dirty, stain.

cleanse *(SYN.)* mop, purify, wash, sweep.
(ANT.) stain, soil, dirty.

clear *(SYN.)* fair, sunny, cloudless,

transparent, apparent, limpid, distinct, intelligible, evident.
(ANT.) obscure, unclear, muddled, confused, dark, cloudy, blocked.

clearly *(SYN.)* plainly, obviously, evidently, definitely.
(ANT.) questionably, dubiously.

clemency *(SYN.)* forgiveness, charity, compassion, grace, mercy, leniency, pity.
(ANT.) punishment, vengeance, retribution.

clerical *(SYN.)* ministerial, pastoral, priestly, celestial, holy, sacred, secretarial.

clerk *(SYN.)* typist, office worker, office girl, saleslady, salesperson, salesclerk.

clever *(SYN.)* apt, dexterous, quick, adroit, quick-witted, talented, bright, skillful, witty, ingenious, smart.
(ANT.) unskilled, slow, stupid, backward, maladroit, bungling, dull, clumsy.

cleverness *(SYN.)* intellect, intelligence, comprehension, mind, perspicacity, sagacity.
(ANT.) sobriety, stupidity, solemnity, commonplace.

client *(SYN.)* patron.

cliff *(SYN.)* scar, tor, bluff, crag, precipice, escarpment.

climate *(SYN.)* aura, atmosphere, air, ambience.

climax *(SYN.)* apex, culmination, peak, summit, consummation, height, acme.
(ANT.) depth, base, anticlimax, floor.

climb *(SYN.)* mount, scale.
(ANT.) descend.

clip *(SYN.)* snip, crop, cut, mow, clasp.

cloak *(SYN.)* conceal, cover, disguise, clothe, cape, guard, envelop, hide, mask.
(ANT.) divulge, expose, reveal, bare, unveil.

clod *(SYN.)* wad, hunk, gobbet, lump, chunk, clot, gob, dunce, dolt, oaf, fool.

clog *(SYN.)* crowd, congest, cram, overfill, stuff.

cloister *(SYN.)* monastery, priory, hermitage, abbey.

close *(SYN.)* adjacent, adjoining, immediate, unventilated, stuffy, abutting.
(ANT.) afar, faraway, removed, distant.

closet *(SYN.)* cabinet, locker, wardrobe, cupboard.

cloth *(SYN.)* fabric, goods, material, textile.

clothe *(SYN.)* garb, dress, apparel.
(ANT.) strip, undress.

clothes *(SYN.)* array, attire, apparel, clothing, dress, garb, dress, garments, raiment, drapery, vestments.
(ANT.) nudity, nakedness.

clothing *(SYN.)* attire, clothes, apparel, array, dress, drapery, garments, garb, vestments.
(ANT.) nudity, nakedness.

cloud *(SYN.)* fog, mist, haze, mass, collection, obscure, dim, shadow.

cloudy *(SYN.)* dim, dark, indistinct, murky, mysterious, indefinite, vague, sunless, clouded, obscure, overcast, shadowy.
(ANT.) sunny, clear, distinct, limpid, lucid, clarified, cloudless, clearheaded, brilliant, bright.

club *(SYN.)* society, association, set, circle, organization, bat, cudgel, stick, blackjack.

clue *(SYN.)* sign, trace, hint, suggestion.

clumsy *(SYN.)* bungling, inept, rough, unpolished, bumbling, awkward, ungraceful, gauche, ungainly, unskillful, untoward.
(ANT.) polished, skillful, neat, graceful, dexterous, adroit.

cluster *(SYN.)* batch, clutch, group, bunch, gather, pack, assemble, crowd.

clutch *(SYN.)* grip, grab, seize, hold.

coalition *(SYN.)* combination, association, alliance, confederacy, entente, league, treaty.
(ANT.) schism, separation, divorce.

coarse *(SYN.)* unpolished, vulgar, refined, rough, smooth, impure, rude, crude, gruff, gross, cultivated, delicate, cultured.
(ANT.) delicate, smooth, refined, polished, genteel, cultivated, suave, fine, cultured.

coast *(SYN.)* seaboard, seashore, beach, shore, drift, glide, ride.

coax *(SYN.)* urge, persuade, wheedle, cajole.
(ANT.) force, bully, coerce.

coddle *(SYN.)* pamper, baby, spoil, indulge.

code *(SYN.)* crypt, cryptogram, cipher.

coerce *(SYN.)* constrain, compel, enforce, force, drive, oblige, impel.
(ANT.) prevent, persuade, convince, induce.

coercion *(SYN.)* emphasis, intensity, energy, dint, might potency, power, vigor, strength, compulsion, force, constraint, violence.
(ANT.) impotence, frailty, feebleness, weakness, persuasion.

cognizance *(SYN.)* apprehension, erudition, acquaintance, information, learning, knowledge, lore, science, scholarship, understanding.
(ANT.) illiteracy, misunderstanding, ignorance.

cognizant *(SYN.)* conscious, aware, apprised informed, mindful, observant, perceptive.
(ANT.) unaware, ignorant, oblivious, insensible.

coherent *(SYN.)* logical, intelligible, sensible, rational, commonsensical, reasonable.

coiffeur *(SYN.)* hairdresser.

coiffure *(SYN.)* haircut, hairdo.

coincide *(SYN.)* acquiesce, agree, accede, assent, consent, comply, correspond, concur, match, tally, harmonize, conform.
(ANT.) differ, disagree, protest, contradict.

coincidence *(SYN.)* accident, chance.
(ANT.) plot, plan, prearrangement, scheme.

coincident *(SYN.)* identical, equal, equivalent, distinguishable, same, like.
(ANT.) distinct, contrary, disparate, opposed.

coincidental *(SYN.)* unpredicted, unexpected, chance, unforeseen, accidental, fortuitous.

cold *(SYN.)* cool, freezing, chilly, frigid, icy, frozen, wintry, arctic, unfriendly, indifferent, phlegmatic, stoical, passionless, chill, unemotional, heartless, unfeeling.
(ANT.) hot, torrid, fiery, burning, ardent, friendly, temperate, warm, passionate.

collapse *(SYN.)* descend, decrease, diminish, fail, downfall, failure, decline, fall, drop, sink, subside, topple.
(ANT.) soar, steady, limb, mount, arise.

colleague *(SYN.)* companion, attendant, comrade, associate, crony, mate, friend, partner.
(ANT.) enemy, stranger, adversary.

collect *(SYN.)* assemble, amass, concentrate, pile, accumulate, congregate, obtain, heap, gather, solicit, secure, procure, raise, get, mass, hoard, consolidate.
(ANT.) divide, dole, assort, dispel, distribute, disperse.

collected *(SYN.)* cool, calm, composed, peaceful, imperturbable, placid, sedate, quiet.
(ANT.) excited, violent, aroused, agitated.

collection *(SYN.)* amount, conglomeration, sum, entirety, aggregation, hoard, accumulation, pile, store, aggregate, total, whole.
(ANT.) part, unit, particular, element, ingredient.

collide *(SYN.)* hit, smash, crash, strike.

collision *(SYN.)* conflict, combat, duel, battle, encounter, crash, smash, fight, contention, struggle, discord.
(ANT.) concord, amity, harmony, consonance.

collusion *(SYN.)* combination, cabal, intrigue, conspiracy, plot, treason, treachery.

color *(SYN.)* hue, paint, pigment, complexion, dye, shade, tone, tincture, stain, tint, tinge.
(ANT.) paleness, transparency, achromatism.

colorful *(SYN.)* impressive, vivid, striking, multicolored, offbeat, weird, unusual.
(ANT.) flat, dull, uninteresting.

colossal *(SYN.)* enormous, elephantine, gargantuan, huge, immense, gigantic, prodigious.
(ANT.) little, minute, small, miniature, diminutive, microscopic, tiny.

combat *(SYN.)* conflict, duel, battle, collision, encounter, fight, contest, oppose, war, contention, struggle, discord.
(ANT.) consonance, harmony, concord, yield, surrender, succumb, amity.

combination *(SYN.)* association, confederacy, alliance, entente, league, com-

pounding, mixture, blend, composite, federation, mixing, compound, blending, union.
(ANT.) *separation, division, schism, divorce.*

combine (SYN.) adjoin, associate, accompany, conjoin, connect, link, mix, blend, couple, unite, join.
(ANT.) *detach, disjoin, divide, separate, disconnect.*

come (SYN.) near, approach, reach, arrive, advance.
(ANT.) *depart, leave, go.*

comedian (SYN.) comic, wit, humorist, gagman, wag.

comely (SYN.) charming, elegant, beauteous, beautiful, fine, lovely, pretty, handsome.
(ANT.) *hideous, repulsive, foul, unsightly.*

come-on (SYN.) lure, inducement, enticement, temptation, premium.

comfort (SYN.) contentment, ease, enjoyment, relieve, consolation, relief, cheer, console, calm, satisfaction, soothe, encourage, succor, luxury, solace.
(ANT.) *depress, torture, discomfort, upset, misery, disturb, agitate, affliction, discompose, uncertainty, suffering.*

comfortable (SYN.) pleasing, agreeable, convenient, cozy, welcome, acceptable, relaxed, restful, cozy, gratifying, easy, contented, rested, satisfying, pleasurable.
(ANT.) *miserable, distressing, tense, strained, troubling, edgy, uncomfortable.*

comical (SYN.) droll, funny, humorous, amusing, ludicrous, witty, ridiculous, odd, queer.
(ANT.) *sober, solemn, sad, serious, melancholy.*

command (SYN.) class, method, plan regularity, rank, arrangement, series, sequence, point, aim, conduct, manage, guide, bid, system, succession, bidding, direct, order, demand, direction, rule, dictate, decree.
(ANT.) *consent, obey, misdirect, distract, deceive, misguide, license, confusion.*

commandeer (SYN.) take, possession, seize, confiscate, appropriate.

commanding (SYN.) imposing, masterful, assertive, authoritative, positive.

commence (SYN.) open, start.
(ANT.) *stop, end, terminate, finish.*

commend (SYN.) laud, praise, applaud, recommend.
(ANT.) *censure, blame, criticize.*

commendable (SYN.) deserving, praiseworthy.
(ANT.) *bad, deplorable, lamentable.*

commendation (SYN.) approval, applause, praise, recommendation, honor, medal.
(ANT.) *criticism, condemnation, censure.*

commensurate (SYN.) keep, celebrate, observe, honor, commend, extol, glorify, laud, praise, honor.
(ANT.) *decry, disgrace, disregard, overlook, profane, dishonor.*

comment (SYN.) assertion, declaration, annotation, explanation, review, commentary, report, remark, observation, utterance, criticism, statement.

commerce (SYN.) business, engagement, employment, art, trade, marketing, enterprise, occupation.
(ANT.) *hobby, pastime, avocation.*

commission (SYN.) board, committee, command, permit, order, permission, delegate, authorize, deputize, entrust.

commit (SYN.) perpetrate, perform, obligate, do, commend, consign, relegate, bind, delegate, empower, pledge, entrust, authorize, trust.
(ANT.) *neglect, mistrust, release, free, miscarry, fail, loose.*

commitment (SYN.) duty, promise, responsibility, pledge.

committee (SYN.) commission, bureau, board, delegate, council.

commodious (SYN.) appropriate, accessible, adapted, favorable, handy, fitting, timely.
(ANT.) *inconvenient, troublesome, awkward.*

commodity (SYN.) article, merchandise, wares, goods.

common (SYN.) ordinary, popular, familiar, mean, low, general, vulgar, communal, mutual, shared, natural, frequent, prevalent, joint, conventional, plain, usual, universal.
(ANT.) *odd, exceptional, scarce, noble, extraordinary, different, separate, outstanding, rare, unusual, distinctive,*

refined.

commonplace *(SYN.)* common, usual, frequent, ordinary, everyday.

(ANT.) distinctive, unusual, original.

commonsense *(SYN.)* perceptible, alive, apprehensible, aware, awake, cognizant, conscious, comprehending, perceptible.

(ANT.) unaware, impalpable, imperceptible.

commotion *(SYN.)* confusion, chaos, disarray, ferment, disorder, stir, tumult, agitation.

(ANT.) tranquillity, peace, certainty, order.

communicable *(SYN.)* infectious, virulent, catching, transferable, contagious.

(ANT.) hygienic, noncommunicable, healthful.

communicate *(SYN.)* convey, impart, inform, confer, disclose, reveal, relate, tell, advertise, publish, transmit, publicize, divulge.

(ANT.) withhold, hide, conceal.

communication *(SYN.)* disclosure, transmission, declaration, announcement, notification, publication, message, report, news, information.

communicative *(SYN.)* unreserved, open, frank, free, straightforward, unrestrained.

(ANT.) close-mouthed, secretive.

communion *(SYN.)* intercourse, fellowship, participation, association, sacrament, union.

(ANT.) nonparticipation, alienation.

community *(SYN.)* public, society, city, town, village, township.

compact *(SYN.)* contracted, firm, narrow, snug, close, constricted, packed, vanity, treaty, agreement, tense, taught, tight, niggardly, parsimonious, compressed, stingy.

(ANT.) slack, open, loose, relaxed, unconfined, unfretted, sprawling, lax.

companion *(SYN.)* attendant, comrade, consort, friend, colleague, partner, crony, mate, associate.

(ANT.) stranger, enemy, adversary.

companionship *(SYN.)* familiarity, cognizance, acquaintance, fellowship, knowledge, intimacy.

(ANT.) unfamiliarity, inexperience, ignorance.

company *(SYN.)* crew, group, band, party, throng, house, assemblage, troop, fellowship, association, business, concern, partnership, corporation, companionship, firm.

(ANT.) seclusion, individual, solitude, dispersion.

comparable *(SYN.)* allied, analogous, alike, akin, like, correspondent, correlative, parallel.

(ANT.) opposed, incongruous, dissimilar, unalike, different, divergent.

compare *(SYN.)* discriminate, match, differentiate, contrast, oppose.

comparison *(SYN.)* likening, contrasting, judgment.

compartment *(SYN.)* division, section.

compassion *(SYN.)* mercy, sympathy, pity, commiseration, condolence.

(ANT.) ruthlessness, hardness, brutality, inhumanity, cruelty.

compassionate *(SYN.)* sympathizing, benign, forbearing, good, tender, affable, humane, indulgent, kind, sympathetic, kindly.

(ANT.) inhuman, merciless, unkind, unsympathetic, cruel.

compatible *(SYN.)* consistent, agreeing, conforming, accordant, congruous, harmonious, cooperative, agreeable, constant, consonant, correspondent.

(ANT.) discrepant, paradoxical, disagreeable, contradictory.

compel *(SYN.)* drive, enforce, coerce, constrain, force, oblige, impel.

(ANT.) induce, coax, prevent, wheedle, persuade, cajole, convince.

compensate *(SYN.)* remunerate, repay, reimburse, recompense, balance.

compensation *(SYN.)* fee, earnings, pay, payment, recompense, allowance, remuneration, remittance, settlement, stipend, repayment, salary, wages.

(ANT.) present, gratuity, gift.

compete *(SYN.)* rival, contest, oppose, vie.

(ANT.) reconcile, accord.

competence *(SYN.)* skill, ability, capability.

competent *(SYN.)* efficient, clever,

capable, able, apt, proficient, skillful, fitted, qualified.

(ANT.) *inept, incapable, unfitted, awkward, incompetent, inadequate.*

competition *(SYN.)* contest, match, rivalry, tournament.

competitor *(SYN.)* rival, contestant, opponent.

(ANT.) *ally, friend, colleague.*

complain *(SYN.)* lament, murmur, protest, grouch, grumble, regret, moan, remonstrate, whine, repine.

(ANT.) *rejoice, praise, applaud, approve.*

complaint *(SYN.)* protest, objection, grievance.

complement *(SYN.)* supplement, complete.

(ANT.) *clash, conflict.*

complete *(SYN.)* consummate, entire, ended, full, thorough, finished, full, whole, concluded, over, done, terminate, unbroken, total, undivided.

(ANT.) *unfinished, imperfect, incomplete, start, partial, begin, commence, lacking.*

completion *(SYN.)* achievement, attainment, end, conclusion, close, finish, accomplishment, realization.

(ANT.) *omission, neglect, failure, defeat.*

complex *(SYN.)* sophisticated, compound, intricate, involved, perplexing, elaborate, complicated.

(ANT.) *basic, simple, rudimentary, uncompounded, uncomplicated, plain.*

complexion *(SYN.)* paint, pigment hue, color, dye, stain, tincture, tinge, tint, shade.

(ANT.) *paleness, transparency, achromatism.*

compliant *(SYN.)* meek, modest, lowly, plain, submissive, simple, unostentatious, unassuming, unpretentious.

(ANT.) *proud, vain, arrogant, haughty, boastful.*

complicated *(SYN.)* intricate, involved, complex, compound, perplexing.

(ANT.) *simple, plain, uncompounded.*

compliment *(SYN.)* eulogy, flattery, praise, admiration, honor, adulation, flatter, commendation, tribute.

(ANT.) *taunt, affront, aspersion, insult, disparage, criticism.*

complimentary *(SYN.)* gratis, free.

comply *(SYN.)* assent, consent, accede, acquiesce, coincide, conform, concur, tally.

(ANT.) *differ, dissent, protest, disagree.*

component *(SYN.)* division, fragment, allotment, moiety, apportionment, scrap, portion, section, share, segment, ingredient, organ.

(ANT.) *whole, entirety.*

comport *(SYN.)* carry, conduct, behave, act, deport, interact, operate, manage.

compose *(SYN.)* forge, fashion, mold, make, construct, create, produce, shape, form, constitute, arrange, organize, make up, write, invent, devise, frame.

(ANT.) *misshape, dismantle, disfigure, destroy.*

composed *(SYN.)* calm, cool, imperturbable, placid, quiet, unmoved, sedate, peaceful, collected, tranquil.

(ANT.) *aroused, violent, nervous, agitated, perturbed, excited.*

composer *(SYN.)* author, inventor, creator, maker, originator.

composition *(SYN.)* paper, theme, work, essay, compound, mixture, mix.

composure *(SYN.)* calmness, poise, control, self-control, self-possession.

(ANT.) *anger, rage, turbulence, agitation.*

compound *(SYN.)* blend, confound, jumble, consort, aggregate, complicated.

(ANT.) *segregate, separate, divide, simple, sort.*

comprehension *(SYN.)* insight, perception, understanding, awareness.

(ANT.) *misconception, insensibility.*

compress *(SYN.)* press, compact, squeeze, pack, crowd.

(ANT.) *spread, stretch, expand.*

compulsion *(SYN.)* might, energy, potency, strength.

(ANT.) *persuasion, impotence, frailty.*

compulsory *(SYN.)* required, obligatory, necessary.

(ANT.) *elective, optional, free, unrestricted.*

compute *(SYN.)* count, calculate, determine, figure.

(ANT.) *conjecture, guess, miscalculate.*

comrade *(SYN.)* attendant, companion, colleague.

(ANT.) stranger, enemy.

con *(SYN.)* cheat, bamboozle, trick, swindle.

conceal *(SYN.)* disguise, cover, hide, mask, screen, secrete, veil, withhold.
(ANT.) reveal, show, disclose.

concede *(SYN.)* permit, suffer, tolerate, grant, give, admit, acknowledge, allow, yield.
(ANT.) forbid, contradict, protest, refuse, deny, negate.

conceit *(SYN.)* pride, vanity, complacency, conception.
(ANT.) humility, meekness, humbleness, modesty.

conceited *(SYN.)* proud, arrogant, vain, smug.
(ANT.) humble, modest, self-effacing.

conceive *(SYN.)* design, create, imagine, understand, devise, concoct, perceive, frame, grasp, invent.
(ANT.) imitate, reproduce.

concentrate *(SYN.)* localize, focus, condense, ponder, meditate, center, scrutinize.
(ANT.) scatter, diffuse, dissipate, disperse.

concept *(SYN.)* fancy, conception, image, notion, idea, sentiment, thought.
(ANT.) thing, matter, substance, entity.

conception *(SYN.)* consideration, deliberation, fancy.

concession *(SYN.)* admission, yielding, granting.
(ANT.) insistence, demand.

concise *(SYN.)* pity, neat, brief, compact, succinct.
(ANT.) wordy, lengthy, verbose, prolix.

conclude *(SYN.)* decide, achieve, close, complete, end, finish, terminate, arrange, determine, settle.
(ANT.) start, begin.

concluding *(SYN.)* extreme, final, last, terminal, utmost.
(ANT.) first, foremost, opening, initial.

conclusion *(SYN.)* end, finale, termination, deduction, close, settlement, decision.
(ANT.) commencement, inception, opening, start.

conclusive *(SYN.)* decisive, eventual, final, terminal.

(ANT.) original, first, inaugural.

concord *(SYN.)* agreement, unison, understanding, accordance, stipulation.
(ANT.) disagreement, discord, dissension.

concrete *(SYN.)* solid, firm, precise, definite, specific.
(ANT.) undetermined, vague, general.

concur *(SYN.)* agree, assent, consent, accede.
(ANT.) dissent, protest, differ.

condemn *(SYN.)* denounce, reproach, blame, upbraid.
(ANT.) condone, forgive, absolve, praise.

condense *(SYN.)* shorten, reduce, abridge, abbreviate, concentrate, digest.
(ANT.) enlarge, increase, swell, expand.

condition *(SYN.)* circumstance, state, situation, case, plight, requirement.

conduct *(SYN.)* control, deportment, supervise, manage, behavior, deed, actions.

confess *(SYN.)* avow, acknowledge, admit, concede.
(ANT.) disown, renounce, deny, conceal.

confession *(SYN.)* defense, justification, excuse.
(ANT.) dissimulation, denial, complaint.

confidence *(SYN.)* firmness, self-reliance, assurance, faith, trust, pledge, declaration, self-confidence, reliance, self-assurance.
(ANT.) distrust, shyness, mistrust, bashfulness.

confident *(SYN.)* certain, sure, dauntless, self-assured.
(ANT.) uncertain, timid, shy.

confine *(SYN.)* enclose, restrict, hinder, fence, limit.
(ANT.) release, expose, free, expand, open.

confirm acknowledge, establish, settle, substantiate, approve, fix, verify, assure.
(ANT.) disclaim, deny.

confirmation *(SYN.)* demonstration, experiment, test, trail, verification.
(ANT.) fallacy, invalidity.

conflict *(SYN.)* duel, combat, fight, collision, discord, encounter, interference, inconsistency, contention.
(ANT.) consonance, harmony, amity.

confiscate *(SYN.)* capture, catch, gain, purloin, steal.

conflagration *(SYN.)* flame, glow, heat, warmth, fervor.

(ANT.) apathy, cold, quiescence.

conform *(SYN.)* adapt, comply, yield, submit, obey, adjust, agree, fit, suit.

(ANT.) misapply, misfit, rebel, vary, disagree, disturb.

conformity *(SYN.)* congruence, accord, agreement.

confound *(SYN.)* confuse, baffle, perplex, puzzle.

confront *(SYN.)* confront, defy, hinder, resist, thwart.

(ANT.) submit, agree, support.

confuse *(SYN.)* confound, perplex, mystify, dumbfound, baffle, puzzle.

(ANT.) explain, instruct, edify, illumine, enlighten.

congregate *(SYN.)* gather, foregather, meet, convene.

(ANT.) scatter, dispel, disperse, dissipate.

congress *(SYN.)* parliament, legislature, assembly.

conjecture *(SYN.)* law, supposition, theory.

(ANT.) proof, fact, certainty.

conjunction *(SYN.)* combination, junction, connection.

(ANT.) separation, disconnection, diversion.

connect *(SYN.)* adjoin, link, combine, relate, join, attach, unite, associate, attribute.

(ANT.) detach, separate, disjoin, untie, dissociation.

conquer *(SYN.)* master, beat, humble, defeat, overcome, rout, win, succeed, achieve.

(ANT.) cede, yield, retreat, surrender.

conquest *(SYN.)* triumph, victory, achievement.

(ANT.) surrender, failure.

conscientious *(SYN.)* upright, straight, honest.

(ANT.) careless, irresponsible.

consecrated *(SYN.)* holy, divine, devout, spiritual.

(ANT.) evil, worldly, secular.

consent *(SYN.)* permission, leave, agree, let, assent, agreement, license, permit.

(ANT.) refusal, opposition, denial, dissent, prohibition.

consequence *(SYN.)* outcome, issue, result, effect, significance, importance.

(ANT.) impetus, cause.

consequential *(SYN.)* significant, important, weighty.

(ANT.) trivial, unimportant, minor, insignificant.

conservative *(SYN.)* conventional, reactionary, cautious, moderate, careful.

(ANT.) radical, liberal, rash, foolhardy, reckless.

consider *(SYN.)* heed, ponder, contemplate, examine, study, weigh, reflect, think.

(ANT.) ignore, overlook, disdain, disregard, neglect.

considerable *(SYN.)* much, noteworthy, worthwhile.

considerate *(SYN.)* careful, considerate, heedful, prudent, kind, thoughtful, polite, introspective, reflective.

(ANT.) thoughtless, heedless, inconsiderate, selfish, rash.

consistent *(SYN.)* conforming, accordant, compatible.

(ANT.) paradoxical, discrepant, contrary, antagonistic, opposed, eccentric, incon

consolation *(SYN.)* enjoyment, sympathy, relief, ease, contentment, comfort.

(ANT.) discomfort, suffering, discouragement, torture.

console *(SYN.)* solace, comfort, sympathize with.

(ANT.) worry, annoy, upset, disturb, distress.

consolidate *(SYN.)* blend, combine, conjoin, fuse, mix, merge, unite.

(ANT.) decompose, separate, analyze, disintegrate.

conspicuous *(SYN.)* distinguished, clear, manifest.

(ANT.) hidden, obscure, neutral, common.

conspiracy *(SYN.)* machination, combination, treason, intrigue, cabal, treachery.

conspire *(SYN.)* plan, intrigue, plot, scheme.

constancy *(SYN.)* devotion, faithfulness, accuracy, precision, exactness.

(ANT.) faithlessness, treachery, perfidy.

constant *(SYN.)* continual, invariable, abiding, permanent, faithful, invariant, true, ceaseless, enduring.

(ANT.) *fickle, irregular, wavering, off-and-on, infrequent, occasional.*

constantly (SYN.) eternally, ever, ever-more, forever.

(ANT.) *rarely, sometimes, never, occasionally.*

consternation (SYN.) apprehension, dismay, alarm.

(ANT.) *bravery, courage, boldness, assurance.*

constitute (SYN.) compose, found, form, establish, organize, create, appoint, delegate, authorize.

constitution (SYN.) law, code, physique, health, vitality.

constrain (SYN.) necessity, indigence, need, want.

(ANT.) *luxury, freedom, uncertainty.*

construct (SYN.) build, form, erect, make, fabricate, raise.

(ANT.) *raze, demolish.*

construction (SYN.) raising, building, fabricating.

constructive (SYN.) useful, helpful, valuable.

(ANT.) *ruinous, destructive.*

construe (SYN.) explain, interpret, solve, render.

(ANT.) *distort, confuse, misconstrue.*

consult (SYN.) discuss, chatter, discourse, gossip, confer, report, rumor, deliberate, speech, talk.

(ANT.) *writing, correspondence, silence.*

consume (SYN.) engulf, absorb, use up, use, expend, exhaust, devour, devastate.

(ANT.) *emit, expel, exude, discharge.*

contagious (SYN.) infectious, virulent, communicable.

(ANT.) *noncommunicable, healthful, hygienic.*

contain (SYN.) embody, hold, embrace, include, accommodate, repress, restrain.

(ANT.) *emit, encourage, yield, discharge.*

contaminate (SYN.) corrupt, sully, taint, defile, soil, pollute, dirty, infect, poison.

(ANT.) *purify.*

contemplative (SYN.) simultaneous, meditative.

(ANT.) *inattentive, indifferent, thoughtless.*

contemporary (SYN.) modern, present,

simultaneous, fashionable, coexisting, contemporaneous, up-to-date.

(ANT.) *old, antecedent, past, ancient, succeeding, bygone.*

contempt (SYN.) detestation, malice, contumely, disdain.

(ANT.) *respect, reverence, admiration, esteem, awe.*

contemptible (SYN.) base, mean, vile, vulgar, nasty, low, detestable, selfish.

(ANT.) *generous, honorable, noble, exalted, admirable.*

contemptuous (SYN.) disdainful, sneering, scornful.

(ANT.) *modest, humble.*

contend (SYN.) dispute, combat, contest, assert, claim, argue, maintain.

content (SYN.) pleased, happy, contented, satisfied.

(ANT.) *restless, dissatisfied, discontented.*

contented (SYN.) delighted, fortunate, gay, happy, joyous, lucky, merry.

(ANT.) *gloomy, blue.*

contention (SYN.) combat, duel, struggle, discord.

(ANT.) *concord, harmony, amity, consonance.*

contentment (SYN.) delight, happiness, gladness, pleasure, satisfaction.

(ANT.) *misery, sorrow, grief, sadness, despair.*

contest (SYN.) dispute, debate, competition.

(ANT.) *allow, concede, agree.*

continence (SYN.) forbearance, temperance.

(ANT.) *self-indulgence, excess, intoxication.*

contingency (SYN.) likelihood, possibility, occasion.

continue (SYN.) proceed, extend, endure, persist, resume, renew, recommence.

(ANT.) *check, cease, discontinue, stop, suspend.*

continuous (SYN.) continuing, uninterrupted, ceaseless, unceasing, incessant.

(ANT.) *intermittent, irregular, sporadic.*

contract (SYN.) condense, diminish, reduce, bargain.

(ANT.) *lengthen, extend, swell, expand, elongate.*

contradict (SYN.) gainsay, counter, oppose, confute, dispute.

(ANT.) verify, confirm, agree, support.

contradictory *(SYN.)* inconsistent, conflicting, incompatible, paradoxical, unsteady.

(ANT.) congruous, consistent, correspondent.

contrary *(SYN.)* disagreeable, perverse, hostile, stubborn, opposite, opposing, opposed, disagreeing, disastrous, conflicting, unlucky.

(ANT.) lucky, agreeable, propitious, favorable, like, obliging, similar, complementary, tractable, fortunate.

contrast *(SYN.)* differentiate, compare, distinction, disagreement, distinguish, differ, discriminate, difference, oppose.

(ANT.) agreement, similarity, likeness.

contribute *(SYN.)* grant, give, donate, bestow, provide, offer.

(ANT.) deny, withhold.

contribution *(SYN.)* grant, gift, offering, donation.

contrition *(SYN.)* grief, regret, self-reproach.

(ANT.) self-satisfaction, complacency.

control *(SYN.)* govern, regulate, rule, command, dominate, direct, manage.

(ANT.) ignore, forsake, follow, submit, abandon.

controversy *(SYN.)* disagreement, dispute, debate.

(ANT.) agreement, harmony, accord, concord, decision.

convenience *(SYN.)* accessibility, aid, benefit, help, service, availability.

(ANT.) inconvenience.

convenient *(SYN.)* adapted, appropriate, fitting, favorable, handy, suitable.

(ANT.) inconvenient, troublesome, awkward.

convention *(SYN.)* meeting, conference, assembly, practice, custom, rule.

conventional *(SYN.)* common, regular, usual, everyday, habitual, routine.

(ANT.) exotic, unusual, bizarre, extraordinary.

conversant *(SYN.)* aware, intimate, familiar, versed, close, friendly, sociable.

(ANT.) affected, distant, cold, reserved.

conversation *(SYN.)* colloquy, dialogue, chat, parley.

converse *(SYN.)* jabber, talk, argue, comment, harangue, plead, rant, spout, discuss, chat, talk, speak, reason.

conversion *(SYN.)* alteration, change, mutation, modification, metamorphosis.

convert *(SYN.)* change, alter, alter, turn, transform, shift, modify, exchange, win over.

(ANT.) establish, stabilize, settle, retain.

convey *(SYN.)* carry, bear, communicate, transport, transmit, support, sustain.

(ANT.) drop, abandon.

conveyance *(SYN.)* van, car, train, truck, plane.

convict *(SYN.)* felon, offender, criminal.

conviction *(SYN.)* opinion, position, view, faith, belief, confidence, feeling.

(ANT.) doubt, heresy, incredulity, denial.

convince *(SYN.)* persuade, assure, exhort, induce.

(ANT.) deter, compel, restrain, dissuade.

convivial *(SYN.)* jolly, social, jovial, gregarious.

(ANT.) solemn, stern, unsociable.

convoy *(SYN.)* with, attend, chaperone.

(ANT.) avoid, desert, quit, leave.

cool *(SYN.)* frosty, chilly, icy, cold, wintry, quiet, composed, collected, distant, unfriendly, quiet, moderate.

(ANT.) hot, warm, heated, overwrought, excited, hysterical, friendly, outgoing.

cooperate *(SYN.)* unite, combine, help, contribute.

coordinate *(SYN.)* attune, harmonize, adapt, match.

copious *(SYN.)* ample, abundant, bountiful, overflowing, plentiful, profuse, rich.

(ANT.) scant, scarce, insufficient, meager, deficient.

copy *(SYN.)* facsimile, exemplar, imitation, duplicate, reproduction, likeness, print, carbon, transcript.

(ANT.) prototype, original.

cordial *(SYN.)* polite, friendly, affable, genial, earnest, gracious, warm, ardent, hearty, sincere.

(ANT.) unfriendly, cool, aloof, hostile, ill-tempered.

core *(SYN.)* midpoint, heart, kernel, center, middle.

(ANT.) outskirts, border, surface, outside, boundary, rim.

corporation *(SYN.)* business, organization, crew, group, troop, society, company, conglomerate, firm.
(ANT.) individual, dispersion, seclusion.

corpse *(SYN.)* cadaver, carcass, remains, body, form.
(ANT.) spirit, soul, mind.

corpulent *(SYN.)* obese, portly, chubby, stout.
(ANT.) slim, thin, slender, lean, gaunt.

correct *(SYN.)* true, set right, faultless, impeccable, proper, accurate, precise.
(ANT.) condone, aggravate, false, inaccurate, wrong, untrue, faulty.

correction *(SYN.)* order, improvement, regulation, instruction, amendment.
(ANT.) confusion, turbulence, chaos.

correlative *(SYN.)* allied, correspondent, like, similar.
(ANT.) different, opposed, divergent.

correspond *(SYN.)* compare, coincide, match, agree, suit, fit, write.
(ANT.) differ, diverge, vary.

correspondent *(SYN.)* allied, alike, comparable, like, parallel, similar.
(ANT.) different, opposed, divergent, dissimilar.

corridor *(SYN.)* hallway, hall, foyer, passage, lobby.

corrode *(SYN.)* erode.

corrupted *(SYN.)* crooked, dishonest, impure, spoiled.

cost *(SYN.)* price, value, damage, charge, loss, sacrifice, penalty, worth.

costly *(SYN.)* dear, expensive.
(ANT.) cheap, inexpensive.

costume *(SYN.)* dress, clothes, apparel, clothing, garb.

couch *(SYN.)* davenport, sofa.

council *(SYN.)* caution, instruction, committee.

counsel *(SYN.)* guidance, attorney, lawyer, counselor, hint, imply, opinion, advice.
(ANT.) declare, dictate, insist.

count *(SYN.)* consider, number, enumerate, total.
(ANT.) conjecture, guess, miscalculate.

countenance *(SYN.)* visage, face, aspect, support, appearance, approval.
(ANT.) forbid, prohibit.

counteract *(SYN.)* thwart, neutralize, offset, counterbalance, defeat.

counterfeit *(SYN.)* false, fraudulent, pretended, pretend, sham, imitate, forgery.
(ANT.) authentic, natural, real, genuine, true.

country *(SYN.)* state, nation, forest, farmland.
(ANT.) city.

couple *(SYN.)* team, pair, accompany, associate, attach.
(ANT.) detach, separate, disjoin, disconnect.

courage *(SYN.)* fearlessness, boldness, chivalry, fortitude, mettle, spirit, daring.
(ANT.) fear, timidity.

course *(SYN.)* passage, advance, path, road, progress.

courteous *(SYN.)* civil, respectful, polite, genteel, well-mannered, gracious.
(ANT.) discourteous, rude, uncivil, impolite, boorish.

courtesy *(SYN.)* graciousness, politeness, respect.
(ANT.) discourtesy, rudeness.

covenant *(SYN.)* agreement, concord, harmony, unison.
(ANT.) variance, discord, dissension, difference.

cover *(SYN.)* clothe, conceal, disguise, curtain, guard, envelop, mask, cloak, shield, hide, screen, protect.
(ANT.) bare, expose, reveal.

covert *(SYN.)* potential, undeveloped, concealed.
(ANT.) explicit, visible, manifest.

covetous *(SYN.)* grasping, greedy, acquisitive.
(ANT.) generous.

cowardice *(SYN.)* dread, dismay, fright, dismay, panic, terror, timidity.
(ANT.) fearlessness, courage, bravery.

crack *(SYN.)* snap, break.

cracker *(SYN.)* wafer, biscuit.

craft *(SYN.)* talent, skill, expertness, ability, cunning, guile, deceit, trade.

crafty *(SYN.)* covert, clever, cunning, skillful, foxy, tricky, sly, underhand.
(ANT.) frank, sincere, gullible, open, guileless, ingenuous.

craggy *(SYN.)* rough, rugged, irregular, uneven.

(ANT.) level, sleek, smooth, fine, polished.

crank (SYN.) cross, irritable, bad-tempered, testy.
(ANT.) cheerful, happy.

crash (SYN.) smash, shatter.

craving (SYN.) relish appetite, desire, liking, longing.
(ANT.) renunciation, distaste, disgust.

create (SYN.) fashion, form, generate, engender, formulate, make, originate.
(ANT.) disband, abolish, terminate, destroy, demolish.

credit (SYN.) believe, accept, belief, trust, faith, merit.
(ANT.) doubt, reject, question, distrust.

credulous (SYN.) trusting, naive, believing, gullible.
(ANT.) suspicious.

creed (SYN.) belief, precept, credo, faith, teaching.
(ANT.) practice, deed, conduct, performance.

creek (SYN.) brook, spring, stream, rivulet.

crime (SYN.) offense, insult, aggression, wrongdoing.
(ANT.) right, gentleness, innocence, morality.

criminal (SYN.) unlawful, crook, gangster, outlaw, illegal, convict, delinquent, offender, malefactor.

cripple (SYN.) hurt, maim, damage, injure.

crippled (SYN.) deformed, disabled, maimed, hobbling, limping, unconvincing.
(ANT.) robust, sound, vigorous, athletic.

crisis (SYN.) conjuncture, emergency, pass, pinch, acme, climax, contingency.
(ANT.) calm, normality, stability, equilibrium.

crisp (SYN.) crumbling, delicate, frail, brittle.
(ANT.) calm, normality.

criterion (SYN.) measure, law, rule, principle, gauge, proof.
(ANT.) fancy guess, chance, supposition.

critic (SYN.) reviewer, judge, commentator, censor, defamer, slanderer.

critical (SYN.) exact, fastidious, caviling, faultfinding, accurate, condemning, reproachful, risky.
(ANT.) shallow, uncritical, approving, insignificant, trivial.

criticize (SYN.) examine, analyze, inspect, blame, censure, appraise, evaluate.
(ANT.) neglect, overlook, approve.

critique (SYN.) criticism, inspection, review.

crony (SYN.) colleague, companion, chum, buddy, comrade, friend, mate.
(ANT.) stranger, enemy, adversary.

crooked (SYN.) twisted, corrupt, hooked, curved, criminal, dishonest, degrade.
(ANT.) improved, raised, straight, honest, vitalized, upright, enhanced.

crop (SYN.) fruit, produce, harvest, cut, mow, reaping, result, yield.

cross (SYN.) mix, mingle, traverse, interbreed, annoyed, irritable, cranky, testy, angry, mean.
(ANT.) cheerful.

crouch (SYN.) duck, stoop.

crow (SYN.) boast, brag.

crowd (SYN.) masses, flock, host, squeeze, mob, multitude, populace, press, cramp, throng, swarm.

crown (SYN.) coronet, apex, crest, circlet, pinnacle, tiara, skull, head, top, zenith.
(ANT.) base, bottom, foundation, foot.

crude (SYN.) rude, graceless, unpolished, green, harsh, rough, coarse, ill-prepared.
(ANT.) finished, refined, polished, cultured, genteel.

cruel (SYN.) ferocious, mean, heartless, unmerciful.
(ANT.) humane, forbearing, kind, compassionate.

cruelty (SYN.) harshness, meanness, savagery.
(ANT.) compassion, kindness.

crumb (SYN.) jot, grain, mite, particle, shred.
(ANT.) mass, bulk, quantity.

crunch (SYN.) champ, gnaw, nibble, pierce.

crush (SYN.) smash, break.

cry (SYN.) yowl, yell, roar, shout, bellow, scream, wail, weep, bawl, sob.

cryptic (SYN.) puzzling, mysterious, enigmatic, hidden, secret, vague, obscure, occult, unclear.

cull *(SYN.)* elect, choose, pick.
(ANT.) reject, refuse.

culpable *(SYN.)* guilty.
(ANT.) innocent.

culprit *(SYN.)* delinquent, felon, offender.

culture *(SYN.)* humanism, cultivation, breeding, education, learning.
(ANT.) illiteracy, vulgarity, ignorance.

cumbersome *(SYN.)* bulky, clumsy, awkward.
(ANT.) handy.

cunning *(SYN.)* clever, wily, crafty, foxy, skillful, tricky, ingenious, foxiness, ability.
(ANT.) gullible, honest, naive, openness.

curb *(SYN.)* check, restraint, hinder, hold, limit, control, stop, suppress.
(ANT.) aid, loosen, incite.

cure *(SYN.)* help, treatment, heal, medicine, restorative, relief, remedy.

curious *(SYN.)* interrogative, interested, peculiar, queer, nosy, peeping, prying.
(ANT.) unconcerned, incurious, ordinary.

current *(SYN.)* up-to-date, contemporary, present.
(ANT.) antiquated, old, ancient, past.

curse *(SYN.)* ban, oath, swear, condemn.
(ANT.) boon, blessing.

cursory *(SYN.)* frivolous, shallow, slight.
(ANT.) complete, deep, profound.

curt *(SYN.)* hasty, short, abrupt, brusque, brief.
(ANT.) friendly, smooth, gradual, polite.

curtail *(SYN.)* condense, contract, diminish, reduce.
(ANT.) lengthen, extend.

curtain *(SYN.)* blind, drape, shade.

curve *(SYN.)* crook, deflect, bend, bow, incline, turn.
(ANT.) resist, stiffen.

cushion *(SYN.)* pillow, pad, check, absorb.

custodian *(SYN.)* guard, keeper.

custom *(SYN.)* fashion, rule, routine, practice, usage.

cut *(SYN.)* slash, gash, prick, slit, sever, cleave, mow, incision, chop, lop, slice.

cut in *(SYN.)* butt in, interfere.

cut off *(SYN.)* cease, end, stop, terminate.

cutthroat *(SYN.)* killer, executioner, murderer, assassin, merciless, ruthless.

dab *(SYN.)* coat, pat, smear.

dabble *(SYN.)* splatter, toy, splash, fiddle, putter.

daft *(SYN.)* crazy, foolish.

daily *(SYN.)* every day, diurnal, regularly.

dainty *(SYN.)* slender, pleasing, delicate, frail, pleasant.
(ANT.) uncouth, vulgar, coarse, tough.

dally *(SYN.)* dawdle, linger, lag, delay, loiter.
(ANT.) rush, hurry, dash, get going, bustle.

damage *(SYN.)* spoil, deface, impair, mar, hurt, injury.
(ANT.) repair, benefit, mend, rebuild, improve, ameliorate.

dame *(SYN.)* woman, lady.

damn *(SYN.)* denounce, descry, doom, curse, reprove.
(ANT.) bless, honor, glorify, praise, accept, applaud.

damp *(SYN.)* humid, dank, moisture, wetness.
(ANT.) arid, dry.

dance *(SYN.)* bounce, flit, skip, sway, prance, bob, glide, caper, cavort, frisk.

dandle *(SYN.)* jounce, joggle, bounce, jiggle, nestle.

dandy *(SYN.)* coxcomb, fop, swell, great, fine, wonderful.
(ANT.) rotten, terrible, awful, miserable, slob.

danger *(SYN.)* jeopardy, risk, threat, hazard, uncertainty.
(ANT.) safety, immunity, security, defense.

dangerous *(SYN.)* risky, insecure, threatening, critical, perilous, unsafe, uncertain.
(ANT.) trustworthy, secure, protected, safe.

dangle *(SYN.)* droop, swing, flap, hang, sag.

dank *(SYN.)* moist, muggy.
(ANT.) dry.

dapper *(SYN.)* spruce, trim, natty, smart, well-tailored, dashing, neat.
(ANT.) untidy, sloppy, shabby, messy, unkempt.

dappled *(SYN.)* spotted, flecked, brindled, variegated, piebald, pied.
(ANT.) uniform, solid.

dare *(SYN.)* brave, call, question, defy,

risk, challenge.

daredevil *(SYN.)* lunatic, madcap.

daring *(SYN.)* foolhardy, chivalrous, rash, fearless, courageous, intrepid, valiant, courage, bravery, brave.
(ANT.) timid, cowardice, timidity, cautious.

dark *(SYN.)* somber, obscure, gloomy, black, unilluminated, dim, evil, hidden, secret, swarthy, murky, opaque, dismal, mournful.
(ANT.) lucid, light, happy, cheerful, illuminated.

darling *(SYN.)* dear, adored, sweetheart, favorite.
(ANT.) uncherished, unlovable, disagreeable, rejected.

darn *(SYN.)* repair, mend.

dart *(SYN.)* scurry, arrow, barb, hurry, dash, throw, missile, run, hasten.

dash *(SYN.)* pound, thump, beat, smite, buffet, thrash, smash, break, scurry, run.
(ANT.) stroke, hearten, encourage, defend.

dashing *(SYN.)* swashbuckling, dapper, flamboyant.
(ANT.) dull, colorless, shabby, lifeless.

dastardly *(SYN.)* craven, cowardly, mean, rotten, villainous.
(ANT.) heroic, brave, high-minded, courageous.

data *(SYN.)* information, statistics, proof, facts.

date *(SYN.)* interview, appointment, commitment.

dated *(SYN.)* out-of-date, old-fashioned, outmoded.
(ANT.) latest, now, current, fashionable, hot.

daub *(SYN.)* coat, grease, soil, scribble, cover, stain, smear.

daunt *(SYN.)* discourage, dishearten, intimidate.
(ANT.) enspirit, encourage.

dauntless *(SYN.)* fearless, brave, bold, courageous, intrepid, valiant.
(ANT.) fearful, timid.

dawn *(SYN.)* sunrise, start, outset, daybreak, origin.
(ANT.) dusk, sunset, nightfall, end, conclusion, finish.

daze *(SYN.)* perplex, stun, puzzle, bewilder, upset, confuse, ruffle, confusion.

dazzle *(SYN.)* surprise, stun, astonish, impress, bewilder.

dead *(SYN.)* departed, lifeless, deceased, insensible, inanimate, dull, defunct, gone.
(ANT.) animate, functioning, active, living, alive, stirring.

deaden *(SYN.)* anesthetize, numb, paralyze.

deadlock *(SYN.)* standstill, impasse, stalemate.

deadly *(SYN.)* lethal, mortal, fatal, deathly, baleful.

deaf *(SYN.)* stone-deaf, unhearing, unheeding, unaware, unheedful, stubborn.
(ANT.) aware, conscious.

deafening *(SYN.)* vociferous, noisy, stentorian.
(ANT.) soft, inaudible, subdued.

deal *(SYN.)* act, treat, attend, cope, barter, trade, bargain, apportion, give, distribute.

dear *(SYN.)* valued, esteemed, expensive, beloved, costly, darling, high-priced, loved.
(ANT.) hateful, reasonable, inexpensive, cheap.

dearth *(SYN.)* shortage, lack, scarcity.

death *(SYN.)* decease, extinction, demise, passing.
(ANT.) life.

debase *(SYN.)* lower, degrade, alloy, adulterate, defile, humiliate, depress, abase, pervert, corrupt.
(ANT.) restore, improve, vitalize, enhance.

debate *(SYN.)* wrangle, discuss, plead, argue, discussion, contend, argument.
(ANT.) agreement, reject, accord, ignore, spurn.

debonair *(SYN.)* urbane, sophisticated, refined.

debris *(SYN.)* rubbish, litter, junk, wreckage, refuse, detritus, ruins, trash, residue.

debt *(SYN.)* amount due, liability, obligation.

decay *(SYN.)* decrease, spoil, ebb, decline, waste, disintegrate, wane, dwindle, molder, deteriorate, perish, wither, rot, collapse, rottenness, putrefy, die.

(ANT.) progress, rise, increase, grow, flourish.

deceased *(SYN.)* lifeless, departed, dead, insensible.

(ANT.) living, alive.

deceit *(SYN.)* duplicity, cheat, fraud, chicanery, trick, cunning, deception, guile, beguilement, deceitfulness.

(ANT.) truthfulness, openness, forthrightness, honesty.

deceitful *(SYN.)* false, fraudulent, insincere, dishonest.

(ANT.) sincere, honest.

deceive *(SYN.)* cheat, defraud, hoodwink, mislead, swindle.

decency *(SYN.)* decorum, dignity, propriety.

decent *(SYN.)* befitting, fit, suitable, becoming, respectable, adequate, seemly, fitting, comely, appropriate, proper, tolerable, decorous.

(ANT.) vulgar, gross, improper, unsuitable, indecorous, reprehensible, indecent, coarse.

deception *(SYN.)* trick, cheat, sham, deceit, trickery, craftiness, treachery.

(ANT.) openness, frankness, candor, probity, truthfulness.

deceptive *(SYN.)* specious, fallacious, deceitful, false, delusive, unreliable, illusive, tricky, dishonest, deceiving.

(ANT.) honest, real, genuine, true, truthful, authentic.

decide *(SYN.)* resolve, determine, terminate, conclude, close, settle, adjudicate.

(ANT.) waver, hesitate, vacillate, doubt, suspend.

decipher *(SYN.)* render, unravel, construe, solve, decode, translate, elucidate.

(ANT.) misconstrue, distort, misinterpret, confuse.

decision *(SYN.)* resolution, determination, settlement.

decisive *(SYN.)* determined, firm, decided, unhesitating.

declaration *(SYN.)* pronouncement, notice, affirmation, statement, announcement, assertion.

declare *(SYN.)* assert, promulate, affirm, tell, broadcast.

(ANT.) deny, withhold, conceal, suppress.

decline *(SYN.)* descend, decay, dwindle, refuse, incline.

(ANT.) accept, ascend, ameliorate, increase.

decompose *(SYN.)* rot, disintegrate, molder, decay.

decorate *(SYN.)* trim, paint, deck, enrich, color, beautify.

(ANT.) uncover, mar, deface, defame, debase.

decoration *(SYN.)* ornamentation, embellishment.

decoy *(SYN.)* lure, bait.

decrease *(SYN.)* lessen, wane, deduct, diminish, curtail.

(ANT.) expansion, increase, enlarge, expand, grow.

decree *(SYN.)* order, edict, statute, declaration.

decrepit *(SYN.)* feeble, puny, weakened, infirm, enfeebled, languid, rickety, weak, run-down, tumble-down.

(ANT.) strong, forceful, vigorous, energetic, lusty.

decry *(SYN.)* lower, belittle, derogate, minimize.

(ANT.) praise, commend, magnify, aggrandize.

dedicate *(SYN.)* sanctify, consecrate, hallow, devote.

dedicated *(SYN.)* disposed, true, affectionate, fond.

(ANT.) indisposed, detached, untrammeled, disinclined.

deduct *(SYN.)* lessen, shorten, abate, remove, eliminate, curtail, subtract.

(ANT.) grow, enlarge, add, increase, amplify, expand.

deed *(SYN.)* feat, transaction, action, performance, act, operation, achievement.

(ANT.) intention, cessation, inactivity, deliberation.

deem *(SYN.)* hold, determine, believe, regard, reckon, judge, consider, account.

deep *(SYN.)* bottomless, low, unplumbed, acute, obscure, involved, absorbed.

(ANT.) shallow.

deface *(SYN.)* spoil, impair, damage, mar, hurt, scratch, mutilate, disfigure, injure.

(ANT.) mend, benefit, repair.

defamation *(SYN.)* invective. reproach,

upbraiding, abuse, insult, outrage.
(ANT.) *respect, approval, laudation, commendation.*

default (SYN.) loss, omission, lack, failure, want.
(ANT.) *victory, achievement, sufficiency, success.*

defeat (SYN.) quell, vanquish, beat, overcome, overthrow, subdue, frustrate, spoil.
(ANT.) *submit, retreat, cede, yield, surrender, capitulate.*

defect (SYN.) shortcoming, fault, omission, blemish, imperfection, forsake, leave.
(ANT.) *perfection, flawlessness, support, join.*

defective (SYN.) faulty, imperfect, inoperative, flawed.
(ANT.) *flawless, perfect.*

defend (SYN.) screen, espouse, justify, protect, vindicate, fortify, assert, guard, safeguard, shield.
(ANT.) *oppose, assault, submit, attack, deny.*

defense (SYN.) resistance, protection, bulwark, fort, barricade, trench, rampart.

defer (SYN.) postpone, delay.
(ANT.) *speed, hurry, expedite.*

deference (SYN.) fame, worship, adoration, reverence, admiration, respect, fame.
(ANT.) *dishonor, derision, reproach, contempt.*

defiant (SYN.) rebellious, antagonistic, obstinate.
(ANT.) *yielding, submissive.*

deficient (SYN.) lacking, short, incomplete, defective, scanty, insufficient, inadequate.
(ANT.) *enough, ample, sufficient, adequate.*

defile (SYN.) pollute, march, corrupt, dirty, file, debase.
(ANT.) *purify.*

define (SYN.) describe, fix, establish, label, designate, set, name, explain.

definite (SYN.) fixed, prescribed, certain, specific, exact, determined, distinct.
(ANT.) *indefinite, confused, undetermined, equivocal.*

definitely (SYN.) certainly, assuredly, absolutely, positively, surely.

definition (SYN.) sense, interpretation, meaning.

deft (SYN.) handy, adroit, clever, adept, dexterous, skillful, skilled.
(ANT.) *inept, clumsy, maladroit, awkward.*

defunct (SYN.) lifeless, dead, departed, expired, extinct, spiritless, inanimate.
(ANT.) *living, alive, stirring.*

defy (SYN.) hinder, oppose, withstand, attack, resist, confront, challenge, flout.
(ANT.) *yield, allow, relent, surrender, submit, accede.*

degenerate (SYN.) dwindle, decline, weaken.
(ANT.) *ascend, ameliorate, increase, appreciate.*

degree (SYN.) grade, amount, step, measure, rank, honor.

deign (SYN.) condescend.

dejected (SYN.) depressed, downcast, sad, disheartened, blue, discouraged.
(ANT.) *cheerful, happy.*

delectable (SYN.) tasty, delicious, savory, delightful, sweet, luscious.
(ANT.) *unsavory, distasteful, unpalatable, acrid.*

delegate (SYN.) emissary, envoy, ambassador, representative, commission.

delete (SYN.) erase, cancel, remove.
(ANT.) *add.*

deleterious (SYN.) evil, unwholesome, sinful, bad, wicked, immoral, destructive, injurious, hurtful, damaging, detrimental.
(ANT.) *moral, excellent, reputable, healthful, healthy, helpful, constructive, good.*

deliberate (SYN.) studied, willful, intended, contemplated, premeditated, planned, methodical.
(ANT.) *fortuitous, hasty, accidental.*

delicate (SYN.) frail, critical, slender, dainty, pleasing, fastidious, exquisite, precarious, demanding, sensitive, savory, fragile, weak.
(ANT.) *tough, strong, coarse, clumsy, hearty, hale, vulgar.*

delicious (SYN.) tasty, luscious, delectable, sweet.

(ANT.) unsavory, distasteful, unpalatable, unpleasant.

delight *(SYN.)* joy, bliss, gladness, pleasure, ecstasy, happiness, rapture.
(ANT.) revolt, sorrow, annoyance, displeasure, disgust, displease, revulsion, misery.

delightful *(SYN.)* pleasing, pleasant, charming, refreshing, pleasurable.
(ANT.) nasty, disagreeable, unpleasant.

delirious *(SYN.)* raving, mad, giddy, frantic, hysterical.

deliver *(SYN.)* impart, publish, rescue, commit, communicate, free, address, offer, save, give, liberate,
(ANT.) restrict, confine, capture, enslave, withhold.

deluge *(SYN.)* overflow, flood.

delusion *(SYN.)* mirage, fantasy, phantasm, vision, dream, illusion, phantom.
(ANT.) substance, actuality.

delve *(SYN.)* dig, look, search, scoop, explore, hunt.

demand *(SYN.)* claim, inquire, ask, need, require, obligation, requirement, ask for.
(ANT.) tender, give, present, waive, relinquish, offer.

demean *(SYN.)* comport, bear, operate, carry, act, manage.

demeanor *(SYN.)* manner, way, conduct, actions.

demented *(SYN.)* insane, crazy, mad, mental.

demolish *(SYN.)* ruin, devastate, ravage, annihilate, wreck, destroy, raze, exterminate, obliterate.
(ANT.) erect, make, save, construct, preserve, build.

demolition *(SYN.)* wrecking, destruction.
(ANT.) erection, construction.

demon *(SYN.)* fiend, monster, devil, ogre, spirit.

demonstrate *(SYN.)* evince, show, prove, display, illustrate, describe, explain, manifest, exhibit.
(ANT.) hide, conceal.

demonstration *(SYN.)* exhibit, show, presentation, exhibition, display, rally.

demur *(SYN.)* waver, falter, delay, stutter, doubt, vacillate, hesitate, scruple.
(ANT.) proceed, decide, resolve, continue.

demure *(SYN.)* meek, shy, modest, diffident, retiring, bashful, coy.

den *(SYN.)* cave, lair, cavern.

denial *(SYN.)* disallowance, proscription, refusal.

denounce *(SYN.)* condemn, blame, reprove, reprehend, censure, reproach, upbraid.
(ANT.) condone, approve, forgive, commend, praise.

dense *(SYN.)* crowded, slow, close, obtuse, compact, dull, stupid, compressed, thick, concentrated, packed.
(ANT.) sparse, quick, dispersed, clever, dissipated, empty, smart, bright.

dent *(SYN.)* notch, impress, pit, nick.

deny *(SYN.)* refuse, withhold, dispute, disavow, forbid.
(ANT.) confirm, affirm, admit, confess, permit, allow, concede, assert.

depart *(SYN.)* quit, forsake, withdraw, renounce, desert, relinquish, die, perish.
(ANT.) tarry, remain, come, abide, stay, arrive.

departure *(SYN.)* valediction, farewell.

depict *(SYN.)* explain, recount, describe, portray, characterize, relate, narrate.

deplore *(SYN.)* repine, lament, bemoan, wail, bewail, weep.

deport *(SYN.)* exile, eject, oust, banish, expel, dismiss, ostracize, dispel, exclude.
(ANT.) receive, admit, shelter, accept, harbor.

deportment *(SYN.)* deed, behavior, manner, action.

deposit *(SYN.)* place, put, bank, save, store, sediment, dregs, addition, entry.
(ANT.) withdraw, withdrawal.

depreciate *(SYN.)* dwindle, decrease, decay, belittle, disparage, weaken, minimize.
(ANT.) ascend, ameliorate, praise, increase, applaud.

depress *(SYN.)* deject, dishearten, sadden, dampen, devaluate, devalue, lessen, lower, cheapen, reduce, dispirit, discourage, sink.
(ANT.) exalt, cheer, exhilarate.

derision *(SYN.)* irony, satire, banter, raillery, sneering, gibe, ridicule.

derivation *(SYN.)* source, birth, inception, start, beginning, spring, commencement, foundation, origin.

(ANT.) issue, end, outcome, harvest, product.

descend *(SYN.)* wane, lower, move, slope, incline, decline, slant, sink.

(ANT.) increase, appreciate, ameliorate, ascend.

descendant *(SYN.)* child, issue, progeny, offspring.

describe *(SYN.)* portray, picture, recount, depict, relate, characterize, represent.

description *(SYN.)* history, record, recital, account, computation, chronicle.

(ANT.) misrepresentation, confusion, caricature.

desecration *(SYN.)* profanation, insult, defamation, reviling, abuse, maltreatment, aspersion, perversion.

(ANT.) respect, commendation, approval, laudation.

desert *(SYN.)* forsake, wilderness, resign, abjure, abandon, wasteland, waste, leave, surrender, abdicate, quit, barren, uninhabited.

(ANT.) uphold, defend, stay, maintain, accompany, join.

deserter *(SYN.)* runaway, renegade, fugitive, defector.

design *(SYN.)* drawing, purpose, outline, devise, intend, draw, contrive, draft, cunning, plan, artfulness, delineation, scheming, sketch.

(ANT.) candor, accident, result, chance.

designate *(SYN.)* manifest, indicate, show, specify, denote, reveal, name, appoint.

(ANT.) divert, mislead, conceal, falsify, distract.

desirable *(SYN.)* coveted, wanted.

desire *(SYN.)* longing, craving, yearning, appetite, lust, long for, crave, covet, want.

(ANT.) hate, aversion, loathing, abomination, detest.

desist *(SYN.)* cork, stop, cease, hinder, terminate, abstain, halt, interrupt, seal, arrest.

(ANT.) promote, begin, speed, proceed, start.

desolate *(SYN.)* forlorn, waste, bare, lonely, abandoned, wild, deserted,

uninhabited, empty, sad, miserable.

(ANT.) crowded, teeming, populous, happy, cheerful, fertile, attended.

despair *(SYN.)* discouragement, pessimism.

(ANT.) elation, optimism, hope, joy, confidence.

desperado *(SYN.)* criminal, crook, thug, gangster.

desperate *(SYN.)* reckless, determined, despairing, wild, daring, hopeless, despondent, audacious.

(ANT.) optimistic, composed, hopeful, collected, calm.

despicable *(SYN.)* vulgar, offensive, base, vile, contemptible, selfish, low, mean, worthless, nasty.

(ANT.) noble, exalted, admirable, generous, worthy, dignified.

despise *(SYN.)* hate, scorn, detest, loathe, disdain, abhor, condemn, dislike. '

(ANT.) honor, love, approve, like, admire.

despite *(SYN.)* notwithstanding.

despoil *(SYN.)* plunder, rob.

despondent *(SYN.)* sad, dismal, depressed, somber, ejected, melancholy, doleful, sorrowful.

(ANT.) joyous, cheerful, merry, happy.

despot *(SYN.)* tyrant, ruler, oppressor, dictator. .

despotic *(SYN.)* authoritative, unconditional, absolute, tyrannous, entire.

(ANT.) dependent, conditional, qualified.

destiny *(SYN.)* fate, portion, outcome, consequence, result, fortune, doom, lot.

destitute *(SYN.)* poor, penurious, needy, impecunious, impoverished, indigent.

(ANT.) opulent, wealthy, affluent, rich.

destroyed *(SYN.)* rent, smashed, interrupted, flattened, wrecked, broken.

(ANT.) whole, repaired, integral, united.

destruction *(SYN.)* ruin, devastation, extinction.

(ANT.) beginning, creation.

detach *(SYN.)* deduct, remove, subtract, curtail, divide, shorten, decrease.

(ANT.) hitch, grow, enlarge, increase, connect, amplify, attack, expand.

detail *(SYN.)* elaborate, commission, part, itemize, portion, division, fragment, assign, circumstance, segment.

detain *(SYN.)* impede, delay, hold back, retard, arrest, restrain, stay.
(ANT.) quicken, hasten, expedite, forward, precipitate.

detect *(SYN.)* discover, reveal, find, ascertain, determine, learn, originate, devise.
(ANT.) hide, screen, lose, cover, mask.

determinant *(SYN.)* reason, incentive, source, agent, principle, inducement.
(ANT.) result, effect, consequence, end.

determine *(SYN.)* decide, settle, end, conclude, ascertain, induce, fix, verify, resolve, establish, necessitate.

detest *(SYN.)* loathe, hate, despise.
(ANT.) savor, appreciate, like, love.

detriment *(SYN.)* injury, harm, disadvantage, damage.
(ANT.) benefit.

detrimental *(SYN.)* hurtful, mischievous, damaging, harmful.
(ANT.) salutary, advantageous, profitable, beneficial.

develop *(SYN.)* evolve, unfold, enlarge, amplify, expand, create, grow, advance, reveal, unfold, mature, elaborate.
(ANT.) wither, contract, degenerate, stunt, deteriorate, compress.

development *(SYN.)* growth, expansion, progress, unraveling, elaboration, evolution, maturing, unfolding.
(ANT.) compression, abbreviation, curtailment.

deviate *(SYN.)* deflect, stray, divert, diverge, wander, sidetrack, digress.
(ANT.) preserve, follow, remain, continue, persist.

device *(SYN.)* tool, utensil, means, channel, machine, agent, vehicle, gadget, apparatus, tools, instrument, contrivance.
(ANT.) preventive, impediment, hindrance, obstruction.

devise *(SYN.)* create, concoct, invent, originate.

devote *(SYN.)* assign, dedicate, give, apply.
(ANT.) withhold, relinquish, ignore, withdraw.

devotion *(SYN.)* piety, zeal, ardor, loyalty, dedication, religiousness, consecration.
(ANT.) unfaithfulness, aversion, alienation, indifference.

devour *(SYN.)* consume, gulp, gorge, waste, eat, ruin.

devout *(SYN.)* sacred, religious, spiritual, holy, theological, pietistic, pious.
(ANT.) profane, skeptical, atheistic, secular, impious.

dexterity *(SYN.)* talent, capability, qualification, aptness, skill, ability.
(ANT.) unreadiness, incapacity, disability.

dexterous *(SYN.)* clever, adroit, handy, deft, facile, skillful, skilled, proficient.
(ANT.) awkward, clumsy.

dialect *(SYN.)* slang, jargon, cant, speech, idiom, tongue, diction, vernacular.
(ANT.) nonsense, drivel, babble, gibberish.

dialogue *(SYN.)* interview, chat, discussion, conference, exchange, talk.

diary *(SYN.)* memo, account, journal, words.

dicker *(SYN.)* haggle, bargain, negotiate.

dictate *(SYN.)* deliver, speak, record, command, order.

dictator *(SYN.)* oppressor, tyrant, despot, persecutor, overlord, autocrat.

die *(SYN.)* fade, wane, cease, depart, wither, decay, decline, sink, expire, perish.
(ANT.) live, begin, grow, survive, flourish.

difference *(SYN.)* inequality, variety, disparity, discord, distinction, dissension.
(ANT.) harmony, similarity, identity, agreement, likeness, compatibility, kinship.

different *(SYN.)* unlike, various, distinct, miscellaneous, divergent, sundry, contrary, differing, diverse, variant.
(ANT.) similar, congruous, same, alike, identical.

differentiate *(SYN.)* separate, discriminate, distinguish, perceive, detect, recognize.
(ANT.) confuse, omit, mingle, confound, overlook.

diffuse *(SYN.)* spread, sparse, scattered, scanty, dispersed.
(ANT.) concentrated.

dig *(SYN.)* burrow, excavate, appreciate, understand.

digest *(SYN.)* consume, eat, reflect on, study, shorten.

dignified *(SYN.)* serious, solemn, noble,

stately.

dignify *(SYN.)* honor, elevate.

(ANT.) shame, degrade, humiliate.

dignity *(SYN.)* stateliness, distinction, bearing.

digress *(SYN.)* divert, wander, bend, stray, deflect.

(ANT.) preserve, continue, remain, follow, persist.

dilate *(SYN.)* increase, widen, amplify, enlarge, augment.

(ANT.) shrink, contract, restrict, abridge.

dilemma *(SYN.)* fix, strait, condition, scrape, difficulty.

(ANT.) ease, calmness, satisfaction, comfort.

diligent *(SYN.)* patient, busy, hardworking, active, perseverant, assiduous.

(ANT.) unconcerned, indifferent, apathetic, lethargic.

dim *(SYN.)* pale, shadowy, faint, faded, unclear, vague, darken, dull, indistinct.

(ANT.) brighten, brilliant, bright, illuminate, glaring.

dimension *(SYN.)* size, importance, measure, extent.

diminish *(SYN.)* suppress, lower, decrease, shrink, wane, abate, reduce, lessen.

(ANT.) enlarge, revive, amplify, increase.

diminutive *(SYN.)* small, wee, tiny, little, minute.

(ANT.) large, big, great, gigantic, huge.

din *(SYN.)* tumult, clamor, sound, babble, outcry, row.

(ANT.) quiet, stillness, hush.

dine *(SYN.)* lunch, eat, sup, feed.

dingy *(SYN.)* dull, dark, dismal, dirty, drab, murky.

(ANT.) cheerful, bright.

dip *(SYN.)* immerse, plunge, submerge, wet, swim.

diplomacy *(SYN.)* knack, dexterity, skill, address, poise, tact, finesse.

(ANT.) vulgarity, blunder, awkwardness, incompetence.

diplomatic *(SYN.)* politic, adroit, tactful, discreet.

(ANT.) rude, churlish, gruff, boorish, impolite, coarse.

dire *(SYN.)* horrible, terrible, appalling, fearful, harrowing, grievous, ghastly, aw-

ful.

(ANT.) lovely, enchanting, fascinating, beautiful.

direct *(SYN.)* rule, manage, bid, order, level, command, conduct, regulate, point.

(ANT.) swerving, untruthful, misguide, distract, indirect.

direction *(SYN.)* way, order, course, instruction, tendency, management, route, trend, guidance.

dirt *(SYN.)* pollution, soil, filthiness, filth.

(ANT.) cleanliness, cleanness.

disability *(SYN.)* inability, weakness, handicap, incapacity, injury, unfitness, incompetence, impotence.

(ANT.) power, ability, strength, capability.

disadvantage *(SYN.)* drawback, hindrance, handicap, inconvenience, obstacle.

(ANT.) advantage, benefit, convenience.

disagree *(SYN.)* quarrel, dispute, differ, conflict.

(ANT.) agree.

disappear *(SYN.)* end, fade out, vanish.

(ANT.) emerge, appear.

disappoint *(SYN.)* fail, displease, mislead, dissatisfy.

(ANT.) please, satisfy, gratify.

disapprove *(SYN.)* object to, disfavor, oppose.

(ANT.) approve.

disarm *(SYN.)* paralyze, demilitarize.

disaster *(SYN.)* casualty, mishap, misfortune, catastrophe, accident, adversity.

(ANT.) fortune, advantage.

disavow *(SYN.)* reject, revoke, disclaim, retract, disown.

(ANT.) recognize.

disband *(SYN.)* scatter, split, dismiss, separate.

disbelief *(SYN.)* doubt, incredulity, skepticism.

(ANT.) certainty, credulity.

discard *(SYN.)* scrap, reject.

discern *(SYN.)* distinguish, see, descry, separate, differentiate, perceive.

(ANT.) omit, confuse, overlook, mingle, confound.

discernment *(SYN.)* perception, sharpness, intelligence, perspicacity, acuity.

(ANT.) dullness, stupidity.

discharge *(SYN.)* remove, relieve, dismiss, banish, unburden, shoot, fire, explosion, eject, detonation.
(ANT.) retain, employ, enlist, hire, accept, recall, detain.

disciple *(SYN.)* learner, follower, student, adherent, supporter, scholar, pupil.
(ANT.) guide, leader.

discipline *(SYN.)* training, order, instruction, drill, restraint, regulation.
(ANT.) carelessness, sloppiness, confusion, negligence, messiness, chaos, turbulence.

disclaim *(SYN.)* retract, reject, deny, renounce, disavow.
(ANT.) recognize.

disclose *(SYN.)* show, divulge, betray, uncover, discover, reveal, expose.
(ANT.) hide, cloak, mask, cover, obscure, conceal.

disconnect *(SYN.)* divide, separate, unhook.
(ANT.) connect, bind, attach, unify, engage.

disconsolate *(SYN.)* depressed, downcast, sorrowful, dejected, dismal, sad.
(ANT.) delightful, merry, glad, cheerful, happy.

discontent *(SYN.)* displeased, disgruntled, unhappy, dissatisfied, vexed.

discontinue *(SYN.)* postpone, delay, adjourn, stay, stop, defer, suspend, end, cease.
(ANT.) prolong, persist, continue, start, begin, proceed.

discord *(SYN.)* disagreement, conflict.
(ANT.) concord, accord, agreement.

discourage *(SYN.)* hamper, obstruct, restrain, block, dishearten, retard, check, dispirit, thwart, depress.
(ANT.) expedite, inspire, encourage, promote, inspirit, assist, further.

discourteous *(SYN.)* gruff, rude, vulgar, blunt, impolite, saucy, uncivil.
(ANT.) stately, courtly, civil, dignified, genteel.

discover *(SYN.)* find out, invent, expose, ascertain, devise, reveal, learn, determine, detect.
(ANT.) hide, screen, cover, conceal, lose.

discredit *(SYN.)* disbelieve, dishonor,

doubt, disgrace.

discreet *(SYN.)* politic, discriminating, judicious, adroit, prudent, cautious.
(ANT.) incautious, rude, coarse, boorish, tactless.

discrepant *(SYN.)* incompatible, wavering, contrary.
(ANT.) correspondent, compatible, consistent.

discriminating *(SYN.)* exact, particular, critical, accurate.
(ANT.) unimportant, shallow, insignificant, superficial.

discrimination *(SYN.)* perspicacity, discernment, racism, wisdom, bias, sagacity, intolerance, prejudice.
(ANT.) thoughtlessness, senselessness, arbitrariness.

discuss *(SYN.)* gossip, plead, discourse, blab, lecture, talk, chat, spout, mutter.

disease *(SYN.)* malady, disorder, ailment, illness, affliction, infirmity, complaint.
(ANT.) soundness, health, vigor.

disentangle *(SYN.)* unwind, untie, clear, unravel, unknot, unsnarl, untangle.

disfigured *(SYN.)* deformed, marred, defaced, scarred.

disgrace *(SYN.)* odium, chagrin, shame, mortification, embarrassment.
(ANT.) renown, glory, respect, praise, dignity, honor.

disgraceful *(SYN.)* ignominious, shameful, discreditable, disreputable, scandalous, dishonorable.
(ANT.) renowned, esteemed, respectable, honorable.

disguise *(SYN.)* excuse, simulation, pretension, hide.
(ANT.) show, reality, actuality, display, reveal, sincerity, fact.

disgust *(SYN.)* offend, repulse, nauseate, revolt.
(ANT.) admiration, liking.

disgusting *(SYN.)* repulsive, nauseating, revolting, nauseous, repugnant.

dish *(SYN.)* serve, container, give, receptacle.

dishonest *(SYN.)* crooked, impure, unsound, false, contaminated, venal, corrupt.
(ANT.) upright, honest, straightforward.

dishonor *(SYN.)* disrepute, scandal, indignity, chagrin, mortification, shame, obloquy, defamation.

(ANT.) renown, glory, praise, honor, dignity.

disinclined *(SYN.)* unwilling, reluctant, loath.

disingenuous *(SYN.)* tricky, deceitful, scheming, dishonest, underhanded.

disintegrate *(SYN.)* decompose, dwindle, spoil, decay, wane, ebb, decline, rot.

(ANT.) increase, flourish, rise.

disinterested *(SYN.)* unbiased, open-minded, neutral, impartial, unprejudiced.

dislike *(SYN.)* aversion, dread, reluctance, abhorrence.

(ANT.) devotion, affection, enthusiasm, attachment.

disloyal *(SYN.)* false, treasonable, apostate, unfaithful, recreant, treacherous.

(ANT.) true, devoted, constant, loyal.

dismal *(SYN.)* dark, lonesome, somber, bleak, dull, sad, doleful, sorrowful.

(ANT.) lively, gay, happy, lighthearted, charming, cheerful.

dismantle *(SYN.)* take apart, wreck, disassemble.

dismay *(SYN.)* disturb, bother, dishearten, horror, alarm, bewilder, frighten, scare.

(ANT.) encourage, hearten.

dismiss *(SYN.)* remove, discharge, discard, release.

(ANT.) retain, detain, engage, hire, accept, recall.

disobedient *(SYN.)* refractory, forward, unruly, insubordinate, defiant, rebellious.

(ANT.) submissive, compliant, obedient.

disobey *(SYN.)* invade, break, violate, infringe, defile.

disorder *(SYN.)* tumult, chaos, jumble, confusion.

(ANT.) organization, neatness, system, order.

disorganization *(SYN.)* jumble, confusion, muddle.

(ANT.) system, order.

disorganized *(SYN.)* muddled, confused, indistinct, bewildered, mixed.

(ANT.) organized, lucid, clear.

disown *(SYN.)* deny, renounce, reject, repudiate, forsake, disinherit.

disparaging *(SYN.)* belittling, deprecatory, discrediting.

disparage *(SYN.)* undervalue, depreciate, lower, belittle.

(ANT.) exalting, praise, aggrandize, magnify.

disparagement *(SYN.)* lowering, decrying, undervaluing, belittling, minimizing.

(ANT.) praise, exalting, aggrandizement.

dispassionate *(SYN.)* calm, cool, composed, controlled, unemotional.

dispatch *(SYN.)* throw, impel, transmit, emit, cast, finish, report, message, send, speed, achieve, conclude, communication.

(ANT.) reluctance, get, retain, bring, slowness, hold.

dispel *(SYN.)* disseminate, scatter, disperse, separate.

(ANT.) collect, accumulate, gather.

dispense *(SYN.)* deal, give, allot, assign, apportion, mete, distribute, grant, allocate.

(ANT.) refuse, withhold, confiscate, retain, keep.

disperse *(SYN.)* dissipate, scatter, disseminate, diffuse, separate, dispel.

(ANT.) collect, amass, gather, assemble, accumulate.

dispirited *(SYN.)* down-hearted, unhappy, dejected, disheartened, sad.

(ANT.) cheerful, happy, optimistic.

displace *(SYN.)* remove, transport, lodge, shift.

(ANT.) retain, leave, stay.

display *(SYN.)* parade, exhibit, show, expose, reveal, demonstrate, showing.

(ANT.) hide, cover, conceal.

displeasure *(SYN.)* dislike, disapproval, dissatisfaction, distaste, discontentment.

disposal *(SYN.)* elimination, adjustment, removal, release, arrangement.

dispose *(SYN.)* settle, adjust.

disposition *(SYN.)* behavior, character, deed, deportment, action, manner, bearing, temperament, nature.

dispossess *(SYN.)* eject, expel, evict, oust, dislodge.

disprove *(SYN.)* refute, deny, invalidate, controvert.

dispute *(SYN.)* squabble, debate, argument, controversy, contention, disagreement, bicker, contest.

(ANT.) harmony, concord, agreement, allow, concur.

disregard (SYN.) slight, omit, ignore, inattention, oversight, skip, neglect.

(ANT.) regard, include.

disrepair (SYN.) ruin, decay, dilapidation, destruction.

disreputable (SYN.) dishonored, notorious, dishonorable, disgraced.

disrespectful (SYN.) fresh, impertinent, rude, impolite.

(ANT.) polite, respectful, courteous.

dissect (SYN.) examine, cut.

disseminate (SYN.) publish, circulate, spread, broadcast.

dissent (SYN.) objection, challenge, disagreement, protest, remonstrance, difference, nonconformity.

(ANT.) assent, acceptance, compliance, agreement.

dissertation (SYN.) thesis, treatise, disquisition.

dissimilar (SYN.) diverse, unlike, various, distinct, contrary, sundry, different.

(ANT.) same, alike, similar, congruous.

dissimulation (SYN.) pretense, deceit, sanctimony, hypocrisy, cant.

(ANT.) honesty, candor, openness, frankness, truth.

dissipate (SYN.) misuse, squander, dwindle, consume, waste, lavish.

(ANT.) save, conserve, preserve, accumulate.

dissolve (SYN.) liquefy, end, cease, melt, fade, disappear.

distant (SYN.) stiff, cold, removed, far, afar, unfriendly, remote, far-away, separated, aloof, reserved.

(ANT.) nigh, friendly, close, cordial, near.

distasteful (SYN.) disagreeable, unpleasant, objectionable.

distend (SYN.) swell, widen, magnify, expand, enlarge.

distinct (SYN.) plain, evident, lucid, visible, apparent, different, separate, individual, obvious, manifest, clear.

(ANT.) vague, indistinct, uncertain, obscure, ambiguous.

distinction (SYN.) importance, peculiarity, trait, honor, fame, characteristic, repute, quality, renown.

(ANT.) nature, substance, essence, being.

distinctive (SYN.) odd, exceptional, rare, individual, eccentric, special, strange.

(ANT.) ordinary, general, common, normal.

distinguish (SYN.) recognize, differentiate, divide, classify, descry, discern, separate, perceive, detect.

(ANT.) mingle, conjoin, blend, found, omit, confuse.

distinguished (SYN.) eminent, illustrious, renowned, celebrated, elevated, noted.

(ANT.) ordinary, common, unknown, undistinguished.

distort (SYN.) contort, falsify, twist, misrepresent.

distract (SYN.) occupy, bewilder, disturb, divert.

(ANT.) focus, concentrate.

distracted (SYN.) abstracted, preoccupied, absent.

(ANT.) attentive, attending, watchful, present.

distraction (SYN.) entertainment, confusion.

distress (SYN.) torment, misery, trouble, worry, pain, agony, torture, anguish, anxiety, disaster, wretchedness, peril, danger.

(ANT.) joy, solace, comfort, relief.

distribute (SYN.) deal, sort, allot, mete, classify, share, issue, dole, apportion, allocate, dispense, group.

district (SYN.) domain, place, territory, country, region.

distrust (SYN.) scruple, unbelief, suspect, mistrust.

(ANT.) faith, conviction, trust, belief, determination.

disturb (SYN.) perturb, vex, confuse, worry, agitate, derange, unsettle, perplex.

(ANT.) quiet, order, calm, settle, pacify, soothe.

disturbance (SYN.) disorder, commotion, confusion, riot, fight, brawl.

(ANT.) calm, tranquillity, serenity.

diverge (SYN.) fork, separate.

(ANT.) converge, join, merge.

diverse (SYN.) unlike, various, different,

several.

divert *(SYN.)* detract, amuse, confuse, distract, deflect.

(ANT.) tire, bore, weary.

divide *(SYN.)* share, split, detach, cleave, apportion, sunder, part, distribute, allocate, disunite, estrange.

(ANT.) merge, unite, convene, join, gather, combine.

divine *(SYN.)* holy, supernatural, godlike, transcendent, celestial, heavenly.

(ANT.) mundane, wicked, blasphemous, profane.

division *(SYN.)* partition, separation, sharing, section, segment, part, portion.

(ANT.) union, agreement.

divorce *(SYN.)* disjoin, disconnect, separate, divide.

divulge *(SYN.)* discover, release, expose, show, betray, reveal, admit, disclose.

(ANT.) hide, conceal, cloak.

dizzy *(SYN.)* staggering, unsteady, giddy, light-headed.

(ANT.) rational, clearheaded, unconfused.

do *(SYN.)* effect, conduct, perform, work, suffice, accomplish, finish, transact, serve, discharge, execute, complete, carry on, make, settle, conclude, fulfill.

docile *(SYN.)* pliant, tame, complaint, obedient, submissive, yielding.

(ANT.) unruly, obstinate, ungovernable, mulish.

doctor *(SYN.)* heal, treat, medic, remedy, cure.

doctrine *(SYN.)* tenet, precept, belief, dogma, teaching, principle, creed.

(ANT.) deed, practice, conduct, perform.

document *(SYN.)* report, minute, memorial, vestige, account, note, trace.

doing *(SYN.)* feat, performance, act, deed, accomplishment, transaction.

(ANT.) intention, inactivity, cessation, inhibition.

doleful *(SYN.)* dark, depressed, sad, dismal, sorrowful, unhappy, morose, lonesome, mournful.

(ANT.) gay, lively, cheerful, joyous.

domain *(SYN.)* place, division, region, territory, empire, realm, quarter, dominion, bailiwick, jurisdiction, land.

domestic *(SYN.)* family, tame, native, servant, homemade, household, internal.

(ANT.) alien, foreign, outside.

domesticate *(SYN.)* train, tame, housebreak, teach.

domicile *(SYN.)* dwelling, residence, home, abode.

dominate *(SYN.)* control, manage, rule, influence, subjugate, command, govern, tyrannize, direct, regulate.

(ANT.) follow, ignore, abandon, submit, forsake.

domination *(SYN.)* mastery, sway, ascendancy, transcendence.

don *(SYN.)* wear, slip on.

donation *(SYN.)* gift, bequest, present, benefaction, grant, contribution, offering, largess, boon.

(ANT.) earnings, purchase, deprivation, loss.

done *(SYN.)* complete, concluded, finished, over, terminated.

doom *(SYN.)* fortune, issue, result, destruction, destiny, consequence, fate, outcome, destine, ruin, death, lot.

doomed *(SYN.)* fated, predestined, destined, foreordained.

dormant *(SYN.)* unemployed, inert, lazy, unoccupied, idle, indolent.

(ANT.) working, employed, occupied, active, industrious.

dose *(SYN.)* quantity, amount, portion.

dote *(SYN.)* indulge, treasure, coddle, pamper, spoil.

(ANT.) ignore.

double *(SYN.)* copy, fold, duplicate.

doubt *(SYN.)* distrust, incredulity, suspicion, hesitation, uncertainty, question, scruple, ambiguity, skepticism, suspect, mistrust, unbelief, suspense.

(ANT.) conviction, belief, determination, trust, certainty.

doubtful *(SYN.)* uncertain, unsettled, dubious, questionable, unsure, undetermined.

doubtless *(SYN.)* certainly, undoubtedly, assuredly, positively, unquestionably.

dour *(SYN.)* gloomy, sulky, crabbed, morose, fretful.

(ANT.) joyous, pleasant, amiable, merry.

douse *(SYN.)* immerse, quench, dip, dunk, extinguish.

dowdy *(SYN.)* messy, unkempt, untidy,

sloppy, shabby, frowzy.

downcast *(SYN.)* sad, disheartened, unhappy, dejected, dispirited, discourage, depressed, glum.

downfall *(SYN.)* destruction, comedown.

downgrade *(SYN.)* reduce, lower, diminish, decrease, depreciate.
(ANT.) improve, upgrade, appreciate.

downhearted *(SYN.)* glum, discouraged, depressed, gloomy, downcast, sad, dejected.
(ANT.) enthusiastic, cheerful, happy.

downpour *(SYN.)* cloudburst, deluge, flood.

downright *(SYN.)* totally, positively, completely, definitely.

dowry *(SYN.)* endowment, gift, settlement, talent, ability.

drab *(SYN.)* flat, dull, lifeless, unattractive.

draft *(SYN.)* air, induction, wind, enrollment, drawing, outline.

drag *(SYN.)* heave, pull, tug, crawl, draw, tarry, tow, haul, delay.

drain *(SYN.)* empty, deprive, dry, filter, spend, tap, exhaust, waste, sap, use.
(ANT.) fulfill, fill.

drama *(SYN.)* show, play, production, piece.

dramatist *(SYN.)* playwright.

drape *(SYN.)* flow, cover, hang.

drastic *(SYN.)* severe, rough, extreme, violent, tough, intense.

draw *(SYN.)* tug, obtain, trace, lure, drag, attract, persuade, induce, haul, write, remove, extend, stretch, take out, allure, pull, prolong, extract, tow, draft, delineate, unsheathe, lure, depict.
(ANT.) shorten, contract, propel, alienate, drive.

drawback *(SYN.)* snag, hitch, disadvantage, handicap, deficiency, difficulty, check, obstacle, hindrance, impediment.
(ANT.) gain, benefit, windfall.

dread *(SYN.)* awe, horror, fear, terror, alarm, reverence, apprehension.
(ANT.) courage, boldness, assurance, confidence.

dreadful *(SYN.)* dire, inspiring, ghastly, appalling, horrid, impressive, terrible.
(ANT.) fascinating, beautiful, enjoyable, enchanting, lovely.

dream *(SYN.)* fantasy, wish, hope, vision, daydream, reverie, imagine, fantasize.

dream up *(SYN.)* cook up, create, think up, concost.

dreary *(SYN.)* dull, sad, bleak, lonesome, gloomy, chilling.
(ANT.) lively, hopeful, gay, cheerful, bright, joyous.

drench *(SYN.)* wet, bathe, flood, soak, saturate.

dress *(SYN.)* garb, frock, gown, clothing, costume, apparel, attire, wardrobe, wear, don, robe, raiment.
(ANT.) undress, strip, divest, disrobe.

dribble *(SYN.)* fall, drip, leak, slaver, slobber.

drift *(SYN.)* roam, tendency, meander, sail, float, direction, wander, intention.

drifter *(SYN.)* hobo, tramp.

drill *(SYN.)* employment, lesson, task, use, activity, operation, training.
(ANT.) relaxation, indolence, rest, idleness, repose.

drink *(SYN.)* gulp, swallow, imbibe, beverage.

drip *(SYN.)* dribble, drop.

drive *(SYN.)* impel, coerce, oblige, force, push, direct, constrain, journey, urge, enforce, trip, handle, ride.

driver *(SYN.)* motorist, operator, teamster, trucker.

droll *(SYN.)* laughable, funny, amusing, witty, comical.
(ANT.) sober, sad, solemn, melancholy.

drone *(SYN.)* buzz, hum, loafer, idler, nonworker.

drool *(SYN.)* drivel, slaver, dribble, spit, gibber, jabber.

droop *(SYN.)* dangle, weaken, hang, sink, fail, settle, sag.
(ANT.) stand, tower, extend, rise, straighten.

drop *(SYN.)* droop, dribble, topple, collapse, downward, drip, trickle, tumble, gob, slip, decrease, fall, dismiss.
(ANT.) ascend, mount, steady, arise, soar.

drown *(SYN.)* sink, inundate, submerge, immerse.

drowse *(SYN.)* nap, doze, catnap, snooze, sleep, slumber.

drowsy *(SYN.)* dozing, torpid, soothing,

dreamy, sleepy, comatose, lethargic.

(ANT.) alert, awake, sharp, keen, acute.

drub *(SYN.)* wallop, thrash, beat, thump, cane, flog, rout, outclass, overcome.

drudge *(SYN.)* work, labor, toiler, flunky, menial.

drudgery *(SYN.)* toil, travail, effort, task, labor.

(ANT.) recreation, indolence, leisure.

drug *(SYN.)* remedy, medicine, stupefy, anesthetize.

drunk *(SYN.)* tight, intoxicated, soused, drunken, inebriated, alcoholic, sozzled, lush, tipsy.

dry *(SYN.)* thirsty, dehydrated, vapid, plain, arid, parched, barren, waterless, dull, desiccated, tiresome.

(ANT.) fresh, wet, soaked, fascinating, attractive, lively.

dubious *(SYN.)* unsure, uncertain, undecided, hesitant, spurious, unreliable, puzzling, ambiguous.

(ANT.) decided, fixed, irrefutable, definite, genuine, authentic, trustworthy.

duck *(SYN.)* douse, dip, submerse, submerge, immerse, plunge, wet, souse, drench, engulf, avoid, shun, lower, bob, hedge, shy, evade, swerve, quail.

(ANT.) raise, confront, face, elevate, cope with, undertake, assume, face up to.

duct *(SYN.)* pipe, tube, passage, vein, canal, funnel, main, trough, artery.

due *(SYN.)* payable, unpaid, owing, owed, imminent, expected.

duel *(SYN.)* competition, contest, engagement, rivalry, combat, strife, encounter, battle, conflict, dispute, strive.

dues *(SYN.)* assessment, fees, cost, levy, admission, fare, toll, contribution.

duffer *(SYN.)* bungler, slouch, blunderer, novice, incompetent, fumbler, lummox.

(ANT.) master, expert, pro.

dull *(SYN.)* commonplace, slow, sad, dreary, boring, stupid, uninteresting, blunt, tedious, dulled, dumb, tiring, monotonous, obtuse, tiresome, dense, unimaginative, unfeeling, dismal.

(ANT.) clear, animated, interesting, lively.

dullard *(SYN.)* dolt, dunce, moron, clod, blockhead, numskull.

dumb *(SYN.)* dull, witless, ignorant, mute, speechless, brainless, dense, stupid, senseless.

(ANT.) discerning, bright, alert, clever, intelligent.

dumbfound *(SYN.)* stagger, stun, nonplus, stupefy, overwhelm, amaze, confuse, startle, surprise, astonish.

dumfounded *(SYN.)* shocked, astonished, flabbergasted, astounded, stunned.

dump *(SYN.)* heap, fling down, drop, empty, unload, clear out, dispose of, tipple, discharge, overturn, upset, dismiss, abandon.

(ANT.) store, fill, load, hoard, pack.

dunk *(SYN.)* plunge, submerge, dip.

(ANT.) uplift, elevate, recover.

duplicate *(SYN.)* replica, replicate, facsimile, copy, twin, transcript.

(ANT.) prototype.

duplicity *(SYN.)* dissimulation, deception, hypocrisy, artifice, cant, guile.

(ANT.) openness, artlessness, genuineness.

durability *(SYN.)* might, strength, force, sturdiness, intensity, potency, vigor.

(ANT.) weakness, frailty, feebleness.

durable *(SYN.)* constant, firm, fixed, unchangeable, enduring, abiding, lasting.

(ANT.) unstable, temporary, perishable, transitory.

duration *(SYN.)* time, term, epoch, interim.

dutiful *(SYN.)* docile, faithful.

(ANT.) disobedient, willful, unruly, headstrong.

duty *(SYN.)* bond, responsibility, accountability, obligation, conscience.

(ANT.) freedom, choice.

dwarf *(SYN.)* midget, runt.

(ANT.) mammoth, colossus, monster, giant.

dwell *(SYN.)* inhabit, roost, settle, abide, live, reside.

dwindle *(SYN.)* decrease, diminish, fade.

(ANT.) enlarge, increase, grow, gain.

dying *(SYN.)* failing, expiring, waning, passing, final.

(ANT.) thriving, booming, flourishing.

dynamic *(SYN.)* active, forceful, kinetic, energetic.

(ANT.) sleepy, stable, inert, ineffectual, listless.

eager *(SYN.)* avid, hot, anxious, fervent, keen, enthusiastic, impatient, ardent, impassioned, yearning.
(ANT.) unconcerned, apathetic, impassioned, dull, uninterested, indifferent.

early *(SYN.)* opportune, first, beforehand, advanced, soon, shortly.
(ANT.) retarded, late, tardy, belated, overdue.

earmark *(SYN.)* peculiarity, characteristic, brand, sign, feature, stamp, trademark.

earn *(SYN.)* attain, win, get, achieve, obtain, gain, deserve, clear, realize, collect, net, acquire, merit.
(ANT.) lose, waste, consume, forfeit.

earnest *(SYN.)* sincere, decided, determined, intent, serious, eager, resolute.
(ANT.) indifferent, frivolous, insincere.

earnings *(SYN.)* wages, pay, salary, income.

earth *(SYN.)* globe, dirt, land, world, turf, soil, sod, ground.

earthly *(SYN.)* mundane, everyday, worldly.
(ANT.) heavenly.

earthy *(SYN.)* earthlike, coarse, earthen, crude, unrefined, vulgar.
(ANT.) tasteful, elegant, polished, refined.

ease *(SYN.)* lighten, alleviate, pacify, soothe, allay, comfort, contentedness, assuage, reduce, rest, facilitate, relaxation, calm, repose, mitigate, contentment, relax.
(ANT.) worry, disturb, confound, aggravate, difficulty, effort, trouble, intensify, distress.

easily *(SYN.)* readily, effortlessly, lightly, smoothly, naturally, facilely, doubtlessly.
(ANT.) hardly, ardously, painfully, laboriously.

easiness *(SYN.)* repose, comfort, satisfaction, contentment, liberty, leisure, facility, simplicity.
(ANT.) unrest, torment, arduousness, difficulty, discomfort.

easy *(SYN.)* light, simple, facile, gentle, effortless, unhurried, comfortable, pleasant, cozy, relaxed, plain, uncomplicated, restful.

(ANT.) hard, demanding, awkward, strict, difficult, formal.

easygoing *(SYN.)* calm, mild, complacent, relaxed, unconcerned, serene, uncritical, cheerful, carefree, unhurried.
(ANT.) severe, demanding, stern, strict, harsh.

eat *(SYN.)* consume, swallow, dine, corrode, chew, lunch, devour, feast, breakfast, erode.

eavesdrop *(SYN.)* spy, listen, snoop, overhear.

eavesdropper *(SYN.)* monitor, listener, snoop, spy.

ebb *(SYN.)* diminish, recede, decline, decrease, retreat, lessen.
(ANT.) wax, grow, thrive, increase, swell.

ebullient *(SYN.)* vivacious, buoyant, exuberant.
(ANT.) lethargic, sad, gloomy, depressed.

eccentric *(SYN.)* odd, irregular, unusual, abnormal, peculiar.
(ANT.) ordinary, conventional, normal.

eccentricity *(SYN.)* kink, idiosyncracy, whim, freak, caprice, foible, quirk, oddness, strangeness, aberration.
(ANT.) normality, conventionality, ordinariness.

ecclesiatical *(SYN.)* religious, churchly, clerical.

echelon *(SYN.)* rank, level, grade, place, status.

echo *(SYN.)* response, imitation, suggestion, trace, reaction, imitate, repeat.

eclectic *(SYN.)* selective, diverse, broad, liberal, comprehensive, general.
(ANT.) limited, narrow, rigid, confined.

eclipse *(SYN.)* conceal, screen, hide, cover, obscure, overcast, veil.

economical *(SYN.)* saving, thrifty, careful, frugal, provident, sparing.
(ANT.) wasteful, extravagant, lavish, improvident, prodigal.

economize *(SYN.)* pinch, scrimp, save.

economy *(SYN.)* saving, thrift.

ecstasy *(SYN.)* frenzy, gladness, delight, madness, joy, glee, exaltation, pleasure, transport, trance, rapture.
(ANT.) misery, melancholy, sadness.

ecstatic *(SYN.)* overjoyed, thrilled, delighted, happy, elated.

edge *(SYN.)* margin, brim, verge, brink,

border, keenness, extremity, boundary, trim, periphery, hem, rim, sting.
(ANT.) dullness, center, bluntness.

edgy *(SYN.)* tense, touchy, nervous, irritable.

edict *(SYN.)* declaration, order, ruling, decree, pronouncement, command, law, proclamation.

edifice *(SYN.)* construction, building, establishment.

edit *(SYN.)* check, revise, correct, amend.

educate *(SYN.)* instruct, teach, school, train.

education *(SYN.)* training, development, knowledge, learning, cultivation, schooling, instruction, study.

eerie *(SYN.)* weird, fearful, ghastly, spooky, strange.

efface *(SYN.)* obliterate, erase.

effect *(SYN.)* produce, consequence, evoke, cause, make, complete, outcome, result, determine.

effective *(SYN.)* efficient, practical, productive.
(ANT.) useless, wasteful, ineffective.

efficiency *(SYN.)* efficacy, capability, effectiveness, competency, ability.
(ANT.) wastefulness, inability.

efficient *(SYN.)* efficacious, skillful, capable, adept, competent, useful, effectual, effective, serviceable, apt, proficient.
(ANT.) inefficient, unskilled, ineffectual, incompetent.

effort *(SYN.)* labor, endeavor, pains, essay, trial, exertion, struggle, strain, trouble, try, attempt, strife, toil.

effortless *(SYN.)* simple, easy.

egg *(SYN.)* stir, ovum, incite, urge, arouse, embryo, provoke.

egghead *(SYN.)* scholar, intellectual, pedant.

egoism *(SYN.)* self-interest, conceit, pride, selfishness, egotism.
(ANT.) modesty, generosity, selflessness.

eject *(SYN.)* expel, remove, oust, eliminate.
(ANT.) include.

elaborate *(SYN.)* detail, develop, decorated, decorative, ornate, complex.
(ANT.) simplify, simple, unadorned.

elapse *(SYN.)* expire.

elastic *(SYN.)* yielding, flexible, adaptable, pliable.

elated *(SYN.)* delighted, rejoicing, overjoyed, jubilant.
(ANT.) sad, unhappy.

elder *(SYN.)* senior.
(ANT.) younger.

elderly *(SYN.)* aged, old.
(ANT.) young, youthful.

elect *(SYN.)* pick, appoint, choose.

electrify *(SYN.)* shock, charge, stir, upset, generate, agitate.

elegant *(SYN.)* tasteful, refined, cultivated, choice, polished, superior, fine.
(ANT.) crude, coarse, unpolished, tasteless.

elementary *(SYN.)* simple, primary, basic, uncomplicated, initial, beginning, fundamental.
(ANT.) involved, complex, sophisticated, complicated.

elevate *(SYN.)* raise, lift.
(ANT.) lower, drop.

elf *(SYN.)* devil, fairy, imp.

elicit *(SYN.)* summon.

eligible *(SYN.)* fit, suitable, qualified.

eliminate *(SYN.)* expel, eject, remove, dislodge, extirpate, erase, oust.
(ANT.) admit, involve.

elite *(SYN.)* nobility, upper-class, aristocracy, gentry.
(ANT.) mob, proletariat.

elongate *(SYN.)* extend, prolong, lengthen.

elope *(SYN.)* escape, flee.

eloquent *(SYN.)* expressive, fluent, articulate, glib, meaningful.
(ANT.) inarticulate.

else *(SYN.)* different, another, other.

elude *(SYN.)* escape, miss, avoid, dodge.
(ANT.) add, include.

emaciated *(SYN.)* wasted, thin, starved, withered, shriveled, gaunt, shrunken, drawn, undernourished.

emancipate *(SYN.)* liberate, free, deliver, save.
(ANT.) restrain.

embankment *(SYN.)* shore, dam, bank, fortification, buttress.

embargo *(SYN.)* prohibition, restriction, restraint.

embark *(SYN.)* board, depart.

embarrass *(SYN.)* discomfit, rattle, distress, hamper, fluster, entangle, abash, mortify, hinder, perplex, confuse, shame, trouble.
(ANT.) relieve, encourage, help.
embassy *(SYN.)* ministry, legation, consulate.
embed *(SYN.)* root, inset, enclose, plant.
embellish *(SYN.)* adorn, decorate, ornament.
embezzle *(SYN.)* pilfer, misuse, rob, misappropriate, steal, take.
embitter *(SYN.)* provoke, arouse, alienate, anger, inflame.
emblem *(SYN.)* token, mark, symbol, badge.
embody *(SYN.)* comprise, cover, embrace, include.
embrace *(SYN.)* espouse, accept, receive, comprehend, contain, welcome, comprise, cover, clasp, include, adopt, hug.
(ANT.) spurn, reject, bar, exclude, repudiate.
embroider *(SYN.)* decorate, adorn, stitch, trim, overstate, embellish, ornament, exaggerate, magnify.
emerge *(SYN.)* surface, show, appear.
emergency *(SYN.)* strait, pass, crisis, urgency, predicament, pinch.
eminent *(SYN.)* renowned, glorious, distinguished, noted, celebrated, elevated, glorious, important, conspicuous, prominent, famous.
(ANT.) ordinary, commonplace, unknown, undistinguished, common.
emissary *(SYN.)* envoy, minister, delegate, agent, spy.
emit *(SYN.)* expel, breathe, shoot, hurl, ooze, vent, belch, discharge.
emotion *(SYN.)* passion, turmoil, perturbation, affection, sentiment, feeling, trepidation, agitation.
(ANT.) dispassion, indifference, tranquillity, calm, restraint.
emotional *(SYN.)* ardent, passionate, stirring, zealous, impetuous, overwrought, enthusiastic.
(ANT.) tranquil, calm, placid.
emphasis *(SYN.)* accent, stress, insistence.
emphatic *(SYN.)* positive, definite, forceful, energetic, strong.

(ANT.) lax, quiet, unforceful.
employ *(SYN.)* avail, use, devote, apply, utilize, engage, sign, hire, retain, service, contract.
(ANT.) reject, discard.
employee *(SYN.)* laborer, worker, servant.
(ANT.) boss, employer.
employer *(SYN.)* owner, boss, management, proprietor, manager, superintendent, supervisor.
(ANT.) employee, worker.
employment *(SYN.)* occupation, work, business, position, job, service, engagement.
(ANT.) leisure, idleness, slothfulness.
empower *(SYN.)* enable, sanction, permit, warrant.
empty *(SYN.)* void, devoid, unfilled, barren, senseless, unoccupied, vain, unfurnished, vacant, blank, evacuate, unload, hollow.
(ANT.) supplied, full, occupied.
emulate *(SYN.)* follow, imitate, copy.
enable *(SYN.)* authorize, empower, sanction, qualify.
enact *(SYN.)* legislate, portray, pass, stage, represent.
enchant *(SYN.)* charm, titillate, fascinate, bewitch, delight, thrill, captivate.
(ANT.) tire, bore.
encircle *(SYN.)* comprise, include, bound, encompass.
enclose *(SYN.)* envelop, confine, bound, surround, encompass, encircle, circumscribe.
(ANT.) open, exclude, distend, expose, develop.
encompass *(SYN.)* include, surround, encircle.
encore *(SYN.)* repetition, repeat, again.
encounter *(SYN.)* battle, meet, oppose, run into, face, collide.
encourage *(SYN.)* incite, favor, cheer, impel, countenance, inspirit, exhilarate, animate, hearten, embolden, support.
(ANT.) deter, dispirit, deject, dissuade.
encroach *(SYN.)* interfere, trespass, intrude, infringe.
encumber *(SYN.)* hamper, load, burden.
end *(SYN.)* completion, object, close,

aim, result, conclusion, finish, extremity, bound, intent, halt, stop, limit, purpose, cessation, expiration, termination.
(ANT.) *opening, start, introduction, beginning, launch, inception.*
endanger *(SYN.)* imperil, hazard, risk.
(ANT.) *secure.*
endear *(SYN.)* allure, charm.
endeavor *(SYN.)* strive, struggle, exertion, attempt, try, labor.
endless *(SYN.)* constant, nonstop, continuous, incessant, everlasting.
endorse *(SYN.)* approve, accept, sign, confirm, pass.
endow *(SYN.)* provide, furnish, bestow, give, contribute.
(ANT.) *divest.*
endure *(SYN.)* experience, undergo, sustain, last, bear, continue, remain, undergo, persist, brook, tolerate, suffer.
(ANT.) *wane, die, perish, succumb, fail.*
enemy *(SYN.)* foe, antagonist, rival, opponent, competitor, adversary, opposition.
(ANT.) *colleague, ally, friend, accomplice.*
energy *(SYN.)* strength, vim, force, power, stamina, vigor, might.
(ANT.) *feebleness, lethargy.*
enervate *(SYN.)* enfeeble, weaken, debilitate, exhaust, devitalize.
(ANT.) *invigorate.*
enfold *(SYN.)* clasp, surround, wrap, embrace, hug.
enforce *(SYN.)* make, drive, compel, execute, force.
engage *(SYN.)* absorb, occupy, employ, hold, involve, hire, agree, engross, retain, promise, commit, entangle.
(ANT.) *fire, disengage, discharge, dismiss.*
engaged *(SYN.)* affianced, betrothed, busy, occupied.
engaging *(SYN.)* fascinating, appealing, enticing, interesting, tempting, lovely, beguiling, charming, enchanting, engrossing, delightful, exquisite.
(ANT.) *ordinary, boring.*
engender *(SYN.)* develop, breed, cause, generate, produce.
engineer *(SYN.)* direct, conduct, guide, lead, manage.

engrave *(SYN.)* print, cut, impress, inscribe, carve, sketch.
engross *(SYN.)* engage, enthrall, occupy, fascinate, absorb.
engulf *(SYN.)* flood, swallow.
enhance *(SYN.)* better, uplift, improve.
enigma *(SYN.)* mystery, stumper, riddle.
enigmatic *(SYN.)* perplexing, confusing, puzzling, baffling, mystifying.
enjoy *(SYN.)* savor, like, relish.
enjoyment *(SYN.)* pleasure, delight, gratification.
(ANT.) *abhorrence, displeasure.*
enlarge *(SYN.)* widen, distend, amplify, broaden, extend, increase, augment, expand, dilate.
(ANT.) *diminish, shrink, contract, decrease, wane, restrict.*
enlighten *(SYN.)* inform, illuminate, clarify, teach, instruct.
(ANT.) *confuse.*
enlist *(SYN.)* enroll, prompt, join, induce, enter, register, persuade.
(ANT.) *quit, leave, abandon.*
enliven *(SYN.)* inspire, brighten, stimulate.
enmity *(SYN.)* antagonism, hatred, animosity, malignity, ill-will, antipathy, hostility, unfriendliness.
(ANT.) *love, like, friendliness.*
enormity *(SYN.)* heinousness, wickedness, barbarity, atrociousness.
enormous *(SYN.)* vast, huge, colossal, immense, gargantuan, elephantine, gigantic, stupendous, large.
(ANT.) *small, slight, tiny, minute, infinitesimal, diminutive, little.*
enough *(SYN.)* ample, adequate, sufficient, plenty.
(ANT.) *inadequate, insufficient.*
enrage *(SYN.)* anger, provoke, madden, inflame.
(ANT.) *appease, soothe, calm.*
enrich *(SYN.)* better, improve.
enroll *(SYN.)* record, list, recruit, register, enlist, write.
(ANT.) *quit, leave, abandon.*
enshrine *(SYN.)* bury, entomb.
ensign *(SYN.)* banner, colors, flag, officer.
enslave *(SYN.)* keep, hold, capture.
ensue *(SYN.)* arise, succeed, follow,

result.

ensure *(SYN.)* guarantee, assure, protect, defend, cover.

entangle *(SYN.)* confuse, snare, involve, ravel, snarl, tangle, trap.

enter *(SYN.)* join, go inside.

enterprise *(SYN.)* fete, deed, venture, project, adventure, undertaking, ambition, business, exploit.

enterprising *(SYN.)* energetic, resourceful.
(ANT.) *lazy, indolent, sluggish, unresourceful.*

entertain *(SYN.)* cheer, gladden, hold, consider, please, contemplate, divert, amuse, harbor, fascinate, interest.
(ANT.) *repulse, tire, bore, disgust, annoy.*

enthrall *(SYN.)* captivate, fascinate, enchant, charm, thrill.

enthusiasm *(SYN.)* fervor, fanaticism, zeal, ardor, intensity, devotion, excitement, eagerness, fervency, earnestness.
(ANT.) *indifference, ennui, apathy, unconcern, detachment.*

enthusiastic *(SYN.)* earnest, zealous, eager.
(ANT.) *aloof, indifferent, unconcerned.*

entice *(SYN.)* lure, attract, seduce.

entire *(SYN.)* complete, intact, whole, undivided.
(ANT.) *divided, separated, incomplete, partial.*

entirely *(SYN.)* altogether, thoroughly, wholly, solely.

entitle *(SYN.)* call, label, name, empower, allow, authorize, license, title.

entourage *(SYN.)* train, company, retinue, escort.

entrance *(SYN.)* inlet, portal, doorway, fascinate, entry, intrigue, door, charm, thrill.
(ANT.) *exit.*

entreat *(SYN.)* implore, beg, plead.

entreaty *(SYN.)* plea, appeal.

entrust *(SYN.)* commit, charge, assign, delegate, consign, commission.

enumerate *(SYN.)* count, tally, list, number.

enunciate *(SYN.)* announce, express, speak, state.

envelop *(SYN.)* embrace, cover, conceal, surround, wrap.

environment *(SYN.)* neighborhood, habitat, surroundings, setting.

envision *(SYN.)* picture, imagine, visualize.

envoy *(SYN.)* delegate, emissary, representative, agent, messenger.

envy *(SYN.)* covetousness, jealousy, spitefulness, covet.
(ANT.) *indifference, generosity.*

epicure *(SYN.)* gourmand, gourmet, connoisseur, gastronome, epicurean, aesthete.

epidemic *(SYN.)* prevalent, scourge, plague, catching, pestilence, infectious.

episode *(SYN.)* happening, affair, occurrence, event, experience.

epoch *(SYN.)* age.

equal *(SYN.)* even, uniform, like, alike, equitable, same, identical, commensurate, equivalent, regular, parallel.
(ANT.) *different, unequal, irregular, uneven.*

equilibrium *(SYN.)* stability, steadiness, balance, firmness.

equip *(SYN.)* fit, rig, provide, outfit, prepare, furnish.

equipment *(SYN.)* utensils, material, apparatus.

equitable *(SYN.)* square, rightful, fair, due, just, fit.
(ANT.) *partial, biased, unjust, uneven.*

equity *(SYN.)* impartiality, fairness, justness, justice, evenandedness.

equivalent *(SYN.)* match, rival, equal, like, replacement.

equivocal *(SYN.)* oblique, ambiguous, vague, indeterminate, uncertain, obscure.
(ANT.) *clear, precise, explicit, certain, clear-cut, definite.*

equivocate *(SYN.)* temporize, evade, hedge, quibble, fudge, waffle, straddle.

era *(SYN.)* epoch, cycle, age, time, period.

eradicate *(SYN.)* remove, demolish, eliminate.

erase *(SYN.)* obliterate, remove, cancel.
(ANT.) *add, include.*

erect *(SYN.)* upright, build, straight, raise, construct, vertical.
(ANT.) *flat, horizontal, raze, flatten, demolish.*

erection (SYN.) building, construction, raising, fabrication.

erode (SYN.) rust, consume, disintegrate.

erotic (SYN.) carnal, fleshy, amatory, prurient, lewd, wanton, passionate, lecherous.

err (SYN.) slip, misjudge.

errand (SYN.) chore, duty, task, exercise.

errant (SYN.) roving, rambling, wandering, vagrant.

erratic (SYN.) irregular, abnormal, uneven, occasional, sporadic, changeable, unsteady, odd, eccentric, strange, extraordinary, queer, unconventional, bizarre, peculiar, uncertain, unusual, unstable.

(ANT.) *regular, steady, normal, ordinary.*

erroneous (SYN.) wrong, mistaken, incorrect, inaccurate, false, untrue.

(ANT.) *true, right, correct, accurate.*

error (SYN.) inaccuracy, fault, slip, oversight, fallacy, mistake, blunder.

erudite (SYN.) sage, wise, learned, deep, profound.

erupt (SYN.) vomit.

escapade (SYN.) caper, antic, stunt, trick, prank.

escape (SYN.) shun, avoid, flee, decamp, elude, flight, avert, departure, abscond, fly, evade.

(ANT.) *meet, confront, invite, catch.*

escort (SYN.) conduct, lead, attend, accompany, protection, guard, guide, convoy, usher, squire.

especially (SYN.) unusually, principally, mainly, particularly, primarily.

essay (SYN.) test, thesis, undertake, paper, try.

essence (SYN.) substance, character, nature, principle, odor, meaning, basis, smell, perfume.

essential (SYN.) vital, intrinsic, basic, requisite, fundamental, indispensable, critical, requirement, necessity, necessary, important.

(ANT.) *dispensable, unimportant, inessential.*

establish (SYN.) prove, fix, found, settle, institute, raise, verify, conform, form, sanction, ordain, begin, organize.

(ANT.) *upset, discontinue, scatter, disperse, refute, abolish, unsettle.*

esteem (SYN.) revere, deem, appreciate, honor, value, think, admire, respect, hold, prize, reverence, regard.

(ANT.) *scorn, disdain, depreciate, disregard, contempt, abhor.*

estimate (SYN.) calculate, gauge, judge, rate, evaluate, compute, value, figure.

estimation (SYN.) judgment, viewpoint, opinion.

etch (SYN.) stamp, engrave, impress.

eternal (SYN.) undying, immortal, ceaseless, infinite, everlasting, deathless, perpetual, endless, timeless.

(ANT.) *mortal, transient, finite, brief, temporary, passing.*

etiquette (SYN.) decorum, formality.

evacuate (SYN.) withdraw, depart, leave, vacate.

evade (SYN.) miss, avoid, bypass.

(ANT.) *confront, meet, face.*

evaluate (SYN.) value, appraise, assay.

evaporate (SYN.) disappear, vanish.

(ANT.) *condense, appear.*

even (SYN.) smooth, level, still, square, same, flat, balanced, equal, parallel, identical.

(ANT.) *irregular, bumpy, unbalanced, unequal, divergent.*

evening (SYN.) twilight, dusk, sunset.

(ANT.) *sunrise, dawn.*

event (SYN.) issue, end, result, circumstance, occurrence, incident, consequence, happening, episode, outcome.

eventual (SYN.) consequent, ultimate.

(ANT.) *present, current.*

eventually (SYN.) ultimately.

ever (SYN.) continuously, constantly.

(ANT.) *never.*

everlasting (SYN.) permanent, ceaseless, endless, continual.

evermore (SYN.) always.

everyday (SYN.) commonplace, common, usual, ordinary, customary.

(ANT.) *rare.*

evict (SYN.) oust, put out, expel.

evidence (SYN.) grounds, clue, facts, testimony, data, sign, proof.

evident (SYN.) apparent, clear, obvious, indubitable, plain, conspicuous, patent, manifest, open, unmistakable.

(ANT.) *hidden, unclear, uncertain, obscure, concealed.*

evil *(SYN.)* immoral, harmful, badness, sinful, injurious, woe, bad, wicked.
(ANT.) goodness, moral, useful, upright, virtuous, beneficial, virtue.

evoke *(SYN.)* summon, prompt.

evolve *(SYN.)* grow, advance, develop, result, emerge, unfold.

exact *(SYN.)* correct, faultless, errorless, detailed, accurate.
(ANT.) inaccurate, inexact, faulty.

exaggerate *(SYN.)* stretch, expand, amplify, embroider, heighten, overstate, caricature, magnify, enlarge.
(ANT.) understate, minimize, diminish, depreciate.

exalt *(SYN.)* erect, consecrate, raise, elevate, extol, dignify.
(ANT.) humble, degrade, humiliate.

examination *(SYN.)* investigation, inspection, test, scrutiny.

examine *(SYN.)* assess, contemplate, question, review, audit, notice, inquire, analyze, check, investigate, dissect, inspect, survey.
(ANT.) omit, disregard, overlook.

example *(SYN.)* pattern, archetype, specimen, illustration, model, instance, prototype, sample.
(ANT.) rule, concept, principle.

exasperate *(SYN.)* aggravate, anger, madden, irritate.

excavate *(SYN.)* unearth, dig, burrow.

exceed *(SYN.)* excel, beat, surpass, top.

exceedingly *(SYN.)* extremely, very, especially, unusually, surprisingly.

excel *(SYN.)* better, beat, surpass.

excellence *(SYN.)* distinction, superiority.
(ANT.) poorness, inferiority, badness.

excellent *(SYN.)* wonderful, fine, marvelous, superior.
(ANT.) poor, terrible, bad, inferior.

except *(SYN.)* omitting, barring, but, reject, excluding, save, exclude.

exception *(SYN.)* affront, offense, exclusion, deviation, omission, anomaly.

exceptional *(SYN.)* different, irregular, strange, unusual, abnormal.

excerpt *(SYN.)* abstract, extract.

excess *(SYN.)* surplus, intemperance, extravagance, immoderation, profusion, abundant, profuse, superfluity.
(ANT.) want, sparse, lack, dearth.

exchange *(SYN.)* barter, interchange, substitute, trade, change, swap.

excite *(SYN.)* arouse, incite, agitate, stimulate, awaken, disquiet.
(ANT.) lull, quiet, bore, pacify.

exclaim *(SYN.)* vociferate, cry, call out, ejaculate, shout.

exclamation *(SYN.)* shout, outcry, clamor.

exclude *(SYN.)* omit, restrain, hinder, bar, except, prevent.
(ANT.) welcome, involve, embrace, admit, accept, include.

exclusion *(SYN.)* exception, rejection.
(ANT.) inclusion.

exclusive *(SYN.)* restricted, limited, restrictive, choice, selective, fashionable.
(ANT.) common, general, ordinary, unrestricted, unfashionable.

excursion *(SYN.)* voyage, tour, trip.

excuse *(SYN.)* exculpate, forgive, remit, acquit, free, pardon, condone, explanation, overlook, exempt, reason, justify, absolve.
(ANT.) revenge, punish, convict.

execute *(SYN.)* complete, accomplish, do, achieve, kill, perform.

exemplify *(SYN.)* show, illustrate.

exempt *(SYN.)* excuse, except, release.

exercise *(SYN.)* drill, task, use, activity, lesson, training, exertion, application, gymnastics, operation, practice, employment.
(ANT.) rest, indolence, repose.

exertion *(SYN.)* attempt, effort, strain, endeavor.

exhale *(SYN.)* blow, breathe out.

exhaust *(SYN.)* drain, tire, empty, wear out, use, finish, fatigue.
(ANT.) renew, refresh, replace.

exhaustive *(SYN.)* comprehensive, thorough, extensive, complete.
(ANT.) incomplete.

exhibit *(SYN.)* demonstrate, display, reveal, betray, present, show, flaunt.
(ANT.) hide conceal, disguise.

exhilarate *(SYN.)* gladden, refresh, cheer, excite, stimulate.

exhort *(SYN.)* advise, coax, press, urge, prompt.

exile *(SYN.)* expulsion, proscription, deportation, banish, ostracism, expatria-

tion, deport, extradition, expel.
(ANT.) retrieval, welcome, recall, admittance, reinstatement.
exist (SYN.) stand, live, occur, be.
exit (SYN.) leave, depart.
exodus (SYN.) leaving, exit, departure.
exonerate (SYN.) acquit, clear.
exorbitant (SYN.) unreasonable, outrageous, overpriced, preposterous, excessive.
(ANT.) normal, reasonable.
exotic (SYN.) strange, vivid, foreign, gay.
(ANT.) dull, native.
expand (SYN.) unfold, enlarge, broaden, spread, inflate, swell, grow.
(ANT.) contract, shrivel, shrink.
expect (SYN.) await, think, hope, anticipate.
expedient (SYN.) helpful, desirable, rush, hasten, useful, fitting, sensible.
(ANT.) delay.
expedition (SYN.) trek, speed, trip, haste, voyage, journey, hurry.
expel (SYN.) exile, dislodge, discharge, excommunicate, eject, dismiss, banish.
(ANT.) favor, recall, invite, admit.
expend (SYN.) consume, waste, exhaust.
(ANT.) ration, reserve, conserve.
expense (SYN.) charge, cost, payment, price.
expensive (SYN.) costly, dear.
(ANT.) modest, inexpensive, cheap.
experience (SYN.) occurrence, episode, sensation, happening, existence, background, feeling, living, encountering.
experienced (SYN.) expert, qualified, accomplished, skilled, practiced.
(ANT.) untutored, inexperienced, naive.
experiment (SYN.) trial, test, prove, research, examine, try, verify.
expert (SYN.) adept, handy, skillful, clever, specialist, authority, skilled, knowledgeable, ingenious.
(ANT.) untrained, unskilled, inexperienced.
expire (SYN.) terminate, die, cease, perish, pass, end, disappear.
(ANT.) commence, continue.
explain (SYN.) illustrate, decipher, expound, clarify, resolve, define, unravel, elucidate, unfold, justify, interpret.
(ANT.) darken, baffle, obscure.

explanation (SYN.) definition, description, interpretation, account, reason, justification, excuse.
explicit (SYN.) lucid, definitive, specific, express, clear, manifest.
(ANT.) vague, implicit, ambiguous.
exploit (SYN.) feat, deed, accomplishment, adventure.
explore (SYN.) research, hunt, probe, search, investigate, look, examine.
explosion (SYN.) bang, boom, blowup, flare-up, blast, detonation, outbreak, convulsion, furor, tantrum.
explosive (SYN.) fiery, rabid, eruptive, volcanic, fulminatory, charged.
(ANT.) stable, inert, peaceful, calm.
exponent (SYN.) explicator, spokesman, supporter, expounder, interpreter.
expose (SYN.) uncover, display, bare, open, unmask, reveal.
(ANT.) hide, conceal, mask, covered.
exposition (SYN.) fair, bazaar, show, expo, exhibition.
expound (SYN.) clarify, present, explain, lecture, demonstrate.
express (SYN.) voice, tell, send, say, ship, declare, state, precise, specific, swift, describe.
expression (SYN.) declaration, statement.
expressive (SYN.) suggestive, meaningful, telling, significant, indicative, thoughtful.
(ANT.) unthinking, meaningless.
expressly (SYN.) precisely, exactly, definitely, clearly.
(ANT.) tentatively, vaguely, ambiguously.
expulsion (SYN.) ejection, discharge, removal, elimination.
expunge (SYN.) blot out, erase, obliterate, delete, efface, remove, cancel.
expurgate (SYN.) cleanse, purge, censor, edit, emasculate, abridge, blip.
exquisite (SYN.) delicate, delightful, attractive, dainty, beautiful, elegant, fine, superb, lovely, excellent, perfect.
(ANT.) vulgar, dull, ugly, unattractive.
extant (SYN.) subsisting, remaining, surviving, present, existing.
(ANT.) lost, defunct, extinct, vanished.
extemporaneous (SYN.) casual, impromptu, offhand.

extemporize *(SYN.)* adlib, improvise, devise.

extend *(SYN.)* lengthen, stretch, increase, offer, give, yield, grant, magnify.
(ANT.) abbreviate, shorten, curtail.

extension *(SYN.)* expansion, increase, stretching, enlargement.

extensive *(SYN.)* vast, wide, spacious.
(ANT.) narrow, cramped, confined, restricted.

extent *(SYN.)* length, degree, range, amount, measure, size, compass, reach, magnitude, scope, expanse, area.

extenuating *(SYN.)* exculpating, excusable, qualifying, justifying, softening.

exterior *(SYN.)* surface, face, outside, covering, outer, external.
(ANT.) inside, lining, interior, internal.

exterminate *(SYN.)* slay, kill, destroy.

external *(SYN.)* outer, exterior, outside.
(ANT.) inner, internal, inside, interior.

externals *(SYN.)* images, effects, look, appearance, veneer, aspect.

extinct *(SYN.)* lost, dead, gone, vanished.
(ANT.) present, flourishing, alive, extant.

extinction *(SYN.)* eclipse, annihilation, obliteration, dissolution, death.

extinguish *(SYN.)* suppress, smother, quench.

extol *(SYN.)* laud, eulogize, exalt, praise.
(ANT.) denounce, discredit, disparage.

extra *(SYN.)* surplus, spare, additional.

extract *(SYN.)* remove, withdraw.
(ANT.) penetrate, introduce.

extraordinary *(SYN.)* unusual, wonderful, marvelous, rare, peculiar, noteworthy, remarkable, exceptional.
(ANT.) commonplace, ordinary, usual.

extravagant *(SYN.)* excessive, exaggerated, lavish, wasteful, extreme.
(ANT.) prudent, frugal, thrifty, provident.

extreme *(SYN.)* excessive, outermost, limit, greatest, utmost, furthest, extremity, endmost, extravagant, ultimate.
(ANT.) reasonable, modest, moderate.

extricate *(SYN.)* rescue, free, clear, release, liberate.

exuberant *(SYN.)* buoyant, ebullient.
(ANT.) sad, depressed.

exult *(SYN.)* rejoice, delight.

eye *(SYN.)* watch, view, stare, look, inspect, glance.

fable *(SYN.)* legend, parable, myth, fib, falsehood, fiction, tale, story.

fabled *(SYN.)* legendary, famous, famed, historic.

fabric *(SYN.)* goods, textile, material, cloth, yard goods.

fabricate *(SYN.)* assemble, make, construct, produce, create, manufacture, form.
(ANT.) raze, destroy, demolish.

fabrication *(SYN.)* deceit, lie, falsehood, untruth, forgery, prevarication, deception.
(ANT.) verity, reality, actuality, truth, fact.

fabulous *(SYN.)* amazing, marvelous, unbelievable, fantastic, astounding, astonishing, striking.
(ANT.) ordinary, commonplace, credible, proven, factual.

facade *(SYN.)* deception, mask, front, show, pose, veneer, guise, affectation.

face *(SYN.)* cover, mug, front, assurance, countenance, audacity, visage, expression, look, features, facade, encounter, meet, surface.
(ANT.) rear, shun, avoid, evade, back, timidity.

facet *(SYN.)* perspective, view, side, phase.

facetious *(SYN.)* jocular, pungent, playful, humorous, funny, clever, droll, witty, jesting.
(ANT.) sober, serious, grave, weighty.

face to face *(SYN.)* opposing, nose to nose, confronting.

facile *(SYN.)* simple, easy, quick, uncomplicated, clever, fluent, skillful, adroit.
(ANT.) complex, difficult, complicated, laborious, hard, ponderous, painstaking, arduous.

facilitate *(SYN.)* help, speed, ease, promote, accelerate, expedite.

facility *(SYN.)* ability, skill, ease, skillfulness, material.
(ANT.) effort, difficulty, labor.

facsimile *(SYN.)* reproduction, likeness, replica.

fact *(SYN.)* reality, deed, certainty, act, incident, circumstance, occurrence, truth, actuality.

(ANT.) falsehood, fiction, delusion.

faction (SYN.) clique, party, sect.

factitious (SYN.) false, sham, artificial, spurious, mannered, unnatural, affected.

(ANT.) natural, real, genuine, artless.

factor (SYN.) part, certain, element, basis, cause.

factory (SYN.) installation, plant, mill, works.

factual (SYN.) true, correct, accurate, genuine, authentic.

(ANT.) incorrect, erroneous, fabricated, invented.

faculty (SYN.) power, capacity, talent, staff, gift, ability, qualification, ability.

fad (SYN.) fashion, vogue, mania, rage.

faddish (SYN.) ephemeral, modish, temporary, passing, fleeting.

(ANT.) lasting, permanent, enduring, classic.

fade (SYN.) pale, bleach, weaken, dim, decline, sink, discolor, fail, diminish, droop.

fagged (SYN.) exhausted, jaded, tired, weary, pooped, worn.

fail (SYN.) neglect, weaken, flunk, miss, decline, founder, disappoint, fade.

(ANT.) succeed, achieve, accomplish.

failing (SYN.) fault, foible, imperfection, frailty, defect, peccadillo, shortcoming.

(ANT.) steadiness, strength, integrity, firmness.

failure (SYN.) miscarriage, omission, decline, deficiency, fiasco, lack, dereliction, failing, unsuccessfulness, loss, default, insufficiency, decay.

(ANT.) conquest, accomplishment, success, triumph, victory, hit, luck, achievement.

faint (SYN.) timid, faded, languid, dim, pale, wearied, feeble, indistinct, weak.

(ANT.) strong, sharp, forceful, glaring, clear, distinct, conspicuous, brave.

faint-hearted (SYN.) shy, cowardly, timid, bashful.

(ANT.) fearless, brave, stouthearted, courageous.

fair (SYN.) pale, average, light, sunny, mediocre, bright, just, affair, clear, lovely, market, blond, honest, attractive, equitable, impartial, reasonable, fete,

exposition.

(ANT.) ugly, fraudulent, foul, outstanding, dishonorable, unfair.

fairly (SYN.) equally, evenly, rather, impartially, passably, justly, squarely, somewhat.

fair-minded (SYN.) reasonable, fair, just, open-minded, honest, unprejudiced, impartial, evenhanded.

(ANT.) bigoted, narrowminded, unjust, close-minded, partisan.

fairness (SYN.) equity, justice, evenhandedness, honesty.

(ANT.) favoritism, partiality, bias, onesidedness.

fairy (SYN.) leprechaun, gnome, elf, pixie, sprite.

faith (SYN.) dependence, trust, reliance, creed, loyalty, doctrine, confidence, tenet, persuasion, constancy, credence, fidelity, religion, belief.

(ANT.) mistrust, disbelief, doubt, infidelity.

faithful (SYN.) staunch, true, devoted, trusty, loyal, constant, credible, steadfast, strict, trustworthy, accurate.

(ANT.) untrustworthy, faithless, inaccurate, wrong, false, disloyal, erroneous, treacherous.

faithless (SYN.) treacherous, unfaithful, disloyal, perfidious.

(ANT.) loyal, true, unwavering, constant, faithful.

fake (SYN.) falsify, distort, pretend, feign, fraud, counterfeit, cheat, false, artificial, phony, imitation, forgery.

(ANT.) honest, pure, real, genuine, authentic.

falderal (SYN.) foolery, jargon, nonsense, gibberish, blather, balderdash.

fall (SYN.) drop, decline, diminish, topple, decrease, sink, hang, extend, descend, subside, plunge, collapse.

(ANT.) soar, climb, steady, rise, ascend.

fallacious (SYN.) untrue, false, wrong, erroneous, deceptive, illusory, delusive.

(ANT.) accurate, true, exact, real, factual.

fallacy (SYN.) mistake, error, illusion, sophism, misconception, deception.

fall back (SYN.) retreat, recede, retire, withdraw, concede.

(ANT.) progress, advance, gain, prosper, proceed.

fallow *(SYN.)* idle, unprepared, unproductive, inactive.

(ANT.) prepared, productive, cultivated.

false *(SYN.)* incorrect, wrong, deceitful, fake, imitation, counterfeit.

(ANT.) genuine, loyal, true, honest.

falsehood *(SYN.)* untruth, lie, fib, story.

(ANT.) truth.

falsify *(SYN.)* misquote, distort, misstate, mislead, adulterate.

falter *(SYN.)* stumble, tremble, waver, hesitate, flounder.

fame *(SYN.)* distinction, glory, honor, mane, eminence, credit, reputation, renown, acclaim, notoriety.

(ANT.) infamy, obscurity, anonymity, disrepute.

famed *(SYN.)* known, renowned, famous.

(ANT.) obscure, unknown, anonymous.

familiar *(SYN.)* informal, intimate, close, acquainted, amicable, knowing, cognizant, versed, unreserved, friendly, sociable, affable, aware, common, known, intimate.

(ANT.) unfamiliar, distant, affected, reserved.

familiarity *(SYN.)* sociability, liberty, acquaintance, comprehension, awareness, frankness, intimacy, understanding, knowledge, fellowship, unreserve.

(ANT.) distance, ignorance, reserve, presumption, constraint, haughtiness.

family *(SYN.)* kin, tribe, folks, group, relatives.

famine *(SYN.)* want, deficiency, starvation, need.

(ANT.) excess, plenty.

famous *(SYN.)* distinguished, noted, glorious, illustrious, famed, celebrated, well-known, eminent, renowned, prominent, esteemed.

(ANT.) obscure, hidden, unknown.

fan *(SYN.)* arouse, spread, admirer, enthusiast, devotee, stir, aficionado, whip, follower.

fanatic *(SYN.)* bigot, enthusiast, zealot.

fancy *(SYN.)* love, dream, ornate, imagine, suppose, imagination, taste, fantasy, ornamented, fussy, elaborate.

(ANT.) plain, undecorated, simple, unadorned.

fantastic *(SYN.)* strange, unusual, odd, wild, unimaginable, incredible, unbelievable, unreal, bizarre, capricious.

(ANT.) mundane, ordinary, staid, humdrum.

fantasy *(SYN.)* illusion, dream, whim, hallucination, delusion, caprice, mirage, daydream.

(ANT.) bore.

far *(SYN.)* removed, much, distant, remote, estranged, alienated.

(ANT.) close, near.

fare *(SYN.)* prosper, eat, passenger, thrive, toll, progress, succeed.

farewell *(SYN.)* goodby, valediction, departure, leaving.

(ANT.) welcome, greeting.

farm *(SYN.)* grow, harvest, cultivate, ranch, hire, charter, plantation.

fascinate *(SYN.)* charm, enchant, bewitch, attract, enthrall.

fashion *(SYN.)* create, shape, style, mode, make, custom, form, manner, method, way, vogue.

fashionable *(SYN.)* chic, smart, stylish, modish, elegant, voguish.

(ANT.) dowdy, unfashionable.

fast *(SYN.)* fleet, firm, quick, swift, inflexible, stable, secure, expeditious, rapid, steady, solid, constant, speedy.

(ANT.) insecure, sluggish, unstable, loose, slow, unsteady.

fasten *(SYN.)* secure, bind, tie, join, fix, connect, attach, unite.

(ANT.) open, loose, free, loosen, release, separate.

fastidious *(SYN.)* choosy, selective, discriminating, picky, meticulous.

fat *(SYN.)* stout, plump, chubby, pudgy, obese, oily, fleshy, greasy, fatty, portly, corpulent, paunchy, wide, thick, rotund.

(ANT.) slim, gaunt, emaciated, thin, slender.

fatal *(SYN.)* killing, lethal, doomed, disastrous, deadly, fateful, mortal.

(ANT.) nonfatal.

fate *(SYN.)* end, fortune, doom, issue, destiny, necessity, portion, result, lot, chance, luck, outcome, consequence, kismet.

father *(SYN.)* cause, sire, breed,

originate, founder, inventor.

fatherly *(SYN.)* protective, paternal, kind, paternalistic.

fathom *(SYN.)* penetrate, understand, interpret, comprehend.

fatigue *(SYN.)* weariness, lassitude, exhaustion, enervation, languor, tiredness. *(ANT.)* vivacity, rejuvenation, energy, vigor.

fault *(SYN.)* defect, flaw, mistake, imperfection, shortcoming, error, weakness, responsibility, omission, blemish, blame, failure. *(ANT.)* perfection, completeness.

faultfinding *(SYN.)* carping, censorious, critical, caviling, nitpicking.

faulty *(SYN.)* imperfect, broken, defective, damaged, impaired. *(ANT.)* flawless, perfect, whole.

favor *(SYN.)* rather, resemble, liking, service, prefer, approval, like, support, patronize, benefit. *(ANT.)* deplore, disapprove.

favorite *(SYN.)* prized, pet, choice, darling, treasured, preferred.

favoritism *(SYN.)* prejudice, bias, partiality. *(ANT.)* fairness, impartiality.

fear *(SYN.)* horror, terror, fright, trepidation, alarm, consternation, dismay, cowardice, panic, anxiety, dread, scare, apprehension. *(ANT.)* fearlessness, boldness, courage, assurance.

fearless *(SYN.)* bold, brave, courageous, gallant, dauntless, confident. *(ANT.)* timid, fearful, cowardly.

feast *(SYN.)* dinner, banquet, barbecue.

feat *(SYN.)* performance, act, operation, accomplishment, achievement, doing, transaction, deed. *(ANT.)* intention, deliberation, cessation.

feature *(SYN.)* trait, quality, characteristic, highlight, attribute.

fee *(SYN.)* payment, pay, remuneration, charge, recompense.

feeble *(SYN.)* faint, puny, exhausted, impair, delicate, weak, enervated, frail, powerless, forceless, sickly, decrepit, ailing. *(ANT.)* strong, forceful, powerful, vigorous, stout.

feed *(SYN.)* satisfy, nourish, food, fodder, forage.

feel *(SYN.)* sense, experience, perceive.

feeling *(SYN.)* opinion, sensibility, tenderness, affection, impression, belief, sensation, sympathy, thought, passion, sentiment, attitude, emotion. *(ANT.)* fact, imperturbability, anesthesia, insensibility.

fellowship *(SYN.)* clan, society, brotherhood, fraternity, camaraderie, brotherliness, companionship, comradeship, association. *(ANT.)* dislike, discord, distrust, enmity, strife, acrimony.

felonious *(SYN.)* murderous, criminal, larcenous.

feminine *(SYN.)* womanly, girlish, ladylike, female, maidenly, womanish. *(ANT.)* masculine, male, virile.

ferocious *(SYN.)* savage, fierce, wild, blood-thirsty, brutal. *(ANT.)* playful, gentle, harmless, calm.

fertile *(SYN.)* rich, fruitful, teeming, plenteous, bountiful, prolific, luxuriant, productive, fecund. *(ANT.)* unproductive, barren, sterile.

festival *(SYN.)* feast, banquet, regalement, celebration.

festive *(SYN.)* joyful, gay, joyous, merry, gala, jovial, jubilant. *(ANT.)* sad, gloomy, mournful, morose.

fetching *(SYN.)* charming, attractive, pleasing, captivating, winsome.

feud *(SYN.)* dispute, quarrel, strife, argument, conflict, controversy. *(ANT.)* amity, understanding, harmony, peace.

fiber *(SYN.)* line, strand, thread, string.

fickle *(SYN.)* unstable, fitful, capricious, restless, changeable, inconstant, variable. *(ANT.)* stable, constant, trustworthy, steady, reliable, dependable.

fiction *(SYN.)* fabrication, romance, falsehood, tale, allegory, narrative, fable, novel, story, invention. *(ANT.)* verity, reality, fact, truth.

fictitious *(SYN.)* invented, imaginary, fabricated, unreal, counterfeit, feigned. *(ANT.)* real, true, genuine, actual, proven.

fidelity (SYN.) fealty, devotion, precision, allegiance, exactness, constancy, accuracy, faithfulness, loyalty.
(ANT.) treachery, disloyalty, perfidy.

fidget (SYN.) squirm, twitch, wriggle.

fiendish (SYN.) devilish, demonic, diabolical, savage, satanic.

fierce (SYN.) furious, wild, savage, violent, ferocious, vehement.
(ANT.) calm, meek, mild, gentle, placid.

fight (SYN.) contend, scuffle, struggle, encounter, battle, wrangle, combat, brawl, quarrel, dispute, war, skirmish, conflict.

figure (SYN.) design, pattern, mold, shape, form, frame, reckon, calculate, compute, determine.

fill (SYN.) glut, furnish, store, stuff, occupy, gorge, pervade, content, stock, fill up, supply, sate, replenish, satisfy.
(ANT.) void, drain, exhaust, deplete, empty.

filter (SYN.) screen, strainer, sieve.

filth (SYN.) pollution, dirt, sewage, foulness.
(ANT.) cleanliness, innocence, purity.

filthy (SYN.) foul, polluted, dirty, stained, unwashed, squalid.
(ANT.) pure, clean, unspoiled.

final (SYN.) ultimate, decisive, concluding, ending, terminal, last, conclusive, eventual, latest.
(ANT.) inaugural, rudimentary, beginning, initial, incipient, first, original.

finally (SYN.) at last, eventually, ultimately.

find (SYN.) observe, detect, discover, locate.

fine (SYN.) thin, pure, choice, small, elegant, dainty, splendid, handsome, delicate, nice, powdered, beautiful, minute, exquisite, subtle, pretty, refined.
(ANT.) thick, coarse, rough, blunt, large.

finicky (SYN.) fussy, meticulous, finical, fastidious, prim.

finish (SYN.) consummate, close, get done, terminate, accomplish, conclude, execute, perform, complete, end, achieve, fulfill, do, perfect.
(ANT.) open, begin, start, beginning.

fire (SYN.) vigor, glow, combustion, passion, burning, conflagration, ardor, flame, blaze, intensity, fervor.
(ANT.) apathy, cold.

firm (SYN.) solid, rigid, inflexible, stiff, unchanging, steadfast, dense, hard, unshakable, business, company, corporation, partnership.
(ANT.) weak, limp, soft, drooping.

first (SYN.) chief, primary, initial, pristine, beginning, foremost, primeval, earliest, prime, primitive, original.
(ANT.) subordinate, last, least, hindmost, latest.

fishy (SYN.) suspicious, questionable, doubtful.
(ANT.) believable, credible.

fit (SYN.) adjust, suit, suitable, accommodate, conform, fitting, robust, harmonize, belong, seizure, spasm, attack, suited, appropriate, healthy, agree, adapt.
(ANT.) misfit, disturb, improper.

fitful (SYN.) variable, restless, fickle, capricious, unstable, changeable.
(ANT.) trustworthy, stable, constant, steady.

fitting (SYN.) apt, due, suitable, proper.
(ANT.) improper, unsuitable, inappropriate.

fix (SYN.) mend, regulate, affix, set, tie, repair, attach, settle, link, bind, determine, establish, define, place, rectify, stick, limit, adjust, fasten.
(ANT.) damage, change, mistreat, displace, alter, disturb, mutilate.

fixation (SYN.) fetish, obsession, infatuation, compulsion.

flair (SYN.) style, dash, flamboyance, drama, gift, knack, aptitude.

flamboyant (SYN.) showy, flashy, ostentatious, gaudy, ostentatious.

flame (SYN.) blaze, fire.

flash (SYN.) flare, flame, wink, twinkling, instant, gleam.

flashy (SYN.) tawdry, tasteless, pretentious, garish, flamboyant.

flat (SYN.) vapid, stale, even, smooth, tasteless, horizontal, dull, level, insipid, uninteresting, lifeless, boring, plane.
(ANT.) tasty, racy, hilly, savory, stimulating, interesting, broken, sloping.

flattery (SYN.) compliment, praise, applause, blarney, acclaim.

flaunt *(SYN.)* exhibit, show off, display, parade.

(ANT.) conceal, hide, disguise.

flavor *(SYN.)* tang, taste, savor, essence, quality, character, season, spice.

flaw *(SYN.)* spot, imperfection, blemish, fault, deformity, blotch.

flee *(SYN.)* fly, abscond, hasten, escape, run away, decamp, evade.

(ANT.) remain, appear, stay, arrive.

fleece *(SYN.)* filch, rob, purloin, swindle, defraud, pilfer, cheat.

fleet *(SYN.)* rapid, swift, quick, fast.

(ANT.) unhurried, sluggish, slow.

fleeting *(SYN.)* brief, swift, passing, temporary.

(ANT.) stable, fixed, lasting, permanent.

fleshy *(SYN.)* overweight, chubby, stocky, plump, obese, stout.

(ANT.) spare, underweight, skinny.

flexible *(SYN.)* lithe, resilient, pliable, tractable, complaint, elastic, yielding, adaptable, agreeable, supple, pliant, easy, ductile.

(ANT.) hard, unbending, firm, brittle, inflexible, rigid, fixed.

flighty *(SYN.)* giddy, light-headed, frivolous, irresponsible.

(ANT.) solid, responsible, steady.

flimsy *(SYN.)* wobbly, weak, frail, fragile, unsteady, delicate, thin..

(ANT.) durable, stable, firm, strong.

fling *(SYN.)* pitch, throw, toss, fun, celebration, party.

flippant *(SYN.)* disrespectful, sassy, insolent, brazen, rude, impertinent.

(ANT.) courteous, polite, mannerly.

flit *(SYN.)* flutter, scurry, hasten, dart, skim.

flock *(SYN.)* gathering, group, flight, swarm, herd, school.

flog *(SYN.)* thrash, lash, switch, strike, paddle.

flood *(SYN.)* overflow, deluge, inundate, cascade.

florid *(SYN.)* gaudy, fancy, ornate, embellished.

(ANT.) spare, simple, plain, unadorned.

flourish *(SYN.)* succeed, grow, prosper, wave, thrive, bloom.

(ANT.) wither, wane, die, decline.

flout *(SYN.)* disdain, scorn, spurn, ignore, taunt, ridicule, mock.

flow *(SYN.)* proceed, abound, spout, come, stream, run, originate, emanate, result, pour, squirt, gush, spurt.

fluctuate *(SYN.)* vary, oscillate, change, waver, hesitate, vacillate.

(ANT.) persist, stick, adhere, resolve.

fluent *(SYN.)* graceful, glib, flowing.

fluid *(SYN.)* liquid, running, liquefied.

flush *(SYN.)* abundant, flat, even, level.

fluster *(SYN.)* rattle, flurry, agitate, upset, perturb, quiver, vibrate.

fly *(SYN.)* flee, mount, shoot, decamp, hover, soar, flit, flutter, sail, escape, rush, spring, glide, abscond, dart, float.

(ANT.) sink, descend, plummet.

foam *(SYN.)* suds, froth, lather.

foe *(SYN.)* opponent, enemy, antagonist, adversary.

(ANT.) associate, ally, friend, comrade.

fog *(SYN.)* haze, mist, cloud, daze, confusion, stupor, vapor, smog.

foible *(SYN.)* frailty, weakness, failing, shortcoming, kink.

foist *(SYN.)* misrepresent, insinuate, falsify.

fold *(SYN.)* lap, double, overlap, clasp, pleat, tuck.

follow *(SYN.)* trail, next, observe, succeed, ensue, obey, chase, comply, accompany, result, imitate, heed, adopt.

(ANT.) elude, cause, precede, avoid, flee.

follower *(SYN.)* supporter, devotee, henchman, adherent, partisan, votary, attendant, disciple, successor.

(ANT.) master, head, chief, dissenter.

following *(SYN.)* public, disciples, supporters, clientele, customers.

folly *(SYN.)* imprudence, silliness, foolishness, indiscretion, absurdity, imprudence, imbecility, stupidity, extravagance.

(ANT.) reasonableness, judgment, sense, prudence, wisdom.

fond *(SYN.)* affectionate, loving, attached, tender, devoted.

(ANT.) hostile, cool, distant, unfriendly.

fondness *(SYN.)* partiality, liking, affection.

(ANT.) hostility, unfriendliness.

food *(SYN.)* viands, edibles, feed, repast, nutriment, sustenance, diet, bread,

provisions, meal, rations, victuals, fare.
(*ANT.*) *want, hunger, drink, starvation.*

fool (*SYN.*) oak, dunce, jester, idiot,
simpleton, buffoon, harlequin, dolt,
blockhead, numskull, clown, dope, trick,
deceive, nincompoop.
(*ANT.*) *scholar, genius, sage.*

foolish (*SYN.*) senseless, irrational, crazy,
silly, brainless, absurd, idiotic, simple,
nonsensical, stupid, preposterous,
asinine.
(*ANT.*) *sane, sound, sensible, rational,
judicious, wise, reasonable, prudent.*

footing (*SYN.*) base, basis, foundation.

footloose (*SYN.*) uncommitted, free,
detached, independent.
(*ANT.*) *engaged, rooted, involved.*

forbearance (*SYN.*) moderation,
abstinence, abstention, continence.
(*ANT.*) *greed, excess, intoxication.*

forbid (*SYN.*) disallow, prevent, ban,
prohibit, taboo, outlaw.
(*ANT.*) *approve, let, allow, permit.*

forbidding (*SYN.*) evil, hostile, unfriendly, sinister, scary, repulsive.
(*ANT.*) *pleasant, beneficent, friendly.*

force (*SYN.*) energy, might, violence,
vigor, intensity, dint, power, constraint,
coercion, vigor, compel, compulsion,
oblige, make, coerce, emphasis,
strength.
(*ANT.*) *weakness, frailty, persuasion,
feebleness, impotence, ineffectiveness.*

forceful (*SYN.*) dynamic, vigorous, energetic, potent, drastic, intense.
(*ANT.*) *lackadaisical, insipid, weak.*

foreboding (*SYN.*) misgiving, suspicion,
apprehension, presage, intuition.

forecast (*SYN.*) prophesy, predict,
predetermine.

foregoing (*SYN.*) above, former, preceding, previous, prior.
(*ANT.*) *later, coming, below, follow.*

foreign (*SYN.*) alien, strange, exotic, different, unfamiliar.
(*ANT.*) *commonplace, ordinary,
familiar.*

foreigner (*SYN.*) outsider, alien, newcomer, stranger.
(*ANT.*) *native.*

foreman (*SYN.*) super, boss, overseer,
supervisor.

forerunner (*SYN.*) harbinger, proclaimer,
informant.

foresee (*SYN.*) forecast, expect, anticipate, surmise, envisage.

forest (*SYN.*) grove, woodland, wood,
copse, woods.

forestall (*SYN.*) hinder, thwart,
prevent, obstruct, repel.

foretell (*SYN.*) soothsay, divine, predict.

forever (*SYN.*) evermore, always, everlasting, hereafter, endlessly.
(*ANT.*) *fleeting, temporarily.*

forfeit (*SYN.*) yield, resign, lose, sacrifice.

forgive (*SYN.*) exonerate, excuse, pardon.
(*ANT.*) *impeach, accuse, blame, censure.*

forgo (*SYN.*) relinquish, release, surrender, abandon.
(*ANT.*) *keep, retain, safeguard.*

forlorn (*SYN.*) pitiable, desolate,
dejected, woeful, wretched.
(*ANT.*) *optimistic, cherished, cheerful.*

form (*SYN.*) frame, compose, fashion, arrange, construct, make up, devise,
create, invent, mold, shape, forge, organize, produce, combine, constitute,
make.
(*ANT.*) *wreck, dismantle, destroy, misshape.*

formal (*SYN.*) exact, stiff, correct, outward, conformist, conventional, affected, regular, proper, ceremonious,
decorous, methodical, precise, external,
perfunctory.
(*ANT.*) *heartfelt, unconstrained, easy,
unconventional.*

former (*SYN.*) earlier, previous,
erstwhile, prior.

formidable (*SYN.*) alarming, frightful,
imposing, terrible, terrifying, dire, fearful.
(*ANT.*) *weak, unimpressive, ordinary.*

forsake (*SYN.*) abandon, desert, forgo,
quit, discard, neglect.

forte (*SYN.*) gift, capability, talent,
specialty, aptitude, bulwark.

forth (*SYN.*) out, onward, forward.

forthright (*SYN.*) honest, direct, frank,
candid, outspoken, blunt, sincere, plain,
explicit.

forthwith (*SYN.*) instantly, promptly, immediately.
(*ANT.*) *afterward, later, ultimately.*

fortify *(SYN.)* bolster strengthen, buttress, barricade, defend.

fortuitous *(SYN.)* successful, benign, lucky, advantageous, propitious, favored, chance.
(ANT.) unlucky, condemned, persecuted.

fortunate *(SYN.)* happy, auspicious, fortuitous, successful, favored, advantageous, benign, charmed, lucky, felicitous, blessed, propitious.
(ANT.) ill-fated, cheerless, unlucky, unfortunate, cursed, condemned.

fortune *(SYN.)* chance, fate, lot, luck, riches, wealth, kismet, destiny.

fortuneteller *(SYN.)* soothsayer, clairvoyant, forecaster, oracle, medium.

forward *(SYN.)* leading, front, promote, elevate, advance, first, ahead, onward, further, foremost, aggrandize.
(ANT.) withhold, retard, hinder, retreat.

foul *(SYN.)* base, soiled, dirty, mean, unclean, polluted, impure, vile, evil, muddy, wicked, rainy, stormy, despicable, filthy.
(ANT.) pure, neat, wholesome, clean.

found *(SYN.)* organize, establish.

foundation *(SYN.)* support, root, base, ground, underpinning, bottom, establishment, substructure, basis.
(ANT.) top, cover, building.

foxy *(SYN.)* cunning, sly, artful, crafty, wily, sharp, shrewd, slick.

fraction *(SYN.)* fragment, part, section, morsel, share, piece.

fracture *(SYN.)* crack, break, rupture.

fragile *(SYN.)* delicate, frail, weak, breakable, infirm, brittle, feeble.
(ANT.) tough, hardy, sturdy, strong, stout.

fragment *(SYN.)* scrap, piece, bit, remnant, part, splinter, segment.

fragrance *(SYN.)* odor, smell, scent, perfume, aroma.

fragrant *(SYN.)* aromatic, scented, perfumed.

frail *(SYN.)* feeble, weak, delicate, breakable, fragile.
(ANT.) sturdy, strong, powerful.

frame *(SYN.)* support, framework, skeleton, molding, border, mount.

frank *(SYN.)* honest, open, unreserved, direct, sincere, straightforward.
(ANT.) tricky, dishonest.

frantic *(SYN.)* frenzied, crazed, raving, panicky.
(ANT.) composed, stoic.

fraud *(SYN.)* deception, guile, swindle, deceit, artifice, imposture, trick, cheat, imposition, duplicity, chicanery.
(ANT.) sincerity, fairness, integrity.

fraudulent *(SYN.)* tricky, fake, dishonest, deceitful

fray *(SYN.)* strife, fight, battle, struggle, tussle, combat, brawl, melee, skirmish.
(ANT.) truce, agreement, peace, concord.

freak *(SYN.)* curiosity, abnormality, monster, oddity.

free *(SYN.)* munificent, clear, autonomous, immune, open, freed, bountiful, liberated, unfastened, immune, emancipated, unconfined, unobstructed, easy, artless, loose, familiar, bounteous, unrestricted, liberal, independent, careless, frank, exempt.
(ANT.) stingy, clogged, illiberal, confined, parsimonious.

freedom *(SYN.)* independence, privilege, familiarity, unrestraint, liberty, exemption, liberation, immunity, license.
(ANT.) servitude, constraint, bondage, slavery, necessity.

freely *(SYN.)* liberally, generously, unstintingly.

freight *(SYN.)* chipping, cargo, load, shipment.

frenzy *(SYN.)* craze, agitation, excitement.

frequent *(SYN.)* usual, habitual, common, often, customary, general.
(ANT.) unique, rare, solitary, uncommon, exceptional, infrequent, scanty.

fresh *(SYN.)* recent, new, additional, modern, further, refreshing, natural, brisk, novel, inexperienced, late, current, sweet, pure, cool.
(ANT.) stagnant, decayed, musty, faded.

fret *(SYN.)* torment, worry, grieve, anguish.

fretful *(SYN.)* testy, irritable, touchy, peevish, short-tempered.
(ANT.) calm.

friend *(SYN.)* crony, supporter, ally, companion, intimate, associate, advocate, comrade, mate, patron, acquaintance, chum, defender.

(ANT.) stranger, adversary.

friendly *(SYN.)* sociable, kindly, affable, genial, companionable, social, neighborly, amicable.

(ANT.) hostile, antagonistic, reserved.

friendship *(SYN.)* knowledge, familiarity, fraternity, acquaintance, intimacy, fellowship, amity, comradeship.

(ANT.) unfamiliarity, ignorance.

fright *(SYN.)* alarm, fear, panic, terror.

frighten *(SYN.)* scare, horrify, daunt, affright, appall, terrify, alarm, terrorize, astound, dismay, startle, panic.

(ANT.) soothe, embolden, compose.

frigid *(SYN.)* cold, wintry, icy, glacial, arctic, freezing.

fringe *(SYN.)* hem, edge, border, trimming, edging.

frisky *(SYN.)* animated, lively, peppy, vivacious.

frolic *(SYN.)* play, romp, frisk, gambol.

front *(SYN.)* facade, face, start, beginning, border, head.

(ANT.) rear, back.

frontier *(SYN.)* border, boundary.

frugal *(SYN.)* parsimonious, saving, stingy, provident, economical.

(ANT.) extravagant, wasteful, self-indulgent, intemperate.

fruitful *(SYN.)* fertile, rich, bountiful, teeming, fecund, productive, luxuriant.

(ANT.) lean, unproductive, sterile.

fruitless *(SYN.)* barren, futile, vain, sterile, unproductive.

(ANT.) fertile, productive.

frustrate *(SYN.)* hinder, defeat, thwart, circumvent, outwit, foil, baffle, disappoint, balk, discourage, prevent.

(ANT.) promote, fulfill, accomplish.

fugitive *(SYN.)* refugee, deserter, runaway.

fulfill *(SYN.)* do, effect, complete, accomplish, realize.

full *(SYN.)* crammed, entire, satiated, flowing, perfect, gorged, soaked, complete, filled, packed, extensive, plentiful, replete, voluminous.

(ANT.) lacking, devoid, partial, empty, depleted.

full-fledged *(SYN.)* schooled, expert, professional, adept, qualified, top-flight, senior, full-blown, trained, able.

(ANT.) inexperienced, untried, untrained.

full-grown *(SYN.)* ripe, adult, full-fledged, mature, developed, complete.

(ANT.) green, young, unripe, adolescent.

fullness *(SYN.)* glut, repletion, enough, satiety, satiation, sufficiency, all, totality, satisfaction, overload, wholeness, aggregate, everything, sum.

(ANT.) need, want, hunger, lack, insufficiency, privation, emptiness.

full-scale *(SYN.)* major, lavish, comprehensive, unlimited, maximum.

(ANT.) indifferent, partial, minor, halfhearted.

fulsome *(SYN.)* disgusting, repulsive, nauseating, nauseous, repellent.

fume *(SYN.)* gas, steam, smoke, rage, rave, vapor.

fun *(SYN.)* merriment, pleasure, enjoyment, gaiety, sport, amusement.

function *(SYN.)* operation, activity, use, affair, ceremony, gathering, party.

fundamental *(SYN.)* basic, essential, primary, elementary.

funny *(SYN.)* odd, droll, ridiculous, farcical, laughable, comic, curious, amusing, humorous, witty.

(ANT.) solemn, sad, sober, melancholy.

furious *(SYN.)* angry, enraged.

(ANT.) serene, calm.

furnish *(SYN.)* yield, give, endow, fit, produce, equip, decorate, supply.

(ANT.) divest, denude, strip.

furor *(SYN.)* commotion, tumult, turmoil.

furthermore *(SYN.)* moreover, also, further.

furtive *(SYN.)* surreptitious, secret, hidden, clandestine.

(ANT.) honest, open.

fury *(SYN.)* wrath, anger, frenzy, rage, violence, fierceness, ferociousness.

(ANT.) calmness, serenity.

fuss *(SYN.)* commotion, bother, pester, annoy, irritate.

futile *(SYN.)* pointless, idle, vain, useless.

(ANT.) weighty, important, worthwhile, serious, valuable.

future *(SYN.)* approaching, imminent, coming, impending.

(ANT.) former, past.

fuzzy *(SYN.)* indistinct, blurred.

(ANT.) lucid, clear.

gab *(SYN.)* jabber, babble, chatter, prattle, gossip.

gabble *(SYN.)* chatter, babble, jabber, blab, prate, gaggle, prattle, blather.

gad *(SYN.)* wander, roam, rove, ramble, meander.

gadget *(SYN.)* contrivance, de-vice, doodad, jigger, thing.

gaffe *(SYN.)* blunder, boner, mistake, gaucherie, error.

gag *(SYN.)* witticism, crack jest, joke.

gaiety *(SYN.)* joyousness, cheerfulness, joyfulness, light-heartedness.

(ANT.) melancholy, sadness, depression.

gain *(SYN.)* acquire, avail, account, good, interest, attain, favor, achieve, get, secure, advantage, earn, profit.

(ANT.) trouble, lose, calamity, forfeit, handicap, lose.

gainful *(SYN.)* lucrative, rewarding, profitable, beneficial, payable, productive.

(ANT.) unproductive, unprofitable.

gainsay *(SYN.)* refute, contradict, controvert, deny, refuse, contravene.

(ANT.) maintain, aver, affirm.

gait *(SYN.)* stride, walk, tread.

gala *(SYN.)* ball, party, carnival, fete.

gale *(SYN.)* burst, surge.

gall *(SYN.)* nerve, audacity, impudence, annoy, vex, anger, provoke, irritate.

gallant *(SYN.)* bold, brave, courageous, valorous, valiant, noble, polite, fearless, heroic, chivalrous.

gallantry *(SYN.)* valor, daring, courage, prowess, heroism, manliness, dauntlessness, graciousness, attentiveness, coquetry, gentleness.

(ANT.) poltroonery, timidity, cowardice, cravenness.

gallery *(SYN.)* passageway, hall, aisle, hallway, passage.

galling *(SYN.)* vexing, irritating, annoying, distressful.

galore *(SYN.)* abounding, plentiful, profuse, rich.

gamble *(SYN.)* game, wager, bet, hazard, risk, venture.

game *(SYN.)* fun, contest, merriment, pastime, match, play, amusement, recreation, diversion.

(ANT.) labor, hardship, work, business.

gangster *(SYN.)* crook, hoodlum, gunman, criminal.

gap *(SYN.)* cavity, chasm, pore, gulf, aperture, abyss, interval, space, hole, void, pore, break, opening.

gape *(SYN.)* ogle, stare, gawk.

garb *(SYN.)* clothing, dress, vesture, array, attire, clothes, drapery, apparel.

(ANT.) nudity, nakedness.

garbage *(SYN.)* refuse, waste.

garbled *(SYN.)* twisted, confused.

gargantuan *(SYN.)* colossal, monumental, giant, huge, large, enormous.

garments *(SYN.)* drapery, dress, garb, apparel, array, attire, clothes, vesture, raiment, clothing.

(ANT.) nakedness, nudity.

garnish *(SYN.)* decorate, embellish, trim, adorn, enrich, beautify, deck, ornament.

(ANT.) expose, strip, uncover, defame.

garrulous *(SYN.)* chatty, glib, verbose, talkative, communicative, voluble.

(ANT.) silent, uncommunicative, laconic, reticent, taciturn.

gash *(SYN.)* lacerate, slash, pierce, cut, hew, slice.

gasp *(SYN.)* pant, puff, wheeze.

gather *(ANT.)* assemble, collect, garner, harvest, reap, deduce, judge, amass, congregate, muster, cull, glean.

(ANT.) scatter, disperse, distribute, disband, separate.

gathering *(SYN.)* meeting, crowd, throng, company.

gaudy *(SYN.)* showy, flashy, loud, bold.

gaunt *(ANT.)* lank, diaphanous, flimsy, gauzy, narrow, rare, scanty, meager, gossamer, emaciated, scrawny, tenuous, thin, fine, lean, skinny, spare, slim.

(ANT.) wide, fat, thick, broad.

gay *(SYN.)* merry, lighthearted, joyful, cheerful, sprightly, jolly, happy, joyous, gleeful, jovial, colorful, bright.

(ANT.) glum, mournful, sad, depressed, sorrowful, somber.

gaze *(SYN.)* look, stare, view, watch, examine, observe, glance, behold, discern, seem, see, survey, witness.

(ANT.) hide, overlook, avert.

geld *(SYN.)* neuter, alter, spay, castrate.

gem *(SYN.)* jewel, semiprecious stone.

general *(SYN.)* ordinary, universal, usual,

common, customary, regular, vague, miscellaneous, indefinite.

(ANT.) definite, particular, exceptional, singular, rare, particular, precise, exact.

generally (SYN.) ordinarily, usually, customarily, normally, mainly.

(ANT.) seldom, infrequently.

generation (SYN.) age, date, era, period, seniority, senescence, senility.

(ANT.) infancy, youth, childhood.

generosity (SYN.) magnanimity, benevolence, humanity, kindness, philanthropy, tenderness, altruism.

(ANT.) selfishness, malevolence, cruelty, inhumanity.

generous (SYN.) giving, liberal, unselfish, magnanimous, bountiful, munificent, charitable, big, noble, beneficent.

(ANT.) greedy, stingy, selfish, covetous.

genesis (SYN.) birth, root, creation, source, origin.

genius (SYN.) intellect, adept, intellectual, sagacity, proficient, creativity, ability, inspiration, faculty.

(ANT.) dullard, stupidity, dolt, shallowness, moron, ineptitude, obtuseness.

genre (SYN.) chaste, order, set, elegance, class, excellence, kind, caste.

genteel (SYN.) cultured, polished, polite, refined.

(ANT.) discourteous, churlish.

gentle (SYN.) peaceful, placid, tame, serene, relaxed, docile, benign, soothing, calm, soft, mild, amiable, friendly.

(ANT.) nasty, harsh, rough, fierce, mean.

genuine (SYN.) real, true, unaffected, authentic, sincere, bona fide, unadulterated, legitimate, actual, veritable.

(ANT.) false, sham, artificial, fake, counterfeit, bogus, pretended, insincere, sham.

genus (SYN.) kind, race, species, type, variety.

germ (SYN.) pest, virus, contamination, disease, pollution, taint, infection.

germinate (SYN.) vegetate, pullulate, sprout, develop.

gesture (SYN.) omen, signal, symbol, emblem, indication, note, token, symptom.

get (SYN.) obtain, receive, attain, gain, achieve, acquire, procure, earn, fetch, carry, remove, prepare, take.

(ANT.) lose, surrender, forfeit, leave, renounce.

ghastly (SYN.) frightful, horrible, horrifying, frightening, grisly, hideous.

ghost (SYN.) phantom, spook, apparition, specter, trace, hint, vestige, spirit.

ghoulish (SYN.) weird, eerie, horrifying, gruesome, sinister, scary.

giant (SYN.) monster, colossus, mammoth, superman.

(ANT.) small, tiny, dwarf, runt, midget, infinitesimal.

gibe (SYN.) sneer, jeer, mock, scoff, boo, hoot, hiss.

(ANT.) approve.

giddy (SYN.) reeling, dizzy, flighty, silly, scatterbrained.

(ANT.) serious.

gift (SYN.) endowment, favor, gratuity, bequest, talent, charity, present.

(ANT.) purchase, loss, ineptitude, deprivation, earnings.

gigantic (SYN.) huge, colossal, immense, large, vast, elephantine, gargantuan.

(ANT.) small, tiny, minute, diminutive, little.

giggle (SYN.) chuckle, jeer, laugh, roar, snicker, titter, cackle, guffaw, mock.

gild (SYN.) cover, coat, paint, embellish, sweeten, retouch.

gird (SYN.) wrap, tie, bind, belt, encircle, surround, get set, prepare.

(ANT.) untie.

girl (SYN.) female, lass, miss.

girth (SYN.) measure, size, width, dimensions, expanse.

gist (SYN.) connotation, explanation, purpose, significance, acceptation.

(ANT.) redundancy.

give (SYN.) bestow, contribute, grant, impart, provide, donate, confer, deliver, present, furnish, yield, develop.

(ANT.) withdraw, take, retain, keep, seize.

glad (SYN.) happy, cheerful, gratified, delighted, joyous, merry, pleased, exulting.

(ANT.) sad, depressed, dejected, melancholy, unhappy, morose, somber.

gladiator (SYN.) battler, fighter, competitor, combatant, contender, contestant.

glamorous (SYN.) spellbinding, fascinating, alluring.

glamour *(SYN.)* charm, allure, attraction, magnetism.

glance *(SYN.)* eye, gaze, survey, view, examine, inspect, discern, look, see, witness.

(ANT.) hide, miss, avert, overlook.

glare *(SYN.)* flash, dazzle, stare, glower, glow, shine.

glaring *(SYN.)* flagrant, obvious, blatant, prominent.

glass *(SYN.)* cup, tumbler, goblet, pane.

glaze *(SYN.)* buff, luster, cover, wax, gloss, coat, polish.

gleam *(SYN.)* flash, glimmer, glisten, shimmer, sparkle.

glean *(SYN.)* reap, gather, select, harvest, pick, separate.

glee *(SYN.)* mirth, joy, gladness, enchantment, delight, cheer, bliss, elation.

(ANT.) depression, misery, dejection.

glen *(SYN.)* ravine, valley.

glib *(SYN.)* smooth, suave, flat, plain, polished, sleek.

(ANT.) rough, rugged, blunt, harsh, bluff.

glide *(SYN.)* sweep, sail, fly, flow, slip, coast, cruise, move easily, skim, slide.

glimmer *(SYN.)* blink, shimmer, flicker, indication, hint, clue, suggestion.

glimpse *(SYN.)* notice, glance, peek, see, impression, look.

glint *(SYN.)* flash, gleam, peek, glance, glimpse, sparkle, glitter.

glisten *(SYN.)* shimmer, shine, glimmer, twinkle, glitter, glister, sparkle.

globe *(SYN.)* orb, ball, world, earth, map, universe.

gloom *(SYN.)* bleakness, despondency, misery, sadness, woe, darkness, dejection.

(ANT.) joy, mirth, exultation, cheerfulness, light, happiness, brightness, frivolity.

gloomy *(SYN.)* despondent, dismal, glum, somber, sorrowful, sad, dejected, disconsolate, dim, dark.

(ANT.) happy, merry, cheerful, high-spirited, bright, sunny.

glorify *(SYN.)* enthrone, exalt, honor, revere, adore, dignify, enshrine, consecrate, praise, worship, laud.

(ANT.) mock, dishonor, debase, abuse.

glorious *(SYN.)* exalted, high, noble, splendid, supreme, elevated, lofty, celebrated, renowned, famed, magnificent, grand, proud.

(ANT.) ridiculous, low, base.

glory *(SYN.)* esteem, praise, respect, reverence, admiration, honor, dignity.

(ANT.) dishonor, disgrace, contempt, reproach, derision.

gloss *(SYN.)* luster, shine, glow, sheen.

glossy *(SYN.)* smooth, glistening, shiny, sleek, polished.

(ANT.) matte, dull.

glow *(SYN.)* beam, glisten, radiate, shimmer, sparkle.

glower *(SYN.)* scowl, stare, frown, glare.

(ANT.) beam, grin, smile.

glowing *(SYN.)* fiery, intense, passionate, zealous, enthusiastic, ardent, eager.

(ANT.) cool, indifferent, apathetic.

glue *(SYN.)* bind, fasten, cement, paste.

glum *(SYN.)* morose, sulky, fretful, crabbed, sullen, dismal, dour, moody.

(ANT.) joyous, merry, amiable.

glut *(SYN.)* gorge, sate, content, furnish, fill, pervade, satiate, stuff, replenish.

(ANT.) empty, exhaust, deplete, void.

glutton *(SYN.)* pig, hog, greedy eater.

gluttony *(SYN.)* ravenousness, piggishness, devouring.

(ANT.) satisfaction, fullness.

gnarled *(SYN.)* twisted, knotted, rugged, knobby.

go *(SYN.)* proceed, depart, flee, move, vanish, exit, leave, suit, harmonize, pass.

(ANT.) stay, arrive, enter, stand, come.

goad *(SYN.)* incite, prod, drive, urge, push, shove, jab, provoke, stimulate.

goal *(SYN.)* craving, destination, desire, longing, objective, finish, end, passion.

godlike *(SYN.)* holy, supernatural, heavenly, celestial, divine, transcendent.

(ANT.) profane, wicked, blasphemous, diabolical.

godly *(SYN.)* pious, religious, holy, pure, divine, spiritual, righteous, saintly.

golden *(SYN.)* shining, metallic, bright, fine, superior, nice, excellent, valuable.

(ANT.) dull, inferior.

good *(SYN.)* honest, sound, valid, cheerful, honorable, worthy, conscientious, moral, genuine, humane, kind, fair, useful, skillful, adequate, friendly, genial.

(ANT.) bad, imperfect, vicious, undesirable, unfriendly, unkind, evil.

goodness *(SYN.)* good, honesty, integrity, virtue.

(ANT.) sin, evil, dishonesty, corruption, badness.

goods *(SYN.)* property, belongings, holdings, possessions, merchandise, wares.

good will *(SYN.)* agreeability, harmony, willingness.

gore *(SYN.)* impale, penetrate, puncture, gouge.

gorge *(SYN.)* ravine, devour, stuff, gobble, valley, defile, pass, cram, fill.

gorgeous *(SYN.)* grand, ravishing, glorious, stunning, brilliant, divine.

(ANT.) homely, ugly, squalid.

gory *(SYN.)* bloody.

gossamer *(SYN.)* dainty, fine, filmy, delicate, sheer.

gossip *(SYN.)* prate, rumor, prattle, hearsay, meddler, tattler, chatter.

gouge *(SYN.)* scoop, dig, carve, burrow, excavate, chisel, notch.

govern *(SYN.)* manage, oversee, reign, preside over, supervise, direct, command, regulate, determine, influence, guide, rule.

(ANT.) assent, submit, acquiesce, obey.

government *(SYN.)* control, direction, rule, command.

governor *(SYN.)* controller, administrator, director.

grab *(SYN.)* snatch, grip, clutch, seize, grasp, capture, pluck.

grace *(SYN.)* charm, beauty, handsomeness, loveliness, dignify, fairness, honor, distinguish, sympathy, attractiveness, elegance, clemency, excuse, pardon.

(ANT.) eyesore, homeliness, deformity, ugliness, disfigurement.

graceful *(SYN.)* elegant, fluid, natural, supple, beautiful, comely, flowing, lithe.

(ANT.) clumsy, awkward, gawky, ungainly, deformed.

gracious *(SYN.)* warm-hearted, pleasing, friendly, engaging, agreeable, kind, amiable, kindly, nice, good, courteous.

(ANT.) surly, hateful, churlish, rude, disagreeable, impolite, thoughtless, discourteous, ill-natured.

grade *(SYN.)* kind, rank, elegance, denomination, sort, arrange, category, classify, rate, group, place, mark.

gradual *(SYN.)* deliberate, sluggish, dawdling, slow, moderate, easy, delaying.

(ANT.) quick, swift, fast, speedy, rapid.

graduate *(SYN.)* pass, finish, advance.

graft *(SYN.)* fraud, theft, cheating, dishonesty, transplant, corruption.

grain *(SYN.)* speck, particle, plant, bit, seed, temper, fiber, character, texture, markings, nature, tendency.

grand *(SYN.)* great, elaborate, splendid, royal, stately, noble, considerable, outstanding, distinguished, impressive, prominent, majestic, fine, dignified.

(ANT.) unassuming, modest, insignificant, unimportant, humble.

grandeur *(SYN.)* resplendence, majesty, distinction, glory.

grandiose *(SYN.)* grand, lofty, magnificent, stately, noble, pompous.

(ANT.) lowly, ordinary, common, undignified, humble.

granite *(SYN.)* stone, rock.

grant *(SYN.)* confer, allocate, deal, divide, mete, appropriation, assign, benefaction, distribute, allowance, donate, award, mete out, deal out.

(ANT.) refuse, withhold, confiscate, keep.

granular *(SYN.)* grainy, sandy, crumbly, rough, gritty.

graph *(SYN.)* design, plan, stratagem, draw up, chart, sketch, cabal, machination, outline, plot, scheme, diagram.

graphic *(SYN.)* vivid, lifelike, significant, meaningful, pictorial, descriptive.

grapple *(SYN.)* grip, seize, clutch, clasp, grasp, fight, struggle.

grasp *(SYN.)* clutch, grip, seize, apprehend, capture, snare, hold, clasp, comprehend, reach, grab, understand, grapple, possession, control.

(ANT.) release, lose, throw, liberate.

grasping *(SYN.)* possessive, greedy, selfish, acquisitive, mercenary.

(ANT.) liberal, unselfish, generous.

grate *(SYN.)* file, pulverize, grind, scrape, scratch, annoy, irritate.

grateful *(SYN.)* beholden, obliged, appreciative, thankful, indebted.

(ANT.) ungrateful, unappreciative, grudging, thankless.

gratify (*SYN.*) charm, gladden, please.
(*ANT.*) *frustrate.*

gratifying (*SYN.*) contentment, solace, relief, comfort, ease, succor.
(*ANT.*) *suffering, torment, affliction, discomfort, torture, misery.*

grating (*SYN.*) harsh, rugged, severe, stringent, coarse, gruff, strict.
(*ANT.*) *smooth, mild, gentle, soft.*

gratis (*SYN.*) complimentary, free.

gratitude (*SYN.*) gratefulness, thankfulness, appreciation.
(*ANT.*) *ungratefulness.*

gratuity (*SYN.*) tip, bonus, gift, donation.

grave (*SYN.*) sober, grim, earnest, serious, important, momentous, sedate, solemn, somber, imposing, vital, essential, staid, consequential, thoughtful.
(*ANT.*) *light, flighty, trivial, insignificant, unimportant, trifling, merry, frivolous.*

gravel (*SYN.*) stones, pebbles, grain.

gravitate (*SYN.*) incline, tend, lean, approach, toward.

gravity (*SYN.*) concern, importance, seriousness, pull, movement.
(*ANT.*) *triviality.*

graze (*SYN.*) scrape, feed, rub, brush, contact, skim.

grease (*SYN.*) fat, oil, lubrication.

greasy (*SYN.*) messy, buttery, waxy, fatty.

great (*SYN.*) large, numerous, eminent, illustrious, big, gigantic enormous, immense, vast, weighty, fine, important, countless, prominent, vital, huge, grand.
(*ANT.*) *minute, common, menial, ordinary, diminutive, small, paltry, unknown.*

greed (*SYN.*) piggishness, lust, desire, greediness, avarice.
(*ANT.*) *unselfishness, selflessness.*

greedy (*SYN.*) selfish, devouring, ravenous, avaricious, covetous, rapacious.
(*ANT.*) *full, generous, munificent, giving.*

green (*SYN.*) inexperienced, modern, novel, recent, naive, fresh, natural.
(*ANT.*) *hackneyed, musty, decayed, faded, stagnant.*

greet (*SYN.*) hail, accost, meet, address, talk to, speak to, welcome, approach.
(*ANT.*) *pass by, avoid.*

gregarious (*SYN.*) outgoing, civil, affable, communicative, hospitable, sociable.

(*ANT.*) *inhospitable, antisocial, disagreeable, hermitic.*

grief (*SYN.*) misery, sadness, tribulation, affliction, heartache, woe, trial, anguish.
(*ANT.*) *happiness, solace, consolation, comfort, joy.*

grievance (*SYN.*) injury, wrong, injustice, detriment, complaint, damage, prejudice, evil, objection.
(*ANT.*) *improvement, benefit, repair.*

grieve (*SYN.*) lament, brood over, mourn, weep, wail, sorrow, distress, bemoan.
(*ANT.*) *revel, carouse, celebrate, rejoice, gladden.*

grievous (*SYN.*) gross, awful, outrageous, shameful, lamentable, regrettable.
(*ANT.*) *agreeable, pleasurable.*

grill (*SYN.*) cook, broil, question, interrogate, barbecue, grating, gridiron.

grim (*SYN.*) severe, harsh, strict, merciless, fierce, horrible, inflexible, adamant, ghastly, frightful, unyielding.
(*ANT.*) *pleasant, lenient, relaxed, amiable, congenial, smiling.*

grimace (*SYN.*) expression, scowl, mope.

grimy (*SYN.*) unclean, grubby, soiled.

grin (*SYN.*) beam, smile, smirk.

grind (*SYN.*) mill, mash, powder, crush, crumble, pulverize, smooth, grate.

grip (*SYN.*) catch, clutch, apprehend, trap, arrest, grasp, hold, bag, suitcase, lay hold of, clench, command, control.
(*ANT.*) *release, liberate, lose, throw.*

gripe (*SYN.*) protest, lament, complaint.

grit (*SYN.*) rub, grind, grate, sand, gravel, pluck, courage, stamina.

groan (*SYN.*) sob, wail, howl, moan, whimper, wail, complain.

groggy (*SYN.*) dazed, dopy, stupefied, stunned, drugged, unsteady.
(*ANT.*) *alert.*

groom (*SYN.*) tend, tidy, preen, curry, spouse, consort.

groove (*SYN.*) furrow, channel, track, routine, slot, scratch.

groovy (*SYN.*) marvelous, delightful, wonderful.

grope (*SYN.*) fumble, feel around.

gross (*SYN.*) glaring, coarse, indelicate, obscene, bulky, great, total, whole, brutal, grievous, aggregate, earthy, rude, vulgar, entire, enormous, plain, crass.

hang-up *(SYN.)* inhibition, difficulty, snag, hindrance.

hanker *(SYN.)* wish, yearn, long, desire, pine, thirst.

haphazard *(SYN.)* aimless, random, purposeless, indiscriminate, accidental.
(ANT.) determined, planned, designed, deliberate.

hapless *(SYN.)* ill-fated, unfortunate, jinxed, luckless.

happen *(SYN.)* occur, take place, bechance, betide, transpire, come to pass, chance, befall.

happening *(SYN.)* episode, event, scene, incident, affair, experience, phenomenon.

happiness *(SYN.)* pleasure, gladness, delight, beatitude, bliss, contentment, satisfaction, joy, joyousness.
(ANT.) sadness, sorrow, misery, grief.

happy *(SYN.)* gay, joyous, cheerful, fortunate, glad, merry, contented, satisfied, lucky, blessed, pleased.
(ANT.) gloomy, morose, sad, sorrowful, miserable, inconvenient, unlucky, depressed.

happy-go-lucky *(SYN.)* easygoing, carefree, unconcerned.
(ANT.) prudent, responsible, concerned.

harangue *(SYN.)* oration, diatribe, lecture, tirade.

harass *(SYN.)* badger, irritate, molest, pester, taunt, torment, provoke, tantalize, worry, aggravate, annoy, nag, plague, vex.
(ANT.) please, soothe, comfort, delight, gratify.

harbinger *(SYN.)* sign, messenger, proclaim.

harbor *(SYN.)* haven, port, anchorage, cherish, entertain, protect, shelter.

hard *(SYN.)* difficult, burdensome, arduous, rigid, puzzling, cruel, strict, unfeeling.
(ANT.) fluid, brittle, effortless, gentle, tender, easy, simple, plastic, soft, lenient, flabby.

hard-boiled *(SYN.)* unsympathetic, tough, harsh.

hardship *(SYN.)* ordeal, test, effort, affliction, misfortune, trouble, experiment.

(ANT.) consolation, alleviation.

hardy *(SYN.)* sturdy, strong, tough, vigorous.
(ANT.) frail, decrepit, feeble, weak, fragile.

harm *(SYN.)* hurt, mischief, misfortune, mishap, damage, wickedness, cripple.
(ANT.) favor, kindness, benefit, boon.

harmful *(SYN.)* damaging, injurious, mischievous, detrimental, hurtful, deleterious.
(ANT.) helpful, salutary, profitable, advantageous.

harmless *(SYN.)* protected, secure, snag, dependable, certain, painless, innocent.
(ANT.) perilous, hazardous, insecure, dangerous, unsafe.

harmonious *(SYN.)* tuneful, melodious, congenial.
(ANT.) dissonant, discordant, disagreeable.

harmony *(SYN.)* unison, bargain, contract, stipulation, pact, agreement, accordance, concord, accord.
(ANT.) discord, dissension, difference, variance.

harness *(SYN.)* control, yoke.

harry *(SYN.)* vex, pester, harass, bother, plague.

harsh *(SYN.)* jarring, gruff, rugged, severe, stringent, blunt, grating, unpleasant.
(ANT.) smooth, soft, gentle, melodious, soothing, easy.

harvest *(SYN.)* reap, gather, produce, yield, crop, gain, acquire, fruit, result, reaping, proceeds, glean, garner.
(ANT.) plant, squander, lose.

haste *(SYN.)* speed, hurry, rush, rapidity, flurry.
(ANT.) sloth, sluggishness.

hasten *(SYN.)* hurry, sprint, quicken, rush, precipitate, accelerate, scurry, run.
(ANT.) retard, tarry, detain, linger, dawdle, delay, hinder.

hasty *(SYN.)* quick, swift, irascible, lively, nimble, brisk, active, speedy, impatient, testy, sharp, fast, rapid.
(ANT.) slow, dull, sluggish.

hat *(SYN.)* helmet, bonnet.

hatch *(SYN.)* breed, incubate.

hate *(SYN.)* loathe, detest, despise, dis-

favor, hatred, abhorrence, abominate.
(ANT.) *love, cherish, admire, like.*

hatred *(SYN.)* detestation, dislike, malevolence, enmity, aversion, animosity.
(ANT.) *friendship, affection, attraction.*

haughty *(SYN.)* proud, stately, vainglorious, arrogant, disdainful, overbearing.
(ANT.) *meek, ashamed, lowly.*

haul *(SYN.)* draw, pull, drag.

have *(SYN.)* own, possess, seize, hold, control, occupy, acquire, undergo, maintain, experience, receive, gain.
(ANT.) *surrender, abandon, renounce, lose.*

havoc *(SYN.)* devastation, ruin, destruction.

hazard *(SYN.)* peril, chance, dare, risk, offer, conjecture.
(ANT.) *safety, defense, protection, immunity.*

hazardous *(SYN.)* perilous, precarious, threatening, unsafe, dangerous, critical.
(ANT.) *protected, secure, safe.*

hazy *(SYN.)* uncertain, unclear, ambiguous, dim.
(ANT.) *specific, clear, lucid, precise, explicit.*

head *(SYN.)* leader, summit, top, culmination, director, chief, master, commander.
(ANT.) *foot, base, bottom, follower, subordinate.*

heady *(SYN.)* thrilling, intoxicating, exciting.

healthy *(SYN.)* wholesome, hale, robust, sound, well, vigorous, strong, hearty, healthful, hygienic.
(ANT.) *noxious, diseased, unhealthy, delicate, frail, infirm, injurious.*

heap *(SYN.)* collection, mound, increase, store, stack, pile, gather, accumulate, amass, accrue.
(ANT.) *dissipate, scatter, waste, diminish, disperse.*

hear *(SYN.)* heed, listen, detect, harken, perceive.

heart *(SYN.)* middle, center, sympathy, nucleus, midpoint, sentiment, core.
(ANT.) *outskirts, periphery, border, rim, boundary.*

heartache *(SYN.)* anguish, mourning, sadness, sorrow, affliction, distress, grief.
(ANT.) *happiness, joy, solace, comfort, consolation.*

heartbroken *(SYN.)* distressed, forlorn, mean, paltry, worthless, contemptible, wretched, crestfallen, disconsolate, low.
(ANT.) *noble, fortunate, contented, significant.*

hearten *(SYN.)* encourage, favor, impel, urge, promote, sanction, animate, cheer, exhilarate, cheer.
(ANT.) *deter, dissuade, deject, discourage, dispirit.*

heartless *(SYN.)* mean, cruel, ruthless, hardhearted.
(ANT.) *sympathetic, kind.*

heart-rending *(SYN.)* heart-breaking, depressing.

hearty *(SYN.)* warm, earnest, ardent, cordial, sincere, gracious, sociable.
(ANT.) *taciturn, aloof, cool.*

heat *(SYN.)* hotness, warmth, temperature, passion, ardor, zeal, inflame, cook.
(ANT.) *cool, chill, coolness, freeze, coldness, chilliness, iciness, cold.*

heated *(SYN.)* vehement, fiery, intense, passionate.

heave *(SYN.)* boost, hoist.

heaven *(SYN.)* empyrean, paradise.

heavenly *(SYN.)* superhuman, godlike, blissful, saintly, holy, divine, celestial.
(ANT.) *wicked, mundane, profane, blasphemous.*

heavy *(SYN.)* weighty, massive, gloomy, serious, ponderous, cumbersome, trying, burdensome, harsh, grave.
(ANT.) *brisk, light, animated.*

heckle *(SYN.)* torment, harass, tease, hector, harry.

heed *(SYN.)* care, alertness, circumspection, consider, watchfulness, study, attention, notice, regard.
(ANT.) *negligence, oversight, over look, neglect, ignore, disregard, indifference.*

heedless *(SYN.)* sightless, headlong, rash, unmindful, deaf, unseeing, oblivious, ignorant, blind.
(ANT.) *perceiving, sensible, aware.*

height *(SYN.)* zenith, peak, summit, tallness, mountain, acme, apex, elevation,

(ANT.) appealing, delicate, refined, proper, polite, cultivated, slight, comely, trivial, decent.

grotesque *(SYN.)* strange, weird, odd, incredible, fantastic, monstrous, absurd, freakish, bizarre, peculiar, deformed.

grotto *(SYN.)* tunnel, cave, hole, cavern.

grouch *(SYN.)* protest, remonstrate, whine, complain, grumble, murmur.
(ANT.) praise, applaud, rejoice, approve.

ground *(SYN.)* foundation, presumption, surface, principle, underpinning.
(ANT.) implication, superstructure.

group *(SYN.)* crowd, clock, party, troupe, swarm, bunch, brook, assembly, lot, collection, pack, horde.
(ANT.) disassemble.

grouse *(SYN.)* mutter, grumble, gripe, scold, growl.

grovel *(SYN.)* creep, crawl, cower, cringe, slouch, stoop.

groveling *(SYN.)* dishonorable, lowly, sordid, vile, mean, abject, ignoble.
(ANT.) lofty, noble, esteemed.

grow *(SYN.)* extend, swell, advance, develop, enlarge, enlarge, germinate, mature, expand, flower, raise.
(ANT.) wane, shrink, atrophy, decay, diminish, contract.

growl *(SYN.)* complain, snarl, grumble, gnarl, roar.

grown-up *(SYN.)* full-grown, adult, of age, mature, big.
(ANT.) little, childish, budding, junior.

growth *(SYN.)* expansion, development, unfolding, maturing, progress, elaboration, evolution.
(ANT.) degeneration, deterioration, curtailment, abbreviation, compression.

grudge *(SYN.)* malevolence, malice, resentment, bitterness, spite, animosity.
(ANT.) kindness, love, benevolence, affection, good will, friendliness, toleration.

grudgingly *(SYN.)* reluctantly, unwillingly, under protest, involuntarily.

grueling *(SYN.)* taxing, exhausting, excruciating, trying, arduous, grinding.
(ANT.) effortless, easy, light, simple.

gruesome *(SYN.)* hideous, frightful, horrible, loathsome, ghastly, horrifying.
(ANT.) agreeable, soothing, delightful, charming.

guarantee *(SYN.)* bond, pledge, token, warrant, earnest, surety, bail, commitment, promise, secure.

guarantor *(SYN.)* voucher, sponsor, warrantor, signatory, underwriter, surety.

guaranty *(SYN.)* warranty, token, deposit, earnest.

guard *(SYN.)* protect, shield, veil, cloak, conceal, disguise, preserve, hide.
(ANT.) unveil, expose, ignore, neglect, bare, reveal, disregard, divulge.

guardian *(SYN.)* curator, keeper, protector, custodian, patron, watchdog.

guess *(SYN.)* estimate, suppose, think, assume, reason, believe, reckon, speculate.
(ANT.) know.

guest *(SYN.)* caller, client, customer, patient, visitor.
(ANT.) host.

guide *(SYN.)* manage, supervise, conduct, direct, lead, steer, escort, pilot, show.
(ANT.) follower, follow.

guild *(SYN.)* association, union, society.

guile *(SYN.)* deceitfulness, fraud, wiliness, trick, deceit.
(ANT.) sincerity, openness, honesty, truthfulness, candor, frankness.

guileless *(SYN.)* open, innocent, naive, sincere, simple, candid.
(ANT.) treacherous, plotting.

guilt *(SYN.)* sin, blame, misstep, fault, offense.

guilty *(SYN.)* culpable, to blame, responsible, at fault, criminal, blameworthy.
(ANT.) blameless, innocent, guiltless.

gulch *(SYN.)* gorge, valley, gully, ravine, canyon.

gullible *(SYN.)* trustful, naive, innocent, unsuspecting, deceivable, unsuspicious.
(ANT.) skeptical, sophisticated.

gulp *(SYN.)* devour, swallow, gasp, repress, choke.

gush *(SYN.)* pour, spurt, stream, rush out, spout, flood, flush, chatter, babble.

gust *(SYN.)* blast, wind, outbreak, outburst, eruption.

gutter *(SYN.)* ditch, groove, drain, channel, trench.

gymnasium *(SYN.)* playground, arena, court, athletic field.

gymnastics *(SYN.)* drill, exercise, acrobatics, calisthenics.

habit *(SYN.)* usage, routine, compulsion, use, wont, custom, disposition, practice.

habitation *(SYN.)* abode, domicile, lodgings.

habitual *(SYN.)* general, usual, common, frequent, persistent, customary, routine. *(ANT.) solitary, unique, exceptional, occasional.*

habituated *(SYN.)* used, accustomed, adapted, acclimated, comfortable.

hack *(SYN.)* cleave, chop, slash, hew, slice, pick, sever.

hackneyed *(SYN.)* stale, stereotyped, trite, commonplace, ordinary, banal. *(ANT.) novel, stimulating, modern, fresh, creative.*

hag *(SYN.)* beldam, crone, vixen, granny, ogress, harridan, virage.

haggard *(SYN.)* drawn, debilitated, spent. *(ANT.) bright, fresh, animated.*

haggle *(SYN.)* dicker, bargain.

hail *(SYN.)* welcome, approach, accost, speak to, address, greet. *(ANT.) pass by, avoid.*

hairless *(SYN.)* shorn, glabrous, bald, baldpated. *(ANT.) hirsute, hairy, unshaven.*

hair-raising *(SYN.)* horrifying, exciting, alarming, thrilling, startling, frightful, scary.

hairy *(SYN.)* bearded, shaggy, hirsute, bewhiskered.

hale *(SYN.)* robust, well, wholesome, hearty, healthy, sound, salubrious. *(ANT.) noxious, frail, diseased, delicate, infirm.*

half-baked *(SYN.)* crude, premature, makeshift, illogical.

half-hearted *(SYN.)* uncaring, indifferent, unenthusiastic. *(ANT.) eager, enthusiastic, earnest.*

half-wit *(SYN.)* dope, simpleton, nitwit, dunce, idiot.

hall *(SYN.)* corridor, lobby, passage, hallway, vestibule.

hallow *(SYN.)* glorify, exalt, dignify, aggrandize, consecrate, elevate, ennoble, raise, erect. *(ANT.) dishonor, humiliate, debase, degrade.*

hallowed *(SYN.)* holy, sacred, beatified, sacrosanct, blessed, divine.

hallucination *(SYN.)* fantasy, mirage, dream, vision, phantasm, appearance.

halt *(SYN.)* impede, obstruct, terminate, stop, hinder, desist, check, arrest, abstain. *(ANT.) start, begin, proceed, speed, beginning, promote.*

halting *(SYN.)* imperfect, awkward, stuttering, faltering, hobbling, doubtful, limping. *(ANT.) decisive, confident, smooth, graceful, facile.*

hammer *(SYN.)* beat, bang, whack, pound, batter, drive.

hamper *(SYN.)* prevent, impede, thwart, restrain, hinder, obstruct. *(ANT.) help, assist, encourage, facilitate.*

hamstrung *(SYN.)* disabled, helpless, paralyzed.

hand *(SYN.)* assistant, helper, support, aid, farmhand.

handicap *(SYN.)* retribution, penalty, disadvantage, forfeiture, hindrance. *(ANT.) reward, pardon, compensation, remuneration.*

handily *(SYN.)* readily, skillfully, easily, dexterously, smoothly, adroitly, deftly.

handkerchief *(SYN.)* bandanna, scarf.

handle *(SYN.)* hold, touch, finger, clutch, grip, manipulate, feel, grasp, control, oversee, direct, treat, steer, supervise, run, regulate.

hand out *(SYN.)* disburse, distribute, deal, mete.

hand over *(SYN.)* release, surrender, deliver, yield, present, fork over.

handsome *(SYN.)* lovely, pretty, fair, comely, beautiful, charming, elegant, good-looking, large, generous, liberal, beauteous, fine. *(ANT.) repulsive, ugly, unattractive, stingy, small, mean, homely, foul, hideous.*

handy *(SYN.)* suitable, adapted, appropriate, favorable, fitting, near, ready, close. *(ANT.) inopportune, troublesome, awkward.*

hang *(SYN.)* drape, hover, dangle, suspend, kill, sag, execute, lynch.

hang in *(SYN.)* continue, endure, remain, perservere, resist, persist.

altitude, prominence.

(ANT.) base, depth, anticlimax.

heighten *(SYN.)* increase, magnify, annoy, chafe, intensify, amplify, aggravate, provoke, irritate.

(ANT.) soothe, mitigate, palliate, soften, appease.

heinous *(SYN.)* abominable, grievous.

hello *(SYN.)* greeting, good evening, good afternoon, good morning.

(ANT.) farewell, good-bye, so long.

help *(SYN.)* assist, support, promote, relieve, abet, succor, back, uphold, further, remedy, encourage, aid, facilitate, mitigate.

(ANT.) afflict, thwart, resist, hinder, impede.

helper *(SYN.)* aide, assistant, supporter.

helpful *(SYN.)* beneficial, serviceable, wholesome, useful, profitable, advantageous, good, salutary.

(ANT.) harmful, injurious, useless, worthless, destructive, deleterious, detrimental.

helpfulness *(SYN.)* assistance, cooperation, usefulness.

(ANT.) antagonism, hostility, opposition.

helpless *(SYN.)* weak, feeble, dependent, disabled, inept, unresourceful.

(ANT.) resourceful, enterprising.

helplessness *(SYN.)* impotence, feebleness, weakness, incapacity, ineptitude, invalidism, shiftless.

(ANT.) power, strength, might, potency.

helter-skelter *(SYN.)* haphazardly, chaotically, irregularly.

hem *(SYN.)* bottom, border, edge, rim, margin, pale, verge, flounce, boundary.

hem in *(SYN.)* enclose, shut in, confine, restrict, limit.

hence *(SYN.)* consequently, thence, therefore, so, accordingly.

herald *(SYN.)* harbinger, crier, envoy, forerunner, precursor, augury, forecast.

herculean *(SYN.)* demanding, heroic, titanic, mighty, prodigious, laborious, arduous.

herd *(SYN.)* group, pack, drove, crowd, flock, gather.

heretic *(SYN.)* nonconformist, sectarian, unbeliever, sectary, schismatic, apostate.

heritage *(SYN.)* birthright, legacy, patrimony.

hermit *(SYN.)* recluse, anchorite.

hero *(SYN.)* paladin, champion, idol.

heroic *(SYN.)* bold, courageous, fearless, gallant, valiant, valorous, brave, chivalrous, adventurous, dauntless, intrepid, magnanimous.

(ANT.) fearful, weak, cringing, timid, cowardly.

heroism *(SYN.)* valor, bravery, gallant, dauntless, bold, courageous, fearless.

hesitant *(SYN.)* reluctant, unwilling, disinclined, loath, slow, averse.

(ANT.) willing, inclined, eager, ready, disposed.

hesitate *(SYN.)* falter, waver, pause, doubt, demur, delay, vacillate, wait, stammer, stutter, scruple.

(ANT.) proceed, resolve, continue, decide, persevere.

hesitation *(SYN.)* distrust, scruple, suspense, uncertainty, unbelief, ambiguity, doubt, incredulity, skepticism.

(ANT.) determination, belief, certainty, faith, conviction.

hidden *(SYN.)* undeveloped, unseen dormant, concealed, quiescent, latent, potential, inactive.

(ANT.) visible, explicit, conspicuous.

hide *(SYN.)* disguise, mask, suppress, withhold, veil, cloak, conceal, screen, camouflage, pelt, skin, leather, cover.

(ANT.) reveal, show, expose, disclose, uncover, divulge.

hideous *(SYN.)* frightful, ugly, shocking, frightening, horrible, terrible, horrifying, terrifying, grisly, gross.

(ANT.) lovely, beautiful, beauteous.

high *(SYN.)* tall, eminent, exalted, elevated, sharp, lofty, proud, shrill, raised, strident, prominent, important, powerful, expensive, dear, costly, grave, serious, extreme, towering.

(ANT.) low, mean, tiny, stunted, short, base, lowly, deep, insignificant, unimportant, inexpensive, reasonable, trivial, petty, small.

highly *(SYN.)* extremely, very, extraordinarily, exceedingly.

high-minded *(SYN.)* lofty, noble, honorable.

(ANT.) dishonorable, base.

high-priced *(SYN.)* dear, expensive,

costly.

(ANT.) economical, cheap.

high-strung *(SYN.)* nervous, tense, intense.

(ANT.) calm.

highway *(SYN.)* parkway, speedway, turnpike, superhighway, freeway.

hilarious *(SYN.)* funny, sidesplitting, hysterical.

(ANT.) depressing, sad.

hinder *(SYN.)* hamper, impede, block, retard, stop, resist, thwart, obstruct, check, prevent, interrupt, delay, slow.

(ANT.) promote, further, assist, expedite, advance, facilitate.

hindrance *(SYN.)* interruption, delay, interference, obstruction, obstacle, barrier.

hinge *(SYN.)* rely, depend, pivot.

hint *(SYN.)* reminder, allusion, suggestion, clue, tip, taste, whisper, implication, intimate, suspicion, mention, insinuation.

(ANT.) declaration, affirmation.

hire *(SYN.)* employ, occupy, devote, apply, enlist, lease, rent, charter, rental, busy, engage, utilize, retain, let, avail.

(ANT.) reject, banish, discard, fire, dismiss, discharge.

history *(SYN.)* narration, relation, computation, record, account, chronicle, detail, description, narrative, annal, tale, recital.

(ANT.) confusion, misrepresentation, distortion, caricature.

hit *(SYN.)* knock, pound, strike, hurt, pummel, beat, come upon, find, discover, blow, smite.

hitch *(SYN.)* tether, fasten, harness, interruption, hindrance, interference.

hoard *(SYN.)* amass, increase, accumulate, gather, save, secret, store, cache, store, accrue, heap.

(ANT.) dissipate, scatter, waste, diminish, squander, spend, disperse.

hoarse *(SYN.)* deep, rough, husky, raucous, grating, harsh.

(ANT.) clear.

hoax *(SYN.)* ploy, ruse, wile, device, cheat, deception, antic, imposture, stratagem, stunt, guile, fraud.

(ANT.) openness, sincerity, candor, ex-posure, honesty.

hobby *(SYN.)* diversion, pastime, avocation.

(ANT.) vocation, profession.

hoist *(SYN.)* heave, lift, elevate, raise, crane, elevator.

hold *(SYN.)* grasp, occupy, possess, curb, contain, stow, carry, adhere, have, clutch, keep, maintain, clasp, grip.

(ANT.) vacate, relinquish, surrender, abandon.

holdup *(SYN.)* heist, robbery, stickup, delay, interruption.

hole *(SYN.)* cavity, void, pore, opening, abyss, chasm, gulf, aperture, tear, pit, burrow.

hollow *(SYN.)* unfilled, vacant, vain, meaningless, flimsy, false, hole, cavity.

(ANT.) sound, solid, genuine, sincere, full.

holy *(SYN.)* devout, divine, blessed, consecrated, sacred, spiritual, pious, sainted, religious, saintly, hallowed.

(ANT.) worldly, sacrilegious, unconsecrated, evil, profane.

home *(SYN.)* dwelling, abode, residence, seat, quarters, house, habitat.

homely *(SYN.)* uncommonly, disagreeable, ill-natured, unattractive, deformed, surly, repellent, spiteful.

(ANT.) fair, handsome, pretty, attractive, comely, beautiful.

honest *(SYN.)* sincere, trustworthy, truthful, fair, ingenuous, candid, conscientious, moral, upright, open, just, straightfoward.

(ANT.) fraudulent, tricky, deceitful, dishonest, lying.

honor *(SYN.)* esteem, praise, worship, admiration, homage, glory, respect.

(ANT.) scorn, dishonor, despise, neglect, abuse, shame, derision, disgrace.

honorable *(SYN.)* fair, noble, creditable, proper, reputable, honest, admirable, true, trusty, eminent.

(ANT.) infamous, disgraceful, shameful.

honorary *(SYN.)* gratuitous, complimentary.

hoodlum *(SYN.)* crook, gangster, criminal, hooligan.

hope *(SYN.)* expectation, faith, optimism, anticipation, expectancy.

(ANT.) pessimism, despair, despondency.

hopeless *(SYN.)* desperate, incurable, disastrous.

(ANT.) promising, hopeful.

horde *(SYN.)* host, masses, press, rabble, swarm, multitude, crowd, populace.

horizontal *(SYN.)* even, level, plane, flat, straight.

(ANT.) upright, vertical.

horrendous *(SYN.)* awful, horrifying, terrible, dreadful.

(ANT.) splendid, wonderful.

horrible *(SYN.)* awful, dire, ghastly, horrid, repulsive, frightful, appalling, horrifying, dreadful, ghastly.

(ANT.) enjoyable, enchanting, beautiful, lovely, fascinating.

horrid *(SYN.)* repulsive, terrible, appalling, dire, awful, frightful, fearful.

(ANT.) fascinating, enchanting, enjoyable, lovely.

horror *(SYN.)* dread, awe, hatred, loathing, foreboding, alarm, apprehension.

(ANT.) courage, boldness, assurance, confidence.

hospital *(SYN.)* infirmary, clinic, sanatorium, rest home, sanitarium.

hospitality *(SYN.)* warmth, liberality, generosity, graciousness, welcome.

hostile *(SYN.)* unfriendly, opposed, antagonistic, inimical, adverse, warlike.

(ANT.) friendly, favorable, amicable.

hot *(SYN.)* scorching, fervent, fiery, impetuous, scalding, heated, sizzling, blazing, frying, roasting, warm.

(ANT.) indifferent, apathetic, bland.

hotbed *(SYN.)* sink, nest, well, den, nursery, cradle, source, incubator, seedbed.

hotel *(SYN.)* hostel, motel, inn, hostelry.

hourly *(SYN.)* frequently, steadily, constantly, unfailingly, perpetually, ceaselessly, continually.

(ANT.) occasionally, seldom.

house *(SYN.)* building, residence, abode, dwelling.

housebreaker *(SYN.)* robber, thief, prowler, cracksman.

housing *(SYN.)* lodgings, shelter.

hovel *(SYN.)* cabin, hut, sty, shack, shed.

hover *(SYN.)* hang, drift, poise, stand by, linger, impend, waver, hand around.

hub *(SYN.)* pivot, center, core, heart, axis, basis, focus.

hubbub *(SYN.)* uproar, tumult, commotion, clamor.

(ANT.) peacefulness, stillness, silence, quiet, quiescence.

huddle *(SYN.)* mass, herd, bunch, crowd, cram, gather, shove, flock, ball.

hue *(SYN.)* pigment, tint, shade, dye, complexion, paint, color, tone, tincture.

(ANT.) transparency, achromatism, paleness.

huffy *(SYN.)* sensitive, vulnerable, testy, offended, thin-skinned, touchy.

(ANT.) tough, placid, stolid, impassive.

hug *(SYN.)* embrace, coddle, caress, kiss, pet, press, clasp, fondle, cuddle.

(ANT.) tease, vex, spurn, buffet, annoy.

huge *(SYN.)* great, immense, vast, ample, big, capacious, extensive, gigantic, enormous, vast, tremendous.

(ANT.) short, small, mean, little, tiny.

hulking *(SYN.)* massive, awkward, bulky.

hum *(SYN.)* whir, buzz, whizz, purr, croon, murmur, intone, vibrate.

human *(SYN.)* manlike, hominid, mortal, fleshly, individual, person, tellurian.

humanist *(SYN.)* scholar, sage, savant.

humanitarianism *(SYN.)* good will, beneficence, philanthropy, humanism.

humble *(SYN.)* modest, crush, mortify, simple, shame, subdue, meek, abase, break, plain, submissive, compliant, unpretentious.

(ANT.) praise, arrogant, exalt, illustrious, boastful, honor.

humbly *(SYN.)* deferentially, meekly, respectfully, unassumingly, diffidently, modestly, subserviently.

(ANT.) insolently, proudly, grandly.

humid *(SYN.)* moist, damp, misty, muggy, wet, watery.

(ANT.) parched, dry.

humiliate *(SYN.)* corrupt, defile, depress, pervert, abase, degrade, disgrace.

(ANT.) restore, raise, improve.

humiliation *(SYN.)* chagrin, dishonor.

(ANT.) honor, praise, dignity, renown.

humor *(SYN.)* jocularity, wit, irony, joking, amusement, facetiousness, joke, disposition, waggery, fun, clowning.

(ANT.) sorrow, gravity, seriousness.

hunger *(SYN.)* desire, longing, zest, craving, liking, passion.

(ANT.) *satiety, repugnance, disgust.*

hunt *(SYN.)* pursuit, investigation, examination, inquiry.

(ANT.) *cession, abandonment.*

hurried *(SYN.)* rushed, hasty, swift, headlong, slipshod, careless, impulsive.

(ANT.) *deliberate, slow, dilatory, thorough.*

hurry *(SYN.)* quicken, speed, ado, rush, accelerate, run, hasten, race, urge.

(ANT.) *retard, tarry, hinder, linger, dawdle, delay.*

hurt *(SYN.)* damage, harm, grievance, detriment, pain, injustice, injure, abuse, distress, disfigured, mar.

(ANT.) *improvement, repair, compliment, help, praise.*

hurtle *(SYN.)* charge, collide, rush, lunge.

husband *(SYN.)* spouse, mate.

husk *(SYN.)* shell, hull, pod, skin, covering, crust, bark.

hustle *(SYN.)* hasten, run, hurry, speed.

hut *(SYN.)* cottage, shanty, cabin, shed.

hutch *(SYN.)* box, chest, locker, trunk, coffer, bin.

hybrid *(SYN.)* mule, mixture, crossbreed, cross, mongrel, mutt, composite.

hypercritical *(SYN.)* faultfinding, captious, censorious.

(ANT.) *lax, easygoing, indulgent, lenient.*

hypnotic *(SYN.)* soothing, opiate, sedative, soporific, entrancing, spellbinding, arresting, charming, engaging, gripping.

hypnotize *(SYN.)* entrance, dazzle, mesmerize, fascinate, spellbind.

hypocrisy *(SYN.)* pretense, deceit, dissembling, fakery, feigning, pharisaism, sanctimony, cant, dissimulation.

(ANT.) *openness, candor, truth, directness, forthrightness, honesty, frankness.*

hypocrite *(SYN.)* cheat, deceiver, pretender, dissembler, fake, charlatan.

hypocritical *(SYN.)* dissembling, two-faced, insincere, dishonest, duplicitous.

(ANT.) *heartfelt, true, genuine, honest.*

hypothesis *(SYN.)* law, theory, supposition, conjecture.

(ANT.) *proof, fact, certainty.*

hypothetical *(SYN.)* conjectural, speculative.

(ANT.) *actual.*

idea *(SYN.)* conception, image, opinion, sentiment, thought, impression.

(ANT.) *thing, matter, entity, object, substance.*

ideal *(SYN.)* imaginary, supreme, unreal, visionary, exemplary, utopian.

(ANT.) *imperfect, actual, material, real, faulty.*

identify *(ANT.)* recollect, apprehend, perceive, remember, confess, acknowledge.

(ANT.) *ignore, forget, overlook, renounce, disown.*

identity *(SYN.)* uniqueness, personality, character.

ideology *(SYN.)* credo, principles, belief.

idiom *(SYN.)* language, speech, vernacular, lingo, dialect, jargon, slang.

(ANT.) *babble, gibberish, drivel, nonsense.*

idiot *(SYN.)* buffoon, harlequin, dolt, jester, dunce, blockhead, imbecile, numbskull, simpleton, oaf.

(ANT.) *philosopher, genius, scholar, sage.*

idle *(SYN.)* unemployed, dormant, lazy, inactive, unoccupied, indolent, slothful.

(ANT.) *occupied, working, employed, active, industrious, busy, engaged.*

ignoble *(SYN.)* dishonorable, ignominious, lowly, menial vile, sordid, vulgar, abject.

(ANT.) *righteous, lofty, honored, esteemed, noble.*

ignorant *(SYN.)* uneducated, untaught, uncultured, illiterate, uninformed, unlearned, unlettered.

(ANT.) *cultured, literate, educated, erudite, informed, cultivated, schooled, learned.*

ignore *(SYN.)* omit, slight, disregard, overlook, neglect.

(ANT.) *notice, regard, include.*

ill *(SYN.)* diseased, ailing, indisposed, morbid, infirm, unwell, unhealthy, sick.

(ANT.) *robust, strong, healthy, well, sound, fit.*

ill-use *(SYN.)* defame, revile, vilify, misemploy, disparage, abuse, traduce, asperse.

(ANT.) *protect, cherish, respect, honor, praise.*

ill-advised *(SYN.)* injudicious, ill-considered, imprudent.

ill-at-ease *(SYN.)* nervous, uncomfortable, uneasy.

(ANT.) comfortable.

illegal *(SYN.)* prohibited, unlawful, criminal, illicit.

(ANT.) permitted, lawful, honest, legal, legitimate.

illiberal *(SYN.)* fanatical, bigoted, intolerant, narrow-minded, dogmatic.

(ANT.) progressive, liberal.

illicit *(SYN.)* illegitimate, criminal, outlawed, unlawful, prohibited, illegal.

(ANT.) legal, honest, permitted, lawful, licit.

ill-natured *(SYN.)* crabby, cranky, grouchy, cross.

illness *(SYN.)* complaint, infirmity, ailment, disorder.

(ANT.) healthiness, health, soundness, vigor.

illogical *(SYN.)* absurd, irrational, preposterous.

ill-tempered *(SYN.)* crabby, cranky, cross, grouchy.

ill-treated *(SYN.)* harmed, mistreated, abused.

illuminate *(SYN.)* enlighten, clarify, irradiate, illustrate, light, lighten, explain, interpret, elucidate, brighten.

(ANT.) obscure, confuse, darken, obfuscate, shadow.

illusion *(SYN.)* hallucination, vision, phantom, delusion, fantasy, dream, mirage.

(ANT.) substance, actuality.

illusive *(SYN.)* fallacious, delusive, false, specious.

(ANT.) real, truthful, authentic, genuine, honest.

illustrate *(SYN.)* decorate, illuminate, adorn, show, picture, embellish.

illustration *(SYN.)* likeness, painting, picture, print, scene, sketch, view, engraving, drawing, panorama.

illustrious *(SYN.)* prominent, eminent, renowned, famed, great, vital, elevated, noble, excellent, dignified, gigantic, enormous, immense.

(ANT.) menial, common, minute, diminutive, small, obscure, ordinary, little.

image *(SYN.)* reflection, likeness, idea, representation, notion, picture, conception.

imaginary *(SYN.)* fanciful, fantastic, unreal, whimsical.

(ANT.) actual, real.

imagine *(SYN.)* assume, surmise, suppose, conceive, dream, pretend, conjecture.

imbecile *(SYN.)* idiot, numskull, simpleton, blockhead, harlequin, nincompoop.

(ANT.) scholar, genius, philosopher, sage.

imbibe *(SYN.)* absorb, consume, assimilate, engulf, engage, occupy, engross.

(ANT.) dispense, exude, discharge, emit.

imitate *(SYN.)* duplicate, mimic, follow, reproduce, mock, counterfeit, copy.

(ANT.) invent, distort, alter.

imitation *(SYN.)* replica, reproduction copy, duplicate, facsimile, transcript.

(ANT.) prototype, original.

immaculate *(SYN.)* clean, spotless, unblemished.

(ANT.) dirty.

immature *(SYN.)* young, boyish, childish, youthful, childlike, puerile, girlish.

(ANT.) old, senile, aged, elderly, mature.

immeasurable *(SYN.)* unlimited, endless, eternal, immense, interminable, unbounded, immeasurable.

(ANT.) limited, confined, bounded, finite.

immediate *(SYN.)* present, instant, instantaneous, near, close, next, prompt, direct.

(ANT.) distant, future.

immediately *(SYN.)* now, presently, instantly, promptly, straightway, directly, instantaneously, forthwith.

(ANT.) sometime, hereafter, later, shortly, distantly.

immense *(SYN.)* enormous, large, gigantic, huge, colossal, elephantine, great.

(ANT.) small, diminutive, little, minuscule, minute.

immensity *(SYN.)* hugeness, enormousness, vastness.

immerse *(SYN.)* plunge, dip, dunk, sink, submerge, engage, absorb, engross.

(ANT.) uplift, elevate, recover.

immigration *(SYN.)* settlement, colonization.

(ANT.) exodus, emigration.

imminent (SYN.) impending, menacing, threatening.

(ANT.) retreating, afar, distant, improbable, remote.

immoderation (SYN.) profusion, surplus, extravagance, excess, intemperance.

(ANT.) lack, want, deficiency, dearth, paucity.

immoral (SYN.) sinful, wicked, corrupt, bad, indecent, profligate, unprincipled.

(ANT.) pure, high-minded, chaste, virtuous, noble.

immortal (SYN.) infinite, eternal, timeless, undying, perpetual, ceaseless.

(ANT.) mortal, transient, finite, ephemeral, temporal.

immune (SYN.) easy, open, autonomous, unobstructed, free, emancipated, clear, independent, unrestricted.

(ANT.) confined, impeded, restricted, subject.

immutable (SYN.) constant, faithful, invariant, persistent, unchanging, unalterable, continual, ceaseless.

(ANT.) mutable, vacillating, wavering, fickle.

impact (SYN.) striking, contact, collision.

impair (SYN.) harm, injure, spoil, deface, destroy, hurt, damage, mar.

(ANT.) repair, mend, ameliorate, enhance, benefit.

impart (SYN.) convey, disclose, inform, tell, reveal, transmit, notify, confer, divulge, communicate, relate.

(ANT.) hide, withhold, conceal.

impartial (SYN.) unbiased, just, honest, fair, reasonable, equitable.

(ANT.) fraudulent, dishonorable, partial.

impartiality (SYN.) indifference, unconcern, impartiality, neutrality.

(ANT.) passion, ardor, fervor, affection.

impasse (SYN.) standstill, deadlock, stalemate.

impede (SYN.) hamper, hinder, retard, thwart, check, encumber, interrupt, bar, clog, delay, obstruct, block, frustrate, restrain, stop.

(ANT.) assist, promote, help, advance, further.

impediment (SYN.) barrier, bar, block, difficulty, check, hindrance, snag, obstruction.

(ANT.) assistance, help, aid, encouragement.

impel (SYN.) oblige, enforce, drive, coerce, force, constrain.

(ANT.) induce, prevent, convince, persuade.

impending (SYN.) imminent, nigh, threatening, overhanging, approaching, menacing.

(ANT.) remote, improbable, afar, distant, retreating.

impenetrable (SYN) rigid, tough, harsh, strict, unfeeling, rigorous, intricate, arduous, penetrable, cruel, difficult, severe, stern, firm, hard, compact.

(ANT.) soft, simple, gentle, tender, brittle, fluid, flabby, elastic, lenient, easy, effortless.

imperative (SYN.) critical, instant, important, necessary, serious, urgent, cogent, compelling, crucial, pressing, impelling, importunate, exigent, insistent.

(ANT.) trivial, insignificant, unimportant, petty.

imperceptible (SYN.) invisible, indiscernible, unseen, indistinguishable.

(ANT.) seen, evident, visible, perceptible.

imperfection (SYN.) flaw, shortcoming, vice, defect, blemish, failure, mistake, omission, fault, error.

(ANT.) correctness, perfection, completeness.

imperil (SYN.) jeopardize, risk, endanger, hazard, risk.

(ANT.) guard, insure.

impersonal (SYN.) objective, detached, disinterested.

(ANT.) personal.

impersonate (SYN.) mock, simulate, imitate, ape, counterfeit, mimic, copy, duplicate.

(ANT.) alter, invent, diverge, distort.

impertinence (SYN) impudence, presumption, sauciness, effrontery, audacity, rudeness, assurance, boldness, insolence.

(ANT.) truckling, politeness, diffidence, subserviency.

impertinent (SYN.) rude, offensive, insolent, disrespectful, arrogant, brazen, impudent, insulting, contemptuous, abusive.

(ANT.) *polite, respectful, considerate, courteous.*

impetuous (SYN.) rash, heedless, quick, hasty, careless, passionate, impulsive.

(ANT.) *cautious, reasoning, careful, prudent, thoughtful, calculating.*

implicate (SYN.) reproach, accuse, blame, involve, condemn, incriminate, rebuke, censure.

(ANT.) *exonerate, absolve, acquit.*

implore (SYN.) beg, pray, request, solicit, crave, entreat, beseech, ask, importune, supplicate, adjure, appeal, petition.

(ANT.) *give, cede, bestow, favor, grant.*

imply (SYN.) mean, involve, suggest, connote, hint, mention, indicate, insinuate, signify.

(ANT.) *state, assert, declare, express.*

impolite (SYN.) rude, unpolished, impudent, boorish, blunt, discourteous, rough, saucy, surly, savage, insolent, gruff, uncivil, coarse, ignorant, crude, illiterate, raw, primitive, vulgar, untaught.

(ANT.) *genteel, courteous, courtly, dignified, polite, stately, noble, civil.*

import (SYN.) influence, significance, stress, emphasis, importance, value, weight.

(ANT.) *triviality, insignificance.*

important (SYN.) critical, grave, influential, momentous, well-known, pressing, relevant, prominent, primary, essential, weighty, material, considerable, famous, principle, famed, sequential, notable, significant, illustrious, decisive.

(ANT.) *unimportant, trifling, petty, trivial, insignificant, secondary, anonymous, irrelevant.*

impose (SYN.) levy, require, demand.

imposing (SYN.) lofty, noble, majestic, magnificent, august, dignified, grandiose, high, grand, impressive, pompous, stately.

(ANT.) *ordinary, undignified, humble, common, lowly.*

imposition (SYN.) load, onus, burden.

impossible (SYN.) preposterous.

impregnable (SYN.) safe, invulnerable, secure, unassailable.

(ANT.) *vulnerable.*

impress (SYN.) awe, emboss, affect, mark, imprint, indent, influence.

impression (SYN.) influence, indentation, feeling, opinion, mark, effect, depression, guess, thought, belief, dent, sensibility.

(ANT.) *fact, insensibility.*

impressive (SYN.) arresting, moving, remarkable, splendid, thrilling, striking, majestic, grandiose, imposing, commanding, affecting, exciting, touching, stirring.

(ANT.) *regular, unimpressive, commonplace.*

impromptu (SYN.) casual, unprepared, offhand, extemporaneous.

improper (SYN.) unfit, unsuitable, inappropriate, naughty, indecent, unbecoming.

(ANT.) *fitting, proper, appropriate.*

improve (SYN.) better, reform, refine, ameliorate, amend, help, upgrade, rectify.

(ANT.) *debase, vitiate, impair, corrupt, damage.*

improvement (SYN) growth, advance, progress, betterment, development, advancement, progression.

(ANT.) *relapse, regression, decline, retrogression, delay.*

imprudent (SYN.) indiscreet, thoughtless, desultory, lax, neglectful, remiss, careless, inattentive, heedless, inconsiderate, reckless, ill-advised, irresponsible, unconcerned.

(ANT.) *careful, meticulous, accurate.*

impudence (SYN.) boldness, insolence, rudeness, sauciness, assurance, effrontery, impertinence, presumption, audacity.

(ANT.) *politeness, truckling, subserviency, diffidence.*

impudent (SYN.) forward, rude, abrupt, prominent, striking, bold, fresh, impertinent, insolent, pushy, insulting, brazen.

(ANT.) *bashful, flinching, polite, courteous, cowardly, retiring, timid.*

impulse (SYN.) hunch, whim, fancy, urge, caprice, surge, pulse.

impulsive (SYN.) passionate, rash, spontaneous, heedless, careless, hasty, quick, impetuous.

(ANT.) reasoning, calculating, careful, prudent, cautious.

impure *(SYN.)* dishonest, spoiled, tainted, contaminated, debased, corrupt, profligate, unsound, putrid, corrupted, crooked, depraved, vitiated, venal.

imputation *(SYN.)* diary, incrimination, arraignment, indictment.

(ANT.) exoneration, pardon, exculpation.

inability *(SYN.)* incompetence, incapacity, handicap, disability, impotence.

(ANT.) power, strength, ability, capability.

inaccurate *(SYN.)* false, incorrect, mistaken, untrue, askew, wrong, awry, erroneous, fallacious.

(ANT.) right, accurate, true, correct.

inactive *(SYN.)* lazy, unemployed, indolent, motionless, still, inert.

(ANT.) employed, working, active, industrious, occupied.

inadequate *(SYN.)* insufficient, lacking, short, incomplete, defective, scanty.

(ANT.) satisfactory, enough, adequate, ample, sufficient.

inadvertent *(SYN.)* careless, negligent, unthinking.

inane *(SYN.)* trite, insipid, banal, absurd, silly, commonplace, vapid, foolish.

(ANT.) stimulating, novel, fresh, original, striking.

inanimate *(SYN.)* deceased, spiritless, lifeless, gone, dull, mineral, departed.

(ANT.) living, stirring, alive, animate.

inattentive *(SYN.)* absentminded, distracted, abstracted, preoccupied.

(ANT.) watchful, attending, attentive.

inaugurate *(SYN.)* commence, begin, open, originate, start, arise, launch, enter.

(ANT.) end, terminate, close, complete, finish.

incentive *(SYN.)* impulse, stimulus, inducement.

(ANT.) discouragement.

inception *(SYN.)* origin, start, source, opening, beginning, outset, commencement.

(ANT.) end, termination, close, comple-

tion.

incessant *(SYN.)* perennial, uninterrupted, continual, ceaseless, continuous, unremitting, eternal, constant.

(ANT.) rare, occasional, periodic, interrupted.

incident *(SYN.)* happening, situation, occurrence, circumstance, condition.

incidental *(SYN.)* casual, contingent, trivial, undesigned.

(ANT.) intended, fundamental, planned, calculated.

incinerate *(SYN.)* sear, char, blaze, scald, singe, consume.

(ANT.) quench, put out, extinguish.

incisive *(SYN.)* neat, succinct, terse, brief, compact, condensed, summary, concise.

(ANT.) wordy, prolix, verbose.

incite *(SYN.)* goad, provoke, urge, arouse, encourage.

(ANT.) quiet, bore, pacify, soothe.

inclination *(SYN.)* bent, preference, desire, slope, affection, bent, bias, disposition, bending, penchant.

(ANT.) nonchalance, apathy, distaste, reluctance, disinclination, repugnance.

include *(SYN.)* contain, hold, accommodate, embody, encompass, involve, comprise, embrace.

(ANT.) omit, exclude, discharge.

income *(SYN.)* earnings, salary, wages, revenue, pay, return, receipts.

incomparable *(SYN.)* peerless, matchless, unequaled.

incompetency *(SYN.)* inability, weakness, handicap, impotence, disability.

(ANT.) strength, ability, power, capability.

incongruous *(SYN.)* inconsistent, contrary, incompatible, irreconcilable, contradictory, unsteady, incongruous.

(ANT.) consistent, compatible, correspondent.

inconsiderate *(SYN.)* unthinking, careless, unthoughtful.

(ANT.) logical, consistent.

inconsistency *(SYN)* discord, variance, contention.

(ANT.) harmony, concord, amity, consonance.

inconsistent *(SYN.)* fickle, wavering, variable, changeable, contrary, unstable, illogical, contradictory.

(ANT.) unchanging, steady, logical, stable, uniform.

inconspicuous *(SYN.)* retiring, unnoticed, unostentatious.

(ANT.) obvious, conspicuous.

inconstant *(SYN.)* fickle, shifting, changeable, fitful, vacillating, unstable, wavering.

(ANT.) stable, constant, steady, uniform, unchanging.

inconvenient *(SYN.)* awkward, inappropriate, untimely.

(ANT.) handy, convenient.

incorrect *(SYN.)* mistaken, wrong, erroneous.

(ANT.) proper, accurate.

increase *(SYN.)* amplify, enlarge, grow, magnify, multiply, augment, enhance, expand, intensify, swell, raise.

(ANT.) diminish, reduce, atrophy, shrink, shrinkage.

incredible *(SYN.)* improbable, unbelievable.

(ANT.) plausible, credible, believable.

incriminate *(SYN.)* charge, accuse, indict, arraign.

(ANT.) release, exonerate, acquit, absolve, vindicate.

incrimination *(SYN.)* imputation, indictment, accusation, charge, arraignment.

(ANT.) exoneration, pardon, exculpation.

indebted *(SYN.)* obliged, grateful, beholden.

(ANT.) unappreciative.

indecent *(SYN.)* impure, obscene, coarse, dirty, filthy, smutty, gross, disgusting.

(ANT.) modest, refined, decent, pure.

indeed *(SYN.)* truthfully, really, honestly, surely.

indefinite *(SYN.)* unsure, uncertain, vague, confused.

(ANT.) decided, definite, equivocal.

independence *(SYN.)* liberation, privilege, freedom, immunity, familiarity.

(ANT.) necessity, constraint, compulsion, reliance, dependence, bondage, servitude.

independent *(SYN.)* free, unrestrained, voluntary, autonomous, self-reliant.

(ANT.) enslaved, contingent, dependent, restricted.

indestructible *(SYN.)* enduring, lasting, permanent, unchangeable, abiding.

(ANT.) unstable, temporary, transitory, ephemeral.

indicate *(SYN.)* imply, denote, signify, specify, intimate, designate, symbolize, show.

(ANT.) mislead, falsify, distract, conceal, falsify.

indication *(SYN.)* proof, emblem, omen, sign, symbol, token, mark, portent.

indict *(SYN.)* charge, accuse, incriminate, censure.

(ANT.) acquit, vindicate, absolve, exonerate.

indictment *(SYN.)* incrimination, arraignment.

(ANT.) pardon, exoneration, exculpation.

indifference *(SYN.)* unconcern, apathy, impartiality.

(ANT.) ardor, passion, affection, fervor.

indifferent *(SYN.)* uncaring, insensitive, cool.

(ANT.) caring, concerned, earnest.

indigence *(SYN.)* necessity, destitution, poverty, want, need, privation, penury.

(ANT.) wealth, abundance, plenty, riches, affluence.

indigenous *(SYN.)* inborn, native, inherent, domestic.

indigent *(SYN.)* wishing, covetous, demanding, lacking, requiring, wanting.

indignant *(SYN.)* irritated, irate, angry, aroused.

(ANT.) calm, serene, content.

indignation *(SYN.)* ire, petulance, passion, choler, anger, wrath, temper.

(ANT.) self-control, peace, forbearance, patience.

indignity *(SYN.)* insolence, insult, abuse, affront, offense.

(ANT.) homage, apology, salutation.

indirect *(SYN.)* winding, crooked, devious, roundabout, cunning, tricky.

(ANT.) straightforward, direct, straight, honest.

indiscretion *(SYN.)* imprudence, folly, absurdity.

(ANT.) prudence, sense, wisdom, reasonableness, judgment.

indispensable *(SYN.)* necessary, fun-

damental, basic, essential, important, intrinsic, vital.
(ANT.) optional, expendable, peripheral, extrinsic.

indistinct *(SYN.)* cloudy, dark, mysterious, vague, blurry, ambiguous, cryptic, dim, obscure, enigmatic, abstruse, hazy, blurred, unintelligible.
(ANT.) clear, lucid, bright, distinct.

indistinguishable *(SYN.)* identical, like, coincident, equal, same, equivalent.
(ANT.) dissimilar, opposed, contrary, disparate, distinct.

individual *(SYN.)* singular, specific, unique, distinctive, single, particular, undivided, human, apart, marked, person, different, special, separate.
(ANT.) universal, common, general, ordinary.

individuality *(SYN.)* symbol, description, mark, kind, character, repute, class, standing, sort, nature, disposition, reputation, sign.

indolent *(SYN.)* slothful, lazy, idle, inactive, slow, sluggish, torpid, supine, inert.
(ANT.) diligent, active, assiduous, vigorous, zestful, alert.

indomitable *(SYN.)* insurmountable, unconquerable, invulnerable, impregnable, unassailable.
(ANT.) weak, puny, powerless, vulnerable.

induce *(SYN.)* evoke, cause, influence, persuade, effect, make, originate, prompt, incite, create.

inducement *(SYN.)* incentive, motive, purpose, stimulus, reason, impulse, cause, principle, spur, incitement.
(ANT.) result, attempt, action, effort, deed.

induct *(SYN.)* instate, establish, install.
(ANT.) eject, oust.

indulge *(SYN.)* humor, satisfy, gratify.

indulgent *(SYN.)* obliging, pampering, tolerant, easy.

indurate *(SYN.)* impenitent, hard, insensible, tough, obdurate, callous, unfeeling.
(ANT.) soft, compassionate, tender, sensitive.

industrious *(SYN.)* perseverant, busy, active, diligent, assiduous, careful, patient.

(ANT.) unconcerned, indifferent, lethargic, careless, apathetic, lazy, indolent, shiftless.

inebriated *(SYN.)* drunk, tight, drunken, intoxicated, tipsy.
(ANT.) sober, clearheaded, temperate.

ineffective *(SYN.)* pliant, tender, vague, wavering, defenseless, weak, inadequate, poor, irresolute, frail, decrepit, delicate, vacillating, assailable, exposed, vulnerable.
(ANT.) sturdy, robust, strong, potent, powerful.

inept *(SYN.)* clumsy, awkward, improper, inappropriate.
(ANT.) adroit, dexterous, adept, appropriate, proper, apt, fitting.

inequity *(SYN.)* wrong, injustice, unfairness, grievance, injury.
(ANT.) righteousness, lawfulness, equity, justice.

inert *(SYN.)* lazy, dormant, slothful, inactive, idle, indolent, motionless, unmoving, fixed, static.
(ANT.) working, active, industrious, occupied.

inertia *(SYN.)* indolence, torpidity, idleness, slothfulness, sluggishness, supineness.
(ANT.) assiduousness, activity, alertness, diligence.

inevitable *(SYN.)* definite, fixed, positive, sure, undeniable, indubitable, certain, assured, unquestionable, secure.
(ANT.) uncertain, probable, doubtful, questionable.

inexpensive *(SYN.)* cheap, inferior, mean, beggarly, common, poor, shabby, modest, economical.
(ANT.) expensive, costly, dear.

inexperienced *(SYN.)* naive, untrained, uninformed.
(ANT.) experienced, skilled, sophisticated, trained, seasoned.

inexplicable *(SYN.)* hidden, mysterious, obscure, secret, dark, cryptic, enigmatical, incomprehensible, occult, recondite, inscrutable, dim.
(ANT.) plain, simple, clear, obvious, explained.

infamous *(SYN.)* shocking, shameful, scandalous.

infantile *(SYN.)* babyish, naive, immature, childish.
(ANT.) mature, grownup, adult.

infect *(SYN.)* pollute, poison, contaminate, defile, sully, taint.
(ANT.) purify, disinfect.

infection *(SYN.)* virus, poison, ailment, disease, pollution, pest, germ, taint, contamination, contagion.

infectious *(SYN.)* contagious, virulent, catching, communicable, pestilential, transferable.
(ANT.) noncommunicable, hygienic, healthful.

infer *(SYN.)* understand, deduce, extract.

inference *(SYN.)* consequence, result, conclusion, corollary, judgment, deduction.
(ANT.) preconception, foreknowledge, assumption, presupposition.

inferior *(SYN.)* secondary, lower, poorer, minor, subordinate, mediocre.
(ANT.) greater, superior, better, higher.

infinite *(SYN.)* immeasurable, interminable, unlimited, unbounded, eternal, boundless, illimitable, immense, endless, vast, innumerable, numberless, limitless.
(ANT.) confined, limited, bounded, circumscribed, finite.

infinitesimal *(SYN.)* minute, microscopic, tiny, submicroscopic.
(ANT.) gigantic, huge, enormous.

infirm *(SYN.)* feeble, impaired, decrepit, forceless, languid, puny, powerless, enervated, weak, exhausted.
(ANT.) stout, vigorous, forceful, lusty, strong.

infirmity *(SYN.)* disease, illness, malady, ailment, sickness, disorder, complaint.
(ANT.) soundness, health, vigor, healthiness.

inflame *(SYN.)* fire, incite, excite, arouse.
(ANT.) soothe, calm.

inflammation *(SYN.)* infection, soreness, irritation.

inflammatory *(SYN.)* instigating, inciting, provocative.

inflate *(SYN.)* expand, swell, distend.
(ANT.) collapse, deflate.

inflexible *(SYN.)* firm, stubborn, headstrong, immovable, unyielding, uncompromising, dogged, contumacious, determined, obstinate, rigid, unbending, unyielding, steadfast.
(ANT.) submissive, compliant, docile, amenable, yielding, flexible, giving, elastic.

inflict *(SYN.)* deliver, deal, give, impose, apply.

influence *(SYN.)* weight, control, effect, sway.

influenced *(SYN.)* sway, affect, bias, control, actuate, impel, stir, incite.

influential *(SYN.)* important, weighty, prominent, significant, critical, decisive, momentous, relevant, material, pressing, consequential, grave.
(ANT.) petty, irrelevant, mean, trivial, insignificant.

inform *(SYN.)* apprise, instruct, tell, notify, advise, acquaint, enlighten, impart, warn, teach, advise, relate.
(ANT.) delude, mislead, distract, conceal.

informal *(SYN.)* simple, easy, natural, unofficial, familiar.
(ANT.) formal, distant, reserved, proper.

informality *(SYN.)* friendship, frankness, liberty, acquaintance, sociability, intimacy, unreserved.
(ANT.) presumption, constraint, reserve, distance, haughtiness.

information *(SYN.)* knowledge, data, intelligence, facts.

informative *(SYN.)* educational, enlightening, instructive.

informer *(SYN.)* tattler, traitor, betrayer.

infrequent *(SYN.)* unusual, rare, occasional, strange.
(ANT.) commonplace, abundant, usual, ordinary, customary, frequent, numerous.

ingenious *(SYN.)* clever, skillful, talented, adroit, dexterous, quick-witted, bright, smart, witty, sharp, apt, resourceful, imaginative, inventive, creative.
(ANT.) dull, slow, awkward, bungling, unskilled, stupid.

ingenuity *(SYN.)* cunning, inventiveness, resourcefulness, aptitude, faculty, cleverness, ingenuousness.
(ANT.) ineptitude, clumsiness, dullness, stupidity.

ingenuous *(SYN.)* open, sincere, honest,

candid, straightforward, plain, frank, truthful, free, naive, simple, innocent, unsophisticated.
(ANT.) *scheming, sly, contrived, wily.*

ingredient (SYN.) component, element, constituent.

inhabit (SYN.) fill, possess, absorb, dwell, occupy, live.
(ANT.) *relinquish, abandon, release.*

inherent (SYN.) innate, native, congenital, inherent, intrinsic, inborn, inbred, natural, real.
(ANT.) *extraneous, acquired, external, extrinsic.*

inhibit (SYN.) curb, constrain, hold back, restrain, bridle, hinder, repress, suppress, stop, limit.
(ANT.) *loosen, aid, incite, encourage.*

inhuman (SYN.) merciless, cruel, brutal, ferocious, savage, ruthless, malignant, barbarous, barbaric, bestial.
(ANT.) *kind, benevolent, forbearing, gentle, compassionate, merciful, humane, humane.*

inimical (SYN.) hostile, warlike, adverse, antagonistic, opposed, unfriendly.
(ANT.) *favorable, amicable, cordial.*

iniquitous (SYN.) baleful, immoral, pernicious, sinfu.,
(ANT.) *moral, good, excellent, honorable, reputable.*

iniquity (SYN.) injustice, wrong, grievance.
(ANT.) *lawful, equity, righteousness, justice.*

initial (SYN.) original, first, prime, beginning, earliest.
(ANT.) *latest, subordinate, last, least, hindmost, final.*

initiate (SYN.) institute, enter, arise, inaugurate.
(ANT.) *terminate, complete, end, finish, close, stop.*

initiative (SYN.) enthusiasm, energy, vigor, enterprise.

injure (SYN.) harm, wound, abuse, dishonor, damage, hurt, impair, spoil.
(ANT.) *praise, ameliorate, help, preserve, compliment.*

injurious (SYN.) detrimental, harmful, mischievous, damaging, hurtful, deleterious.

(ANT.) *profitable, helpful, advantageous, salutary, beneficial, useful.*

injury (SYN.) harm, detriment, damage, injustice, wrong, prejudice, grievance.
(ANT.) *repair, benefit, improvement.*

injustice (SYN.) unfairness, grievance, iniquity, wrong.
(ANT.) *righteousness, justice, equity, lawfulness.*

innate (SYN.) native, inherent, congenital, innate, real, inborn, natural, intrinsic.
(ANT.) *extraneous, acquired, external, extrinsic.*

innocent (SYN.) pure, sinless, blameless, innocuous, lawful, naive, faultless, virtuous.
(ANT.) *guilty, corrupt, sinful, culpable, sophisticated, wise.*

innocuous (SYN.) naive, pure, innocent, blameless, virtuous, lawful, faultless.
(ANT.) *sinful, corrupt, unrighteous, culpable, guilty.*

inquire (SYN.) ask, solicit, invite, demand, claim, entreat, interrogate, query, beg.
(ANT.) *dictate, insist, reply, command, order.*

inquiry (SYN.) investigation, quest, research, examination, interrogation.
(ANT.) *inattention, inactivity, disregard, negligence.*

inquisitive (SYN.) meddling, peeping, nosy, interrogative, peering, searching, prying.
(ANT.) *unconcerned, indifferent, incurious.*

insane (SYN.) deranged, mad, foolish, idiotic, demented.
(ANT.) *sane, rational, reasonable, sound, sensible.*

insensitive (SYN.) unfeeling, impenitent, callous, hard.
(ANT.) *soft, compassionate, tender, sensitive.*

insight (SYN.) intuition, acumen, penetration.
(ANT.) *obtuseness.*

insignificant (SYN.) trivial, paltry, petty, small, frivolous, unimportant.
(ANT.) *momentous, serious, important, weighty.*

insist *(SYN.)* command, demand, require.

insolence *(SYN.)* boldness, presumption, sauciness, effrontery, audacity.
(ANT.) politeness, truckling, diffidence, subserviency.

insolent *(SYN.)* arrogant, impertinent, insulting, rude.
(ANT.) respectful, courteous, polite, considerate.

inspect *(SYN.)* observe, discern, eye, behold, glance, scan, stare, survey, view.
(ANT.) overlook, miss, avert.

inspection *(SYN.)* examination, retrospect, survey.

inspiration *(SYN.)* creativity, aptitude, genius, originality.
(ANT.) dullard, moron, shallowness, ineptitude, stupidity.

instance *(SYN.)* occasion, illustration, occurrence.

instant *(SYN.)* flash, moment.

instantaneous *(SYN.)* hasty, sudden unexpected, rapid, abrupt, immediate.
(ANT.) slowly, anticipated.

instantly *(SYN.)* now, presently, directly, forthwith, immediately, rapidly.
(ANT.) sometime, distantly, hereafter, later, shortly.

institute *(SYN.)* ordain, establish, raise, form, organize, begin, initiate.
(ANT.) overthrow, upset, demolish, abolish, unsettle.

instruct *(SYN.)* teach, tutor, educate, inform, school, instill, train, inculcate, drill.
(ANT.) misinform, misguide.

instrument *(SYN.)* channel, device, utensil, tool, agent, medium, agent, implement.
(ANT.) obstruction, hindrance, preventive.

insubordinate *(SYN.)* rebellious, unruly, defiant, disorderly, disobedient, undutiful, refractory, intractable, mutinous.
(ANT.) obedient, compliant, submissive, dutiful.

insufficient *(SYN.)* limited, lacking, deficient, short, inadequate.
(ANT.) ample, protracted, abundant, big, extended.

insulation *(SYN.)* quarantine, segregation, seclusion, withdrawal, isolation, loneliness, alienation, solitude.
(ANT.) union, communion, association, fellowship, connection.

insult *(SYN.)* insolence, offense, abuse, dishonor, affront, insult, indignity, offend, humiliate, outrage.
(ANT.) compliment, homage, apology, salutation, flatter, praise.

integrated *(SYN.)* mingled, mixed, combined, interspersed, desegregated, nonsectarian, interracial.
(ANT.) separated, divided, segregated.

integrity *(SYN.)* honesty, openness, trustworthiness, fairness, candor, justice, rectitude, sincerity, uprightness, soundness, wholeness, honor, principle, virtue.
(ANT.) fraud, deceit, cheating, trickery, dishonesty.

intellect *(SYN.)* understanding, judgment.

intellectual *(SYN.)* intelligent.

intelligence *(SYN.)* reason, sense, intellect, understanding, mind, ability, skill, aptitude.
(ANT.) feeling, passion, emotion.

intelligent *(SYN.)* clever, smart, knowledgeable, alert, discerning, astute, quick, enlightened, smart, bright, wise.
(ANT.) insipid, obtuse, dull, stupid, slow, foolish, unintelligent, dumb.

intend *(SYN.)* plan, prepare, scheme, contrive, outline, design, sketch, plot, project, delineate.

intense *(SYN.)* brilliant, animated, graphic, lucid, bright, expressive, vivid, deep, profound, concentrated, serious, earnest.
(ANT.) dull, vague, dusky, dim, dreary.

intensify *(SYN.)* accrue, augment, amplify, enlarge, enhance, extend, expand, heighten, grow, magnify, raise, multiply.
(ANT.) reduce, decrease, contract, diminish.

intent *(SYN.)* purpose, design, objective, intention, aim.
(ANT.) accidental, result, chance.

intensity *(SYN.)* force, potency, power, toughness, activity, durability, fortitude, vigor, stamina.
(ANT.) weakness, feebleness, infirmity,

frailty.

intention *(SYN.)* intent, purpose, objective, plan, expectation, aim, object.

(ANT.) chance, accident.

intentional *(SYN.)* deliberate, intended, studied, willful, contemplated, premeditated, designed, voluntary, purposeful, planned.

(ANT.) fortuitous, accidental, chance.

intentionally *(SYN.)* purposefully, deliberately, maliciously.

(ANT.) accidentally.

interest *(SYN.)* attention, concern, care, advantage, benefit, profit, ownership, credit, attract, engage, amuse, entertain.

(ANT.) apathy, weary, disinterest.

interested *(SYN.)* affected, concerned.

(ANT.) unconcerned, indifferent, uninterested.

interesting *(SYN.)* engaging, inviting, fascinating, attractive.

(ANT.) boring, tedious, uninteresting, wearisome.

interfere *(SYN.)* meddle, monkey, interpose, interrupt, tamper, butt in, intervene.

interference *(SYN.)* prying, intrusion, meddling, obstacle, obstruction.

interior *(SYN.)* internal, inmost, inner, inward, inside, center.

(ANT.) outer, adjacent, exterior, external, outside.

interject *(SYN.)* intrude, introduce, insert, inject, interpose.

(ANT.) overlook, avoid, disregard.

interminable *(SYN)* immense, endless, immeasurable, unlimited, vast, unbounded, boundless, eternal, infinite.

(ANT.) limited, bounded, circumscribed, confined.

internal *(SYN.)* inner, interior, inside, intimate, private.

(ANT.) outer, external, surface.

interpose *(SYN.)* arbitrate, inject, intervene, meddle, insert, interject, introduce, intercede, intrude, interfere.

(ANT.) overlook, avoid, disregard.

interpret *(SYN.)* explain, solve, translate, construe, elucidate, decode, explicate, render, unravel, define, understand.

(ANT.) misinterpret, falsify, confuse, distort, misconstrue.

interrogate *(SYN.)* quiz, analyze, inquire, audit, question, contemplate, assess, dissect, notice, scan, review, view, check, survey, scrutinize, examine.

(ANT.) overlook, omit, neglect, disregard.

interrupt *(SYN.)* suspend, delay, postpone, defer, adjourn, stay, discontinue, intrude, interfere.

(ANT.) prolong, persist, continue, maintain, proceed.

interval *(SYN.)* pause, gap.

intervene *(SYN.)* insert, intercede, meddle, inject, introduce, interpose, mediate, interfere, interrupt, intrude.

(ANT.) overlook, avoid, disregard.

intimacy *(SYN.)* fellowship, friendship, acquaintance, frankness, familiarity, unreserved, liberty.

(ANT.) presumption, distance, haughtiness, constraint, reserve.

intimate *(SYN.)* chummy, confidential, friendly, loving, affectionate, close, familiar, near, personal, private, secret.

(ANT.) conventional, formal, ceremonious, distant.

intimation *(SYN.)* reminder, implication, allusion, hint, insinuation.

(ANT.) declaration, statement, affirmation.

intolerant *(SYN.)* fanatical, narrow-minded, prejudice.

(ANT.) tolerant, radical, liberal, progressive.

intoxicated *(SYN.)* inebriated, tipsy, drunk, tight, drunken.

(ANT.) sober, temperate, clearheaded.

intrepid *(SYN.)* brave, fearless, insolent, abrupt, rude, pushy, adventurous, daring.

(ANT.) timid, bashful, flinching, cowardly, retiring.

intricate *(SYN.)* compound, perplexing, complex, involved, complicated.

(ANT.) simple, plain.

intrigue *(SYN.)* design, plot, cabal, machination..

intrinsic *(SYN.)* natural, inherent, inbred, congenital.

(ANT.) extraneous, acquired, external, extrinsic.

introduce *(SYN.)* acquaint, submit, present, offer.

introduction (SYN.) preamble, prelude, beginning, prologue, start, preface. (ANT.) finale, conclusion, end, epilogue, completion.

intrude (SYN.) invade, attack, encroach, trespass. (ANT.) vacate, evacuate, abandon, relinquish.

intruder (SYN.) trespasser, thief, prowler, robber.

intuition (SYN.) insight, acumen, perspicuity, penetration, discernment.

invade (SYN.) intrude, violate, infringe, attack, penetrate, encroach, trespass. (ANT.) vacate, abandon, evacuate, relinquish.

invalidate (SYN.) annul, cancel, abolish, revoke. (ANT.) promote, restore, sustain, establish, continue.

invaluable (SYN.) priceless, precious, valuable. (ANT.) worthless.

invasion (SYN.) assault, onslaught, aggression, attack. (ANT.) surrender, opposition, resistance, defense.

invective (SYN.) insult, abuse, disparagement, upbraiding. (ANT.) laudation, plaudit, commendation.

invent (SYN.) devise, fabricate, conceive, contrive, create. (SYN.) reproduce, copy.

inventive (SYN.) fanciful, poetical, clever, creative. (ANT.) unromantic, literal, dull, prosaic.

inventiveness (SYN) cunning, cleverness, ingeniousness. (ANT.) ineptitude, clumsiness, dullness, stupidity.

invert (SYN.) upset, turn about, transpose. (ANT.) maintain, stabilize, endorse.

investigate (SYN.) look, probe, search, scour, inspect, study.

invisible (SYN.) indistinguishable, unseen, imperceptible. (ANT.) evident, visible, seen, perceptible.

invite (SYN.) bid, ask, encourage, request, urge.

involuntary (SYN.) reflex, uncontrolled, automatic. (SYN.) voluntary, willful.

involve (SYN.) include, embrace, entangle, envelop. (ANT.) separate, extricate, disengage.

involved (SYN.) compound, intricate, complicated, complex, perplexing. (ANT.) plain, uncompounded, simple.

invulnerable (SYN.) indomitable, unassailable, invincible, unconquerable, insurmountable, impregnable. (ANT.) weak, puny, vulnerable.

irate (SYN.) incensed, enraged, angry.

ire (SYN.) indignation, irritation, wrath, anger, animosity, fury, passion. (ANT.) peace, patience, self-control.

irk (SYN.) irritate, bother, disturb, pester, trouble, vex, tease, chafe, annoy. (ANT.) console, soothe, accommodate.

irrational (SYN.) inconsistent, preposterous, self-contradictory, unreasonable. (ANT.) sensible, sound, rational consistent, reasonable.

irregular (SYN.) eccentric, unusual, aberrant, devious, abnormal, unnatural. (ANT.) regular, methodical, fixed, usual, ordinary, even.

irrelevant (SYN.) foreign, unconnected, remote, alien. (ANT.) germane, relevant, akin, kindred.

irresolute (SYN.) frail, pliant, vacillating, ineffective, wavering, weak, yielding. (ANT.) robust, potent, sturdy, strong.

irritable (SYN.) hasty, hot, peevish, testy, irascible, choleric, excitable, touchy. (ANT.) composed, agreeable, tranquil.

irritate (SYN.) irk, molest, bother, annoy, tease, disturb, inconvenience, vex. (ANT.) console, gratify, accommodate, soothe, pacify.

irritable (SYN.) peevish, testy, sensitive. (ANT.) happy, cheerful.

irritation (SYN.) chagrin, mortification, vexation, annoyance, exasperation. (ANT.) pleasure, comfort, appeasement.

isolate (SYN.) detach, segregate. (ANT.) happy, cheerful.

isolated (SYN.) lone, single, alone, desolate, secluded, solitary, deserted, sole. (ANT.) surrounded, accompanied.

issue (SYN.) flow, result, come, emanate, originate, abound, copy, distribute.

jab *(SYN.)* thrust, poke, nudge, prod, push.

jabber *(SYN.)* mumble, gossip, prattle, chatter, gab, palaver.

jack *(SYN.)* fellow, guy, boy, toiler, guy, man, worker.

jackal *(SYN.)* puppet, drone, slave, legman, flunky, tool, vassal.

jackass *(SYN.)* fool, idiot, dope, dunce, ignoramus, imbecile, ninny, simpleton, blockhead.

jacket *(SYN.)* wrapper, envelope, coat, sheath, cover, casing, folder, enclosure, skin.

jade *(SYN.)* hussy, wanton, trollop, harlot, whore, wench, hag, shrew.

jaded *(SYN.)* exhausted, bored, tired, fatigued, satiated, weary, hardened.

jag *(SYN.)* notch, snag, protuberance, barb, point.

jagged *(SYN.)* ragged, pointy, notched, serrated.

(ANT.) smooth.

jail *(SYN.)* stockade, prison, reformatory, penitentiary, keep, dungeon, brig, confine, lock up, detain, imprison, hold captive, incarcerate.

jailbird *(SYN.)* convict, parolee, con, inmate, prisoner.

jailer *(SYN.)* guard, keeper, turnkey, warden.

jam *(SYN.)* force, pack, ram, crowd, push, wedge, squeeze, stuff, load, cram, press, crush, marmalade, jelly, conserve, preserve.

jamboree *(SYN.)* celebration, fete, spree, festival, festivity, carousal.

jangle *(SYN.)* rattle, vibrate, clank, clatter, dissonance, discord, quarrel, din, discord, dispute.

janitor *(SYN.)* custodian, doorkeeper, caretaker, gatekeeper.

jape *(SYN.)* lampoon, banter, joke, jest, tease, ridicule.

jar *(SYN.)* rattle, shake, bounce, jolt.

jargon *(SYN.)* speech, idiom, dialect, vernacular, diction, argot, phraseology, language, patois, parlance, slang.

(ANT.) gibberish, babble, nonsense, drivel.

jaundiced *(SYN.)* biased, prejudiced.

(ANT.) fair.

jaunt *(SYN.)* journey, trip, tour, excursion, outing, voyage, expedition.

jaunty *(SYN.)* lively, vivacious, bouyant, winsome, frisky, showy, dapper, breezy, airy.

jazzy *(SYN.)* garish, vivacious, loud, splashy, exaggerated, flashy.

jealous *(SYN.)* covetous, desirous of, envious.

jealousy *(SYN.)* suspicion, envy, resentfulness, greed, covetousness.

(ANT.) tolerance, indifference, geniality, liberality.

jeer *(SYN.)* taunt, mock, scoff, deride, make fun of, gibe, sneer.

(ANT.) flatter, praise, compliment, laud.

jeering *(SYN.)* mockery, sneering, derision, sarcasm, irony, ridicule.

jell *(SYN.)* finalize, congeal, set, solidify, shape up, take form.

jeopardize *(SYN.)* risk, dare, expose, imperil, chance, venture, conjecture, hazard, endanger.

(ANT.) know, guard, determine.

jerk *(SYN.)* quiver, twitch, shake, spasm, jolt, yank, fool.

jerkwater *(SYN.)* remote, hick, backwoods, unimportant.

jest *(SYN.)* mock, joke, tease, fun, witticism, quip.

jester *(SYN.)* fool, buffoon, harlequin, clown.

(ANT.) sage, genius, scholar, philosopher.

jettison *(SYN.)* heave, discharge, throw, eject, cast off, dismiss.

jetty *(SYN.)* pier, breakwater, bulwark, buttress.

jewel *(SYN.)* ornament, gem, bauble, stone.

jib *(SYN.)* shrink, shy, dodge, retreat, balk.

jig *(SYN.)* caper, prance, jiggle, leap, skip.

jiggle *(SYN.)* shimmy, agitate, jerk, twitch, wiggle.

jilt *(SYN.)* abandon, get rid of, reject, desert, forsake, leave.

jingle *(SYN.)* chime, ring, tinkle.

jinx *(SYN.)* hex, whammy, nemesis, curse, evil eye.

jittery *(SYN.)* jumpy, nervous, quivering, shaky, skittery.

job *(SYN.)* toil, business, occupation, post, chore, stint, career, duty, employment, profession, trade, work, situation, labor, assignment, position, undertaking, calling, task.

jobless *(SYN.)* idle, unoccupied, inactive, unemployed.

jocularity *(SYN.)* humor, wit, joke, facetiousness, waggery.

(ANT.) sorrow, gravity.

jocund *(SYN.)* mirthful, elated, pleasant, cheerful, merry, gay, jovial, frolicsome.

jog *(SYN.)* gait, trot, sprint, run, lope.

join *(SYN.)* conjoin, unite, attach, accompany, associate, assemble, fit, couple, combine, fasten, unite, clasp, put together, go with, adjoin, link, connect.

(ANT.) separate, disconnect, split, sunder, part, divide, detach.

joint *(SYN.)* link, union, connection, junction, coupling, common, combined, mutual, connected.

(ANT.) divided, separate.

joke *(SYN.)* game, jest, caper, prank, anecdote, quip, tease, antic, banter, laugh.

joker *(SYN.)* wisecracker, humorist, comedian, trickster, comic, jester, wit, punster.

jolly *(SYN.)* merry, joyful, gay, happy, sprightly, pleasant, jovial, gleeful, spirited, cheerful, glad.

(ANT.) mournful, depressed, sullen, glum.

jolt *(SYN.)* sway, waver, startle, rock, jar, totter, jerk, bounce, quake, bump, shake.

josh *(SYN.)* poke fun at, kid, tease, ridicule.

jostle *(SYN.)* shove, push, bump, thrust.

jot *(SYN.)* note, write, record.

jounce *(SYN.)* bounce, jolt, bump, jostle, jar, shake.

journal *(SYN.)* account, diary, log, chronicle, magazine, newspaper, record.

journey *(SYN.)* tour, passage, cruise, tion, serum, fluid.

jumble *(SYN.)* disarrangement, tumult, agitation, ferment, mix, turmoil, commotion, confuse, scramble, disorder.

(ANT.) peace, arrange, compose, certainty, tranquillity.

jumbo *(SYN.)* huge, big, immense, enormous, giant, colossal, monstrous, mammoth, gigantic, tremendous.

(ANT.) mini, midget, dwarf, small, little, tiny.

jump *(SYN.)* leap, caper, skip, bound, vault, hop, spring.

jumpy *(SYN.)* touchy, excitable, nervous, sensitive.

(ANT.) tranquil, calm, unruffled.

junction *(SYN.)* coupling, joining, union, crossroads, intersection, weld, connection, linking, seam, joint.

(ANT.) separation.

jungle *(SYN.)* woods, thicket, undergrowth, forest, bush.

junior *(SYN.)* secondary, inferior, minor, lower, younger.

junk *(SYN.)* rubbish, scraps, trash, waste, dump, discard, castoffs, debris.

junky *(SYN.)* tawdry, ramshackle, tattered, tacky, shoddy.

jurisdiction *(SYN.)* power, commission, warrant, authority, authorization, magistacy, sovereignty.

just *(SYN.)* fair, trustworthy, precise, exact, candid, upright, honest, impartial, lawful, rightful, proper, legal, truthful, only, conscientious.

(ANT.) tricky, dishonest, unjust, corrupt, lying, deceitful.

justice *(SYN.)* justness, rectitude, equity, law, impartiality, right.

(ANT.) unfairness, inequity, wrong, partiality.

justifiable *(SYN.)* allowable, tolerable, admissible.

(ANT.) unsuitable, inadmissible.

justify *(SYN.)* uphold, excuse, defend, acquit, exonerate, clear, vindicate.

(ANT.) convict.

jut *(SYN.)* project, protrude, stick out.

(ANT.) indent, recess.

juvenile *(SYN.)* puerile, youthful, childish, youngster, youth, young, child.

(ANT.) old, aged, adult, mature.

voyage, pilgrimage, jaunt, trip, outing, expedition, junket, excursion, travel.

joust *(SYN.)* tournament, contest, skirmish, competition, fight.

jovial *(SYN.)* good-natured, kindly, merry, good-humored, joyful, jolly, gleeful.

(ANT.) solemn, sad, serious, grim.

joy *(SYN.)* pleasure, glee, bliss, elation, mirth, felicity, rapture, delight, transport, exultation, gladness, happiness, festivity, satisfaction, merriment, ecstasy.

(ANT.) grief, depression, unhappiness, sorrow, misery, gloom, sadness, affliction.

joyful *(SYN.)* gay, lucky, opportune, cheerful, happy, blissful, jovial, merry, gleeful, delighted, glad, contented, fortunate.

(ANT.) gloomy, sad, blue, solemn, serious, grim, morose, glum, depressed.

joyous *(SYN.)* jolly, gay, blithe, merry, gleeful, cheerful, jovial.

(ANT.) sad, gloomy, sorrowful, melancholy.

jubilant *(SYN.)* exulting, rejoicing, overjoyed, triumphant, gay, elated, delighted.

(ANT.) dejected.

jubilee *(SYN.)* gala, holiday, celebration, festival, fete.

judge *(SYN.)* umpire, think, estimate, decide, arbitrator, condemn, decree, critic, appreciate, adjudicator, determine, arbiter, magistrate, arbitrate, justice, mediate, referee, evaluate.

judgment *(SYN.)* wisdom, perspicacity, discernment, decision, common sense, estimation, verdict, understanding, intelligence, discretion, opinion, sense, discrimination.

(ANT.) thoughtlessness, senselessness, arbitrariness.

judicial *(SYN.)* legal, judicatory, forensic.

judicious *(SYN.)* sensible, wise, well-advised, thoughtful.

(ANT.) ignorant.

jug *(SYN.)* bottle, jar, flask, flagon, pitcher.

juice *(SYN.)* broth, liquid, sap, distilla-

keen *(SYN.)* clever, cunning, acute, penetrating, exact, severe, shrewd, wily, astute, sharp, bright, intelligent, smart, sharp-witted, witty, cutting, fine, quick.

(ANT.) stupid, shallow, dull, blunted, slow, bland, gentle, obtuse, blunt.

keep *(SYN.)* maintain, retain, observe, protect, confine, sustain, continue, preserve, save, guard, restrain, reserve.

(ANT.) abandon, dismiss, discard, ignore, neglect, lose, reject, relinquish.

keeper *(SYN.)* warden, jailer, guard, custodian.

keepsake *(SYN.)* souvenir, memento.

keg *(SYN.)* container, drum, tub, barrel, tank.

ken *(SYN.)* field, view, vision, range, scope.

kennel *(SYN.)* pound, dog-house.

kernel *(SYN.)* heart, core, nucleus.

kettle *(SYN.)* pan, caldron, vat, pot, teapot, tureen.

key *(SYN.)* opener, explanation, tone, lead, note, pitch, answer, clue.

kick *(SYN.)* punt, remonstrate, boot.

kickback *(SYN.)* repercussion, backfire, rebound.

kickoff *(SYN.)* beginning, opening, commencement, outset, start.

kid *(SYN.)* joke, tease, fool, jest, tot, child.

kidnap *(SYN.)* abduct, snatch, shanghai.

kill *(SYN.)* execute, put to death, slay, butcher, assassinate, murder, cancel, destroy, slaughter, annihilate, massacre.

(ANT.) save, protect, animate, resuscitate, vivify.

killing *(SYN.)* massacre, genocide, slaughter, carnage, bloodshed.

kin *(SYN.)* relatives, family, folks, relations.

kind *(SYN.)* humane, affable, compassionate, benevolent, merciful, tender, sympathetic, breed, indulgent, forbearing, kindly, race, good, thoughtful.

(ANT.) unkind, cruel, merciless, severe, mean, inhuman.

kindle *(SYN.)* fire, ignite, light, arouse, excite, set trigger, move, provoke, inflame.

(ANT.) pacify, extinguish, calm.

kindred *(SYN.)* family, relations, rela-

tives, consanguinity, kinsfolk, affinity.
(ANT.) *strangers, disconnection, foreigners.*

kinetic (SYN.) vigorous, active, dynamic, energetic, mobile, forceful.

kingdom (SYN.) realm, empire, monarchy, domain.

kingly (SYN.) kinglike, imperial, regal, royal, majestic.

kink (SYN.) twist, curl, quirk, complication.

kinship (SYN.) lineage, blood, family, stock, relationship.

kismet (SYN.) fate, end, fortune, destiny.

kiss (SYN.) pet, caress, fondle, cuddle, osculate, embrace.
(ANT.) *vex, spurn, annoy, tease, buffet.*

kit (SYN.) outfit, collection, furnishings, equipment, rig, gear, set.

knack (SYN.) cleverness, readiness, deftness, ability, ingenuity, skill, aptitude, talent, adroitness, skillfulness.
(ANT.) *inability, clumsiness, awkwardness, ineptitude.*

knave (SYN.) rogue, rascal, villain.

knead (SYN.) combine, mix, blend.

knife (SYN.) sword, blade.

knightly (SYN.) valiant, courageous, gallant, chivalrous, noble.

knit (SYN.) unite, join, mend, fasten, connect, combine.

knock (SYN.) thump, tap, rap, strike, hit, punch, beat, pound, hammer, thwack.

knoll (SYN.) hill, elevation, hump.

knot (SYN.) cluster, gathering, collection.

know (SYN.) perceive, comprehend, apprehend, recognize, understand, discern.
(ANT.) *doubt, suspect, dispute, ignore.*

knowing (SYN.) smart, wise, clever, sagacious, shrewd.

knowledge (SYN.) information, wisdom, erudition, learning, apprehension.
(ANT.) *misunderstanding, ignorance, stupidity, illiteracy.*

knurl (SYN.) gnarl, knot, projection, burl, node, lump.

kosher (SYN.) permitted, okay, fit, proper, acceptable.

kowtow (SYN.) stoop, bend, kneel, genuflect, bow.

kudos (SYN.) acclaim, praise, approbation, approval.

label (SYN.) mark, tag, title, name, marker, stamp, sticker, ticket, docket, identity.

labor (SYN.) toil, travail, effort, task, childbirth, work, parturition, striving, workers, effort, industry, workingmen, strive, exertion, employment, drudgery, endeavor.
(ANT.) *recreation, indolence, idleness, leisure.*

laboratory (SYN.) lab, workroom, workshop.

laborer (SYN.) wage earner, helper, worker, toiler, coolie.

laborious (SYN.) tiring, difficult, hard, burdensome, industrious, painstaking.
(ANT.) *simple, easy, relaxing, restful.*

labyrinth (SYN.) complex, maze, tangle.

lace (SYN.) openwork, fancywork, embroidery, edging.

lacerate (SYN.) mangle, tear roughly.

laceration (SYN.) cut, wound, puncture, gash, lesion, injury.

lack (SYN.) want, need, shortage, dearth, scarcity, require.
(ANT.) *profusion, quantity, plentifulness.*

lackey (SYN.) yesman, stooge, flatterer, flunky.

lacking (SYN.) insufficient, short, deficient, incomplete, defective, scanty.
(ANT.) *satisfactory, enough, ample, sufficient, adequate.*

lackluster (SYN.) dull, pallid, flat, lifeless, drab, dim.

laconic (SYN.) short, terse, compact, brief, curt, succinct, concise.

lacquer (SYN.) polish, varnish, gild.

lad (SYN.) youth, boy, chap, fellow, stripling.

laden (SYN.) burdened, loaded, weighted.

ladle (SYN.) scoop, dipper.

lady (SYN.) matron, woman, dame, gentlewoman.

ladylike (SYN.) feminine, womanly, maidenly, womanish, female, girlish.
(ANT.) *masculine, male, virile, mannish, manly.*

lag (SYN.) dawdle, loiter, linger, poke, dillydally, straggle, delay, tarry, slowdown.

laggard (SYN.) dallier, idler, lingerer,

slowpoke, dawdler.

lair *(SYN.)* retreat, burrow, den, nest, mew, hole.

lambaste *(SYN.)* berate, castigate, scold, censure.

lame *(SYN.)* feeble, maimed, disabled, crippled, deformed, hobbling, unconvincing, weak, poor, inadequate, halt, defective, limping, unsatisfactory.
(ANT.) vigorous, convincing, plausible, athletic, robust, agile, sound.

lament *(SYN.)* deplore, wail, bemoan, bewail, regret, grieve, mourning, lamentation, moaning, wailing, weep, mourn, sorrow, repine.
(ANT.) celebrate, rejoice.

lamentable *(SYN.)* unfortunate, deplorable.

lamp *(SYN.)* light, beam, illumination, shine, insight, knowledge, understanding, radiance, luminosity, incandescence.
(ANT.) shadow, darkness, obscurity, gloom.

lampoon *(SYN.)* skit, tirade, burlesque, parody, satire.

lance *(SYN.)* cut, pierce, perforate, stab, puncture, impale, knife.

land *(SYN.)* earth, continent, ground, soil, domain, estate, field, realm, plain, surface, arrive, descend, country, island, region, alight, shore, sod, tract, touch down, farm.

landlord *(SYN.)* owner, landholder, landowner, proprietor.

landmark *(SYN.)* keystone, monument, milestone, point, cornerstone.

landscape *(SYN.)* panorama, environs, countryside, scenery, scene.

landslide *(SYN.)* rockfall, glissade, avalanche.

lane *(SYN.)* alley, way, road, path, aisle, pass, channel, avenue, artery, passage.

language *(SYN.)* dialect, tongue, speech, lingo, jargon, cant, diction, idiom, patter, phraseology, vernacular, words, lingo, talk, slang.
(ANT.) gibberish, nonsense, babble, drivel.

languid *(SYN.)* feeble, drooping, irresolute, debilitated, dull, lethargic, weak, faint, listless, wearied.
(ANT.) forceful, strong, vigorous.

languish *(SYN.)* decline, sink, droop, wither, waste, fail, wilt, wizen, weaken.
(ANT.) revive, rejuvenate, refresh, renew.

languor *(SYN.)* weariness, depression, torpor, inertia, apathy.

lanky *(SYN.)* skinny, gaunt, lean, scrawny, slender, thin.
(ANT.) chunky, stocky, obese, fat.

lantern *(SYN.)* torch, light, lamp, flashlight.

lap *(SYN.)* drink, lick, fold over.

lapse *(SYN.)* decline, sink, go down, slump.

larceny *(SYN.)* pillage, robbery, stealing, theft, burglary, plunder.

lard *(SYN.)* grease, fat.

large *(SYN.)* great, vast, colossal, ample, extensive, capacious, sizable, broad, massive, grand, immense, big, enormous, huge, giant, mammoth, wide.
(ANT.) tiny, little, short, small.

largely *(SYN.)* chiefly, mainly, principally, mostly.

lariat *(SYN.)* lasso, rope.

lark *(SYN.)* fling, frolic, play, fun, spree, joke, revel, celebration, sport.

lascivious *(SYN.)* lecherous, raunchy, lustful, wanton, lewd.

lash *(SYN.)* thong, whip, rod, cane, blow, strike, hit, beat, knout.

lass *(SYN.)* maiden, girl, damsel.
(ANT.) woman.

lasso *(SYN.)* lariat, rope, noose, snare.

last *(SYN.)* terminal, final, ultimate, remain, endure, concluding, latest, utmost, end, conclusive, hindmost, continue, extreme.
(ANT.) first, initial, beginning, opening, starting, foremost.

latch *(SYN.)* clasp, hook, fastener, lock, closing, seal, catch.

late *(SYN.)* overdue, tardy, behind, advanced, delayed, new, slow, recent.
(ANT.) timely, early.

lately *(SYN.)* recently, yesterday.

latent *(SYN.)* potential, undeveloped, unseen, dormant, secret, concealed, inactive, hidden, obscured, covered, quiescent.
(ANT.) visible, evident, conspicuous, explicit, manifest.

lather *(SYN.)* suds, foam, froth.

lateral *(SYN.)* sideways, glancing, tangential, marginal, skirting, side.

latitude *(SYN.)* range, scope, freedom, extent.

latter *(SYN.)* more recent, later.
(ANT.) former.

lattice *(SYN.)* grating, screen, frame, trellis, openwork, framework, grid.

laud *(SYN.)* commend, praise, extol, glorify, compliment.
(ANT.) criticize, belittle.

laudable *(SYN.)* creditable, praiseworthy, commendable, admirable.

laudation *(SYN.)* applause, compliment, flattery, praise, commendation, acclaim, extolling, glorification.
(ANT.) criticizing, condemnation, reproach, disparagement, censure.

laugh *(SYN.)* chuckle, giggle, snicker, cackle, titter, grin, smile, roar, guffaw, jeer, mock.

laughable *(SYN.)* funny, amusing, comical, humorous, ridiculous.

launch *(SYN.)* drive, fire, propel, start, begin, originate, set afloat, initiate.
(ANT.) finish, stop, terminate.

launder *(SYN.)* bathe, wash, scrub, scour.

laurels *(SYN.)* glory, distinction, recognition, award, commendation, honor.

lavatory *(SYN.)* toilet, washroom, bathroom, latrine.

lavish *(SYN.)* squander, waste, dissipate, scatter, abundant, free, plentiful, liberal, extravagant, ample, wear out, prodigal, generous, spend.
(ANT.) economize, save, conserve, accumulate, sparing, stingy, preserve.

law *(SYN.)* decree, formula, statute, act, rule, ruling, standard, principle, ordinance, proclamation, regulation, order, edict.

lawful *(SYN.)* legal, permissible, allowable, legitimate, authorized, constitutional.
(ANT.) prohibited, criminal, illicit, illegal, illegitimate.

lawless *(SYN.)* uncivilized, uncontrolled, wild, savage, untamed, violent.
(ANT.) obedient, tame.

lawlessness *(SYN.)* chaos, anarchy.

lawn *(SYN.)* grass, grounds, meadow, turf.

lawyer *(SYN.)* counsel, attorney, counselor.

lax *(SYN.)* slack, loose, careless, vague, lenient, lazy.
(ANT.) firm, rigid.

lay *(SYN.)* mundane, worldly, temporal, place, dispose, bet, wager, hazard, risk, stake, site, earthly, profane, laic, arrange, location, put, set, ballad, deposit, position, song, secular.
(ANT.) spiritual, unworldly, remove, misplace, disturb, mislay, disarrange, ecclesiastical, religious.

lay off *(SYN.)* discharge, bounce, fire, dismiss.

layout *(SYN.)* plan, arrangement, design.

lazy *(SYN.)* slothful, supine, idle, inactive, sluggish, inert, indolent, torpid.
(ANT.) alert, ambitious, forceful, diligent, active, assiduous.

lea *(SYN.)* pasture, meadow.

leach *(SYN.)* remove, extract, seep, dilute, wash out.

lead *(SYN.)* regulate, conduct, guide, escort, direct, supervise, command, come first, steer, control.
(ANT.) follow.

leader *(SYN.)* master, ruler, captain, chief, commander, principal, director, head, chieftain.
(ANT.) follower, servant, disciple, subordinate, attendant.

leading *(SYN.)* dominant, foremost, principal, first, main, primary.

league *(SYN.)* entente, partnership, association, confederacy, coalition, society, alliance, federation, union.
(ANT.) separation, schism.

leak *(SYN.)* dribble, flow, drip, opening, perforation.

lean *(SYN.)* rely, tilt, slim, slender, slope, incline, tend, trust, bend, tendency, slant, depend, spare, scant, lanky, thin, meager, inclination, narrow, sag.
(ANT.) rise, heavy, fat, erect, straighten, portly, raise.

leaning *(SYN.)* trend, proclivity, bias, tendency, bent, predisposition, proneness.
(ANT.) disinclination, aversion.

leap *(SYN.)* vault, skip, caper, dive, hurdle, jump, bound, start, hop, plunge, spring.

learn *(SYN.)* gain, find out, memorize, acquire, determine.

learned *(SYN.)* erudite, knowing, enlightened, deep, wise, discerning, scholarly, intelligent, educated, sagacious.
(ANT.) simple, uneducated, ignorant, illiterate, unlettered, foolish.

learning *(SYN.)* science, education, lore, apprehension, wisdom, knowledge, scholarship, erudition.
(ANT.) misunderstanding, ignorance, stupidity.

lease *(SYN.)* charter, let, rent, engage.

leash *(SYN.)* chain, strap, shackle, collar.

least *(SYN.)* minutest, smallest, tiniest, trivial, minimum, fewest, slightest.
(ANT.) most.

leave *(SYN.)* give up, retire, desert, abandon, withdraw, relinquish, will, depart, quit, liberty, renounce, go, bequeath, consent, allowance, permission, freedom, forsake.
(ANT.) come, stay, arrive, tarry, remain, abide.

lecherous *(SYN.)* lustful, sensual, carnal, lascivious.

lecture *(SYN.)* talk, discussion, lesson, instruct, speech, conference, sermon, report, recitation, address, oration, discourse.
(ANT.) writing, meditation, correspondence.

ledge *(SYN.)* eaves, ridge, shelf, rim, edge.

lee *(SYN.)* shelter, asylum, sanctuary, haven.

leech *(SYN.)* barnacle, bloodsucker, parasite.

leer *(SYN.)* eye, grimace, ogle, wink, squint.

leeway *(SYN.)* reserve, allowance, elbowroom, slack, clearance.

leftovers *(SYN.)* scraps, remains, residue, remainder.

legacy *(SYN.)* bequest, inheritance, heirloom.

legal *(SYN.)* legitimate, rightful, honest, allowable, allowed, permissible, lawful, permitted, authorized.
(ANT.) illicit, illegal, prohibited, illegitimate.

legalize *(SYN.)* authorize, ordain, approve, sanction.

legate *(SYN.)* envoy, agent, representative, emissary.

legend *(SYN.)* saga, fable, allegory, myth, parable, tale, story, folklore, fiction, chronicle.
(ANT.) history, facts.

legendary *(SYN.)* fictitious, traditional, mythical, imaginary, fanciful.

legible *(SYN.)* plain, readable, clear, distinct.
(ANT.) illegible.

legion *(SYN.)* outfit, unit, troop, regiment, company, battalion, force, army, team, division.

legislation *(SYN.)* resolution, ruling, lawmaking, regulation, enactment, statute, decree.

legislator *(SYN.)* statesman, congressman, senator, politician, lawmaker.

legitimate *(SYN.)* true, real, bona fide, lawful, proper, right, valid, correct, unadulterated, authentic, rightful, legal, sincere.
(ANT.) sham, counterfeit, artificial, false.

leisure *(SYN.)* respite, intermission, ease, relaxation, rest, calm, tranquillity, recreation, peace, pause.
(ANT.) motion, commotion, tumult, agitation, disturbance.

leisurely *(SYN.)* sluggish, laggard, unhurried, relaxed, casual, dawdling, slow, deliberate.
(ANT.) hurried, swift, pressed, rushed, forced, fast, speedy, quick.

lend *(SYN.)* entrust, advance, loan, confer.

length *(SYN.)* reach, measure, extent, distance, span, longness, stretch.

lengthen *(SYN.)* stretch, prolong, draw, increase, grow, protract, extend.
(ANT.) shrink, contract, shorten.

leniency *(SYN.)* grace, pity, compassion, mercy, mildness, charity, mercy, clemency.
(ANT.) vengeance, punishment, cruelty.

lenient *(SYN.)* tender, humane, clement, tolerant, compassionate, merciful, relaxed, forgiving, gentle, mild, lax, kind.
(ANT.) unfeeling, pitiless, brutal, remorseless.

leprechaun *(SYN.)* gnome, imp, goblin, fairy, elf, sprite, banshee.

lesion *(SYN.)* wound, blemish, sore, trauma, injury.

less *(SYN.)* fewer, smaller, reduced, negative, stinted.
(ANT.) more.

lessen *(SYN.)* shorten, reduce, deduct, subtract, curtail, diminish, shrink, dwindle, decline, instruction, teaching, remove, decrease.
(ANT.) swell, grow, enlarge, increase, expand, multiply, amplify.

lesson *(SYN.)* exercise, session, class, assignment, section, recitation.

let *(SYN.)* admit, hire out, contract, allow, permit, consent, leave, grant, rent.
(ANT.) deny.

letdown *(SYN.)* disillusionment, disappointment.

lethal *(SYN.)* mortal, dangerous, deadly, fatal, devastating.

lethargic *(SYN.)* sluggish, logy, slow, listless, phlegmatic, lazy.
(ANT.) vivacious, energetic.

lethargy *(SYN.)* numbness, stupor, daze, insensibility, torpor.
(ANT.) wakefulness, liveliness, activity, readiness.

letter *(SYN.)* note, letter, mark, message, character, symbol, sign, memorandum.

letup *(SYN.)* slowdown, slackening, lessening, abatement, reduction.

levee *(SYN.)* dike, breakwater, dam, embankment.

level *(SYN.)* smooth, even, plane, equivalent, uniform, horizontal, equal, flatten, equalize, raze, destroy, demolish, flat.
(ANT.) uneven, sloping, hilly, broken.

level-headed *(SYN.)* reasonable, sensible, calm, collected, cool.

leverage *(SYN.)* clout, power, influence, weight, rank.

levity *(SYN.)* humor, triviality, giddiness, hilarity, fun, frivolity.

levy *(SYN.)* tax, duty, tribute, rate, assessment, exaction, tool, charge, custom.
(ANT.) wages, remuneration, gift.

lewd *(SYN.)* indecent, smutty, course, gross, disgusting, impure.
(ANT.) pure, decent, refined.

liability *(SYN.)* indebtedness, answerability, obligation, vulnerability.

liable *(SYN.)* answerable, responsible, likely, exposed to, subject, amenable, probable, accountable.
(ANT.) immune, exempt, independent.

liaison *(SYN.)* union, coupling, link, connection, alliance.

liar *(SYN.)* fibber, falsifier, storyteller, fabricator, prevaricator.

libel *(SYN.)* slander, calumny, vilification, aspersion, defamation.
(ANT.) defense, praise, applause, flattery.

liberal *(SYN.)* large, generous, unselfish, kind, openhanded, broad, tolerant, unprejudiced, open-minded, lavish, plentiful, ample, abundant, extravagant, extensive.
(ANT.) restricted, conservative, stingy, confined.

liberality *(SYN.)* kindness, philanthropy, beneficence, humanity, altruism, benevolence, generosity.
(ANT.) selfishness, cruelty, malevolence.

liberate *(SYN.)* emancipate, loose, release, let go, deliver, free, discharge.
(ANT.) subjugate, oppress, jail, confine, restrict, imprison.

liberated *(SYN.)* loose, frank, emancipated, careless, liberal, freed, autonomous, exempt, familiar.
(ANT.) subject, clogged, restricted, impeded.

liberty *(SYN.)* permission, independence, autonomy, license, privilege, emancipation, freedom.
(ANT.) constraint, imprisonment, bondage, captivity.

license *(SYN.)* liberty, freedom, liberation, permission, exemption, authorization, warrant, allow, consent, permit, sanction, approval, unrestraint.
(ANT.) servitude, constraint, bondage, necessity.

lick *(SYN.)* taste, lap, lave.

lid *(SYN.)* top, cover, cap, plug, cork, stopper.

lie *(SYN.)* untruth, fib, illusion, delusion, falsehood, fiction, equivocation, prevarication, repose, location, perjury, misinform, recline, similitude.
(ANT.) variance, truth, difference.

life *(SYN.)* sparkle, being, spirit, vivacity, animation, buoyancy, vitality, existence, biography, energy, vigor.

(ANT.) demise, lethargy, death, languor.

lift *(SYN.)* hoist, pick up, elevate, raise, heft.

light *(SYN.)* brightness, illumination, beam, gleam, lamp, knowledge, brilliance, fixture, bulb, candle, fire, ignite, burn, dawn, incandescence, flame, airy, unsubstantial, dainty, luminosity, shine, radiance, giddy, enlightenment, weightless.

(ANT.) darken, gloom, shadow, extinguish, darkness.

lighten *(SYN.)* diminish, unburden, reduce, brighten.

light-headed *(SYN.)* giddy, silly, dizzy, frivolous.

(ANT.) sober, clearheaded, rational.

lighthearted *(SYN.)* carefree, merry, gay, cheerful, happy, glad.

(ANT.) somber, sad, serious, melancholy.

like *(SYN.)* fancy, esteem, adore, love, admire, care for, prefer, cherish.

(ANT.) disapprove, loathe, hate, dislike.

likely *(SYN.)* liable, reasonable, probable, possible.

likeness *(SYN.)* similarity, resemblance, representation, image, portrait.

(ANT.) difference.

likewise *(SYN.)* besides, as well, also, too, similarly.

liking *(SYN.)* fondness, affection, partiality.

(ANT.) antipathy, dislike.

limb *(SYN.)* arm, leg, member, appendage, part, bough.

limber *(SYN.)* bending, flexible, elastic, pliable.

(ANT.) inflexible, stiff.

limbo *(SYN.)* exile, banishment, purgatory.

limelight *(SYN.)* spotlight, notice, notoriety, fame, prominence.

limerick *(SYN.)* jingle, rhyme.

limit *(SYN.)* terminus, bound, extent, confine, border, restriction, boundary, restraint, edge, frontier, check, end.

(ANT.) endlessness, vastness, boundlessness.

limn *(SYN.)* depict, portray, sketch, paint, illustrate.

limp *(SYN.)* soft, flabby, drooping, walk, limber, supple, flexible, hobble, stagger.

(ANT.) stiff.

limpid *(SYN.)* clear, open, transparent, unobstructed.

(ANT.) cloudy.

line *(SYN.)* row, file, series, array, sequence, wire, seam, wrinkle, crease, boundary, arrangement, kind, division.

lineage *(SYN.)* race, family, tribe, nation, strain, folk, people, ancestry, clan.

linger *(SYN.)* wait, rest, bide, delay, dwadle, stay, loiter, remain, dillydally, tarry.

(ANT.) leave, expedite.

lingo *(SYN.)* vernacular, dialect, language, jargon, speech.

link *(SYN.)* unite, connector, loop, couple, attach, connective, connection, coupling, juncture, bond.

(ANT.) separate, disconnect, split.

lip *(SYN.)* edge, brim, rim.

liquid *(SYN.)* watery, fluent, fluid, flowing.

(ANT.) solid, congealed.

liquidate *(SYN.)* defray, pay off, settle, defray.

liquor *(SYN.)* spirits, alcohol, drink, booze.

lissom *(SYN.)* nimble, quick, lively, flexible, agile.

list *(SYN.)* roll, register, slate, enumeration, series.

listen *(SYN.)* overhear, attend to, heed, hear, list, hearken.

(ANT.) ignore, scorn, disregard, reject.

listless *(SYN.)* uninterested, tired, lethargic, unconcerned, apathetic.

(ANT.) active.

literal *(SYN.)* exact, verbatim, precise, strict, faithful.

literally *(SYN.)* actually, exactly, really.

literate *(SYN.)* informed, educated, learned, intelligent, versed, knowledgeable.

(ANT.) unread, illiterate, ignorant, unlettered.

literature *(SYN.)* books, writings, publications.

lithe *(SYN.)* supple, flexible, bending, limber, pliable.

(ANT.) stiff.

litigious *(SYN.)* quarrelsome, disputatious, argumentative.

litter *(SYN.)* rubbish, trash, scatter, clutter, strew, debris, rubble, disorder.

little *(SYN.)* tiny, petty, miniature, diminutive, puny, wee, significant, small, short, brief, bit, trivial.

(ANT.) huge, large, big, long, immense.

liturgy *(SYN.)* ritual, sacrament, worship, service.

live *(SYN.)* dwell, reside, abide, survive, exist, alive, occupy, stay, active, surviving.

(ANT.) die.

livelihood *(SYN.)* keep, sustenance, support, subsistence, job, trade, profession, vocation.

lively *(SYN.)* blithe, vivaciousness, clear, vivid, active, frolicsome, brisk, fresh, animated, energetic, live, spry, vigorous, quick, nimble, bright, exciting, supple.

(ANT.) stale, dull, listless, slow, vapid.

livestock *(SYN.)* animals, cattle.

livid *(SYN.)* grayish, furious, pale, enraged.

living *(SYN.)* support, livelihood, existent, alive.

load *(SYN.)* oppress, trouble, burden, weight, freight, afflict, encumber, pack, shipment, cargo, lade, tax.

(ANT.) lighten, console, unload, mitigate, empty, ease.

loafer *(SYN.)* loiterer, bum, idler, sponger, deadbeat.

loan *(SYN.)* credit, advance, lend.

loath *(SYN.)* reluctant, unwilling, opposed.

loathe *(SYN.)* dislike, despise, hate, abhor, detest, abominate.

(ANT.) love, approve, like, admire.

loathsome *(SYN.)* foul, vile, detestable, revolting, abominable, atrocious, offensive.

(ANT.) pleasant, commendable, alluring, agreeable, delightful.

lob *(SYN.)* toss, hurl, pitch, throw, heave.

lobby *(SYN.)* foyer, entry, entrance, vestibule, passageway, entryway.

local *(SYN.)* limited, regional, restricted, particular.

locality *(SYN.)* nearness, neighborhood, district, vicinity.

(ANT.) remoteness.

locate *(SYN.)* discover, find, unearth, site, situate, place.

located *(SYN.)* found, residing, positioned, situated, placed.

location *(SYN.)* spot, locale, station, locality, situation, place, area, site, vicinity, position, zone, region.

lock *(SYN.)* curl, hook, bolt, braid, ringlet, plait, close, latch, tuft, fastening, bar, hasp, fasten, tress.

(ANT.) open.

locker *(SYN.)* wardrobe, closet, cabinet, chest.

locket *(SYN.)* case, lavaliere, pendant.

locomotion *(SYN.)* movement, travel, transit, motion.

locution *(SYN.)* discourse, cadence, manner, accent.

lodge *(SYN.)* cabin, cottage, hut, club, chalet, society, room, reside, dwell, live, occupy, inhabit, abide, board, fix, settle.

lodger *(SYN.)* guest, tenant, boarder, occupant.

lofty *(SYN.)* high, stately, grandiose, grand, towering, elevated, exalted, sublime, majestic, scornful, proud, tall, pompous.

(ANT.) undignified, lowly, common, ordinary.

log *(SYN.)* lumber, wood, board, register, record, album, account, journal.

logical *(SYN.)* strong, effective, telling, convincing, reasonable, sensible, rational, sane, sound, cogent.

(ANT.) crazy, illogical, irrational, unreasonable, weak.

logy *(SYN.)* tired, inactive, lethargic, sleepy, weary.

loiter *(SYN.)* idle, linger, wait, stay, tarry, dillydally, dawdle.

loll *(SYN.)* hang, droop, recline, repose, relax.

lone *(SYN.)* lonely, sole, unaided, single, deserted, isolated, secluded, apart, alone, solitary.

(ANT.) surrounded, accompanied.

loner *(SYN.)* recluse, maverick, outsider, hermit.

loneliness *(SYN.)* solitude, isolation, seclusion, alienation.

lonely *(SYN.)* unaided, isolated, single, solitary, lonesome, alone, unaccompanied, deserted, desolate.
(ANT.) surrounded, attended.

lonesome *(SYN.)* secluded, remote, unpopulated, barren, empty, desolate.

long *(SYN.)* lengthy, prolonged, wordy, elongated, extended, lingering, drawn out, lasting, protracted, extensive, length, prolix, farreaching, extended.
(ANT.) terse, concise, abridged, short.

long-standing *(SYN.)* persistent, established.

long-winded *(SYN.)* boring, dull, wordy.
(ANT.) curt, terse.

look *(SYN.)* gaze, witness, seem, eye, behold, see, watch, scan, view, appear, stare, discern, glance, examine, examination, peep, expression, appearance, regard, study, contemplation, survey.
(ANT.) overlook, hide, avert, miss.

loom *(SYN.)* emerge, appear, show up.

loop *(SYN.)* ringlet, noose, spiral, fastener.

loose *(SYN.)* untied, unbound, lax, vague, unrestrained, dissolute, limp, undone, baggy, disengaged, indefinite, slack, careless, heedless, unfastened, free, wanton.
(ANT.) restrained, steady, fastened, secure, tied, firm, fast, definite, inhibited.

loosen *(SYN.)* untie, undo, loose, unchain.
(ANT.) tie, tighten, secure.

loot *(SYN.)* booty, plunder, take, steal, rob, sack, rifle, pillage, ravage, devastate.

lope *(SYN.)* sprint, run, race, bound, gallop.

lopsided *(SYN.)* unequal, twisted, uneven, askew, distorted.

loquacious *(SYN.)* garrulous, wordy, profuse, chatty.

lord *(SYN.)* peer, ruler, proprietor, boss, nobleman, master, owner, governor.

lore *(SYN.)* learning, knowledge, wisdom, stories, legends, beliefs, teachings.

lose *(SYN.)* misplace, flop, fail, sacrifice, forfeit, mislay, vanish, surrender.
(ANT.) succeed, locate, place, win, discover, find.

loss *(SYN.)* injury, damage, want, hurt, need, bereavement, trouble, death, failure, deficiency.

lost *(SYN.)* dazed, wasted, astray, forfeited, preoccupied, used, adrift, bewildered, missing, distracted, consumed, misspent, absorbed, confused, mislaid, gone, destroyed.
(ANT.) found, anchored.

lot *(SYN.)* result, destiny, bunch, many, amount, fate, cluster, group, sum, portion, outcome, number, issue.

lotion *(SYN.)* cosmetic, salve, balm, cream.

lottery *(SYN.)* wager, chance, drawing, raffle.

loud *(SYN.)* vociferous, noisy, resounding, shrill, stentorian, clamorous, sonorous, thunderous, blaring, roaring, deafening.
(ANT.) soft, inaudible, murmuring, subdued, quiet, dulcet.

lounge *(SYN.)* idle, loaf, laze, sofa, couch, davenport, relax, rest, lobby, salon, divan.

louse *(SYN.)* scoundrel, knave, cad, rat.

lousy *(SYN.)* revolting, grimy, rotten, dirty, disgusting.

lovable *(SYN.)* charming, attractive, delightful, amiable, sweet, cuddly, likeable.

love *(SYN.)* attachment, endearment, affection, adoration, liking, devotion, warmth, tenderness, like, friendliness, adore, worship, cherish.
(ANT.) loathing, detest, indifference, dislike, hate, hatred.

loveliness *(SYN.)* grace, pulchritude, elegance, charm, attractiveness, comeliness, fairness, beauty.
(ANT.) ugliness, eyesore, disfigurement, deformity.

lovely *(SYN.)* handsome, fair, charming, pretty, attractive, delightful, beautiful, beauteous, exquisite, comely.
(ANT.) ugly, unsightly, homely, foul, hideous, repulsive.

lover *(SYN.)* fiance, suitor, courter, sweetheart, beau.

loving *(SYN.)* close, intimate, confidential, affectionate, friendly.
(ANT.) formal, conventional,

ceremonious, distant.

low *(SYN.)* mean, vile, despicable, vulgar, abject, groveling, contemptible, lesser, menial.
(ANT.) righteous, lofty, esteemed, noble.

lower *(SYN.)* subordinate, minor, secondary, quiet, soften, disgrace, degrade, decrease, reduce, diminish, lessen, inferior.
(ANT.) greater, superior, increase, better.

low-key *(SYN.)* subdued, muted, calm, controlled, restrained, understated, gentle.

lowly *(SYN.)* lowborn, humble, base, low, mean, common, average, simple, modest.
(ANT.) royal, noble.

loyal *(SYN.)* earnest, ardent, addicted, inclined, faithful, devoted, affectionate, fond, patriotic, dependable, true.
(ANT.) indisposed, detached, disloyal, traitorous, untrammeled.

loyalty *(SYN.)* devotion, steadfastness, constancy, faithfulness, fidelity, patriotism, allegiance.
(ANT.) treachery, falseness, disloyalty.

lubricate *(SYN.)* oil, grease, anoint.

lucent *(SYN.)* radiant, beaming, vivid, illuminated, lustrous.

lucid *(SYN.)* plain, visible, clear, intelligible, unmistakable, transparent, limpid, translucent, open, explicit, understandable, distinct.
(ANT.) unclear, vague, obscure.

luck *(SYN.)* chance, fortunate, fortune, lot, fate, fluke, destiny, karma, providence.
(ANT.) misfortune.

lucky *(SYN.)* favored, favorable, auspicious, fortunate, successful, felicitous, benign.
(ANT.) unlucky, condemned, unfortunate, persecuted.

lucrative *(SYN.)* profitable, productive, beneficial.

ludicrous *(SYN.)* absurd, ridiculous, preposterous.

lug *(SYN.)* pull, haul, drag, tug.

lugubrious *(SYN.)* mournful, sad, gloomy, somber, melancholy.

lukewarm *(SYN.)* unenthusiastic, tepid, spiritless, detached, apathetic, mild.

lull *(SYN.)* quiet, calm, soothe, rest, hush, stillness, pause, break, intermission, recess, respite, silence.

luminous *(SYN.)* beaming, lustrous, shining, glowing, gleaming, bright, light, alight, clear, radiant.
(ANT.) murky, dull, dark.

lummox *(SYN.)* yokel, bumpkin, clown, oaf, klutz.

lunacy *(SYN.)* insanity, derangement, aberration, psychosis, craziness.
(ANT.) stability, rationality.

lunge *(SYN.)* charge, stab, attack, thrust, push.

lurch *(SYN.)* topple, sway, toss, roll, rock, tip, pitch.

lure *(SYN.)* draw, tug, drag, entice, attraction, haul, attract, temptation, persuade, pull, draw on, allure.
(ANT.) drive, alienate, propel.

lurid *(SYN.)* sensational, terrible, melodramatic, startling.

lurk *(SYN.)* sneak, hide, prowl, slink, creep.

luscious *(SYN.)* savory, delightful, juicy, sweet, pleasing, delectable, palatable, delicious, tasty.
(ANT.) unsavory, nauseous, acrid.

lush *(SYN.)* tender, succulent, ripe, juicy.

lust *(SYN.)* longing, desire, passion, appetite, craving, aspiration, urge.
(ANT.) hate, aversion, loathing, distaste.

luster *(SYN.)* radiance, brightness, glister, fame, effulgence, gloss, sheen, shine, gleam, glow, glitter, brilliance.
(ANT.) dullness, obscurity, darkness.

lustful *(SYN.)* amorous, sexy, desirous, passionate, wanton.

lusty *(SYN.)* healthy, strong, mighty, powerful, sturdy, strapping, hale, hardy.
(ANT.) weak.

luxuriant *(SYN.)* abundant, flourishing, dense, lush, rich.

luxurious *(SYN.)* rich, lavish, deluxe, splendid.
(ANT.) simple, crude, sparse.

luxury *(SYN.)* frills, comfort, extravagance, elegance, splendor, prosperity, swankiness, grandeur.
(ANT.) poverty.

lyric *(SYN.)* musical, text, words, libretto.

lyrical *(SYN.)* poetic, musical.

macabre *(SYN.)* grim, horrible, gruesome.

machination *(SYN.)* hoax, swindle, card-sharping, plot, cabal, conspriracy.

machine *(SYN.)* motor, mechanism, device, contrivance.

macilent *(SYN.)* gaunt, lean, lank, meager, emaciated.

maculation *(SYN.)* irisation, striae, iridescence.

mad *(SYN.)* incensed, crazy, insane, angry, furious, delirious, provoked.

(ANT.) sane, calm, healthy, rational, lucid, cheerful.

madam *(SYN.)* dame, woman, lady, matron, mistress.

madden *(SYN.)* anger, annoy, convulse, asperate.

(ANT.) please, mollify, calm.

madness *(SYN.)* derangement, delirium, aberration, frenzy, psychosis.

(ANT.) stability, rationality.

maelstrom *(SYN.)* surge, rapids, eddy, riptide.

magazine *(SYN.)* journal, periodical, arsenal, armory.

magical *(SYN.)* mystical, marvelous, magic, miraculous.

magician *(SYN.)* conjuror, sorcerer, wizard, witch, artist, trickster.

magnanimous *(SYN.)* giving, bountiful, beneficent.

(ANT.) stingy, greedy, selfish.

magnate *(SYN.)* leader, bigwig, tycoon, chief, giant.

magnetic *(SYN.)* pulling, attractive, alluring, drawing, enthralling, seductive.

magnetism *(SYN.)* allure, irresistibility, attraction.

magnificence *(SYN.)* luxury, majesty, dynamic.

magnificent *(SYN.)* rich, lavish, luxurious, splendid, wonderful, impressive.

(ANT.) simple, plain.

magnify *(SYN.)* heighten, exaggerate, amplify, expand, stretch, caricature, increase.

(ANT.) compress understate, depreciate, belittle.

magnitude *(SYN.)* mass, bigness, size, area, volume, dimensions, greatness, extent, measure, importance.

maid *(SYN.)* chambermaid, servant, maidservant.

maiden *(SYN.)* original, foremost, first, damsel, lass.

(ANT.) accessory, secondary.

mail *(SYN.)* dispatch, send, letters, post.

maim *(SYN.)* disable, cripple, hurt, wound, injure, mangle.

main *(SYN.)* essential, chief, highest, principal, first, leading, cardinal.

(ANT.) supplemental, subordinate.

mainstay *(SYN.)* buttress, pillar, refuge, reinforcement, support, backbone.

maintain *(SYN.)* claim, support, uphold, defend, vindicate, sustain, continue.

(ANT.) neglect, oppose, discontinue, resist, deny.

maintenance *(SYN.)* subsistence, livelihood, living, support, preservation.

majestic *(SYN.)* magnificent, stately, noble, august, grand, imposing, sublime, lofty.

(ANT.) humble, lowly, undignified, common, ordinary.

majesty *(SYN.)* grandeur, dignity, nobility, splendor, distinction, eminence.

major *(SYN.)* important, superior, larger, chief, greater.

(ANT.) minor.

make *(SYN.)* execute, cause, produce, establish, assemble, create, shape, compel, build, fabricate.

(ANT.) unmake, break, undo, demolish.

make-believe *(SYN.)* pretend, imagined, simulated, false, fake, unreal.

maker *(SYN.)* inventor, creator, producer, builder.

makeshift *(SYN.)* proxy, deputy, understudy, expedient, agent, lieutenant, alternate, substitute.

(ANT.) sovereign, head, principal.

make-up *(SYN.)* composition, formation, structure.

malady *(SYN.)* disease, illness, sickness, ailment, infirmity, disorder, affliction.

(ANT.) vigor, healthiness, health.

malaise *(SYN.)* anxiety, apprehension, dissatisfaction, uneasiness, nervousness.

male *(SYN.)* masculine, virile.

(ANT.) female, womanly, feminine.

malcontent *(SYN.)* displeased, ill-humored, querulous, discontented.

malevolence *(SYN.)* spite, malice, enmity, rancor.

(ANT.) love, affection, toleration, kindness.

malfunction *(SYN.)* flaw, breakdown, snag, glitch.

malice *(SYN.)* spite, grudge, enmity, ill will, malignity, animosity, rancor, resentment, grudge.

(ANT.) love, affection, toleration, benevolence, charity.

malicious *(SYN.)* hostile, malignant, virulent, bitter, rancorous, evilminded, malevolent, spiteful, wicked.

(ANT.) kind, benevolent, affectionate.

malign *(SYN.)* misuse, defame, revile, abuse, asperse, misapply.

(ANT.) praise, cherish, protect, honor.

malignant *(SYN.)* harmful, deadly, mortal, destructive, hurtful, malicious.

(ANT.) benign, harmless.

malingerer *(SYN.)* quitter, idler, goldbrick.

malleable *(SYN.)* meek, tender, soft, lenient.

(ANT.) tough, rigid, unyielding, hard.

malodorous *(SYN.)* reeking, fetid, smelly, noxious, vile, rancid, offensive.

malpractice *(SYN.)* wrongdoing, misdeed, abuse, malfeasance, error.

maltreatment *(SYN.)* disparagement, perversion, aspersion, invective, defamation, profanation.

(ANT.) respect, approval, laudation, commendation.

mammoth *(SYN.)* enormous, gigantic, gargantuan, ponderous.

(ANT.) minuscule, tiny, small.

man *(SYN.)* person, human being, society, folk, soul, individual, mortal, fellow, male, gentleman.

(ANT.) woman.

manageable *(SYN.)* willing, obedient, docile, controllable, tractable, submissive, governable, untroublesome.

(ANT.) recalcitrant, unmanageable, wild.

management *(SYN.)* regulation, administration, supervision, direction.

manager *(SYN.)* overseer, superintendent, supervisor, director, boss.

mandate *(SYN.)* order, injunction, command, referendum, dictate, writ, directive.

mandatory *(SYN.)* compulsory, required, obligatory, imperative, necessary.

(ANT.) optional.

maneuver *(SYN.)* execution, effort, proceeding, enterprise, working, action, operation, agency.

(ANT.) rest, inaction, cessation.

mangle *(SYN.)* tear apart, cut, maim, wound, mutilate, injure, break.

mangy *(SYN.)* shoddy, frazzled, seedy, threadbare, shabby, ragged, sordid.

manhandle *(SYN.)* maltreat, maul, abuse, ill-treat.

mania *(SYN.)* insanity, enthusiasm, craze, desire.

manic *(SYN.)* excited, hyped up, agitated.

manifest *(SYN.)* open, evident, lucid, clear, distinct, unobstructed, cloudless, apparent, intelligible.

(ANT.) vague, overcast, unclear, cloudy, hidden.

manifesto *(SYN.)* pronouncement, edict, proclamation, statement.

manifold *(SYN.)* various, many, multiple, numerous, abundant, copious, profuse.

(ANT.) few.

manipulate *(SYN.)* manage, feel, work, operate, handle, touch, maneuver.

manly *(SYN.)* strong, brave, masculine, manful, courageous, stalwart.

manner *(SYN.)* air, demeanor, way, behavior, fashion.

mannerism *(SYN.)* eccentricity, quirk, habit, peculiarity, trait.

mannerly *(SYN.)* well-bred, gentlemanly, courteous, suave, polite, genteel.

manor *(SYN.)* land, mansion, estate, domain, villa, castle, property, palace.

mantle *(SYN.)* serape, garment, overgarment, cover, cloak, wrap.

manual *(SYN.)* directory, guidebook, handbook, physical, laborious, menial.

manufacture *(SYN.)* construct, make, assemble, fabricate, produce, build.

manuscript *(SYN.)* copy, writing, work, paper, composition, document.

many *(SYN.)* numerous, various, divers, multitudinous, sundry, multifarious, several, manifold.

(ANT.) infrequent, meager, few, scanty.

map   115   matter

map *(SYN.)* sketch, plan, chart, graph, itinerary.

mar *(SYN.)* spoil, hurt, damage, impair, harm, deface, injure.

(ANT.) repair, benefit, mend.

march *(SYN.)* promenade, parade, pace, hike, walk.

marginal *(SYN.)* unnecessary, nonessential, borderline.

(ANT.) essential.

marine *(SYN.)* naval, oceanic, nautical, ocean, maritime.

mariner *(SYN.)* seafarer, gob, seaman, sailor.

maritime *(SYN.)* shore, coastal, nautical.

mark *(SYN.)* stain, badge, stigma, vestige, sign, feature, label, characteristic, trace, stamp, brand.

marked *(SYN.)* plain, apparent, noticeable, evident, noteworthy.

m a r k e t   *(S Y N .)*   supermarket, marketplace, plaza.

maroon *(SYN.)* desert, leave behind, forsake, abandon.

marriage *(SYN.)* wedding, matrimony, nuptials, espousal, union, alliance.

(ANT.) divorce, celibacy, separation.

marrow *(SYN.)* center, core, gist, essential, soul.

marsh *(SYN.)* bog, swamp, mire, everglade, estuary.

marshal *(SYN.)* adjutant, officer, order, arrange, rank.

martial *(SYN.)* warlike, combative, militant, belligerent.

(ANT.) peaceful.

martyr *(SYN.)* victim, sufferer, tortured, torment, plague, harass, persecute.

marvel *(SYN.)* phenomenon, wonder, miracle, astonishment, sensation.

marvelous *(SYN.)* rare, wonderful, extraordinary, unusual, exceptional, miraculous, wondrous.

(ANT.) usual, common, ordinary. commonplace.

masculine *(SYN.)* robust, manly, virile, strong, bold.

(ANT.) weak, emasculated, feminine, female.

mash *(SYN.)* mix, pulverize, crush, grind, crumble.

mask *(SYN.)* veil, disguise, cloak, secrete, withhold, hide, cover, protection, protector, camouflage.

(ANT.) uncover, reveal, disclose, show, expose.

masquerade *(SYN.)* pretend, disguise, pose, impersonate, costume party.

mass *(SYN.)* society, torso, body, remains, association, carcass, bulk, company, pile.

(ANT.) spirit, mind, intellect.

massacre *(SYN.)* butcher, murder, carnage, slaughter, execute, slay, genocide.

(ANT.) save, protect, vivify, animate.

massive *(SYN.)* grave, cumbersome, heavy, sluggish, ponderous, serious, burdensome, huge, immense.

(ANT.) light, animated, small, tiny, little.

masterful *(SYN.)* commanding, bossy, domineering, dictatorial, cunning, wise.

masterpiece *(SYN.)* prizewinner, classic, perfection.

mastery *(SYN.)* sway, domination, transcendence, ascendancy, influence, jurisdiction, prestige.

mat *(SYN.)* cover, rug, pallet, bedding, pad.

match *(SYN.)* equivalent, equal, contest, balance, resemble, peer, mate.

matchless *(SYN.)* peerless, incomparable, unequaled, unrivaled, excellent.

(ANT.) ordinary.

mate *(SYN.)* friend, colleague, associate, partner, companion, comrade.

(ANT.) stranger, adversary.

material *(SYN.)* sensible, momentous, bodily, palpable, important, physical.

(ANT.) metaphysical, spiritual, insignificant, mental.

materialize *(SYN.)* take shape, finalize, embody, incarnate, emerge, appear.

mathematics *(SYN.)* measurements, computations, numbers, calculation, figures.

matrimony *(SYN.)* marriage, wedding, espousal, union.

(ANT.) virginity, divorce.

matrix *(SYN.)* template, stamp, negative, stencil, mold, form, die, cutout.

matted *(SYN.)* tangled, clustered, rumpled, shaggy, knotted, gnarled, tousled.

matter *(SYN.)* cause, thing, substance, occasion, material, moment, topic, stuff, consequence, affair.

(ANT.) spirit, immateriality.

mature *(SYN.)* ready, matured, complete, ripe, consummate, mellow, aged, seasoned, fullgrown.

(ANT.) raw, crude, undeveloped, young, immature.

mausoleum *(SYN.)* shrine, tomb, vault.

maverick *(SYN.)* nonconformist, oddball, outsider, dissenter, loner.

maxim *(SYN.)* rule, code, law, proverb, principle, saying, adage, motto.

maximum *(SYN.)* highest, largest, head, greatest, supremacy, climax.

(ANT.) minimum.

maybe *(SYN.)* feasibly, perchance, perhaps, possibly.

(ANT.) definitely.

mayhem *(SYN.)* brutality, viciousness, ruthlessness.

maze *(SYN.)* complex, labyrinth, network, muddle, confusion, snarl, tangle.

meadow *(SYN.)* field, pasture, lea, range, grassland.

meager *(SYN.)* sparse, scanty, mean, frugal, deficient, slight, paltry, inadequate.

(ANT.) ample, plentiful, abundant, bountiful.

meal *(SYN.)* refreshment, dinner, lunch, repast.

mean *(SYN.)* sordid, base, intend, plan, propose, expect, indicate, denote, say, signify.

(ANT.) dignified, noble, openhanded, kind, generous.

meander *(SYN.)* wind, stray, wander, twist

meaning *(SYN.)* gist, connotation, intent, purport, drift, signification, explanation, purpose, significance.

meaningful *(SYN.)* profound, deep, expressive, important.

meaningless *(SYN.)* nonsensical, senseless, unreasonable.

measure *(SYN.)* law, bulk, rule, criterion, size, volume, weight, standard, dimension, breadth, depth, test.

(ANT.) guess, chance, supposition.

mechanism *(SYN.)* device, contrivance, tool, machine.

medal *(SYN.)* decoration, award, badge, medallion, reward, ribbon, prize, honor.

meddle *(SYN.)* tamper, interpose, pry, snoop, intrude, interrupt, interfere.

mediate *(SYN.)* settle, intercede, umpire, intervene, negotiate, arbitrate, referee.

medicinal *(SYN.)* helping, healing, remedial, therapeutic, corrective.

medicine *(SYN.)* drug, medication, remedy, cure, prescription, potion.

mediocre *(SYN.)* medium, mean, average, moderate, fair, ordinary.

(ANT.) outstanding, exceptional.

meditate *(SYN.)* remember, muse, think, judge, mean, conceive, contemplate, consider, picture, reflect, believe, plan, reckon.

medium *(SYN.)* modicum, average, middling, median.

(ANT.) extreme.

medley *(SYN.)* hodgepodge, mixture, assortment.

meek *(SYN.)* subdued, dull, tedious, flat, docile, domesticated, tame, domestic.

(ANT.) spirited, exciting, savage, wild.

meet *(SYN.)* fulfill, suffer, find, collide, gratify, engage, connect, converge.

(ANT.) scatter, disperse, separate, cleave.

melancholy *(SYN.)* disconsolate, dejected, despondent, glum, somber, pensive.

(ANT.) happy, cheerful, merry.

meld *(SYN.)* unite, mix, combine, fuse, merge, blend, commingle, amalgamate.

melee *(SYN.)* battle royal, fight, brawl, free-for-all.

mellow *(SYN.)* mature, ripe, aged, cured, sweet, smooth, melodious.

(ANT.) unripened, immature.

melodious *(SYN.)* lilting, musical, lyric, dulcet, mellifluous, tuneful, melodic.

melodramatic *(SYN.)* dramatic, ceremonious, affected, stagy, histrionic.

(ANT.) unemotional, subdued, modest.

melody *(SYN.)* strain, concord, music, air, song, tune, harmony.

melt *(SYN.)* dissolve, liquefy, blend, fade out, vanish, dwindle, disappear, thaw.

(ANT.) freeze, harden, solidify.

member *(SYN.)* share, part, allotment, moiety, element, concern, interest, lines, faction, role, apportionment.

(ANT.) whole.

membrane *(SYN.)* layer, sheath, tissue.

memento *(SYN.)* keepsake, token, reminder, trophy, sign, souvenir.

memoirs *(SYN.)* diary, reflections, experiences, autobiography, journal.

memorable *(SYN.)* important, historic, significant, unforgettable, noteworthy, momentous, crucial, impressive.

(ANT.) passing, forgettable, transitory, commonplace.

memorandum *(SYN.)* letter, mark, token, note, indication, remark, message.

memorial *(SYN.)* monument, souvenir, memento, remembrance, reminiscent, ritual, testimonial.

memorize *(SYN.)* study, remember.

memory *(SYN.)* renown, reminiscence, fame, retrospection, recollection, reputation.

(ANT.) oblivion.

menace *(SYN.)* warning, threat, intimidation, warn, threaten, imperil, forebode.

menagerie *(SYN.)* collection, zoo, kennel.

mend *(SYN.)* restore, better, refit, sew, remedy, patch, correct, repair, rectify, ameliorate, improve, reform, recover.

(ANT.) hurt, deface, rend, destroy.

mendacious *(SYN.)* dishonest, false, lying, deceitful, deceptive, tricky.

(ANT.) honest, truthful, sincere, creditable.

mendicant *(SYN.)* ragamuffin, vagabond, beggar.

menial *(SYN.)* unskilled, lowly, degrading, tedious, humble, routine.

mental *(SYN.)* reasoning, intellectual, rational, thinking, conscious, thoughtful.

(ANT.) physical.

mentality *(SYN.)* intellect, reason, understanding, liking, disposition, judgment, brain, inclination, faculties, outlook.

(ANT.) materiality, corporeality.

mention *(SYN.)* introduce, refer to, reference, allude, enumerate, speak of.

mentor *(SYN.)* advisor, tutor, sponsor, guru, teacher, counselor, master, coach.

mercenary *(SYN.)* sordid, corrupt, venal, covetous, grasping, avaricious, greedy.

(ANT.) liberal, generous.

merchandise *(SYN.)* stock, wares, goods, sell, commodities, promote, staples.

merchant *(SYN.)* retailer, dealer, trader, storekeeper, salesman, businessman.

merciful *(SYN.)* humane, kindhearted, tender, clement, sympathetic, forgiving, tolerant, forbearing, lenient, compassionate, tenderhearted, kind.

(ANT.) remorseless, cruel, unjust, mean, harsh, unforgiving, vengeful, brutal, unfeeling, pitiless.

merciless *(SYN.)* carnal, ferocious, brute, barbarous, gross, ruthless, cruel, remorseless, bestial, savage, rough, pitiless, inhuman.

(ANT.) humane, courteous, merciful, openhearted, kind, civilized.

mercurial *(SYN.)* fickle, unstable, volatile, changeable, inconstant, capricious.

mercy *(SYN.)* grace, consideration, kindness, clemency, mildness, forgiveness, pity, charity, sympathy, leniency.

(ANT.) punishment, retribution, ruthlessness, cruelty, vengeance.

mere *(SYN.)* only, simple, scant, bare.

(ANT.) substantial, considerable.

merely *(SYN.)* only, barely, simply.

meretricious *(SYN.)* gaudy, sham, bogus, tawdry, flashy, garish.

merge *(SYN.)* unify, fuse, combine, unite, blend, commingle.

(ANT.) separate, decompose, analyze.

merger *(SYN.)* cartel, union, conglomerate, trust, incorporation, combine.

meridian *(SYN.)* climax, summit, pinnacle, zenith, peak, acme, apex.

merit *(SYN.)* worthiness, earn, goodness, effectiveness, power, value, virtue, goodness, quality, deserve, excellence, worth.

(ANT.) sin, fault, lose, consume.

merited *(SYN.)* proper, deserved, suitable, adequate, earned.

(ANT.) unmerited, improper.

meritorious *(SYN.)* laudable, excellent, good, deserving.

merry *(SYN.)* hilarious, lively, festive, joyous, sprightly, mirthful, blithe, gay, cheery, joyful, jolly, happy, gleeful, jovial, cheerful.

(ANT.) sorrowful, doleful, morose, gloomy, sad, melancholy.

mesh *(SYN.)* grid, screen, net, complex.

mesmerize *(SYN.)* enthrall, transfix,

spellbind, charm, fascinate, hypnotize.

mess *(SYN.)* dirtiness, untidiness, disorder, confusion, muddle, trouble, jumble, difficulty, predicament, confuse, dirty.

message *(SYN.)* letter, annotation, memo, symbol, indication, sign, note, communication, memorandum, observation, token.

messenger *(SYN.)* bearer, agent, runner, courier, liaison, delegate, page.

messy *(SYN.)* disorderly, dirty, confusing, confused, disordered, sloppy, slovenly.
(ANT.) orderly, neat, tidy.

metallic *(SYN.)* grating, harsh, clanging, brassy, brazen.

metamorphosis *(SYN.)* transfiguration, change, alteration, rebirth, mutation.

mete *(SYN.)* deal, assign, apportion, divide, give, allocate, allot, measure.
(ANT.) withhold, keep, retain.

meteoric *(SYN.)* flashing, blazing, swift, brilliant, spectacular, remarkable.

meter *(SYN.)* record, measure, gauge.

method *(SYN.)* order, manner, plan, way, mode, technique, fashion, approach, design, procedure.
(ANT.) disorder.

methodical *(SYN.)* exact, definite, ceremonious, stiff, accurate, distinct, unequivocal.
(ANT.) easy, loose, informal, rough.

meticulous *(SYN.)* precise, careful, exacting, fastidious, fussy, perfectionist.

metropolitan *(SYN.)* civic, city, municipal.

mettle *(SYN.)* intrepidity, resolution.
(ANT.) fear, timidity, cowardice.

microscopic *(SYN.)* tiny, precise, fine, detailed, minute, infinitesimal, minimal.
(ANT.) general, huge, enormous.

middle *(SYN.)* midpoint, nucleus, center, midst, median, central, intermediate.
(ANT.) end, rim, outskirts, beginning, border, periphery.

middleman *(SYN.)* dealer, agent, distributor, broker, representative.

midget *(SYN.)* gnome, shrimp, pygmy, runt, dwarf.
(ANT.) giant.

midst *(SYN.)* center, heart, middle, thick.

midway *(SYN.)* halfway, midmost, inside, central, middle.

mien *(SYN.)* way, semblance, manner, behavior, demeanor, expression, deportment.

miff *(SYN.)* provoke, rile, chagrin, irk, irritate, affront, offend, annoy, exasperate.

might *(SYN.)* force, power, vigor, potency, ability, strength.
(ANT.) frailty, vulnerability, weakness.

mighty *(SYN.)* firm, fortified, powerful, athletic, potent, muscular, robust, strong, cogent.
(ANT.) feeble, weak, brittle, insipid, frail, delicate.

migrant *(SYN.)* traveling, roaming, straying, roving, rambling, transient, meandering.
(ANT.) stationary.

migrate *(SYN.)* resettle, move, emigrate, immigrate, relocate, journey.
(ANT.) stay, remain, settle.

migratory *(SYN.)* itinerant, roving, mobile, vagabond, unsettled, nomadic.

mild *(SYN.)* soothing, moderate, gentle, tender, bland, pleasant, kind, meek, calm, compassionate, temperate, peaceful, soft.
(ANT.) severe, turbulent, stormy, excitable, violent, harsh, bitter.

milieu *(SYN.)* environment, background, locale, setting, scene, circumstances.

militant *(SYN.)* warlike, belligerent, hostile, fighting, aggressive, combative.
(ANT.) peaceful.

military *(SYN.)* troops, army, soldiers.

millstone *(SYN.)* load, impediment, burden, encumbrance, hindrance.

mimic *(SYN.)* simulate, duplicate, copy, imitate, mock, counterfeit, simulate.
(ANT.) invent, distort, alter.

mind *(SYN.)* intelligence, psyche, disposition, intention, understanding, intellect, spirit, brain, inclination, mentality, soul, wit.
(ANT.) matter, corporeality.

mindful *(SYN.)* alert, aware, watchful, cognizant, watchful, sensible, heedful.

mingle *(SYN.)* unite, coalesce, fuse, merge, combine, amalgamate, unify, conjoin, mix, blend, commingle.
(ANT.) analyze, sort, disintegrate.

miniature *(SYN.)* small, little, tiny, midget, minute, minuscule, wee, petite.

(ANT.) outsize.

minimize *(SYN.)* shorten, deduct, belittle, decrease, reduce, curtail, lessen, diminish, subtract.

(ANT.) enlarge, increase, amplify.

minimum *(SYN.)* lowest, least, smallest, slightest.

(ANT.) maximum.

minister *(SYN.)* pastor, clergyman, vicar, parson, curate, preacher, prelate, chaplain, cleric, deacon, reverend.

minor *(SYN.)* poorer, lesser, petty, youth, inferior, secondary, smaller, unimportant, lower.

(ANT.) higher, superior, major, greater.

minority *(SYN.)* youth, childhood, immaturity.

minstrel *(SYN.)* bard, musician.

mint *(SYN.)* stamp, coin, strike, punch.

minus *(SYN.)* lacking, missing, less, absent, without.

minute *(SYN.)* tiny, particular, fine, precise, jiffy, instant, moment, wee, exact, detailed, microscopic.

(ANT.) large, general, huge, enormous.

miraculous *(SYN.)* spiritual, wonderful, marvelous, incredible, preternatural.

(ANT.) natural, common, plain, everyday, human.

mirage *(SYN.)* vision, illusion, fantasy, dream, phantom.

(ANT.) reality, actuality.

mirror *(SYN.)* glass, reflector.

mirth *(SYN.)* joy, glee, jollity, joyousness, gaiety, joyfulness, laughter, merriment.

(ANT.) sadness, gloom.

misappropriate *(SYN.)* embezzle, steal, purloin, plunder, cheat, filch.

miscarriage *(SYN.)* omission, want, decay, fiasco, default, deficiency, loss, abortion.

(ANT.) success, sufficiency, achievement.

miscellaneous *(SYN.)* diverse, motley, indiscriminate, assorted, sundry, heterogeneous, mixed, varied.

(ANT.) classified, selected, homogeneous, alike, ordered.

mischief *(SYN.)* injury, harm, damage, evil, ill, prankishness, rascality, roguishness.

(ANT.) kindness, boon.

mischievous *(SYN.)* roguish, prankish, naughty, playful.

(ANT.) well-behaved, good.

miscreant *(SYN.)* rascal, wretch, rogue, sinner, criminal, villain, scoundrel.

miscue *(SYN.)* blunder, fluff, mistake, error, lapse.

misdemeanor *(SYN.)* infringement, transgression, violation, offense, wrong.

miserable *(SYN.)* abject, forlorn, comfortless, low, worthless, pitiable, distressed, heartbroken.

(ANT.) fortunate, happy, contented, joyful, content, wealthy, honorable, lucky, noble, significant.

miserly *(SYN.)* stingy, greedy, acquisitive, tight, tightfisted, cheap, mean, parsimonious, avaricious.

(ANT.) bountiful, generous, spendthrift, munificent, extravagant, openhanded, altruistic.

misery *(SYN.)* suffering, woe, evil, agony, torment, trouble, distress, anguish, grief, unhappiness, anguish, tribulation, calamity, sorrow.

(ANT.) fun, pleasure, delight, joy.

misfit *(SYN.)* crank, loner, deviate, fifth wheel, individualist.

misfortune *(SYN.)* adversity, distress, mishap, calamity, accident, catastrophe, hardship, ruin, disaster, affliction.

(ANT.) success, blessing, prosperity.

misgiving *(SYN.)* suspicion, doubt, mistrust, hesitation, uncertainty.

misguided *(SYN.)* misdirected, misled, misinformed, wrong, unwise, foolish, erroneous, unwarranted, ill-advised.

mishap *(SYN.)* misfortune, casualty, accident, disaster, adversity, reverse.

(ANT.) intention, calculation, purpose.

mishmash *(SYN.)* medley, muddle, gallimaufry, hodgepodge, hash.

misjudge *(SYN.)* err, mistake, miscalculate.

mislay *(SYN.)* misplace, lose.

(ANT.) discover, find.

mislead *(SYN.)* misdirect, deceive, misinform, deceive, delude.

misleading *(SYN.)* fallacious, delusive, deceitful, false, deceptive, illusive.

(ANT.) real, genuine, truthful, honest.

mismatched *(SYN.)* unfit, unsuitable, incompatible.

misrepresent *(SYN.)* misstate, garble, disguise.

miss *(SYN.)* lose, want, crave, yearn for, fumble, drop, error, slip, default, omit, lack.

(ANT.) suffice, have, achieve.

missing *(SYN.)* wanting, lacking, absent, lost, gone.

mission *(SYN.)* business, task, job, stint, work, errand, assignment, delegation.

missionary *(SYN.)* publicist, evangelist, propagandist.

mistake *(SYN.)* slip, misjudge, fault, blunder, misunderstand, confuse.

(ANT.) truth, accuracy.

mistaken *(SYN.)* false, amiss, incorrect, awry, wrong, misinformed, confused, inaccurate, askew.

(ANT.) true, correct, suitable, right.

mister *(SYN.)* young man, gentleman, esquire, fellow.

mistreat *(SYN.)* wrong, pervert, oppress, harm, maltreat, abuse.

mistrust *(SYN.)* suspect, doubt, distrust, dispute, question, apprehension.

(ANT.) trust.

misunderstand *(SYN.)* misjudge, misinterpret, jumble, confuse, mistake.

(ANT.) perceive, comprehend.

mite *(SYN.)* particle, mote, smidgen, trifle, iota.

mitigate *(SYN.)* soften, soothe, abate, assuage, relieve, allay, diminish.

(ANT.) irritate, agitate, increase.

mixture *(SYN.)* diversity, variety, strain, sort, change, kind, confusion.

(ANT.) likeness, sameness, homogeneity, monotony.

moan *(SYN.)* wail, groan, cry, lament.

moat *(SYN.)* fortification, ditch, trench.

mob *(SYN.)* crowd, host, populace, swarm, riot, bevy, horde, rabble, throng.

mock *(SYN.)* taunt, jeer, deride, scoff, scorn, fleer, ridicule, tease, fake, imitation, sham, gibe, sneer.

(ANT.) praise, applaud, real, genuine, honor, authentic.

mode *(SYN.)* method, fashion, procedure, design, manner, technique, way, style.

(ANT.) disorder, confusion.

model *(SYN.)* copy, prototype, type, example, ideal, imitation, version, fac-

simile.

(ANT.) reproduction.

moderate *(SYN.)* lower, decrease, average, fair, reasonable, abate, medium.

(ANT.) intensify, enlarge.

moderation *(SYN.)* sobriety, forbearance, self-control, restraint, continence.

(ANT.) greed, excess.

moderator *(SYN.)* referee, leader, arbitrator, chairman.

modern *(SYN.)* modish, current, recent, novel, fresh, contemporary, new.

(ANT.) old, antiquated, past, bygone, ancient.

modernize *(SYN.)* refurnish, refurbish, improve, rebuild, renew, renovate.

modest *(SYN.)* unassuming, virtuous, bashful, meek, shy, humble, decent, demure.

(ANT.) forward, bold, ostentatious, conceited, immodest.

modesty *(SYN.)* decency, humility, propriety, simplicity, shyness.

modification *(SYN.)* alternation, substitution, variety, change, alteration.

(ANT.) uniformity, monotony.

modify *(SYN.)* shift, vary, alter, change, convert, adjust, temper, moderate, curb.

(ANT.) settle, establish.

module *(SYN.)* unit, measure, norm, dimension, component, gauge.

moiety *(SYN.)* part, scrap, share, allotment, piece, division, portion.

moisture *(SYN.)* wetness, mist, dampness, condensation.

(ANT.) aridity, dryness.

mold *(SYN.)* make, fashion, organize, produce, forge, constitute, create, combine.

(ANT.) wreck, dismantle, destroy.

moldy *(SYN.)* dusty, crumbling, dank.

molest *(SYN.)* irk, disturb, trouble, annoy, pester, bother, vex, inconvenience.

(ANT.) console, accommodate.

moment *(SYN.)* flash, jiffy, instant, twinkling, gravity, importance, consequence.

momentary *(SYN.)* concise, pithy, brief, curt, terse, laconic, compendious.

(ANT.) long, extended, prolonged.

momentous *(SYN.)* critical, serious, essential, grave, material, weighty.

(ANT.) unimportant, trifling, mean, trivial, tribial.

momentum *(SYN.)* impetus, push, thrust, force, impulse, drive, vigor, propulsion.

monarch *(SYN.)* ruler, king, queen, empress, emperor.

monastic *(SYN.)* withdrawn, dedicated, austere, unworldly, celibate, abstinent.

monastery *(SYN.)* convent, priory, abbey.

money *(SYN.)* cash, bills, coin, notes, currency, funds, specie, capital.

monkey *(SYN.)* tamper, interfere, interrupt, interpose.

monogram *(SYN.)* mark, stamp, signature

monologue *(SYN.)* discourse, lecture, sermon, talk.

monomania *(SYN.)* obsessiveness, passion, single-mindedness, extremism.

monotonous *(SYN.)* dull, slow, tiresome, boring, humdrum, burdensome.
(ANT.) interesting, riveting, quick.

monster *(SYN.)* brute, beast, villain, demon, wretch.

monument *(SYN.)* remembrance, memento, commemoration, statue.

mood *(SYN.)* joke, irony, waggery, temper, disposition, temperament.
(ANT.) sorrow, gravity.

moody *(SYN.)* morose, fretful, crabbed, changeable, sulky, dour, short-tempered, testy, temperamental, irritable, peevish, glum.
(ANT.) good natured, merry, pleasant.

moor *(SYN.)* tether, fasten, tie, dock, anchor, bind.

moorings *(SYN.)* marina, slip, harbor, basin, landing, dock, wharf, pier.

moot *(SYN.)* unsettled, questionable, problematical, controversial.

mop *(SYN.)* wash, wipe, swab, scrub.

mope *(SYN.)* gloom, pout, whine, grumble, grieve, sulk, fret.
(ANT.) rejoice.

moral *(SYN.)* just, right, chaste, good, virtuous, pure, decent, honest, upright, ethical, righteous, honorable.
(ANT.) libertine, immoral, unethical, licentious, amoral, sinful.

morale *(SYN.)* confidence, spirit.

morality *(SYN.)* virtue, strength, worth, chastity, probity, force, merit.
(ANT.) fault, sin, corruption, vice.

morals *(SYN.)* conduct, scruples, guidelines, behavior, life style, standards.

morass *(SYN.)* fen, march, swamp, mire.

morbid *(SYN.)* sickly, unhealthy, ghastly, awful, horrible, shocking.
(ANT.) pleasant, healthy.

more *(SYN.)* further, greater, farther, extra, another.
(ANT.) less.

moreover *(SYN.)* further, in addition, also, furthermore, besides.

mores *(SYN.)* standards, rituals, rules, customs, conventions, traditions.

moron *(SYN.)* subnormal, dunce, blockhead, imbecile, retardate, simpleton.

morose *(SYN.)* gloomy, moody, fretful, crabbed, downcast, sad, unhappy.
(ANT.) merry, gay, amiable, joyous.

morsel *(SYN.)* portion, fragment, bite, bit, scrap.
(ANT.) whole, all, sum.

mortal *(SYN.)* fatal, destructive, human.
(ANT.) superficial, divine.

mortified *(SYN.)* embarrassed, humiliated, ashamed.

mortuary *(SYN.)* morgue, crematory, funeral parlor.

most *(SYN.)* extreme, highest, supreme, greatest, majority.
(ANT.) least.

mostly *(SYN.)* chiefly, generally, largely, mainly, principally, especially.

mother *(SYN.)* bring about, produce, breed, mom, mama, watch, foster, mind, nurse, originate.
(ANT.) father.

motion *(SYN.)* change, activity, movement, proposition, action, signal.
(ANT.) stability, immobility, equilibrium.

motionless *(SYN.)* still, undisturbed, rigid, fixed, stationary, unresponsive.

motivate *(SYN.)* move, prompt, stimulate, induce, activate, propel, arouse.

motive *(SYN.)* inducement, purpose, cause, incentive, reason, incitement.
(ANT.) deed, result, attempt.

motley *(SYN.)* heterogeneous, mixed, assorted, sundry, diverse, miscellaneous.
(ANT.) ordered, classified.

motto *(SYN.)* proverb, saying, adage, byword, saw, slogan, catchword, aphorism.

mound *(SYN.)* hillock, hill, heap, pile,

stack, knoll, accumulation, dune.

mount (SYN.) scale, climb, increase, rise, prepare, ready, steed, horse, tower. (ANT.) sink, descend.

mountain (SYN.) alp, mount, pike, peak, ridge, height.

mountebank (SYN.) faker, rascal, swindler, cheat.

mounting (SYN.) backing, pedestal, easel, support, framework, background.

mourn (SYN.) suffer, grieve, bemoan, sorrow, lament, weep, bewail. (ANT.) revel, celebrate, carouse.

mourning (SYN.) misery, trial, distress, affliction, tribulation, sorrow, woe. (ANT.) happiness, solace, comfort, joy.

move (SYN.) impel, agitate, persuade, induce, push, instigate, advance, stir, transfer, budge, actuate. (ANT.) halt, stop, deter, rest.

movement (SYN.) activity, effort, gesture, move, proposition, crusade, action. (ANT.) stillness, immobility, equilibrium.

mow (SYN.) prune, cut, shave, crop, clip.

much (SYN.) abundance, quantity, mass, ample, plenty, sufficient.

muddled (SYN.) disconcerted, confused. (ANT.) plain, lucid, organized.

muff (SYN.) blunder, bungle, spoil, mess.

muffle (SYN.) soften, deaden, mute, quiet, drape, shroud, veil, cover. (ANT.) louden, amplify.

mulish (SYN.) obstinate, stubborn, headstrong, rigid, tenacious, willful.

multifarious (SYN.) various, many, numerous, diversified, several. (ANT.) scanty, infrequent, scarce, few.

multiply (SYN.) double, treble, increase, triple, propagate, spread, expand. (ANT.) lessen, decrease.

multitude (SYN.) crowd, throng, mass, swarm, host, mob, army, legion. (ANT.) scarcity, handful.

mumble (SYN.) stammer, whisper, hesitate, mutter. (ANT.) shout, yell.

munificent (SYN.) bountiful, full, generous, forthcoming. (ANT.) voracious, insatiable, grasping.

murder (SYN.) homicide, kill, slay, slaughter, butcher, killing, massacre. (ANT.) save, protect, vivify, animate.

murderer (SYN.) slayer, killer, assassin.

murky (SYN.) gloomy, dark, obscure. (ANT.) cheerful, light.

murmur (SYN.) mumble, whine, grumble, whimper, lament, mutter, complaint, remonstrate, repine. (ANT.) praise, applaud.

muscle (SYN.) brawn, strength, power, fitness, vigor, vim, stamina.

muse (SYN.) ponder, brood, think, meditate, ruminate.

museum (SYN.) exhibit hall, treasure house, gallery.

mushroom (SYN.) multiply, proliferate, flourish, spread, grow, pullulate.

music (SYN.) symphony, harmony.

muss (SYN.) mess, disarray, rumple, litter, clutter. (ANT.) fix, arrange.

must (SYN.) ought to, should, duty, obligation, ultimatum.

muster (SYN.) cull, pick, collect, harvest, accumulate, garner, reap, deduce. (ANT.) separate, disband, scatter.

musty (SYN.) mildewed, rancid, airless, dank, stale, decayed, rotten, funky.

mute (SYN.) quiet, noiseless, dumb, taciturn, hushed, peaceful, speechless. (ANT.) raucous, clamorous, noisy.

mutilate (SYN.) tear, cut, clip, amputate, lacerate, dismember, deform, castrate.

mutiny (SYN.) revolt, overthrow, rebellion, rebel, coup, uprising, insurrection.

mutter (SYN.) complain, mumble, whisper, grumble.

mutual (SYN.) correlative, interchangeable, shared, alternate, joint, common. (ANT.) unshared, unrequited, separate.

muzzle (SYN.) restrain, silence, bridle, bind, curb, suppress, gag, stifle, censor.

myopia (SYN.) incomprehension, folly.

mysterious (SYN.) hidden, mystical, secret, cryptic, incomprehensible, dim. (ANT.) simple, obvious, clear.

mystery (SYN.) riddle, difficulty, enigma, puzzle, strangeness, conundrum. (ANT.) solution, key, answer, resolution.

mystify (SYN.) puzzle, confound, bewilder, stick, get, floor, bamboozle.

myth (SYN.) fable, parable, allegory, fiction, tradition, lie, saga, legend. (ANT.) history.

nag *(SYN.)* badger, harry, provoke, tease, bother, annoy, molest, taunt, vex, torment, worry, annoy, pester, irritate, horse, torment.
(ANT.) please, comfort, soothe, delight.

nail *(SYN.)* hold, fasten, secure, fix, seize, snare, capture, apprehend.
(ANT.) release.

naive *(SYN.)* frank, unsophisticated, natural, ingenuous, simple, innocent.
(ANT.) worldly, cunning, crafty.

naked *(SYN.)* uncovered, unfurnished, nude, bare, open, unclad, stripped, exposed, plain, mere, simple, barren, unprotected, bald, defenseless.
(ANT.) covered, protected, dressed, clothed, concealed, suppressed.

name *(SYN.)* title, reputation, appellation, style, fame, repute, renown, denomination, appoint, character, designation, surname, distinction, christen, entitle, specify, denominate, mention, epithet, label, designate.
(ANT.) anonymity, misnomer, hint, misname.

nap *(SYN.)* nod, doze, sleep, snooze, catnap, siesta, slumber, drowse, forty winks.

narcissistic *(SYN.)* egotistical, egocentric, self-centered.

narcotics *(SYN.)* opiates, drugs, sedatives, tranquilizers, barbiturates.

narrate *(SYN.)* recite, relate, declaim, detail, rehearse, deliver, review, tell, describe, recount, report.

narrative *(SYN.)* history, relation, account, record, chronicle, detail, recital, description, story, tale.
(ANT.) distortion, caricature, misrepresentation.

narrow *(SYN.)* narrow-minded, illiberal, bigoted, fanatical, prejudiced, close, restricted, slender, cramped, confined, meager, thin, tapering, tight.
(ANT.) tolerant, progressive, liberal, wide, broad.

narrow-minded *(SYN.)* close-minded, intolerant, biased, partisan, arbitrary, bigoted.
(ANT.) tolerant, liberal, broadminded.

nascent *(SYN.)* prime, introductory, elementary.

nasty *(SYN.)* offensive, malicious, selfish, mean, disagreeable, unpleasant, foul, dirty, filthy, loathsome, disgusting, polluted, obscene, indecent, sickening, nauseating, obnoxious, revolting, odious, repulsive, vile.
(ANT.) generous, dignified, noble, admirable, pleasant.

nation *(SYN.)* state, community, realm, nationality, commonwealth, land, kingdom, country, republic, society, tribe.

native *(SYN.)* domestic, inborn, inherent, natural, aboriginal, endemic, innate, inbred, indigenous, hereditary, original, local.
(ANT.) alien, stranger, foreigner, outsider, foreign.

natty *(SYN.)* chic, well-dressed, sharp, dapper.

natural *(SYN.)* innate, genuine, real, unaffected, characteristic, native, normal, regular, inherent, original, simple, inbred, inborn, hereditary, typical, authentic, honest, legitimate, pure, customary.
(ANT.) irregular, false, unnatural, formal, abnormal.

naturally *(SYN.)* typically, ordinarily, usually, indeed, normally, plainly, of course, surely, certainly, customarily.
(ANT.) artificially.

nature *(SYN.)* kind, disposition, reputation, character, repute, world, quality, universe, essence, variety, features, traits.

naught *(SYN.)* nought, zero, nothing, nil.

naughty *(SYN.)* unmanageable, insubordinate, disobedient, mischievous, unruly, bad, misbehaving, disorderly, wrong, evil, rude, improper, indecent.
(ANT.) obedient, good, well-behaved.

nausea *(SYN.)* sickness, vomiting, upset, queasiness.

nauseated *(SYN.)* unwell, sick, queasy, squeamish.

nautical *(SYN.)* naval, oceanic, marine, ocean.

naval *(SYN.)* oceanic, marine, nautical,

maritime.

navigate *(SYN.)* sail, cruise, pilot, guide, steer.

near *(SYN.)* close, nigh, dear, adjacent, familiar, neighboring, nearby, approaching, impending, proximate, imminent, bordering, adjoining.

(ANT.) removed, distant, far, remote.

nearly *(SYN.)* practically, close to, approximately, almost.

neat *(SYN.)* trim, orderly, precise, clear, spruce, nice, tidy, clean, well-kept, clever, skillful, adept, apt, tidy, dapper, smart, proficient, expert, handy, well-done, shipshape, elegant, well-organized.

(ANT.) unkempt, sloppy, dirty, slovenly, messy, sloppy, disorganized.

nebulous *(SYN.)* fuzzy, indistinct, indefinite, clouded, hazy.

(ANT.) definite, distinct, clear.

necessary *(SYN.)* needed, expedient, unavoidable, required, essential, indispensable, urgent, imperative, inevitable, compelling, compulsory, obligatory, needed, exigent, important.

(ANT.) optional, nonessential, contingent, casual, accidental, unnecessary, dispensable, unneeded.

necessity *(SYN.)* requirement, fate, destiny, constraint, requisite, poverty, exigency, compulsion, want, essential, prerequisite.

(ANT.) option, luxury, freedom, choice, uncertainty.

necromancy *(SYN.)* charm, sorcery, conjuring, wizardry.

need *(SYN.)* crave, want, demand, claim, desire, covet, wish, lack, necessity, requirement, poverty, require, pennilessness.

needed *(SYN.)* necessary, indispensable, essential, requisite.

(ANT.) optional, contingent.

needle *(SYN.)* goad, badger, tease, nag, prod, provoke.

needless *(SYN.)* nonessential, unnecessary, superfluous, useless, purposeless.

needy *(SYN.)* poor, indigent, impoverished penniless, destitute.

(ANT.) affluent, well-off, wealthy, well-to-do.

nefarious *(SYN.)* detestable, vicious, wicked, atrocious, horrible, vile, dreadful.

negate *(SYN.)* revoke, void, cancel, nullify.

neglect *(SYN.)* omission, default, heedlessness, carelessness, thoughtlessness, disregard, negligence, oversight, omission, ignore, slight, failure, overlook, omit, skip, pass over, be inattentive.

(ANT.) diligence, do, protect, watchfulness, care, attention, careful, attend, regard, concern.

negligent *(SYN.)* imprudent, thoughtless, lax, careless, inattentive, indifferent, remiss, neglectful.

(ANT.) careful, nice, accurate, meticulous.

negligible *(SYN.)* trifling, insignificant, trivial, inconsiderable, minute.

(ANT.) major, vital, important.

negotiate *(SYN.)* intervene, talk over, mediate, transact, umpire, referee, arbitrate, arrange, settle, bargain.

neighborhood *(SYN.)* environs, nearness, locality, district, vicinity, area, section, locality.

(ANT.) remoteness.

neighboring *(SYN.)* bordering, near, adjacent, next to, surrounding, adjoining.

neighborly *(SYN.)* friendly, sociable, amiable, affable, companionable, congenial, kind, cordial, amicable, warm, social.

(ANT.) distant, reserved, cool, unfriendly, hostile.

neophyte *(SYN.)* greenhorn, rookie, amateur, beginner, apprentice, tyro, student.

nepotism *(SYN.)* bias, prejudice, partronage, favoritism.

nerve *(SYN.)* bravery, spirit, courage, boldness, rudeness, strength, stamina, bravado, daring, impudence, mettle, impertinence.

(ANT.) frailty, cowardice, weakness.

nervous *(SYN.)* agitated, restless, excited, shy, timid, upset, disturbed,

shaken, rattle, high-strung, flustered, tense, jittery, strained, edgy, perturbed, fearful.
(ANT.) placid, courageous, confident, calm, tranquil, composed, bold.
nest *(SYN.)* den, refuge, hideaway.
nestle *(SYN.)* cuddle, snuggle.
net *(SYN.)* snare, trap, mesh, earn, gain, web, get, acquire, secure, obtain.
nettle *(SYN.)* irritate, vex, provoke, annoy, disturb, irk, needle, pester.
neurotic *(SYN.)* disturbed, psychoneurotic.
neutral *(SYN.)* nonpartisan, uninvolved, detached, impartial, cool, unprejudiced, indifferent, inactive.
(ANT.) involved, biased, partisan.
neutralize *(SYN.)* offset, counteract, nullify, negate.
nevertheless *(SYN.)* notwithstanding, however, although, anyway, but, regardless.
new *(SYN.)* modern, original, newfangled, late, recent, novel, young, firsthand, fresh, unique, unusual.
(ANT.) antiquated, old, ancient, obsolete, outmoded.
newborn *(SYN.)* baby, infant, cub, suckling.
news *(SYN.)* report, intelligence, information, copy, message, advice, tidings, knowledge, word, story, data.
next *(SYN.)* nearest, following, closest, successive, succeeding, subsequent.
nibble *(SYN.)* munch, chew, bit.
nice *(SYN.)* pleasing, pleasant, agreeable, thoughtful, satisfactory, friendly, enjoyable, gratifying, desirable, fine, good, cordial.
(ANT.) nasty, unpleasant, disagreeable, unkind, inexact, careless, thoughtless.
niche *(SYN.)* corner, nook, alcove, cranny, recess.
nick *(SYN.)* cut, notch, indentation, dash, score, mark.
nickname *(SYN.)* byname, sobriquet.
nigh *(SYN.)* close, imminent, near, adjacent, approaching, bordering, neighboring, impending.
(ANT.) removed, distant.
nightmare *(SYN.)* calamity, horror, tor-

ment, bad dream.
nil *(SYN.)* zero, none, nought, nothing.
nimble *(SYN.)* brisk, quick, active, supple, alert, lively, spry, light, fast, speedy, swift, agile.
(ANT.) slow, heavy, sluggish, clumsy.
nincompoop *(SYN.)* nitwit, idiot, fool, moron, blockhead, ninny, idiot, simpleton.
nip *(SYN.)* bite, pinch, chill, cold, squeeze, crispness, sip, small.
nippy *(SYN.)* chilly, sharp, bitter, cold, penetrating.
nit-picker *(SYN.)* fussbudget, precise, purist, perfectionist.
nitty-gritty *(SYN.)* essentials, substance, essence.
noble *(SYN.)* illustrious, exalted, dignified, stately, eminent, lofty, grand, elevated, honorable, honest, virtuous, great, distinguished, majestic, important, prominent, magnificent, grandiose, aristocratic, upright, well-born.
(ANT.) vile, low, base, mean, dishonest, common, ignoble.
nocturnal *(SYN.)* nightly.
nod *(SYN.)* bob, bow, bend, tip, signal.
node *(SYN.)* protuberance, growth, nodule, cyst, lump, wen.
noise *(SYN.)* cry, sound, din, babel, racket, uproar, clamor, tumult, outcry, sounds, bedlam, commotion.
(ANT.) quiet, stillness, hush, silence, peace.
noisome *(SYN.)* repulsive, disgusting, revolting, obnoxious, malodorous, rotten, rancid.
noisy *(SYN.)* resounding, loud, clamorous, vociferous, stentorian, tumultuous.
(ANT.) soft, dulcet, subdued, quiet, silent, peaceful.
nomad *(SYN.)* gypsy, rover, traveler, roamer, migrant, vagrant, wanderer.
nominate *(SYN.)* propose, choose, name, select.
nomination *(SYN.)* appointment, naming, choice, selection, designation.
nominee *(SYN.)* sapirant, contestant, candidate, competitor.
nonbeliever *(SYN.)* skeptic, infidel, atheist, heathen.

nonchalant *(SYN.)* unconcerned, indifferent, cool, lackadaisical, casual.

noncommittal *(SYN.)* neutral, tepid, undecided, cautious.

nonconformist *(SYN.)* protester, rebel, radical, dissenter, renegade, dissident, eccentric.

nondescript *(SYN.)* unclassifiable, indescribable, indefinite.

nonentity *(SYN.)* nothing, menial, nullity.

nonessential *(SYN.)* needless, unnecessary.

nonpareil *(SYN.)* unsurpassed, exceptional, paramount, unrivaled.

nonplus *(SYN.)* confuse, perplex, dumfound, mystify, confound, puzzle, baffle, bewilder.

(ANT.) *illumine, clarify, solve, explain.*

nonsense *(SYN.)* balderdash, rubbish, foolishness, folly, ridiculousness, stupidity, absurdity, poppycock, trash.

nonsensical *(SYN.)* silly, preposterous, absurd, unreasonable, foolish, irrational, ridiculous, stupid, senseless.

(ANT.) *sound, consistent, reasonable.*

nonstop *(SYN.)* constant, continuous, unceasing, endless.

nook *(SYN.)* niche, corner, recess, cranny, alcove.

noose *(SYN.)* snare, rope, lasso, loop.

normal *(SYN.)* ordinary, uniform, natural, unvaried, customary, regular, healthy, sound, whole, usual, typical, characteristic, routine, standard.

(ANT.) *rare, erratic, unusual, abnormal.*

normally *(SYN.)* regularly, frequently, usually, customarily.

nosy *(SYN.)* inquisitive, meddling, peering, searching, curious, prying.

(ANT.) *unconcerned, incurious, uninterested.*

notable *(SYN.)* noted, unusual, uncommon, noteworthy, remarkable, conspicuous, distinguished, distinctive, celebrity, starts, important, striking, special, memorable, extraordinary, rare, exceptional, personality.

(ANT.) *commonplace, ordinary, usual.*

notch *(SYN.)* cut, nick, indentation, gash.

note *(SYN.)* sign, annotation, letter, indication, observation, mark, symbol, comment, remark, token, message, memorandum, memo, record, write, list, inscribe, notice.

noted *(SYN.)* renowned, glorious, celebrated, famous, illustrious, well-known, distinguished, famed, notable.

(ANT.) *unknown, hidden, infamous, ignominious.*

noteworthy *(SYN.)* consequential, celebrated, exceptional, outstanding, prominent.

notice *(SYN.)* heed, perceive, hold, mark, behold, descry, recognize, observe, attend to, remark, note, regard, see, sign, announcement, poster, note, advertisement, observation, warning.

(ANT.) *overlook, disregard, skip.*

notify *(SYN.)* apprise, acquaint, instruct, tell, advise, warn, teach, inform, report, remind, mention.

(ANT.) *mislead, delude, conceal.*

notion *(SYN.)* image, conception, sentiment, abstraction, thought, idea, impression, fancy, understanding, view, opinion, concept.

(ANT.) *thing, matter, substance, entity.*

notorious *(SYN.)* celebrated, renowned, famous, well-known, popular, infamous.

nourish *(SYN.)* strengthen, nurse, feed, supply, nurture, sustain, support.

nourishment *(SYN.)* nutriment, food, sustenance, support.

(ANT.) *starvation, deprivation.*

novel *(SYN.)* fiction, narrative, allegory, tale, fable, story, romance, invention, new, different, unusual, strange, original, new, unique, fresh.

(ANT.) *verity, history, truth, fact.*

novice *(SYN.)* beginner, amateur, newcomer, greenhorn, learner, apprentice, freshman, dilettante.

(ANT.) *expert, professional, adept, master.*

now *(SYN.)* today, at once, right away, immediately, at this time, present.

(ANT.) *later.*

noxious *(SYN.)* poisonous, harmful, damaging, toxic, detrimental.

(ANT.) harmless.

nucleus *(SYN.)* core, middle, heart, focus, hub, kernel.

nude *(SYN.)* naked, unclad, plain, open, defenseless, mere, bare, exposed, unprotected, simple, stripped, uncovered.
(ANT.) dressed, concealed, protected, clothed, covered.

nudge *(SYN.)* prod, push, jab, shove, poke, prompt.

nugget *(SYN.)* clump, mass, lump, wad, chunk, hunk.

nuisance *(SYN.)* annoyance, bother, irritation, pest.

nullify *(SYN.)* abolish, cross out, delete, invalidate, obliterate, cancel, expunge, repeal, annul, revoke, quash, rescind.
(ANT.) perpetuate, enact, confirm, enforce.

numb *(SYN.)* unfeeling, dull, insensitive, deadened, paralyzed, anesthetized.

number *(SYN.)* quantity, sum, amount, volume, aggregate, total, collection, sum, numeral, count, measure, portion, bulk, figure, multitude, digit.
(ANT.) zero, nothing, nothingness.

numeral *(SYN.)* figure, symbol, digit, number.

numerous *(SYN.)* many, several, manifold, multifarious, various, multitudinous, diverse, abundant, sundry, numberless, infinite.
(ANT.) scanty, infrequent, meager, few, scarce.

nuptials *(SYN.)* marriage, wedding, espousal, wedlock, matrimony, union.
(ANT.) virginity, divorce, celibacy.

nurse *(SYN.)* tend, care for, nourish, nurture, feed, foster, mind, attend.

nurture *(SYN.)* hold dear, foster, sustain, appreciate, prize, bring up, rear, value, treasure, cherish.
(ANT.) reject, neglect, dislike, disregard, abandon.

nutriment *(SYN.)* food, diet, sustenance, repast, meal, fare, edibles.
(ANT.) hunger, want, starvation, drink.

nutrition *(SYN.)* nourishment, sustenance, food, nutriment.

oaf *(SYN.)* boor, clod, clown, lummox, fool, lout, dunce, bogtrotter, hillbilly.

oasis *(SYN.)* shelter, haven, retreat, refuge.

oath *(SYN.)* promise, pledge, vow, profanity, curse, agreement, commitment, swearword.

obdurate *(SYN.)* insensible, callous, hard, tough, unfeeling, insensitive, impenitent, indurate.
(ANT.) soft, compassionate, tender, sensitive.

obedience *(SYN.)* docility, submission, subservience, compliance, conformability.
(ANT.) rebelliousness, disobedience.

obedient *(SYN.)* dutiful, yielding, tractable, compliant, submissive, deferential.
(ANT.) rebellious, intractable, insubordinate, obstinate.

obese *(SYN.)* portly, fat, pudgy, chubby, plump, rotund, stout, thickset, corpulent, stocky, paunchy.
(ANT.) slim, gaunt, lean, thin, slender.

obey *(SYN.)* submit, yield, mind, comply, listen to, serve, conform, concur.
(ANT.) resist, disobey.

obfuscate *(SYN.)* bewilder, complicate, fluster, confuse.

object *(SYN.)* thing, aim, intention, design, end, objective, particular, mark, purpose, goal, target, article.
(ANT.) assent, agree, concur, approve, acquiesce.

objection *(SYN.)* disagreement, protest, rejection, dissent, challenge, noncompliance, difference, nonconformity, recusancy, disapproval, criticism, variance, remonstrance.
(ANT.) acceptance, compliance, agreement, assent.

objectionable *(SYN.)* improper, offensive, unbecoming, deplorable.

objective *(SYN.)* aspiration, goal, passion, desire, aim, hope, purpose, drift, design, ambition, end, object, intention, intent, longing, craving.
(ANT.) biased, subjective.

objectivity *(SYN.)* disinterest, neutrality, impartiality, indifference.

obligate *(SYN.)* oblige, require, pledge,

bind, force, compel.

obligation *(SYN.)* duty, bond, engagement, compulsion, account, contract, ability, debt, responsibility.

(ANT.) freedom, choice, exemption.

oblige *(SYN.)* constrain, force, impel, enforce, coerce, drive, compel, gratify.

(ANT.) persuade, convince, allure, free, induce, disoblige, prevent.

obliging *(SYN.)* considerate, helpful, thoughtful, well-meaning, accommodating.

(ANT.) discourteous.

obliterate *(SYN.)* terminate, destroy, eradicate, raze, extinguish, exterminate, annihilate, devastate, wipe out, ravage, blot out, erase, ruin, demolish.

(ANT.) make, save, construct, establish, preserve.

oblivious *(SYN.)* sightless, unmindful, headlong, rash, blind, senseless, ignorant, forgetful, undiscerning, preoccupied, unconscious.

(ANT.) sensible, aware, calculated, perceiving, discerning.

oblong *SYN.)* rectangular, elliptical, elongated.

obloquy *(SYN.)* defamation, rebuke, censure.

obnoxious *(SYN.)* hateful, offensive, nasty, disagreeable, repulsive, loathsome, vile, disgusting, detestable, wretched, terrible, despicable, dreadful.

obscene *(SYN.)* indecent, filthy, impure, dirty, gross, lewd, pornographic, coarse, disgusting, bawdy, offensive, smutty.

(ANT.) modest, pure, decent, refined.

obscure *(SYN.)* cloudy, enigmatic, mysterious, abstruse, cryptic, dim, indistinct, dusky, ambiguous, dark, indistinct, unintelligible, unclear, shadowy, fuzzy, blurred, vague.

(ANT.) clear, famous, distinguished, noted, illumined, lucid, bright, distinct.

obsequious *(SYN.)* fawning, flattering, ingratiating.

observance *(SYN.)* protocol, ritual, ceremony, rite, parade, pomp, solemnity, formality.

(ANT.) omission.

observant *(SYN.)* aware, alert, careful, mindful, watchful, heedful, considerate, attentive, anxious, circumspect, cautious, wary.

(ANT.) unaware, indifferent, oblivious.

observation *(SYN.)* attention, watching, comment, opinion, remark, notice, examination.

observe *(SYN.)* note, behold, discover, notice, perceive, eye, detect, inspect, keep, commemorate, mention, utter, watch, examine, mark, view, express, see, celebrate.

(ANT.) neglect, overlook, disregard, ignore.

observer *(SYN.)* examiner, overseer, lookout, spectator, bystander, witness, watcher.

obsession *(SYN.)* preoccupation, mania, compulsion, passion, fetish, infatuation.

obsolete *(SYN.)* old, out-of-date, ancient, archaic, extinct, old-fashioned, discontinued, obsolescent, venerable, dated, antiquated.

(ANT.) modern, stylish, current, recent, fashionable, extant.

obstacle *(SYN.)* block, hindrance, barrier, impediment, snag, check, deterrent, stoppage, hitch, bar, difficulty, obstruction.

(ANT.) help, aid, assistance, encouragement.

obstinate *(SYN.)* firm, head-strong, immovable, stubborn, determined, dogged, intractable, uncompromising, inflexible, willful, bullheaded, contumacious, obdurate, unbending, unyielding.

(ANT.) yielding, docile, amenable, submissive, pliable, flexible, compliant.

obstruct *(SYN.)* clog, barricade, impede, block, delay, hinder, stop, close, bar.

(ANT.) promote, clear, aid, help, open, further.

obstruction *(SYN.)* block, obstacle, barrier, blockage, interference.

obtain *(SYN.)* get, acquire, secure, win, procure, attain, gain, receive, assimilate.

(ANT.) surrender, forfeit, lose, forego, miss.

obtrusive *(SYN.)* blatant, garish, conspicuous.

obtuse *(SYN.)* blunt, dull, slow-witted, unsharpened, stupid, dense, slow.

(ANT.) clear, interesting, lively, bright, animated, sharp.

obviate (SYN.) prevent, obstruct, forestall, preclude, intercept, avert, evade.

obvious (SYN.) plain, clear, evident, palpable, patent, self-evident, apparent, distinct, understandable, manifest, unmistakable.

(ANT.) concealed, hidden, abstruse, obscure.

obviously (SYN.) plainly, clearly, surely, evidently, certainly.

occasion (SYN.) occurrence, time, happening, excuse, opportunity, chance.

occasional (SYN.) random, irregular, sporadic, infrequent, periodically, spasmodic.

(ANT.) chronic, regular, constant.

occasionally (SYN.) seldom, now and then, infrequently, sometimes, irregularly.

(ANT.) regularly, often.

occlude (SYN.) clog, obstruct, choke, throttle.

occupant (SYN.) tenant, lodger, boarder, dweller, resident, inhabitant.

occupation (SYN.) employment, business, enterprise, job, trade, vocation, work, profession, matter, interest, concern, affair, activity, commerce, trading, engagement.

(ANT.) hobby, pastime, avocation.

occupy (SYN.) dwell, have, inhabit, absorb, hold, possess, fill, busy, keep.

(ANT.) relinquish, abandon, release.

occur (SYN.) take place, bechance, come about, befall, chance, transpire, happen.

occurrence (SYN.) episode, event, issue, end, result, consequence, happening, circumstance, outcome.

ocean (SYN.) deep, sea, main, briny.

odd (SYN.) strange, bizarre, eccentric, unusual, single, uneven, unique, queer, quaint, peculiar, curious, unmatched, remaining, singular.

(ANT.) matched, common, typical, normal, familiar, even, usual, regular.

odious (SYN.) obscene, depraved, vulgar, despicable, mean, wicked, sordid, foul, base, loathsome, depraved, vicious, displeasing, hateful, revolting, offensive, repulsive, horrible, obnoxious, vile.

(ANT.) decent, upright, laudable, attractive, honorable.

odor (SYN.) fume, aroma, fragrance, redolence, smell, stink, scent, essence, stench.

odorous (SYN.) scented, aromatic, fragrant.

odyssey (SYN.) crusade, quest, journey, voyage.

offbeat (SYN.) uncommon, eccentric, strange, unconventional, peculiar.

off-color (SYN.) rude, improper, earthy, suggestive, salty.

offend (SYN.) annoy, anger, vex, irritate, displease, provoke, hurt, grieve, pain, disgust, wound, horrify, stricken, insult, outrage.

(ANT.) flatter, please, delight.

offender (SYN.) criminal, culprit, lawbreaker, miscreant.

offense (SYN.) indignity, injustice, transgression, affront, outrage, misdeed, sin, insult, atrocity, aggression, crime.

(ANT.) morality, gentleness, innocence, right.

offensive (SYN.) attacking, aggressive, unpleasant, revolting, disagreeable, nauseous, disgusting.

(ANT.) pleasing, defending, defensive, pleasant, attractive, agreeable.

offer (SYN.) suggestion, overture, proposal, present, suggest, propose, try, submit, attempt, tender.

(ANT.) withdrawal, denial, rejection.

offhand (SYN.) informal, unprepared, casual, impromptu, spontaneous.

(ANT.) considered, planned, calculated.

office (SYN.) position, job, situation, studio, berth, incumbency, capacity, headquarters, duty, task, function, work, post.

officiate (SYN.) regulate, administer, superintend, oversee, emcee.

offset (SYN.) compensate, counterbalance, cushion, counteract, neutralize, soften, balance.

offshoot (SYN.) outgrowth, addition, byproduct, supplement, appendage, accessory, branch.

offspring (SYN.) issue, children, progeny, descendants.

often (SYN.) frequently, repeatedly, commonly, generally, many times, recurrently.

(ANT.) seldom, infrequently, rarely, occasionally, sporadically.

ogle (SYN.) gaze, stare, eye, leer.

ogre (SYN.) fiend, monster, devil, demon.

ointment (SYN.) lotion, pomade, balm, emollient.

old (SYN.) antique, senile, ancient, archaic, old-fashioned, superannuated, obsolete, venerable, antiquated, elderly, discontinued, abandoned, aged.

(ANT.) new, youthful, recent, modern, young.

old-fashioned (SYN.) outmoded, old, dated, ancient.

(ANT.) modern, fashionable, current, new.

olio (SYN.) potpourri, variety, mixture, jumble.

omen (SYN.) sign, gesture, indication, proof, portent, symbol, token, emblem, signal.

ominous (SYN.) unfavorable, threatening, sinister, menacing.

omission (SYN.) failure, neglect, oversight, default.

(ANT.) inclusion, notice, attention, insertion.

omit (SYN.) exclude, delete, cancel, eliminate, ignore, neglect, skip, leave out, drop, miss, bar, overlook, disregard.

(ANT.) insert, notice, enter, include, introduce.

omnipotent (SYN.) almighty, divine.

oncoming (SYN.) imminent, approaching, arriving, nearing.

onerous (SYN.) intricate, arduous, hard, perplexing, difficult, burdensome, puzzling.

(ANT.) simple, easy, facile, effortless.

one-sided (SYN.) unfair, partial, biased, prejudiced.

(ANT.) impartial, neutral.

ongoing (SYN.) advancing, developing, continuing, progressive.

onlooker (SYN.) witness, spectator, observer, bystander.

only (SYN.) lone, sole, solitary, single, merely, but, just.

onset (SYN.) commencement, beginning,

opening, start, assault, attack, charge, offense, onslaught.

(ANT.) end.

onslaught (SYN.) invasion, aggression, attack, assault, offense, drive, criticism, onset, charge, denunciation.

(ANT.) vindication, defense, surrender, opposition, resistance.

onus (SYN.) load, weight, burden, duty.

onward (SYN.) ahead, forward, frontward.

(ANT.) backward.

ooze (SYN.) seep, leak, drip, flow, filter.

opacity (SYN.) obscurity, thickness, imperviousness.

opaque (SYN.) murky, dull, cloudy, filmy, unilluminated, dim, obtuse, indistinct, shadowy, dark, obscure.

(ANT.) light, clear, bright.

open (SYN.) uncovered, overt, agape, unlocked, passable, accessible, unrestricted, candid, plain, clear, exposed, unclosed, unobstructed, free, disengaged, frank, unoccupied, public, honest, ajar, available.

open (SYN.) unbar, unfold, exhibit, spread, unseal, expand, unfasten.

(ANT.) close, shut, conceal, hide.

open-handed (SYN.) kind, generous, charitable, lavish, extravagant, bountiful.

(ANT.) mean, stingy.

openhearted (SYN.) frank, honest, candid, sincere, ingenuous, straightforward.

(ANT.) insincere, devious.

opening (SYN.) cavity, hole, void, abyss, aperture, chasm, pore, gap, loophole.

openly (SYN.) sincerely, frankly, freely.

(ANT.) secretly.

open-minded (SYN.) tolerant, fair, just, liberal, impartial, reasonable, unprejudiced.

(ANT.) prejudiced, bigoted.

operate (SYN.) comport, avail, behave, interact, apply, manage, utilize, demean, run, manipulate, employ, act, exploit, exert, exercise, practice, conduct.

(ANT.) neglect, waste.

operation (SYN.) effort, enterprise, mentality, maneuver, action, instrumentality, performance, working, proceeding, agency.

(ANT.) inaction, cessation, rest, inactivity.

operative *(SYN.)* busy, active, industrious, working, effective, functional.
(ANT.) inactive, dormant.

opiate *(SYN.)* hypnotic, tranquilizer, narcotic.

opinion *(SYN.)* decision, feeling, notion, view, idea, conviction, belief, judgment, sentiment, persuasion.
(ANT.) knowledge, fact, misgiving, skepticism.

opinionated *(SYN.)* domineering, overbearing, arrogant, dictatorial, dogmatic, positive, magisterial, obstinate, pertinacious.
(ANT.) questioning, fluctuating, indecisive, skeptical, open-minded, indecisive.

opponent *(SYN.)* competitor, foe, adversary, contestant, enemy, rival, contender, combatant, antagonist.
(ANT.) comrade, team, ally, confederate.

opportune *(SYN.)* fitting, suitable, appropriate, proper, favorable, felicitous.

opportunity *(SYN.)* possibility, chance, occasion, time, spell, turn, contingency, opening.
(ANT.) obstacle, disadvantage, hindrance.

oppose *(SYN.)* defy, resist, withstand, combat, bar, counteract, confront, hinder, thwart, struggle, fight, contradict, hinder, obstruct.
(ANT.) submit, support, agree, cooperate, succumb.

opposed *(SYN.)* opposite, contrary, hostile, adverse, counteractive, unlucky, antagonistic, unfavorable, disastrous.
(ANT.) lucky, benign, propitious, fortunate, favorable.

opposite *(SYN.)* reverse, contrary, different, unlike, opposed.
(ANT.) like, same, similar.

opposition *(SYN.)* combat, struggle, discord, collision, conflict, battle, fight, encounter, discord, controversy, inconsistency, variance.
(ANT.) harmony, amity, concord, consonance.

oppress *(SYN.)* harass, torment, vex, afflict, annoy, harry, pester, hound, worry, persecute.
(ANT.) encourage, support, comfort, assist, aid.

oppression *(SYN.)* cruelty, tyranny, persecution, injustice, despotism, brutality, abuse.
(ANT.) liberty, freedom.

oppressive *(SYN.)* difficult, stifling, burdensome, severe, domineering, harsh, unjust, overbearing, hard, overwhelming.

oppressor *(SYN.)* bully, scourge, slavedriver.

opprobrium *(SYN.)* disgrace, contempt, reproach, shame, discredit.

opt *(SYN.)* choose, prefer, pick, select.

optical *(SYN.)* seeing, visual.

optimism *(SYN.)* faith, expectation, optimism, anticipation, trust, expectancy, confidence, hope.
(ANT.) despair, pessimism, despondency.

optimistic *(SYN.)* happy, cheerful, bright, glad, pleasant, radiant, jaunty.
(ANT.) pessimistic.

option *(SYN.)* preference, choice, selection, alternative, election.

optional *(SYN.)* selective, elective, voluntary.
(ANT.) required.

opulence *(SYN.)* luxury, abundance, fortune, riches, wealth, plenty, possessions, affluence.
(ANT.) need, indigence, want, poverty.

opulent *(SYN.)* wealthy, rich, prosperous, well-off, affluent, well-heeled.

oracle *(SYN.)* authority, forecaster, wizard, seer, mastermind, clairvoyant.

oral *(SYN.)* voiced, sounded, vocalized, said, uttered, verbal, vocal, spoken.
(ANT.) recorded, written, documentary.

orate *(SYN.)* preach, lecture, sermonize.

oration *(SYN.)* address, lecture, speech, sermon, discourse, recital, declamation.

orb *(SYN.)* globe, sphere, ball, moon.

orbit *(SYN.)* path, lap, course, circuit, revolution, revolve, circle.

orchestra *(SYN.)* ensemble, band.

orchestrate *(SYN.)* coordinate, direct, synchronize, organize.

ordain *(SYN.)* constitute, create, order, decree, decide, dictate, command, rule, bid, sanction, appoint.

(ANT.) terminate, disband.

ordeal *(SYN.)* hardship, suffering, test, affliction, trouble, fortune, proof, examination, trial, experiment, tribulation.
(ANT.) consolation, alleviation.

order *(SYN.)* plan, series, decree, instruction, command, system, method, aim, arrangement, class, injunction, mandate, instruct, requirement, dictate, bidding.
(ANT.) consent, license, confusion, disarray, irregularity, permission.

order *(SYN.)* guide, command, rule, direct, govern, manage, regulate, bid, conduct.
(ANT.) misguide, deceive, misdirect, distract.

orderly *(SYN.)* regulated, neat, well-organized, disciplined, methodical, shipshape.
(ANT.) sloppy, messy, haphazard, disorganized.

ordinarily *(SYN.)* commonly, usually, generally, mostly, customarily, normally.

ordinary *(SYN.)* common, habitual, normal, typical, usual, conventional, familiar, accustomed, customary, average, standard, everyday, inferior, mediocre, regular, vulgar, plain.
(ANT.) uncommon, marvelous, extraordinary, remarkable, strange.

ordance *(SYN.)* munitions, artillery, weapons.

organ *(SYN.)* instrument, journal, voice.

organic *(SYN.)* living, biological, animate.

organism *(SYN.)* creature, plant, microorganism.

organization *(SYN.)* order, rule, system, arrangement, method, plan, regularity, scheme, mode, process.
(ANT.) irregularity, chaos, disarrangement, chance, disorder, confusion.

organize *(SYN.)* assort, arrange, plan, regulate, systematize, devise, categorize, classify, prepare.
(ANT.) jumble, disorder, disturb, confuse, scatter.

organized *(SYN.)* planned, neat, orderly, arranged.

orient *(SYN.)* align, fit, accustom, adjust.

orifice *(SYN.)* vent, slot, opening, cavity, hole.

origin *(SYN.)* birth, foundation, source, start, commencement, inception, beginning, derivation, infancy, parentage, spring, cradle.
(ANT.) product, issue, outcome, end.

original *(SYN.)* primary, fresh, new, initial, pristine, creative, first, primordial, inventive, primeval, novel, introductory.
(ANT.) banal, trite, subsequent, derivative, later, modern, terminal.

originality *(SYN.)* unconventionality, genius, novelty, creativity, imagination.

originate *(SYN.)* fashion, invent, cause, create, make, initiate, inaugurate, organize, institute, produce, engender, commence, found, establish, form, begin, arise, generate.
(ANT.) demolish, terminate, annihilate, disband, destroy.

originator *(SYN.)* creator, inventor, discoverer.
(ANT.) follower, imitator.

ornament *(SYN.)* decoration, ornamentation, adornment, embellishment, trimming.

ornamental *(SYN.)* ornate, decorative.

ornate *(SYN.)* florid, overdone, elaborate, showy, flowery, pretentious.

ornery *(SYN.)* disobedient, firm, unruly, stiff, rebellious, stubborn, headstrong, willful, contrary, rigid, mean, difficult, malicious, disagreeable.
(ANT.) pleasant.

orthodox *(SYN.)* customary, usual, conventional, correct, proper, accepted.
(ANT.) different, unorthodox.

oscillate *(SYN.)* vary, change, hesitate, waver, undulate, fluctuate, vacillate.
(ANT.) persist, resolve, adhere, stick, decide.

ostentation *(SYN.)* parade, show, boasting, pageantry, vaunting, pomp, display, flourish.
(ANT.) reserve, humility, unobtrusiveness, modesty.

ostentatious *(SYN.)* flashy, showy, overdone, fancy, pretentious, swanky, garish.

ostracize *(SYN.)* hinder, omit, bar, exclude, blackball, expel, prohibit, prevent, except.
(ANT.) welcome, accept, include, admit.

other *(SYN.)* distinct, different, extra, further, new, additional, supplementary.

ought *(SYN.)* must, should, need to, be obliged.

oust *(SYN.)* eject, banish, exclude, expatriate, ostracize, dismiss, exile, expel. *(ANT.) shelter, accept, receive, admit, harbor.*

ouster *(SYN.)* expulsion, banishment, ejection, overthrow.

outbreak *(SYN.)* riot, revolt, uprising, disturbance, torrent, eruption, outburst.

outburst *(SYN.)* outbreak, eruption, torrent, ejection, discharge.

outcast *(SYN.)* friendless, homeless, deserted, abandoned, forsaken, disowned, derelict, forlorn, rejected.

outclass *(SYN.)* outshine, dominate, surpass.

outcome *(SYN.)* fate, destiny, necessity, doom, portion, consequence, result, end, fortune, effect, issue, aftermath.

outcry *(SYN.)* scream, protest, clamor, noise, uproar.

outdo *(SYN.)* outshine, defeat, excel, beat, surpass.

outer *(SYN.)* remote, outside, exterior, external.

outfit *(SYN.)* garb, kit, gear, furnish, equip, rig, clothing, provisions.

outgoing *(SYN.)* leaving, departing, friendly, congenial, amicable. *(ANT.) unfriendly, incoming.*

outgrowth *(SYN.)* effect, outcome, upshot, fruit, result, consequence, product, byproduct, development.

outing *(SYN.)* journey, trip, excursion, jaunt, expedition, junket.

outlandish *(SYN.)* peculiar, odd, weird, curious, strange, queer, exotic, bazaar. *(ANT.) ordinary, common.*

outlast *(SYN.)* survive, endure, outlive.

outlaw *(SYN.)* bandit, outcast, badman, convict, criminal, fugitive, desperado.

outlay *(SYN.)* expense, costs, spending, disbursement, expenditure, charge.

outlet *(SYN.)* spout, opening, pore, passage.

outline *(SYN.)* form, sketch, brief, draft, figure, profile, contour, chart, diagram, skeleton, delineation, plan, silhouette.

outlook *(SYN.)* viewpoint, view, prospect, opportunity, position, attitude, future.

outlying *(SYN.)* external, remote, outer, out-of-the-way, surburban, rural.

outmoded *(SYN.)* unfashionable, old-fashioned. *(ANT.) up-to-date, modern.*

outnumber *(SYN.)* exceed.

output *(SYN.)* yield, crop, harvest, proceeds, productivity, production, achievement, accomplishment.

outrage *(SYN.)* aggression, transgression, vice, affront, offense, insult, indignity, atrocity, misdeed, trespass, wrong. *(ANT.) morality, right, gentleness, innocence.*

outrageous *(SYN.)* shameful, shocking, disgraceful, insulting, nonsensical, absurd, foolish, crazy, excessive, ridiculous, bizarre, preposterous, offensive. *(ANT.) prudent, reasonable, sensible.*

outright *(SYN.)* entirely, altogether, completely, openly, freely, quite, fully, thoroughly.

outset *(SYN.)* inception, origin, start, beginning, commencement, opening. *(ANT.) end, completion, termination, consummation, close.*

outside *(SYN.)* covering, exterior, surface, facade, externals, appearance. *(ANT.) intimate, insider.*

outsider *(SYN.)* immigrant, stranger, foreigner, alien, newcomer, bystander. *(ANT.) countryman, friend, acquaintance, neighbor, associate.*

outsmart *(SYN.)* outmaneuver, outwit.

outspoken *(SYN.)* rude, impolite, unceremonious, brusque, unrestrained, vocal, open, straightfoward, blunt, unreserved, frank, forthright. *(ANT.) suave, tactful, shy, polished, polite, subtle.*

outstanding *(SYN.)* well-known, famous, important, prominent, leading, eminent, distinguished, great, significant, conspicuous. *(ANT.) insignificant, unimportant.*

outward *(SYN.)* apparent, outside, exterior, visible.

outweigh *(SYN.)* predominate, supersede, counteract, dwarf.

outwit *(SYN.)* baffle, trick, outsmart, bewilder, outdo, outmaneuver, confuse.

oval *(SYN.)* egg-shaped, elliptical, ovular.

ovation *(SYN.)* fanfare, homage, applause, tribute, cheers, acclamation.

overall *(SYN.)* comprehensive, complete, general, extensive, widespread, entire.

overbearing *(SYN.)* domineering, masterful, autocratic, dictatorial, bossy, arrogant, imperious, haughty.
(ANT.) humble.

overcast *(SYN.)* dim, shadowy, cloudy, murky, dark, mysterious, gloomy, somber, dismal, hazy, indistinct.
(ANT.) sunny, bright, distinct, limpid, clear.

overcome *(SYN.)* quell, beat, crush, master, surmount, rout, humble, conquer, subjugate, defeat, subdue, upset.
(ANT.) retreat, surrender, capitulate, cede, lose.

overconfident *(SYN.)* egotistical, headstrong, arrogant, conceited.

overdo *(SYN.)* stretch, exaggerate, enlarge, magnify, exhaust, overexert, strain.

overflow *(SYN.)* run over, flood, spill, cascade, inundate.

overflowing *(SYN.)* ample, plentiful, teeming, abundant, copious, plenteous, profuse.
(ANT.) insufficient, scant, deficient, scarce.

overhang *(SYN.)* protrude, extend, projection.

overhaul *(SYN.)* recondition, rebuild, service, repair, condition, mend, revamp.

overhead *(SYN.)* high, above, aloft, expenses, costs.

overjoyed *(SYN.)* enchanted, delighted, ecstatic, enraptured, elated, blissful.
(ANT.) depressed.

overlap *(SYN.)* overhang, extend, superimpose.

overlook *(SYN.)* miss, disregard, exclude, cancel, omit, skip, ignore, drop, delete.
(ANT.) notice, enter, introduce, insert.

overly *(SYN.)* exceedingly, needlessly, unreasonably.

overpass *(SYN.)* span, bridge, viaduct.

overpower *(SYN.)* overcome, conquer, master, defeat, surmount, vanquish.
(ANT.) surrender.

overrated *(SYN.)* exaggerated, mis-represented.

overrule *(SYN.)* disallow, nullify, cancel, override, repeal.

overrun *(SYN.)* spread, exceed, beset, infest, abound.

oversee *(SYN.)* direct, run, operate, administer, superintend, manage, supervise.

overseer *(SYN.)* leader, ruler, master, teacher, chief, commander, employer, manager.
(ANT.) slave, servant.

overshadow *(SYN.)* dominate, control, outclass, surpass, domineer, outshine.

oversight *(SYN.)* omission, charge, superintendence, surveillance, inattention, error, inadvertence, neglect, mistake, control, slip, negligence, management.
(ANT.) scrutiny, care, attention, observation.

overstep *(SYN.)* surpass, exceed, trespass, transcend, impinge, violate, intrude.

overt *(SYN.)* honest, candid, frank, plain, open, apparent, straightforward.

overtake *(SYN.)* outdistance, reach, catch, pass.

overthrow *(SYN.)* defeat, demolish, overcome, destroy, ruin, rout, vanquish, subvert, reverse, supplant, overturn, overpower, upset.
(ANT.) revive, restore, construct, regenerate, reinstate.

overture *(SYN.)* offer, bid, proposal, prelude, presentation, recommendation.
(ANT.) finale.

overturn *(SYN.)* demolish, overcome, vanquish, upset, destroy, overthrow.
(ANT.) uphold, construct, build, preserve, conserve.

overweight *(SYN.)* pudgy, stout, heavy, obese, fat.

overwhelm *(SYN.)* crush, surmount, vanquish, conquer, astonish, surprise, bewilder, astound, startle, overcome, overpower, defeat.

overwrought *SYN.)* frantic, distraught, hysterical.

owe *(SYN.)* be liable, be indebted.

own *(SYN.)* monopolize, hold, possess, maintain, have.

owner *(SYN.)* landholder, partner, proprietor, possessor.

pace *(SYN.)* rate, gait, step.

pacific *(SYN.)* peaceful, calm, serene, undisturbed.
(ANT.) turbulent, wild, excited, frantic.

pacify *(SYN.)* appease, lull, relieve, quell, soothe, allay.
(ANT.) incense, inflame, arouse, excite.

pack *(SYN.)* prepare, stow, crowd, stuff, bundle, parcel.

package *(SYN.)* parcel, packet, load, bundle, box, bottle.

packed *(SYN.)* filled, complete, plentiful, crammed, full, replete, gorged.
(ANT.) lacking, depleted, devoid, vacant, insufficient, partial, empty.

pain *(SYN.)* twinge, ache, anguish, throe, paroxysm, suffering, misery.
(ANT.) happiness, pleasure, comfort, relief, solace, ease.

painful *(SYN.)* hurting, galling, poignant, bitter, grievous, agonizing, aching.
(ANT.) sweet, pleasant.

painting *(SYN.)* image, picture, portrayal, scene, illustration, panorama, likeness.

pale *(SYN.)* colorless, white, pallid, dim, faint, whiten.
(ANT.) flushed, ruddy, bright.

panic *(SYN.)* fear, terror, fright, alarm, apprehension, trembling, horror, dread.
(ANT.) tranquillity, composure, serenity.

paper *(SYN.)* journal, newspaper, document, article.

parable *(SYN.)* fable, saga, legend, myth, allegory, chronicle, fiction.
(ANT.) history, fact.

parade *(SYN.)* procession, cavalcade, succession, train, file, cortege, retinue.

paradoxical *(SYN.)* vacillating, wavering.
(ANT.) correspondent, compatible.

parallel *(SYN.)* allied, analogous, comparable, corresponding, akin, similar.
(ANT.) opposed, different, incongruous.

paraphernalia *(SYN.)* effect, gear, belonging, equipment.

parcel *(SYN.)* packet, package, bundle.

parched *(SYN.)* dry, arid, thirsty, drained.
(ANT.) moist, damp.

pardon *(SYN.)* absolution, forgiveness, remission, acquittal, amnesty, excuse.
(ANT.) sentence, penalty, conviction, punishment.

pardon *(SYN.)* condone, overlook, remit,

absolve, acquit, forgive, excuse.
(ANT.) punish, chastise, accuse, condemn, convict.

parley *(SYN.)* interview, talk, conference, chat, dialogue.

parsimonious *(SYN.)* avaricious, miserly, penurious, stingy, acquisitive, greedy.
(ANT.) munificent, extravagant, bountiful, altruistic.

part *(SYN.)* piece, section, allotment, portion, segment, side, interest, organ, section, fraction, participation.
(ANT.) whole, entirety.

partake *(SYN.)* dispense, parcel, allot, assign, distribute, partition, appropriate.
(ANT.) condense, aggregate, combine.

partial *(SYN.)* unfinished, undone, incomplete, prejudiced, unfair.

partiality *(SYN.)* preconception, bias, predisposition.
(ANT.) reason, fairness, impartiality.

participant *(SYN.)* associate, colleague.

particle *(SYN.)* mite, crumb, scrap, atom, corpuscle, grain, speck, bit, spot.
(ANT.) quantity, bulk, mass.

particular *(SYN.)* peculiar, fastidious, individual, distinctive, singular, exact.
(ANT.) general, rough, universal, comprehensive.

partisan *(SYN.)* follower, successor, adherent, attendant, henchman.
(ANT.) leader, chief, master, head.

partition *(SYN.)* distribution, division, separation, screen.
(ANT.) unification, joining.

partner *(SYN.)* colleague, comrade, friend, crony, consort, associate, companion, mate, participant.
(ANT.) stranger, enemy, adversary.

pass *(SYN.)* proceed, continue, move, go, disregard, ignore, exceed, gap, permit, throw, toss.
(ANT.) note, consider, notice.

passable *(SYN.)* fair, average, mediocre, acceptable, adequate, satisfactory.
(ANT.) worst, excellent, first-rate, exceptional.

passage *(SYN.)* section, passageway, corridor, section, voyage, tour, crossing.

passenger *(SYN.)* traveler, tourist, rider, voyager.

passion *(SYN.)* feeling, affection, turmoil,

sentiment, rapture, excitement, desire, love, liking, fondness.
(ANT.) tranquillity, indifference, calm, restraint, dispassion, apathy, coolness.

passive *(SYN.)* relaxed, idle, stoical, enduring, inert, inactive, submissive.
(ANT.) dynamic, active, aggressive.

past *(SYN.)* done, finished, over, former.
(ANT.) future, present, ahead.

pastime *(SYN.)* match, amusement, diversion, fun, play, recreation, entertainment.
(ANT.) quiescence, labor, apathy.

patch *(SYN.)* restore, fix, repair, ameliorate, correct.
(ANT.) rend, deface, hurt.

patent *(SYN.)* conspicuous, apparent, obvious, clear, evident, unmistakable.
(ANT.) hidden, concealed, obscure.

path *(SYN.)* avenue, street, trail, walk, course, road.

pathetic *(SYN.)* piteous, sad, affecting, moving, poignant, pitiable, touching, pitiful.
(ANT.) funny, comical, ludicrous.

patience *(SYN.)* perseverance, composure, endurance, fortitude, forbearance, calmness, passiveness, persistence.
(ANT.) restlessness, nervousness, impatience, unquite, impetuosity.

patron *(SYN.)* purchaser, buyer, client, customer.

pattern *(SYN.)* guide, example, original, model, design, figure, decoration.

pause *(SYN.)* falter, hesitate, waver, demur, doubt, scruple, delay, vacillate, hesitation, rest, interruption.
(ANT.) proceed, continue, decide, resolve, persevere, continuity, perpetuate.

pay *(SYN.)* earnings, salary, allowance, stipend, wages.
(ANT.) gratuity, present, gift.

peace *(SYN.)* hush, repose, serenity, tranquillity, silence, stillness, calmness.
(ANT.) noise, tumult, agitation, disturbance.

peaceable *(SYN.)* mild, calm, friendly, peaceful, amiable, gentle, pacific.
(ANT.) aggressive, hostile, warlike.

peaceful *(SYN.)* pacific, calm, undisturbed, quiet, serene, mild, placid, gentle.

(ANT.) noisy, violent, agitated, turbulent, disturbed, disrupted, riotous.

peak *(SYN.)* climax, culmination, summit, zenith, height, acme, consummation, apex.
(ANT.) depth, floor, base, anticlimax, base, bottom.

peculiar *(SYN.)* odd, eccentric, extraordinary, unusual, individual, particular, striking, rare, exceptional, distinctive, outlandish.
(ANT.) ordinary, common, normal, general, regular.

peculiarity *(SYN.)* characteristic, feature, mark, trait, quality, attribute, property.

pedigree *(SYN.)* descent, line, parentage, lineage, ancestry.

peek *(SYN.)* glimpse, look, peer, peep.

peer *(SYN.)* match, rival, equal, parallel, peep, glimpse, examine.

peeve *(SYN.)* nettle, irk, irritate, annoy, vex.

peevish *(SYN.)* ill-natured, irritable, waspish, touchy, petulant, snappish, fractious, ill-tempered, fretful.
(ANT.) pleasant, affable, good-tempered, genial.

penalty *(SYN.)* fine, retribution, handicap, punishment, forfeiture, forfeit.
(ANT.) remuneration, compensation, reward, pardon.

penchant *(SYN.)* disposition, propensity, tendency, partiality, inclination, bent, tendency, slant, bias.
(ANT.) justice, fairness, equity.

penetrating *(SYN.)* profound, recondite, abstruse, deep, solemn, piercing, puncturing, boring, sharp, acute.
(ANT.) superficial, shallow, slight.

penitent *(SYN.)* remorseful, sorrowful, regretful, contrite, sorry, repentant.
(ANT.) remorseless, objurgate.

penniless *(SYN.)* poor, destitute, impecunious, needy.
(ANT.) rich, wealthy, affluent, opulent, prosperous, well-off.

pensive *(SYN.)* dreamy, meditative, thoughtful, reflective.
(ANT.) thoughtless, heedless, inconsiderate, precipitous.

penurious *(SYN.)* avaricious, greedy, parsimonious, miserly, stingy, acquisitive.

(ANT.) munificent, extravagant, bountiful, generous, altruistic.

perceive *(SYN.)* note, conceive, see, comprehend, understand, discern, recognize, apprehend, notice, observe, distinguish.

(ANT.) overlook, ignore, miss.

perceptible *(SYN.)* sensible, appreciable, apprehensible.

(ANT.) imperceptible, absurd.

perception *(SYN.)* understanding, apprehension, conception, insight.

(ANT.) misconception, ignorance, misapprehension, insensibility.

perceptive *(SYN.)* informed, observant, apprised, cognizant, aware, conscious.

(ANT.) unaware, ignorant, oblivious.

perfect *(SYN.)* ideal, whole, faultless, immaculate, complete, superlative.

(ANT.) incomplete, defective, imperfect, deficient.

perform *(SYN.)* impersonate, pretend, act, play, do, accomplish, achieve.

performance *(SYN.)* parade, entertainment, demonstration, movie, show, production, ostentation, spectacle, presentation, offering.

perfunctory *(SYN.)* decorous, exact, formal, external, correct, affected, methodical.

(ANT.) unconventional, easy, unconstrained, natural.

perhaps *(SYN.)* conceivable, possible.

(ANT.) absolutely, definitely.

peril *(SYN.)* jeopardy, danger.

(ANT.) safety, immunity, protection, defense, security.

perilous *(SYN.)* menacing, risky, hazardous, critical.

(ANT.) safe, firm, protected, secure.

period *(SYN.)* era, age, interval, span, tempo, time.

periodical *(SYN.)* uniform, customary, orderly, systematic, regular, steady.

(ANT.) exceptional, unusual, abnormal, rare, erratic.

perish *(SYN.)* die, sink cease, decline, decay, depart, wane, wither, languish, expire, cease, pass away.

(ANT.) grow, survive, flourish.

permanent *(SYN.)* constant, fixed, changeless, unchangeable, lasting, indestructible, stable, continuing, long-lived, persistent, persisting.

(ANT.) unstable, transient, ephemeral, temporary, transitory, passing, inconstant.

permeate *(SYN.)* penetrate, pervade, run through, diffuse, fill, saturate.

permissible *(SYN.)* allowable, fair, tolerable, admissible, justifiable, probable.

(ANT.) inadmissible, irrelevant.

permission *(SYN.)* authorization, liberty, permit, license.

(ANT.) refusal, denial, opposition.

permissive *(SYN.)* easy, tolerant, openminded, unrestrictive.

(ANT.) restrictive.

permit *(SYN.)* let, tolerate, authorize, sanction, allow.

(ANT.) refuse, resist, forbid, protest, object, prohibit.

perpendicular *(SYN.)* standing, upright, vertical.

(ANT.) horizontal.

perpetrate *(SYN.)* commit, perform, do.

(ANT.) neglect, fail, miscarry.

perpetual *(SYN.)* everlasting, immortal, ceaseless, endless, timeless, undying.

(ANT.) transient, mortal, finite, temporal ephemeral.

perpetually *(SYN.)* continually, ever, incessantly, eternally, always, constantly.

(ANT.) rarely, sometimes, never, occasionally, fitfully.

perplex *(SYN.)* confuse, dumbfound, mystify, puzzle.

(ANT.) solve, explain, illumine, instruct, clarify.

perplexed *(SYN.)* confused, disorganized, mixed, bewildered, deranged.

(ANT.) plain, obvious, clear, lucid.

perplexing *(SYN.)* intricate, complex, involved, compound, complicated.

(ANT.) uncompounded, plain, simple.

persecute *(SYN.)* harass, hound, torment, worry, vex, torture, harry, afflict, annoy.

(ANT.) support, comfort, assist, encourage, aid.

persevere *(SYN.)* remain, abide, endure, last, persist.

(ANT.) vacillate, desist, discontinue, cease, waver, lapse.

perseverance *(SYN.)* persistency, constancy, pertinacity, steadfastness, tenacity.

(ANT.) sloth, cessation, laziness, idleness, rest.

persist *(SYN.)* endure, remain, abide, persevere, continue, last.

(ANT.) vacillate, waver, desist, cease, discontinue, stop.

persistence *(SYN.)* persistency, constancy, perseverance, tenacity.

(ANT.) cessation, rest, sloth, idleness.

persistent *(SYN.)* lasting, steady, obstinate, stubborn.

(ANT.) wavering, unsure, vacillating.

person *(SYN.)* human, individual, somebody, someone.

personality *(SYN.)* make-up, nature, disposition.

perspicacity *(SYN.)* intelligence, understanding, discernment, judgment, wisdom, sagacity.

(ANT.) thoughtlessness, stupidity, arbitrariness, senselessness.

persuade *(SYN.)* entice, coax, exhort, prevail upon, urge.

(ANT.) restrain, deter, compel, dissuade, coerce.

persuasion *(SYN.)* decision, notion, view, sentiment, conviction, belief, opinion.

(ANT.) knowledge, skepticism, fact.

persuasive *(SYN.)* winning, alluring, compelling, convincing, stimulating.

(ANT.) dubious, unconvincing.

pertinent *(SYN.)* apt, material, relevant, relating, applicable, to the point, germane, apropos, apposite.

(ANT.) unrelated, foreign, alien.

perturbed *(SYN.)* agitated, disturbed, upset, flustered.

pervade *(SYN.)* penetrate, saturate, fill, diffuse, infiltrate, run through.

perverse *(SYN.)* obstinate, ungovernable, sinful, contrary, fractious, forward.

(ANT.) docile, agreeable, obliging.

perversion *(SYN.)* maltreatment, outrage, desecration.

(ANT.) respect.

pervert *(SYN.)* deprave, humiliate, impair, debase, corrupt, degrade, defile.

(ANT.) improve, raise, enhance.

perverted *(SYN.)* wicked, perverse, sinful.

pest *(SYN.)* annoyance, nuisance, bother, irritant.

pester *(SYN.)* disturb, annoy, irritate, tease, bother, chafe, inconvenience, trouble, harass, torment, worry.

(ANT.) console, accommodate, gratify.

petition *(SYN.)* invocation, prayer, request, appeal, plea, application.

petty *(SYN.)* paltry, trivial, frivolous, small, unimportant, insignificant.

(ANT.) important, serious, weighty, momentous, vital, significant, generous.

petulant *(SYN.)* irritable, ill-natured, fretful, snappish.

(ANT.) pleasant, affable, good-tempered, genial.

phenomenon *(SYN.)* occurrence, fact, happening, incident.

philanthropy *(SYN.)* kindness, benevolence, charity, generosity, tenderness, liberality, humanity, magnanimity.

(ANT.) unkindness, inhumanity, cruelty, malevolence, selfishness.

phlegmatic *(SYN.)* unfeeling, sluggish, slow, lazy.

(ANT.) passionate, ardent, energetic.

phony *(SYN.)* counterfeit, artificial, ersatz, fake, synthetic, unreal, spurious.

(ANT.) real, genuine, natural, true.

picture *(SYN.)* etching, image, representation, sketch, appearance, cinema, engraving, scene, view, illustration, likeness, drawing.

piece *(SYN.)* portion, bit, fraction, morsel, scrap, fragment, amount, part, quantity, unit, section, portion.

(ANT.) sum, whole, entirety, all, total.

pigment *(SYN.)* shade, tint, tincture, stain, tinge.

(ANT.) transparency, paleness.

pile *(SYN.)* accumulation, heap, collection, amass.

pilgrimage *(SYN.)* trip, tour, expedition.

pinnacle *(SYN.)* crown, zenith, head, summit, chief, apex.

(ANT.) bottom, foundation, base, foot.

pious *(SYN.)* devout, religious, spiritual, consecrated, divine, hallowed, holy, saintly, sacred.

(ANT.) worldly, sacrilegious, evil, secular, profane.

pitch *(SYN.)* throw, cast, toss, propel, hurl, fling, thrust.

(ANT.) retain, draw, hold, pull, haul.

piteous *(SYN.)* poignant, pitiable, sad, pathetic.
(ANT.) funny, ludicrous, comical.

pitfall *(SYN.)* lure, snare, wile, ambush, bait, intrigue, trick, trap, net, snare.

pitiable *(SYN.)* poignant, touching, moving, affecting.
(ANT.) ludicrous, funny.

pitiless *(SYN.)* unmerciful, mean, unpitying, merciless.
(ANT.) gentle, kind.

pity *(SYN.)* sympathy, commiseration, condolence, mercy, compassion, charity.
(ANT.) ruthlessness, hardness, cruelty, inhumanity, brutality, vindictiveness.

place *(SYN.)* lay, arrange, put, deposit, space, region, location, plot, area, spot.
(ANT.) mislay, remove, disarrange, disturb, misplace.

placid *(SYN.)* pacific, serene, tranquil, calm, imperturbable, composed, peaceful.
(ANT.) wild, frantic, stormy, excited.

plagiarize *(SYN.)* recite, adduce, cite, quote, paraphrase, repeat, extract.
(ANT.) retort, contradict.

plague *(SYN.)* hound, pester, worry, harass, annoy, persecute, vex, afflict, badger.
(ANT.) encourage, aid, assist.

plain *(SYN.)* candid, simple, flat, smooth, clear, evident, sincere, unpretentious, level, distinct, absolute, visible, open, frank, palpable.
(ANT.) embellished, abstruse, abrupt, rough, broken, insincere, adorned, fancy.

plan *(SYN.)* design, purpose, sketch, devise, invent, contrive, intend, draw, create.

plane *(SYN.)* level, airplane.

plastic *(SYN.)* pliable, moldable, supple, flexible.

plausible *(SYN.)* likely, practical, credible, feasible, possible, probable.
(ANT.) impracticable.

play *(SYN.)* entertainment, amusement, pastime, sport, game, fun, recreation, show.
(ANT.) work, labor, boredom.

plea *(SYN.)* invocation, request, appeal, entreaty, supplication, petition, suit.

plead *(SYN.)* beseech, defend, beg, appeal, ask, implore, argue, entreat.
(ANT.) deprecate, deny, refuse.

pleasant *(SYN.)* agreeable, welcome, suitable, charming, pleasing, amiable, gratifying, acceptable, pleasurable, enjoyable, nice.
(ANT.) offensive, disagreeable, obnoxious, unpleasant, horrid, sour, difficult, nasty.

please *(SYN.)* satisfy, suffice, fulfill, content, appease, gratify, satiate, compensate.
(ANT.) dissatisfy, annoy, tantalize, frustrate, displease.

pleasing *(SYN.)* luscious, melodious, sugary, delightful, agreeable, pleasant.
(ANT.) repulsive, sour, acrid, bitter, offensive, irritating.

pleasure *(SYN.)* felicity, declight, amusement, enjoyment gratification.
(ANT.) suffering, pain, vexation, trouble, affliction, discomfort, torment.

pledge *(SYN.)* promise, statement, assertion, declaration, assurance, agreement.

plenty *(SYN.)* fruitfulness, bounty, fullness, abundance.
(ANT.) want, scarcity, need.

pliable *(SYN.)* elastic, supple, resilient, ductile.
(ANT.) rigid, unbending, brittle, stiff.

plight *(SYN.)* dilemma, situation, difficulty, condition, fix, scrape, state.
(ANT.) satisfaction, ease, calmness.

plot *(SYN.)* design, plan, scheme, cabal, conspiracy, chart, machination.

plotting *(SYN.)* cunning, scheming, objective, artfulness, contrivance, purpose.
(ANT.) accident, chance, result, candor.

ploy *(SYN.)* ruse, guile, antic, deception, hoax, subterfuge.
(ANT.) honesty, sincerity, openness, exposure, candor.

plump *(SYN.)* obese, portly, corpulent, pudgy, stout.
(ANT.) slim, thin, gaunt, lean, slender.

plunder *(SYN.)* ravage, strip, sack, rob, pillage, raid, loot.

pogrom *(SYN.)* massacre, carnage, slaughter, butchery.

poignant *(SYN.)* pitiable, touching, affecting, impressive, sad, tender, moving.

point *(SYN.)* direct, level, spot.

(ANT.) distract, misguide, deceive.

pointed *(SYN.)* keen, sharp, quick, acute, cutting.

(ANT.) shallow, stupid, bland.

poise *(SYN.)* composure, self-equilibrium, carriage, calmness, balance, self-control.

(ANT.) rage, turbulence, agitation, anger, excitement.

poison *(SYN.)* corrupt, sully, taint, infect, befoul, defile.

(ANT.) purify, disinfect.

polished *(SYN.)* glib, diplomatic, urbane, refined, sleek, suave, slick.

(ANT.) rough, blunt, bluff.

polite *(SYN.)* civil, refined, well-mannered, accomplished, courteous, genteel, urbane, well-bred, cultivated.

(ANT.) uncouth, impertinent, rude, boorish, uncivil.

pollute *(SYN.)* contaminate, poison, taint, sully, infect, befoul, defile, dirty.

(ANT.) purify, disinfect, clean.

pompous *(SYN.)* high, magnificent, stately, august, dignified, grandiose, noble.

(ANT.) lowly, undignified, humble, common, ordinary.

ponder *(SYN.)* examined, study, contemplate, investigate, meditate, muse, weigh, deliberate, consider.

ponderous *(SYN.)* burdensome, trying, gloomy, serious, sluggish, massive, heavy, cumbersome, grievous, grave, dull, weighty.

(ANT.) light, animated, brisk.

poor *(SYN.)* penniless, bad, deficient, destitute, inferior, shabby, wrong, scanty, unfavorable, impoverished.

(ANT.) wealthy, prosperous, rich, fortunate, good.

poppycock *(SYN.)* rubbish, babble, twaddle, nonsense.

popular *(SYN.)* favorite, general, common, familiar, well-liked, approved, accepted, celebrated, admired.

(ANT.) unpopular, restricted.

pornographic *(SYN.)* impure, dirty, filthy, lewd, smutty, offensive, disgusting.

(ANT.) refined, modest, pure.

portentous *(SYN.)* significant, critical, momentous.

(ANT.) trivial.

portion *(SYN.)* share, bit, parcel, part, piece, section, segment, allotment.

(ANT.) whole, bulk.

portly *(SYN.)* majestic, grand, impressive, dignified, stout, fat, heavy, obese.

(ANT.) slender, thin, slim.

portrait *(SYN.)* painting, representation, picture, likeness.

portray *(SYN.)* depict, picture, represent, sketch, describe, delineate, paint.

(ANT.) misrepresent, caricature, suggest.

pose *(SYN.)* model.

position *(SYN.)* caste, site, locality, situation, condition, standing, incumbency, office, bearing, posture, berth, place, job, pose, rank, attitude, location, place, spot, station, situation, occupation.

positive *(SYN.)* sure, definite, fixed, inevitable, undeniable, indubitable, assured, certain, unquestionable.

(ANT.) uncertain, doubtful, questionable, probably, unsure, dubious, confused, negative, adverse.

positively *(SYN.)* unquestionably, surely, certainly, absolutely.

possess *(SYN.)* own, obtain, control, have, seize, hold, occupy, affect, hold, control.

(ANT.) surrender, abandon, lose.

possessed *(SYN.)* entranced, obsessed, consumer, haunted, enchanted.

possession *(SYN.)* custody, ownership, occupancy.

possessions *(SYN.)* commodities, effects, goods, property, merchandise, wares, wealth, belongings, stock.

possible *(SYN.)* likely, practical, probable, feasible, plausible, credible.

(ANT.) visionary, impossible, improbable.

possibility *(SYN.)* opportunity, chance, contingency, occasion.

(ANT.) obstacle, disadvantage.

possible *(SYN.)* feasible, practical, practicable, doable.

possibly *(SYN.)* perhaps, maybe.

post *(SYN.)* position, job, berth, incumbency, situation, shaft, pole, fort, base.

postpone *(SYN.)* delay, stay, suspend, discontinue, defer, adjourn, interrupt.

(ANT.) persist, prolong, maintain, con-

tinue, proceed.

postulate *(SYN.)* principle, adage, saying, proverb, truism, byword, aphorism, axiom, maxim.

potency *(SYN.)* effectiveness, capability, skillfulness, efficiency, competency.

(ANT.) wastefulness, inability.

potent *(SYN.)* mighty, influential, convincing, effective.

(ANT.) feeble, weak, powerless.

potential *(SYN.)* likely, possible, dormant, hidden, latent.

pouch *(SYN.)* container, bag, sack.

pound *(SYN.)* buffet, beat, punch, strike, thrash, defeat, subdue, pulse, smite, belabor, knock, thump, overpower, palpitate, rout, vanquish.

(ANT.) fail, surrender, defend, shield.

pour *(SYN.)* flow.

pout *(SYN.)* brood, sulk, mope.

poverty *(SYN.)* necessity, need, want, destitution, indigence, distress.

(ANT.) plenty, abundance, wealth, riches, affluence, richness, comfort.

power *(SYN.)* potency, might, authority, control, predominance, capability, faculty, validity, force, vigor, command, influence, talent, ability, dominion.

(ANT.) incapacity, fatigue, weakness, disablement, impotence, ineptitude.

powerful *(SYN.)* firm, strong, concentrated, enduring, forcible, robust, sturdy, tough, athletic, forceful, hale, impregnable, hardy, mighty, potent.

(ANT.) feeble, insipid, brittle, delicate, fragile, weak, ineffectual, powerless.

practical *(SYN.)* sensible, wise, prudent, reasonable, sagacious, sober, sound, workable, attainable.

(ANT.) stupid, unaware, impalpable, imperceptible, absurd, impractical.

practically *(SYN.)* almost, nearly.

practice *(SYN.)* exercise, habit, custom, manner, wont, usage, drill, tradition, performance, action, repetition.

(ANT.) inexperience, theory, disuse, idleness, speculation.

practiced *(SYN.)* able, expert, skilled.

(ANT.) inept.

prairie *(SYN.)* plain, grassland.

praise *(SYN.)* applaud, compliment, extol, laud, glorify, commend, acclaim, eulogize, flatter, admire, celebrate, commendation, approval.

(ANT.) criticize, censure, reprove, condemn, disparage, disapprove, criticism.

pray *(SYN.)* supplicate, importune, beseech, beg.

prayer *(SYN.)* plea, suit, appeal, invocation, supplication, petition, entreaty.

preach *(SYN.)* teach, urge, lecture.

preamble *(SYN.)* overture, prologue, beginning, introduction, prelude, start, foreword, preface.

(ANT.) end, finale, completion, conclusion, epilogue.

precarious *(SYN.)* dangerous, perilous, threatening, menacing, critical, risky, unsafe, hazardous.

(ANT.) secure, firm, protected, safe.

precaution *(SYN.)* foresight, forethought, care.

precedence *(SYN.)* preference, priority.

precedent *(SYN.)* model, example.

precept *(SYN.)* doctrine, tenet, belief, creed, teaching, dogma.

(ANT.) practice, conduct, performance.

precious *(SYN.)* dear, useful, valuable, costly, esteemed, profitable, expensive, priceless, dear.

(ANT.) poor, worthless, mean, trashy.

precipice *(SYN.)* bluff, cliff.

precipitate *(SYN.)* swift, hasty, sudden.

precipitous *(SYN.)* unannounced, sudden, harsh, rough, unexpected, sharp, abrupt, hasty, craggy, steep.

(ANT.) expected, anticipated, gradual.

precise *(SYN.)* strict, exact, formal, rigid, definite, unequivocal, prim, ceremonious, distinct, accurate, correct.

(ANT.) loose, easy, vague, informal, careless, erroneous.

precisely *(SYN.)* specifically, exactly.

precision *(SYN.)* correction, accuracy.

preclude *(SYN.)* hinder, prevent, obstruct, forestall, obviate, thwart.

(ANT.) permit, aid, encourage, promote.

preclusion *(SYN.)* omission, exception.

(ANT.) standard, rule, inclusion.

predicament *(SYN.)* dilemma, plight, situation, condition, fix, difficulty.

(ANT.) satisfaction, comfort, calmness.

predict *(SYN.)* forecast, foretell.

prediction *(SYN.)* forecast, prophecy.

predilection *(SYN.)* attachment, inclination, affection, bent, desire, penchant, disposition, preference.
(ANT.) repugnance, aversion, apathy, distaste, nonchalance.

predominant *(SYN.)* highest, paramount, cardinal, foremost, main, first, leading, supreme, principal, essential, prevalent, dominant, prevailing.
(ANT.) subsidiary, auxiliary, supplemental, minor, subordinate.

predominate *(SYN.)* prevail, outweigh.

preface *(SYN.)* foreword, introduction, preliminary, prelude, prologue.

prefer *(SYN.)* select, favor, elect, fancy.

preference *(SYN.)* election, choice, selection, alternative, option.

prejudice *(SYN.)* bias, favoritism, unfairness, partiality.

prejudiced *(SYN.)* fanatical, narrow-minded, dogmatic, bigoted, intolerant.
(ANT.) radical, liberal, progressive.

preliminary *(SYN.)* introductory, preparatory, prelude, preface.

premature *(SYN.)* early, untimely, unexpected.
(ANT.) timely.

premeditated *(SYN.)* intended, voluntary, contemplated, designed, intentional, willful, deliberate, studied.
(ANT.) fortuitous, accidental.

premeditation *(SYN.)* intention, deliberation, forethought, forecast.
(ANT.) hazard, accident, impromptu, extemporization.

premise *(SYN.)* basis, presupposition, assumption, postulate, principle.
(ANT.) superstructure, derivative, trimming, implication.

preoccupied *(SYN.)* abstracted, distracted, absorbed, meditative, inattentive, absent, absent-minded.
(ANT.) attentive, alert, conscious, present, attending, watchful.

prepare *(SYN.)* contrive, furnish, ready, predispose, condition, fit, arrange, plan, qualify, make ready, get ready.

preposterous *(SYN.)* foolish, nonsensical, silly, contradictory, unreasonable, absurd, inconsistent, irrational.
(ANT.) sensible, rational, consistent, sound, reasonable.

prerequisite *(SYN.)* essential, requirement, necessity, demand.

prerogative *(SYN.)* grant, right, license, authority, privilege.
(ANT.) violation, encroachment, wrong, injustice.

prescribe *(SYN.)* order, direct, designate.

presence *(SYN.)* nearness, attendance, closeness, vicinity, appearance, bearing.

present *(SYN.)* donation, gift, today, now, existing, current, largess, donate, acquaint, introduce, being, give, gratuity, boon, grant.
(ANT.) reject, accept, retain, receive.

presentable *(SYN.)* polite, well-bred, respectable, well-mannered.

presently *(SYN.)* shortly, soon, directly, immediately.

preserve *(SYN.)* protect, save, conserve, maintain, secure, rescue, uphold, spare, keep, can, safeguard, defend, rescue.
(ANT.) impair, abolish, destroy, abandon, squander, injure.

preside *(SYN.)* officiate, direct, administrate.

press *SYN.)* impel, shove, urge, hasten, push, compress, squeeze, hug, crowd, propel, force, drive, embrace, smooth, iron, insist on, pressure, promote jostle.
(ANT.) oppose, drag, retreat, ignore.

pressing *(SYN.)* impelling, insistent, necessary, urgent, compelling imperative, instant, serious, important, cogent, exigent, importunate.
(ANT.) unimportant, trifling, insignificant, petty, trivial.

pressure *(SYN.)* force, influence, stress, press, compulsion, urgency, constraint.
(ANT.) relaxation, leniency, ease.

prestige *(SYN.)* importance, reputation, weight, influence, renown, fame.

presume *(SYN.)* guess, speculate, surmise, imagine, conjecture, apprehend, believe, think, assume, suppose, deduce.
(ANT.) prove, ascertain, demonstrate, know, conclude.

presumption *(SYN.)* boldness, impertinence, insolence, rudeness, assurance, effrontery, impudence, assumption, audacity, supposition, sauciness.
(ANT.) politeness, truckling, diffidence.

presumptuous *(SYN.)* bold, impertinent, fresh, imprudent, rude, forward.

presupposition *(SYN.)* basis, principle, premise, assumption, postulate.
(ANT.) superstructure, derivative.

pretend *(SYN.)* feign, stimulate, act, profess, make believe, imagine, sham.
(ANT.) expose, reveal, display, exhibit.

pretense *(SYN.)* mask, pretext, show, affection, disguise, garb, semblance, simulation, fabrication, lie, excuse, falsification, deceit, subterfuge.
(ANT.) sincerity, actuality, truth, fact, reality.

pretentious *(SYN.)* gaudy, ostentatious.
(ANT.) simple, humble.

pretty *(SYN.)* charming, handsome, lovely, beauteous, fair, comely, attractive, beautiful, elegant.
(ANT.) repulsive, foul, unsightly, homely, plain, hideous.

prevail *(SYN.)* win, succeed, predominate, triumph.
(ANT.) yield, lose.

prevailing *(SYN.)* common, current, general, steady, regular, universal.

prevalent *(SYN.)* ordinary, usual, common, general, familiar, popular, prevailing, widespread, universal, frequent.
(ANT.) odd, scarce, extraordinary.

prevent *(SYN.)* impede, preclude, forestall, stop, block, check, halt, interrupt, deter, slow, obviate, hinder, obstruct.
(ANT.) expedite, help, allow, abet, aid, permit, encourage, promote.

previous *(SYN.)* former, anterior, preceding, prior, antecedent, earlier.
(ANT.) subsequent, following, consequent, succeeding, later.

prey *(SYN.)* raid, seize, victimize.

price *(SYN.)* worth, cost, expense, charge, value.

pride *(SYN.)* self-respect, vanity, glory, superciliousness, haughtiness, conceit, arrogance, self-importance, pretension, egotism, satisfaction, fulfillment, enjoyment, self-esteem.
(ANT.) modesty, shame, humbleness, lowliness, meekness, humility.

prim *(SYN.)* formal, puritanical, priggish, prudish.

primarily *(SYN.)* mainly, chiefly, firstly, essentially, originally.
(ANT.) secondarily.

primary *(SYN.)* first, principal, primeval, pristine, beginning, original, initial, fundamental, elementary, chief, foremost, earliest, main, prime.
(ANT.) subordinate, last, secondary, least, hindmost, latest.

prime *(SYN.)* first, primary, chief, excellent, best, superior, ready.

primeval *(SYN.)* fresh, primary, novel, inventive, creative, primordial, original, first, new, initial.
(ANT.) trite, modern, subsequent, banal, later, terminal, derivative.

primitive *(SYN.)* antiquated, early, primeval, prehistoric, uncivilized, uncultured, simple, pristine, old, aboriginal, unsophisticated, rude, rough, primary.
(ANT.) sophisticated, modish, civilized, cultured, cultivated, late.

primordial *(SYN.)* novel, creative, original, first, initial, new, primary.
(ANT.) trite, terminal, banal, modern, derivative, subsequent, later.

principal *(SYN.)* first, leading, main, supreme, predominant, chief, foremost, highest, prime, primary, leader, headmaster, paramount, essential, cardinal.
(ANT.) supplemental, secondary, auxiliary, accessory, minor, subordinate.

principle *(SYN.)* law, method, axiom, rule, propriety, regulation, maxim, formula, order, statute.
(ANT.) exception, hazard, chance.

print *(SYN.)* issue, reprint, publish, letter, sign, fingerprint, mark, picture, lithograph, engraving, etching.

prior *(SYN.)* previous, antecedent, sooner, earlier, preceding, former.
(ANT.) succeeding, following, later, consequent, subsequent.

prison *(SYN.)* brig, jail, stockade.

pristine *(SYN.)* primordial, creative, first, original, fresh, inventive, novel, primary, initial.
(ANT.) trite, terminal, derivative, modern, banal, subsequent, plagiarized.

private *(SYN.)* concealed, hidden, secret, clandestine, unknown, personal, surreptitious, covert, individual, special.
(ANT.) exposed, known, closed, general,

public, conspicuous, disclosed, obvious.

privation *(SYN.)* necessity, penury, destitution, need, poverty, want.

(ANT.) wealth, affluence, abundance, plenty, riches.

privilege *(SYN.)* liberty, right, advantage, immunity, freedom, license, favor.

(ANT.) restriction, inhibition, prohibition, disallowance.

prize *(SYN.)* compensation, bonus, award, premium, remuneration, reward, bounty, esteem, value, rate, recompense, requital.

(ANT.) charge, punishment, wages, earnings, assessment.

probable *(SYN.)* presumable, likely.

probe *(SYN.)* stretch, reach, investigate, examine, examination, scrutiny, scrutinize, inquire, explore, inquiry, investigation, extend.

(ANT.) miss, short.

problem *(SYN.)* dilemma, question, predicament, riddle, difficulty, puzzle.

procedure *(SYN.)* process, way, fashion, form, mode, conduct, practice, manner, habit, system, operation, management.

proceed *(SYN.)* progress, continue, issue, result, spring, thrive, improve, advance, emanate, rise.

(ANT.) retard, withhold, withdraw, hinder, retreat, oppose.

proceeding *(SYN.)* occurrence, business, affair, deal, negotiation, transaction.

proceedings *(SYN.)* record, document.

proceeds *(SYN.)* result, produce, income, reward, intake, fruit, profit, store, yield, product, return, harvest, crop.

process *(SYN.)* method, course, system.

procession *(SYN.)* cortege, parade, sequence, train, cavalcade, succession.

proclaim *(SYN.)* declare, assert, make known, promulgate, state, assert, broadcast, express, announce, aver, advertise, tell, publish, profess.

proclamation *(SYN.)* declaration, announcement, promulgation.

procrastinate *(SYN.)* waver, vacillate, defer, hesitate, delay, postpone.

procreate *(SYN.)* generate, produce, beget, engender, originate, propagate, sire, create, father.

(ANT.) murder, destroy, abort, kill.

procure *(SYN.)* secure, gain, win, attain, obtain, get, acquire, earn.

(ANT.) lose.

prod *(SYN.)* goad, nudge, jab, push.

prodigious *(SYN.)* astonishing, enormous, immense, monstrous, remarkable, marvelous, huge, amazing, stupendous, monumental.

(ANT.) insignificant, commonplace.

produce *(SYN.)* harvest, reaping, bear, result, originate, bring about, store, supply, make, create, crop, proceeds, bring forth, occasion, breed, generate, cause, exhibit, show, demonstrate, fabricate, hatch, display, manufacture, exhibit, give, yield.

(ANT.) conceal, reduce, destroy, consume, waste, hide.

product *(SYN.)* outcome, result, output, produce, goods, commodity, stock.

productive *(SYN.)* fertile, luxuriant, rich, bountiful, fruitful, creative, fecund, teeming, plenteous, prolific.

(ANT.) wasteful, unproductive, barren, impotent, useless, sterile.

profanation *(SYN.)* dishonor, insult, outrage, aspersion, defamation, invective, misuse, abuse, reviling, maltreatment, desecration, perversion.

(ANT.) plaudit, commendation, laudation, respect, approval.

profane *(SYN.)* deflower, violate, desecrate, pollute, dishonor, ravish.

profess *(SYN.)* declare, assert, make known, state, protest, announce, aver, express, broadcast, avow, tell.

(ANT.) suppress, conceal, withhold.

profession *(SYN.)* calling, occupation, vocation, employment.

(ANT.) hobby, avocation, pastime.

proffer *(SYN.)* extend, tender, volunteer, propose, advance.

(ANT.) reject, spurn, accept, retain.

proficient *(SYN.)* competent, adept, clever, able, cunning, practiced, skilled, versed, ingenious, accomplished.

(ANT.) untrained, inexpert, bungling, awkward, clumsy.

profit *(SYN.)* gain, service, advantage, return, earnings, emolument, improvement, benefit, better, improve.

(ANT.) waste, loss, detriment, debit, lose,

damage, ruin.

profitable *(SYN.)* beneficial, advantageous, helpful, wholesome, useful, gainful, favorable, beneficial, serviceable, salutary, productive, good.
(ANT.) harmful, destructive, injurious, deleterious, detrimental.

profligate *(SYN.)* corrupt, debased, tainted, unsound, vitiated, contaminated, crooked, depraved, impure.

profound *(SYN.)* deep, serious, knowing, wise, intelligent, knowledgeable, recondite, solemn, abstruse, penetrating.
(ANT.) trivial, slight, shallow.

profuse *(SYN.)* lavish, excessive, extravagant, improvident, luxuriant, prodigal, wasteful, exuberant, immoderate, plentiful.
(ANT.) meager, poor, economical, sparse, skimpy.

profusion *(SYN.)* immoderation, superabundance, surplus, extravagance, intemperance, superfluity.
(ANT.) lack, paucity, death, want, deficiency.

program *(SYN.)* record, schedule, plan, agenda, calendar.

progress *(SYN.)* advancement, betterment, advance, movement, improve, progression.
(ANT.) delay, regression, relapse, retrogression.

progression *(SYN.)* gradation, string, train, chain, arrangement, following.

prohibit *(SYN.)* hinder, forbid, disallow, obstruct, prevent.
(ANT.) help, tolerate, allow, sanction, encourage, permit.

project *(SYN.)* design, proposal, scheme, contrivance, throw, cast, device, plan.
(ANT.) production, accomplishment, performance.

prolong *(SYN.)* extend, increase, protract, draw, stretch, lengthen.
(ANT.) shorten.

promise *(SYN.)* assurance, guarantee, pledge, undertaking, agreement, bestowal.

promote *(SYN.)* advance, foster, encourage, assist.
(ANT.) obstruct, demote, hinder, impede.

prompt *(SYN.)* punctual, timely, exact,

arouse, evoke, occasion, induce, urge, ineffect, cite, suggest, hint. *(ANT.) laggardly, slow, tardy, dilatory.*

promptly *(SYN.)* immediately, instantly, straightway, directly.
(ANT.) later, sometime, here-after, distantly, shortly.

promulgate *(SYN.)* declare, known, protest, affirm, broadcast, profess, assert.
(ANT.) repress, conceal, withhold.

prone *(SYN.)* apt, inclined, disposed, likely.

pronounce *(SYN.)* proclaim, utter, announce, articulate.

proof *(SYN.)* evidence, verification, confirmation, experiment, demonstration.
(ANT.) fallacy, invalidity, failure.

propagate *(SYN.)* create, procreate, sire, beget, breed, father, originate, produce.
(ANT.) extinguish, kill, abort.

propel *(SYN.)* drive, push, transfer, actuate, induce.
(ANT.) stay, deter, halt, rest.

propensity *(SYN.)* leaning, proneness, trend, drift, aim, inclination, bias, proclivity.
(ANT.) disinclination, aversion.

proper *(SYN.)* correct, suitable, decent, peculiar, legitimate, right, conventional.

prophet *(SYN.)* fortuneteller, oracle, seer, soothsayer.

propitious *(SYN.)* lucky, opportune, advantageous, favorable, fortunate.

proportion *(SYN.)* steadiness, poise, composure, relation, balance, equilibrium.
(ANT.) unsteadiness, imbalance, fall.

proposal *(SYN.)* plan, proposition, tender, scheme, program, suggestion.
(ANT.) rejection, acceptance, denial.

propose *(SYN.)* offer, proffer, recommend, plan, mean, expect, move, design.
(ANT.) fulfill, perform, effect.

prosaic *(SYN.)* commonplace, common, everyday, ordinary, routine.
(ANT.) exciting, different, extraordinary.

prosper *(SYN.)* succeed, flourish, thrive.
(ANT.) miscarry, wane, miss.

prosperous *(SYN.)* rich, wealthy, affluent, well-to-do, sumptuous, well-off.
(ANT.) impoverished, indigent, beggarly, needy.

protect *(SYN.)* defend, preserve, save, keep, conserve.

(ANT.) impair, abandon, destroy, abolish, injure.

protuberance *(SYN.)* prominence, projection, bulge.

proud *(SYN.)* overbearing, arrogant, haughty, stately, vain, glorious.

(ANT.) humble, meek, ashamed, lowly.

prove *(SYN.)* manifest, verify, confirm, demonstrate, establish, show, affirm.

(ANT.) contradict, refute, disprove.

proverb *(SYN.)* maxim, saying, adage, saw, motto, apothegm.

provide *(SYN.)* supply, endow, afford, produce, yield, give.

(ANT.) strip, denude, divest, despoil.

provident *(SYN.)* saving, thrifty, economical, frugal.

(ANT.) wasteful, lavish, extravagant.

provoke *(SYN.)* excite, stimulate, agitate, arouse, incite, excite, irritate, annoy, anger.

(ANT.) quell, allay, pacify, calm, quiet.

proximate *(SYN.)* nigh, imminent, adjacent, neighboring, bordering, close.

(ANT.) removed, distant, far.

prudence *(SYN.)* watchfulness, care, heed, vigilance, judgment, wisdom.

(ANT.) rashness, recklessness, abandon, foolishness.

prying *(SYN.)* inquisitive, meddling, curious, inquiring, nosy, peering.

(ANT.) unconcerned, incurious, indifferent.

psyche *(SYN.)* judgment, reason, understanding, brain, intellect, mentality.

(ANT.) materiality, body.

psychosis *(SYN.)* derangement, insanity, madness, delirium, dementia, frenzy.

(ANT.) stability, rationality, sanity.

public *(SYN.)* common, civil, governmental, federal, unrestricted.

publish *(SYN.)* distribute, issue, declare, announce, reveal, proclaim, publicize.

pull *(SYN.)* attract, induce, prolong, draw, tow, drag, allure, entice, extract.

(ANT.) shorten, alienate, drive, propel.

pummel *(SYN.)* punish, correct, castigate, discipline, chastise, strike.

(ANT.) release, acquit, free, exonerate.

punctual *(SYN.)* timely, prompt, exact, ready, nice.

(ANT.) laggardly, tardy, dilatory, late.

punish *(SYN.)* correct, pummel, chasten, reprove, strike, castigate, chastise.

(ANT.) release, exonerate, reward, pardon, acquit, free.

puny *(SYN.)* feeble, impaired, exhausted, infirm, unimportant, weak, decrepit.

(ANT.) strong, forceful, lusty.

pupil *(SYN.)* student, undergraduate.

purchase *(SYN.)* get, procure, buy, shopping, acquire, obtain.

(ANT.) sell, dispose of, vend.

pure *(SYN.)* chaste, absolute, clean, immaculate, untainted, spotless, guiltless, modest, virgin, bare, unmixed, simple.

(ANT.) corrupt, mixed, defiled, foul, tainted, adulterated, polluted, tarnished.

purely *(SYN.)* entirely, completely.

purify *(SYN.)* cleanse, wash, clean, mop.

(ANT.) soil, dirty, sully, stain, pollute.

puritanical *(SYN.)* prim, stiff.

(ANT.) permissive.

purloin *(SYN.)* loot, plagiarize, steal, pilfer, burglarize, plunder, pillage, snitch, embezzle, swipe.

(ANT.) repay, return, refund, buy.

purpose *(SYN.)* intention, end, goal, aim, objective, application, use, drift, object, intent, design.

(ANT.) hazard, accident, fate.

pursue *(SYN.)* persist, track follow, hunt, hound, chase, trail.

(ANT.) evade, abandon, flee, elude.

pursuit *(SYN.)* hunt, chase.

push *(SYN.)* jostle, shove, urge, press, thrust, force, drive, crowd, hasten.

(ANT.) ignore, falter, halt, drag, oppose.

pushy *(SYN.)* impudent, abrupt, prominent, insolent, forward, brazen, conspicuous, bold, striking.

(ANT.) retiring, timid, cowardly, bashful.

put *(SYN.)* set, place, state, express, say, assign, attach, establish.

putrefy *(SYN.)* disintegrate, decay, rot, waste, spoil, decompose.

(ANT.) grow, increase, luxuriate.

puzzle *(SYN.)* mystery, mystify, confound, perplex, riddle, conundrum, confusion, question, bewilder, confuse.

(ANT.) key, solution, solve, explain, answer, resolution.

quack *(SYN.)* faker, fake, fraud, gaggle, clack, gabble, bluffer, cackle, dissembler, charlatan, impostor.

quackery *(SYN.)* charlatanism, deceit, make-believe, fakery, duplicity, dissimulation, pretense, fraudulence, sham. *(ANT.)* integrity, probity, veracity, sincerity, honesty.

quaff *(SYN.)* swig, swill, swallow, lap up, sip, drink, ingurgitate, guzzle, imbibe.

quagmire *(SYN.)* swamp, bog, fen, ooze, morass, slough, marsh, plight, predicament, dilemma, impasse, fix.

quail *(SYN.)* recoil, cower, flinch, blench, wince, falter, shrink, shake, hesitate. *(ANT.)* brave, resist, defy, withstand.

quaint *(SYN.)* odd, uncommon, old-fashioned, antique, antiquated, queer, unusual, curious, eccentric, peculiar. *(ANT.)* usual, normal, common, novel, ordinary, modern, current, familiar.

quake *(SYN.)* shake, tremble, shudder, quiver, pulsate, stagger, shiver, temblor, vibrate, quaver, throb, earth-quake.

qualification *(SYN.)* efficiency, adaptation, restriction, aptness, skill, ability, faculty, talent, power, aptitude, competence, capability, fitness, condition. *(ANT.)* unreadiness, incapacity, disability.

qualified *(SYN.)* clever, skillful, efficient, suitable, able, capable, fit, fitted, suited, bounded, limited, contingent, eligible, delimited, adept, circumscribed. *(ANT.)* deficient, inept, impotent, categorical, unlimited, unfitted, unfit, incapable, unsuitable, inadequate.

qualify *(SYN.)* fit, suit, befit, ready, prepare, empower, lessen, moderate, soften, capacitate, condition, adapt, label, designate, name, call, equip, train, restrict, restrict, limit, change. *(ANT.)* unfit, incapacitate, disable, disqualify, enlarge, reinforce, aggravate.

quality *(SYN.)* trait, feature, attribute, value, peculiarity, grade, caliber, character, distinction, rank, condition, status, characteristic, kind, nature, constitution, mark, type, property. *(ANT.)* nature, inferiority, mediocrity, triviality, indifference, inferior, shoddy, secondrate, being, substance, essence.

qualm *(SYN.)* doubt, uneasiness, anxiety, suspicion, skepticism, question, pang, compunction, twinge, regret, uncertainty, demur, fear, remorse, misgiving. *(ANT.)* security, comfort, confidence, easiness, invulnerability, firmness.

quandary *(SYN.)* predicament, perplexity, confusion, uncertainty, puzzle, plight, bewilderment, fix, difficulty, entanglement, impasse, doubt, dilemma. *(ANT.)* ease, relief, certainty, assurance.

quantity *(SYN.)* sum, measure, volume, content, aggregate, bulk, mass, portion, amount, number, multitude, extent. *(ANT.)* zero, nothing.

quarantine *(SYN.)* segregate, separate, confine, isolate, seclude.

quarrel *(SYN.)* contention, argument, affray, dispute, altercation, squabble, feud, difference, disagree, bicker, differ, spar, fight, bickering, tiff, argue, disagreement, spat. *(ANT.)* peace, friendliness, reconciliation, amity, agreement, sympathy, accord, concur, support, agree, unity, harmony.

quarrelsome *(SYN.)* testy, contentious, edgy, peevish, irritable, snappish, argumentative, cross, disputatious, cranky, belligerent, combative, disagreeable. *(ANT.)* genial, friendly, peaceful, easygoing, peaceable, tempered.

quarry *(SYN.)* prey, quest, game, victim, goal, aim, prize, objective.

quarter *(SYN.)* place, source, fount, well, origin, mainspring, ruth, mercy, pity, compassion, clemency, benevolence, forbearance. *(ANT.)* ruthlessness, brutality, cruelty, barbarity, harshness, ferocity.

quarters *(SYN.)* residence, rooms, lodgings, dwelling, flat, billets, chambers, accommodations.

quash *(SYN.)* void, annul, overthrow, nullify, suppress, cancel, quench, quell, repress, invalidate. *(ANT.)* reinforce, sustain, authorize, sanction, validate, incite.

quasi *(SYN.)* wouldbe, partial, synthetic, nominal, imitation, bogus, sham, counterfeit. *(ANT.)* certified, real, genuine, legitimate.

quaver *(SYN.)* tremble, shake, hesitate, trill, oscillate, waver, vibrate, shiver, quiver, falter, quake.

quay *(SYN.)* dock, wharf, pier, jetty, bank.

queasy *(SYN.)* sick, squeamish, nauseated, uneasy, restless, nauseous, uncomfortable.

(ANT.) untroubled, comfortable, easy, relaxed.

queen *(SYN.)* empress, diva, doyenne, goddess, star.

queer *(SYN.)* odd, quaint, curious, unusual, droll, strange, peculiar, extraordinary, singular, uncommon, eccentric, weird, funny, nutty, screwy, wacky, deviant.

(ANT.) familiar, usual, normal, commonplace, plain, patent, conventional, ordinary.

queerness *(SYN.)* oddity, oddness, freakishness, strangeness, singularity, outlandishness, anomaly, weirdness, aberration.

(ANT.) normality, familiarity, commonness, standardization.

quell *(SYN.)* subdue, calm, pacify, quiet, cool, hush, appease, lull, mollify, reduce, crush, smother, suppress, stifle, extinguish.

(ANT.) encourage, foment, arouse, foster, incite.

quench *(SYN.)* extinguish, stop, suppress, sate, allay, abate, stifle, slacken, put out, slake, satisfy.

(ANT.) set, light, begin, start, kindle.

querulous *(SYN.)* faultfinding, fretful, carping, critical, complaining, censorious, captious, petulant.

(ANT.) pleased, easygoing, contented, carefree.

query *(SYN.)* inquire, interrogate, demand, investigate, probe, examine, question, inquiry, ask.

(ANT.) answer.

quest *(SYN.)* investigation, interrogation, research, examination, search, question, exploration, seek, pursue, journey, hunt, pursuit, explore, query.

(ANT.) negligence, inactivity, disregard.

question *(SYN.)* interrogate, quiz, doubt, ask, pump, challenge, inquiry, uncer-

tainty, interview, suspect, inquire, dispute, demand, examine.

(ANT.) accept, solution, reply, assurance, rejoinder, state, answer, result, response, attest, avow, confidence, respond.

questionable *(SYN.)* uncertain, doubtful, dubious, implausible, debatable, hypothetical, unlikely.

(ANT.) obvious, assured, indubitable, proper, unimpeachable, seemly, conventional, sure, certain.

queue *(SYN.)* file, row, line, series, chain, tier, sequence.

quibble *(SYN.)* cavil, shift, evasion, equivocation, dodge, sophism, prevaricate, quiddity, palter.

quick *(SYN.)* rapid, touchy, shrewd, active, hasty, testy, nimble, irascible, discerning, fast, swift, precipitate, excitable, speedy, sharp, impatient, acute, abrupt, curt, brisk, clever, keen, lively.

(ANT.) inattentive, dull, gradual, patient, slow, unaware, unhurried, backward, deliberate, sluggish.

quicken *(SYN.)* expedite, forward, rush, hurry, accelerate, push, hasten, dispatch, facilitate, speed.

(ANT.) slow, impede, hinder, hamper, delay, kill, deaden, retard, block.

quickly *(SYN.)* soon, rapidly, fast, at once, promptly, presently, swiftly, hastily, fleety, headlong.

(ANT.) deliberately, slowly, later, gradually.

quick-witted *(SYN.)* astute, shrewd, alert, keen, penetrating, quick, knowing.

(ANT.) slow, dull, unintelligent, plodding.

quiescent *(SYN.)* latent, resting, silent, tranquil, undeveloped, still, quiet, dormant, secret, concealed, inactive.

(ANT.) visible, aroused, evident, active, patent, astir, manifest.

quiet *(SYN.)* meek, passive, hushed, peaceful, calm, patient, quiescent, motionless, tranquil, gentle, undisturbed.

(ANT.) disturbed, agitation, excitement, loud, disturbance, restless, noisy, boisterous, anxious, noise, agitated.

quietness *(SYN.)* tranquillity, repose, calm, silence, quietude, calmness, still-

ness, quietism, muteness, seclusion.
(ANT.) flurry, disturbance, fuss, turbulence, hubbub, agitation, uproar, tumult.
quintessence *(SYN.)* heart, soul, extract, essence, distillation, core.
(ANT.) contingency, adjunct, excrescence, nonessential.
quip *(SYN.)* jest, sally, wisecrack, witticism, joke, jibe, pleasantry.
quirk *(SYN.)* mannerism, idiosyncrasy, foible, peculiarity, oddity, quiddity.
quirky *(SYN.)* odd, weird, whimsical, peculiar, pixilated, erratic, kinky.
(ANT.) usual, normal, conventional, steady.
quisling *(SYN.)* collaborationist, traitor, betrayer.
(ANT.) partisan, loyalist.
quit *(SYN.)* leave, stop, desist, depart, abandon, resign, withdraw, refrain.
(ANT.) persevere, remain, stay, endure, persist, abide, continue.
quite *(SYN.)* somewhat, rather, completely, truly, wholly, really, entirely.
(ANT.) hardly, merely, barely, somewhat.
quitter *(SYN.)* shirker, dropout, defeatist, loser, malingerer.
quiver *(SYN.)* quake, shake, shudder, tremble, shiver.
quixotic *(SYN.)* unrealistic, romantic, visionary, impractical, idealistic, chimerical, lofty, fantastic, fey.
(ANT.) pragmatic, realistic, prosaic, practical.
quiz *(SYN.)* challenge, interrogate, inquire, pump, doubt, question, ask, dispute, test, query, examine.
(ANT.) reply, say, inform, respond, answer, state.
quizzical *(SYN.)* teasing, coy, mocking, derisive, insolent, arch, bantering.
(ANT.) respectful, obsequious, normal, everyday, usual, serious, attentive.
quota *(SYN.)* share, portion, apportionment, ratio, proportion, allotment.
quotation *(SYN.)* quote, selection, excerpt, repetition, cutting, reference.
quote *(SYN.)* refer to, recite, paraphrase, adduce, repeat, illustrate, cite, echo.
(ANT.) retort, misquote, contradict, refute.

rabble *(SYN.)* throng, mob, crowd.
race *(SYN.)* meet, run, clan, stock, lineage, strain, match, hurry, speed.
(ANT.) linger, dawdle, dwell.
racket *(SYN.)* sound, cry, babel, noise, uproar, hubbub, clamor, fuss, disturbance, din, tumult, fracas.
(ANT.) stillness, hush, silence, quiet, tranquillity, peace.
racy *(SYN.)* interesting, vigorous, lively, spirited, animated, entertaining.
radiance *(SYN.)* luster, brilliancy, brightness, splendor, effulgence, glowing.
(ANT.) gloom, darkness, obscurity.
radiate *(SYN.)* spread, emit, shine, gleam, illuminate.
raft *(SYN.)* pontoon, platform, float.
ragamuffin *(SYN.)* tatterdemalion, wretch, beggar, vagabond, mendicant.
rage *(SYN.)* passion, ire, exasperation, fashion, fad, rant, storm, fume, overflow.
(ANT.) peace, forbearance, conciliation, patience.
raging *(SYN.)* raving, severe, passionate, boisterous, violent, fierce, wild, passionate, acute, intense, powerful.
(ANT.) feeble, soft, calm, quiet.
ragged *(SYN.)* tattered, torn, worn, shredded, seedy, threadbare, shabby.
rain *(SYN.)* shower, drizzle, rainstorm, sprinkle, deluge, downpour.
raise *(SYN.)* grow, muster, awake, rouse, excite, enlarge, increase, rise, breed, exalt, lift.
(ANT.) destroy, decrease, lessen, cut, depreciate, lower, abase, debase, drop, demolish, level.
rally *(SYN.)* muster, convoke, summon, convene, convention, assemblage.
ramble *(SYN.)* err, amble, walk, deviate, stroll, digress.
(ANT.) stop, linger, stay, halt.
rambunctious *(SYN.)* stubborn, defiant, unruly, aggressive, contrary.
rampage *(SYN.)* tumult, outbreak, uproar, rage, frenzy, ebullition, storm.
rampant *(SYN.)* excessive, flagrant, boisterous.
(ANT.) bland, calm, mild.
ramshackle *(SYN.)* rickety, decrepit, flimsy, dilapidated, shaky.

rancid *(SYN.)* spoiled, rank, tainted, sour, musty, putrid, rotten, purtrescent.
(ANT.) pure, fresh, wholesome, fragrant.

rancor *(SYN.)* spite, grudge, malice, animosity, malevolence, hostility.
(ANT.) kindness, toleration, affection.

random *(SYN.)* haphazard, chance, unscheduled, unplanned, casual.
(ANT.) intentional, specific, particular.

range *(SYN.)* expanse, extent, limit, area, grassland, pasture, plain, change, wander, roam, travel, rove.

ransack *(SYN.)* pillage, loot, ravish, search.

ransom *(SYN.)* release, deliverance, compensation, redeem.

rapacious *(SYN.)* greedy, wolfish, avaricious, ravenous, grasping, predatory.

rapid *(SYN.)* speedy, quick, swift, fast.
(ANT.) deliberate, halting, sluggish, slow.

rapine *(SYN.)* destruction, pillage, robbery, marauding.

rapport *(SYN.)* harmony, fellowship, agreement, mutuality, accord, empathy.

rapture *(SYN.)* joy, gladness, ecstasy, bliss, transport, exultation, delight, happiness, enchantment, ravishment.
(ANT.) woe, misery, wretch, depression.

rare *(SYN.)* unique, strange, precious, uncommon, infrequent, choice, singular, occasional, unusual, fine.
(ANT.) worthless, common, commonplace, usual, everyday, customary.

rarely *(SYN.)* scarcely, hardly infrequently, occasionally.
(ANT.) usually, continually, often.

rascal *(SYN.)* scoundrel, villain, trickster, rogue, scamp, swindler, imp, prankster.

rash *(SYN.)* quick, careless, passionate, thoughtless, hotheaded, reckless, foolhardy, eruption.
(ANT.) thoughtful, considered, prudent, reasoning, calculating, careful.

raspy *(SYN.)* gruff, harsh, dissonant, grinding, hoarse, grating, strident.

ratify *(SYN.)* validate, certify, endorse, uphold.

rating *(SYN.)* assessment, position, status, classification.

ration *(SYN.)* portion, allowance, distribute, measure, allotment, share.

rationality *(SYN.)* cause, aim, understanding, ground, argument, mind, sense.

raucous *(SYN.)* raspy, harsh, grating, hoarse, discordant.
(ANT.) dulcet, pleasant, sweet.

ravage *(SYN.)* ruin, despoil, strip, waste, destroy, pillage, plunder, sack, havoc.
(ANT.) conserve, save, accumulate.

ravine *(SYN.)* chasm, gorge, crevasse, canyon, abyss.

raw *(SYN.)* harsh, rough, coarse, unrefined, undone, crude, unpolished, natural.
(ANT.) finished, refined, processed.

raze *(SYN.)* ravage, wreck, destroy, flatten, annihilate, obliterate, demolish.
(ANT.) make, erect, construct, preserve, establish, save.

reach *(SYN.)* overtake, extent, distance, scope, range, extend, attain, stretch.
(ANT.) fail, miss.

reaction *(SYN.)* result, response, reception.

readable *(SYN.)* understandable, distinct, legible, plain, clear, comprehensible.
(ANT.) obliterated, illegible.

ready *(SYN.)* mature, ripe, arrange, prompt, prepared, completed, quick, mellow.
(ANT.) undeveloped, immature, green.

real *(SYN.)* true, actual, positive, authentic, genuine, veritable.
(ANT.) counterfeit, unreal, fictitious, false, sham, supposed.

realize *(SYN.)* discern, learn, perfect, actualize, understand, apprehend, know.
(ANT.) misunderstand, misapprehend.

really *(SYN.)* truly, actually, honestly, undoubtedly, positively, genuinely.
(ANT.) questionably, possibly, doubtfully.

realm *(SYN.)* land, domain, kingdom, sphere, department, estate, world.

reap *(SYN.)* gather, harvest, pick, acquire, garner.
(ANT.) plant, seed, sow, lose, squander.

rear *(SYN.)* posterior, raise, lift, train, nurture, rump, build, foster.

reason *(SYN.)* intelligence, objective, understanding, aim, judgment, common sense, sanity, gather, assume, sake.

reasonable *(SYN.)* prudent, rational, logical, sage, sound, moderate, intelligent, sensible, discreet.

(ANT.) unaware, imperceptible, insane, absurd, stupid, illogical, irrational.

rebel *(SYN.)* revolutionary, traitor, mutineer, mutiny, revolt, disobey.

rebellious *(SYN.)* unruly, forward, defiant, undutiful.

(ANT.) obedient, compliant, submissive.

rebuild *(SYN.)* restore, renew, refresh, reconstruct.

rebuke *(SYN.)* chide, scold, reproach, censure, upbraid, scolding, condemn.

(ANT.) praise, exonerate, absolve.

recall *(SYN.)* recollect, remembrance, withdraw, retract, remember, recollection, reminisce, mind, memory, remind.

(ANT.) forget, overlook, ignore.

receive *(SYN.)* entertain, acquire, admit, accept, shelter, greet, obtain, welcome.

(ANT.) reject, offer, give, bestow, discharge, impart.

recent *(SYN.)* novel, original, late, new, newfangled, fresh, modern, current.

(ANT.) old, antiquated, ancient.

recess *(SYN.)* hollow, opening, nook, cranny, dent, respite, rest, break, pause.

(ANT.) gather, convene.

recipe *(SYN.)* instructions, formula, prescriptions, procedure, method.

recital *(SYN.)* history, account, relation, chronicle, narrative, detail, narration.

(ANT.) distortion, confusion.

recite *(SYN.)* describe, narrate, declaim, rehearse, tell, mention, repeat, detail.

reckless *(SYN.)* thoughtless, inconsiderate, careless, imprudent, rash, indiscreet.

(ANT.) careful, nice, accurate.

reclaim *(SYN.)* reform, rescue, reinstate, regenerate.

recline *(SYN.)* stretch, sprawl, repose, rest, lounge, loll.

recluse *(SYN.)* hermit, eremite, loner, anchorite.

recognize *(SYN.)* remember, avow, own, know, admit, apprehend, recollect, recall.

(ANT.) disown, ignore, renounce.

recollection *(SYN.)* remembrance, retrospection, impression, recall.

(ANT.) forgetfulness, oblivion.

recommend *(SYN.)* hind, suggest, counsel, allude, praise, approve, intimate, advocate.

(ANT.) disapprove, declare, insist.

recommendation *(SYN.)* instruction, justice, trustworthiness, counsel, admonition, caution, integrity.

(ANT.) fraud, deceit, trickery, cheating.

reconcile *(SYN.)* meditate, unite, adapt, adjust, settle, reunite, appease.

reconsider *(SYN.)* ponder, reevaluate, mull over, reflect.

record *(SYN.)* enter, write, register, chronicle, history, account, document.

recount *(SYN.)* report, convey, narrate, tell, detail, recite, describe, repeat.

recover *(SYN.)* regain, redeem, recapture, retrieve, mend, heal.

(ANT.) debilitate, succumb, worsen.

recreation *(SYN.)* entertainment, amusement, enjoyment, diversion, fun.

recruit *(SYN.)* trainee, beginner, volunteer, draftee, select, enlist, novice.

recuperate *(SYN.)* regain, retrieve, cure, recapture, revive, recover, repossess.

(ANT.) sicken, weaken, lose, forfeit.

redeem *(SYN.)* claim, recover, repossess, regain, reclaim, cash in, retrieve.

reduce *(SYN.)* lessen, decrease, lower, downgrade, degrade, suppress, lower, abate, diminish.

(ANT.) enlarge, swell, raise, elevate, revive, increase.

reduction *(SYN.)* shortening, abridgment, abbreviation.

(ANT.) amplification, extension.

reek *(SYN.)* odor, stench, stink, smell.

refer *(SYN.)* recommend, direct, commend, regard, concern, mention.

referee *(SYN.)* judge, arbitrator, umpire, arbiter, moderator, mediator.

reference *(SYN.)* allusion, direction, mention, concern, respect, referral.

refine *(SYN.)* purify, clarify.

(ANT.) pollute, debase, muddy, downgrade.

refined *(SYN.)* purified, cultured, cultivated, courteous.

(ANT.) rude, coarse, crude, vulgar.

refinement *(SYN.)* culture, enlightenment, education.

(ANT.) vulgarity, ignorance, boorishness.

reflect *(SYN.)* muse, mirror, deliberate,

cogitate, think, reproduce, ponder, consider, reason, meditate.

reflection *(SYN.)* warning, conception, intelligence, appearance, likeness, image, cogitation, notification.

reform *(SYN.)* right, improve, correction, change, amend.
(ANT.) spoil, damage, aggravate, vitiate.

refuge *(SYN.)* safety, retreat, shelter, asylum, sanctuary.
(ANT.) peril, exposure, jeopardy, danger.

refuse *(SYN.)* spurn, rebuff, decline, reject, trash, rubbish, withhold, disallow, waste, garbage, deny.
(ANT.) allow, accept, welcome, grant.

refute *(SYN.)* rebut, disprove, confute, falsify, controvert.
(ANT.) prove, confirm, accept, establish.

regain *(SYN.)* redeem, retrieve, recover, repossess.
(ANT.) lose.

regalement *(SYN.)* feast, dinner, celebration.

regard *(SYN.)* estimate, value, honor, affection, notice, care, consideration, consider, relation, respect, attend, thought, reference, care, concern, liking.
(ANT.) neglect, disgust, antipathy.

regenerate *(SYN.)* improve, reconstruct, remedy, reestablish, rebuild.

regimented *(SYN.)* ordered, directed controlled, orderly, rigid, disciplined.
(ANT.) loose, free, unstructured.

region *(SYN.)* belt, place, spot, territory, climate, area, zone, locality, station.

register *(SYN.)* catalog, record, book, list, roll, enter, roster, chronicle.

regret *(SYN.)* sorrow, qualm, lament, grief, compunction, misgiving, remorse.
(ANT.) obduracy, complacency.

regular *(SYN.)* steady, orderly, natural, normal, customary, methodical, symmetrical.
(ANT.) odd, exceptional, unusual, irregular, abnormal.

regulate *(SYN.)* control, manage, govern, direct, legislate, set, adjust, systematize.

rehabilitate *(SYN.)* renew, restore, rebuild, reestablish, repair, reconstruct.

rehearse *(SYN.)* repeat, practice, train, learn, coach, prepare, perfect, direct.

reimburse *(SYN.)* recompense, remunerate, compensate, remit.

reinforce *(SYN.)* brace, strengthen, fortify, intensify.

reiterate *(SYN.)* reproduce, recapitulate, duplicate, repeat, rephrase.

reject *(SYN.)* spurn, rebuff, decline, renounce, expel, discard, withhold.
(ANT.) endorse, grant, welcome, accept.

rejoice *(SYN.)* celebrate, delight, enjoy, revel, exhilarate, elate.

relapse *(SYN.)* worsen, deteriorate, regress, weaken, fade, worsen, sink, fail.
(ANT.) strengthen, progress, advance, get well.

relate *(SYN.)* refer, beat, report, describe, tell, correlate, narrate, recount, compare, connect.

relationship *(SYN.)* link, tie, bond, affinity, conjunction.
(ANT.) separation, disunion.

relative *(SYN.)* dependent, proportional, about, pertinent, regarding.

relax *(SYN.)* slacken, loosen, repose, rest, recline.
(ANT.) increase, tighten, intensify.

relaxation *(SYN.)* comfort, recess, breather, loafing.

release *(SYN.)* liberate, emancipate, relinquish, proclaim, publish, liberation, announce, deliver, free.
(ANT.) restrict, imprison, subjugate.

relegate *(SYN.)* entrust, authorize, remand, refer.

relent *(SYN.)* cede, yield, surrender, give, relax, abdicate.
(ANT.) strive, assert, struggle.

relentless *(SYN.)* eternal, dogged, ceaseless, incessant, persistent, determined.

relevant *(SYN.)* related, material, apt, applicable, fit, relating, germane.
(ANT.) foreign, alien, unrelated.

reliable *(SYN.)* trusty, tried, certain, secure, trustworthy.
(ANT.) unreliable, eccentric, questionable, erratic.

reliance *(SYN.)* faith, confidence, trust.
(ANT.) mistrust, doubt, skepticism.

relic *(SYN.)* remains, fossil, throwback, heirloom, souvenir, keepsake.

relief *(SYN.)* help, aid, comfort, ease, backing, patronage, alms, support.
(ANT.) hostility, defiance, antagonism,

resistance.

relieve (SYN.) diminish, soothe, calm, abate, pacify, lighten, comfort, alleviate. (ANT.) disturb, irritate, agitate, trouble, aggravate.

religion (SYN.) tenet, belief, dogma, faith, creed.

religious (SYN.) godly, reverent, faithful, devout, zeal, pious, divine, holy, devoted, sacred, theological. (ANT.) profane, irreligious, skeptical, impious, lax.

religiousness (SYN.) love, zeal, affection, devoutness, fidelity, ardor. (ANT.) indifference, apathy.

relinquish (SYN.) capitulate, submit, yield, abandon, cede, sacrifice, disclaim. (ANT.) overcome, conquer, rout, resist.

reluctance (SYN.) disgust, hatred, repulsion, abhorrence, distaste, repugnance. (ANT.) enthusiasm, affection, devotion.

reluctant (SYN.) slow, averse, hesitant, unwilling, loath, disinclined, balky. (ANT.) ready, eager, willing, disposed.

remain (SYN.) survive, rest, stay, abide, halt, endure, dwell, tarry, continue. (ANT.) finish, leave, terminate, dissipate.

remainder (SYN.) leftover, residue, rest, surplus, balance, excess.

remark (SYN.) comment, note, observe, observation, annotation, declaration.

remedy (SYN.) redress, help, cure, relief, medicine, restorative, rectify, alleviate, medication, correct.

remember (SYN.) recollect, reminisce, recall, memorize, mind, retain, remind. (ANT.) forget, overlook.

remembrance (SYN.) monument, memory, recollection, souvenir, retrospection.

remiss (SYN.) delinquent, lax, careless, negligent, oblivious, forgetful, absent-minded, sloppy.

remit (SYN.) send, pay, forward, forgive, pardon, overlook, excuse, reimburse.

remnant (SYN.) remains, remainder, rest, residue, trace, relic.

remonstrate (SYN.) grouch, protest, complain, grumble, murmur, repine. (ANT.) rejoice, applaud, praise.

remorse (SYN.) sorrow, compunction, repentance.

(ANT.) obduracy, complacency.

remote (SYN.) inconsiderable, removed, slight, far, unlikely, distant, inaccessible, unreachable, isolated. (ANT.) visible, nearby, current, close.

remove (SYN.) transport, eject, move, vacate, withdraw, dislodge, transfer, murder, kill, oust, extract. (ANT.) insert, retain, leave, stay, keep.

remuneration (SYN.) wages, payment, pay, salary, compensation, reimbursement.

render (SYN.) become, make, perform, do, offer, present, give, submit.

renegade (SYN.) defector, insurgent, dissenter, rebel, maverick, betrayer.

renew (SYN.) restore, renovate, overhaul, revise, modernize, reshape, redo.

renounce (SYN.) resign, disown, revoke, abandon, quit, retract, forgo, leave, forsake, abdicate, reject. (ANT.) assert, uphold, recognize.

renovate (SYN.) restore, rehabilitate, rebuild, refresh, renew, overhaul.

renowned (SYN.) noted, famous, distinguished, wellknown, celebrated. (ANT.) unknown, infamous, hidden, obscure.

rent (SYN.) payment, rental, lease, hire.

repair (SYN.) rebuilding, mend, renew, tinker, correct, patch, restore, adjust, amend, rehabilitation. (ANT.) harm, break.

repeal (SYN.) end, cancel, nullify, annul, quash, abolish, cancellation, rescind, abolition, abrogate.

repeat (SYN.) reiterate, restate, redo, rehearse, quote, reproduce.

repellent (SYN.) sickening, offensive, disgusting, nauseating, obnoxious.

repentance (SYN.) penitence, remorse, sorrow, compunction, qualm, grief. (ANT.) obduracy, complacency.

repentant (SYN.) regretful, sorrowful, contrite, sorry. (ANT.) remorseless, obdurate.

repetitious (SYN.) repeated, monotonous, boring.

repine (SYN.) protest, lament, complain, whine, regret, grouch, grumble. (ANT.) rejoice, applaud, praise.

replacement (SYN.) understudy, proxy,

alternate, substitute, replica, surrogate.

reply *(SYN.)* retort, rejoinder, answer, retaliate, respond, confirmation.

(ANT.) summoning, inquiry.

report *(SYN.)* declare, herald, publish, announce, summary, publish, advertise.

(ANT.) suppress, conceal.

represent *(SYN.)* picture, draw, delineate, portray, depict, denote.

(ANT.) misrepresent, caricature.

representative *(SYN.)* delegate, agent, substitute.

repress *(SYN.)* limit, stop, check, bridle, curb, restrain, constrain, suppress.

(ANT.) loosen, aid, incite, liberate.

reproach *(SYN.)* defamation, dishonor, insult, profanation, abuse, disparagement, misuse, reviling.

(ANT.) respect, laudation.

reproduction *(SYN.)* replica, copy, exemplar, transcript.

repugnance *(SYN.)* disgust, hatred, reluctance, abhorrence, aversion, loathing.

(ANT.) devotion, affection, enthusiasm, attachment.

repulsive *(SYN.)* repellent, ugly, homely, deformed, horrid, offensive, plain.

(ANT.) fair, pretty, attractive.

reputation *(SYN.)* class, nature, standing, name, fame, character, distinction.

repute *(SYN.)* class, nature, reputation, disposition.

require *(SYN.)* exact, need, lack, claim, demand, want.

requisite *(SYN.)* vital, necessary, basic, fundamental, indispensable, essential.

(ANT.) casual, nonessential, accidental.

rescind *(SYN.)* annul, quash, revoke, abolish, invalidate, abrogate, withdraw.

rescue *(SYN.)* liberate, ransom, release, deliver, deliverance, liberation.

research *(SYN.)* exploration, interrogation, query, examination, study.

(ANT.) inattention, disregard, negligence.

resemblance *(SYN.)* parity, similitude, analogy, likeness, correspondence.

(ANT.) distinction, difference.

resentment *(SYN.)* displeasure, bitterness, indignation, rancor, outrage, hostility.

(ANT.) complacency, understanding, good will.

reservation *(SYN.)* skepticism, restriction, objection, limitation, doubt.

reserve *(SYN.)* fund, hold, save, stock, maintain.

(ANT.) waste, squander.

residence *(SYN.)* home, dwelling, stay, seat, abode, quarters, domicile.

residue *(SYN.)* balance, remainder, rest, ashes, remnants, dregs, leftovers, ends.

resign *(SYN.)* vacate, withdraw, leave, surrender, quit.

resigned *(SYN.)* forbearing, accepting, composed, uncomplaining.

(ANT.) turbulent, chafing.

resist *(SYN.)* defy, attack, withstand, hinder, confront.

(ANT.) relent, allow, yield.

resolute *(SYN.)* firm, resolved, set, determined, decided.

(ANT.) irresolute, wavering, vacillating.

resolve *(SYN.)* determination, decide, persistence, determine, confirm, decision.

(ANT.) integrate, indecision, inconstancy.

resourceful *(SYN.)* inventive, imaginative, skillful.

respect *(SYN.)* honor, approval, revere, heed, value, admiration, reverence.

(ANT.) disrespect, neglect, abuse, scorn, disregard.

respectable *(SYN.)* becoming, tolerable, decent.

(ANT.) unsavory, vulgar, gross, disreputable.

response *(SYN.)* reply, acknowledgment, answer, retort, rejoinder.

(ANT.) summoning, inquiry.

responsibility *(SYN.)* duty, trustworthiness, trust, liability, commitment.

restitution *(SYN.)* recompense, satisfaction, refund, amends, retrieval.

restive *(SYN.)* balky, disobedient, fractious, impatient, unruly, fidgety.

restore *(SYN.)* repair, recover, rebuild, reestablish, renovate, return, renew, mend, reinstall, revive, rehabilitate.

restraint *(SYN.)* order, self-control, reserve, control, regulation, limitation.

(ANT.) freedom, liberty.

restrict *(SYN.)* fetter, restrain, confine, limit, engage, attach, connect, link, tie.

(ANT.) broaden, enlarge, loose, free.

result *(SYN.)* effect, issue, outcome, resolve, end, consequence, happen, determination, conclusion.

(ANT.) cause, beginning, origin.

resume *(SYN.)* restart, continue, recommence.

retain *(SYN.)* keep, hold, recall, remember, employ, hire, engage.

retard *(SYN.)* detain, slacken, defer, impede, hold back, delay, postpone.

(ANT.) accelerate, speed, hasten, rush.

retention *(SYN.)* reservation, acquisition, holding, tenacity, possession.

reticent *(SYN.)* reserved, subdued, quiet, shy, withdrawn, restrained, bashful.

(ANT.) outspoken, forward, opinionated.

retire *(SYN.)* resign, quit, abdicate, depart, vacate.

retiring *(SYN.)* timid, bashful, withdrawn, modest, quiet, reserved.

(ANT.) gregarious, assertive, bold.

retort *(SYN.)* reply, answer, response, respond, rejoin, rejoinder, retaliate.

(ANT.) summoning, inquiry.

retreat *(SYN.)* leave, depart, retire, withdraw, retirement, withdrawal, departure, shelter, refuge.

(ANT.) advanced.

retrench *(SYN.)* reduce, scrape, curtail.

retribution *(SYN.)* justice, vengeance, reprisal, punishment, comeuppance, vindictiveness, revenge, retaliation.

retrieve *(SYN.)* regain, recover, recapture, reclaim, salvage, recoup.

retrograde *(SYN.)* regressive, backward, declining, deteriorating, worsening.

(ANT.) onward, progression, advanced.

return *(SYN.)* restoration, replace, revert, recur, restore, retreat.

(ANT.) keep, take, retain.

reveal *(SYN.)* discover, publish, communicate, impart, uncover, tell, betray, divulge, disclose.

(ANT.) conceal, cover, obscure, hide.

revel *(SYN.)* rejoice, wallow, bask, enjoy, delight, savor, gloat, luxuriate, relish.

revelation *(SYN.)* hallucination, dream, phantoms, apparition, ghost, mirage, specter, daydream, suprise, shocker.

(ANT.) verity, reality.

revelry *(SYN.)* merriment, merrymaking, carousal, feasting, gala, festival.

revenge *(SYN.)* vindictiveness, reprisal, requital, vengeance, repayment, repay, retribution, reparation.

(ANT.) reconcile, forgive, pity.

revenue *(SYN.)* take, proceeds, income, profit, return.

revere *(SYN.)* admire, honor, worship, respect, venerate, adore.

(ANT.) ignore, despise.

reverence *(SYN.)* glory, worship, homage, admiration, dignity, renown, respect, esteem, veneration, adoration, honor.

(ANT.) dishonor, derision, reproach.

reverent *(SYN.)* honoring, respectful, adoring, pious, devout, humble.

(ANT.) impious, disrespectful.

reverse *(SYN.)* overthrow, unmake rescind, opposite, invert, contrary, rear, back, misfortune, defeat, catastrophe, upset, countermand, revoke.

(ANT.) vouch, stabilize, endorse, affirm.

revert *(SYN.)* revive, relapse, backslide, rebound, retreat, recur, go back.

(ANT.) keep, take, appropriate.

review *(SYN.)* reconsideration, examination, commentary, retrospection, restudy, journal, synopsis, study, reexamine, critique, inspection.

revile *(SYN.)* defame, malign, vilify, abuse, traduce, scandalize, smear.

(ANT.) honor, respect, cherish, protect.

revise *(SYN.)* change, alter, improve, correct, amend, update, rewrite, polish.

revision *(SYN.)* inspection, survey, retrospection, commentary, critique.

revival *(SYN.)* renaissance, exhumation, resurgence, renewal, revitalization.

revive *(SYN.)* refresh, lessen, decrease, renew, reduce, lower, abate, reanimate, diminish, rejuvenate, suppress.

(ANT.) increase, amplify, intensify.

revoke *(SYN.)* nullify, cancel, abolish, quash, rescind, abrogate.

revolt *(SYN.)* mutiny, rebel, disgust, revolution, uprising, rebellion, upheaval, takeover, insurgence, abolish.

revolting *(SYN.)* hateful, odious, abominable, foul, vile, detestable, loathsome, repugnant, sickening.

(ANT.) delightful, agreeable, pleasant.

revolution *(SYN.)* rebellion, mutiny, turn, coup, revolt, overthrow, cycle.

revolutionary *(SYN.)* insurgent, extremist, radical, subversive, mutinous.

revolve *(SYN.)* spin, wheel, rotate, circle, circle, turn, whirl, gyrate.

(ANT.) *travel, proceed, wander.*

revolver *(SYN.)* gun, pistol.

revulsion *(SYN.)* reversal, rebound, backlash, withdrawal, recoil.

reward *(SYN.)* bounty, premium, meed, award, compensation, prize, recompense, bonus, remuneration, wages.

(ANT.) *charge, wages, punishment.*

rewarding *(SYN.)* pleasing, productive, fruitful, profitable, favorable, satisfying, gratifying, fulfilling.

rhetoric *(SYN.)* style, verbosity, expressiveness, eloquence, flamboyance.

rhyme *(SYN.)* poem, verse, poetry, ballad, ditty, rhapsody, sonnet.

ribald *(SYN.)* suggestive, offcolor, indecent, spicy, rude, vulgar.

rich *(SYN.)* ample, costly, wealthy, fruitful, prolific, abundant, well-off, affluent, plentiful, fertile, bountiful, luxuriant.

(ANT.) *poor, unfruitful, beggarly, barren, impoverished, scarce, scanty, unproductive, destitute.*

rickety *(SYN.)* unsound, unsteady, flimsy, unstable, shaky, decrepit, wobbly.

(ANT.) *steady, solid, sturdy.*

ricochet *(SYN.)* recoil, backfire, rebound, bounce, deviate, boomerang.

rid *(SYN.)* free, clear, shed, delivered, eliminate, disperse, unload, purge.

riddle *(SYN.)* puzzle, mystery, conundrum, problem, question, enigma.

(ANT.) *key, solution, answer, resolution.*

ride *(SYN.)* tour, journey, motor, manage, drive, control, guide.

ridge *(SYN.)* hillock, backbone, spine, crest, mound, hump.

ridicule *(SYN.)* gibe, banter, mock, jeering, deride, tease, taunt, satire, mockery, derision.

(ANT.) *praise, respect.*

ridiculous *(SYN.)* silly, nonsensical, absurd, accurate, inconsistent, proper, laughable, apt, preposterous, foolish.

(ANT.) *sound, reasonable, consistent.*

rife *(SYN.)* widespread, abundant, innumerable, rampant, teeming.

rifle *(SYN.)* plunder, pillage, rummage, ransack, rob, steal.

rift *(SYN.)* crevice, fault, opening, crack, flaw, fissure, split, breach, opening.

right *(SYN.)* correct, appropriate, suitable, ethical, fit, real, legitimate, justice, factual, just, directly, virtue, true, definite, straight, honorably, seemly.

(ANT.) *immoral, unfair, wrong, bad, improper.*

righteous *(SYN.)* ethical, chaste, honorable, good, virtuous, good, noble.

(ANT.) *sinful, libertine, amoral, licentious.*

rigid *(SYN.)* strict, unyielding, stiff, stern, austere, rigorous, inflexible, stringent, unbendable, severe, harsh, unbending.

(ANT.) *supple, flexible, mild, compassionate, pliable, limp, relaxed.*

rigorous *(SYN.)* unfeeling, rough, strict, blunt, cruel, hard, severe, grating, coarse, jarring, stern, stringent.

(ANT.) *soft, mild, tender, gentle, smooth.*

rile *(SYN.)* irritate, nettle, hector, exasperate, provoke, gripe.

rim *(SYN.)* verge, frontier, boundary, fringe, brim.

(ANT.) *core, mainland, center.*

ring *(SYN.)* fillet, band, loop, circlet, circle, surround, encircle, peal, sound, resound.

rinse *(SYN.)* launder, cleanse, wash, soak, immerse, laundering, rinsing, immerse, bathe, clean.

riot *(SYN.)* disturbance, disorder, outburst, commotion, insurgence, uproar, confusion, tumult, revolt.

rip *(SYN.)* tear, rend, wound, lacerate, shred, scramble, dart, dash, split, disunite.

(ANT.) *unite, join, repair.*

ripe *(SYN.)* ready, finished, mature, complete, fullgrown, develop, mellow, avid, consummate.

(ANT.) *raw, crude, undeveloped, premature, unprepared, unripe, immature.*

riposte *(SYN.)* rejoinder, comeback, quip, retort, response, reply, wisecrack.

ripple *(SYN.)* wave, ruffle, gurgle, corrugation, rumple, crumple, dribble, bubble.

rise *(SYN.)* thrive, awaken, ascend, climb, mount, tower, prosper, advance, proceed.

(ANT.) *fall, drop, plunge, fade, slump, decline, sinking, setback, retrogression.*

risk (SYN.) hazard, peril, jeopardy, threat, vulnerability, contingency.

(ANT.) *protection, immunity, defense.*

risky (SYN.) menacing, chancy, threatening, critical, dicey, unsound, dangerous.

(ANT.) *guarded, safe, firm, secure.*

rite (SYN.) pomp, solemnity, ceremony, observance, ceremonial, formality.

ritual (SYN.) pomp, solemnity, ceremony, parade, rite, ritualism, prescription, routine, custom, tradition.

rival (SYN.) enemy, opponent, adversary, oppose, competitor, contest, antagonist.

(ANT.) *colleague, confederate, allay, collaborator, helpmate, teammate.*

rivalry (SYN.) contest, struggle, duel, race, vying, opposition, competition.

(ANT.) *alliance, collaboration, partnership, cooperation, teamwork, coalition.*

river (SYN.) brook, stream, tributary, creek.

road (SYN.) street, way, highway, pike, drive, highway, expressway, boulevard.

roam (SYN.) err, saunter, deviate, rove, range, wander, digress, ramble, stroll.

(ANT.) *stop, linger, stay, halt.*

roar (SYN.) cry, bellow, yell, blare, scream, whoop, holler, yelp.

roast (SYN.) deride, ridicule, parody, burlesque.

rob (SYN.) fleece, steal, loot, plunder, burglarize, ransack, hold up, rip off, thieve.

robbery (SYN.) larceny, plundering, thievery, stealing, snatching, burglary.

robe (SYN.) housecoat, bathrobe, dressing gown, caftan, smock, cape.

robust (SYN.) well, hearty, hale, sound, healthy, strong.

(ANT.) *fragile, feeble, debilitated, reserved, refined, puny, frail, delicate.*

rock (SYN.) pebble, boulder, stone, gravel, granite, roll, sway, limestone.

rod (SYN.) bar, pole, wand, stick, pike, staff, billy, baton.

rogue (SYN.) criminal, rascal, good-for-nothing.

roister (SYN.) bluster, swagger, swashbuckle, vaunt, bluff, flourish, rollick.

role (SYN.) task, part, function, characterization, portrayal, face, character.

roll (SYN.) revolve, rotate, reel, lumber, swagger, stagger, progress, proceed, turn.

rollicking (SYN.) spirited, frolicsome, exuberant, lighthearted, carefree.

romance (SYN.) affair, enchantment, novel, tale, adventure, enterprise, daring.

romantic (SYN.) poetic, mental, dreamy, fanciful, imaginative, extravagant, impractical, exaggerated, wild.

(ANT.) *homely, fainthearted, familiar, unromantic, pessimistic, unemotional, cynical, literal, prosaic, factual.*

room (SYN.) enclosure, cell, cubicle, reside.

roost (SYN.) coop, henhouse, hearth, lodgings.

rooted (SYN.) fixed, fast, firm, steadfast, immovable, stationary.

rope (SYN.) string, wire, cord, cable, line, strand, rigging, ropework, cordage.

roster (SYN.) list, census, muster, enrollment, listing.

rosy (SYN.) reddish, pink, healthy, fresh, cheerful, flushed, promising, favorable.

(ANT.) *pale, pallid, gray, wan, disheartening, ashen, unfavorable, gloomy.*

rot (SYN.) putrefy, waste, dwindle, spoil, decline, decomposition, wane, rotting.

(ANT.) *increase, rise, grow, luxuriate.*

rotary (SYN.) axial, rotating, rolling, rotational.

rotation (SYN.) turning, rolling, succession, gyration, swirling, spinning, whirling.

rote (SYN.) repetition, system, convention, routine, mechanization, habitude, habit, custom, perfunctoriness.

rotten (SYN.) decayed, decomposed, spoiled, putrid, contaminated, tainted.

(ANT.) *unspoiled, pure, sweet.*

rough (SYN.) jagged, scratchy, craggy, stormy, rugged, unpolished, approximate, uneven, irregular, bumpy, coarse, unpolished, rude.

(ANT.) *calm, polished, civil, smooth, sleek, sophisticated.*

round (SYN.) rotund, chubby, complete, spherical, circular, bowed.

(ANT.) slender, trim, slim, thin, lean.

rouse *(SYN.)* waken, awaken, stimulate, excite, summon, arise, stir.

(ANT.) rest, calm, sleep, restrain, sedate.

rout *(SYN.)* defeat, beat, quell, vanquish, conquer, humble, subdue, scatter.

(ANT.) cede, retreat.

route *(SYN.)* street, course, thoroughfare, track, road.

routine *(SYN.)* way, habit, use, method, system, channel, circuit.

(ANT.) unusual, rate, uncommon.

row *(SYN.)* file, order, series, rank, progression, sequence, arrangement.

royal *(SYN.)* lordly, regal, noble, courtly, ruling, stately, dignified, supreme, majestic, sovereign, imperial.

(ANT.) servile, common, low, humble.

rub *(SYN.)* shine, polish, scour, scrape.

rubbish *(SYN.)* debris, garbage, trash, waste, junk.

rude *(SYN.)* gruff, impudent, blunt, impolite, boorish, insolent, saucy, rough, crude, unmannerly, coarse, impertinent.

(ANT.) courtly, civil, stately, polished, courteous, cultivated, polite.

rudimentary *(SYN.)* essential, primary, fundamental, original, imperfect.

ruffle *(SYN.)* rumple, disarrange, disorder, disturb, trimming, frill.

rugged *(SYN.)* jagged, craggy, harsh, severe, tough.

(ANT.) smooth, level, even.

ruin *(SYN.)* wreck, exterminate, devastate, annihilate, raze, demolish, spoil, wreck, destroy, destruction.

(ANT.) save, establish, preserve.

ruination *(SYN.)* obliteration, annihilation, havoc, catastrophe.

rule *(SYN.)* law, guide, order, sovereignty, control.

ruling *(SYN.)* judgment, decision, decree.

ruminate *(SYN.)* brood, reflect, meditate, ponder, consider, speculate, mull.

rumple *(SYN.)* tousle, furrow, crease, wrinkle, dishevel.

run *(SYN.)* race, hurry, speed, hasten, sprint, dart.

rush *(SYN.)* dash, speed, hurry, hasten, run, scoot, hustle, scurry.

(ANT.) tarry, linger.

sacrament *(SYN.)* communion, fellowship, association, participation, union.

(ANT.) nonparticipation, alienation.

sacred *(SYN.)* consecrated, blessed, devout, divine, holy, spiritual, saintly.

(ANT.) profane, evil, sacrilegious, worldly, secular, blasphemous.

sad *(SYN.)* dejected, cheerless, despondent, depressed, disconsolate, doleful, down-hearted, glum, saddening.

(ANT.) happy, cheerful, glad, merry.

safe *(SYN.)* dependable, certain, harmless, secure, snug.

(ANT.) hazardous, dangerous, unsafe, insecure, perilous.

sage *(SYN.)* intellectual, disciple, learner, savant, judicious, sagacious, rational, logical, scholar, expert.

(ANT.) dunce, fool, dolt, idiot.

saintly *(SYN.)* virtuous, moral, holy, devout, righteous.

sake *(SYN.)* motive, reason, purpose, benefit, advantage.

salary *(SYN.)* compensation, fee, payment, wages.

(ANT.) gratuity, present, gift.

salubrious *(SYN.)* healthy, well, hygienic, wholesome.

(ANT.) diseased, delicate, frail, injurious, infirm.

salutary *(SYN.)* beneficial, advantageous, profitable.

(ANT.) destructive, deleterious, detrimental, injurious, harmful.

sample *(SYN.)* example, case, illustration, model, instance, pattern, prototype, specimen, token.

sanctuary *(SYN.)* harbor, haven, asylum, refuge, retreat, shelter.

(ANT.) danger, hazard, exposure, peril.

sane *(SYN.)* balanced, rational, normal, sound.

(ANT.) crazy, insane, irrational.

sarcastic *(SYN.)* biting, acrimonious, cutting, caustic, ironic, sneering.

(ANT.) agreeable, affable, pleasant.

satiate *(SYN.)* compensate, please, gratify, remunerate.

(ANT.) displease, dissatisfy, annoy, frustrate, tantalize.

satire *(SYN.)* cleverness, fun, banter, humor, irony, raillery, pleasantry.

(ANT.) platitude, sobriety, stupidity.

satirical *(SYN.)* biting, caustic, derisive, sarcastic, sneering, sardonic, taunting.

(ANT.) agreeable, affable, pleasant.

satisfaction *(SYN.)* blessedness, beatitude, bliss, delight, contentment, felicity, pleasure, enjoyment.

(ANT.) grief, misery, sadness, despair.

satisfy *(SYN.)* compensate, appease, content, gratify, fulfill, suitable.

(ANT.) displease, dissatisfy, annoy, frustrate, tantalize.

savage *(SYN.)* brutal, cruel, barbarous, ferocious, inhuman, merciless, malignant.

(ANT.) compassionate, forbearing, benevolent, gentle, tame, cultivated.

save *(SYN.)* defend, conserve, keep, maintain, guard, preserve, protect, safeguard, spare, free, liberate, salvage.

(ANT.) abolish, destroy, abandon, impair, injure.

say *(SYN.)* converse, articulate, declare, express, discourse, harangue, talk, state.

(ANT.) hush, refrain, be silent.

scale *(SYN.)* balance, proportion, ration, range, climb.

scandal *(SYN.)* chagrin, mortification, dishonor, disgrace, disrepute, odium.

(ANT.) glory, honor, dignity.

scandalous *(SYN.)* disgraceful, discreditable, dishonorable, ignominious.

(ANT.) honorable, renowned, esteemed.

scant *(SYN.)* succinct, summary, concise, terse, inadequate, deficient.

(ANT.) ample, big, extended, abundant.

scarce *(SYN.)* occasional, choice, infrequent, exceptional, incomparable.

(ANT.) frequent, ordinary, usual, customary, abundant, numerous, worthless.

scare *(SYN.)* alarm, papal, affright, astound, dismay, horrify, terrorize, shock.

(ANT.) compose, reassure, soothe.

scared *(SYN.)* apprehensive, afraid, fainthearted, frightened, fearful, timid.

(ANT.) bold, assured, courageous, composed, sanguine.

scent *(SYN.)* fragrance, fume, stench, stink, smell.

scheme *(SYN.)* conspiracy, cabal, design, machination, design, devise.

scope *(SYN.)* area, compass, expanse, amount, extent, reach, size, range.

score *(SYN.)* reckoning, tally, record, mark, rating.

scramble *(SYN.)* combine, mix, blend, hasten, clamber.

scrap *(SYN.)* fragment, rag, apportionment, part, portion, piece, section, share, segment, crumb, junk.

(ANT.) whole, entirety.

scrape *(SYN.)* difficulty, dilemma, condition, fix, predicament, plight, situation.

(ANT.) comfort, ease, calmness.

script *(SYN.)* penmanship, hand, handwriting, text, lines.

scrupulous *(SYN.)* conscientious, candid, honest, truthful, upright, painstaking, critical.

(ANT.) dishonest, fraudulent, lying, deceitful, tricky.

scurry *(SYN.)* scamper, scramble, hasten, hustle.

seal *(SYN.)* emblem, stamp, symbol, crest, signet.

search *(SYN.)* exploration, inquiry, pursuit, quest, explore, scrutinize, investigate, hunt, probe, rummage, ransack, seek, scour.

(ANT.) resignation, abandonment.

season *(SYN.)* mature, perfect, ripen, develop, age.

seclusion *(SYN.)* insulation, isolation, loneliness, alienation, quarantine, segregation, separation, retirement.

(ANT.) fellowship, union, communion.

secondary *(SYN.)* minor, poorer, inferior, lower, subordinate.

(ANT.) greater, higher, superior.

secret *(SYN.)* concealed, hidden, latent, covert, private, surreptitious, unknown.

(ANT.) disclosed, exposed, known, obvious, conspicuous, open, public.

section *(SYN.)* district, country, domain, dominion, division, land, place, province, territory, subdivision.

security *(SYN.)* bond, earnest, token, surety.

sedate *(SYN.)* controlled, serene, calm, composed, unruffled.

seize *(SYN.)* check, detain, withhold, grab, grasp.

(ANT.) free, liberate, release, activate, discharge, loosen.

select *(SYN.)* cull, opt, pick, choose, elect, prefer.

(ANT.) reject, refuse.

self-important *(SYN.)* egotistical, proud, conceited, egocentric.

selfish *(SYN.)* illiberal, narrow, self-centered, self-seeking, mercenary, stingy, ungenerous, mean, miserly.

(ANT.) charitable.

sell *(SYN.)* market, retail, merchandise, vend, trade.

send *(SYN.)* discharge, emit, dispatch, cast, propel, impel, throw, transmit, forward, ship, convey, mail.

(ANT.) get, hold, retain, receive, bring.

senile *(SYN.)* antiquated, antique, aged, ancient, archaic, obsolete, old, elderly, old-fashioned, venerable.

(ANT.) new, youthful, young, modern.

sensation *(SYN.)* feeling, image, impression, apprehension, sense, sensibility, perception, sensitiveness.

(ANT.) insensibility, stupor, apathy.

sensational *(SYN.)* exciting, startling, spectacular.

sense *(SYN.)* drift, connotation, acceptation, explanation, gist, implication, intent, import, interpretation, sensation, perception.

senseless *(SYN.)* dense, dull, crass, brainless, dumb, obtuse, foolish, stupid.

(ANT.) discerning, intelligent, alert, clever, bright.

sensible *(SYN.)* apprehensible, perceptible, appreciable, alive, aware, awake, perceiving, conscious, sentient, intelligent, discreet, judicious, prudent, sagacious, reasonable.

(ANT.) impalpable, imperceptible, absurd, stupid, unaware, foolish.

sensual *(SYN.)* lascivious, earthy, lecherous, carnal, sensory, voluptuous, wanton, erotic, lustful, sexual.

(ANT.) chaste, ascetic, abstemious, virtuous.

sentiment *(SYN.)* affection, sensibility, passion, impression, opinion, attitude.

(ANT.) coldness, imperturbability, anesthesia, insensibility, fact.

separate *(SYN.)* part sever, sunder, divide, allot, dispense, share, distribute, disconnect, split, isolate, segregate, different, distinct.

(ANT.) convene, join, gather, combine.

separation *(SYN.)* insulation, isolation, loneliness, alienation, seclusion, retirement, solitude, segregation.

(ANT.) communion, fellowship, union, association.

sequence *(SYN.)* chain, graduation, order, progression, arrangement, series, succession, train, string.

serene *(SYN.)* composed, imperturbable, calm, dispassionate, pacific, placid.

(ANT.) frantic, turbulent, wild, excited, stormy, agitated, turbulent.

series *(ANT.)* following, chain, arrangement, graduation, progression, order, sequence, train, string.

servant *(SYN.)* attendant, butler, domestic, valet, manservant, maid.

serve *(SYN.)* assist, attend, help, succor, advance, benefit, forward, answer, promote, content, satisfy, suffice, wait on, aid.

(ANT.) command, direct, dictate, rule.

servile *(SYN.)* base, contemptible, despicable, abject, groveling, dishonorable, ignominious, ignoble, lowly, low, menial, mean, sordid, vulgar, vile.

(ANT.) honored, exalted, lofty, esteemed, righteous, noble.

set *(SYN.)* deposit, dispose, position, pose, station, appoint, fix, assign, settle, establish.

(ANT.) mislay, misplace, disturb, remove, disarrange.

settle *(SYN.)* close, conclude, adjudicate, decide, end, resolve, agree upon, establish.

(ANT.) suspend, hesitate, doubt, vacillate, waver.

sever *(SYN.)* part, divide, sunder, split, cut, separate.

(ANT.) convene, connect, gather, join, unite, combine.

severe *(SYN.)* arduous, distressing, acute, exacting, hard, harsh, intense, relentless, rigorous, sharp, stern.

(ANT.) genial, indulgent, lenient, yielding, merciful, considerate.

sew *(SYN.)* mend, patch, fix, stitch, refit, restore, repair.

(ANT.) destroy, hurt, deface, injure.

shabby *(SYN.)* indigent, impecunious, needy, penniless, worn, ragged, destitute, poor, threadbare, deficient, inferior, scanty.
(ANT.) rich, wealthy, ample, affluent, opulent, right, sufficient, good.

shack *(SYN.)* hovel, hut, shanty, shed.

shackle *(SYN.)* chain, fetter, handcuff.

shade *(SYN.)* complexion, dye, hue, paint, color, stain, pigment, darkness, shadow, tincture, dusk, gloom, blacken, darken, conceal, screen, tint, tinge.
(ANT.) transparency, paleness.

shadowy *(SYN.)* dark, dim, gloomy, murky, black, obscure, dusky, unilluminated, dismal, evil, gloomy, sinister, indistinct, hidden, vague, undefined, wicked, indefinite, mystic, secret, occult.
(ANT.) bright, clear, light, pleasant, lucid.

shady *(SYN.)* shifty, shaded, questionable, doubtful, devious.

shaggy *(SYN.)* hairy, unkempt, uncombed, woolly.

shake *(SYN.)* flutter, jar, jolt, quake, agitate, quiver, shiver, shudder, rock, totter, sway, tremble, vibrate, waver.

shaky *(SYN.)* questionable, uncertain, iffy, faltering, unsteady.
(ANT.) sure, definite, positive, certain.

shallow *(SYN.)* exterior, cursory, flimsy, frivolous, slight, imperfect, superficial.
(ANT.) complete, deep, abstruse, profound, thorough.

sham *(SYN.)* affect, act, feign, assume, pretend, simulate, profess.
(ANT.) exhibit, display, reveal, expose.

shame *(SYN.)* chagrin, humiliation, abashment, disgrace, mortification, dishonor, ignominy, embarrassment, disrepute, odium mortify, humiliate, abash, humble, opprobrium, scandal.
(ANT.) pride, glory, praise, honor.

shameful *(SYN.)* disgraceful, dishonorable, disreputable, discreditable, humiliating, ignominious, scandalous.
(ANT.) honorable, renowned, respectable, esteemed.

shameless *(SYN.)* unembarrassed, unashamed, brazen, bold, impudent.

(ANT.) demure, modest.

shape *(SYN.)* create, construct, forge, fashion, form, make, produce, mold, constitute, compose, arrange, combine, organize, frame, outline, figure, invent, appearance, pattern, cast, model, devise.
(ANT.) disfigure, misshape, wreck.

shapeless *(SYN.)* rough, vague.

shapely *(SYN.)* attractive, well-formed, curvy, alluring.
(ANT.) shapeless.

share *(SYN.)* parcel, bit, part, division, portion, ration, piece, fragment, allotment, partake, apportion, participate, divide, section.
(ANT.) whole.

shared *(SYN.)* joint, common, reciprocal, correlative, mutual.
(ANT.) unrequited, dissociated.

sharp *(SYN.)* biting, pointed, cunning, acute, keen, rough, fine, cutting, shrill, cutting, pungent, witty, acrid, blunt, steep, shrewd.
(ANT.) gentle, bland, shallow, smooth, blunt.

sharpen *(SYN.)* whet, hone, strop.

shatter *(SYN.)* crack, rend, break, pound, smash, burst, demolish, shiver, infringe.
(ANT.) renovate, join, repair, mend.

shattered *(SYN.)* fractured, destroyed, reduced, separated, broken, smashed, flattened, rent, wrecked.
(ANT.) united, integral, whole.

shawl *(SYN.)* stole, scarf.

sheepish *(SYN.)* coy, embarrassed, shy, humble, abashed, diffident, timid, modest, timorous.
(ANT.) daring, outgoing, adventurous.

sheer *(SYN.)* thin, transparent, clear, simple, utter, absolute, abrupt, steep.

sheet *(SYN.)* leaf, layer, coating, film.

shelter *(SYN.)* retreat, safety, cover, asylum, protection, sanctuary, harbor, guard, haven, security.
(ANT.) unveil, expose, bare, reveal.

shield *(SYN.)* envelop, cover, clothe, curtain, protest, protection, cloak, guard, conceal, defense, shelter, hide, screen.
(ANT.) unveil, divulge, reveal, bare.

shift *(SYN.)* move, modify, transfer, substitute, vary, change, alter, spell, turn, transfigure.

(ANT.) settle, establish, stabilize.

shifting (SYN.) wavering, inconstant, changeable, fitful, variable, fickle.

(ANT.) uniform, stable, unchanging.

shiftless (SYN.) idle, lazy, slothful.

(ANT.) energetic.

shifty (SYN.) shrewd, crafty, tricky.

shilly-shally (SYN.) fluctuate, waver, hesitate, vacillate.

shimmer (SYN.) glimmer, shine, gleam.

(ANT.) dull.

shine (SYN.) flicker, glisten, glow, blaze, glare, flash, beam, shimmer, glimmer, radiate, brush, polish, twinkle, buff, luster, gloss, scintillate, radiance, gleam.

shining (SYN.) dazzling, illustrious, showy, superb, brilliant, effulgent, magnificent, splendid, bright.

(ANT.) ordinary, dull, unimpressive.

shiny (SYN.) bright, glossy, polished, glistening.

(ANT.) lusterless, dull.

shipshape (SYN.) clean, neat.

(ANT.) sloppy, messy.

shiver (SYN.) quiver, quake, quaver, tremble, shudder, shake, break, shatter.

shock (SYN.) disconcert, astonish, surprise, astound, amaze, clash, disturbance, bewilder, outrage, horrify, revolt, agitation, stagger, blow, impact, collision, surprise, startle, upset, stun.

(ANT.) prepare, caution, admonish.

shocking (SYN.) hideous, frightful, severe, appalling, horrible, awful, terrible, dire, fearful.

(ANT.) safe, happy, secure, joyous.

shore (SYN.) seaside, beach, coast.

(ANT.) inland.

short (SYN.) abrupt, squat, concise, brief, low, curtailed, dumpy, terse, inadequate, succinct, dwarfed, small, abbreviated.

(ANT.) extended, ample, protracted.

shortage (SYN.) deficiency, deficit.

(ANT.) surplus, enough.

shortcoming (SYN.) error, vice, blemish, failure, flaw, omission, failing.

(ANT.) perfection, completeness.

shorten (SYN.) curtail, limit, cut, abbreviate, reduce, abridge, lessen.

(ANT.) lengthen, elongate.

shortening (SYN.) reduction, abridgment, abbreviation.

(ANT.) enlargement, amplification.

shortly (SYN.) soon, directly, presently.

shortsighted (SYN.) myopic, nearsighted, unimaginative, unthinking, thoughtless.

shout (SYN.) cry, yell, roar, vociferate, bellow, exclaim.

(ANT.) whisper, intimate.

shove (SYN.) propel, drive, urge, crowd, jostle, force, push, promote.

(ANT.) retreat, falter, oppose, drag, halt.

shovel (SYN.) spade.

show (SYN.) flourish, parade, point, reveal, explain, movie, production, display, exhibit, spectacle, demonstrate, entertainment, tell, guide, prove, indicate, present, lead, demonstration.

showy (SYN.) ceremonious, stagy, affected, theatrical, artificial.

(ANT.) unaffected, modest, unemotional, subdued.

shred (SYN.) particle, speck, iota, mite, bit, smidgen, tear, slit, cleave, rip, disunite, wound, rend, mince, tatter.

(ANT.) bulk, unite, quantity, mend, aggregate, repair.

shrewd (SYN.) cunning, covert, artful, stealthy, foxy, astute, ingenious, guileful, crafty, sly, surreptitious, wily, tricky, clever, intelligent, clandestine.

(ANT.) frank, sincere, candid, open.

shriek (SYN.) screech, scream, howl, yell.

shrill (SYN.) keen, penetrating, sharp, acute, piercing, severe.

(ANT.) gentle, bland, shallow.

shrink (SYN.) diminish, shrivel, dwindle.

shrivel (SYN.) wizen, waste, droop, decline, sink, dry, languish, wither.

(ANT.) renew, refresh, revive, rejuvenate.

shun (SYN.) escape, avert, forestall, avoid, forbear, evade, ward, free.

(ANT.) encounter, confront, meet.

shut (SYN.) seal, finish, stop, close, terminate, conclude, clog, end, obstruct.

(ANT.) begin, open, start, unbar, inaugurate, unlock, commence.

shy (SYN.) reserved, fearful, bashful, retiring, cautious, demure, timid, shrinking, wary, chary.

(ANT.) brazen, bold, immodest, selfconfident, audacious.

sick (SYN.) ill, morbid, ailing, unhealthy, diseased, unwell, infirm.

(ANT.) sound, well, robust, strong.

sinful *(SYN.)* bad, corrupt, dissolute, antisocial, immoral, licentious, profligate, evil, indecent, unprincipled. *(ANT.)* pure, noble, virtuous.

single *(SYN.)* individual, marked, particular, distinctive, separate, special, sole, unwed, unmarried, singular, unique. *(ANT.)* ordinary, universal, general.

sink *(SYN.)* diminish, droop, extend, downward, drop, descend. *(ANT.)* mount, climb, soar, steady, arise.

situation *(SYN.)* circumstance, plight, state, site, location, placement, locale, predicament, position, state, condition.

size *(SYN.)* bigness, bulk, dimensions, expanse, amplitude, measurement, area.

skeptic *(SYN.)* doubter, infidel, agnostic, deist, questioner, unbeliever. *(ANT.)* believer, worshiper, adorer.

sketch *(SYN.)* draft, figure, form, outline, contour, delineation, drawing, picture.

skill *(SYN.)* cunning, deftness, cleverness, talent, readiness, skillfulness. *(ANT.)* ineptitude, inability.

skin *(SYN.)* outside, covering, peel, rind, shell, pare.

skip *(SYN.)* drop, eliminate, ignore, exclude, cancel, delete, disregard, omit, overlook neglect, miss. *(ANT.)* notice, introduce, include, insert.

slander *(SYN.)* libel, calumny, backbiting, aspersion, scandal, vilification. *(ANT.)* praise, flattery, commendation, defense.

slant *(SYN.)* disposition, inclination, bias, bent, partiality, slope, tilt, pitch, penchant, prejudice, proneness, lean, tendency. *(ANT.)* justice, fairness, impartiality, equity.

slaughter *(SYN.)* butcher, kill, massacre, slay, butchering.

sleep *(SYN.)* drowse, nap, nod, slumber, snooze.

slight *(SYN.)* lank, lean, meager, emaciated, gaunt, fine, tenuous, unimportant, slim. *(ANT.)* regard, notice, enormous, large, major, huge.

slim *(SYN.)* thin, slender, lank, slight,

weak.

slip *(SYN.)* error, fault, inaccuracy, shift, err, slide, mistake, glide, blunder. *(ANT.)* precision, truth, accuracy.

slit *(SYN.)* slash, cut, tear, slot.

slothful *(SYN.)* indolent, idle, inactive, lazy, inert, supine, sluggish, torpid. *(ANT.)* alert, diligent, active, assiduous.

slovenly *(SYN.)* sloppy, unkempt, messy. *(ANT.)* meticulous, neat.

slow *(SYN.)* deliberate, dull, delaying, dawdling, gradual, leisurely, tired, sluggish, unhurried, late, behindhand. *(ANT.)* rapid, quick, swift, speedy, fast.

sluggish *(SYN.)* dull, deliberate, dawdling, delaying, laggard, gradual, leisurely, tired, slow, lethargic. *(ANT.)* quick, rapid, fast, speedy, swift, energetic, vivacious.

slumber *(SYN.)* drowse, catnap, nod, doze, repose, sleep, rest, snooze.

slump *(SYN.)* drop, decline, descent.

small *(SYN.)* little, minute, petty, diminutive, puny, wee, tiny, trivial, slight, miniature. *(ANT.)* immense, enormous, large, huge.

smart *(SYN.)* dexterous, quick, skillful, adroit, apt, clever, bright, witty, ingenious, sharp, intelligent. *(ANT.)* foolish, stupid, unskilled, awkward, clumsy, bungling, slow, dumb.

smell *(SYN.)* fragrance, fume, odor, perfume, incense, stink, scent, sniff, detect, bouquet.

smite *(SYN.)* knock, hit, dash, overpower, subdue, vanquish, rout. *(ANT.)* surrender, fail, defend, shield.

smooth *(SYN.)* polished, sleek, slick, glib, diplomatic, flat, level, plain, suave, urbane, even, unwrinkled. *(ANT.)* rugged, harsh, rough, blunt, bluff, uneven.

smother *(SYN.)* suffocate, asphyxiate, stifle.

smutty *(SYN.)* disgusting, filthy, impure, coarse, dirty, lewd, offensive, obscene, pornographic. *(ANT.)* modest, refined, decent, pure.

snappish *(SYN.)* ill-natured, ill-tempered, fractious, irritable, fretful, peevish, testy, touchy, petulant. *(ANT.)* good-tempered, pleasant, good-natured, affable, genial.

snare *(SYN.)* capture, catch, arrest, clutch, grasp, grip, lay, apprehend, seize, trap, net.

(ANT.) throw, release, lose, liberate.

sneer *(SYN.)* fleer, flout, jeer, mock, gibe, deride, taunt.

(ANT.) laud, flatter, praise, compliment.

sneering *(SYN.)* derision, gibe, banter, jeering, mockery, raillery, sarcasm, ridicule, satire.

sniveling *(SYN.)* whimpering, sniffling, weepy, whining, blubbering.

snug *(SYN.)* constricted, close, contracted, compact, firm, narrow, taut, tense, stretched, tight, cozy, comfortable, sheltered.

(ANT.) loose, lax, slack, relaxed, open.

soak *(SYN.)* saturate, drench, steep, wet.

soar *(SYN.)* flutter, fly, flit, float, glide, sail, hover, mount.

(ANT.) plummet, sink, fall, descend.

sober *(SYN.)* sedate, serious, staid, earnest, grave, solemn, moderate.

(ANT.) ordinary, joyful, informal, boisterous, drunk, fuddled, inebriated.

social *(SYN.)* friendly, civil, gregarious, affable, communicative, hospitable, sociable, group, common, genial, polite.

(ANT.) inhospitable, hermitic, antisocial, disagreeable.

society *(SYN.)* nation, community, civilization, organization, club, association, fraternity, circle, association, company.

soft *(SYN.)* gentle, lenient, flexible, compassionate, malleable, meek, mellow, subdued, mild, tender, supple, yielding, pliable, elastic, pliant.

(ANT.) unyielding, rough, hard, rigid.

soil *(SYN.)* defile, discolor, spot, befoul, blemish, blight, dirty.

(ANT.) purify, honor, cleanse, bleach.

solace *(SYN.)* contentment, ease, enjoyment, comfort, consolation, relief.

(ANT.) torture, torment, misery, affliction, discomfort.

sole *(SYN.)* isolated, desolate, deserted, secluded, unaided, lone, alone, only, single, solitary.

(ANT.) surrounded, accompanied.

solemn *(SYN.)* ceremonious, imposing, formal, impressive, reverential, ritualis-

tic, grave, sedate, earnest, sober, staid, serious, dignified.

(ANT.) ordinary, joyful, informal, boisterous, cheerful, gay, happy.

solitary *(SYN.)* isolated, alone, lonely, deserted, unaided, sole.

(ANT.) surrounded, attended, accompanied.

somatic *(SYN.)* corporeal, corporal, natural, material, bodily, physical.

(ANT.) spiritual, mental.

somber *(SYN.)* dismal, dark, bleak, doleful, cheerless, natural, physical, serious, sober, gloomy, grave.

(ANT.) lively, joyous, cheerful, happy.

soon *(SYN.)* shortly, early, betimes, beforehand.

(ANT.) tardy, late, overdue, belated.

soothe *(SYN.)* encourage, console, solace, comfort, cheer, pacify.

(ANT.) dishearten, depress, antagonize, aggravate, disquiet, upset, unnerve.

soothing *(SYN.)* gentle, benign, docile, calm, mild, tame.

(ANT.) violent, savage, fierce, harsh.

sorcery *(SYN.)* enchantment, conjuring, art, charm, black, magic, voodoo, witchcraft, wizardry.

sorrow *(SYN.)* grief, distress, heartache, anguish, misery, tribulation, gloom, depression.

(ANT.) consolation, solace, joy, happiness, comfort.

sorrowful *(SYN.)* dismal, doleful, dejected, despondent, depressed, disconsolate, gloomy, melancholy, grave, aggrieved.

(ANT.) merry, happy, cheerful, joyous.

sorry *(SYN.)* hurt, pained, sorrowful, afflicted, grieved, mean, shabby, contemptible, worthless, vile, regretful, apologetic.

(ANT.) delighted, impenitent, cheerful, unrepentant, splendid.

sour *(SYN.)* glum, sullen, bitter, peevish, acid, rancid, tart, acrimonious, sharp, bad-tempered, unpleasant, cranky.

(ANT.) wholesome, kindly, genial, benevolent, sweet.

source *(SYN.)* birth, foundation, agent, determinant, reason, origin, cause, start, incentive, motive, spring, inducement, principle, beginning.

(ANT.) product, harvest, outcome, issue, consequence, end.

souvenir *(SYN.)* memento, monument, commemoration, remembrance.

sovereign *(SYN.)* monarch, king, emperor, queen, empress.

sovereignty *(SYN.)* command, influence, authority, predominance, control, sway.

(ANT.) debility, incapacity, disablement, ineptitude, impotence.

space *(SYN.)* room, area, location.

spacious *(SYN.)* capacious, large, vast, ample, extensive, wide, roomy, large.

(ANT.) limited, confined, narrow, small, cramped.

span *(SYN.)* spread, extent.

spare *(SYN.)* preserve, safeguard, uphold, conserve, protect, defend, rescue, reserve, additional, unoccupied.

(ANT.) impair, abolish, injure, abandon.

sparing *(SYN.)* economical, thrifty, frugal.

(ANT.) lavish.

sparkle *(SYN.)* gleam, glitter, twinkle, beam, glisten, radiate, shine, blaze.

spat *(SYN.)* quarrel, dispute, affray, wrangle, altercation.

(ANT.) peace, friendliness, agreement, reconciliation.

spawn *(SYN.)* yield, bear.

speak *(SYN.)* declare, express, say, articulate, harangue, converse, talk, utter.

(ANT.) refrain, hush, quiet.

special *(SYN.)* individual, uncommon, distinctive, peculiar, exceptional, unusual, extraordinary, different.

(ANT.) general, widespread, broad, prevailing, average, ordinary.

specialist *(SYN.)* authority, expert.

species *(SYN.)* variety, type, kind, class.

specific *(SYN.)* limited, characteristic, definite, peculiar, explicit, categorical, particular, distinct, precise.

(ANT.) generic, general, nonspecific.

specify *(SYN.)* name, call, mention, appoint, denominate, designate, define.

(ANT.) miscall, hint.

specimen *(SYN.)* prototype, example, sample, model, pattern, type.

speck *(SYN.)* scrap, jot, bit, mite, smidgen, crumb, iota, particle, spot.

(ANT.) quantity, bulk, aggregate.

spectacle *(SYN.)* demonstration, ostentation, movie, array, exhibition, show, display, performance, parade, splurge.

spectator *(SYN.)* viewer, observer.

speculate *(SYN.)* assume, deduce, surmise, apprehend, imagine, consider, view, think, guess, suppose, conjecture.

(ANT.) prove, demonstrate, conclude.

speech *(SYN.)* gossip, discourse, talk, chatter, lecture, conference, discussion, address, dialogue, articulation, accent.

(ANT.) silence, correspondence, writing.

speed *(SYN.)* forward, push, accelerate, hasten, rapidity, dispatch, swiftness.

(ANT.) impede, slow, block, retard.

spellbound *(SYN.)* fascinated, entranced, hypnotized, mesmerized, rapt.

spend *(SYN.)* pay, disburse, consume.

(ANT.) hoard, save.

spendthrift *(SYN.)* squanderer, profligate.

sphere *(SYN.)* globe, orb, ball, environment, area, domain.

spherical *(SYN.)* round, curved, globular.

spicy *(SYN.)* indecent, off-color.

spin *(SYN.)* revolve, turn, rotate, whirl, twirl, tell, narrate, relate.

spine *(SYN.)* vertebrae, backbone.

spineless *(SYN.)* weak, limp, cowardly.

(ANT.) brave, strong, courageous.

spirit *(SYN.)* courage, phantom, verve, fortitude, apparition, mood, soul, ghost.

(ANT.) listlessness, substance, languor.

spirited *(SYN.)* excited, animated, lively, active, vigorous, energetic.

(ANT.) indolent, lazy, sleepy.

spiritless *(SYN.)* gone, lifeless, departed, dead, insensible, deceased, unconscious.

(ANT.) stirring, alive, living.

spiritual *(SYN.)* sacred, unearthly, holy, divine, immaterial, supernatural.

(ANT.) material, physical, corporeal.

spite *(SYN.)* grudge, rancor, malice, animosity, malevolence, malignity.

(ANT.) kindness, toleration, affection.

spiteful *(SYN.)* vicious, disagreeable, surly, ill-natured.

(ANT.) pretty, beautiful, attractive, fair.

splendid *(SYN.)* glorious, illustrious, radiant, brilliant, showy, superb, bright.

(ANT.) ordinary, mediocre, dull.

splendor *(SYN.)* effulgence, radiance,

brightness, luster, magnificence, display.
(ANT.) darkness, obscurity, dullness.

splinter *(SYN.)* fragment, piece, sliver, chip, shiver.

split *(SYN.)* rend, shred, cleave, disunite, sever, break, divide, opening, lacerate.
(ANT.) repair, unite, join, sew.

spoil *(SYN.)* rot, disintegrate, waste, decay, ruin, damage, mold, destroy.
(ANT.) luxuriate, grow, flourish.

spoken *(SYN.)* verbal, pronounced, articulated, vocal, uttered, oral.
(ANT.) written, documentary.

spokesman *(SYN.)* agent, representative.

spontaneous *(SYN.)* impulsive, voluntary, automatic, instinctive, willing, extemporaneous, natural, unconscious.
(ANT.) planned, rehearsed, forced, studied, prepared.

sport *(SYN.)* match, play, amusement, fun, pastime, entertainment, athletics.

sporting *(SYN.)* considerate, fair, sportsmanlike.

spot *(SYN.)* blemish, mark, stain, flaw, blot, location, place, site, splatter.

spotty *(SYN.)* erratic, uneven, irregular.
(ANT.) regular, even.

spout *(SYN.)* spurt, squirt, tube, nozzle.

spray *(SYN.)* splash, spatter, sprinkle.

spread *(SYN.)* unfold, distribute, open, disperse, unroll, unfurl, scatter, jelly.
(ANT.) shut, close, hide, conceal.

sprightly *(SYN.)* blithe, hopeful, vivacious, buoyant, lively, light, nimble.
(ANT.) hopeless, depressed, sullen, dejected, despondent.

spring *(SYN.)* commencement, foundation, start, beginning, inception, jump, cradle, begin, birth, bound, originate.
(ANT.) issue, product, end.

sprinkle *(SYN.)* strew, scatter, rain.

spruce *(SYN.)* orderly, neat, trim, clear.
(ANT.) unkempt, sloppy, dirty.

spry *(SYN.)* brisk, quick, agile, nimble, energetic, supple, alert, active, lively.
(ANT.) heavy, sluggish, inert, clumsy.

spur *(SYN.)* inducement, purpose, cause, motive, impulse, reason, incitement.
(ANT.) effort, action, result, attempt.

squabble *(SYN.)* bicker, debate, altercate, contend, discuss, argue, quarrel.
(ANT.) concede, agree, assent.

squalid *(SYN.)* base, indecent, grimy, dirty, pitiful, filthy, muddy, nasty.
(ANT.) wholesome, clean, pure.

squander *(SYN.)* scatter, lavish, consume, dissipate, misuse.
(ANT.) preserve, conserve, save.

squeamish *(SYN.)* particular, careful.

stab *(SYN.)* stick, gore, pierce, knife, spear, bayonet.

stability *(SYN.)* steadiness, balance, proportion, composure, symmetry.
(ANT.) imbalance, fall, unsteadiness.

stable *(SYN.)* firm, enduring, constant, fixed, unwavering, steadfast, steady.
(ANT.) irresolute, variable, changeable.

stagger *(SYN.)* totter, sway, reel, vary, falter, alternate.

stain *(SYN.)* blight, dye, tint, befoul, spot, defile, mark, color, tinge.
(ANT.) honor, bleach, decorate, purify.

stale *(SYN.)* tasteless, spoiled, old, inedible, dry, uninteresting, trite, flat, dull.
(ANT.) new, fresh, tasty.

stamp *(SYN.)* crush, trample, imprint, mark, brand, block.

stand *(SYN.)* tolerate, suffer, stay, remain, sustain, rest.
(ANT.) run, yield, advance.

standard *(SYN.)* law, proof, pennant, emblem, touchstone, measure, example.
(ANT.) guess, chance, irregular, unusual.

start *(SYN.)* opening, source, commence, onset, surprise, shock, beginning, origin, begin, initiate, jerk, jump.
(ANT.) completion, termination, close.

starved *(SYN.)* longing, voracious, hungry, craving, avid.
(ANT.) satisfied, sated, gorged.

state *(SYN.)* circumstance, predicament, case, situation, condition, affirm.
(ANT.) imply, conceal, retract.

stately *(SYN.)* lordly, elegant, regal, sovereign, impressive, magnificent, courtly, grand.
(ANT.) low, common, mean, servile, humble, vulgar.

statement *(SYN.)* announcement, mention, allegation, declaration, thesis.

station *(SYN.)* post, depot, terminal, position, place.

statuesque *(SYN.)* imposing, stately,

regal, majestic.

status *(SYN.)* place, caste, standing, condition, state.

staunch *(SYN.)* faithful, true, constant, reliable, loyal.

(ANT.) *treacherous, untrustworthy.*

stay *(SYN.)* delay, continue, hinder, check, hold, hindrance, support, brace, line, rope, linger, sojourn, abide, halt, stand, rest, remain, tarry, arrest, wait.

(ANT.) *hasten, progress, go, depart, advance, leave.*

stead *(SYN.)* place.

steadfast *(SYN.)* solid, inflexible, constant, stable, unyielding, secure.

(ANT.) *unstable, insecure, unsteady.*

steadfastness *(SYN.)* persistence, industry, tenacity, constancy, persistency.

(ANT.) *laziness, sloth, cessation.*

steady *(SYN.)* regular, even, unremitting, stable, steadfast, firm, reliable, solid.

steal *(SYN.)* loot, rob, swipe, burglarize, pilfer, shoplift, embezzle, snitch.

(ANT.) *restore, buy, return, refund.*

stealthy *(SYN.)* sly, secret, furtive.

(ANT.) *direct, open, obvious.*

steep *(SYN.)* sharp, hilly, sheer, abrupt, perpendicular, precipitous.

(ANT.) *gradual, level, flat.*

steer *(SYN.)* manage, guide, conduct, lead, supervise, escort, navigate, drive, control, direct.

stem *(SYN.)* stalk, trunk, arise, check, stop, originate, hinder.

stench *(SYN.)* odor, fetor, fetidness, stink, aroma, smell, fume, scent.

step *(SYN.)* stride, pace, stage, move, action, measure, come, go, walk.

stern *(SYN.)* harsh, rigid, exacting, rigorous, sharp, severe, strict, hard, unyielding, unmitigated, stringent.

(ANT.) *indulgent, forgiving, yielding, lenient, considerate.*

stew *(SYN.)* ragout, goulash, boil, simmer.

stick *(SYN.)* stalk, twig, rod, staff, pole, pierce, spear, stab, puncture, gore, cling, adhere, hold, catch, abide, remain, persist.

stickler *(SYN.)* nitpicker, perfectionist, disciplinarian.

sticky *(SYN.)* tricky, delicate, awkward.

stiff *(SYN.)* severe, unbendable, unyielding, harsh, inflexible, unbending, rigid, firm, hard, solid, rigorous.

(ANT.) *supple, yielding, compassionate, mild, lenient, resilient.*

stifle *(SYN.)* choke, strangle, suffocate.

stigma *(SYN.)* trace, scar, blot, stain, mark, vestige.

still *(SYN.)* peaceful, undisturbed, but, mild, hushed, calm, patient, modest, nevertheless, motionless, meek, quiescent, stationary, besides, however, quiet, hush, tranquil, serene, placid.

(ANT.) *agitated, perturbed, loud.*

stimulate *(SYN.)* irritate, excite, arouse, disquiet, rouse, activate, urge, invigorate, animate, provoke.

(ANT.) *quell, calm, quiet, allay.*

stimulus *(SYN.)* motive, goad, arousal, provocation, encouragement.

(ANT.) *discouragement, depressant.*

stipend *(SYN.)* payment, earnings, salary, allowance, pay, compensation, wages.

(ANT.) *gratuity, gift.*

stipulate *(SYN.)* require, demand.

stir *(SYN.)* instigate, impel, push, agitate, induce, mix, rouse, move, propel.

(ANT.) *halt, stop, deter.*

stock *(SYN.)* hoard, store, strain, accumulation, supply, carry, keep, provision, fund, breed, sort.

(ANT.) *sameness, likeness, homogeneity, uniformity.*

stoical *(SYN.)* passive, forbearing, uncomplaining, composed, patient.

(ANT.) *turbulent, chafing, hysterical.*

stolid *(SYN.)* obtuse, unsharpened, dull, blunt, edgeless.

(ANT.) *suave, tactful, polished, subtle.*

stone *(SYN.)* pebble, gravel, rock.

stony *(SYN.)* insensitive, cold.

stoop *(SYN.)* bow, bend, lean, crouch.

stop *(SYN.)* terminate, check, abstain, hinder, arrest, close, bar, cork, halt, end, conclude, obstruct, finish, quit, pause, discontinue, stay, impede, cease.

(ANT.) *start, proceed, speed, begin.*

store *(SYN.)* amass, hoard, collect, market, shop, reserve, supply, deposit, bank, save, accrue, increase, stock.

(ANT.) *dissipate, waste, disperse.*

storm *(SYN.)* gale, tempest, tornado, thunderstorm, hurricane, rage, rant, assault, besiege.

stormy *(SYN.)* rough, inclement, windy, blustery, roaring, tempestuous.

(ANT.) quiet, calm, tranquil, peaceful.

story *(SYN.)* yarn, novel, history, tale, falsehood, account, fable, anecdote.

stout *(SYN.)* plump, obese, chubby, fat, paunchy, overweight, portly, heavy.

(ANT.) thin, slender, flimsy, gaunt, slim.

straight *(SYN.)* erect, honorable, square, just, direct, undeviating, unbent, right.

(ANT.) dishonest, bent, circuitous, twisted, crooked.

straightforward *(SYN.)* direct, open, candid, aboveboard.

(ANT.) devious.

strait *(SYN.)* fix, situation, passage, condition, dilemma, channel, trouble, predicament, difficulty, distress, crisis.

(ANT.) ease, calmness, satisfaction, comfort.

strange *(SYN.)* bizarre, peculiar, odd, abnormal, irregular, unusual, curious.

(ANT.) regular, common, familiar, conventional.

stranger *(SYN.)* foreigner, outsider, newcomer, alien, outlander, immigrant.

(ANT.) friend, associate, acquaintance.

strap *(SYN.)* strip, belt, thong, band.

stratagem *(SYN.)* design, ruse, cabal, plot, machination, subterfuge, trick, wile.

stream *(SYN.)* issue, proceed, flow, come, abound, spout, run, brook.

strength *(SYN.)* power, might, toughness, durability, lustiness, soundness, vigor.

(ANT.) weakness, frailty, feebleness.

stress *(SYN.)* urgency, press, emphasize, accentuate, accent, weight, strain, importance, compulsion.

(ANT.) relaxation, lenience, ease.

stretch *(SYN.)* strain, expand, elongate, extend, lengthen, spread, protract.

(ANT.) tighten, loosen, slacken, contract.

strict *(SYN.)* rough, stiff, stringent, harsh.

(ANT.) easygoing, lenient.

strike *(SYN.)* pound, hit, smite, beat, assault, attack, affect, impress, overwhelm, sitdown, walkout, slowdown.

striking *(SYN.)* arresting, imposing, splendid, august, impressive, thrilling, stirring, awesome, aweinspiring.

(ANT.) ordinary, unimpressive, commonplace, regular.

stringent *(SYN.)* harsh, rugged, grating, severe, gruff.

strip *(SYN.)* disrobe, undress, remove, uncover, peel, ribbon, band, piece.

stripped *(SYN.)* open, simple, bare, nude, uncovered, exposed, bald, plain, naked, barren, defenseless.

(ANT.) protected, dressed, concealed.

strive *(SYN.)* aim, struggle, attempt, undertake, design, endeavor, try.

(ANT.) omit, abandon, neglect, decline.

stroke *(SYN.)* rap, blow, tap, knock, feat, achievement, accomplishment, caress.

stroll *(SYN.)* amble, walk, ramble.

strong *(SYN.)* potent, hale, athletic, mighty, sturdy, impregnable, resistant.

(ANT.) feeble, insipid, brittle, weak, bland, fragile.

structure *(SYN.)* construction, framework, arrangement.

struggle *(SYN.)* fray, strive, fight, contest, battle, skirmish, oppose, clash.

(ANT.) peace, agreement, truce.

stubborn *(SYN.)* obstinate, firm, determined, inflexible, obdurate, uncompromising, pigheaded, contumacious, rigid, unbending, intractable.

(ANT.) docile, yielding, amenable.

student *(SYN.)* pupil, observer, disciple, scholar, learner.

study *(SYN.)* weigh, muse, master, contemplate, reflect, examination, examine.

stuff *(SYN.)* thing, subject, material, theme, matter, substance, fill, ram, cram, pack, textile, cloth, topic.

(ANT.) spirit, immateriality.

stumble *(SYN.)* sink, collapse, tumble, drop, topple, lurch, trip, fall.

(ANT.) steady, climb, soar, arise.

stun *(SYN.)* shock, knock out, dumbfound, take, amaze, alarm.

(ANT.) forewarn, caution, prepare.

stunning *(SYN.)* brilliant, dazzling, exquisite, ravishing.

(ANT.) drab, ugly.

stunt *(SYN.)* check, restrict, hinder.

stupid *(SYN.)* dull, obtuse, half-witted, brainless, foolish, dumb, witless, idiotic.

(ANT.) smart, intelligent, clever, quick, bright, alert, discerning.

stupor (SYN.) lethargy, torpor, daze, languor, drowsiness, numbness.
(ANT.) *wakefulness, liveliness, activity.*

sturdy (SYN.) hale, strong, rugged, stout, mighty, enduring, hardy, well-built.
(ANT.) *fragile, brittle, insipid, delicate.*

style (SYN.) sort, type, kind, chic, smartness, elegance.

subdue (SYN.) crush, overcome, rout, beat, reduce, lower, defeat, vanquish.
(ANT.) *retreat, cede, surrender.*

subject (SYN.) subordinate, theme, case, topic, dependent, citizen, matter.

sublime (SYN.) lofty, raised, elevated, supreme, exalted, splendid, grand.
(ANT.) *ordinary, vase, low, ridiculous.*

submerge (SYN.) submerse, dunk, sink, dip, immerse, engage, douse, engross.
(ANT.) *surface, rise, uplift, elevate.*

submissive (SYN.) deferential, yielding, dutiful, compliant.
(ANT.) *rebellious, intractable.*

submit (SYN.) quit, resign, waive, yield, tender, offer, abdicate, cede, surrender.
(ANT.) *fight, oppose, resist, struggle, deny, refuse.*

subordinate (SYN.) demean, reduce, inferior, assistant, citizen, liegeman.
(ANT.) *superior.*

subsequent (SYN.) later, following.
(ANT.) *preceding, previous.*

subside (SYN.) decrease, lower, sink, droop, hang, collapse, downward.
(ANT.) *mount, steady, arise, climb.*

subsidy (SYN.) support, aid, grant.

substance (SYN.) stuff, essence, importance, material, moment, matter.
(ANT.) *spirit, immaterial.*

substantial (SYN.) large, considerable, sizable, actual, real, tangible, influential.
(ANT.) *unimportant, trivial.*

substantiate (SYN.) strengthen, corroborate, confirm.

substitute (SYN.) proxy, expedient, deputy, makeshift, replacement, alternate, lieutenant, representative, surrogate, displace, exchange, equivalent.
(ANT.) *sovereign, master, head.*

subterfuge (SYN.) pretext, excuse, cloak, simulation, disguise, garb, pretension.
(ANT.) *reality, truth, actuality, sincerity.*

subtle (SYN.) suggestive, indirect.

(ANT.) *overt, obvious.*

subtract (SYN.) decrease, reduce, curtail, deduct, diminish, remove, lessen.
(ANT.) *expand, increase, add, enlarge, grow.*

succeed (SYN.) thrive, follow, replace, achieve, win, flourish, prevail, inherit.
(ANT.) *miscarry, anticipate, fail, precede.*

successful (SYN.) fortunate, favorable, lucky, triumphant.

succor (SYN.) ease, solace, comfort, enjoyment, consolation.
(ANT.) *suffering, discomfort, torture, affliction, torment.*

sudden (SYN.) rapid, swift, immediate, abrupt, unexpected, unforeseen, hasty.
(ANT.) *slowly, anticipated.*

suffer (SYN.) stand, experience, endure, bear, feel, allow, let, permit, sustain.
(ANT.) *exclude, banish, overcome.*

suggest (SYN.) propose, offer, recommend, allude.
(ANT.) *dictate, declare, insist.*

suggestion (SYN.) exhortation, recommendation, intelligence, caution, admonition, warning, advice.

suitable (SYN.) welcome, agreeable, acceptable, gratifying.
(ANT.) *offensive, disagreeable.*

sullen (SYN.) moody, fretful, surly, crabbed, morose, dour.
(ANT.) *merry, gay, pleasant, amiable.*

sum (SYN.) amount, total, aggregate, whole, increase, append, add.
(ANT.) *sample, fraction, reduce, deduct.*

summit (SYN.) peak, top, crown, pinnacle.
(ANT.) *bottom, foundation, base, foot.*

sunny (SYN.) cheery, cheerful, fair, joyful, happy, cloudless.
(ANT.) *overcast, cloudy.*

superficial (SYN.) flimsy, shallow, cursory, slight, exterior.
(ANT.) *thorough, deep, abstruse, profound.*

superior (SYN.) greater, finer, better, employer, boss.
(ANT.) *inferior.*

superiority (SYN.) profit, mastery, advantage, good, service, edge, utility.
(ANT.) *obstruction, harm, detriment, impediment.*

supernatural *(SYN.)* unearthly, preter-natural, marvelous, miraculous.
(ANT.) plain, human, physical, common.

supervise *(SYN.)* rule, oversee, govern, command, direct, superintend, control.
(ANT.) submit, forsake, abandon.

supervision *(SYN.)* oversight, charge, management.

supervisor *(SYN.)* manager, boss, foreman, director.

supple *(SYN.)* lithe, pliant, flexible, lim-ber, elastic, pliable.
(ANT.) stiff, brittle, rigid, unbending.

supplication *(SYN.)* invocation, plea, ap-peal, request, entreaty.

supply *(SYN.)* provide, inventory, hoard, reserve, store, accumulation, stock, fur-nish, endow, give.

support *(SYN.)* groundwork, aid, favor, base, prop, assistance, comfort, basis, succor, living, subsistence, encourage-ment, backing, help.
(ANT.) discourage, abandon, oppose, opposition, attack.

suppose *(SYN.)* believe, presume, deduce, apprehend, speculate, guess, conjecture.
(ANT.) prove, demonstrate, ascertain.

suppress *(SYN.)* diminish, reduce, over-power, abate, lessen, decrease, subdue.
(ANT.) revive, amplify, intensify, enlarge.

sure *(SYN.)* confident, fixed, trustwor-thy, reliable, unquestionable, convinced, stable, firm, safe, solid, destined, fated, inevitable, indubitable.
(ANT.) probable, uncertain, doubtful.

surface *(SYN.)* outside, exterior, cover, covering.

surly *(SYN.)* disagreeable, hostile, un-friendly, ugly, antagonistic.

surname *(SYN.)* denomination, epithet, title, name, appellation, designation.

surpass *(SYN.)* pass, exceed, excel, out-strip, outdo.

surplus *(SYN.)* extravagance, intem-perance, superabundance, excess, im-moderation, remainder, extra, pro-fusion, superfluity.
(ANT.) want, lack, dearth, paucity.

surprise *(SYN.)* miracle, prodigy, wonder, awe, phenomenon, marvel.
(ANT.) expectation, triviality, indif-ference, familiarity.

surrender *(SYN.)* relinquish, resign, yield, abandon, sacrifice, submit, cede.
(ANT.) overcome, rout, conquer.

surround *(SYN.)* confine, encompass, circle, encircle, girdle, fence, cir-cumscribe, limit, envelop.
(ANT.) open, distend, expose, enlarge.

suspect *(SYN.)* waver, disbelieve, presume, suppose, suspected, assume, defendant suspicious, doubt.
(ANT.) decide, believe, trust.

suspend *(SYN.)* delay, hang, withhold, in-terrupt, postpone, dangle, adjourn, poise, defer, swing.
(ANT.) persist, proceed, maintain.

suspicious *(SYN.)* suspecting, distrustful, doubtful, doubting, questioning, suspect, skeptical, unusual.

sustain *(SYN.)* bear, carry, help, advo-cate, back, encourage, maintain, assist.
(ANT.) discourage, betray, oppose, destroy.

sway *(SYN.)* control, affect, stir, ac-tuate, impel, impress, bend, wave, swing, persuade, influence.

swear *(SYN.)* declare, state, affirm, vouchsafe, curse, maintain.
(ANT.) demur, oppose, deny, contradict.

sweeping *(SYN.)* extensive, wide, general, broad, tolerant, comprehensive, vast.
(ANT.) restricted, confined.

sweet *(SYN.)* engaging, luscious, pure, clean, fresh, melodious, winning, un-salted, pleasant, agreeable.
(ANT.) bitter, harsh, nasty, irascible, dis-cordant, irritable, acrid.

swift *(SYN.)* quick, fast, fleet, speedy, rapid, expeditious.

swindle *(SYN.)* bilk, defraud, con, deceive, cheat, guile, imposture.
(ANT.) sincerity, honesty, fairness.

sympathetic *(SYN.)* considerate, compas-sionate, gentle, affable, merciful.
(ANT.) unkind, merciless, unsympathetic, indifferent, intolerant, cruel.

sympathy *(SYN.)* compassion, commisera-tion, pity.
(ANT.) indifference, unconcern, an-tipathy, malevolence.

system *(SYN.)* organization, procedure, regularity, arrangement, mode, order.
(ANT.) confusion, chance, disorder.

table 171 **tantrum**

table *(SYN.)* catalog, list, schedule, postpone, chart, index, shelve, delay.

tablet *(SYN.)* pad, notebook, capsule, sketchpad, pill, lozenge.

taboo *(SYN.)* banned, prohibited, forbidden, restriction.

(ANT.) accepted, allowed, sanctioned.

tacit *(SYN.)* understood, assumed.

taciturn *(SYN.)* quiet, withdrawn.

tack *(SYN.)* add, join, attach, clasp.

tackle *(SYN.)* rigging, gear, apparatus, equipment, grab, seize, catch, down, throw, try, undertake.

tacky *(SYN.)* gummy, sticky, gooey.

tact *(SYN.)* dexterity, poise, diplomacy, judgment, savoirfaire, skill, finesse, sense, prudence, adroitness, address.

(ANT.) incompetence, vulgarity, blunder, rudeness, awkwardness, insensitivity.

tactful *(SYN.)* discreet, considerate, judicious, adroit, sensitive, diplomatic, skillful, discriminating, politic.

(ANT.) coarse, gruff, tactless, boorish, unfeeling, churlish, rude.

tactical *(SYN.)* foxy, cunning, proficient, deft, adroit, clever, expert.

(ANT.) blundering, gauche, clumsy, inept.

tactics *(SYN.)* plan, strategy, approach, maneuver, course, scheme.

tag *(SYN.)* sticker, label, mark, identification, marker, name.

tail *(SYN.)* rear, back, follow, end, shadow, pursue, trail, heel.

tailor *(SYN.)* modiste, couturier, modify, redo, shape, fashion.

taint *(SYN.)* spot, stain, tarnish, soil, mark, discolor.

(ANT.) cleanse, disinfect, clean.

tainted *(SYN.)* crooked, impure, vitiated, profligate, debased, spoiled, corrupted, depraved, dishonest, contaminated, putrid, unsound.

take *(SYN.)* accept, grasp, catch, confiscate, clutch, adopt, assume, receive, bring, attract, claim, necessitate, steal, ensnare, capture, demand, select, appropriate, obtain, captivate, hold, seize, win, escort, note, record, rob, shoplift, get, remove, gain.

taking *(SYN.)* charming, captivating, winning, attractive.

takeover *(SYN.)* revolution, merger, usurpation, confiscation.

tale *(SYN.)* falsehood, history, yarn, chronicle, account, fable, fiction, narration, story, narrative, anecdote.

talent *(SYN.)* capability, knack, skill, endowment, gift, cleverness, aptitude, ability, cleverness, genius.

(ANT.) ineptitude, incompetence, stupidity.

talented *(SYN.)* skillful, smart, adroit, dexterous, clever, apt, quick-witted, witty, ingenious.

(ANT.) dull, clumsy, awkward, unskilled, stupid, slow.

talk *(SYN.)* conversation, gossip, report, speech, communicate, discuss, confer, chatter, conference, preach, dialogue, reason, jabber, discourse, lecture, communication, consul, plead, argue.

(ANT.) silence, correspondence, meditation, writing.

talkative *(SYN.)* glib, communicative, chattering, loquacious, voluble, garrulous, chatty.

(ANT.) uncommunicative, laconic, reticent, silent.

tall *(SYN.)* elevated, high, towering, big, lofty, imposing, gigantic.

(ANT.) tiny, low, short, small, stunted.

tally *(SYN.)* score, count, compute, reckon, calculate, estimate, list, figure.

tame *(SYN.)* domesticated, dull, insipid, docile, broken, uninteresting, gentle, subdued, insipid, flat, unexciting, boring, empty, break, domesticate, mild, tedious, domestic, submissive.

(ANT.) spirited, savage, wild, exciting, animated, undomesticated.

tamper *(SYN.)* mix in, interrupt, interfere, meddle, interpose.

tang *(SYN.)* zest, sharpness, tartness.

tangible *(SYN.)* material, sensible, palpable, corporeal, bodily.

(ANT.) metaphysical, mental, spiritual.

tangle *(SYN.)* confuse, knot, snarl, twist, ensnare, embroil, implicate.

tangy *(SYN.)* pungent, peppery, seasoned, sharp, tart.

tantalize *(SYN.)* tease, tempt, entice, titillate, stimulate, frustrate.

tantrum *(SYN.)* outburst, fit, fury, flare-up, conniption, rampage.

tap *(SYN.)* pat, rap, hit, strike, blow, faucet, spout, spigot, bunghole.

tape *(SYN.)* ribbon, strip, fasten, bandage, bind, record, tie.

taper *(SYN.)* narrow, decrease, lessen.

tardy *(SYN.)* slow, delayed, overdue, late.
(ANT.) prompt, timely, punctual, early.

target *(SYN.)* aim, goal, object, objective.

tariff *(SYN.)* duty, tax, levy, rate.

tarnish *(SYN.)* discolor, blight, defile, sully, spot, befoul, disgrace, stain.
(ANT.) honor, purify, cleanse, bleach, decorate, shine, gleam, sparkle.

tarry *(SYN.)* dawdle, loiter, linger, dally, remain, delay, procrastinate.

tart *(SYN.)* sour, acrid, pungent, acid, sharp, distasteful, bitter.
(ANT.) mellow, sweet, pleasant.

task *(SYN.)* work, job, undertaking, labor, chore, duty, stint.

taste *(SYN.)* tang, inclination, liking, sensibility, flavor, savor, try, sip, sample, zest, experience, undergo, appreciation, relish, discrimination, discernment, judgment.
(ANT.) indelicacy, disinclination, antipathy, insipidity.

tasteful *(SYN.)* elegant, choice, refined, suitable, artistic.
(ANT.) offensive, unbecoming.

tasteless *(SYN.)* flavorless, insipid, unpalatable, rude, unrefined, uncultivated, boorish, uninteresting.

tasty *(SYN.)* delectable, delicious, luscious, palatable, tempting.

tattered *(SYN.)* ragged, torn, shoddy, shabby, frazzled, frayed, tacky, seedy.

tattle *(SYN.)* inform, divulge, disclose, blab, reveal.

taunt *(SYN.)* tease, deride, flout, scoff, sneer, mock, annoy, pester, bother, ridicule, jeer.
(ANT.) praise, compliment, laud, flatter.

taunting *(SYN.)* ironic, caustic, cutting, sardonic, derisive, biting, acrimonious, sarcastic, satirical, sneering.
(ANT.) pleasant, agreeable, affable.

taut *(SYN.)* tight, constricted, firm, stretched, snug, tense, extended.
(ANT.) slack, loose, relaxed, open, lax.

tavern *(SYN.)* pub, bar, cocktail lounge.

tawdry *(SYN.)* pretentious, showy, vulgar, tasteless, sordid, garish.

tax *(SYN.)* duty, assessment, excise, levy, toll, burden, strain, tribute, tariff, assess, encumber, overload, impost, custom, exaction, rate.
(ANT.) reward, gift, remuneration.

taxi *(SYN.)* cab, taxicab.

teach *(SYN.)* inform, school, educate, train, inculcate, instruct, instill, tutor.
(ANT.) misinform, misguide.

teacher *(SYN.)* tutor, instructor, professor, lecturer.

team *(SYN.)* company, band, party, crew, gang, group.

teamwork *(SYN.)* collaboration.

tear *(SYN.)* rend, shred, sunder, cleave, rip, lacerate, teardrop, disunite, rend, divide, drop, wound, split, slit, sever.
(ANT.) mend, repair, join, unite, sew.

tearful *(SYN.)* sad, weeping, crying, sobbing, weepy, lachrymose.

tease *(SYN.)* badger, harry, bother, irritate, nag, pester, taunt, vex, annoy, disturb, harass, worry, tantalize, plague, aggravate, provoke, torment.
(ANT.) please, delight, soothe, comfort, gratify.

technical *(SYN.)* industrial, technological, specialized, mechanical.

technique *(SYN.)* system, method, routine, approach, procedure.

tedious *(SYN.)* boring, dilatory, humdrum, sluggish, monotonous, irksome, dreary, dull, tiring, burdensome, tiresome, wearisome, tardy.
(ANT.) interesting, entertaining, engaging, exciting, amusing, quick.

teem *(SYN.)* abound, swarm.

teeming *(SYN.)* overflowing, bountiful, abundant, ample, profuse, plenteous, rich, copious.
(ANT.) scant, scarce, deficient, insufficient.

teeter *(SYN.)* sway, hesitate, hem and haw, waver.

telecast *(SYN.)* broadcast.

televise *(SYN.)* telecast.

tell *(SYN.)* report, mention, state, betray, announce, recount, relate, narrate, rehearse, mention, utter, confess, disclose, direct, request, acquaint, instruct, notify, inform, discover, determine, reveal, divulge.

telling *(SYN.)* persuasive, convincing, forceful, effective.

telltale *(SYN.* revealing, informative, suggestive, meaningful.

temerity *(SYN.)* rashness, foolhardiness, audacity, boldness, recklessness.

(ANT.) prudence, wariness, caution, hesitation, timidity.

temper *(SYN.)* fury, choler, exasperation, anger, passion, petulance, disposition, nature, rage, soothe, soften, wrath, indignation, irritation, pacify, animosity, mood, resentment.

(ANT.) peace, self-control, forbearance, conciliation.

temperament *(SYN.)* humor, mood, temper, nature, disposition.

temperamental *(SYN.)* testy, moody, touchy, sensitive, irritable.

(ANT.) calm, unruffled, serene.

temperance *(SYN.)* abstinence, sobriety, self-denial, forbearance, abstention.

(ANT.) intoxication, excess, self-indulgence, gluttony, wantonness.

temperate *(SYN.)* controlled, moderate, cool, calm, restrained.

(ANT.) excessive, extreme, prodigal.

tempest *(SYN.)* draft, squall, wind, blast, gust, storm, hurricane, commotion, tumult, zephyr.

(ANT.) calm, tranquillity, peace.

tempo *(SYN.)* measure, beat, cadence, rhythm.

temporal *(SYN.)* mundane, earthly, lay, profane, worldly, terrestrial, laic.

(ANT.) spiritual, ecclesiastical, unworldly, religious, heavenly.

temporary *(SYN.)* brief, momentary, shortlived, fleeting, ephemeral, passing, short, transient.

(ANT.) lasting, permanent, immortal, everlasting, timeless, abiding.

tempt *(SYN.)* entice, allure, lure, attract, seduce, invite, magnetize.

tenacious *(SYN.)* persistent, determined, unchanging, unyielding.

tenable *(SYN.)* correct, practical, rational, reasonable, sensible, defensible.

tenacity *(SYN.)* perseverance, steadfastness, industry, constancy, persistence, pertinacity.

(ANT.) laziness, rest, cessation, idleness.

tenant *(SYN.)* renter, lessee, lodger, lease-holder, dweller, resident.

tend *(SYN.)* escort, follow, care for, lackey, watch, protect, take care of, attend, guard, serve.

tendency *(SYN.)* drift, inclination, proneness, leaning, bias, aim, leaning, disposition, predisposition, propensity, trend, impulse.

(ANT.) disinclination, aversion.

tender *(SYN.)* sympathetic, sore, sensitive, painful, gentle, meek, delicate, fragile, proffer, bland, mild, loving, offer, affectionate, soothing, propose, moderate, soft.

(ANT.) rough, severe, fierce, chewy, tough, cruel, unfeeling, harsh.

tenderfoot *(SYN.)* novice, apprentice, beginner, amateur.

tenderhearted *(SYN.)* kind, sympathetic, merciful, softhearted, understanding, sentimental, affectionate, gentle.

tenderness *(SYN.)* attachment, kindness, love, affection, endearment.

(ANT.) repugnance, indifference, aversion, hatred, repulsive.

tenet *(SYN.)* dogma, belief, precept, doctrine, creed, opinion.

(ANT.) deed, conduct, practice, performance.

tense *(SYN.)* strained, stretched, excited, tight, nervous.

(ANT.) loose, placid, lax, relaxed.

tension *(SYN.)* stress, strain, pressure, anxiety, apprehension, distress.

tentative *(SYN.)* hypothetical, indefinite, probationary, conditional.

tenure *(SYN.)* administration, time, regime, term.

tepid *(SYN.)* temperate, mild, lukewarm.

(ANT.) boiling, scalding, passionate, hot.

term *(SYN.)* period, limit, time, boundary, duration, name, phrase, interval, session, semester, expression, word.

terminal *(SYN.)* eventual, final, concluding, decisive, ending, fatal, latest, last, ultimate, conclusive.

(ANT.) original, first, rudimentary, incipient, inaugural.

terminate *(SYN.)* close, end, finish, abolish, complete, cease, stop, conclude, expire, culminate.

(ANT.) *establish, begin, initiate, start, commence.*

terminology *(SYN.)* vocabulary, nomenclature, terms, phraseology.

terms *(SYN.)* stipulations, agreement, conditions, provisions.

terrible *(SYN.)* frightful, dire, awful, gruesome, horrible shocking, horrifying, terrifying, horrid, hideous, appalling.

(ANT.) *secure, happy, joyous, pleasing, safe.*

terrific *(SYN.)* superb, wonderful, glorious, great, magnificent, divine, colossal, sensational, marvelous.

terrify *(SYN.)* dismay, intimidate, startle, terrorize, appall, frighten, petrify, astound, alarm, affright, horrify, scare.

(ANT.) *soothe, allay, reassure, compose, embolden.*

territory *(SYN.)* dominion, province, quarter, section, country, division, region, domain, area, place, district.

terror *(SYN.)* fear, alarm, dismay, horror, dread, consternation, fright, panic.

(ANT.) *calm, security, assurance, peace.*

terse *(SYN.)* concise, incisive, succinct, summary, condensed, compact, neat, pithy, summary.

(ANT.) *verbose, wordy, lengthy, prolix.*

test *(SYN.)* exam, examination, trial, quiz, analyze, verify, validate.

testify *(SYN.)* depose, warrant, witness, state, attest, swear.

testimony *(SYN.)* evidence, attestation, declaration, proof, witness.

(ANT.) *refutation, argument, disproof, contradiction.*

testy *(SYN.)* ill-natured, irritable, snappish, waspish, fractious, fretful, touchy, ill-tempered, peevish, petulant.

(ANT.) *pleasant, affable, good-tempered, genial, good-natured.*

tether *(SYN.)* tie, hamper, restraint.

text *(SYN.)* textbook, book, manual.

textile *(SYN.)* material, cloth, fabric.

texture *(SYN.)* construction, structure, make-up, composition, grain, finish.

thankful *(SYN.)* obliged, grateful, appreciative.

(ANT.) *thankless, ungrateful, resenting.*

thaw *(SYN.)* liquefy, melt, dissolve.

(ANT.) *solidify, freeze.*

theater *(SYN.)* arena, playhouse, battlefield, stadium, hall.

theatrical *(SYN.)* ceremonious, melodramatic, stagy, artificial, affected, dramatic, showy, dramatic, compelling.

(ANT.) *unemotional, subdued, modest, unaffected.*

theft *(SYN.)* larceny, robbery, stealing, plunder, burglary, pillage, thievery.

theme *(SYN.)* motive, topic, argument, subject, thesis, text, point, paper.

theoretical *(SYN.)* bookish, learned, scholarly, pedantic, academic, formal, erudite, scholastic.

(ANT.) *practical, ignorant, common-sense, simple.*

theory *(SYN.)* doctrine, guess, presupposition, postulate, assumption, hypothesis, speculation.

(ANT.) *practice, verity, fact, proof.*

therefore *(SYN.)* consequently, thence so, accordingly, hence, then.

thick *(SYN.)* compressed, heavy, compact, viscous, close, concentrated, crowded, syrupy, dense.

(ANT.) *watery, slim, thin, sparse, dispersed, dissipated.*

thief *(SYN.)* burglar, robber, criminal.

thin *(SYN.)* diluted, flimsy, lean, narrow, slender, spare, emaciated, diaphanous, gauzy, meager, slender, tenuous, slim, rare, sparse, scanty, lank, gossamer, scanty, slight.

(ANT.) *fat, wide, broad, thick, bulky.*

think *(SYN.)* picture, contemplate, ponder, esteem, intend, mean, imagine, deliberate, contemplate, recall, speculate, recollect, deem, apprehend, consider, devise, plan, judge, purpose, reflect, suppose, assume, meditate.

(ANT.) *forget, conjecture, guess.*

thirst *(SYN.)* desire, craving, longing.

thirsty *(SYN.)* arid, dry, dehydrated, parched, craving, desirous.

(ANT.) *satisfied.*

thorn *(SYN.)* spine, barb, prickle, nettle, bramble.

thorough *(SYN.)* entire, complete, perfect, total, finished, unbroken, perfect, careful, consummate, undivided.

(ANT.) *unfinished, careless, slapdash,*

imperfect, haphazard, lacking.

thoroughfare *(SYN.)* avenue, street, parkway, highway, boulevard.

(ANT.) byway.

though *(SYN.)* in any case, notwithstanding, however, nevertheless.

thought *(SYN.)* consideration, pensive, attentive, heedful, prudent, dreamy, reflective, introspective, meditation, notion, view, deliberation, sentiment, fancy, idea, impression, reasoning, contemplation, judgment, regard.

(ANT.) thoughtlessness.

thoughtful *(SYN.)* considerate, attentive, dreamy, pensive, provident, introspective, meditative, cautious, heedful, kind, courteous, friendly, pensive.

(ANT.) thoughtless, heedless, inconsiderate, rash, precipitous, selfish.

thoughtless *(SYN.)* inattentive, unconcerned, negligent, lax, desultory, inconsiderate, careless, imprudent, inaccurate, neglectful, indiscreet, remiss.

(ANT.) meticulous, accurate, nice.

thrash *(SYN.)* whip, beat, defeat, flog, punish, flog, strap, thresh.

thread *(SYN.)* yarn, strand, filament, fiber, string, cord.

threadbare *(SYN.)* shabby, tacky, worn, ragged, frayed.

threat *(SYN.)* menace, warning, danger, hazard, jeopardy, omen.

threaten *(SYN.)* caution, warning, forewarn, menace, intimidate, loom.

threatening *(SYN.)* imminent, nigh, approaching, impending, overhanging, sinister, foreboding.

(ANT.) improbable, retreating, afar, distant, remote.

threshold *(SYN.)* edge, verge, start, beginning, doorsill, commencement.

thrift *(SYN.)* prudence, conservation, saving, economy.

thrifty *(SYN.)* saving, economical, sparing, frugal, provident, stingy, saving, parsimonious.

(ANT.) wasteful, spendthrift, intemperate, self-indulgent, extravagant.

thrill *(SYN.)* arouse, rouse, excite, stimulation, excitement, tingle.

(ANT.) bore.

thrive *(SYN.)* succeed, flourish, grow,

prosper.

(ANT.) expire, fade, shrivel, die, fail, languish.

throb *(SYN.)* pound, pulsate, palpitate, beat, pulse.

throe *(SYN.)* pang, twinge, distress, suffering, pain, ache, grief, agony.

(ANT.) pleasure, relief, ease, solace, comfort.

throng *(SYN.)* masses, press, crowd, bevy, populace, swarm, rabble, horde, host, mass, teem, mob, multitude.

throttle *(SYN.)* smother, choke, strangle.

through *(SYN.)* completed, done, finished, over.

throughout *(SYN.)* all over, everywhere.

throw *(SYN.)* propel, cast, pitch, toss, hurl, send, thrust, fling.

(ANT.) retain, pull, draw, haul, hold

thrust *(SYN.)* jostle, push, promote, crowd, force, drive, hasten, push, press, shove, urge.

(ANT.) ignore, falter, retreat, drag, oppose, halt.

thug *(SYN.)* mobster, hoodlum, mugger, gangster, assassin, gunman.

thump *(SYN.)* blow, strike, knock, jab, poke, pound, beat, clout, bat, rap, bang.

thunderstruck *(SYN.)* amazed, astounded, astonished, awed, flabbergasted, surprised, dumbfounded, bewildered, spellbound.

thus *(SYN.)* hence, therefore, accordingly, so, consequently.

thwart *(SYN.)* defeat, frustrate, prevent, foil, stop, baffle, circumvent hinder, obstruct, disappoint, balk, outwit.

(ANT.) promote, accomplish, fulfill, help, further.

ticket *(SYN.)* stamp, label, tag, seal, token, pass, summons, certificate, ballot, sticker, slate, citation.

tickle *(SYN.)* delight, entertain, thrill, amuse, titillate, excite.

ticklish *(SYN.)* fragile, delicate, tough.

tidings *(SYN.)* message, report, information, word, intelligence, news.

tidy *(SYN.)* trim, clear, neat, precise, spruce, orderly, shipshape.

(ANT.) disheveled, unkempt, sloppy, dirty, slovenly.

tie *(SYN.)* bond, join, relationship, bind,

restrict, fetter, connect, conjunction, association, alliance, union, fasten, engage, attach, restrain, oblige, link.
(ANT.) separation, disunion, unfasten, open, loose, untie, free, isolation.

tier *(SYN.)* line, row, level, deck, layer.

tiff *(SYN.)* bicker, squabble, argue, row, clash, dispute, altercation.

tight *(SYN.)* firm, taut, penny-pinching, constricted, snug, taut, parsimonious, secure, fast, strong, sealed, fastened, watertight, locked, close, compact.
(ANT.) slack, lax, open, relaxed, loose.

till *(SYN.)* plow, work, moneybox, depository, cultivate, vault.

tilt *(SYN.)* slant, slope, incline, tip, lean.

timber *(SYN.)* lumber, wood, logs.

time *(SYN.)* epoch, span, term, age, duration, interim, period, tempo, interval, space, spell, season.

timeless *(SYN.)* unending, lasting, perpetual, endless, immemorial.
(ANT.) temporary, mortal, temporal.

timely *(SYN.)* prompt, exact, punctual, ready, precise.
(ANT.) slow, dilatory, tardy, late.

timepiece *(SYN.)* clock, watch.

timetable *(SYN.)* list, schedule.

timid *(SYN.)* coy, humble, sheepish, abashed, embarrassed, modest, bashful, diffident, shamefaced, retiring, fearful, faint-hearted, shy, timorous.
(ANT.) gregarious, bold, daring, adventurous, fearless, outgoing.

tinge *(SYN.)* color, tint, dye, stain, flavor, imbue, season, impregnate.

tingle *(SYN.)* shiver, chime, prickle.

tinker *(SYN.)* potter, putter, fiddle with, dawdle, dally, dabble.

tinkle *(SYN.)* sound, ring, jingle, chime.

tint *(SYN.)* color, tinge, dye, stain, hue, tone, shade.

tiny *(SYN.)* minute, little, petty, wee, slight, diminutive, miniature, small, insignificant, trivial, puny.
(ANT.) huge, large, immense, big, enormous.

tip *(SYN.)* point, end, top, peak, upset, tilt, reward, gift, gratuity, clue, hint, suggestion, inkling.

tirade *(SYN.)* outburst, harangue.

tire *(SYN.)* jade, tucker, bore, weary, exhaust, weaken, wear out, fatigue.
(ANT.) restore, revive, exhilarate, amuse, invigorate, refresh.

tired *(SYN.)* weary, exhausted, fatigued, run-down, sleepy, faint, spent, wearied, worn, jaded.
(ANT.) rested, fresh, hearty, invigorated, energetic, tireless, eager.

tireless *(SYN.)* active, enthusiastic, energetic, strenuous.
(ANT.) exhausted, wearied, fatigued.

tiresome *(SYN.)* dull, boring, monotonous, tedious.
(ANT.) interesting.

titan *SYN.)* colossus, powerhouse, mammoth.

title *(SYN.)* epithet, privilege, name, appellation, claim, denomination, due, heading, ownership, right, deed, designation.

toast *(SYN.)* pledge, celebration.

toddle *(SYN.)* stumble, wobble, shuffle.

toil *(SYN.)* labor, drudgery, work, travail, performance, business, achievement, employment, occupation, sweat, effort.
(ANT.) recreation, ease, vacation, relax, loll, play, leisure, repose.

token *(SYN.)* mark, sign, sample, indication, evidence, symbol.

tolerant *(SYN.)* extensive, vast, considerate, broad, patient, large, sweeping, liberal, wide.
(ANT.) intolerant, bigoted, biased, restricted, narrow, confined.

tolerate *(SYN.)* endure, allow, bear, authorize, permit, brook, stand, abide.
(ANT.) forbid, protest, prohibit, discriminating, unreasonable.

toll *(SYN.)* impost, burden, rate, assessment, duty, custom, excise, tribute, levy, burden, strain.
(ANT.) reward, wages, gift.

tomb *(SYN.)* vault, monument, catacomb, grave, mausoleum.

tone *(SYN.)* noise, sound, mood, manner, expression, cadence.

tongs *(SYN.)* tweezers, hook, grapnel, forceps.

tongue *(SYN.)* diction, lingo, cant, jargon, vernacular, dialect, idiom, speech.
(ANT.) nonsense, babble, gibberish.

too *(SYN.)* furthermore, moreover,

similarly, also, besides, likewise.

tool *(SYN.)* devise, medium, apparatus, agent, implement, utensil, agent, vehicle, instrument.

(ANT.) preventive, hindrance, impediment, obstruction.

top *(SYN.)* crown, pinnacle, peak, tip, cover, cap, zenith, chief, head, summit.

(ANT.) bottom, foundation, base, foot.

topic *(SYN.)* subject, thesis, issue, argument, matter, theme, point.

topple *(SYN.)* collapse, sink, fall, tumble.

torment *(SYN.)* pain, woe, pester, ache, distress, misery, harass, throe, annoy, vex, torture, anguish, suffering, misery.

(ANT.) relief, comfort, ease, gratify, delight.

torpid *(SYN.)* sluggish, idle, lazy, inert, inactive, supine, slothful, indolent, motionless, lethargic.

(ANT.) alert, assiduous, diligent, active.

torpor *(SYN.)* lethargy, daze, numbness, stupor, drowsiness, insensibility.

(ANT.) wakefulness, liveliness, activity, alertness, readiness.

torrent *(SYN.)* flood, downpour, deluge.

torrid *(SYN.)* scorching, ardent, impetuous, passionate, scalding, warm, fiery, hot-blooded, sultry, tropical, intense, sweltering, burning, hot.

(ANT.) passionless, impassive, cold, frigid, apathetic, freezing, phlegmatic, indifferent, temperate.

torso *(SYN.)* form, frame, body.

(ANT.) soul, mind, spirit, intellect.

torture *(SYN.)* anguish, badger, plague, distress, ache, torment, pester, pain, hound, agony, woe, worry, vex, persecute, suffering, throe, afflict, misery.

(ANT.) aid, relief, comfort, ease, support, encourage, mitigation.

toss *(SYN.)* throw, cast, hurl, pitch, tumble, thrust, pitch, fling, propel.

(ANT.) retain, pull, draw, haul, hold.

total *(SYN.)* entire, complete, concluded, finished, thorough, whole, entirely, collection, aggregate, conglomeration, unbroken, perfect, undivided, full.

(ANT.) part, element, imperfect, unfinished, ingredient, particular, lacking.

tote *(SYN.)* move, transfer, convey, carry.

totter *(SYN.)* falter, stagger, reel, sway, waver, stumble, wobble.

touch *(SYN.)* finger, feel, handle, move, affect, concern, mention, hint, trace, suggestion, knack, skill, ability, talent.

touch-and-go *(SYN.)* dangerous, risky, perilous, hazardous.

touching *(SYN.)* pitiable, affecting, moving, sad, adjunct, bordering, tangent, poignant, tender, effective.

(ANT.) removed, enlivening, animated, exhilarating.

touchy *(SYN.)* snappish, irritable, fiery, choleric, testy, hot, irascible, nervous, excitable, petulant, sensitive, short-tempered, jumpy, peevish.

(ANT.) composed, agreeable, tranquil, calm, serene, stolid, cool.

tough *(SYN.)* sturdy, difficult, trying, vicious, incorrigible, troublesome, hard, stout, leathery, strong, laborious, inedible, sinewy, cohesive, firm, callous, obdurate, vicious.

(ANT.) vulnerable, submissive, easy, brittle, facile, weak, fragile, compliant, tender, frail.

toughness *(SYN.)* stamina, sturdiness, fortitude, durability, intensity, might, stoutness, power, sturdiness, vigor.

(ANT.) weakness, feebleness, infirmity.

tour *(SYN.)* rove, travel, go, visit, excursion, ramble, journey, roam.

(ANT.) stop, stay.

tourist *(SYN.)* traveler, sightseer, vagabond, voyager.

tournament *(SYN.)* tourney, match, contest, competition.

tout *(SYN.)* vend, importune, peddle, solicit, sell, hawk.

tow *(SYN.)* tug, take out, unsheathe, haul, draw, remove, extract, pull, drag.

(ANT.) propel, drive.

towering *(SYN.)* elevated, exalted, high, lofty, tall, proud, eminent.

(ANT.) base, stunted, small, tiny, low.

town *(SYN.)* hamlet, village, community, municipality.

toxic *(SYN.)* deadly, poisonous, fatal, lethal, harmful.

(ANT.) beneficial.

toy *(SYN.)* play, romp, frolic, gamble, stake, caper, plaything, wager, revel.

trace *(SYN.)* stigma, feature, indication,

trait, mark, stain, scar, sign, trial, trace, suggestion, characteristic, vestige, symptoms.

track (SYN.) persist, pursue, follow, sign, mark, spoor, trace, path, route, road, carry, hunt, chase.

(ANT.) escape, abandon, flee, elude.

tract (SYN.) area, region, territory, district, expanse, domain.

tractable (SYN.) yielding, deferential, submissive, compliant, obedient.

(ANT.) rebellious, intractable, insubordinate, obstinate.

trade (SYN.) business, traffic, commerce, dealing, craft, occupation, profession, livelihood, swap, barter, exchange.

trademark (SYN.) logo, brand name, identification, emblem, insignia.

tradition (SYN.) custom, legend, folklore, belief, rite, practice.

traduce (SYN.) defame, malign, vilify, revile, abuse, asperse, scandalize.

(ANT.) protect, honor, cherish, praise, respect, support, extol.

tragedy (SYN.) unhappiness, misfortune, misery, adversity, catastrophe.

tragic (SYN.) miserable, unfortunate, depressing, melancholy, mournful.

(ANT.) happy, cheerful, comic.

trail (SYN.) persist, pursue, chase, follow, drag, draw, hunt, track.

(ANT.) evade, flee, abandon, elude.

train (SYN.) direct, prepare, aim, point, level, teach, drill, tutor, bid, instruct, order, command.

(ANT.) distract, deceive, misdirect.

traipse (SYN.) roam, wander, saunter, meander.

trait (SYN.) characteristic, feature, attribute, peculiarity, mark, property.

traitor (SYN.) turncoat, betrayer, spy, double-dealer, conspirator.

traitorous (SYN.) disloyal, faithless, apostate, false, recreant, perfidious, treasonable, treacherous.

(ANT.) devoted, true, loyal, constant.

tramp (SYN.) bum, beggar, rover, hobo, march, stamp, stomp, vagabond.

(ANT.) laborer, worker, gentleman.

trample (SYN.) crush, stomp, squash.

tranquil (SYN.) composed, calm, dispassionate, imperturbable, peaceful,

pacific, placid, quiet, still, serene, undisturbed, unruffled.

(ANT.) frantic, stormy, excited, disturbed, upset, turbulent, wild.

tranquillity (SYN.) calmness, calm, hush, peace, quiet, quiescence, quietude, repose, serenity, rest, stillness, silence.

(ANT.) disturbance, agitation, excitement, tumult, noise.

transact (SYN.) conduct, manage, execute, treat, perform.

transaction (SYN.) business, deal, affair, deed, settlement, occurrence, negotiation, proceeding.

transcend (SYN.) overstep, exceed.

transcribe (SYN.) write, copy, record.

transfer (SYN.) dispatch, send, transmit, remove, transport, transplant, consign, move, shift, reasign, assign, relegate.

transform (SYN.) change, convert, alter, modify, transfigure, shift, vary, veer.

(ANT.) establish, continue, settle, preserve, stabilize.

transgression (SYN.) atrocity, indignity, offense, insult, outrage, aggression, injustice, crime, misdeed, trespass, sin, wrong, vice.

(ANT.) innocence, gentleness, right.

transient (SYN.) ephemeral, evanescent, brief, fleeting, momentary, temporary, short-lived.

(ANT.) immortal, abiding, permanent, lasting, timeless, established.

transition (SYN.) change, variation, modification.

translate (SYN.) decipher, construe, decode, elucidate, explicate, explain, interpret, solve, render, unravel.

(ANT.) distort, falsify, misinterpret, confuse, misconstrue.

transmit (SYN.) confer, convey, communicate, divulge, disclose, impart, send, inform, relate, notify, reveal, dispatch, tell.

(ANT.) withhold, hide, conceal.

transparent (SYN.) crystalline, clear, limpid, lucid, translucent, thin, evident, manifest, plain, evident, explicit, obvious, open.

(ANT.) opaque, muddy, turbid, thick, questionable, ambiguous.

transpire (SYN.) befall, bechance, betide,

happen, chance, occur.

transport *(SYN.)* carry, bear, convey, remove, move, shift, enrapture, transfer, lift, entrance, ravish, stimulate.

transpose *(SYN.)* change, switch, reverse.

trap *(SYN.)* artifice, bait, ambush, intrigue, net, lure, pitfall, ensnare, deadfall, snare, ruse, entrap, bag, trick, stratagem, wile.

trash *(SYN.)* garbage, rubbish, waste.

trashy *(SYN.)* insignificant, worthless, slight.

trauma *(SYN.)* ordeal, upheaval, jolt, shock, disturbance.

travail *(SYN.)* suffering, torment, anxiety, anguish, misery, ordeal.

travel *(SYN.)* journey, go, touring, ramble, voyage, cruise, tour, roam.
(ANT.) stop, stay, remain, hibernate.

travesty *(SYN.)* farce, joke, misrepresentation, counterfeit, mimicry.

treachery *(SYN.)* collusion, cabal, combination, intrigue, conspiracy, machination, disloyalty, betrayal, treason, plot.
(ANT.) allegiance, steadfastness, loyalty.

treason *(SYN.)* cabal, combination, betrayal, sedition, collusion, intrigue, conspiracy, machination, disloyalty, treachery, plot.

treasure *(SYN.)* cherish, hold dear, abundance, guard, prize, appreciate, value, riches, wealth, foster, sustain, nurture.
(ANT.) disregard, neglect, dislike, abandon, reject.

treat *(SYN.)* employ, avail, manipulate, exploit, operate, utilize, exert, act, exercise, practice, handle, manage, deal, entertain, indulge, host, negotiate, tend, attend, heal, use.
(ANT.) neglect, overlook, ignore, waste.

treaty *(SYN.)* compact, agreement, pact, bargain, covenant, alliance, marriage.
(ANT.) schism, separation, divorce.

trek *(SYN.)* tramp, hike, plod, trudge.

tremble *(SYN.)* flutter, jolt, jar, agitate, quake, quiver, quaver, rock, shake shudder, shiver, totter, vibrate, waver.

trembling *(SYN.)* apprehension, alarm, dread, fright, fear, horror, terror, panic.
(ANT.) composure, calmness, tranquility, serenity.

tremendous *(SYN.)* enormous, huge,

colossal, gigantic, great, large.

tremor *(SYN.)* flutter, palpitation.

trench *(SYN.)* gully, gorge, ditch, gulch, moat, dugout, trough.

trenchant *(SYN.)* clear, emphatic, forceful, impressive, meaningful.

trend *(SYN.)* inclination, tendency, drift, course, tendency, direction.

trendy *(SYN.)* modish, faddish, stylish, voguish, popular, current.

trepidation *(SYN.)* apprehension, alarm, dread, fright, fear, horror, panic, terror.
(ANT.) boldness, bravery, fearlessness, courage, assurance.

trespass *(SYN.)* atrocity, indignity, affront, insult, outrage, offense, aggression, crime, misdeed, injustice, vice, wrong, sin.
(ANT.) evacuate, relinquish, abandon.

trespasser *(SYN.)* invader, intruder.

trial *(SYN.)* experiment, ordeal, proof, test, examination, attempt, effort, endeavor, essay, affliction, misery, hardship, suffering, difficulty, misfortune, tribulation, trouble.
(ANT.) consolation, alleviation.

tribe *(SYN.)* group, race, clan, bunch.

tribulation *(SYN.)* anguish, distress, agony, grief, misery, sorrow, torment, suffering, woe, disaster, calamity, evil, trouble, misfortune.
(ANT.) elation, joy, fun, pleasure.

tribunal *(SYN.)* arbitrators, judges, decision-makers, judiciary.

trick *(SYN.)* artifice, antic, deception, device, cheat, fraud, hoax, guile, imposture, ruse, ploy, stratagem, trickery, deceit, jest, joke, prank, defraud, subterfuge, wile, stunt.
(ANT.) exposure, candor, openness, honesty, sincerity.

trickle *(SYN.)* drip, dribble, leak, seep.

tricky *(SYN.)* artifice, antic, covert, cunning, foxy, crafty, furtive, guileful, insidious, sly, shrews, stealthy, surreptitious, subtle, underhand, wily.
(ANT.) frank, candid, ingenuous, sincere, open.

trifling *(SYN.)* insignificant, frivolous, paltry, petty, trivial, small, unimportant.
(ANT.) momentous, serious, important.

trigger *(SYN.)* generate, provoke,

prompt, motivate, activate.

trim *(SYN.)* nice, clear, orderly, precise, tidy, spruce, adorn, bedeck, clip, shave, prune, cut, shear, compact, neat, decorate, embellish, garnish.

(ANT.) deface, deform, spoil, mar, important, serious, momentous, weighty.

trimmings *(SYN.)* accessories, adornments, decorations, garnish, ornaments.

trinket *(SYN.)* bead, token, memento, bauble, charm, knickknack.

trio *(SYN.)* threesome, triad, triple.

trip *(SYN.)* expedition, cruise, stumble, err, journey, jaunt, passage, blunder, bungle, slip, excursion, tour, pilgrimage, voyage, travel.

trite *(SYN.)* common, banal, hackneyed, ordinary, stereotyped, stale.

(ANT.) modern, fresh, momentous, stimulating, novel, new.

triumph *(SYN.)* conquest, achievement, success, prevail, win, jubilation, victory.

(ANT.) succumb, failure, defeat.

triumphant *(SYN.)* celebrating, exultant, joyful, exhilarated, smug.

trivial *(SYN.)* insignificant, frivolous, paltry, petty, trifling, small.

(ANT.) momentous, important weighty, serious.

troops *(SYN.)* militia, troopers, recruits, soldiers, enlisted men.

trophy *(SYN.)* award, memento, honor, testimonial, prize.

tropical *(SYN.)* sultry, sweltering, humid.

trouble *(SYN.)* anxiety, affliction, calamity, distress, hardship, grief, pain, misery, sorrow, woe, bother, annoyance, care, embarrassment, irritation, torment, pains, worry, disorder, problem, disturbance, care, effort, exertion, toil, inconvenience, misfortune, labor.

(ANT.) console, accommodate, gratify, soothe, joy, peace.

troublemaker *(SYN.)* rebel, scamp, agitator, demon, devil, ruffian.

troublesome *(SYN.)* bothersome, annoying, distressing, irksome, disturbing, trying, arduous, vexatious, arduous, difficult, burdensome, laborious, tedious.

(ANT.) amusing, accommodating, gratifying, easy, pleasant.

trounce *(SYN.)* lash, flog, switch, whack,

punish, whip, stomp.

truant *(SYN.)* delinquent, absentee, vagrant, malingerer.

truce *(SYN.)* armistice, cease-fire, interval, break, intermission, respite.

trudge *(SYN.)* march, trek, lumber, hike.

true *(SYN.)* actual, authentic, accurate, correct, exact, genuine, real, veracious, veritable, constant, honest, faithful, loyal, reliable, valid, legitimate, steadfast, sincere, trustworthy.

(ANT.) erroneous, counterfeit, false, spurious, fictitious, faithless, inconstant, fickle.

truly *(SYN.)* indeed, actually, precisely, literally, really, factually.

truncate *(SYN.)* prune, clip, shorten.

truss *(SYN.)* girder, brace, framework.

trust *(SYN.)* credence, confidence, dependence, reliance, faith, trust, depend on, rely on, reckon on, believe, hope, credit, commit, entrust, confide.

(ANT.) incredulity, doubt, skepticism, mistrust.

trusted *(SYN.)* trustworthy, reliable, true, loyal, staunch, devoted.

trustworthy *(SYN.)* dependable, certain, reliable, secure, safe, sure, tried.

(ANT.) fallible, dubious, questionable, unreliable, uncertain.

truth *(SYN.)* actuality, authenticity, accuracy, correctness, exactness, honesty, fact, rightness, truthfulness, veracity, verisimilitude, verity.

(ANT.) falsehood, fiction, lie, untruth.

truthful *(SYN.)* frank, candid, honest, sincere, open, veracious, accurate, correct, exact, reliable.

(ANT.) misleading, sly, deceitful.

try *(SYN.)* endeavor, attempt, strive, struggle, undertake, afflict, test, prove, torment, trouble, essay, examine, analyze, investigate, effort, aim, design, aspire, intend, mean.

(ANT.) decline, ignore, abandon, omit, neglect, comfort, console.

trying *(SYN.)* bothersome, annoying, distressing, irksome, disturbing, troublesome, arduous, vexatious, burdensome, difficult, tedious.

(ANT.) amusing, easy, accommodating, pleasant, gratifying.

tryout *(SYN.)* audition, trial, chance, test.

tryst *(SYN.)* rendezvous, meeting, appointment.

tub *(SYN.)* basin, vessel, sink, bowl.

tube *(SYN.)* hose, pipe, reed.

tubular *(SYN.)* hollow, cylindrical.

tuck *(SYN.)* crease, fold, gather, bend.

tuft *(SYN.)* bunch, group, cluster.

tug *(SYN.)* pull, wrench, tow, haul, draw, yank, jerk.

tuition *(SYN.)* instruction, schooling, teaching, education.

tumble *(SYN.)* toss, trip, fall, sprawl, wallow, lurch, flounder, plunge, topple, stumble.

tumble-down *(SYN.)* ramshackle, decrepit, dilapidated, rickety.

tumult *(SYN.)* chaos, agitation, commotion, confusion, disarray, disarrangement, disorder, noise, hubbub, ferment, stir, jumble, disturbance, uproar.

(ANT.) peacefulness, order, peace, certainty, tranquillity.

tune *(SYN.)* song, concord, harmony, air, melody, strain.

(ANT.) aversion, discord, antipathy.

tunnel *(SYN.)* passage, grotto, cave.

turbid *(SYN.)* dark, cloudy, thick, muddy.

turbulent *(SYN.)* gusty, blustery, inclement, rough, roaring, stormy, tempestuous, disorderly, violent, tumultuous, unruly, windy.

(ANT.) clear, calm, quiet, peaceful, tranquil.

turf *(SYN.)* lawn, grassland, sod, grass.

turmoil *(SYN.)* chaos, agitation, commotion, confusion, disarray, disarrangement, disorder, jumble, uproar.

(ANT.) order, peace, certainty, quiet, tranquillity.

turn *(SYN.)* circulate, circle, invert, rotate, revolve, spin, twist, twirl, whirl, wheel, avert, reverse, become, sour, spoil, ferment, deviate, deflect, divert, swerve, change, alter, transmute.

(ANT.) fix, stand, arrest, stop, continue, endure, proceed, perpetuate.

turncoat *(SYN.)* renegade, defector, deserter, rat, betrayer, traitor.

(ANT.) loyalist.

turret *(SYN.)* watchtower, belfry, steeple, tower, cupola, lookout.

tussle *(SYN.)* wrestle, struggle, contend, battle, fight, scuffle.

tutor *(SYN.)* instruct, prime, school, teach, train, prepare, drill.

tweak *(SYN.)* squeeze, pinch, nip.

twig *(SYN.)* sprig, branch, shoot, stem.

twilight *(SYN.)* sunset, sundown, nightfall, eventide, dusk.

twin *(SYN.)* lookalike, imitation, copy, double, replica.

twine *(SYN.)* string, cordage, rope, cord.

twinge *(SYN.)* smart, pang, pain.

twinkle *(SYN.)* shine, gleam, glisten, sparkle, glitter, shimmer, scintillate.

twirl *(SYN.)* rotate, spin, wind, turn, pivot, wheel, swivel, whirl.

twist *(SYN.)* bow, bend, crook, intertwine, curve, incline, deflect, lean, braid, distort, contort, warp, interweave, stoop, turn.

(ANT.) resist, break, straighten, stiffen.

twitch *(SYN.)* fidget, shudder, jerk.

two-faced *(SYN.)* deceitful, insincere, hypocritical, false, untrustworthy.

(ANT.) straightforward, honest.

tycoon *(SYN.)* millionaire, industrialist, businessman.

tyke *(SYN.)* rascal, urchin, brat, imp.

type *(SYN.)* mark, emblem, sign, category, symbol, character, class, description, nature, kind, variety, example, sample, sort, stamp, model, exemplar, pattern.

(ANT.) deviation, monstrosity, eccentricity, peculiarity.

typhoon *(SYN.)* hurricane, cyclone, storm, tornado, whirlwind, twister.

typical *(SYN.)* common, accustomed, conventional, familiar, customary, habitual ordinary, characteristic.

(ANT.) marvelous, extraordinary, remarkable, odd, uncommon, strange.

typify *(SYN.)* symbolize, illustrate, signify, represent, incarnate, indicate.

tyrannize *(SYN.)* oppress, victimize, threaten, brutalize, coerce.

tyrannous *(SYN.)* arbitrary, absolute, authoritative, despotic.

(ANT.) conditional, accountable, contingent, qualified, dependent.

tyrant *(SYN.)* dictator, autocrat, despot, oppressor, slave driver, martinet, disciplinarian, persecutor.

ugly *(SYN.)* hideous, homely, plain, deformed, repellent, uncomely, repulsive, ill-natured, unsightly, nasty, unpleasant, wicked, disagreeable, spiteful.
(ANT.) beautiful, fair, pretty, attractive, handsome, comely, good.

ultimate *(SYN.)* extreme, latest, final, concluding, decisive, hindmost, last.

umbrage *(SYN.)* anger, displeasure, rancor.

umpire *(SYN.)* judge, referee, arbitrator.

unadulterated *(SYN.)* genuine, clear, clean, immaculate, spotless, pure, absolute, untainted, sheer, bare.
(ANT.) foul, sullied, corrupt, tainted, polluted, tarnished, defiled.

unalterable *(SYN.)* fixed, unchangeable, steadfast, inflexible.

unanimity *(SYN.)* accord, unity, agreement.

unannounced *(SYN.)* hasty, precipitate, abrupt, unexpected.
(ANT.) courteous, expected, anticipated.

unassuming *(SYN.)* humble, lowly, compliant, modest, plain, meek, simple, unostentatious, retiring, submissive, unpretentious.
(ANT.) haughty, showy, pompous, proud, vain, arrogant, boastful.

unattached *(SYN.)* apart, separate, unmarried, single, free, independent.
(ANT.) committed, involved, entangled.

unavoidable *(SYN.)* inescapable, certain, inevitable, unpreventable.

unawares *(SYN.)* abruptly, suddenly, unexpectedly, off guard.

unbalanced *(SYN.)* crazy, mad, insane, deranged.

unbearable *(SYN.)* insufferable, intolerable.
(ANT.) tolerable, acceptable.

unbeliever *(SYN.)* dissenter, apostate, heretic, schismatic, nonconformist, sectary, sectarian.

unbending *(SYN.)* firm, inflexible, decided, determined, obstinate.
(ANT.) flexible.

unbiased *(SYN.)* honest, equitable, fair, impartial, reasonable, just, unprejudiced, just.
(ANT.) partial, fraudulent, dishonorable.

unbroken *(SYN.)* complete, uninter-

rupted, continuous, whole.

unburden *(SYN.)* clear, disentangle, divest, free.

uncanny *(SYN.)* amazing, remarkable, extraordinary, strange.

uncertain *(SYN.)* dim, hazy, indefinite, obscure, indistinct, unclear, undetermined, unsettled, ambiguous, unsure, doubtful, questionable, dubious, vague.
(ANT.) explicit, lucid, specific, certain, unmistakable, precise, clear.

uncertainty *(SYN.)* distrust, doubt, hesitation, incredulity, scruple, ambiguity, skepticism, uncertainty, suspense, suspicion, unbelief.
(ANT.) faith, belief, certainty, conviction, determination.

uncivil *(SYN.)* impolite, rude, discourteous.
(ANT.) polite.

uncivilized *(SYN.)* barbaric, barbarous, barbarian, brutal, crude, inhuman, cruel, merciless, rude, remorseless, ruthless, uncultured, savage, unrelenting.
(ANT.) humane, kind, polite, civilized, refined.

unclad *(SYN.)* exposed, nude, naked, bare, stripped, defenseless, uncovered, open, unprotected.
(ANT.) concealed, protected, clothed, covered, dressed.

uncommon *(SYN.)* unusual, rare, odd, scarce, strange, peculiar, queer, exceptional, remarkable.
(ANT.) ordinary, usual.

uncompromising *(SYN.)* determined, dogged, firm, immovable, contumacious, head-strong, inflexible, obdurate, intractable, obstinate, pertinacious, stubborn, unyielding.
(ANT.) docile, compliant, amenable, yielding, submissive, pliable.

unconcern *(SYN.)* disinterestedness, impartiality, indifference, apathy, insensibility, neutrality.
(ANT.) affection, fervor, passion, ardor.

unconditional *(SYN.)* unqualified, unrestricted, arbitrary, absolute, pure, complete, actual, authoritative, perfect, entire, ultimate, tyrannous.
(ANT.) conditional, contingent, account-

able, dependent, qualified.

unconscious *(SYN.)* lethargic, numb, comatose.

uncouth *(SYN.)* green, harsh, crude, coarse, ill-prepared, rough, raw, unfinished, unrefined, vulgar, rude, impolite, discourteous, unpolished, ill-mannered, crass.

(ANT.) well-prepared, cultivated, refined, civilized, finished.

uncover *(SYN.)* disclose, discover, betray, divulge, expose, reveal, impart, show.

(ANT.) conceal, hide, cover, obscure, cloak.

undependable *(SYN.)* changeable, unstable, uncertain, shifty, irresponsible.

(ANT.) stable, dependable, trustworthy.

under *(SYN.)* beneath, underneath, following, below, lower, downward.

(ANT.) over, above, up, higher.

undercover *(SYN.)* hidden, secret.

undergo *(SYN.)* endure, feel, stand, bear, indulge, suffer, sustain, experience, let, allow, permit, feel, tolerate.

(ANT.) overcome, discard, exclude, banish.

underhand *(SYN.)* sly, secret, sneaky, secretive, stealthy, crafty.

(ANT.) honest, open, direct, frank.

undermine *(SYN.)* demoralize, thwart, erode, weaken, subvert, sabotage.

underscore *(SYN.)* emphasize, stress.

understand *(SYN.)* apprehend, comprehend, appreciate, conceive, discern, know, grasp, hear, learn, realize, see, perceive.

(ANT.) misunderstand, mistake, misapprehend, ignore.

understanding *(SYN.)* agreement, coincidence, concord, accordance, concurrence, harmony, unison, compact, contract, arrangement, bargain, covenant, stipulation.

(ANT.) variance, difference, discord, dissension, disagreement.

understudy *(SYN.)* deputy, agent, proxy, representative, agent, alternate, lieutenant, substitute.

(ANT.) head, principal, sovereign, master.

undertake *(SYN.)* venture, attempt.

undertaking *(SYN.)* effort, endeavor, attempt, experiment, trial, essay.

(ANT.) laziness, neglect, inaction.

undersigned *(SYN.)* casual, chance, contingent, accidental, fortuitous, incidental, unintended.

(ANT.) decreed, planned, willed, calculated.

undesirable *(SYN.)* obnoxious, distasteful, objectionable, repugnant.

(ANT.) appealing, inviting, attractive.

undivided *(SYN.)* complete, intact, entire, integral, total, perfect, unimpaired, whole.

(ANT.) partial, incomplete.

undoing *(SYN.)* ruin, downfall, destruction, failure, disgrace.

undying *(SYN.)* endless, deathless, eternal, everlasting, ceaseless, immortal, infinite, perpetual, timeless.

(ANT.) transient, mortal, temporal, ephemeral, finite, impermanent.

unearthly *(SYN.)* metaphysical, ghostly, miraculous, marvelous, preternatural, superhuman, spiritual, foreign, strange, weird, supernatural.

(ANT.) physical, plain, human, natural, common, mundane.

uneducated *(SYN.)* uncultured, ignorant, illiterate, uninformed, unlearned, untaught, unlettered.

(ANT.) erudite, cultured, educated, literate, formed.

unemployed *(SYN.)* inert, inactive, idle, jobless, unoccupied.

(ANT.) working, occupied, active, industrious, employed.

uneven *(SYN.)* remaining, single, odd, unmatched, rugged, gnarled, irregular.

(ANT.) matched, even, flat, smooth.

unexceptional *(SYN.)* commonplace, trivial, customary.

unexpected *(SYN.)* immediate, hasty, surprising, instantaneous, unforeseen, abrupt, rapid, startling, sudden.

(ANT.) slowly, expected, gradual, predicted, anticipated, planned.

unfaithful *(SYN.)* treacherous, disloyal, deceitful, capricious.

(ANT.) true, loyal, steadfast, faithful.

unfasten *(SYN.)* open, expand, spread, exhibit, unbar, unlock, unfold, unseal.

(ANT.) shut, hide, conceal, close.

unfavorable *(SYN.)* antagonistic, contrary, adverse, opposed, opposite, disastrous, counteractive, unlucky.
(ANT.) benign, fortunate, lucky, propitious.

unfeeling *(SYN.)* hard, rigorous, cruel, stern, callous, numb, hard, strict, unsympathetic, severe.
(ANT.) tender, gentle, lenient. humane.

unfold *(SYN.)* develop, create, elaborate, amplify, evolve, mature, expand.
(ANT.) wither, restrict, contract, stunt, compress.

unfurnished *(SYN.)* naked, mere, bare, exposed, stripped, plain, open, simple.
(ANT.) concealed, protected, covered.

ungainly *(SYN.)* clumsy, awkward, bungling, clownish, gawky.
(ANT.) dexterous, graceful, elegant.

unhappy *(SYN.)* miserable, wretched, melancholy, distressed, sad, depressed, wretched.
(ANT.) joyful, happy, joyous, cheerful.

unhealthy *(SYN.)* infirm, sick, diseased, sickly.
(ANT.) vigorous, well, healthy, hale.

uniform *(SYN.)* methodical, natural, customary, orderly, normal, consistent, ordinary, regular, unvarying, unchanging, systematic, steady, unvaried.
(ANT.) rare, unusual, erratic, abnormal, exceptional, changeable.

unimportant *(SYN.)* petty, trivial, paltry, trifling, insignificant, indifferent, minor, petty.

uninformed *(SYN.)* illiterate, uncultured, uneducated, ignorant, unlearned, untaught, unlettered.
(ANT.) informed, literate, erudite, cultured, educated.

uninhibited *(SYN.)* loose, open, liberated, free.
(ANT.) constrained, tense, suppressed.

unintelligible *(SYN.)* ambiguous, cryptic, dark, cloudy, abstruse, dusky, mysterious, indistinct, obscure, vague.
(ANT.) lucid, distinct, bright, clear.

uninteresting *(SYN.)* burdensome, dilatory, dreary, dull, boring, slow humdrum, monotonous, sluggish, tedious, tardy, wearisome, tiresome.
(ANT.) entertaining, exciting, quick, amusing.

union *(SYN.)* fusion, incorporation, combination, joining, concurrence, solidarity, agreement, unification, concord, harmony, alliance, unanimity, coalition, confederacy, amalgamation, league, concert, marriage.
(ANT.) schism, disagreement, separation, discord.

unique *(SYN.)* exceptional, matchless, distinctive, choice, peculiar, singular, rare, sole, single, incomparable, uncommon, solitary, unequaled.
(ANT.) typical, ordinary, commonplace, frequent, common.

unison *(SYN.)* harmony, concurrence, understanding, accordance, concord, agreeable, coincidence.
(ANT.) disagreement, difference, discord, variance.

unite *(SYN.)* attach, blend, amalgamate, combine conjoin, associate, connect, embody, consolidate, join, link, fuse, unify, merge.
(ANT.) sever, divide, separate, sever, disrupt, disconnect.

universal *(SYN.)* frequent, general, popular, common, familiar, prevailing, prevalent, usual.
(ANT.) scarce, odd, regional, local, extraordinary, exceptional.

unkempt *(SYN.)* sloppy, rumpled, untidy, messy, bedraggled.
(ANT.) presentable, well-groomed, tidy, neat.

unkind *(SYN.)* unfeeling, unsympathetic, unpleasant, cruel, harsh.
(ANT.) considerate, sympathetic, amiable, kind.

unlawful *(SYN.)* illegitimate, illicit, illegal, outlawed, criminal, prohibited.
(ANT.) permitted, law, honest, legal, legitimate, authorized.

unlike *(SYN.)* dissimilar, different, distinct, contrary, diverse, divergent, opposite, incongruous, variant, miscellaneous, divers.
(ANT.) conditional, accountable, contingent, qualified, dependent.

unlucky *(SYN.)* cursed, inauspicious, unfortunate.
(ANT.) prosperous, fortunate, blessed.

unmerciful *(SYN.)* cruel, merciless, heartless, brutal.

unmistakable *(SYN.)* clear, patent, plain, visible, obvious.

unnecessary *(SYN.)* pointless, needless, superfluous, purposeless.

unoccupied *(SYN.)* empty, vacant, uninhabited.

unparalleled *(SYN.)* peerless, unequaled, rare, unique, unmatched.

unpleasant *(SYN.)* offensive, disagreeable, repulsive, obnoxious, unpleasing.

unqualified *(SYN.)* inept, unfit, incapable, incompetent, unquestioned, absolute, utter.

unreasonable *(SYN.)* foolish, absurd, irrational, inconsistent, nonsensical, ridiculous, silly.
(ANT.) reasonable, sensible, sound, consistent, rational.

unruffled *(SYN.)* calm, smooth, serene, unperturbed.

unruly *(SYN.)* unmanageable, disorganized, disorderly, disobedient.
(ANT.) orderly.

unsafe *(SYN.)* hazardous, insecure, critical, dangerous, perilous, menacing, risky, precarious, threatening.
(ANT.) protected, secure, firm, safe.

unselfish *(SYN.)* bountiful, generous, liberal, giving, beneficent, magnanimous, openhanded, munificent.
(ANT.) miserly, stingy, greedy, selfish, covetous.

unsightly *(SYN.)* ugly, unattractive, hideous.

unsophisticated *(SYN.)* frank, candid, artless, ingenuous, naive, open, simple, natural.
(ANT.) sophisticated, worldly, cunning, crafty.

unsound *(SYN.)* feeble, flimsy, weak, fragile, sick, unhealthy, diseased, invalid, faulty, false.

unstable *(SYN.)* fickle, fitful, inconstant, capricious, changeable, restless, variable.
(ANT.) steady, stable, trustworthy, constant.

unswerving *(SYN.)* fast, firm, inflexible, constant, secure, stable, solid, steady, steadfast, unyielding.

(ANT.) sluggish, insecure, unsteady, unstable, loose, slow.

untainted *(SYN.)* genuine, pure, spotless, clean, clear, unadulterated, guiltless, innocent, chaste, modest, undefiled, sincere, virgin.
(ANT.) polluted, tainted, sullied, tarnished, defiled, corrupt, foul.

untamed *(SYN.)* fierce, savage, uncivilized, barbarous, outlandish, rude, undomesticated, desert, wild, frenzied, mad, turbulent, impetuous, wanton.
(ANT.) quiet, gentle, calm, civilized, placid.

untidy *(SYN.)* messy, sloppy, disorderly, slovenly.

untoward *(SYN.)* disobedient, contrary, peevish, fractious, forward, petulant.
(ANT.) docile, tractable, obliging, agreeable.

unusual *(SYN.)* capricious, abnormal, devious, eccentric, aberrant, irregular, variable, remarkable, extraordinary, odd, peculiar, uncommon, strange.
(ANT.) methodical, regular, usual, fixed, ordinary.

unyielding *(SYN.)* fast, firm, inflexible, constant, solid, secure, stable, steadfast.
(ANT.) sluggish, slow, insecure, loose, unsteady, unstable.

upbraid *(SYN.)* blame, censure, berate, admonish, rate, lecture, rebuke, reprimand, reprehend, scold, vituperate.
(ANT.) praise, commend, approve.

uphold *(SYN.)* justify, espouse, assert, defend, maintain, vindicate.
(ANT.) oppose, submit, assault, deny, attack.

upright *(SYN.)* undeviating, right, unswerving, direct, erect, unbent, straight, fair, vertical.
(ANT.) bent, dishonest, crooked, circuitous, winding.

uprising *(SYN.)* revolution, mutiny, revolt, rebellion.

uproar *(SYN.)* noise, disorder, commotion, tumult, disturbance.

upset *(SYN.)* disturb, harass, bother, annoy, haunt, molest, inconvenience, perplex, pester, tease, plague, trouble.
(ANT.) soothe, relieve, please, gratify.

urbane *(SYN.)* civil, considerate, cul-

tivated, courteous, genteel, polite, accomplished, refined, well-mannered.
(ANT.) *rude, uncouth, boorish, uncivil.*

urge (SYN.) craving, desire, longing, lust, appetite, aspiration, yearning, incite, coax, entice, force, drive, prod, press.
(ANT.) *loathing, hate, distaste, aversion, coerce, deter, restrain, compel, dissuade, discourage.*

urgency (SYN.) emergency, exigency, pass, pinch, strait, crisis.

urgent (SYN.) critical, crucial, exigent, imperative, impelling, insistent.
(ANT.) *trivial, unimportant, petty, insignificant.*

usage (SYN.) use, treatment, custom, practice, tradition.

use (SYN.) custom, practice, habit, training, usage, manner, apply, avail employ, operate, utilize, exert, exhaust, handle, manage, accustom, inure, train, exploit.
(ANT.) *disuse, neglect, waste, ignore, overlook, idleness.*

useful (SYN.) beneficial, helpful, good, serviceable, wholesome, advantageous.
(ANT.) *harmful, injurious, deleterious, destructive, detrimental.*

usefulness (SYN.) price, merit, utility, value, excellence, virtue, worth.
(ANT.) *useless, cheapness, valuelessness, uselessness.*

useless (SYN.) bootless, empty, idle, pointless, vain, valueless, worthless, abortive, unavailing, ineffectual, vapid.
(ANT.) *profitable, potent, effective.*

usher (SYN.) guide, lead.

usual (SYN.) customary, common, familiar, general, normal, habitual, accustomed, everyday, ordinary, regular.
(ANT.) *irregular, exceptional, rare, extraordinary, abnormal.*

utilize (SYN.) use, apply, devote, busy, employ, occupy, avail.
(ANT.) *reject, banish, discharge, discard.*

utopian (SYN.) perfect, ideal, faultless, exemplary, supreme, visionary, unreal.
(ANT.) *real, material, imperfect, actual, faulty.*

utter (SYN.) full, perfect, whole, finished, entire, speak, say, complete, superlative.
(ANT.) *imperfect, deficient, lacking, faulty, incomplete.*

vacancy (SYN.) void, emptiness, vacuum, hollowness.
(ANT.) *plenitude, fullness, profusion, completeness.*

vacant (SYN.) barren, empty, blank, bare, unoccupied.
(ANT.) *filled, packed, employed, full, replete, busy.*

vacate (SYN.) abjure, relinquish, abdicate, renounce, resign, surrender.
(ANT.) *stay, support, uphold.*

vacillate (SYN.) hesitate, oscillate, undulate, change, fluctuate, vary, waver.
(ANT.) *adhere, persist, stick.*

vacillating (SYN.) contrary, illogical, contradictory, contrary, inconsistent, incongruous, incompatible.
(ANT.) *correspondent, congruous, consistent.*

vacuity (SYN.) space, emptiness, vacuum, void, blank, nothingness, ignorance, unawareness, senselessness.
(ANT.) *matter, fullness, content, substance, knowledge.*

vacuous (SYN.) dull, blank, uncomprehending, foolish, thoughtless.
(ANT.) *responsive, alert, attentive, bright, intelligent.*

vacuum (SYN.) void, gap, emptiness, hole, chasm, nothingness, abyss.

vagabond (SYN.) pauper, ragamuffin, scrub, beggar, starveling, wretch.
(ANT.) *responsible, established, rooted, installed.*

vagary (SYN.) notion, whim, fantasy, fancy, daydream, caprice, conceit, quirk.

vague (SYN.) indefinite, hazy, obscure, unclear, unsure, unsettled.
(ANT.) *certain, spelled out, specific, lucid, clear, distinct, explicit, precise.*

vain (SYN.) fruitless, empty, bootless, futile, idle, abortive, ineffectual, unavailing, vapid, pointless, valueless.
(ANT.) *meek, modest, potent, rewarding, diffident, profitable, effective.*

vainglory (SYN.) conceit, pride, self-esteem, arrogance, self-respect.
(ANT.) *shame, modesty, meekness, humility, lowliness.*

valid (SYN.) cogent, conclusive, effective, convincing, weighty, well-founded, real, strong, telling, logical.

(ANT.) weak, unconvincing, void, unproved, null, spurious, counterfeit.

valley *(SYN.)* dale, dell, low-land, basin, gully, vale.

(ANT.) highland, hill, upland, headland.

valor *(SYN.)* courage, heroism, bravery, boldness, intrepidity, fearlessness.

value *(SYN.)* price, merit, usefulness, value, virtue, utility, appreciate, prize, hold dear, worth, worthiness.

vanity *(SYN.)* complacency, conception, notion, haughtiness, self-respect, whim, smugness, vainglory, arrogance.

(ANT.) meekness, humility, diffidence.

vanquish *(SYN.)* defeat, crush, rout, quell, subjugate.

(ANT.) surrender, cede, lose, retreat, capitulate.

vapid *(SYN.)* hackneyed, inane, insipid, trite, banal.

(ANT.) striking, novel, fresh, original, stimulating.

variable *(SYN.)* fickle, fitful, inconstant, unstable, shifting, changeable, unsteady.

(ANT.) unchanging, uniform, stable, unwavering, steady.

variant *(SYN.)* dissimilar, different, distinct, contrary, sundry, various.

(ANT.) similar, same, congruous, identical, alike.

variety *(SYN.)* dissimilarity, diversity, heterogeneity, medley, mixture, miscellany, variousness, form.

(ANT.) likeness, monotony, uniformity, sameness, homogeneity.

various *(SYN.)* miscellaneous, sundry, divers, several, contrary, distinct, dissimilar.

(ANT.) identical, similar, same, alike, congruous.

vassalage *(SYN.)* confinement, captivity, imprisonment, slavery, thralldom.

(ANT.) liberation, freedom.

vast *(SYN.)* big, capacious, extensive, huge, great, ample, enormous.

(ANT.) tiny, small, short, little.

vault *(SYN.)* caper, jerk, jump, leap, bound, crypt, sepulcher, hop, spring, safe, start, tomb, grave, catacomb, skip.

vehement *(SYN.)* excitable, fiery, glowing, impetuous, hot, irascible, passionate.

(ANT.) calm, quiet, cool, apathetic,

deliberate.

veil *(SYN.)* clothe, conceal, cover, cloak, web, hide, curtain, disguise, gauze, film, shield, film.

(ANT.) reveal, unveil, bare.

velocity *(SYN.)* quickness, rapidity, speed, swiftness.

venerable *(SYN.)* antiquated, aged, antique, ancient, old-fashion.

(ANT.) young, new, youthful.

venerate *(SYN.)* approve, esteem, admire, appreciate, wonder, respect.

(ANT.) dislike, despise.

vengeance *(SYN.)* requital, reprisal, reparation, retribution, revenge.

(ANT.) forgiveness, remission, pardon, mercy.

venom *(SYN.)* toxin, poison, bitterness, spite, hate.

verbal *(SYN.)* oral, spoken, literal, unwritten, vocal.

(ANT.) printed, written, recorded.

verbose *(SYN.)* communicative, glib, chattering, chatty, garrulous, loquacious.

(ANT.) uncommunicative.

verdict *(SYN.)* judgment, finding, opinion, decision.

verge *(SYN.)* lip, rim, edge, margin, brink, brim.

verification *(SYN.)* confirmation, demonstration, evidence, proof, test.

(ANT.) terseness, laconic, conciseness.

verify *(SYN.)* confirm, substantiate, acknowledge, determine, assure, establish, approve, fix, settle, ratify, strengthen, corroborate, affirm, sanction.

veritable *(SYN.)* authentic, correct, genuine, real, true, accurate, actual.

(ANT.) false, fictitious, spurious, erroneous, counterfeit.

very *(SYN.)* exceedingly, extremely, greatly.

vestige *(SYN.)* stain, scar, mark, brand, stigma, characteristic, trace, feature, trait, suggestion, indication.

veto *(SYN.)* refusal, denial, refuse, deny, negate, forbid.

(ANT.) approve, approval.

vexation *(SYN.)* chagrin, irritation, annoyance, mortification, irritation, pique.

(ANT.) comfort, pleasure, appeasement, gratification.

vibrate *(SYN.)* flutter, jar, ungodliness, tremble, wrong.

vice *(SYN.)* iniquity, crime, offense, evil, guilt, sin, ungodliness, wickedness, depravity, corruption, wrong.

(ANT.) righteousness, virtue, goodness, innocence, purity.

vicinity *(SYN.)* district, area, locality, neighborhood, environs, proximity, nearness, adjacency.

(ANT.) remoteness, distance.

vicious *(SYN.)* bad, evil, wicked, sinful, corrupt, cruel, savage, dangerous.

victimize *(SYN.)* cheat, dupe, swindle, deceive, take advantage of.

victor *(SYN.)* champion, winner.

(ANT.) loser.

victory *(SYN.)* conquest, jubilation, triumph, success, achievement, ovation.

(ANT.) defeat, failure.

view *(SYN.)* discern, gaze, glance, behold, eye, discern, stare, watch, examine, witness, prospect, vision, vista, sight, look, panorama, opinion, judgment, belief, impression, perspective, range, regard, thought, observation, survey, scene, conception, outlook, inspect, observe.

(ANT.) miss, overlook, avert, hide.

viewpoint *(SYN.)* attitude, standpoint, aspect, pose, disposition, position, stand, posture.

vigilant *(SYN.)* anxious, attentive, careful, alert, circumspect, cautious, observant, wary, watchful, wakeful.

(ANT.) inattentive, neglectful, careless.

vigor *(SYN.)* spirit, verve, energy, zeal, fortitude, vitality, strength, liveliness.

(ANT.) listlessness.

vigorous *(SYN.)* brisk, energetic, active, blithe, animated, frolicsome, strong, spirited, lively, forceful, sprightly, vivacious, powerful, supple.

(ANT.) vapid, dull, listless, insipid.

vile *(SYN.)* foul, loathsome, base, depraved, debased, sordid, vulgar, wicked, abject, ignoble, mean, worthless, sinful, bad, low, wretched, evil, offensive, objectionable, disgusting.

(ANT.) honorable, upright, decent, laudable, attractive.

vilify *(SYN.)* asperse, defame, disparage, abuse, malign, revile, scandalize.

(ANT.) protect, honor, praise, cherish.

village *(SYN.)* hamlet, town.

(ANT.) metropolis, city.

villain *(SYN.)* rascal, rogue, cad, brute, scoundrel, devil, scamp.

villainous *(SYN.)* deleterious, evil, bad, base, iniquitous, unsound, sinful, unwholesome, wicked.

(ANT.) honorable, reputable, moral, good, excellent.

violate *(SYN.)* infringe, break.

violent *(SYN.)* strong, forcible, forceful.

(ANT.) gentle.

vindicate clear, assert, defend, absolve, excuse, acquit, uphold, support.

(ANT.) accuse, convict, abandon.

violate *(SYN.)* disobey, invade, defile, break, desecrate, pollute, dishonor, debauch, profane, deflower, ravish.

violence *(SYN.)* constraint, force, compulsion, coercion.

(ANT.) weakness, persuasion, feebleness, impotence, frailty.

violent *(SYN.)* strong, forceful, powerful, forcible, angry, fierce, savage, passionate, furious.

(ANT.) gentle.

virgin *(SYN.)* immaculate, genuine, spotless, clean, clear, unadulterated, chaste, untainted, innocent, guiltless, pure, untouched, modest, maid, maiden, sincere, unused, undefiled, pure.

(ANT.) foul, tainted, defiled, sullied, polluted, corrupt.

virile *(SYN.)* hardy, male, mannish, lusty, bold, masculine, strong, vigorous.

(ANT.) feminine, unmanly, weak, effeminate, womanish, emasculated.

virtue *(SYN.)* integrity, probity, purity, chastity, goodness, rectitude, effectiveness, force, honor, power, efficacy, quality, strength, merit, righteousness, advantage, excellence, advantage.

(ANT.) fault, vice, lewdness, corruption.

virtuous *(SYN.)* good, ethical, chaste, honorable, moral, just, pure, righteous.

(ANT.) licentious, unethical, amoral, sinful, libertine, immoral.

virulent *(SYN.)* hostile, malevolent, malignant, bitter, spiteful, wicked.

(ANT.) kind, affectionate, benevolent.

vision *(SYN.)* dream, hallucination,

mirage, eyesight, sight, fantasy, illusion, specter, revelation, phantom.
(ANT.) verity, reality.

visionary *(SYN.)* faultless, ideal, perfect, unreal, supreme.
(ANT.) real, actual, imperfect, faulty.

visit *(SYN.)* attend, see, call on, appointment.

visitor *(SYN.)* caller, guest.

vista *(SYN.)* view, scene, aspect.

vital *(SYN.)* cardinal, living, paramount, alive, essential, critical, indispensable.
(ANT.) lifeless, unimportant, inanimate, nonessential.

vitality *(SYN.)* buoyancy, being, life, liveliness, existence, spirit, vigor.
(ANT.) death, lethargy, dullness, demise.

vitiate *(SYN.)* allay, abase, corrupt, adulterate, debase, defile, depress, deprave.

vivid *(SYN.)* brilliant, striking, strong, graphic.
(ANT.) dim, dusky, vague, dull, dreary.

vocal *(SYN.)* said, uttered, oral, spoken, definite, outspoken, specific.

void *(SYN.)* barren, emptiness, bare, unoccupied, meaningless, invalid, useless.
(ANT.) employed, full, replete.

volition *(SYN.)* desire, intention, pleasure, preference, choice, decision, resolution.
(ANT.) disinterest, compulsion, indifference.

voluble *(SYN.)* glib, communicative, verbose, loquacious, chatty, chattering.
(ANT.) uncommunicative, laconic, taciturn, silent.

volume *(SYN.)* capacity, skill, power, talent, faculty, magnitude, mass, book, dimensions, quantity, amount, size.
(ANT.) stupidity, inability, impotence, incapacity.

voluntary *(SYN.)* extemporaneous, free, automatic, spontaneous, offhand.
(ANT.) forced, planned, required, rehearsed, compulsory, prepared.

volunteer *(SYN.)* extend, offer, present, advance, propose.
(ANT.) receive, spurn, reject, accept, retain.

voyage *(SYN.)* tour, journey, excursion.

vulnerable *(SYN.)* unguard, defenseless, unprotected.

wafer *(SYN.)* cracker, lozenge.

waft *(SYN.)* convey, glide, sail, float.

wage *(SYN.)* conduct, pursue.

wager *(SYN.)* stake, bet, play, gamble, speculate, risk, chance.

wagon *(SYN.)* carriage, buggy, cart, surrey, stagecoach.

waif *(SYN.)* guttersnipe, ragamuffin, tramp, vagrant, urchin.

wail *(SYN.)* mourn, moan, cry, bewail, lament, bemoan.

wait *(SYN.)* linger, tarry, attend, bide, watch, delay, await, abide, stay, serve.
(ANT.) hasten, act leave, expedite.

waive *(SYN.)* renounce, abandon, surrender, relinquish.
(ANT.) uphold, maintain.

wake *(SYN.)* awaken, rouse, waken, arouse, stimulate.
(ANT.) doze, sleep.

walk *(SYN.)* step, stroll, march, amble, saunter, hike, lane, path, passage.

wall *(SYN.)* barricade, divider, partition, panel, stockade.

wallow *(SYN.)* plunge, roll, flounder, grovel.

wan *(SYN.)* colorless, haggard, gaunt, pale, pallid, pasty, pale.

wander *(SYN.)* rove, stroll, deviate, ramble, roam, traipse, range, err.
(ANT.) linger, stop, settle.

wane *(SYN.)* abate, weaken, fade, ebb, decrease, wither.

want *(SYN.)* penury, destitution, crave, desire, requirement, poverty, wish.
(ANT.) wealth, plenty, abundance.

wanton *(SYN.)* lecherous, immoral, loose, lewd, salacious.

war *(SYN.)* battle, hostilities, combat, fight, strife.

warble *(SYN.)* sing, trill, chirp.

ward *(SYN.)* annex, wing.

warden *(SYN.)* custodian, guard, guardian, keeper, turnkey, jailer, curator.

wardrobe *(SYN.)* chiffonier, bureau, closet, armoire.

wares *(SYN.)* merchandise, staples, inventory, commodities, goods.

wariness *(SYN.)* heed, care, watchfulness, caution.
(ANT.) carelessness, abandon.

warlike *(SYN.)* hostile, unfriendly, com-

bative, belligerent, antagonistic.
(ANT.) cordial, peaceful, amicable.

warm (SYN.) sincere, cordial, hearty, earnest, sympathetic, ardent, heated.
(ANT.) cool, aloof, brisk, indifferent.

warmhearted (SYN.) loving, kind, kindhearted, friendly.

warmth (SYN.) friendliness, cordiality, geniality, understanding, compassion.

warn (SYN.) apprise, notify, admonish, caution, advise.

warning (SYN.) advice, information, caution, portent, admonition, indication.

warp (SYN.) turn, bend, twist, distort, deprave.

warrant (SYN.) pledge, assurance, warranty, guarantee, authorize, approve.

warrior (SYN.) combatant, fighter, soldier, mercenary.

wary (SYN.) careful, awake, watchful, attentive, alive, mindful, cautious.
(ANT.) unaware, indifferent, careless, apathetic.

wash (SYN.) launder, cleanse, rub, touch, reach, border, wet, clean, scrub, bathe.
(ANT.) soil, dirty, stain.

waste (SYN.) forlorn, bleak, wild, solitary, dissipate, abandoned, spend, deserted.
(ANT.) cultivated, attended.

wasteful (SYN.) wanton, costly, lavish, extravagant.

watch (SYN.) inspect, descry, behold, distinguish, guard, attend, observe, contemplate, watchman, sentry, discern.

watchful (SYN.) alert, careful, attentive, vigilant, wary, cautious.

watertight (SYN.) impregnable, firm, solid.

wave (SYN.) ripple, whitecap, undulation, breaker, surf, swell, sea, surge, tide, flow.

waver (SYN.) question, suspect, flicker, deliberate, doubt, distrust, hesitate, falter.
(ANT.) confide, trust, believe, decide.

wavering (SYN.) fickle, shifting, variable, changeable, vacillating, fitful.
(ANT.) unchanging, constant, uniform.

wavy (SYN.) rippling, serpentine, curly.

wax (SYN.) raise, heighten, expand, accrue, enhance, extend, multiply, enlarge, augment.

(ANT.) contract, reduce, atrophy, diminish.

way (SYN.) habit, road, course, avenue, route, mode, system, channel, track, fashion, method, walk, approach, manner, technique, means.

wayward (SYN.) stubborn, headstrong, contrary, obstinate, naughty, disobedient, rebellious, refractory.

weak (SYN.) frail, debilitated, delicate, poor, wavering, infirm, bending, lame, defenseless, vulnerable, fragile, pliant, feeble, watery, diluted.
(ANT.) strong, potent, sturdy, powerful.

weakness (SYN.) incompetence, inability, impotence, handicap, fondness, liking, affection, disability, incapacity.
(ANT.) strength, ability, dislike, power.

wealth (SYN.) fortune, money, riches, possessions, means, abundance, opulence, affluence, property, quantity, profession, luxury.
(ANT.) want, need.

wealthy (SYN.) rich, exorbitant, affluent.
(ANT.) poverty-stricken, poor, indigent, impoverished, beggarly, destitute, needy.

wear (SYN.) erode, fray, grind, apparel, clothes, garb, attire.

weary (SYN.) faint, spent, worn, tired, fatigued, exhausted, tiresome, bored, wearied, tedious, jaded.
(ANT.) rested, hearty, fresh.

weave (SYN.) lace, interlace, plait, intertwine, braid, knit.

web (SYN.) netting, network, net, cobweb, trap, entanglement.

wedlock (SYN.) marriage, union, espousal, wedding.

wee (SYN.) small, tiny, miniature, petite, microscopic.

weep (SYN.) mourn, sob, bemoan, cry, lament, whimper.

weigh (SYN.) heed, deliberate, consider, study, reflect, evaluate.
(ANT.) neglect, ignore.

weight (SYN.) importance, emphasis, load, burden, import, stress, influence, gravity, significance.
(ANT.) triviality, levity, insignificance, lightness.

weird (SYN.) odd, eerie, strange, unnatural, peculiar.

welcome *(SYN.)* take, entertain, greet, accept, receive, reception, gain, greeting.
(ANT.) reject, bestow, impart.

welfare *(SYN.)* good, well-being, prosperity.

well *(SYN.)* hearty, happy, sound, hale, beneficial, good, convenient, expedient, healthy, favorably, fully, thoroughly, surely, competently, certainly, undoubtedly, fit, profitable.
(ANT.) infirm, depressed.

well-bred *(SYN.)* cultured, polite, genteel, courtly.
(ANT.) crude, vulgar, boorish.

well-known *(SYN.)* famous, illustrious, celebrated, noted, eminent, renowned.
(ANT.) unknown, ignominious, obscure, hidden.

wet *(SYN.)* moist, dank, soaked, damp, drenched, dampen, moisten.
(ANT.) arid, dry, parched.

whimsical *(SYN.)* quaint, strange, curious, odd, unusual, droll, queer.
(ANT.) normal, common, usual, familiar.

whole *(SYN.)* total, sound, all, intact, complete, well, hale, healed, entire, uncut, undivided, unbroken, undamaged, intact.
(ANT.) partial, defective, imperfect, deficient.

wholesome *(SYN.)* robust, well, hale, healthy, sound, salutary, nourishing.
(ANT.) frail, noxious, infirm, delicate, injurious, diseased.

wicked *(SYN.)* deleterious, iniquitous, immoral, bad, evil, base, ungodly, unsound, sinful, bitter, blasphemous.
(ANT.) moral, good, reputable, honorable.

wide *(SYN.)* large, broad, sweeping, extensive, vast.
(ANT.) restricted, narrow.

wild *(SYN.)* outlandish, uncivilized, untamed, irregular, wanton, foolish, mad, barbarous, rough, waste, desert, uncultivated.
(ANT.) quiet, gentle, placid, tame, restrained, civilized.

will *(SYN.)* intention, desire, volition, decision, resolution, wish, resoluteness.
(ANT.) disinterest, coercion, indifference.

win *(SYN.)* gain, succeed, prevail, achieve, thrive, obtain, get, acquire, earn, flourish.
(ANT.) lose, miss, forfeit, fail.

winsome *(SYN.)* winning, charming, agreeable.

wisdom *(SYN.)* insight, judgment, learning, sense, discretion, reason, prudence, erudition, foresight.
(ANT.) nonsense, foolishness, stupidity, ignorance.

wise *(SYN.)* informed, sagacious, learned, penetrating, enlightened, advisable, prudent, profound, deep, erudite, scholarly, knowing, sound, intelligent, expedient.
(ANT.) simple, shallow, foolish.

wish *(SYN.)* crave, hanker, long, hunger, yearning, lust, craving, yearn, want, appetite, covet, longing, desire, urge.
(ANT.) hate, aversion, loathing, distaste.

wit *(SYN.)* sense, humor, pleasantry, satire, intelligence, comprehension, banter, mind, wisdom, intellect, wittiness, fun, drollery, humorist, wag, comedian, raillery, irony, witticism.
(ANT.) solemnity, commonplace, sobriety.

witch *(SYN.)* magician, sorcerer, enchanter, sorceress, enchantress, warlock.

witchcraft *(SYN.)* enchantment, magic, wizardry, conjuring, voodoo.

withdraw *(SYN.)* renounce, leave, abandon, recall, retreat, go, quit, retire, depart, retract, remove, forsake.
(ANT.) enter, tarry, abide, place, stay.

wither *(SYN.)* wilt, languish, dry, shrivel, decline, fade, decay, sear, shrink.
(ANT.) renew, refresh, revive.

withhold *(SYN.)* forbear, abstain, repress, check, refrain.
(ANT.) persist, continue.

withstand *(SYN.)* defy, contradict, bar, thwart, oppose, hinder, combat, resist.
(ANT.) succumb, cooperate, support.

witness *(SYN.)* perceive, proof, spectator, confirmation, see, attestation, watch, observe, eyewitness, declaration, notice.
(ANT.) refutation, contradiction, argument.

wizardry *(SYN.)* voodoo, legerdemain,

conjuring, witchcraft, charm.

woe *(SYN.)* sorrow, disaster, trouble, evil, agony, suffering, distress, misery.
(ANT.) pleasure, delight, fun.

womanly *(SYN.)* girlish, womanish, female, ladylike.
(ANT.) mannish, virile, male, masculine.

wonder *(SYN.)* awe, curiosity, surprise, wonderment, conjecture, amazement.
(ANT.) expectation, familiarity, indifference, apathy.

wonderful *(SYN.)* extraordinary, marvelous.

wont *(SYN.)* practice, use, custom, training, habit, usage.
(ANT.) inexperience, disuse.

word *(SYN.)* term, utterance, expression.

work *(SYN.)* opus, employment, achievement, performance, toil, business, exertion, travail, effort.
(ANT.) recreation, leisure, vacation, ease.

worldly *(SYN.)* gross, voluptuous, base.
(ANT.) refined, exalted, spiritual.

worth *(SYN.)* value, price, deserving, excellence, usefulness, utility, worthiness.
(ANT.) uselessness, cheapness.

worthless *(SYN.)* empty, idle, abortive, ineffectual, bootless, pointless, vain.
(ANT.) meek, effective, modest, potent.

wound *(SYN.)* mar, harm, damage, hurt, dishonor, injure, injury, spoil, wrong.
(ANT.) compliment, preserve, help.

wrangle *(SYN.)* spat, bickering, affray, argument, dispute, quarrel, altercation.
(ANT.) peace, friendliness, reconciliation, harmony.

wrap *(SYN.)* cover, protect, shield, cloak, mask, clothe, curtain, guard, conceal.
(ANT.) reveal, bare, unveil.

wreck *(SYN.)* ravage, devastation, extinguish, destroy, annihilate, damage, raze.
(ANT.) construct, preserve, establish.

wretched *(SYN.)* forlorn, miserable, comfortless, despicable, paltry, low.
(ANT.) noble, contented, happy, significant.

writer *(SYN.)* creator, maker, inventor, author, father, composer.

wrong *(SYN.)* awry, incorrect, improper, amiss, naughty, faulty, inaccurate, askew, sin, incorrectness, false, unsuitable.
(ANT.) proper, true, correct, suitable.

yacht *(SYN.)* sailboat, boat, cruiser.

yank *(SYN.)* pull, wrest, draw, haul, tug, jerk, wrench, heave, extract.

yap *(SYN.)* howl, bark.

yard *(SYN.)* pen, confine, court, enclosure, compound, garden.

yardstick *(SYN.)* measure, criterion, gauge.

yarn *(SYN.)* wool, tale, narrative, thread, story, fiber, anecdote, spiel.

yaw *(SYN.)* tack, change course, pitch, toss. roll.

yawn *(SYN.)* open, gape.

yearly *(SYN.)* annually.

yearn *(SYN.)* pine, long for, want, desire, crave, wish.

yearning *(SYN.)* hungering, craving, desire, longing, appetite, lust, urge, aspiration, wish.
(ANT.) distaste, loathing, abomination, hate.

yell *(SYN.)* call, scream, shout, whoop, howl, roar, holler, wail, bawl.

yellow *(SYN.)* fearful, cowardly, chicken.
(ANT.) bold, brave.

yelp *(SYN.)* screech, squeal, howl, bark.

yen *(SYN.)* longing, craving, fancy, appetite, desire, lust, hunger.

yet *(SYN.)* moreover, also, additionally, besides.

yield *(SYN.)* produce, afford, breed, grant, accord, cede, relent, succumb, bestow, allow, permit, give way, submit, bear, surrender, supply, fruits, give up, abdicate, return, impart, harvest, permit, accede, acquiesce, crop, capitulate, pay, concede, generate, relinquish.
(ANT.) assert, deny, refuse, resist, struggle, oppose, strive.

yielding *(SYN.)* dutiful, submissive, compliant, obedient, tractable.
(ANT.) rebellious, intractable, insubordinate.

yoke *(SYN.)* tether, leash, bridle, harness.

yokel *(SYN.)* hick, peasant, hayseed, innocent.

young *(SYN.)* immature, undeveloped, youthful, underdeveloped, juvenile, junior, underage.
(ANT.) old, mature, elderly.

youngster *(SYN.)* kid, lad, stripling,

minor, youth, child, fledgling.
(ANT.) *adult, elder.*
youthful *(SYN.)* childish, immature, young, boyish, childlike, callow, girlish, puerile.
(ANT.) *old, elderly, senile, aged, mature.*
yowl *(SYN.)* yell, shriek, cry, wail, whoop, howl, scream.

zany *(SYN.)* clownish, comical, foolish, silly, scatter-brained.
zap *(SYN.)* drive, vim, pep, determination.
zeal *(SYN.)* fervor, eagerness, passion, feverency, vehemence, devotion, intensity, excitement, earnestness, inspiration, warmth, ardor, fanaticism, enthusiasm.
(ANT.) *unconcern, ennui, apathy, indifference.*
zealot *(SYN.)* champion, crank, fanatic, bigot.
zealous *(SYN.)* enthusiastic, fiery, keen, eager, fervid, ardent, intense, vehement, fervent, glowing, hot, impassioned, passionate.
(ANT.) *cool, nonchalant, apathetic.*
zenith *(SYN.)* culmination, apex, height, acme, consummation, top, summit, pinnacle, climax, peak.
(ANT.) *floor, nadir, depth, base, anticlimax.*
zero *(SYN.)* nonexistent, nil, nothing, none.
zest *(SYN.)* enjoyment, savor, eagerness, relish, satisfaction, gusto, spice, tang, pleasure, exhilaration.
zestful *(SYN.)* delightful, thrilling, exciting, stimulating, enjoyable.
zip *(SYN.)* vigor, vim, energy, vitality, spirited, animation, provocative.
zone *(SYN.)* region, climate, tract, belt, sector, section, district, locality, precinct, territory.
zoo *(SYN.)* menagerie.
zoom *(SYN.)* zip, fly, speed, whiz, roar, race.

GREEK ALPHABET	HEBREW ALPHABET	
ALPHA	ALEF	SIN
BETA	BET	TAV
GAMMA	VET	SOV
DELTA	GIMEL	
EPSILON	DALET	
ZETA	HAY	
ETA	VAV	
THETA	ZAYIN	
IOTA	HET	
KAPPA	TET	
LAMBDA	YOD	
MU	KAF	
NU	HAF	
XI	LAHED	
OMICRON	MEM	
PI	NVN	
RHO	SAMEH	
SIGMA	AYIN	
TAU	PAY	
UPSILON	FAY	
PHI	TZADEE	
CHI	KOF	
PSI	RESH	
OMEGA	SHIN	

A.A. Alcoholics Anonymous; Associate in, of, or, Arts; Antiaircraft Artillery.

A.A.A. American Automobile Association.

a.a.r. against all risks.

Ab *Chem.* alabamine.

A.B.A. American Booksellers Association; American Bar Association.

abbr. abbreviation; abbreviated.

ABC American Broadcasting Company; American Bowling Congress.

ABM Anti-ballistic missile.

Abp. Archbishop.

abr. abridgement; abridged.

abs. abstract; absent; absolute.

A.B.S. American Bible Socity.

Ac *Chem.* acetate; acetyl; actinium.

A.C. Automobile Club; Army Corps; Athletic Club.

acad academy; academic.

acc. acceptance; accompanied; account; accusative; according.

acct. account.

ack. acknowledge.

A.C.L.U. American Civil Liberties Union.

A.C.S. American Cancer Society; American Chemical Society.

act. active.

ad. advertisement; adapted.

AD Active Duty.

A.D.A. American Dental Association; American Dairy Association.

adj. adjective; adjourned; adjustment.

adm. administrator; admission; administration.

Adm. Admiral.

adv. adverb; advertisement; against; advise; advocate.

advt. advertisement.

A.E. Associate in Engineering; Associate in Education.

aeron. aeronautics.

a.f. audio frequency control.

AFB air force base.

AFC automatic frequency control; automatic flight control.

aff. affirmatively; affirmative; affectionate.

afft. affidavit.

A.F.L. American Federation of Labor.

AFL-CIO American Federation of Labor-Congress of Industrial Organizations.

AFM American Federation of Musicians.

Aft. African; Africa.

aft. afternoon.

A.F.T. American Federation of Teachers.

Ag *Chem.* silver.

agcy. agency.

agric. agriculture; agricultural.

agt. agent.

A.H.A. American Hospital Association.

A.I. artificial insemination.

A.I.D.S. Acquired Immune Deficiency Syndrome.

AJ Associate Justice.

A.K.C. American Kennel Club.

Al *Chem.* aluminum.

A.L. *Baseball* American League.

AL. Alabama.

A.L.A. American Library Association; Automobile Legal Association.

AK. Alaska.

a.m. *ante meridiem* before noon.

AM *Chem.* americium.

Am American; America.

amt. amount.

anal. analyze; analogy; analytical.

anat. anatomy; anatomical.

anc. ancient.

anon. anonymous.

ans. answer

ant. antonym.

anth. anthology.

antiq. antiquity.

AOL absent over leave.

ap account payable; account paid.

A.P. Associated Press.

A.P.A American Pharmaceutical Association; American Psychiatric Association;

APO Army Post Office.

app. apparent; appeal; apparatus; appendix; appointed; approximate.

approx. approximately.

apt. apartment.

apx appendix.

Ar *Chem.* argon.

A.S. Anglo-Saxon.

A.S.A. American Standards Association.

ASCAP American Society of Composers, Authors and Publishers.

A.S.C.E. American Society of Civil Engineers.

A.S.M.E. American Society of Mechanical

Engineers.
assn. association.
assoc. associate; association; associated.
asst. assistant.
astr. astronomer; astronomy; astronomical.
At *Chem.* astatine.
ATC Air Traffic Control.
Atl. Atlantic.
ATM Automatic Teller Machine.
att. attention; attorney.
Atty. Gen. Attorney General.
at. wt. atomic weight.
Au *aurum Chem.* gold.
A.U.C. American Unitarian Association.
aud. auditor.
Aug. August.
Aus. Austrian; Austria.
auth author; authorized.
auto. automobile; automotive.
aux. auxiliary.
av. average; avenue;
ave. avenue.
avg. average.
avn. aviation.
A.W.L. absent with leave.
A.W.O.L. absent without leave.
ax. axiom.
AZT Azidothymidine.

B.A. Bachelor of Arts; British America.
B.A.A. Bachelor of Applied Arts.
B.A.E. Bachelor of Arts in Education.
bal. balance.
bap. baptized.
Bapt. Baptist.
B.A.S. Bachelor of applied Science; Bachelor of Agricultural Sciences.
batt. battery; battalion.
B.B.C. British Broadcasting Corporation.
bbl. barrel.
B.C. before Christ; British Columbia; Bachelor of Chemistry.
BCD bad conduct discharge.
B.C.E. Bachelor of Christian Education.
B.C.L. Bachelor of Civil Law.
B.C.S. Bachelor of Chemical Science.
bd. board; bound; bond.
BD bank draft.
bdry. boundary.
Be *Chem.* beryllium.

b.e. bill of entry; bill of exchange.
B.E. Bachelor of Education; Board of Education.
B.E.E. Bachelor of Electrical Enginerring.
bef. before.
Belg. Belgian; Belgium.
bet. between.
bf *Printing* bold face.
B.F.A. Bachelor of Fine Arts.
bg. background; being; bag.
bh *Baseball* base hits.
bhp brake horse power.
Bi *Chem.* bismuth.
Bib. Bible; Biblical.
b.i.d. *Medication* twice a day.
biochem. biochemistry.
biog. biographer; biography; biographical.
biol. biological; biology; biologist.
bk. bank; bark; book; brake.
BK *Chem.* berkelium.
bkcy. *Legal* bankruptcy.
bkg. banking.
bkpr. bookkeeper.
bkry. bakery.
bkt. basket; bucket; bracket;.
bl barrel; blue; block; bale.
B/L bill of lading.
bldg. building.
bldr. builder.
blk. bulk; block; black.
bls. barrels.
B.L.S. Bachelor of Library Science.
blvd. boulevard.
B.M. Bachelor of Medicine.
B.M.E. Bachelor of Music Education.
B.M.S. Bachelor of Marine Science.
B.M.T. bachelor of Medical Technology.
B.N. Bachelor of Nursing.
b.o. back order; branch office.
B. of E. Board of Education.
B. of H. Board of Health.
B. of T. Board of Trade.
bor. borough.
bot. botanical; bought; botany.
Bp. Bishop.
b.p. boiling point.
B.P. blood pressure; Bachelor of Pharmacy; Bachelor or Philosophy.
B.P.A. Bachelor of Professional Arts.
b.p.d. barrels per day.

bpl. birthplace.

B.P.O.E. Benevolent and Protective Order of Elks.

Br *Chem.* bromine.

br. branch; brother; brig.

Br. British; Britain.

b.s. bill of sale; balance sheet.

B.S. Bachelor of Science.

B.S.A. Boy Scouts of America; Bachelor of Science in Agriculture.

B.S.A.A. Bachelor of Science in Applied Arts.

B.S.B.A. Bachelor of Science in Business Administration.

B.S.C.E. Bachelor of Science in Civil Engineering.

B.S.E. Bachelor of Science in Education.

bsh. bushel.

B.S.I.E. Bachelor of Science in Industrial Engineering.

B.S.J. Bachelor of Science in Journalism.

baskt. basket.

B.S.L. Bachelor of Science in Law.

B.S.M. Bachelor of Science in Music.

bsmt. basement.

B.S.N. Bachelor of Science in Nursing.

B.S.P. Bachelor of Science in Pharmacy.

B.S.P.H. Bachelor of Science in Public Health.

B.S.R.T. Bachelor of Science in Radiological Technology.

bt. bought.

Bt. Baronet.

btwn. between.

bty. battery.

bu. bushel; bureau.

bul. bulletin.

bull. bulletin.

bus. bushel; business.

b.v. book value.

B.W.I. British West Indies.

bx. box.

c. centimeter; chapter; copywrite; cubic; cycle; current.

C. Chairman; Church; Congress; Court.

Ca. California.

Ca. *Chem.* calcium.

C.A. Central America; Chief Accountant; Controller of Accounts; Court of Appeals.

CAA Civil Aeronautics Administration.

CAB Civil Aeronautics Administration.

cal. calendar; caliber; calorie.

Camb. Cambridge.

can. canceled; cannon.

Can. Canada; Canadian.

cap. capital; capitalize.

C.A.P. Civil Air Patrol.

Capt. Captain.

Card. Cardinal.

cash. cashier.

cath. Cathedral.

Cath. Catholic.

cav. cavalry; cavity.

C.B.C. Canadian Broadcasting Corporation.

c.c. carbon copy; cubic centimeter.

C.C. cashier's check; Circuit Court; Civil Court; Country Club; County Clerk; County Court.

C.C.A. Circuit Court of Appeals; County Court of Appeals.

C.C.P. Court of Common Pleas.

cd. cord.

Cd *Chem.* cadmium.

C.D. Civil Defense; Coast Dsefense

Ce *Chem.* cerium.

C.E. Chief Engineer; Church of England; Civil Engineer; customs and excise.

CEA Council of Economic Advisors.

Celt. Celtic.

cent. centigrade; century.

cert. certificate.

Cf *Chem.* californium.

C.F. cost and freight.

cg. centigram.

C.G. Center of Gravity; Coast Gurad.

ch. chapter; chief; church.

C.H. Clearing House; Courthouse.

Chanc. Chancellor.

chap. chapter.

chem. chemist; chemistry.

Chev. Chevalier.

chf. chief.

Chin. Chinese.

chron. chronological.

CI cast iron; cost and insurance.

C.I. Chief Inspector; Counter Intelligence.

C.I.A. Central Intelligence Agency.

Cin. Cincinnati.

C. in C. Commander-in-Chief.

cit. cited; citizen.

C.J. Chief Justice.

cl. carload; clause; clergyman.

Cl *Chem.* chlorine.

class. classical; classified.

cld. canceled; colored; cooled.

clk. clerk.

CLU Civil Liberties Union.

cm. centimeter.

Cm *Chem.* curium.

cml commercial.

CNO Chief of Naval Operations

CNS central nervous system.

Co *Chem.* cobalt.

C.O. Commanding Officer; conscientious objector.

C. of C. Chamber of Commerce.

C. of S. Chief of Staff.

col. Colony; color; column.

Col. Colorado; Colombia.

coll. collateral; collected; collection; college; collegiate.

colloq. colloquial; colloquially.

Colo. Colorado.

com. comedy; common; communication.

Com. commander; commission; committee

Com.-in-Chf Commander-in-Chief

comp. comparative; composer; compositor; compound.

Comr. commissioner.

con. consolidated; continued.

Cong. Congregational Congress.

conj. conjunction; conjunctive.

Conn. Connecticut.

consgt. consignment.

const. constant; constituent; constitutional.

cont. containing; continent; continued.

contr. contracted; contralto; contrary.

conv. convalescent; convention; convertible.

cor. corpus; correction; correspondent.

Cor. Corinthians; coroner.

cor. corporal; corporation.

corr. correspond; corruptiion.

cos cosine.

cot cotangent.

c.p. candle power; cerebal palsy; chemically pure.

C.P. Common Pleas; Common Prayer; Court of Probate.

C.P.A. Certified Public Accountant.

CPI Consumer Price Index.

Cpl. Corporal.

C.P.O. Chief Petty Officer.

cr. center; circular; creek; crown.

Cr *Chem.* chromium.

C.R. Costa Rica.

craniol. craniology.

crit. critical.

cs. census; consciousness.

Cs *Chem.* caesium.

C.S. Chief of Staff; Civil Service; court of sessions.

CSC Civil Service Commission.

csk. cask.

CST Central Standard Time.

ct. cent; court; current.

Ct. Connecticut.

C.T. Central Time.

ctf. certificate.

ctl. central.

cu. cubic; cumulus.

cur. currency.

C.W. Child welfare; continuous wave.

C.W.O. Chief Warrant Officer..

cy. capacity; cycle; cyclopedia.

C.Z. Canal Zone.

Czech. Czechoslovakia.

d. daughter; day; degree; date.

D Roman numeral for 500.

D. Democrat; Deacon; Duke; Duchess.

D.A. District Attorney.

D.A.R. Daughters of the American Revolution.

DAV Disabled American Veterans.

db decibel.

D & B Dun and Bradstreet.

DBA doing business as.

dbk. drawback.

dbl. double.

d.c. direct current.

dd. delivered.

DD dishonorable discharge.

D.D.S. Doctor of Dental Surgery.

De. Delaware.

D.E. Doctor of Engineering.

Dea. Deacon.

deb. debutante; debenture;

dec. deceased.

Dec. December.

decd. declared; decreased.

decl. declension.

ded. dedication.

def defective; definite; deferred; definition.

deft. defendant.

deg. degree.

del. delegate; delete; deliver.

Dem. Democrat; democratic.

dent. dentist; dental; dentistry.

dep. department; departed; depot; deputy; departs.

der. derivative; derived; derivation.

deriv. derivative; derivation.

det. detachment.

Deut. Deuteronomy.

D.F. Dean of Faculty.

dft. defendant; draft.

Di *Chem.* didymium.

dial. dialectical; dialect.

diam. diameter.

dict. dictionary; dictation; dictator.

diff. different; difference.

dig. digest.

dipl. diploma; diplomatic.

dir. director; direction.

dis. discount; distance; distribute.

disc. discount; discovered.

disp. dispatch; dispenser.

dist. district; distance; distinguish.

Dist. Atty. District Attorney.

Dist. Ct. district court.

div. divide; dividend; divinity; division;

D.J. disc jockey.

dk deck; dock.

dl. deciliter.

D.L.O. dead letter office.

dly. delivery; daily.

dm decimeter.

D.M.D. Doctor of Dental Medicine.

D.M.S. Doctor of Medical Science.

DMZ demilitarized zone.

D.O.A. dead on arrival.

doc. document.

dol. dollars.

dom. domestic; dominion.

doz. dozen.

D. Ph. Doctor of Philosophy.

dpt. department.

D.P.W. Department of Public Works.

dr. debtor; dram; drawer; draw.

Dr. Doctor; drive.

D.R. Daughters of the Revolution;

d.s. daylight saving;

D.S. Doctor of Science.

D.S.T. Daylight Saving Time.

D.V.M. Doctor of Veterinary Medicine.

d.w.t. deadweight tonnage.

Dy *Chem.* dysprosium.

dyn dynamics.

dz. dozen.

E. east; eastern; English; ecvellent; earth.

ea. each.

E.C. East Central.

eccl ecclesiastical.

ECG electrocardiogram.

econ. economic; economy; economics.

Ecua. Ecuador.

ed. educated; editor; edition; edited.

Ed. B. Bachelor of Education.

Ed. D. Doctor of Education.

edit. edition; editor; edited.

Ed. M. Master of Education.

EDP Electronic Data Processing.

eds. editors.

EDT. Eastern Daylight Time.

educ. educational; educated; education.

E.E. Electrical Engineer.

Eg. Egypt.

E.I. East Indies; East India.

EKG electrocardiogram.

elem. elementary; element; elements.

e.m.h. educable mentally handicapped.

Emp. Empire; Empress; Emperor.

EMU electro magnetic unit.

ency. encyclopedia.

E.N.E. east-northeast.

eng. engineering; engraving; engineer; engraver.

Eng. English; England.

enl. enlarge; enlarged; enlist; enlisted.

E.O. executive officer.

e.o.m. end of the month.

Eph. Epiphany.

epil epilogue.

epit. epitome; epitaph.

eq. equal; equivalent; equation.

EQ educational quotient.

equiv. equivalent.

Er. *Chem.* erbium.

Es. *Chem.* einsteinium.

esp. especially.

e.s.p. estrasensory perception.
est. establisher; estate; estuary; estimated.
E.S.T. Eastern Standard Time.
ETA estimated time of arrival.
etc. and so forth.
Eth. Ethiopia.
et. seq. and the following.
Eu *Chem.* europium.
Eur. European; Europe.
Evang. Evangelical.
evg. evening.
ex. examination; example; except; exception; excursion; executive.
Ex. Exodus.
exam. examined; examination.
exc. except; excellent; exception.
ex int. without interest.
exp. expired; export; exporter; express; expense.
ext. extension; external; extra; extract; extreme; extended.

F. Fahrenheit.
FAA Federal Aviation agency; Federal Alcohol Administration.
fac. facsimile; factory; factor;
Fahr. Fahrenheit.
fam. family; familiar.
fath. fathom.
fb. *Football* fullback.
F.B.I. Federal Bureau of Investigation.
f.c. *Baseball* fielders choice.
F.C.A. Farm Credit administration.
F.C.C. first-class certificate; Federal Communications Commission.
fd. fund.
FDA Food and Drug Administration.
F.D.I.C. Federal Deposit Insurance Corporation.
Feb. February.
fem. feminine; female.
F.E.T. Federal Excise Tax.
feud. feudalism; feudal.
FFA Future Farmers of America.
fgn. foreign.
FHA Future Homemakers of America.
F.H.A. Federal Housing Administration.
F.I. Falkland Islands.
F.I.C.A. Federal Insurance Contributions Act.

fict. fiction.
FIFO First-in, First-Out.
fig. figuratively; figure; figurative.
fin. financial.
Fin. Finland.
FL. Florida.
flor. flourished.
fl oz fluid ounce.
Fm *Chem.* fermium.
F.M. Field Marshal; frequency modulation; Foreign Mission.
fn. footnote.
F.O. Foreign Office; Field Officer.
f.o.b. free on board.
F.O.E. Fraternal Order of Eagles.
fol. following.
for. foreign.
fort. fortified; fortification.
FPHA Federal Public Housing Authority.
FPO field post office.
f.p.m. feet per minute.
f.p.s. feet per second.
fr. franc; fragment;
Fr. *Chem.* francium.
Fr. France; Friday; French; Father.
F.R.B. Federal Reserve Bank.
freq. frequent; frequently; frequentative.
Fri. Friday.
frs. francs.
FRS Federal Reserve System.
frt. freight.
f.s foot-second.
ft. feet; fort; foot.
FTC Federal Trade Commission.
fth. fathom.
furl. furlough.
fut. future.
fwd. forward.
FYI for your information.

g. gender; gram; gauge; guinea; guide.
g.a. general average.
Ga *Chem.* gallium
Ga. Georgia.
G.A. General Assembly.
gal gallon.
galv. galvanized; galvanism.
G.A.W. guaranteed annual wage.
G.B. Great Britain.
Gd *Chem.* gadolinium.
g.d. granddaughter.

G.D. Grand Duchess; Grand Duke.

gdn. guardian; garden.

gen. general; gender; genus; genitive.

Gen. General.

gent. gentleman.

geog. geographer; geography.

geol. geology; geologist.

geom. geometry; geometrical.

Ger. Germany; German.

G.F.T.U. General Federation of Trade Unions.

GHQ *Mil.* general headquarters.

G.I. general issue; government issue; galvanized iron; an enlisted man of the U.S. armed forces.

gloss. glossary.

gm grams; gram.

G.M. general manager; grand master; guided missile; grand marshal.

G.N. graduate nurse.

GNP gross national product.

G.O. general order; general office.

G.O.P. Grand Old Party, relating to the Republican Party.

gov. government.

Gov. Governor.

govt. government.

G.P. general practitioner.

gpm gallons per minute.

G.P.O. General Post Office.

G.Q. general quarters.

gr. grain; great; grand.

gram. grammar; grammatical.

gro. gross.

gr. wt. gross weight.

g.s. grandson.

G.S. general secretary.

G.S.A. Girl Scouts of America.

Gt.Br. Great Britain.

Guia. Guinea.

gun. gunnery.

ha. hectare.

Hal *Chem.* halogen.

hb *Football* halfback.

H.C. Holy Communion.

h.c.l. high cost of living.

hd. head; hand.

hdkf. handkerchief.

hdqrs. headquarters.

He *Chem.* helium.

H.E. high explosive.

Heb. Hebrews; Hebrew.

her. heraldry.

H.E.W. Department of Health Education and Welfare.

hf. half.

Hf *Chem.* hafnium.

HF high frequency.

hg hectogram.

Hg *Chem.* mercury.

hgt. height.

H.I. Hawaiian Islands.

hist. history; historical; historian; histology.

hl. hectoliter.

Ho *Chem.* holmium.

H.O. home office; head office.

H.O.L.C. Home Owners' Loan Corporation.

Hon. honorable; honorary.

hort. horticulture; horticultural.

hosp. hospital.

H.P. horsepower; high pressure.

H.Q. headquarters.

hr. hour.

H.R. House of Representatives.

H.S. High School.

Hun. Hungary.

hund. hundred.

H.V. high voltage.

h.w.m. high water mark.

hdy. hydraulics.

hyp. hypothetical.

i interest; intransitive.

I *Chem.* iodine.

Ia. Iowa.

I. & R. intelligence and reconnaissance.

i.b. invoice book.

ICBM intercontinental ballistic missile.

Ice. Iceland; Icelandic.

ICJ International Court of Justice.

Id. Idaho.

IFC International finance Corporation.

ign. ignition.

i.h.p. indicated horsepower.

IL *Chem.* Illinium.

I.L.G.W.U. International Ladies Garment Workers Union.

ill. illustrated; illustration.

Ill. Illinois.
ILO International Labor Organization.
IMF International Monetary Fund.
imit. imitative.
imp. imperfect; impersonal; important; importer.
imperf. imperfect.
impers. imperfect.
in. inch.
In. *Chem.* indium.
inc. income; incorporated; incumbent.
incl. including; inclusive.
incog. incognito.
ind. index; indirect; industry.
Ind. India; Indiana.
indiv. individual.
inf. inferior; information.
infin. infinitive.
infl. influenced.
in. Hg. *Chem.* inch of mercury.
ins. inches; insulated; insurance.
I.N.S. International News Service.
insp. inspector.
inst. instantaneous; institution; instrumental.
int. interior; internal; interpreter;.
intens. intensive.
inter. intermediate; interrogative.
interrog. interrogation; interrogatively.
Int. Rev. Internal Revenue.
invt. inventory.
Io *Chem.* ionium.
Io. Iowa.
IPA. International Press Association.
IPBM interplanetary ballistic missile.
Ir. *Chem.* iridium.
Ir. Ireland; Irish.
I.R. Internal Revenue.
Ire. Ireland.
I.R.O. Internal Revenue Office.
irreg. irregular.
IRS Internal Revenue Service.
Is. Isaiah; Island.
iss. issue.
It. Italy.
ital. italic.
ITO International Trade Organization.
ITU International Telecommunication Union.
i.v. increased value; intravenous; invoice value.
I.W. Isle of Wight.

I.W.W. Industrial Workers of the World.

j.a. joint account.
J.A. Judge Advocate.
J.A.G. Judge Advocate General.
Jam. Jamaica.
J.A.M.A. Journal of the American Medical Association.
Jan. January.
Jap. Japanese; Japan.
J.C. Jesus Christ.
J.C.C. Junior Chamber of Commerce.
J.C.S. Joint Chief of Staff.
Jct. Junction.
Jer. Jerusalem; Jeremiah.
j-g. junior grade.
J.J. judges;
jnt. joint.
jour. journal.
J.P. Justice of the Peace.
Jr. junior.
jt. joint.
Jud. Judges.
junc. junction.
JV Junior Varsity.

K. *Chem.* potassium.
kal. kalands.
Ks. Kansas.
kc. kilocycle.
K.C. Knight of Columbus.
kg. kilogram; keg.
KIA killed in action.
kil. kilometer; kilogram.
kilom. kilometers; kilometer.
K.J.V. King James' Version.
K.K.K. Ku Klux Klan.
kl. kiloliter.
km. kilometer; kingdom.
K.O. knock-out.
K.P. kitchen police.
Kr. *Chem.* krypton.
kt. karat.
kw. kilowatt.
Ky. Kentucky.

La *Chem.* lanthanum.
La. Louisiana.

L.A. Latin America; Los angeles.
lab. laboratory.
Lab. Labrador.
lam. laminated.
lang. language.
lat. latitude.
Lat. Latin.
lb. pound.
l.c. letter of credit.
L.C. Library of Congress.
l.c.d. lowest common multiple.
LCD *Computer Science* Liquid Crystal Display.
l.c.m. least common multiple.
ld. land.
Ld. Lord.
L.D.S. Latter-Day Saints.
lea. league.
leath. leather.
LED *Computer Science* Light-Emitting Diode.
LF Key *Computer Science* Line Feed Key.
leg. legal; legislative; legislature.
lex. lexicon; lexical.
lf low frequency.
l.g. *Football* left guard.
L.G. life guard.
l.h. left hand.
L.H. lighthouse.
l.h.b. *Football* left halfback.
Li *Chem.* lithium.
L.I. light infantry.
Lieut. Lieutenant.
LIFO *Computer Science* last in, first out.
lin linear; liniment; lineal.
l.i.p. life insurance policy.
liq. liquor; liquid.
L.J. Lord Justice.
L.M.T. local mean time.
log. logarithm.
lon. longitude.
L.O.O.M. Loyal Order of Moose.
LP *Computer Science* line Printer; linear programming.
L.P. low pressure.
lpm *Computer Science* lines per minute.
lps *Computer Science* lines per second.
L.s. left side.
LSD lysergic acid diethylamide.
lsd *Computer Science* least-significant digit.

LSI *Computer Science* Large Scale Integration.
L.S.T. local standard time.
l.t. *Football* left tackle.
Lt. Lieutenant.
ltd. limited.
Lt. Inf. light infantry.
Lu *Chem.* lutetium.
Luth. Lutheran.
Lw *Chem.* lawrencium.
lwop leave without pay.
lwp leave with pay.

M. Roman numeral for 1000.
Ma *Chem.* masurium.
Ma Massachusetts.
M.A. Master of Arts; Military Academy.
MAC *Computer Science* Multiple Access Computer.
MADD Mothers against drunk drivers.
mag. magazine; magnitude.
Maj. Major.
man. manual.
manuf. manufacturing; manufacturer.
mar. maritime; married.
marg. margin.
mas. masculine.
mat. matured.
math. mathematical; mathematics.
max. maximum.
M.B.A. Master of Business Administration.
M.B.S. Master of Business Science.
M.C. Marine Corps.
mcht. merchant.
M.C.L. Master of Civil Law.
Md *Chem.* mendelevium.
Md. Maryland.
M.D.S. Master in Dental Surgery.
mdse. merchandise.
Me *Chem.* methyl.
Me. Maine.
meas. measure.
mech. mechanical; mechanics.
mensur. mensuration.
mer. meridian.
mere. mercury.
meteor. meteorology.
Mex. Mexico.
M.F.A. Master of Fine Arts.

mfg. manufacturing.
mfr. manufacturer.
mg. milligram; milligrams.
Mg Chem. magnesium.
mgr. manager.
M.H. Medal of Honor.
M.H.E. Master of Home Economics.
mi. mile; mill.
M.I. military intelligence.
Mi. Michigan.
micros. microscopy.
mid. middle.
Mid. Midshipman.
M.I.D. Military Intelligence Division.
mil. military.
Mn. Minnesota.
M.I.S. Master of International Service.
miles. miscellaneous.
Ms. Mississippi.
M.J. Master of Journalism.
mks. meter-kilogram-second.
mkt. market.
ml. mail; milliliter.
mm. millimeter;
M.M.E. Master of Music Education.
Mn Chem. manganese.
M.N.A. Master of Nursing Administration.
mng. managing.
Mo Chem. molybdenum.
Mo. Missouri.
mod. moderate.
M.O.H. Medical Officer of Health.
mol. wt molecular weight.
mon. monsastery.
Mon. Monday.
Mons. Monsieur.
morph. morphological.
m.p. melting point.
M.P.E. Master of Physical Education.
m.p.g. miles per gallon.
M.PH. Master of Philosophy.
Mr. Mister.
M.R.C. Medical Reserve Corps.
Mrs. Mistress.
ms. manuscript.
M.S. Master of Science.
M.S.B.A. Master of Science in Business Administration.
M.S.D. Master of Science in Dentistry.
MSG monosodium glutamate.
M.S.J. Master of Science in Journalism.

Ms-Th Chem. mesothorium.
mt. mountain.
Mt. Montana.
MT mechanical translation.
M.T. metric ton.
mtg. meeting; mortgage.
mtg. mortgaged.
mtge. mortgage.
M. Th. Master of Theology.
MTI moving target indicator.
mus. museum; musical; musician; music.
m.v. market value.
myl. myrialiters.
mym myriameter.
myth mythology.

n neutron.
N Chem. nitrogen.
N.A. National Academy; North America; Nautical Almanac.
NAA National Aeronautic Association; National Automobile Association.
NAACP National Association for the Advancement of Colored People.
NAB National Association of Broadcasters.
NAM National Association of Manufacturers.
N.Amer. North America.
NASA National Aeronautics and Space Administration.
nat. native; naturalist.
natl. national; natural; naturalist.
NATO North Atlantic Treaty Organization.
nat. sc. natural science.
naut. nautical.
nav. naval; navigation.
navig. navigation.
Nb. Chem. niobium.
Nb. Nebraska.
NB Naval Base.
NBA National Basketball Association.
N.B.S. National Bureau of Statistics.
N.C. North Carolina.
N.C.A.A. National Conference of Christians and Jews.
N.C.C.M. National Council of Catholic Men.
N.C.C.W. National Council of Catholic Women.

N.C.O. noncommissioned officer.

n.c.v. no commercial value.

Nd *Chem.* Neodymium.

N.D. North Dakota.

NDAC National Defense Advisory Commission.

Ne *Chem.* neon.

N.E. New England; northeastern; northeast.

N.E.A. National Editorial Association; National Education Association.

neg. negatively; negative.

N. Eng. New England.

n.e.s. not elsewhere specified.

neut. neuter.

Newf. Newfoundland

n.f. no funds.

Nfld. Newfoundland.

n.g. no good.

NG *Chem.* nitroglycerin.

N.H.S. National Health Service.

Ni *Chem.* nickel.

N.J. New Jersey.

n.l. *Printing* new line.

N.L. *Baseball* National League.

N. Lat. north latitude.

nm nautical mile.

N.M. New Mexico.

N.M.U. National Maritime Union.

N.N.E. north-northeast.

NNP net national product.

N.N.W. north-northwest.

no. north; northern.

No *Chem.* nobelium.

nom. nominative.

noncom. noncommissioned officer.

n.o.p. not otherwise provided for.

nor. northern; north.

nos. numbers.

n.o.s. not otherwise specified.

Nov. November.

N.P. new paragraph.

n.p. or d. no place or date of publication.

N.R.A. National Recovery Administration; National Recovery Act.

N.S. not specified.

NSA National Shipping Authority; National Students Association.

NSC National Security Council.

n.s.f. not sufficient funds.

NSF National Science Foundation.

N.S.P.C.A. National Society for the Prevention of Cruelty to Animals.

N.S.P.C.C. National · Society for the Prevention of Cruelty to Children.

Nit *Chem.* niton.

nt. wt. net weight.

n.u. name unknown.

num. numbers; number.

N.U.R. National Union of Railway Men.

N.U.T. Nation Union of Teachers.

Nv. Nevada.

N.W. northwest; northwestern.

N.W.T. Northwest Territories.

N.Y. New York.

N.Y.C. New York City.

NYP not yet published.

N.Z. New Zealand.

o. old; only; *Baseball* outs; out.

O. ocean; October; Ontario; Oregon.

o.a. on account.

OAS Organization of American States.

obdt. obedient.

O.B.E. Officer of the Order of the British Empire.

obj. objection; objective; object.

obl. oblique; oblong.

obs. observation; obsolete; obstetrics.

obstet. obstetrics; obstetrical.

oc. ocean.

occas. occasional; occasionally.

Oct. October.

o.d. on demand; over-drive; outside diameter.

O.D. Officer of the Day; olive drab.

ODT Organization of Defense Transportation.

o.e. omissions expected.

O.E. Old English.

OECD Organization for Economic Cooperation and Development.

OEO Officer of Economic Opportunity.

O.E.S. Order of the Eastern Star.

off. officer; official; office.

O.K. correct; all right.

Ok. Oklahoma.

O.L. Old Latin

Ont. Ontario.

o.p. out put.

ophthalm. ophthalmology.

opp. opposite; opposed.

opt. optics; optative; optical; optional.

o.r. owner's risk.

O.R.C. Officer;s Reserve Corps.

ord. order; ordinal; ordinance; ordnance; ordinary; ordained.

ordn. ordnance.

org. organized; organic.

orig. originally; original.

OR. Oregon.

Os *Chem.* osmium.

O.S.A. Order of St. Augustine.

O.S.F. Order of St. Francis.

OSRD Office of Scientific Research and Development.

OSS Office of Strategic Services.

O.T. occupational therapy.

O.T.C. Officer Training Corps.

Oxf. Oxford.

oz. ounce.

p. page; participle; past; pitcher;

P. Pope; president; pressure; Priest; progressive.

p.a. participial adjective.

Pa *Chem.* protactinium.

Pa. Pennsylvania.

Pa public address system.

P.A. power of attorney; purchasing agent; press agent.

PABA *Chem.* paraaminobenzoic acid.

Pac. Pacific.

Pal. Palestine.

paleog. paleography.

paoleoa. paleontology.

pam pamphlet.

p. & l. profit and loss.

par. paragraph; parallel; parish.

paren. parenthesis.

Parl. Parliament; Parliamentary.

part. participle; particular.

pass. passenger.

pat. patent; patented.

PAT *Football* point, or points, after the touchdown.

path. pathological; pathology.

Pat. Off. patent office.

P.A.U. Pan American Union.

P.A.Y.E. pay as you earn.

payt. payment.

p.b. *Baseball* passed ball.

pb *Chem.* lead.

PBA Public Buildings Administration.

pc. price; piece.

p.c. per cent; petty cash; price current.

P.C. penal code; Police Constable; Privy Councilor.

pd. paid.

pd *Chem.* palladium.

P.D. Police Department.

P.E. Physical Education; printer;s error.

ped. *Music* pedal; pedestal.

pen. peninsula.

Pent. Pentecost.

perf. perfect; perforated.

herh. perhaps.

perp. perpendicular.

pers. person; personal.

persp. perspective.

pert. pertaining.

petrog. petrography.

pertol. petrology.

pf. perfect.

Pfc. *Mil.* private first class.

pg. page.

Pg. Portugal.

P.G. post-graduate.

PGA Professional Golfer's Association.

P.G.M. Past Grand Master.

Ph *Chem.* phenyl.

P.H. Public Health.

PHA Public Housing Administration.

Phar. pharmaceutical; pharmacy.

Phar.D Doctor of Pharmacy.

Ph.B Bachelor of Philosophy.

Ph.D Doctor of Philosophy.

Phil. Philadelphia; Philippine.

philol. philology.

phon. phonetics.

phot. photography.

phr. phrase.

PHS Public Health Service.

phys. physical; physician; physiology; physiological; physics.

physiol. physiology.

P.I. Philippine Islands.

PIO public information office.

pk. pack; park; peck.

pkg. package.

pkt. packet.

pl. plural; plate; place.

plat. platoon; plateau.

plf. plaintiff.

plur. plural; plurality.

pm. premium.

Pm *Chem.* promethium.

P.M. afternoon; post mortem; past master.

P.M.G. Paymaster General; Postmaster General.

p.n. please note; promissory note.

PNA *Chem.* pentose nucleic acid.

pneum. pneumatic; pneumatics.

Po *Chem.* polonium.

P.O. Petty Officer; post office; postal order.

P.O.B. post office box.

poet. poetry; poetic.

pol. political; politics.

polit. political; politics.

pop. popular; population.

P.O.P. print-out paper.

pos. position; possession; possessive; positive.

poss. possessive; possible.

pot. potential.

POW prisoner of war.

p.p. past participle; prepaid.

P.P. parcel post.

pph. pamphlet.

ppr. present participle.

P.Q. previous question.

pr. pair; present; priest; price; preference.

Pr. *Chem.* praseodymium.

PRA Public Roads Administration.

prec. preceding.

pred. predicate.

pref. preface; preferred; prefix; prefatory.

prelim. preliminary.

prem. premium.

prep. preparation; preposition; preparatory.

pres. present; presumptive; pressure.

Pres. President.

Presb. Presbyterian.

prin. principle; principally; principal.

print. printing.

priv. privative; private.

PRO Public Relations Officer.

prob. probably; problem; probable.

proc. proceedings; process; procedure; proclamation; proctor.

prod. production; produced;

prof. Professor.

Prog. Progressive.

prom. promoted; promontory.

pron. pronominal; pronounced;

pronunciation..

prop. properly; proper; proposition; property; proprietary.

propr. proprietor.

pros. prosody; proscenium.

Prot. Protestant.

pro. tem. temporarily; for the time being.

prov. provident; provincial; province; provisional.

Prov. Proverbs; Province; Provencal; Provost.

prx. pain.

ps. pieces.

Ps. Psalms.

PSAT Preliminary Scholastic Aptitude Test.

PSC Public Service Commission.

P.S.T. Pacific Standard Time.

p.t. past tense; temporarily.

Pt. *Chem.* platinum.

P.T. physical therapist; patrol torpedo boat.

P.T.A. Parent-Teacher Association.

p.t.o. please turn over.

Pu *Chem.* plutonium.

pub. public; publisher; publishing; published; publication.

punct. punctuation.

PVC polyvinyl chloride.

P.W.A. Public Works Administration.

P.W.D. Public Works Department.

pwt. pennyweight.

PX post exchange.

q. query; quart; question.

Q. Queen; question.

q.b. *Football* quarterback.

Q.B. Queen's Bench.

Q.C. Queen's Counsel.

ql. quintal.

Q.M. Quartermaster Corps.

Q.M.G. Quartermaster General.

qr quarter; quire.

q.s. quarter section.

qt. quart; quality.

qu query; question.

quar quarter; quarterly.

ques. question.

quot. quotation.

qy query.

r. railroad; radius; rare; received; rod; ruble.

r. *Chem.* radical; *Elect.* resistance.

Ra *Chem.* radium.

R.A. Rear admiral; Royal Academician; Royal Artillery.

rad *Math.* radix; radical.

Rad. Radical

R.A.F. Royal Air Force.

rail. railways; railroad;

R & D research and development.

Rb *Chem.* rubidium.

R.B.I. *Baseball* run, or runs, batted in.

R.C. Red Cross; Reserve Corps; Roman Catholic.

F.C.A.F. Royal Canadian Air Force.

R.C.P. Royal College of Physicians.

Ret. *Mil.* recruit.

rd. road; rod; round; rendered.

Rd. *Chem.* radium.

Re *Chem.* rhenium.

r.e. *Football* right end.

rec. receipt; record; recipe; recorder; recorded.

recd. received.

rec. sec. recording secretary.

rect. receipt; rectory; rector; rectangle; redupl. reduplication; reduplicated.

ref. referee; referred; reference; refund.

refl. reflexive; reflex.

reg. region; registered; regular; register.

regd. registered.

regr. registrar.

regt. regiment.

rel. relatively; religion; relative; religious.

relig. religion.

rep. representative; repair; repeat; reporter; report; republic.

Rep. Republican.

repr. reprint; reprinted; represented; representing.

repts. reports.

res reserve; resigned; resides; residence.

ret returned; retained;

rev. reverse; revenue; revised; revolution; revolving.

Rev. revelation; reverend.

rf *Baseball* right field.

R.F.D. rual free delivery.

r.g. *Football* right guard.

r.h. right hand; relative humidity.

r.h.b. *Football* right halfback.

rhet. rhetorical; rhetoric.

R.I. Rhode Island; religious instructions.

riv. river.

rm room; ream.

Rn *Chem.* radon.

R.N. Registered Nurse.

r.p.m. revolutions per minute.

R.P.O. Railway Post Office.

rpt. report.

r.s. right side.

R.S. Recording Secretary.

R.S.V.P. reply, if you please.

rt. right.

r.t. *Football* right tackle.

Ru. *Chem.* ruthenium.

Rum. Rumanian.

Russ. Russian; Russia.

R.V. Revised Version.

Rwy. Railway.

s. second; see; singular; section.

S. *Chem.* sulfur.

S. Sabbath; Saturday; Saxon; school; Saint; south; southern; Sunday.

S.A. Salvation Army.

Sab. Sabbath.

S.A.E. Society of automotive Engineers.

S. Afr. South Africa.

Salv. Salvador.

S. Amer. South America.

S.A.R. Sons of the American Revolution.

Sat. Saturn; Saturday.

SAT Scholastic Aptitude Test.

sax. Saxony.

sb. substantive.

SBA Small Business Administration.

sc. scale; science; scene; scientific.

s.c. small capitals.

Se *CHem.* scandium.

S.C. Security Council; Signal Corps; South Carolina; Supreme Court.

Scand. Scandinavia.

Sch. school; schooner.

sie. scientific; science.

Scot. Scotland; Scottish; Scotch.

scr. scruple.

Script. Scripture; Scriptural.

SCS Soil Conservation Service.

sculp. sculpture; sculptor.

sd. sound.

s.d. sight draft.

S.D. South Dakota.

S.D.S. Students for a Democratic Society.

Se *Chem.* selenium.

sec secant.

sect. section.

secy. secretary.

Sen. Senator; Senior; Senate;

sep. separate; sepal.

Sept. September.

seq. sequel.

ser. series; sermon.

Serg Sergeant.

s.f. sinking fund.

SF Science Fiction.

S.F. San Francisco.

Sfc. *Mil.* sergeant first class.

s.g. specific gravity.

sgd. signed.

Sgt. Sergeant.

sh. shilling; shillings; share.

Shp shaft house power.

shpt. shipment.

Si *Chem.* silicon.

Sib. Siberian; Siberia.

Sic. Sicily; Sicilian.

sing. singular.

S.J. society of Jesus.

sld. sailed; sold; sealed.

Sm *Chem.* samarium.

so. southern; south.

s.o. seller's option; shipping order.

soc. society; socialist.

sociol sociological.

SOS (...—...) international distress call.

sou. southern; south.

sp. special; specimen; spirit; spelling.

Sp. Spain.

s.P. Shore Patrol; submarine patrol.

S.P.C.A. Society for the Prevention of Cruelty to Animals.

S.P.C.C. Society for the Prevention of Cruelty to Children.

spec. specially; specific; special; specifically.

sp. gr. specific gravity.

Spgs. springs.

spt. seaport.

Sq. Squadron; square.

Sr *Chem.* strontium.

Sr. Senior.

SRBM short-range ballistic missile.

S.R.O. standing room only.

S.S. Secret Service; Sunday School.

S.S.E. south-southeast.

SSM surface-to-surface missile.

SSS Selective Service System.

S.S.W. south-southwest.

st. statute; stanza.

s.t. short ton.

St. Street; Saint; Strait.

sta. station.

stat. statute.

std. standard.

ster. sterling.

St. Ex. Stock Exchange.

stg. sterling.

str. steamer.

sub. subscription; suburb; substitute; subway; suburban.

suff. suffix.

Sun. Sunday.

sup. superlative; supplement; superior.

Sup. Ct. Supreme Court; Superior Court.

superl. superlative.

supp. supplement.

supt. superintendent.

Sur. Surrey.

surg. surgery; surgical; surgeon.

surv. surveyor, surviving; surveying.

S.W. southwest; southwestern.

Swed. Swedish; Sweden.

Switz. Switzerland.

syll. syllabus; syllable.

sym. symbol.

syn. synonym.

syst. system.

t. teaspoon; temperature; tense; tenor.

T. Tablespoon; Tuesday; Territory.

Ta *Chem.* tantalum.

tab. tablet; table.

TAC *Mil.* Tactical Air Command.

t.b. trial balance.

Tb *Chem.* terbium.

T.B. tuberculosis; turbercle bacillus.

tbs. tablespoons.

Te *Chem.* technetium.

TD *Football.* touchdown.

Te *Chem.* tellurium.

tech. technology; technical.

technol. technology.

tel. telegraph; telephone; telegram.

teleg. telegraph; telegraphy; telegram.

temp. temperature.
ter. territory; terrace.
term. terminal; termination.
Test. Testament.
Th *Chem.* thorium.
Th Thursday.
T.H. Territory of Hawaii.
theat. theatrical.
theol. theological; theology; theologian.
theor. theorem.
theos. therapeutics; therapeutic.
Thurs. Thursday.
Ti *Chem.* titanium.
tinct. tincture.
tit. title.
TKO *Boxing* technical knockout.
Tl *Chem.* thallium.
Tm *Chem.* thulium.
tn. ton.
Tn. Tennessee.
Tn *Chem.* thoron.
TNT trinitrotoluene.
t.o. telegraph office.
topog. topographical.
tox. toxicology.
tp. township.
t.p. title page.
tr. tincture; train; transaction; transitive; trace; transpose; translated; treasurer.
Tr *Chem.* terbium.
trans. transfer; transformer; transitive; translation; transaction; transverse.
transf. transferred.
trav. traveler; traveling.
treas. treasurer; treasury.
trop. tropical; tropic.

u. uncle; upper; unit; uniform.
U *Chem.* uranium.
U. Union; University.
UAM underwater to air missile.
UAW United Automobile Workers.
U.B. United Brethren.
UFO unidentified flying object.
UHF ultra high frequency.
U.K. United KIngdom.
Ukr. Ukraine.
ult. ultimate.
UMW United MIne Workers.
UN United Nations.

UNICEF United Nations Relief and Rehabilitation Agency.
up. upper.
U.P. United Press.
U.P.I. United Press International.
U.S. United States.
U.S.A. United States of America.
U.S.A.E.C. United States Atomic Energy Commission.
U.S.A.F. United States Air Force.
U.S.A.R. United States Army Reserve.
U.S.C.G. United States Coast Guard.
U.S.D.A. United States Department of Agriculture.
U.S.I.S. United States Information Service.
U.S.M. United States Mail.
U.S.M.C. United States Marine Corps; United States Maritime Commission.
U.S.N. United States Navy.
U.S.N.A. United States National Army; United Sates Naval Academy.
U.S.N.G. United States National Guard.
U.S.O. United Service Organization.
U.S.P.O. United States Post Office.
U.S.P.H.S. United States Public Health Service.
usu. usually; usual.
Ut. Utah.
UV ultraviolet.

v. verb; vector; verse; version.
V Roman numeral for 5.
v.a. verb active.
Va. Virginia.
val. valuation.
var. variation; variety; various; variant.
Vat. Vatican.
v. aux. verb auxiliary.
vb. verb.
vb. n. verbal noun.
v.d. various dates.
V.D. venereal disease.
Venez. Venezuela.
V.F.W. Veterans of Foreign Wars.
VHF very high frequency.
v.i. verb intransitive.
Vi *Chem.* virginium.
V.I. Virgin Islands.
Vic. Victoria.

vil. village.
VISTA Volunteer in Service to America.
V.M.D. Doctor of Veterinary Medicine.
v.n. verb neuter.
VOA Voice of America.
vocab. vocabulary.
vocat. vocative.
vol. volume; volcanic; volcano; volunteer.
v.p. verb passive.
V.P. Vice-President.
v.r. verb reflexive.
vs. verse.
V.S. Veterinary Surgeon.
v.t. verb transitive.
Vt. VErmont.
VTO vertical take-off.
VTOL vertical take-off and landing.
vulg. vulgarly; vulgar.
vv. verses.

w. warehouse; week; wide; wanting; won; with; width; wife.
W. Wednesday; west; western;
W.A. West Africa.
Wash. Washington.
WCC World Council of Churches.
wd. word; ward.
W.D. War Department.
Wed. Wednesday.
WFTU World Federation of Trade Unions.
WHO World Health Organization.
W.I. West Indian; West Indies.
Wi. Wisconsin.
wk. work; week.
wkly. weekly.
w.l. wave length; water line.
WMO World Meteorological Organization.
W.N.W. west-northwest.
W.O. warrant officer.
WRAC Women's Royal Army Corps.
WRAF Women's Royal Air Force.
WRNS Women's Royal Navy Service.
W.S.W. west-southwest.
wt. weight.
W. Va. West Virginia.
WW World War.
WWI World War I.
WWII World War II.
Wy Wyoming.

X Roman numeral for 10.
xe *Chem.* xenon.
XL extra large.
Xmas Christmas.
Xnty. Christianity.
Xtian Christian.

y. year; years; yard; yards.
Y *Chem.* yttrium.
Yb *Chem.* ytterbium.
Y.B. yearbook.
yd. yard.
yeo. yeomanry; yeoman.
Y.M.C.A. Young Men's Christian Association.
Y.M.C.U. Young Men's Christian Union.
Y.M.H.A. Young Men's Hebrew Association.
yr. year; younger; your.
yrs. years; yours.
Yt *Chem.* yttrium.
Yugo. Yugoslavia.
Y.W.C.A. Young Women's Christian Association.
Y.W.H.A. YOung Women's Hebrew Association.

z. zinc; zero.
Zn *Chem.* zinc.
zod. zodiac.
zoogeog. zoogeography.
zool. zoological.
Zr *Chem.* zirconium.

A	B	C	DAM	EEL	FIL
			DAP	EFF	FIN
AAH	BAA	CAB	DAW	EFT	FIR
AAL	BAD	CAD	DAY	EGG	FIT
ABA	BAG	CAL	DEB	EGO	FIX
ABO	BAH	CAM	DEE	ELD	FIZ
ABY	BAL	CAN	DEI	ELF	FLU
ACE	BAM	CAP	DEL	ELK	FLY
ACT	BAN	CAR	DEN	ELL	FOB
ADD	BAP	CAT	DES	ELM	FOE
ADO	BAR	CAW	DEV	EME	FOG
ADZ	BAT	CAY	DEW	EMU	FOH
AFF	BAW	CEE	DEX	END	FON
AFT	BAY	CET	DEY	ENG	FOP
AGA	BEA	CHA	DIB	ENS	FOR
AGE	BED	CHE	DID	EON	FOU
AGO	BEE	CHI	DIE	ERA	FOX
AHA	BEG	CID	DIG	ERE	FOY
AID	BEL	CIE	DIM	ERG	FRO
AIL	BEN	CIG	DIN	ERN	FRY
AIM	BET	COB	DIP	ERR	FUB
AIN	BEY	COD	DIT	ERS	FUD
AIR	BIB	COE	DOC	ESS	FUG
ALA	BID	COG	DOE	ETA	FUN
ALE	BIG	COL	DOG	ETH	FUR
ALL	BIM	CON	DOL	EVE	
ALP	BIN	COO	DOM	EWE	G
ALT	BIO	COP	DON	EYE	
AMI	BIS	COS	DOR		GAB
AMP	BIT	COT	DOT	F	GAD
AND	BOA	COW	DOW		GAE
ANT	BOB	COX	DRY	FAD	GAG
ANY	BOD	COY	DUB	FAG	GAL
APE	BOG	COZ	DUC	FAN	GAM
APT	BOH	CRY	DUD	FAR	GAN
ARC	BOK	CUB	DUE	FAT	GAP
ARE	BON	CUD	DUG	FAX	GAR
ARF	BOO	CUE	DUI	FAY	GAS
ARK	BOP	CUM	DUN	FED	GAT
ARM	BOT	CUP	DUO	FEE	GAY
ART	BOW	CUR	DUP	FEN	GED
ASH	BOX	CUT	DYE	FER	GEE
ASK	BRA	CWM		FET	GEL
ASS	BUD		E	FEU	GET
ATE	BUG	D		FEW	GEY
AVA	BUM		EAR	FEY	GHI
AVO	BUN	DAB	EAT	FEZ	GIB
AWA	BUS	DAD	EAU	FIB	GIG
AWE	BUT	DAG	EBB	FID	GIN
AWN	BUY	DAH	ECU	FIE	GIP
AZO	BYE	DAK	EDH	FIG	GIT

GNU	HUE	**K**	LID	MUD	OHO
GOB	HUG		LIE	MUG	OIL
GOD	HUH	KAB	LIN	MUM	OKA
GOO	HUN	KAE	LIP	MUN	OKE
GOR	HUP	KAS	LIT	MUT	OLD
GOT	HUT	KAT	LOB		OLE
GOX	HYP	KAY	LOG	**N**	ONE
GOY		KEA	LOO		OOH
GUL	**I**	KEF	LOP	NAB	OOT
GUM		KEG	LOT	NAE	OPE
GUN	ICE	KEN	LOW	NAG	OPT
GUT	ICH	KEP	LOX	NAP	ORA
GUY	ICY	KEX	LUG	NAY	ORB
GYM	ILK	KEY	LUX	NEB	ORC
GYP	ILL	KHI	LYE	NEE	ORE
	IMP	KID		NET	ORT
H	INK	KIF	**M**	NEW	OSE
	INN	KIN		NIB	OUD
HAD	ION	KIP	MAC	NIL	OUR
HAE	IRE	KIT	MAD	NIM	OUT
HAG	IRK	KOA	MAE	NIP	OWE
HAH	ISM	KOP	MAG	NIT	OWL
HAJ	ITS	KOR	MAN	NIX	OWN
HAM	IVY	KOS	MAP	NOB	OXY
HAP		KUE	MAR	NOD	
HAS	**J**		MAT	NOG	**P**
HAT		**L**	MAW	NOH	
HAW	JAB		MAY	NOM	PAC
HAY	JAG	LAB	MEL	NOO	PAD
HEM	JAM	LAC	MEM	NOR	PAH
HEN	JAR	LAD	MEN	NOT	PAL
HEP	JAW	LAG	MET	NOW	PAM
HER	JAY	LAM	MEW	NTH	PAN
HET	JEE	LAP	MHO	NUB	PAP
HEW	JET	LAR	MIB	NUN	PAR
HEX	JEU	LAT	MID	NUT	PAS
HEY	JEW	LAW	MIG		PAT
HIC	JIB	LAX	MIL	**O**	PAW
HID	JIG	LAY	MIN		PAX
HIE	JIN	LEA	MIR	OAF	PAY
HIM	JOB	LED	MIX	OAK	PEA
HIP	JOE	LEE	MOA	OAR	PED
HIS	JOG	LEG	MOB	OAT	PEE
HIT	JOT	LEI	MOD	OBE	PEG
HOB	JOW	LEK	MOG	OBI	PEN
HOD	JOY	LET	MOL	OCA	PEP
HOE	JUG	LEU	MOM	ODD	PER
HOG	JUN	LEV	MOO	ODE	PET
HOP	JUS	LEX	MOP	OFF	PEW
HOT	JUT	LEY	MOR	OFT	PHI
HOY		LIB	MOW	OHM	PHT

PIA	REP	SHY	TEN	VEE	
PIC	RES	SIB	TEW	VEG	Y
PIE	RET	SIM	THE	VET	
PIG	REV	SIN	THY	VEX	YAH
PIN	REX	SIP	TIC	VIA	YAK
PIP	RHO	SIR	TIE	VIE	YAM
PIT	RIB	SIS	TIL	VIM	YAP
PIX	RID	SIT	TIN	VIN	YAR
PLY	RIM	SIX	TIP	VIS	YAW
POD	RIN	SKI	TIT	VOE	YAY
POH	RIP	SKY	TOD	VON	YEA
POL	ROB	SLY	TOE	VOW	YEH
POP	ROC	SOB	TOG	VOX	YEN
POT	ROD	SOD	TOM	VUG	YEP
POW	ROE	SOL	TOO	W	YES
POX	ROT	SON	TOP		YET
PRO	ROW	SOP	TOR	WAB	YEW
PRY	RUB	SOT	TOT	WAD	YID
PUB	RUE	SOW	TOW	WAE	YIN
PUD	RUG	SOX	TOY	WAG	YIP
PUG	RUM	SOY	TRY	WAN	YOD
PUN	RUN	SPA	TDK	WAP	YOM
PUP	RUT	SPY	TUB	WAR	YON
PUT	RYA	STY	TUG	WAS	YOU
PYX	RYE	SUB	TUI	WAT	YOW
		SUE	TUN	WAW	YUK
Q	S	SUM	TUP	WAX	YUP
		SUN	TUT	WAY	
QUA	SAB	SUP	TUX	WEB	Z
	SAC	SYN	TWA	WED	
R	SAD		TWO	WEE	ZAG
	SAE	T	TYE	WEN	ZAP
RAD	SAG			WET	ZAX
RAG	SAL	TAB	U	WHA	ZED
RAH	SAP	TAD		WHO	ZEE
RAJ	SAT	TAE	UDO	WHY	ZIG
RAM	SAU	TAG	UGH	WIG	ZIP
RAN	SAW	TAJ	UIT	WIN	ZOA
RAP	SAX	TAM	UMP	WIS	ZOO
RAS	SAY	TAN	UPO	WIT	
RAT	SEA	TAO	URD	WIZ	A
RAW	SEC	TAP	URN	WOE	
RAX	SEE	TAR	USE	WOK	ABBE
RAY	SEI	TAT	UTA	WON	ABED
REB	SEN	TAU		WOO	ABET
REC	SER	TAV	V	WOP	ABLE
RED	SET	TAW		WOT	ABLY
REE	SEW	TEA	VAT	WOW	ABRI
REF	SEX	TED	VAU	WRY	ABUT
REI	SHE	TEE	VAV	WUD	ABYE
REM	SHH	TEG	VAW	WYE	ACHE

ACID	AMEN	AWED	BATE	BITE	BOWL
ACME	AMIA	AWEE	BATH	BITT	BOXY
ACRE	AMID	AWOL	BATT	BIZE	BOYO
ACTA	AMIE	AWRY	BAUD	BLAB	BOZO
ACYL	AMIN	AXAL	BAWD	BLAE	BRAD
ADIT	AMIR	AXEL	BAWL	BLAH	BRAE
ADZE	AMMO	AXES	BEAD	BLAT	BRAG
AERO	AMOK	AXIL	BEAK	BLAW	BRAN
AERY	AMYL	AXIS	BEAM	BLEB	BRAT
AFAR	ANAL	AXLE	BEAN	BLIN	BRAW
AGAR	ANEW	AXON	BEAR	BLIP	BRAY
AGER	ANGA	AYAH	BEAT	BLOB	BRED
AGHA	ANIL	AYIN	BEAU	BLOT	BREE
AGIN	ANKH	AZAN	BECK	BLOW	BREW
AGIO	ANNA	AZON	BEEF	BLUE	BRIE
AGMA	ANQA		BEEN	BLUR	BRIG
AGOG	ANON	B	BEEP	BOAR	BRIM
AGOM	ANTA		BEER	BOAT	BRIN
AGUE	ANTE	BAAL	BEET	BOCK	BRIO
AHEM	ANTI	BABA	BELL	BODE	BRIT
AHOY	ANUS	BABU	BELT	BODY	BROO
AIDE	APER	BABY	BEMA	BOFF	BROW
AINE	APEX	BACH	BEND	BOGY	BRUT
AIRN	APSE	BACK	BENE	BOIL	BUBO
AIRT	AQUA	BADE	BENT	BOLA	BUCK
AJAR	ARAK	BAFF	BERG	BOLD	BUFF
AJEE	ARCH	BAHT	BERM	BOLE	BUHL
AKEE	ARCO	BAIL	BEST	BOLL	BUHR
AKIN	AREA	BAIT	BETA	BOLO	BULB
ALAE	ARIA	BAKE	BEVY	BOLT	BULK
ALAN	ARID	BALD	BHUT	BOMB	BULL
ALAR	ARIL	BALE	BIAS	BOND	BUMF
ALAS	ARMY	BALK	BIBB	BONE	BUMP
ALBA	ARSE	BALL	BICE	BONG	BUND
ALEC	ARTY	BALM	BIDE	BONY	BUNG
ALEE	ARUM	BAND	BIER	BOOB	BUNK
ALFA	ARYO	BANE	BIFF	BOOK	BUNN
ALGA	ARLY	BANG	BIKE	BOOM	BUNT
ALIF	ASCI	BANK	BILE	BOON	BUOY
ALIT	ASEA	BARB	BILK	BOOR	BURA
ALLY	ASHY	BARD	BILL	BOOT	BURD
ALMA	ATNA	BARE	BIMA	BORA	BURG
ALME	ATOM	BARF	BIND	BORE	BURL
ALMS	ATOP	BARK	BINE	BORN	BURN
ALOE	AULD	BARM	BINT	BORT	BURP
ALOW	AURA	BARN	BIRD	BOSH	BURR
ALSO	AUTO	BASE	BIRK	BOSK	BURY
ALTO	AVER	BASH	BIRL	BOSS	BUSH
ALUM	AVID	BASK	BIRR	BOTH	BUSK
AMAH	AVOW	BASS	BISE	BOTT	BUSS
AMBO	AWAY	BAST	BISK	BOUT	BUST

BUSY	CERO	COCO	CRAM	DARN	DINE
BUTT	CESS	CODA	CRAP	DART	DING
BUZZ	CETE	CODE	CRAW	DASH	DINK
BYRE	CHAD	COED	CREW	DATA	DINT
BYRL	CHAM	COFF	CRIB	DATE	DIOL
BYTE	CHAP	COFT	CRIS	DATO	DIPT
	CHAR	COHO	CROP	DAUB	DIRE
C	CHAT	COIF	CROW	DAUT	DIRL
	CHAW	COIL	CRUD	DAVY	DIRT
CADE	CHEF	COIN	CRUS	DAWK	DISC
CADI	CHEW	COIR	CRUX	DAWT	DISH
CAFE	CHEZ	COKE	CUBE	DAZE	DISK
CAGE	CHIA	COLA	CUFF	DEAD	DITA
CAGY	CHIC	COLD	CUKE	DEAF	DITE
CAID	CHIN	COLE	CULL	DEAL	DIVA
CAIN	CHIP	COLT	CULM	DEAN	DIVE
CAKE	CHIT	COLY	CULT	DEAR	DJIN
CALF	CHON	COMA	CURB	DEBT	DOAT
CALK	CHOP	COMB	CURD	DEEM	DOBY
CALL	CHUB	COME	CURE	DEEP	DOCK
CALM	CHUG	COMP	CURF	DEER	DODO
CALX	CHUM	CONE	CURL	DEFI	DOER
CAME	CIAO	CONI	CURN	DEFT	DOES
CAMP	CINE	CONK	CURR	DEFY	DOFF
CANE	CION	CONN	CURT	DEIL	DOGE
CANT	CIST	CONY	CUSK	DEKE	DOGY
CAPE	CITE	COOF	CUSP	DELE	DOIT
CAPH	CITY	COOK	CUSS	DELF	DOJO
CAPO	CLAD	COOL	CUTE	DELI	DOLE
CARD	CLAG	COON	CYAN	DELL	DOLL
CARE	CLAM	COOP	CYME	DEME	DOLT
CARK	CLAN	COOT	CYST	DEMO	DOME
CARL	CLAP	COPE	CZAR	DEMY	DONA
CARN	CLAW	COPY		DENT	DONE
CARP	CLAY	CORD	D	DENY	DONG
CART	CLEF	CORK		DERE	DOOM
CASA	CLEW	CORM	DACE	DERM	DOOR
CASE	CLIP	CORN	DADA	DESK	DOPA
CASH	CLOD	COSH	DADO	DEVA	DOPE
CASK	CLOG	COSS	DAFF	DEWY	DOPY
CAST	CLON	COST	DAFT	DHAK	DORM
CATE	CLOP	COSY	DAGO	DIAL	DOPY
CAVE	CLOT	COTE	DAIS	DICE	DORM
CAVY	CLOY	COUP	DAME	DICK	DORY
CEDE	CLUB	COVE	DAMN	DIDO	DOSE
CEDI	CLUE	COWL	DAMP	DIDY	DOSS
CEIL	COAL	COWY	DANG	DIES	DOST
CELL	COAT	COXA	DANK	DIET	DOTE
CELT	COBB	COZY	DARB	DIKE	DOTH
CENT	COCA	CRAB	DARE	DILL	DOTY
CERE	COCK	CRAG	DARK	DIME	DOUR

DOVE	EARL		FIFE	FOND	GADI
DOWN	EARN	F	FILA	FONT	GAFF
DOXY	EASE		FILE	FOOD	GAGA
DOZE	EAST	FACE	FILL	FOOL	GAGE
DOZY	EASY	FACT	FILM	FOOT	GAIN
DRAB	EATH	FADE	FIND	FORA	GAIT
DRAG	EAVE	FADO	FINE	FORB	GALA
DRAM	EBON	FAIL	FINK	FORD	GALE
DRAW	ECHE	FAIN	FIRE	FORE	GALL
DRAY	ECHO	FAIR	FIRM	FORK	GAMB
DREE	EDDO	FAKE	FIRN	FORM	GAME
DREG	EDDY	FALL	FISC	FORT	GAMP
DREK	EDGE	FAME	FISH	FOSS	GAMY
DREW	EDGY	FANE	FIST	FOUL	GANE
DRIB	EDIT	FANG	FIVE	FOUR	GANG
DRIP	EELY	FANO	FIZZ	FOWL	GAOL
DROP	EERY	FARD	FLAB	FOXY	GAPE
DRUB	EGAD	FARE	FLAG	FRAE	GAPY
DRUG	EGAL	FARL	FLAK	FRAG	GARB
DRUM	EGER	FARM	FLAM	FRAP	GASH
DUAD	EGIS	FARO	FLAN	FRAT	GASP
DUAL	EIDE	FART	FLAP	FRAY	GAST
DUCE	ELAN	FASH	FLAT	FREE	GATE
DUCI	ELHI	FAST	FLAW	FRET	GAUD
DUCK	ELMY	FATE	FLAX	FRIG	GAUM
DUCT	ELSE	FAUN	FLAY	FRIT	GAUR
DUDE	EMEU	FAWN	FLEA	FRIZ	GAVE
DUEL	EMIR	FAZE	FLED	FROE	GAWK
DUET	EMIT	FEAR	FLEE	FROG	GAZE
DUFF	EMYD	FEAT	FLEW	FROM	GEAR
DUIT	ENOL	FECK	FLEX	FRUG	GECK
DULL	ENOW	FEED	FLEY	FUCI	GEEK
DULY	ENVY	FEEL	FLIC	FUEL	GELD
DUMB	EPEE	FEET	FLIP	FUJI	GELT
DUMP	EPHA	FELL	FLIT	FULL	GENE
DUNE	EPIC	FELT	FLOC	FUME	GENS
DUNG	EPOS	FEME	FLOE	FUMY	GENT
DUNK	ERNE	FEND	FLOG	FUND	GENU
DUNT	ERST	FEOD	FLOP	FUNK	GERM
DUPE	ESPY	FERE	FLOW	FURL	GEST
DURA	ETCH	FERN	FLUB	FURY	GEUM
DURN	ETNA	FESS	FLUE	FUSE	GHAT
DUSK	ETUI	FETA	FLUX	FUSS	GIBE
DUST	EVEN	FETE	FOAL	FUZE	GIFT
DUTY	EVIL	FEUD	FOAM	FUZZ	GIGA
DYER	EXAM	FIAR	FOGY	FYCE	GILD
DYKE	EXEC	FIAT	FOHN	FYKE	GILL
	EXPO	FICE	FOIL		GILT
E	EYED	FICO	FOIN	G	GIMP
	EVEN	FIDO	FOLD		GINK
EACH	EVER	FIEF	FOLK	GABY	GIRD

GIRL	GREE	HALF	HEST	HOWL	IOTA
GIRN	GREW	HALL	HETH	HUCK	IRIS
GIRO	GREY	HALM	HICK	HUFF	IRON
GIRT	GRID	HALO	HIDE	HUGE	ISBA
GIST	GRIG	HALT	HIGH	HUIC	ISLE
GIVE	GRIM	HAME	HIKE	HULA	ITCH
GLAD	GRIN	HAND	HILA	HULK	ITEM
GLED	GRIP	HANG	HILI	HULL	IWIS
GLEE	GRIT	HANK	HILL	HUMP	IXIA
GLEG	GROG	HANT	HILT	HUNK	IZAR
GLEN	GROT	HARD	HIND	HUNT	
GLEY	GROW	HARE	HINT	HURL	J
GLIB	GRUB	HARK	HIRE	HURT	
GLIM	GRUM	HARL	HISN	HUSH	JACK
GLOB	GUAN	HARM	HISS	HUSK	JADE
GLOM	GUAR	HARP	HIST	HWAN	JAGG
GLOP	GUCK	HART	HIVE	HYMN	JAIL
GLOW	GUDE	HASH	HOAR	HYPE	JIKE
GLUE	GUFF	HASP	HOAX	HYPO	JAMB
GLUT	GUID	HAST	HOBO	HYTE	JAPE
GNAR	GULF	HATE	HOCK		JARL
GNAT	GULL	HATH	HOER	I	JATO
GNAW	GULP	HAUL	HOGG		JAUK
GOAD	GURU	HAVE	HOKE	IAMB	JAUP
GOAL	GUSH	HAWK	HOLD	IBEX	JAVA
GOAT	GUST	HAZE	HOLE	IBIS	JAZZ
GOBO	GYBE	HAZY	HOLK	ICED	JEAN
GOBY	GYRE	HEAD	HOLM	ICKY	JEEP
GOER	GYRI	HEAL	HOLP	ICON	JEER
GOGO	GYRO	HEAP	HOLT	IDEM	JEEZ
GOLD	GYVE	HEAR	HOLY	IDES	JEFE
GOLF		HEAT	HOME	IDLE	JELL
GONE	H	HECK	HOMO	IDLY	JERK
GONG		HEED	HOMY	IDOL	JESS
GOOD	HAAF	HEEL	HONE	IDYL	JEST
GOOF	HAAR	HEFT	HONG	IFFY	JETE
GOOK	HABU	HEIR	HONK	IGLU	JIBB
GOON	HACK	HELD	HOOD	IKON	JIBE
GOOP	HADE	HELL	HOOF	ILEA	JIFF
GORE	HADJ	HELM	HOOK	ILEX	JILL
GORY	HAEM	HELP	HOOP	ILIA	JILT
GOSH	HAEN	HEME	HOOT	ILLY	JIMP
GOUT	HAET	HEMP	HOPE	IMID	JINK
GOWD	HAFT	HENT	HORA	IMMY	JINN
GOWK	HAIK	HERB	HORN	IMPI	JINZ
GOWN	HAIL	HERD	HOSE	INBY	JIVE
GRAB	HAIR	HERL	HOST	INCH	JOCK
GRAD	HAJI	HERM	HOUR	INFO	JOEY
GRAM	HAJJ	HERN	HOVE	INKY	JOHN
GRAT	HAKE	HERO	HOWF	INLY	JOIN
GRAY	HALE	HERS	HOWK	INTO	JOKE

JOLT	KEPT	KYAR	LEET	LOBO	LUNT
JOSS	KERB	KYAT	LEFT	LOCA	LUNY
JOTA	KERF	KYTE	LEHR	LOCH	LURE
JOUK	KERN		LEND	LOCI	LURK
JOWL	KETO	L	LENO	LOCK	LUSH
JUBA	KHAN		LENS	LOCO	LUST
JUBE	KHAT	LACE	LENT	LODE	LUXE
JUDO	KIBE	LACK	LESS	LOFT	LYNX
JUJU	KICK	LACY	LEST	LOGE	LYRE
JUKE	KIEF	LADE	LEUD	LOGO	LYSE
JUNK	KILL	LADY	LEVO	LOGY	
JURA	KILN	LAIC	LEVY	LOIN	M
JURY	KILO	LAID	LEWD	LOLL	
JUST	KILT	LAIN	LIAR	LONE	MARR
JUTE	KIND	LAIR	LICE	LONG	MACE
	KINE	LAKE	LICK	LOOF	MACH
K	KING	LAKH	LIDO	LOOK	MACK
	KINK	LAKY	LIED	LOOM	MADE
KAAS	KINO	LALL	LIEF	LOON	MAGE
KADI	KIRK	LAMA	LIEN	LOOP	MAGI
KAGU	KIRN	LAMB	LIER	LOOT	MAID
KAIF	KISS	LAME	LIEU	LOPE	MAIL
KAIL	KIST	LAMP	LIFE	LORD	MAIM
KAIN	KITE	LAND	LIFT	LORE	MAIN
KAKA	KITH	LANE	LIKE	LORN	MAIR
KAKI	KIVA	LANK	LILT	LORY	MAKE
KALE	KIWI	LARD	LILY	LOSE	MAKO
KAME	KNAP	LARK	LIMA	LOSS	MALE
KAMI	KNAR	LASE	LIMB	LOST	MALL
KANA	KNEE	LASH	LIME	LOTA	MALM
KANE	KNEW	LASS	LIMN	LOTH	MALT
KAON	KNIT	LAST	LIMO	LOUD	MAMA
KAPA	KNOB	LATE	LIMP	LOUP	MANA
KAPH	KNOP	LATH	LIMY	LOUR	MANE
KARN	KNOT	LATI	LINE	LOUT	MANO
KART	KNOW	LAUD	LING	LOVE	MANY
KAVA	KNUR	LAVA	LINK	LOWE	MARC
KAYO	KOAN	LAVE	LINN	LOWN	MARE
KECK	KOEL	LAWN	LINO	LUAU	MARK
KEEF	KOHL	LAZE	LINT	LUBE	MARL
KEEK	KOLA	LAZY	LINY	LUCK	MART
KEEL	KOLO	LEAD	LION	LUES	MASH
KEEN	KOOK	LEAF	LIRA	LUFF	MASK
KEEP	KOPH	LEAK	LISP	LUGE	MASS
KEET	KOSS	LEAL	LIST	LULL	MAST
KEIR	KOTO	LEAN	LITU	LULU	MATE
KELP	KRIS	LEAP	LOAD	LUMP	MATH
KEMP	KUDO	LEAR	LOAF	LUNA	MATT
KENO	KUDU	LECH	LOAM	LUNE	MAUL
KENT	KURU	LEEK	LOAN	LUNG	MAUN
KEPI	KVAS	LEER	LOBE	LUNK	MAUT

MAXI	MIRY	MULE	NICE	OFAY	OYES
MAYA	MISE	MULL	NICK	OGAM	OYEZ
MAZE	MISO	MUMP	NIDE	OGEE	
MAZY	MISS	MUON	NIDI	OGRE	P
MEAD	MIST	MURA	NIGH	OILY	
MEAL	MITE	MURK	NILL	OINK	PACA
MEAN	MITT	MURR	NINE	OKAY	PACE
MEAT	MITY	MUSE	NIPA	OKRA	PACK
MEED	MIXT	MUSH	NISI	OLEA	PACT
MEET	MOAN	MUSK	NIXY	OLEO	PAGE
MELD	MOAT	MUSS	NOCK	OLIO	PAID
MELL	MOCK	MUST	NODE	OLLA	PAIK
MELT	MODE	MUTE	NODI	OMEN	PAIL
MEMO	MODI	MUTE	NOEL	OMER	PAIN
MEND	MOIL	MUTT	NOGG	OMIT	PAIR
MENO	MOKE	MYNA	NOIL	ONCE	PALE
MENU	MOLA	MYTH	NOIR	ONLY	PALL
MEOW	MOLD		NOLO	ONTO	PALM
MERE	MOLE	N	NOMA	ONUS	PALP
MERK	MOLL		NOME	ONYX	PALY
MERL	MOLT	NAIF	NONA	OOPS	PANE
MESA	MOLY	NAIL	NONE	OOZE	PANG
MESH	MOME	NANA	NOOK	OOZY	PANT
MESS	MOMI	NAOS	NOON	OPAH	PAPA
META	MONK	NAPE	NORM	OPAL	PARA
METE	MONO	NARC	NOSE	OPEN	PARD
MEWL	MONS	NARD	NOSH	OPUS	PARE
MICA	MONY	NARK	NOSY	ORAL	PARK
MICE	MOOD	NARY	NOTA	ORCA	PARR
MICK	MOOL	NAVE	NOTE	ORDO	PART
MIDI	MOON	NAVY	NOWN	ORGY	PASE
MIEN	MOOR	NAZI	NOUS	ORLE	PASH
MIFF	MOOT	NEAP	NOVA	ORRA	PASS
MIGG	MOPE	NEAR	NOWT	ORYX	PAST
MIKE	MORA	NEAT	NUDE	OSSA	PATE
MILD	MORE	NECK	NUKE	OTIC	PATH
MILE	MORN	NEED	NULL	OTTO	PATY
MILK	MORT	NEEM	NUMB	OUCH	PAVE
MILL	MOSK	NEEP	NURL	OUPH	PAWL
MILO	MOSS	NEIF		OURS	PAWN
MILT	MOST	NEMA	O	OUST	PEAG
MIME	MOTE	NENE		OUZO	PEAK
MINA	MOTH	NEON	OAST	OVAL	PEAL
MIND	MOTT	NESS	OBEY	OVEN	PEAN
MINE	MOVE	NEST	OBIA	OVER	PEAR
MINI	MOXA	NETT	OBIT	OVUM	PEAT
MINK	MOZO	NEUM	OBOE	OWSE	PECH
MINT	MUCH	NEVE	OBOL	OXEN	PECK
MIRE	MUCK	NEWS	ODIC	OXID	PEEK
MIRI	MUFF	NEWT	ODOR	OXIM	PEEL
MIRK	MUGG	NEXT	ODYL	OYER	PEEN

PEEP	PITH	PRAM	QUAY	REDO	ROOD
PEER	PITY	PRAT	QUEY	REED	ROOF
PEIN	PIXY	PRAU	QUID	REEF	ROOK
PEKE	PLAN	PRAY	QUIP	REEK	ROOM
PELE	PLAT	PREE	QUIT	REEL	ROOT
PELF	PLAY	PREP	QUIZ	REFT	ROPE
PELT	PLEA	PREX	QUOD	REIF	ROPY
PEND	PLEB	PREY		REIN	ROSE
PENT	PLED	PRIG	R	REIS	ROSY
PEON	PLIE	PRIM		RELY	ROTA
PEPO	PLOD	PROA	RACE	REND	ROTE
PERE	PLOP	PROD	RACK	RENT	ROTL
PERI	PIOT	PROF	RACY	REPP	ROTO
PERK	PLOY	PROG	RAFF	RESH	ROUE
PERM	PLUG	PROM	RAGA	REST	ROUP
PERT	PLUM	PROP	RAGE	RETE	ROUT
PESO	PLUS	PROW	RAGI	RHEA	ROUX
PEST	POCK	PSST	RAIA	RHUS	ROVE
PHAT	POCO	PUCE	RAID	RIAL	RUBE
PHEW	POEM	PUCK	RAIL	RICE	RUBY
PHIZ	POET	PUFF	RAIN	RICH	RUCK
PHON	POGY	PUGH	RAJA	RICK	RUDD
PHOT	POKE	PUKE	RAKE	RIDE	RUDE
PIAL	POKY	PULE	RAKI	RIEL	RUER
PIAN	POLE	PULI	RAMI	RIFE	RUFF
PICA	POLL	PULL	RAMP	RIFF	RUGA
PICE	POLO	PULP	RAND	RIFT	RUIN
PICK	POLY	PUMA	RANG	RILE	RULE
PIED	POME	PUMP	RANI	RILL	RUMP
PIER	POMP	PUNA	RANK	RIME	RUNE
PIKA	POND	PUNG	RANT	RIMY	RUNG
PIKE	PONS	PUNK	RAPE	RIND	RUNT
PILE	PONY	PUNT	RAPT	RING	RUSE
PILI	POOD	PUNY	RARE	RINK	RUSH
PILL	POOH	PUPA	RASE	RIOT	RUSK
PILY	POOL	PURE	RASH	RIPE	RUST
PIMA	POON	PURL	RASP	RISE	RUTH
PIMP	POOP	PURR	RATE	RISK	RYKE
PINA	POOR	PUSH	RATH	RITE	RYND
PINE	POPE	PUSS	RATO	RITZ	RYOT
PING	PORE	PUTT	RAVE	RIVE	
PINK	PORK	PYIC	RAYA	ROAD	S
PINT	PORN	PYIN	RAZE	ROAM	
PINY	PORT	PYRE	RAZZ	ROAN	SABE
PION	POSE		READ	ROBE	SACK
PIPE	POSH	Q	REAL	ROCK	SADE
PIPY	POST		REAM	RODE	SAFE
PIRN	POSY	QAID	REAP	ROIL	SAGA
PISH	POUF	QOPH	RECK	ROLE	SAGE
PISS	POUR	QUAD	REDD	ROLL	SAGO
PITA	POUT	QUAI	REDE	ROMP	SAGY

SAID	SELF	SILT	SNED	SPIC	SWAG
SAIL	SELL	SIMA	SNIB	SPIK	SWAM
SAIN	SEME	SIMP	SNIP	SPIN	SWAN
SAKE	SEMI	SINE	SNIT	SPIT	SWAP
SAKI	SEND	SING	SNOB	SPIV	SWAT
SALE	SENT	SINH	SNOT	SPOT	SWAY
SALL	SEPT	SINK	SNOW	SPRY	SWIM
SALP	SERA	SIPE	SNUB	SPUD	SWOB
SALT	SERE	SIRE	SNUG	SPUE	SWOP
SAME	SETA	SITH	SNYE	SPUN	SWOT
SAMP	SEWN	SITI	SOAK	SPUR	SYBO
SAND	SEXT	SIZE	SOAP	STAB	SYCE
SANE	SEXY	SIZY	SOAR	STAG	SYNC
SANG	SHAD	SKAT	SOCK	STAR	SYNE
SANK	SHAG	SKEE	SODA	STAW	
SANS	SHAH	SKEG	SOFA	STAY	T
SARD	SHAM	SKEP	SOFT	STEM	
SARI	SHAW	SKEW	SOJA	STEP	TABU
SARK	SHAY	SKID	SOKE	STET	TACE
SASH	SHEA	SKIM	SOLA	STEW	TACH
SASS	SHED	SKIN	SOLD	STEY	TACK
SATE	SHEW	SKIP	SOLE	STIR	TACO
SATI	SHIM	SKIT	SOLI	STOA	TACT
SAUL	SHIN	SKUA	SOLD	STOB	TAEL
SAVE	SHIP	SLAB	SOMA	STOP	TAHR
SAWN	SHIV	SLAG	SOME	STOW	TAIL
SCAB	SHMO	SLAM	SONE	STUB	TAIN
SCAD	SHOD	SLAP	SONG	STUD	TAKE
SCAG	SHOE	SLAT	SOON	STUM	TALA
SCAN	SHOG	SLAW	SOOT	STUN	TALC
SCAR	SHOO	SLED	SOPH	STYE	TALE
SCAT	SHOP	SLIM	SORA	SUBA	TALI
SCOP	SHOT	SLIP	SORB	SUCH	TALK
SCOW	SHOW	SLIT	SORD	SUCK	TALL
SCUD	SHRI	SLOB	SORE	SUDD	TAME
SCUM	SHUL	SLOE	SORI	SUDS	TAMP
SCUP	SHUN	SLOG	SORN	SUER	TANG
SCUT	SHUT	SLOP	SORT	SUET	TANK
SEAL	SIAL	SLOT	SOTH	SUGH	TAPA
SEAM	SIBB	SLOW	SOUL	SUIT	TAPE
SEAR	SICE	SLUB	SOUP	SULK	TARE
SEAT	SICK	SLUE	SOUR	SUMO	TARN
SECT	SIDE	SLUG	SOWN	SUMP	TARO
SEED	SIFT	SLUR	SOYA	SUNG	TARP
SEEK	SIGH	SLUT	SPAE	SUNK	TART
SEEL	SIGN	SMOG	SPAN	SUNN	TASK
SEEM	SIKE	SMUG	SPAR	SUPE	TASS
SEEN	SILD	SMUT	SPAT	SURA	TATE
SEEP	SILK	SNAG	SPAY	SURD	TAUT
SEER	SILL	SNAP	SPED	SURF	TAXA
SEGO	SILO	SNAW	SPEW	SWAB	TAXI

TEAK	TINY	TRAP	UMBO	VEST	WANT
TEAL,	TIPI	TRAY	UNAI	VETO	WANY
TEAM	TIRE	TREE	UNAU	VEXT	WARD
TEAR	TIRL	TREF	UNBE	VIAL	WARE
TEAT	TIRO	TREK	UNCI	VICE	WARK
TEEM	TITI	TRET	UNCO	VIDE	WARM
TEEN	TIVY	TRIG	UNDE	VIER	WARN
TEFF	TOAD	TRIM	UNDO	VIEW	WARP
TELA	TOBY	TRIO	UNDY	VILE	WART
TELE	TODY	TRIP	UNIT	VILL	WARY
TELL	TOFF	TROP	UNTO	VINA	WASH
TEND	TOFT	TROT	UPAS	VINE	WASP
TENT	TOFU	TROW	UPBY	VINO	WAST
TEPA	TOGA	TROY	UPDO	VINY	WATT
TERM	TOIL	TRUE	UPON	VIOL	WAUK
TERN	TOKE	TUBA	UREA	VIRL	WAUL
TEST	TOLA	TUBE	URGE	VISA	WAUR
TETH	TOLD	TUCK	URIC	VISE	WAVE
TEXT	TOLE	TUFA	URSA	VITA	WAVY
THAE	TOLL	TUFF	URUS	VIVA	WAWL
THAN	TOLU	TUFT	USER	VIVE	WAXY
THAT	TONE	TULE	UVEA	VOID	WEAK
THAW	TONG	TUMP		VOLE	WEAL
THEE	TONY	TUNA	V	VOLT	WEAN
THEM	TOOK	TUNE		VOTE	WEAR
THEN	TOOL	TUNG	VAGI	VROW	WEED
THEW	TOOM	TURD	VAIL	VUGG	WEEK
THEY	TOON	TURF	VAIN	VUGH	WEEL
THIN	TOOT	TURN	VAIR		WEEN
THIO	TOPE	TUSH	VALE	W	WEER
THIS	TOPI	TUSK	VAMP		WEFT
THOU	TORA	TUTU	VANE	WACK	WEIR
THRO	TORC	TWAT	VANG	WADE	WEKA
THRU	TORE	TWIG	VARA	WADI	WELD
THUD	TORI	TWIN	VARY	WADY	WELL
THUG	TORN	TWIT	VASE	WAFF	WELT
THUS	TORO	TYKE	VAST	WAFT	WENT
TICK	TORR	TYNE	VEAL	WAGE	WEPT
TIDE	TORT	TYPE	VEEP	WAIF	WERE
TIDY	TORY	TYPO	VEER	WAIL	WERT
TIED	TOSH	TYPY	VEIL	WAIN	WEST
TIER	TOSS	TYRE	VEIN	WAIR	WHAM
TIFF	TOST	TYRO	VELA	WAIT	WHAP
TIKE	TOTE	TZAR	VELD	WAKE	WHAT
TILE	TOUR		VENA	WALE	WHEE
TILL	TOUT	U	VEND	WALK	WHEN
TILT	TOWN		VENT	WALL	WHET
TIME	TOWY	UGLY	VERA	WALY	WHEW
TINE	TOYO	ULAN	VERB	WAME	WHEY
TING	TRAD	ULNA	VERT	WAND	WHID
TINT	TRAM	ULVA	VERY	WANE	WHIM

WHIN	WREN	YOUR	ABOVE	AGAIN	ALIAS
WHIP	WRIT	YOWE	ABUSE	AGAMA	ALIBI
WHIR	WYCH	YOWL	ABUZZ	AGAPE	ALIEN
WHIT	WYND	YUAN	ABYSM	AGATE	ALIGN
WHIZ	WYNN	YUGA	ABYSS	AGAVE	ALIKE
WHOA	WYTE	YULE	ACARI	AGAZE	ALINE
WHOM		YURT	ACERB	AGENE	ALIST
WHOP	X	YWIS	ACETA	AGENT	ALIVE
WICH			ACHOO	AGGER	ALKYD
WICK	XYST	Z	ACIDY	AGGIE	ALKYL
WIDE			ACING	AGILE	ALLAY
WIFE	Y	ZANY	ACOCK	AGING	ALLEY
WILD		ZARF	ACOLD	AGIST	ALLOD
WILE	YACK	ZEAL	ACORN	AGLEE	ALLOT
WILL	YAFF	ZEBU	ACRED	AGLET	ALLOW
WILT	YAGI	ZEIN	ACRID	AGLEY	ALLOY
WILY	YALD	ZERO	ACTIN	AGONE	ALLYL
WIND	YANG	ZEST	ACTOR	AGONY	ALMEH
WINE	YANK	ZETA	ACUTE	AGORA	ALMUD
WING	YARD	ZINC	ADAGE	AGREE	ALMUG
WINK	YARE	ZING	ADAPT	AHEAD	ALOFT
WINO	YARN	ZITI	ADDAX	AHOLD	ALOHA
WINY	YAUD	ZOIC	ADDER	AHULL	ALOIN
WIPE	YAUP	ZONE	ADDLE	AIDER	ALONE
WIRE	YAWL	ZOOM	ADEEM	AIMER	ALONG
WISE	YAWN	ZOON	ADEPT	AINEE	ALOOF
WISH	YAWP	ZORI	ADIEU	AIRTH	ALOUD
WISP	YEAH	ZYME	ADIOS	AISLE	ALPHA
WISS	YEAR		ADMAN	AITCH	ALTAR
WIST	YEGG	A	ADMIT	AIVER	ALTER
WITE	YELD		ADMIX	AJIVA	ALTHO
WITH	YELK	ABACA	ADOBE	AKELA	ALULA
WIVE	YELL	ABACK	ADOPT	AKENE	ALWAY
WOAD	YELP	ABAFT	ADORE	ALACK	AMAIN
WOKE	YERK	ABASE	ADORN	ALAMO	AMASS
WOLD	YETI	ABASH	ADOWN	ALAND	AMAZE
WOLF	YETT	ABATE	ADOZE	ALANE	AMBER
WOMB	YEUK	ABBOT	ADULT	ALANG	AMBIT
WONT	YILL	ABEAM	ADUNC	ALANT	AMBLE
WOOD	YIPE	ABELE	ADUST	ALARM	AMBRY
WOOF	YIRD	ABHOR	AECIA	ALARY	AMEBA
WOOL	YIRR	ABIDE	AEDES	ALATE	AMEER
WORD	YODH	ABLER	AEGIS	ALBUM	AMEND
WORE	YOGA	ABMHO	AERIE	ALDER	AMENT
WORK	YOGH	ABODE	AFFIX	ALDOL	AMICE
WORM	YOGI	ABOHM	AFIRE	ALEPN	AMIDE
WORN	YOKE	ABOIL	AFOOT	ALERT	AMIDO
WORT	YOLK	ABOMA	AFORE	ALGID	AMIGA
WOST	YOND	ABOON	AFOUL	ALGIN	AMIGO
WOVE	YONI	ABORT	AFRIT	ALGOR	AMINE
WRAP	YORE	ABOUT	AFTER	ALGUM	AMINO

AMISS	APNEA	ASPEN	AXIOM	BASIS	BEMIX
AMITY	APORT	ASPER	AXITE	BASSI	BENCH
AMOLE	APPAL	ASPIC	AZOTE	BASSO	BENDY
AMONG	APPEL	ASPIS	AZURE	BASSY	BENNE
AMORT	APPLE	ASSAI		BASTE	BENNI
AMOUR	APPLY	ASSAY	B	BATCH	BENNY
AMPLE	APRON	ASSET		BATHE	BERET
AMPUL	APSIS	ASTER	BABEL	BATIK	BERME
AMUCK	APTLY	ASTIR	BABKA	BATON	BERRY
AMUSE	ARBOR	ATAXY	BABOO	BATTU	BERTH
ANCON	ARCUS	ATILT	BABUL	BATTY	BERYL
ANEAR	ARDEB	ATLAS	BACCA	BAULK	BESET
ANELE	ARDOR	ATOLL	BACON	BAWDY	BESOM
ANENT	ARECA	ATOMY	BADDY	BAWTY	BESOT
ANGEL	AREIC	ATONE	BADGE	BAYOU	BETEL
ANGER	ARENA	ATONY	BADLY	BAZAR	BETON
ANGLE	ARETE	ATOPY	BAFFY	BEACH	BETTA
ANGRY	ARGAL	ATRIA	BAGEL	BEADY	BEVEL
ANGST	ARGIL	ATRIP	BAGGY	BEAKY	BEVOR
ANILE	ARGLE	ATTAR	BAIRN	BEAMY	BEWIG
ANIMA	ARGOL	ATTIC	BAITH	BEANO	BEZIL
ANIME	ARGON	AUDAD	BAIZA	BEARD	BHANG
ANIMI	ARGOT	AUDIO	BAIZE	BEAST	BHOOT
ANION	ARGUE	AUDIT	BAKER	BEAUT	BIALY
ANISE	ARGUS	AUGER	BALER	BEAUX	BIBLE
ANKLE	ARHAT	AUGHT	BALKY	BEBOP	BIDDY
ANKUS	ARIEL	AUGUR	BALLY	BECAP	BIDER
ANLAS	ARISE	AUNTY	BALMY	BEDEL	BIDET
ANNAL	ARLES	AURAR	BALSA	BEDEW	BIFFY
ANNEX	ARMER	AUREI	BANAL	BEDIM	BIFID
ANNOY	ARMET	AURES	BANCO	BEECH	BIGHT
ANNUL	ARMOR	AURIC	BANDY	BEEFY	BIGLY
ANODE	AROID	AURIS	BANJO	BEERY	BIGOT
ANOLE	AROMA	AURUM	BANNS	BEFIT	BIJOU
ANOMY	AROSE	AUXIN	BARBE	BEFOG	BIKER
ANTED	ARPEN	AVAIL	BARDE	BEGAN	BILBO
ANTIC	ARRAS	AVAST	BARER	BEGET	BILGE
ANTRA	ARRAY	AVENS	BARGE	BEGIN	BILGY
ANTRE	ARRIS	AVERT	BARIC	BEGOT	BILLY
ANVIL	ARROW	AVGAS	BARKY	BEGUM	BINAL
AORTA	ARSIS	AVIAN	BARMY	BEGUN	BINGE
APACE	ARSON	AVION	BARON	BEIGE	BINGO
APART	ARTAL	AVOID	BARRE	BEIGY	BINIT
APEAK	ARTEL	AWAIT	BARYE	BEING	BIOME
APEEK	ARVAL	AWAKE	BASAL	BELAY	BIONT
APERY	ASCOT	AWARD	BASED	BELCH	BIOTA
APHID	ASCUS	AWARE	BASER	BELGA	BIPED
APHIS	ASDIC	AWING	BASES	BELIE	BIPOD
APIAN	ASHEN	AWOKE	BASIC	BELLE	BIRCH
APING	ASIDE	AXIAL	BASIL	BELLY	BIRLE
APISH	ASKER	AXILE	BASIN	BELOW	BIRSE

BIRTH	BLYPE	BOUND	BROIL	BURSA	CANER
BISON	BOARD	BOURG	BROKE	BURSE	CANNA
BITCH	BOART	BOURN	BROME	BURST	CANNY
BITER	BOAST	BOUSE	BROMO	BUSBY	CANOE
BITSY	BOBBY	BOVID	BRONC	BUSHY	CANON
BITTE	BOCCE	BOWER	BROOD	BUSTY	CANSO
BITTY	BOCCI	BOWSE	BROOK	BUTCH	CANST
BLACK	BOCHE	BOXER	BROOM	BUTEO	CANTO
BLADE	BOFFO	BOYAR	BROSE	BUTTE	CANTY
BLAIN	BOGAN	BOYLA	BROSY	BUTTY	CAPER
BLAME	BOGEY	BRACE	BROTH	BUTUT	CAPON
BLAND	BOGGY	BRACH	BROWN	BUTYL	CAPUT
BLANK	BOGIE	BRACT	BRUGH	BUXOM	CARAT
BLARE	BOGLE	BRAID	BRUIN	BUYER	CARER
BLASE	BOGUS	BRAIL	BRUIT	BWANA	CARET
BLAST	BOHEA	BRAIN	BRUME	BYLAW	CAREX
BLATE	BOITE	BRAKE	BRUNT	BYWAY	CARLE
BLAZE	BOLAR	BRAKY	BRUSH		CARNY
BLEAK	BOLAS	BRAND	BRUSK	C	CAROB
BLEAR	BOLUS	BRANK	BRUTE		CAROL
BLEAT	BOMBE	BRANT	BUBAL	CABAL	CAROM
BLEND	BONER	BRASH	BUBBY	CABBY	CARPI
BLENT	BONEY	BRASS	BUCKO	CABER	CARRY
BLESS	BONGO	BRAVA	BUDDY	CABIN	CARSE
BLEST	BONNE	BRAVE	BUDGE	CABLE	CARTE
BLIMP	BONNY	BRAVO	BUFFO	CABOB	CARVE
BLIMY	BONUS	BRAWL	BUFFY	CACAO	CASED
BLINI	BONZE	BRAWN	BUGGY	CACHE	CASKY
BLINK	BOOBY	BRAWS	BUGLE	CADDY	CASTE
BLISS	BOOMY	BRAXY	BUILD	CADET	CASUS
BLITE	BOOST	BRAZA	BUILT	CADGE	CATCH
BLITZ	BOOTH	BRAZE	BULGE	CADGY	CATER
BLOAT	BOOTY	BREDE	BULGY	CADRE	CATTY
BLOCK	BOOZE	BREED	BULKY	CAGEY	CAULD
BLOKE	BOOZY	BRENT	BULLA	CAHOW	CAULK
BLOND	BORAX	BREVE	BULLY	CAIRD	CAUSE
BLOOD	BORED	BRIAR	BUMPY	CAIRN	CAVED
BLOOM	BORER	BRIBE	BUNCH	CAJON	CAVER
BLOOP	BORIC	BRICK	BUNCO	CALIF	CAVIL
BLOWN	BORNE	BRIDE	BUNKO	CALIX	CEASE
BLOWY	BORON	BRIEF	BUNNY	CALLA	CEBID
BLUED	BORTZ	BRIER	BUNYA	CALVE	CECUM
BLUER	BOSKY	BRILL	BURAN	CALYX	CEDAR
BLUET	BOSOM	BRINE	BURET	CAMAS	CEDER
BLUEY	BOSON	BRING	BURGH	CAMEL	CEIBA
BLUFF	BOSSY	BRINK	BURIN	CAMEO	CELLA
BLUME	BOSUN	BRINY	BURKE	CAMPI	CELLO
BLUNT	BOTCH	BRISK	BURLY	CAMPO	CELOM
BLURB	BOTEL	BRITT	BURNT	CAMPY	CENSE
BLURT	BOUGH	BROAD	BURRO	CANAL	CENTO
BLUSH	BOULE	BROCK	BURRY	CANDY	CEORL

CERED	CHINK	CLASH	CODEX	CORGI	CREEL
CERIA	CHINO	CLASP	CODON	CORKY	CREEP
CERIC	CHIRK	CLASS	COGON	CORNU	CREPE
CHAFE	CHIRM	CLAST	COHOG	CORNY	CREPT
CHAFF	CHIRO	CLAVE	COIGN	CORPS	CREPY
CHAIN	CHIRP	CLEAN	COLIC	CORSE	CRESS
CHAIR	CHIRR	CLEAR	COLIN	COSEC	CREST
CHALK	CHIVE	CLEAT	COLLY	COSET	CRICK
CHAMP	CHIVY	CLEFT	COLOG	COSEY	CRIED
CHANG	CHOIR	CLEPE	COLON	COSIE	CRIER
CHANT	CHOKE	CLICK	COLOR	COSTA	CRIES
CHAOS	CHOKY	CLIFF	COLZA	COTAN	CRIME
CHAPE	CHOMP	CLIFT	COMAL	COUCH	CRIMP
CHAPT	CHORD	CLIMB	COMBE	COUDE	CRISP
CHARD	CHORE	CLIME	COMBO	COUGH	CROAK
CHARE	CHOSE	CLINE	COMER	COULD	CROCI
CHARK	CHOTT	CLING	COMET	COUNT	CROCK
CHARM	CHUCK	CLINK	COMFY	COUPE	CROFT
CHARR	CHUFA	CLIPT	COMIC	COURT	CRONE
CHART	CHUFF	CLOAK	COMMA	COUTH	CRONY
CHARY	CHUMP	CLOCK	COMMY	COVEN	CROOK
CHASE	CHUNK	CLOMB	COMPO	COVER	CROON
CHASM	CHURL	CLOMP	COMPT	COVET	CRORE
CHEAP	CHURN	CLONE	COMTE	COVEY	CROSS
CHEAT	CHURR	CLONK	CONCH	COWER	CROUP
CHECK	CHUTE	CLOOT	CONEY	COWRY	CROWD
CHEEK	CHYLE	CLOSE	CONGA	COYLY	CROWN
CHEEP	CHYME	CLOTH	CONGE	COYPU	CROZE
CHEER	CIBOL	CLOUW	CONGO	COZEN	CRUDE
CHELA	CIDAR	CLOUT	CONIC	COZEY	CRUEL
CHERT	CIGAR	CLOVE	CONIN	COZIE	CRUET
CHESS	CILIA	CLOWN	CONKY	CRAAL	CRUMB
CHEST	CIMEX	CLOZE	CONTE	CRACK	CRUMP
CHETH	CINCH	CLUCK	CONTO	CRAFT	CRUOR
CHEVY	CIRCA	CLUMP	CONUS	CRAKE	CRUSE
CHEWY	CIRRI	CLUNG	COOCH	CRAMP	CRUSH
CHIAO	CISCO	CLUNK	COOEE	CRANE	CRUST
CHICK	CITER	COACT	COOER	CRANK	CRWTH
CHICO	CIVET	COALA	COOEY	CRAPE	CRYPT
CHIDE	CIVIC	COAPT	COOKY	CRASH	CUBBY
CHIEF	CIVIE	COAST	COOLY	CRASS	CUBEB
CHIEL	CIVIL	COATI	COOMB	CRATE	CUBER
CHILD	CIVVY	COBBY	COOPT	CRAVE	CUBIC
CHILE	CLACH	COBIA	COPAL	CRAWL	CUBIT
CHILI	CLACK	COBLE	COPEN	CRAZE	CUDDY
CHILL	CLAIM	COBRA	COPER	CRAZY	CUING
CHIMB	CLAMP	COCCI	COPPA	CREAK	CUISH
CHIME	CLANG	COCKY	COPSE	CREAM	CULCH
CHIMP	CLANK	COCOA	CORAL	CREDO	CULET
CHINA	CLARO	CODEN	CORBY	CREED	CULEX
CHINE	CLARY	CODER	CORER	CREEK	CULLY

CULPA	DAMAN	DELVE	DISCI	DOUCE	DROWN
CULTI	DAMAR	DEMIT	DISCO	DOUGH	DRUID
CUMIN	DANCE	DEMOB	DISHY	DOUMA	DRUNK
CUPEL	DANDY	DEMON	DISME	DOURA	DRUPE
CUPID	DANIO	DEMOS	DITCH	DOUSE	DRUSE
CUPPA	DARER	DEMUR	DITTO	DOVEN	DRYAD
CUPPY	DARIC	DENIM	DITTY	DOWDY	DRYER
CURCH	DARKY	DENSE	DIVAN	DOWER	DRYLY
CURDY	DASHY	DEPOT	DIVER	DOWIE	DUCAL
CURER	DATER	DEPTH	DIVOT	DOWNY	DUCKY
CURET	DATTO	DERAT	DIVVY	DOWRY	DUCKY
CURIA	DATUM	DERAY	DIXIT	DOWSE	DUDDY
CURIE	DAUBE	DERBY	DIZEN	DOXIE	DULIA
CURIO	DAUBY	DERMA	DIZZY	DOYEN	DULSE
CURLY	DAUNT	DERRY	DJINN	DOYLY	DUMKA
CURRY	DAVEN	DESEX	DOBBY	DOZEN	DUMMY
CURSE	DAVIT	DETER	DOBIE	DOZER	DUNCE
CURST	DAWEN	DEUCE	DOBLA	DRAFF	DUNCH
CURVE	DEAIR	DEVEL	DOBRA	DRAFT	DUNGY
CURVY	DEALT	DEVIL	DODGE	DRAIL	DUOMO
CUSEC	DEARY	DEVON	DODGY	DRAIN	DUPER
CUSHY	DEASH	DEWAN	DOEST	DRAKE	DUPLE
CUSSO	DEATH	DEWAX	DOETH	DRAMA	DURAL
CUTCH	DEAVE	DHOTI	DOGEY	DRANK	DUROC
CUTES	DEBAR	DHUTI	DOGGO	DRAPE	DURRA
CUTEY	DEBIT	DIARY	DOGGY	DRAVE	DURUM
CUTIE	DEBUG	DIAZO	DOGIE	DRAWL	DUSKY
CUTIN	DEBUT	DICER	DOGMA	DRAWN	DUSTY
CUTIS	DEBYE	DICEY	DOILY	DREAD	DUTCH
CUTTY	DECAL	DICKY	DOING	DREAM	DWARF
CYANO	DECAY	DICOT	DOLCE	DREAR	DWELL
CYCAD	DECOR	DICTA	DOLLY	DRECK	DWELT
CYCAS	DECOY	DIDST	DOLOR	DRESS	DWINE
CYCLE	DECRY	DIENE	DOMAL	DREST	DYING
CYCLO	DEDAL	DIGHT	DOMIC	DRIED	
CYDER	DEEDY	DIGIT	DONEE	DRIER	E
CYLIX	DEFAT	DIKER	DONNA	DRIES	
CYMAR	DEFER	DILDO	DONSY	DRIFT	EAGER
CYMOL	DEFOG	DILLY	DONUT	DRILL	EAGLE
CYNIC	DEGAS	DIMER	DOOLY	DRILY	EAGRE
CYTON	DEGUM	DIMLY	DOOZY	DRIPT	EARED
	DEICE	DINAB	DOPER	DRIVE	EARLY
D	DEIFY	DINER	DOPEY	DROIT	EARTH
	DEIGN	DINGO	DORMY	DROLL	EATER
	DEISM	DINGY	DORSA	DRONE	EBBET
DACHA	DEIST	DINKY	DORTY	DROOL	EBONY
DADDY	DEITY	DIODE	DOSER	DROOP	ECLAT
DAFFY	DELAY	DIPPY	DOTAL	DROPT	ECOLE
DAILY	DELFT	DIRER	DOTER	DROSS	EDEMA
DAIRY	DELLY	DIRGE	DOTTY	DROUK	EDGER
DALLY	DELTA	DIRTY	DOUBT	DROVE	EDICT

EDIFY	ENFIN	EVICT	FATSO	FIFTH	FLIED
EDUCE	ENJOY	EVITE	FATTY	FIFTY	FLIER
EDUCT	ENORM	EVOKE	FAUGH	FIGHT	FLIES
EERIE	ENROL	EXACT	FAULD	FILAR	FLING
EGADS	ENSKY	EXALT	FAULT	FILCH	FLINT
EGEST	ENSUE	EXCEL	FAUNA	FILER	FLIRT
EGGAR	ENTER	EXERT	FAUVE	FILET	FLITE
EGGER	ENTIA	EXILE	FAVOR	FILLE	FLOAT
EGRET	ENTRY	EXINE	FAVUS	FILLY	FLOCK
EIDER	ENURE	EXIST	FAWNY	FILMY	FLONG
EIDOS	ENVON	EXPEL	FEASE	FILTH	FLOOD
EIGHT	ENVOY	EXTOL	FEAST	FILUM	FLOOR
EJECT	ENZYM	EXTRA	FEAZE	FINAL	FLORA
ELAIN	EOSIN	EXUDE	FECAL	FINCH	FLOSS
ELAND	EPACT	EXULT	FECES	FINER	FLOTA
ELATE	EPHAH	EXURB	FEEZE	FINIS	FLOUR
ELBOW	EPHOD	EYING	FEIGN	FINNY	FLOUT
ELDER	EPHOR	EYRIE	FEINT	FIORD	FLOWN
ELECT	EPOCH	EYRIR	FEIST	FIQUE	FLUFF
ELEGY	EPODE		FELID	FIRED	FLUID
ELEMI	EPOXY	F	FELLA	FIRER	FLUKE
ELFIN	EQUAL		FELLY	FIRRY	FLUKY
ELIDE	EQUIP	FABLE	FEMME	FIRST	FLUME
ELITE	ERASE	FACER	FEMUR	FIRTH	FLUMP
ELOIN	ERECT	FACET	FENCE	FISHY	FLUNG
ELOPE	ERGOT	FACIA	FENNY	FITCH	FLUNK
ELUDE	ERICA	FADDY	FEOFF	FITLY	FLUOR
ELUTE	ERODE	FADGE	FERAL	FIVER	FLUSH
ELVER	EROSE	FAENA	FERIA	FIXER	FLUTE
ELVES	ERROR	FAERY	FERLY	FIZZY	FLUTY
EMBAR	ERUCT	FAGIN	FERMI	FJELD	FLUYT
EMBAY	ERUGO	FAGOT	FERNY	FJORD	FLYBY
EMBED	ERUPT	FAINT	FERRY	FLACK	FLYER
EMBER	ERVIL	FAIRY	FESSE	FLAIL	FLYTE
EMBOW	ESCAR	FAITH	FETAL	FLAIR	FOAMY
EMCEE	ESCOT	FAKER	FETCH	FLAKE	FOCAL
EMEER	ESKAR	FAKIR	FETID	FLAKY	FOCUS
EMEND	ESSAY	FALSE	FETOR	FLAME	FOEHN
EMERY	ESTER	FANCY	FETUS	FLAMY	FOGEY
EMMER	ESTOP	FANGA	FEUAR	FLANK	FOGGY
EMMET	ETAPE	FANON	FEVER	FLARE	FOGIE
EMOTE	ETHER	FANUM	FIBER	FLASH	FOIST
EMPTY	ETHIC	FAQIR	FIBRE	FLASK	FOLIA
EMYDE	ETHOS	FARAD	FICHE	FLAWY	FOLIO
ENACT	ETHYL	FARCE	FICHU	FLAXY	FOLLY
ENATE	ETUDE	FARCI	FICIN	FLEAM	FONDU
ENDER	ETWEE	FARCY	FIDGE	FLECK	FOOTY
ENDOW	EVADE	FARER	FIELD	FLEER	FORAM
ENDUE	EVENT	FARLE	FIEND	FLEET	FORAY
ENEMA	EVERT	FATAL	FIERY	FLECH	FORBY
ENEMY	EVERY	FATLY	FIFER	FLICK	FORCE

FORDO	FUGGY	GAUNT	GIRON	GOLEM	GRIFF
FORGE	FUGIO	GAUSS	GIRSH	GOLLY	GRIFT
FORGO	FUGLE	GAUZE	GIRTH	GOMBO	GRILL
FORKY	FUGUE	GAUZY	GISMO	GONAD	GRIME
FORME	FULLY	GAVEL	GIVEN	GONER	GRIMY
FORTE	FUMER	GAVOT	GIVER	GONIA	GRIND
FORTH	FUMET	GAWKY	GIZMO	GONIF	GRIPE
FORTY	FUNGI	GAWSY	GLACE	GONOF	GRIPT
FOSSA	FUNGO	GAYAL	GLADE	GOODY	GRIPY
FOSSE	FUNKY	GAYLY	GLADY	GOOEY	GRIST
FOUND	FURAN	GAZER	GLAIR	GOOFY	GRITH
FOUNT	FUROR	GECKO	GLAND	GOONY	GROAN
FOVEA	FURRY	GEESE	GLANS	GOOSE	GROAT
FOYER	FURZE	GEEST	GLARE	GOOSY	GROIN
FRAIL	FUSSY	GELID	GLARY	GORAL	GROOM
FRAME	FUSTY	GEMMA	GLASS	GORGE	GROPE
FRANC	FUZEE	GENNY	GLAZE	GORSE	GROSS
FRANK	FUZZY	GEMOT	GLAZY	GORSY	GROSZ
FREAK		GENET	GLEAM	GOUGE	GROUP
FREED	G	GENII	GLEAN	GOURD	GROUT
FREER		GENIP	GLEBA	GOUTY	GROVE
FREMD	GABBY	GENOA	GLEBE	GOWAN	GROWL
FRENA	GABLE	GENRE	GLEDE	GRAAL	GROWN
FRERE	GADDI	GENUS	GLEED	GRACE	GRUEL
FRESH	GADID	GEODE	GLEEK	GRADE	GRUFF
FRIAR	GAFFE	GEOID	GLEET	GRAFT	GRUME
FRIED	GAGER	GERAH	GLAIL	GRAIL	GRUMP
FRIER	GAILY	GERMY	GLIDE	GRAIN	GRUNT
FRIES	GALAH	GESSO	GLIFF	GRAMA	GUACO
FRILL	GALAX	GESTE	GLINT	GRAMP	GUANO
FRISE	GALEA	GETUP	GLOAM	GRANA	GUARD
FRISK	GALLY	GHAST	GLOAT	GRAND	GUAVA
FRITH	GALOP	GHAUT	GLOBE	GRANT	GUESS
FRITT	GAMBA	GHAZI	GLOGG	GRAPE	GUEST
FRIZZ	GAMBE	GHOST	GLOOM	GRAPH	GUIDE
FROCK	GAMER	GHOUL	GLORY	GRAPY	GUILD
FROND	GAMEY	GHYLL	GLOSS	GRASP	GUILE
FRONS	GAMIN	GIANT	GLOST	GRASS	GUILT
FRONT	GAMMA	GIBER	GLOVE	GRATE	GUIRO
FRORE	GAMUT	GIDDY	GLOZE	GRAVE	GUISE
FROSH	GANEF	GIGAS	GLUER	GRAVY	GULAR
FROST	GANEV	GIGHE	GLUEY	GRAZE	GULCH
FROTH	GANJA	GIGOT	GLUME	GREAT	GULES
FROZE	GANOF	GIGUE	GLYPH	GREBE	GULFY
FRUIT	GAPER	GILLY	GNARL	GREED	GULLY
FRUMP	GAPPY	GIMEL	GNASH	GREEK	GULPY
FRYER	GARTH	GIMPY	GNAWN	GREEN	GUMBO
FUBSY	GASSY	GINNY	GNOME	GREET	GUMMA
FUCUS	GAUDY	GIPON	GOBAN	GREGO	GUMMY
FUDGE	GAUGE	GIPSY	GODLY	GRIDE	GUNNY
FUGAL	GAULT	GIRLY	GOING	GRIEF	GUPPY

GURGE	HAULM	HILLY	HOVER	IMAGE	IRING
GURRY	HAUNT	HILUS	HOWDY	IMAGO	IRONE
GURSH	HAVEN	HINGE	HOWFF	IMAUM	IRONY
GUSHY	HAVER	HINNY	HOYLE	IMBED	ISLET
GUSTO	HAVOC	HIPPO	HUBBY	IMBUE	ITCHY
GUSTY	HAWSE	HIPPY	HUFFY	IMIDE	ITHER
GUTSY	HAYER	HIRER	HUGER	IMIDO	IXTLE
GUTTA	HAZAN	HITCH	HULKY	IMINE	
GUTTY	HAZEL	HOAGY	HULLO	IMINO	J
GUYOT	HAZER	HOARD	HUMAN	IMMIX	
GYPSY	HEADY	HOARY	HUMIC	IMPEL	JABOT
GYRON	HEART	HOBBY	HUMID	IMPLY	JACAL
GYRUS	HEATH	HOCUS	HUMOR	INANE	JACKY
	HEAVE	HODAD	HUMPH	INAPT	JAGER
H	HEAVY	HOICK	HUMPY	INARM	JAGGY
	HEDER	HOISE	HUNCH	INBYE	JAGRA
HABIT	HEDGE	HOIST	HUNKY	INCOG	JAKES
HACEK	HEDGY	HOKEY	HURDS	INCUR	JALAP
HADAL	HEEZE	HOKKU	HURLY	INCUS	JAMBE
HADJI	HEFTY	HOKUM	HURRY	INDEX	JANTY
HADST	HEIGH	HOLEY	HUSKY	INDOL	JAPER
HAFIZ	HEIST	HOLLA	HUSSY	INDOW	JAUNT
HAIKU	HELIO	HOLLO	HUTCH	INDRI	JAWAN
HAIRY	HELIX	HOLLY	HUZZA	INDUE	JAZZY
HAJJI	HELLO	HOMED	HYDRA	INEPT	JEBEL
HAKIM	HELOT	HOMEY	HYDRO	INERT	JEHAD
HALER	HELVE	HONAN	HYENA	INFER	JELLY
HALID	HEMAL	HONDA	HYING	INFIX	JEMMY
HALLO	HEMIC	HONER		INFRA	JENNY
HALVA	HEMIN	HONEY	I	INGLE	JERID
HALVE	HEMPY	HONKY		INION	JERKY
HAMAL	HENCE	HONOR	ICHOR	INKER	JERRY
HAMMY	HENNA	HOOCH	ICIER	INKLE	JESSE
HAMZA	HENRY	HOOEY	ICILY	INLAY	JETTY
HANCE	HERBY	HOOKA	ICING	INLET	JIBER
HANDY	HERES	HOOKY	ICTUS	INNED	JIFFY
HANKY	HERMA	HOOLY	IDEAL	INNER	JIHAD
HANSE	HERON	HOPER	IDIOM	INPUT	JIMMY
HAOLE	HERRY	HORAH	IDIOT	INSET	JIMPY
HAPAX	HERTZ	HORAL	IDLER	INTER	JINGO
HAPLY	HEUCH	HORNY	IDYLL	INTRO	JINNI
HAPPY	HEUGH	HORSE	IGLOO	INURE	JNANA
HARDY	HEWER	HORST	IHRAM	INURN	JOCKO
HAREM	HEXAD	HORSY	ILEAC	INVAR	JOINT
HARPY	HEXER	HOSEL	ILEAL	IODIC	JOIST
HARRY	HEXYL	HOTCH	ILEUM	IODID	JOKER
HARSH	HIDER	HOTEL	ILEUS	IODIN	JOLLY
HASTE	HIGHT	HOTLY	ILIAC	IODOL	JOLTY
HATCH	HIKER	HOUND	ILIAD	IONIC	JORAM
HATER	HILAR	HOURI	ILIAL	IRADE	JORUM
HAUGH	HILLO	HOUSE	ILIUM	IRATE	JOTTY

JOULE	KEMPT	KRAUT	LARKY	LETCH	LITER
JOUST	KENAF	KRILL	LARVA	LETHE	LITHE
JOWLY	KENCH	KRONA	LASER	LETUP	LITHO
JUDAS	KENDO	KROON	LASSO	LEVEE	LITRE
JUDGE	KERNE	KRUBI	LATED	LEVEL	LIVEN
JUGAL	KERRY	KUDZU	LATEN	LEVER	LIVER
JUICE	KETCH	KULAK	LATER	LEVIN	LIVES
JUICY	KEVEL	KURTA	LATEX	LEWIS	LIVID
JULEP	KEVIL	KUSSA	LATHE	LIANA	LIVRE
JUMBO	KHADI	KVASS	LATHY	LIANE	LLAMA
JUMPY	KHAKI	KYACK	LAUAN	LIANG	LLANO
JUNCO	KHEDA	KYLIZ	LAUGH	LIARD	LOAMY
JUNKY	KIANG	KYRIE	LAURA	LIBER	LOATH
JUNTA	KIBLA	KYTHE	LAVER	LIBRA	LOBAR
JUNTO	KIDDO		LAYER	LIBRI	LOBBY
JUPON	KIDDY	L	LAZAR	LICHI	LOCAL
JURAL	KILIM		LEACH	LIGHT	LOCUM
JURAT	KILTY	LABEL	LEADY	LICIT	LOCUS
JUREL	KININ	LABIA	LEAFY	LIDAR	LODEN
JUROR	KINKY	LABOR	LEAKY	LIFER	LODGE
JUTTY	KIOSK	LABRA	LEANT	LIGAN	LOESS
	KITER	LACER	LEAPT	LIGHT	LOFTY
K	KITHE	LACEY	LEARN	LIKED	LOGAN
	KITTY	LADEN	LEASE	LIKEN	LOGGY
KABAB	KLONG	LADER	LEARY	LIKER	LOGIA
KABAR	KLOOF	LADLE	LEASH	LILAC	LOGIC
KABOB	KLUTZ	LAEVO	LEAST	LIMAN	LOGOS
KAFIR	KNACK	LAGAN	LEAVE	LIMBA	LOLLY
KAIAK	KNAVE	LAGER	LEAVY	LIMBI	LONER
KALAM	KNEAD	LAICH	LEBEN	LIMBO	LONGE
KALIF	KNEEL	LAIGH	LEDGE	LIMEN	LOOBY
KALPA	KNELL	LAIRD	LEDGY	LIMES	LOOEY
KAMIK	KNELT	LAITH	LEECH	LIMEY	LOOFA
KANJI	KNIFE	LAITY	LEERY	LIMIT	LOOIE
KAPOK	KNISH	LAKED	LEFTY	LINAC	LOONY
KAPUT	KNOCK	LAKER	LEGAL	LINDY	LOOSE
KARAT	KNOLL	LAMED	LEGER	LINED	LOPER
KARMA	KNOSP	LAMER	LEGES	LINEN	LOPPY
KAROO	KNOUT	LAMIA	LEGGY	LINER	LORAL
KARST	KNOWN	LANAI	LEGIT	LINEY	LORAN
KASHA	KNURL	LANCE	LEHUA	LINGA	LORIS
KAURI	KOALA	LANKY	LEMAN	LINGO	LORRY
KAURY	KOINE	LAPEL	LEMMA	LINGY	LOSEL
KAYAK	KOOKY	LAPIN	LEMON	LININ	LOSER
KAZOO	KOPEK	LAPIS	LEMUR	LINKY	LOSSY
KEBAB	KOPJE	LAPSE	LENES	LINTY	LOTAH
KEBAR	KOPPA	LARCH	LENIS	LIPID	LOTIC
KEBOB	KOTOW	LARDY	LENSE	LIPIN	LOTOS
KEDGE	KRAAL	LARES	LENTO	LIPPY	LOTTO
KEEVE	KRAFT	LARGE	LEONE	LISLE	LOTUS
KELPY	KRAIT	LARGO	LEPER	LITAS	LOUGH

LOUIE	MACHO	MASHY	METIS	MOIRA	MOUTH
LOUIS	MACLE	MASON	METRE	MOIST	MOVED
LOUPE	MACRO	MASSA	METRO	MOLAL	MOVER
LOURY	MADAM	MASSE	MEZZO	MOLAR	MOVIE
LOUSE	MADLY	MASSY	MIAUL	MOLDY	MOWER
LOUSY	MADRE	MATCH	MICRA	MOLLY	MOXIE
LOVED	MAFIA	MATER	MICRO	MOLTO	MUCID
LOWER	MAFIC	MATEY	MIDDY	MOMMA	MUCIN
LOWLY	MAGIC	MATIN	MIDGE	MOMMY	MUCKY
LOWSE	MAGMA	MATTE	MIDST	MOMUS	MUCOR
LOYAL	MAGOT	MATZA	MIFFY	MONAS	MUCRO
LUCES	MAGUS	MATZO	MIGHT	MONDE	MUCUS
LUCID	MAHOE	MAUND	MILCH	MONDO	MUDDY
LUCKY	MAILE	MAUVE	MILER	MONEY	MUDRA
LUCRE	MAILL	MAVEN	MILIA	MONGO	MUFTI
LUFFA	MAIST	MAVIE	MILKY	MONIE	MUGGY
LUMEN	MAIZE	MAVIN	MILLE	MONTE	MUHLY
LUMPY	MAJOR	MAVIS	MILPA	MONTH	MUJIK
LUNAR	MAKAR	MAXIM	MILTY	MOOCH	MULCH
LUNCH	MAKER	MAYOR	MIMER	MOODY	MULCT
LUNET	MALAR	MAYST	MIMIC	MOOLA	MULEY
LUNGE	MALIC	MAZER	MINCE	MOONY	MULLA
LUNGI	MALMY	MBIRA	MINCY	MOORY	MUMMY
LUPIN	MALTY	MEALY	MINER	MOOSE	MUNCH
LUPUS	MAMBA	MEANT	MINGY	MOPED	MUNGO
LURCH	MAMBO	MEANY	MINIM	MOPER	MURAL
LURER	MAMEY	MEATY	MINNY	MORAL	MUREX
LURID	MAMIE	MECCA	MINOR	MORAY	MURKY
LUSTY	MAMMA	MEDAL	MINTY	MOREL	MURRE
LUSUS	MAMMY	MEDIA	MINUS	MORON	MURRY
LUTEA	MANGE	MEDIC	MIREX	MORPH	MUSER
LUTED	MANGO	MEDII	MIRKY	MORRO	MUSHY
LYARD	MANGY	MEINY	MIRTH	MOSEY	MUSIC
LYART	MANIA	MELEE	MIRZA	MOSSO	MUSSY
LYASE	MANIC	MELIC	MISDO	MOOSY	MUSTY
LYCEA	MANLY	MELON	MISER	MOSTE	MUTCH
LYCEE	MANNA	MENAD	MISSY	MOTEL	MUTER
LYING	MANOR	MENSA	MISTY	MOTET	MUZZY
LYMPH	MANSE	MENTA	MITER	MOTEY	MYNAH
LYNCH	MANTA	MERCY	MITIS	MOTHY	MYOID
LYRIC	MANUS	MERGE	MITRE	MOTIF	MYOMA
LYSIN	MAPLE	MERIT	MIXER	MOTOR	MYOPE
LYSIS	MAQUI	MERLE	MIXUP	MOTTE	
LYSSA	MARCH	MERRY	MIZEN	MOTTO	N
LYTIC	MARGE	MESHY	MOCHA	MOUCH	
LYTTA	MARIA	MESIC	MODAL	MOULT	NABOB
	MARLY	MESNE	MODEL	MOUND	NADIR
M	MARRY	MESON	MODUS	MOUNT	NAIAD
	MARSE	MESSY	MOGUL	MOURN	NAIVE
MACAW	MARSH	METAL	MOHEL	MOUSE	NAKED
MACER	MASER	MEYER	MOHUR	MOUSY	NAMER

NANCE	NISUS		OPINE	OXIME	PARLE
NANNY	NITER	OAKUM	OPING	OXLIP	PAROL
NAPPE	NITID	OASIS	OPIUM	OXTER	PARRY
NAPPY	NITON	OATEN	OPSIN	OZONE	PARSE
NARCO	NITRE	OATER	OPTIC		PARTY
NARES	NITRO	OAVES	ORACH	P	PARVE
NARIS	NITTY	OBEAH	ORANG		PASEO
NASAL	NIVAL	OBELI	ORATE	PACER	PASHA
NÁSTY	NIXIE	OBESE	ORBIT	PACHA	PASSE
NATAL	NIZAM	OBOLE	ORCIN	PADDY	PASTA
NATES	NOBBY	OCCUR	ORDER	PADLE	PASTE
NATTY	NOBLE	OCEAN	OREAD	PADRE	PASTY
NAVAL	NOBLY	OCHER	ORGAN	PAEAN	PATCH
NAVAR	NODAL	OCHRE	ORGIC	PAEON	PATEN
NAVEL	NODDY	OCHRY	ORIBI	PAGAN	PATER
NAVVY	NODUS	OCREA	ORIEL	PAGED	PATIN
NAWAB	NOHOW	OCTAD	ORLOP	PAGOD	PATIO
NEATH	NOISE	OCTAL	ÓRMER	PAINT	PATSY
NEEDY	NOISY	OCTET	ORNIS	PAISA	PATTY
NEGRO	NOMAD	OCTYL	ORPIN	PAISE	PAUSE
NEGUS	NOMEN	ODDLY	ORRIS	PALEA	PAVAN
NEIGH	NOMOS	ODEON	ORTHO	PALER	PAVER
NEIST	NONCE	ODEUM	OSIER	PALET	PAVID
NEROL	NOOKY	ODIUM	OSMOL	PALLY	PAVIN
NERTS	NOOSE	ODOUR	OSSIA	PALMY	PAVIS
NERTZ	NOPAL	ODYLE	OSTIA	PALSY	PAWER
NERVY	NORIA	OFFAL	OTHER	PAMPA	PAWKY
NETOP	NORTH	OFFER	OTTAR	PANDA	PAYER
NETTY	NOSED	OFTEN	OTTER	PANDY	PAYOR
NEUME	NOSEY	OGHAM	OUGHT	PANEL	PEACE
NEVER	NOTAL	OGIVE	OUPHE	PANGA	PEACH
NEVUS	NOTCH	OGLER	OURIE	PANIC	PEAGE
NEWEL	NOTED	OILER	OUSEL	PANNE	PEAKY
NEWLY	NOTER	OKAPI	OUTBY	PANSY	PEARL
NEWSY	NOTUM	OLDEN	OUTDO	PANTY	PEART
NEXUS	NOVEL	OLDIE	OUTER	PAPAL	PEASE
NGWEE	NOWAY	OLEIC	OUTGO	PAPAW	PEATY
NICHE	NUBBY	OLEIN	OUTRE	PAPER	PEAVY
NICOL	NUBIA	OLIVE	OUZEL	PAPPI	PECAN
NIDAL	NUCHA	OLOGY	OVARY	PAPPY	PECKY
NIDUS	NUDER	OMBER	OVATE	PARCH	PEDAL
NIECE	NUDGE	OMEGA	OVERT	PARDI	PEDES
NIEVE	NUDIE	ONERY	OVINE	PARDY	PEDRO
NIFTY	NUMEN	ONION	OVOID	PARDI	PEERY
NIGHT	NURSE	ONIUM	OVOLO	PARDY	PEEVE
NIHIL	NUTTY	ONSET	OVULE	PARER	PEISE
NINNY	NYALA	ONTIC	OWLET	PAREU	PEKAN
NINON	NYLON	OOMPH	OWNER	PARGE	PEKIN
NINTH	NYMPH	OORIE	OXBOW	PARGO	PEKOE
NIPPY		OOTID	OXEYE	PARIS	PELON
NISEI	O	OPERA	OXIDE	PARKA	PENAL

PENCE	PILED	PLONK	PRANK	PUBES	QUELL
PENES	PILEI	PLUCK	PRASE	PUBIC	QUERN
PENGO	PILOT	PLUBM	PRATE	PUBIS	QUERY
PENIS	PILUS	PLUME	PRAWN	PUCKA	QUEST
PENNA	PINCH	PLUMP	PREEN	PUDGY	QUEUE
PENNI	PINED	PLUMY	PRESA	PUDIC	QUICK
PENNY	PINEY	PLUNK	PRESE	PUFFY	QUIET
PEONY	PINGO	PLUSH	PRESS	PUGGY	QUIFF
PEPPY	PINKO	PLYER	PREST	PUKKA	QUILL
PERCH	PINKY	POACH	PREXY	PULER	QUILT
PERDU	PINNA	POCKY	PRICE	PULIK	QUINT
PERDY	PINON	PODGY	PRICK	PULPY	QUIPU
PERIL	PINTA	PODIA	PRICY	PULSE	QUIRE
PERKY	PINTO	POESY	PRIDE	PUNCH	QUIRK
PERRY	PINUP	POGEY	PRIED	PUNKA	QUIRT
PERSE	PIOUS	POILU	PRIER	PUNKY	QUITE
PESKY	PIPAL	POIND	PRIES	PUNNY	QUOIT
PETAL	PIPER	POINT	PRIMA	PUNTO	QUOTA
PETER	PIPET	POISE	PRIME	PUNTY	QUOTE
PETIT	PIPIT	POKER	PRIMI	PUPIL	QUOTH
PETTI	PIQUE	POKEY	PRIMO	PUPPY	QURSH
PETTO	PIROG	POLAR	PRIMP	PURDA	
PETTY	PITCH	POLED	PRINK	PUREE	R
PEWEE	PITHY	POLER	PRINT	PURER	
PEWIT	PITON	POLIO	PRIOR	PURGE	RABBI
PHAGE	PIVOT	POLKA	PRISE	PURIN	RABIC
PHASE	PIXIE	POLYP	PRISM	PURSE	RABID
PHIAL	PIZZA	PONCE	PRISS	PURSY	RACER
PHLOX	PLACE	POOCH	PRIVY	PUSHY	RACON
PHONE	PLACK	POORI	PRIZE	PUSSY	RADAR
PHONY	PLAGE	POPPA	PROBE	PUTON	RADII
PHOTO	PLAID	POPPY	PROEM	PUTTY	RADIO
PHPHT	PLAIN	PORCH	PROLE	PYLON	RADIX
PHYLA	PLAIT	PORGY	PRONE	PYXIS	RADON
PHYLE	PLANE	PORKY	PRONG		RAGEE
PIANO	PLANK	PORNO	PROOF	Q	RAGGY
PICAL	PLANT	POSER	PROSE		RAINY
PICKY	PLASH	POSIT	PROST	QUACK	RAISE
PICOT	PLASM	POSSE	PROSY	QUAFF	RAJAH
PICUL	PLATE	POTSY	PROUD	QUAIL	RAKEE
PIECE	PLATY	POTTO	PROVE	QUALM	RAKER
PIETA	PLAYA	POTTY	PROWL	QUARE	RALLY
PEITY	PLAZA	POUFF	PROXY	QUARK	RAMEE
PIGGY	PLEAD	POULT	PRUDE	QUART	RAMET
PIGNY	PLEAT	POUND	PRUNE	QUASH	RAMIE
PIKER	PLENA	POUTY	PRUTA	QUASI	RAMMY
PILAF	PLICA	POWER	PRYER	QUASS	RAMUS
PILAR	PLIED	POYOU	PSALM	QUATE	RANCE
PILAU	PLIER	PRAAM	PSHAW	QUEAN	RANCH
PILAW	PLIES	PRAHU	PSOAS	QUEEN	RANDY
PILEA	PLINK	PRANG	PSYCH	QUEER	RANEE

RANGY	REFER	RILLE	ROYAL	SALPA	SCART
RANID	REFIT	RIMER	RUBLE	SALTY	SCARY
RAPER	REGAL	RINSE	RUBUS	SALVE	SCATT
RAPID	REGES	RIPEN	RUCHE	SALVO	SCAUP
RARER	REGMA	RIPER	RUDDY	SAMBA	SCAUR
RASPY	REGNA	RISHI	RUFFE	SAMBO	SCENA
RATAL	REIFY	RISKY	RUGBY	SAMEK	SCEND
RATAN	REIVE	RISUS	RUING	SANDY	SCENE
RATCH	RELAX	RITZY	RULER	SANER	SCENT
RATEL	RELAY	RIVAL	RUMBA	SANGA	SCHAV
RATER	RELIC	RIVER	RUMEN	SANGH	SCHMO
RATHE	REMAN	RIVET	RUMMY	SAPID	SCHUL
RATIO	REMEX	RIYAL	RUMOR	SAPOR	SCHWA
RATTY	REMIT	ROAST	RUNIC	SAPPY	SCION
RAVEL	RENAL	ROBIN	RUNNY	SAREE	SCOFF
RAVER	RENEW	ROBLE	RUNTY	SARIN	SCOLD
RAVIN	RENIN	ROBOT	RUPEE	SAROD	SCONE
RAWLY	RENTE	ROCKY	RURAL	SASIN	SCOOP
RAYAH	REPAY	RODEO	RUSHY	SASSY	SCOOT
RAYON	REPLY	ROGER	RUSTY	SATEM	SCOPE
RAZEE	REPRO	ROGUE	RUTTY	SATIN	SCORE
RAZER	RERAN	ROILY		SATYR	SCORN
RAZOR	RERUN	ROMAN	S	SAUCE	SCOUR
REACH	RESID	RONDO		SAUCH	SCOUT
REACT	RESIN	ROOKY	SABER	SAUCY	SCOWL
READY	RETCH	ROOMY	SABIN	SAUGH	SCRAG
REALM	RETEM	ROOSE	SABIR	SAULT	SCRAM
REATA	RETIA	ROOST	SABLE	SAUNA	SCRAP
REAVE	REVEL	ROOTY	SABOT	SAURY	SCREE
REBBE	REVET	ROPER	SABRE	SAUTE	SCREW
REBEC	REVUE	ROQUE	SACRA	SAVER	SCRIM
REBEL	RHEUM	ROSED	SADHE	SAVIN	SCRIP
REBOP	RHINO	ROSET	SADHU	SAVOR	SCROD
REBUS	RHOMB	ROSIN	SADLY	SAVOY	SCRUB
REBUT	RHUMB	ROTOR	SAFER	SAVVY	SCRUM
RECAP	RHYME	ROUEN	SAGER	SAWER	SCUBA
RECON	RHYTA	ROUGE	SAGUM	SAYER	SCUDO
RECTA	RIANT	ROUGH	SAHIB	SAYID	SCULK
RECTI	RIATA	ROUND	SAICE	SAYID	SCULL
RECTO	RIBBY	ROUPY	SAIGA	SAYST	SCULP
RECUR	RIBES	ROUSE	SAINT	SCALD	SCURF
REDAN	RICER	ROUST	SAITH	SCALE	SCUTA
REDIA	RICIN	ROUTE	SAJOU	SCALL	SCUTE
REDLY	RIDER	ROUTH	SAKER	SCALP	SEAMY
REDOX	RIDGE	ROVEN	SALAD	SCALY	SEBUM
REEDY	RIDGY	ROWEN	SALEP	SCAMP	SECCO
REEFY	RIFLE	ROWDY	SALIC	SCANT	SEDAN
REEKY	RIGHT	ROWEL	SALLY	SCAPE	SEDER
REEST	RIGID	ROWEN	SALMI	SCARE	SEDGE
REEVE	RIGOR	ROWER	SALOL	SCARF	SEDGY
REFEL	RILEY	ROWTH	SALON	SCARP	SEDUM

SEEDY	SHALT	SHOOL	SIXTH	SLOJD	SNOOK
SEELY	SHALY	SHOON	SIXTY	SLOOP	SNOOL
SEEPY	SHAME	SHOOT	SIZAR	SLOPE	SNOOP
SEGNO	SHANK	SHORE	SIZER	SLOTH	SNOOT
SEGUE	SHAPE	SHORL	SKALD	SLOYD	SNORE
SEINE	SHARD	SHORN	SKATE	SLUFF	SNORT
SEISE	SHARE	SHORT	SKEAN	SLUMP	SNOUT
SEISM	SHARK	SHOTE	SKEEN	SLUNG	SNOWY
SEIZE	SHARN	SHOTT	SKEET	SLURB	SNUCK
SELAH	SHARP	SHOUT	SKEIN	SLUSH	SNUFF
SELLE	SHAUL	SHOVE	SKELP	SLYPE	SOAPY
SEMEN	SHAVE	SNOWY	SKENE	SMACK	SOAVE
SEMIS	SHAWL	SHRED	SKILL	SMALT	SOBER
SENGI	SHAWN	SHREW	SKIMO	SMARM	SOCLE
SENNA	SHEAF	SHRUB	SKINK	SMART	SODDY
SENOR	SHEAL	SHRUG	SKINT	SMASH	SOFAR
SENSA	SHEAR	SHUCK	SKIRL	SMAZE	SOFTA
SENSE	SHEEN	SHUNT	SKIRR	SMEAR	SOFTY
SENTI	SHEEP	SHUSH	SKITE	SMEEK	SOGGY
SEPAL	SHEER	SHUTE	SKIVE	SMELL	SOLAN
SEPIA	SHEEN	SHYER	SKOAL	SMELT	SOLAR
SEPOY	SHEER	SIBYL	SKULK	SMERK	SOLDI
SERAC	SHEET	SIDED	SKULL	SMILE	SOLDO
SERAI	SHEIK	SIDLE	SKUNK	SMIRK	SOLED
SERAL	SHELF	SIEGE	SKYEY	SMITE	SOLID
SERER	SHELL	SIEUR	SLACK	SMITH	SOLON
SERGE	SHEND	SIEVE	SLAIN	SMOCK	SOLUM
SERIF	SHEOL	SIGHT	SLAKE	SMOKE	SOLUS
SERIN	SHERD	SIGIL	SLANG	SMOKY	SOLVE
SEROW	SHIED	SIGMA	SLANK	SMOLT	SONAR
SERRY	SHIEL	SIKER	SLANT	SMOTE	SONDE
SERUM	SHIER	SILEX	SLASH	SNACK	SONIC
SERVE	SHIES	SILKY	SLATE	SNAFU	SONLY
SERVO	SHILL	SILLY	SLATY	SNAIL	SONNY
SETON	SHILY	SILTY	SLAVE	SNAKE	SONSY
SETUP	SHINE	SILVA	SLEEK	SNAKY	SOOEY
SEVEN	SHINY	SIMAR	SLEEP	SNARE	SOOTH
SEVER	SHIRE	SINCE	SLEET	SNARK	SOOTY
SEWAN	SHIRK	SINEW	SLEPT	SNARL	SOPHY
SEWAR	SHIRR	SINGE	SLICE	SNASH	SOREL
SEWER	SHIRT	SINUS	SLICK	SNATH	SORER
SEXTO	SHIST	SIREE	SLIDE	SNEAK	SORGO
SHACK	SHIVA	SIRRA	SLIER	SNEAP	SORRY
SHADE	SHIVE	SIRUP	SLILY	SNECK	SORUS
SHADY	SHOAL	SISAL	SLIME	SNEER	SOTOL
SHAFT	SHOAT	SISSY	SLIMY	SNELL	SOUGH
SHAKE	SHOCK	SITAR	SLING	SNICK	SOUND
SHAKO	SHOER	SITUS	SLINK	SNIDE	SOUPY
SHAKY	SHOJI	SIVER	SLIPE	SNIFF	SOUSE
SHALE	SHONE	SIXMO	SLIPT	SNIPE	SOUTH
SHALL	SHOOK	SIXTE	SLOID	SNOOD	SOWAR

SOWER	SPITE	STANK	STOOL	SULKY	SWIVE
SOZIN	SPITZ	STAPH	STOOP	SULLY	SWOON
SPACE	SPLAT	STARE	STOPE	SUMAC	SWOOP
SPADE	SPLAY	STARK	STOPT	SUMMA	SWORD
SPADO	SPLIT	START	STORE	SUNNA	SWORE
SPAHI	SPODE	STASH	STORK	SUNNY	SWORN
SPAIL	SPOIL	STATE	STORM	SUNUP	SWOUN
SPAIT	SPOKE	STAVE	STORY	SUPER	SWUNG
SPAKE	SPOOF	STEAD	STOSS	SUPRA	SYCEE
SPALE	SPOOK	STEAK	STOUP	SURAH	SYLPH
SPALL	SPOOL	STEAL	STOUR	SURAL	SYLVA
SPANG	SPOON	STEAM	STOUT	SURER	SYNCH
SPANK	SPOOR	STEED	STOVE	SURFY	SYNOD
SPARE	SPORE	STEEK	STOWP	SURGE	SYREN
SPARK	SPORT	STEEL	STRAP	SURGY	SYRUP
SPASM	SPOUT	STEEP	STRAW	SURLY	
SPATE	SPRAG	STEER	STRAY	SURRA	T
SPAWN	SPRAT	STEIN	STREP	SUTRA	
SPEAK	SPRAY	STELA	STREW	SUTTA	TABBY
SPEAN	SPREE	STELE	STRIA	SWAGE	TABER
SPEAR	SPRIG	STENO	STRIP	SWAIL	TABES
SPECK	SPRIT	STERE	STROP	SWAIN	TABID
SPECS	SPRUE	STERN	STROW	SWALE	TABLA
SPEED	SPRUG	STICH	STROY	SWAMP	TABLE
SPEEL	SPUME	STICK	STRUM	SWAMY	TABOO
SPEER	SPUMY	STIED	STRUT	SWANG	TABOR
SPEIL	SPUNK	STIES	STUCK	SWANK	TACET
SPEIR	SPURN	STIFF	STUDY	SWARD	TACHE
SPELL	SPURT	STILE	STUFF	SWARE	TACIT
SPELT	SPUTA	STILL	STULL	SWARF	TACKY
SPEND	SQUAB	STILT	STUMP	SWARM	TAFFY
SPENT	SQUAT	STIME	STUNG	SWART	TAFIA
SPERM	SQUAW	STIMY	STUNK	SWATH	TAIGA
SPICA	SQUEG	STING	STUNT	SWEAR	TAINT
SPICE	SQUIB	STINK	STUPA	SWEAT	TAKER
SPICK	SQUID	STINT	STUPE	SWEDE	TAKIN
SPICY	STACK	STIPE	STURT	SWEEP	TALAR
SPIED	STADE	STIRK	STYLE	SWEER	TALER
SPEIL	STAFF	STIRP	STYLI	SWEET	TALKY
SPIER	STAGE	STOAT	STYMY	SWELL	TALLY
SPIES	STAGY	STOCK	SUAVE	SWEPT	TALON
SPIKE	STAID	STOGY	SUBAH	SWIFT	TALUK
SPIKY	STAIN	STOIC	SUBER	SWILL	TALUS
SPILE	STAIR	STOKE	SUCRE	SWINE	TAMAL
SPILL	STALE	STOLE	SUDOR	SWING	TAMER
SPILT	STALK	STOMA	SUDSY	SWINK	TAMIS
SPINE	STALL	STOMP	SUING	SWIPE	TAMMY
SPINY	STAMP	STONE	SUINT	SWIRL	TANGO
SPIRE	STAND	STONY	SUITE	SWISH	TANGY
SPIRT	STANE	STOOD	SULFA	SWISS	TANKA
SPIRY	STANG	STOOK	SULFO	SWITH	TANSY

TANTO	TENSE	THRIL	TONAL	TRANS	TRUTH
TAPER	TENTH	THRIP	TONDO	TRAPT	TRYMA
TAPIR	TENTY	THROE	TONER	TRASH	TRYST
TAPIS	TEPAL	THROW	TONGA	TRASS	TSADE
TARDO	TEPEE	THUJA	TONIC	TRAVE	TSADI
TARDY	TEPID	THUMB	TONNE	TRAWL	TSUBA
TARGE	TERAI	THUMP	TONUS	TREAD	TUBAL
TAROC	TERCE	THURL	TOOTH	TREAT	TUBBY
TAROK	TERGA	THUYA	TOOTS	TREND	TUBER
TAROT	TERNE	THYME	TOPAZ	TRESS	TUFTY
TARRE	TERRA	THYMI	TOPEE	TREWS	TULIP
TARRY	TERRY	THYMY	TOPER	TRIAD	TULLE
TARSI	TERSE	TIARA	TOPHE	TRIAL	TUMID
TASSE	TESLA	TIBIA	TOPIC	TRIBE	TUMMY
TASTE	TESTA	TICAL	TOPOI	TRICE	TUMOR
TASTY	TESTY	TIDAL	TOPOS	TRICK	TUNER
TATER	TETRA	TIGER	TOQUE	TRIED	TUNIC
TATTY	TEUCH	TIGHT	TORAR	TRIER	TUNNY
TAUNT	TEXAS	TIGON	TORCH	TRIES	TUPIK
TAUPE	THACK	TILDE	TORIC	TRIGO	TUQUE
TAWER	THANE	TILER	TORII	TRILL	TURBO
TAWIE	THANK	TILTH	TORSE	TRINE	TURFY
TAWNY	THARM	TIMER	TORSI	TRIOL	TURPS
TAWSE	THECA	TIMID	TORSK	TRIPE	TUTEE
TAXER	THEFT	TINCT	TORSO	TRITE	TUTOR
TAXON	THEIN	TINEA	TORTE	TROAK	TUTTI
TAXUS	THEIR	TINGE	TORUS	TROCK	TUTTY
TAZZA	THEME	TINNY	TOTAL	TRODE	TWAIN
TEACH	THERE	TIPPY	TOTEM	TRODE	TWANG
TEARY	THERM	TIPSY	TOTER	TROIS	TWEAK
TEASE	THESE	TIRED	TOUCH	TROKE	TWEED
TECHY	THETA	TITAN	TOUGH	TROLL	TWEET
TECTA	THICK	TITER	TOUSE	TROMP	TWICE
TEDDU	THIEF	TITHE	TOWEL	TRONA	TWILL
TEENY	THIGH	TITLE	TOWER	TRONE	TWINE
TEETH	THILL	TITRE	TOWIE	TROOP	TWIRL
TEGUA	THINE	TITTY	TOWNY	TROOZ	TWIRP
TEIID	THING	TIZZY	TOXIC	TROPE	TWIST
TEIND	THINK	TOADY	TOXIN	TROTH	TWIXT
TELEX	THIOL	TOAST	TOYER	TROUT	TYING
TELIA	THIRD	TODAY	TOYON	TROVE	TYPAL
TELIC	THIRL	TODDY	TRACE	TRUCE	TYPED
TELLY	THOLE	TOFFY	TRACK	TRUCK	TYPEY
TELOS	THONG	TOGUE	TRACT	TRUED	TYPIC
TEMPI	THORN	TOILE	TRADE	TRUER	TYTHE
TEMPO	THORO	TOKAY	TRAGI	TRULL	
TEMPT	THORP	TOKEN	TRAIK	TRULY	U
TENET	THOSE	TOLAN	TRAIL	TRUMP	
TENIA	THRAW	TOLYL	TRAIN	TRUNK	UDDER
TENON	THREE	TOMAN	TRAIT	TRUSS	UHLAN
TENOR	THREW	TOMMY	TRAMP	TRUST	UKASE

ULCER	URBAN	VENOM	VOLTE	WECHT	WHIDY
ULEMA	UREDO	VENUE	VOLVA	WEDGE	WIDEN
ULTRA	UREIC	VERGE	VOMIT	WEDGY	WIDER
UMBEL	URGER	VERSE	VOTER	WEEDY	WIDOW
UMBER	URINE	VERSO	VOUCH	WEENY	WIDTH
UMBRA	USAGE	VERST	VOWEL	WEEPY	WIELD
UMIAC	USHER	VERTU	VOWER	WEEST	WIGAN
UMIAK	USING	VERVE	VULVA	WEIGH	WIGHT
UNARM	USNEA	VESTA	VYING	WEIRD	WILCO
UNBAR	USQUE	VETCH		WELCH	WILLY
UNBID	USURP	VEXER		WELSH	WINCE
UNBOX	USURY	VEXIL	W	WENCH	WINCH
UNCAP	UTILE	VIAND		WENNY	WINDY
UNCIA	UTTER	VIBES		WETLY	WINEY
UNCLE	UVULA	VICAR	WACKE	WHACK	WINGY
UNCUS		VICHY	WACKY	WHALE	WINZE
UNDEE	V	VIDEO	WADDY	WHANG	WIPER
UNDER		VIEWY	WADER	WHARF	WIRER
UNDID	VACUA	VIGIL	WAEFU	WHAUP	WIRRA
UNDUE	VAGUE	VIGOR	WAFER	WHEAL	WISED
UNFIT	VAGUS	VILLA	WAGER	WHEAT	WISER
UNFIX	VAKIL	VIMEN	WAGON	WHEEL	WISHA
UNGOT	VALET	VINAL	WAHOO	WHEEN	WISPY
UNHAT	VALID	VINCA	WAIST	WHEEP	WITAN
UNIFY	VALOR	VINIC	WAIVE	WHELK	WITCH
UNITE	VALSE	VINLY	WAKEN	WHELM	WITEN
UNITY	VALUE	VIOLA	WAKER	WHELP	WITHE
UNLAY	VALVE	VIPER	WALER	WHERE	WITHY
UNLET	VANDA	VIRAL	WALLA	WHICH	WITTY
UNPEG	VAPID	VIREO	WALLY	WHIFF	WIVER
UNPEN	VAPOR	VIRES	WALTZ	WHILE	WIVES
UNPIN	VARIA	VIRGA	WAMUS	WHINE	WIZEN
UNRIG	VARIX	VIRID	WANEY	WHINY	WOALD
UNRIP	VARNA	VIRTU	WANLY	WHIPT	WOFUL
UNSAY	VARUS	VIRUS	WARTY	WHIRL	WOKEN
UNSET	VARVE	VISIT	WASHY	WHIRR	WOMAN
UNSEW	VASTY	VISTA	WASPY	WHISH	WOMBY
UNSEX	VATIC	VITAL	WASTE	WHISK	WOMEN
UNTIE	VAULT	VITTA	WATAP	WHIST	WONKY
UNTIL	VAUNT	VIVID	WATCH	WHITE	WOODY
UNWIT	VEALY	VIXEN	WATER	WHITY	WOOER
UNZIP	VEENA	VIZIR	WAUGH	WHIZZ	WOOLY
UPDRY	VEERY	VIZOR	WAVER	WHOLE	WOOPS
UPEND	VEGAN	VOCAL	WAVEY	WHOMP	WOOSH
UPPED	VEINY	VOCES	WAXEN	WHOOP	WOOZY
UPPER	VELAR	VODKA	WAXER	WHORE	WORDY
UPSET	VELDT	VODUM	WEALD	WHORL	WORLD
URAEI	VELUM	VOICE	WEARY	WHORT	WORMY
URARE	VENAL	VOILE	WEAVE	WHOSE	WORKY
URARI	VENGE	VOLAR	WEBBY	WHOSO	WORSE
URASE	VENIN	VOLTA	WEBER	WHUMP	WORST

WORTH	YOLKY	A	ADJOIN	ALIDAD	ANNEAL
WOULD	YOUNG		ADJUST	ALIGHT	ANNUAL
WOUND		ABACUS	ADMIRE	ALINER	ANOINT
WOVEN	YOURS	ABASER	ADORER	ALIPED	ANSWER
WRACK	YOUSE	ABATER	ADRIFT	ALKANE	ANTHEM
WRAPT	YOUTH	ABATIS	ADROIT	ALKINE	ANTICK
WREAK	YOWIE	ABATOR	ADVENT	ALKYNE	ANTING
WRECK	YUCCA	ABBACY	ADVERB	ALLEGE	ANTLER
WREST	YULAN	ABBESS	ADVERT	ALLIED	ANURIA
WRIED	YUMMY	ABDUCE	ADVISE	ALLIES	ANYHOW
WRING	YUPON	ABDUCT	AERATE	ALLUDE	ANYONE
WRIST		ABIDER	AERIAL	ALLURE	ANYWAY
WRITE	Z	ABJECT	AEROBE	ALMOND	APACHE
WRONG		ABJURE	AFEARD	ALMOST	APATHY
WROTE	ZAIRE	ABLATE	AFFAIR	ALMUDE	APHTHA
WROTH	ZAMIA	ABLAUT	AFFECT	ALPACA	APICAL
WRUNG	ZANZA	ABLAZE	AFFINE	ALPINE	APIECE
WURST	ZAYIN	ABLEST	AFFIRM	ALSIKE	APNOEA
	ZEBEC	ABLINS	AFFORD	ALTHEA	APOGEE
X	ZEBRA	ABOARD	AFFRAY	ALUMIN	APOLLO
	ZESTY	ABOLLA	AFLOAT	ALVINE	APOLOG
XEBEC	ZILCH	ABORAL	AFRESH	ALWAYS	APPEAL
XENIA	ZINCY	ABOUND	AFTERS	AMADOU	APPEAR
XYLEM	ZINGY	ABRADE	AGAMIC	AMAZON	APPEND
XYLOL	ZIPPY	ABROAD	AGEDLY	AMBEER	APPOSE
XYLYL	ZOMBI	ABRUPT	AGEING	AMBLER	ARABLE
	ZONER	ABSENT	AGENCY	AMBUSH	ARBOUR
Y	ZOOID	ABSORB	AGHAST	AMERCE	ARCADE
	ZOOKS	ABSURD	AGLEAM	AMIDOL	ARCTIC
YACHT	ZORIL	ABULIA	AGNATE	AMIDST	ARDOUR
YAGER	ZOWIE	ACAJOU	AGONIC	AMMINE	AREOLA
YAHOO		ACCEDE	AGRAFE	AMMINO	ARGALI
YAIRD		ACCENT	AHCHOO	AMNION	ARGENT
YAMEN		ACCEPT	AHORSE	AMOEBA	ARGYLE
YAMUN		ACCESS	AIDMAN	AMOUNT	ARGYLL
YAPOK		ACCOST	AIGRET	AMPULE	ARIGHT
YAPON		ACCUSE	AIKIDO	AMTRAC	ARISTA
YAULD		ACETIC	AIMFUL	AMULET	ARMADA
YEARN		ACHIER	AIRBUS	AMYLIC	ARMFUL
YEAST		ACIDIC	AIRILY	ANABAS	ARMLET
YENTA		ACIDLY	AIRING	ANALLY	ARMORY
YEUKY		ACNODE	AIRWAY	ANALOG	ARMOUR
YIELD		ACQUIT	ALANIN	ANARCH	ARMPIT
YINCE		ACROSS	ALASKA	ANCHOR	AROUND
YIPES		ACTING	ALATED	ANCONE	AROUSE
YIRTH		ACTION	ALBINO	ANEMIA	ARRACK
YODLE		ACTIVE	ALCADE	ANGINA	ARREAR
YOGEE		ACUITY	ALCOVE	ANGLER	ARREST
YOGIC		ADAGIO	ALDOSE	ANIMAL	ARRIVE
YOGIN		ADDICT	ALEXIA	ANKLET	ARSENO
YOKEL		ADENYL	ALGOID	ANLAGE	ARSINE

ARTERY	AVAUNT	BALLON	BAULKY	BEMEAN	BIRLER
ARTFUL	AVENGE	BALLOT	BAWDRY	BEMOCK	BISHOP
ARTIST	AVENUE	BAMBOO	BAWLER	BENAME	BISQUE
ASCEND	AVERSE	BANANA	BAZAAR	BENDER	BISTRE
ASCENT	AVIDIN	BANDER	BEACHY	BENIGN	BIZONE
ASHLER	AVIDLY	BANDOG	BEACON	BENNET	BLAMER
ASHMAN	AVOCET	BANGLE	BEADLE	BENZIN	BLANCH
ASHORE	AVOUCH	BANING	BEAGLE	BENZOL	BLASTY
ASKING	AVULSE	BANISH	BEAKER	BENZYL	BLAZER
ASLANT	AWAKEN	BANKER	BEARER	BERATE	BLAZON
ASLEEP	AWEARY	BANNED	BEAUTY	BERLIN	BLEARY
ASLOPE	AWEIGH	BANNER	BEAVER	BESEEM	BLENCH
ASPIRE	AWHIRL	BANNET	BECAME	BESIDE	BLIMEY
ASSAIL	AWLESS	BANTER	BECKET	BESTOW	BLINTZ
ASSENT	AWNING	BARBAL	BECOME	BESTUD	BLITHE
ASSERT	AXEMAN	BARBEL	BEDBUG	BETAKE	BLOCKY
ASSESS	AXILLA	BARBER	BEDDED	BETIDE	BLOODY
ASSIGN	AXLIKE	BARBET	BEDDER	BETISE	BLOTCH
ASSOIL	AZALEA	BARDIC	BEDELL	BETOOK	BLOTTO
ASSUME	AZONAL	BARELY	BEDLAM	BETRAY	BLOUSE
ASSURE	AZOTIC	BARFLY	BEDPAN	BETTER	BLOUSY
ASTHMA	AZYGOS	BARGEE	BEDRID	BETTOR	BLOWER
ASTRAY		BARHOP	BEDRUG	BEVIES	BLOWSY
ASTUTE	B	BARIUM	BEEBEE	BEWARE	BLOWZY
ASWIRL		BARKER	BEECHY	BHAKTI	BLUEST
ASYLUM	BABBLE	BARLOW	BEEPER	BIAXAL	BLUISH
ATAVIC	BABIED	BARONY	BEETLE	BIBBER	BOATEL
ATAXIC	BABIES	BARQUE	BEFALL	BICARB	BOBBIN
ATLATL	BABOON	BARRED	BEFLEA	BICKER	BOBBLE
ATONAL	BACKER	BARREL	BEFOOL	BICRON	BOCCIA
ATONIC	BACKUP	BARREN	BEFORE	BIDING	BODICE
ATRIUM	BADDIE	BARRET	BEFOUL	BIFFIN	BODIED
ATTACH	BADGER	BARROW	BEGAZE	BIFLEX	BODILY
ATTACK	BADMAN	BARTER	BEGGAR	BIFOLD	BODKIN
ATTAIN	BAFFLE	BASING	BEGLAD	BIFORM	BOFFIN
ATTEND	BAGASS	BASELY	BEGONE	BIKING	BOGGED
ATTEST	BAGFUL	BASHER	BEGULF	BIKINI	BOGGLE
ATTIRE	BAGGED	BASIFY	BEHALF	BILBOA	BOILER
ATTORN	BAGGIE	BASKET	BEHAVE	BILKER	BOLERO
ATWAIN	BAGUET	BASSET	BEHELD	BILLET	BOLIDE
AUBURN	BAILEE	BASSLY	BEHEST	BILLON	BOLLOX
AUDILE	BAILER	BASTER	BEHOLD	BINARY	BOLSON
AUGEND	BAILOR	BATBOY	BEHOVE	BINDER	BOMBER
AUGITE	BAITER	BATHER	BEHOWL	BINDLE	BONBON
AUNTIE	BAKERY	BATHOS	BEKNOT	BINNED	BONDER
AURIST	BAKING	BATING	BELAUD	BIOGEN	BONDUC
AUROUS	BALATA	BATMAN	BELFRY	BIOPSY	BONING
AUTHOR	BALDLY	BATTEN	BELIKE	BIOTIC	BONSAI
AUTISM	BALING	BATTER	BELIVE	BIOTIN	BONZER
AUTUMN	BALKER	BATTLE	BELLOW	BIRDIE	BOOTEE
AVATAR	BALLET	BAUBLE	BELONG	BIREME	BOOTIE

BORAGE	BROLLY		CAPOTE	CAYMAN	CHETAH
BORANE	BROMAL	CABALA	CAPRIC	CAYUSE	CHIASM
BORDER	BROMID	CABANA	CARAFE	CEBOID	CHIDER
BOREAL	BROMIN	CABLET	CARATE	CEDING	CHIMAR
BORING	BRONZY	CABMAN	CARBOY	CEILER	CHIMER
BORSCH	BROOMY	CACHET	CARCEL	CELERY	CHINCH
BORSHT	BROWNY	CACKLE	CARDIA	CELIAC	CHINTZ
BOSKER	BROWSE	CACTUS	CAREER	CELLAR	CHISEL
BOSQUE	BRUISE	CADDIS	CARESS	CEMENT	CHIVVY
BOSTON	BRUNET	CADENT	CARIBE	CENSOR	CHOICE
BOTANY	BRYONY	CAECUM	CARIES	CENTAL	CHOLER
BOTCHY	BUBBLY	CAEOMA	CARINA	CENTER	CHOOSY
BOUCLE	BUCCAL	CAGIER	CARING	CENTRE	CHORAL
BOUFFE	BUCKRA	CAGILY	CARNAL	CENTUM	CHORIC
BOUGIE	BUDDER	CAHIER	CARNEY	CERATE	CHORUS
BOUNCE	BUDDLE	CAJOLE	CARNIE	CERCIS	CHRISM
BOUNCY	BUDGET	CALASH	CAROCH	CEREAL	CHROME
BOVINE	BUGLER	CALCAR	CARPER	CERING	CHUKKA
BOWERY	BULBIL	CALCIC	CARPUS	CERITE	CHURCH
BOWFIN	BULBUL	CALESA	CARREL	CEROUS	CHYMIC
BOWLER	BULLET	CALICO	CARROT	CERUSE	CICADA
BOWPOT	BUMKIN	CALKER	CARTON	CERVIX	CICELY
BOWYER	BUMPER	CALKIN	CARVEL	CESIUM	CICERO
BOXFUL	BUNCHY	CALLAN	CARVER	CESTOS	CILIUM
BOXIER	BUNGLE	CALLET	CASAVA	CETANE	CINDER
BOXING	BUNION	CALLUS	CASEIN	CHACMA	CINEMA
BOYISH	BUNTER	CALPAC	CASERN	CHAETA	CIRQUE
BRACER	BURBLY	CALVES	CASING	CHAFER	CIRRUS
BRAGGY	BUREAU	CAMBIA	CASINO	CHAINE	CITHER
BRAISE	BURGER	CAMION	CASQUE	CHAISE	CITIED
BRAIZE	BURIAL	CAMISE	CASSIS	CHALET	CITIFY
BRANCH	BURIED	CAMLET	CASTLE	CHALLY	CITRAL
BRANNY	BURLEY	CAMPER	CASUAL	CHALOT	CITRIC
BRASHY	BURRED	CAMPUS	CATALO	CHAMMY	CITRUS
BRASIL	BURROW	CANAPE	CATCHY	CHAMPY	CIVISM
BRAVER	BURTON	CANARY	CATENA	CHANCY	CLAMOR
BRAWLY	BUSHEL	CANCER	CATION	CHANGE	CLAQUE
BRAYER	BUSILY	CANDID	CATKIN	CHANTY	CLARET
BRAZEN	BUSTER	CANDOR	CATNIP	CHAPEL	CLAUSE
BRAZIL	BUSTLE	CANFUL	CATSUP	CHARKA	CLAVER
BREATH	BUTANE	CANINE	CAUCUS	CHARRO	CLAWER
BREECH	BUTENE	CANING	CAUDAD	CHASER	CLAXON
BREEZY	BUTTER	CANKER	CAUDEX	CHASSE	CLEAVE
BREWIS	BUZZER	CANNOT	CAUGHT	CHASTE	CLEOME
BRIARD	BYGONE	CANOPY	CAULIS	CHAUNT	CLERIC
BRIDLE	BYPAST	CANTER	CAUSAL	CHEBEC	CLERID
BRINER	BYPLAY	CANTLE	CAUSEY	CHEDER	CLEVER
BRIONY	BYROAD	CANTOR	CAVEAT	CHEESE	CLIENT
BROACH	BYZANT	CANULA	CAVERN	CHEGOE	CLIMAX
BROCHE		CAPIAS	CAVIAR	CHEQUE	CLINAL
BROGUE	C	CAPITA	CAVORT	CHESTY	CLINCH

CLINIC	COLOUR	CORRAL	CUBAGE	DACTYL	DECENT
CLIQUE	COLUMN	CORSET	CUBING	DADDLE	DECIDE
CLIQUY	COLURE	CORTEX	CUDDLY	DAEMON	DECILE
CLOACA	COMATE	CORYMB	CUDGEL	DAGGER	DECKEL
CLODDY	COMBAT	COSHER	CUISSE	DAHLIA	DECKLE
CLOGGY	COMEDO	COSIES	CULLET	DAIKER	DECODE
CLONIC	COMEDY	COSIGN	CULTCH	DAIMIO	DECREE
CLOSER	COMELY	COSINE	CULVER	DAINTY	DECURY
CLOSET	COMING	COSMOS	CUMBER	DAKOIT	DEDUCE
CLOTTY	COMITY	COTEAU	CUMMIN	DALLES	DEEJAY
CLOUGH	COMMIE	COTTAR	CUNEAL	DAMAGE	DEEPLY
CLOVEN	COMMON	COTYPE	CUPOLA	DAMASK	DEFACE
CLUBBY	COMOUS	COUGAR	CUPPER	DAMMED	DEFEAT
CLUMPY	COMPEL	COULEE	CUPRIC	DAMMER	DEFIES
CLUMSY	COMPLY	COUPON	CUPULA	DAMPEN	DEFINE
CLUTCH	CONCHA	COUTER	CURACY	DAMPER	DEFOAM
COALER	CONCUR	COVERT	CURARI	DAMSEL	DEFRAY
COARSE	CONDOR	COVING	CURATE	DAMSON	DEFUSE
COATEE	CONFAB	COWPEA	CURBER	DANDLE	DEGAMI
COAXAL	CONFER	COYISH	CURING	DANGLE	DEGREE
COAXER	CONGER	COYOTE	CURIUM	DAPHNE	DEHORT
COBALT	CONIES	COZIES	CURLEW	DAPPLE	DEIFIC
COCAIN	CONING	CRACKY	CURRAN	DARING	DELATE
COCCIC	CONKER	CRAGGY	CURRIE	DARKEN	DELEAD
COCCID	CONNER	CRANCH	CURSER	DARKLY	DELETE
COCCYX	CONOID	CRANNY	CURULE	DARNED	DELIME
COCKER	CONSOL	CRASES	CURVET	DARNEL	DELUGE
COCOON	CONSUL	CRATON	CUSHAW	DARTER	DEMAND
CODDLE	CONTRA	CRAVAT	CUSPIS	DASSIE	DEMARK
CODEIN	CONVEY	CRAVER	CUSTOS	DATARY	DEMENT
CODGER	CONVOY	CRAYON	CUTESY	DATCHA	DEMISE
COELOM	COOKEY	CREAKY	CUTLAR	DATIVE	DEMODE
COEMPT	COOLIE	CREATE	CUTOUT	DATURA	DEMOTE
COERCE	COOLLY	CREDAL	CUTTLE	DAUBER	DENARY
COEVAL	COOPER	CREESH	CYANID	DAUTIE	DENGUE
COFFEE	COOTIE	CREOLE	CYANIN	DAWDLE	DENIES
COFFER	COPECK	CRESOL	CYBORG	DAYBED	DENOTE
CPGENT	COPIES	CRETIN	CYCLIC	DAZZLE	DENTAL
COGITO	COPING	CRIMPY	CYESIS	DEACON	DENTIN
COGNAC	COPPER	CRINGE	CYMBAL	DEADEN	DEODAR
COHEIR	COPULA	CRISIS	CYMOID	DEAFEN	DEPEND
COHERE	COQUET	CRISTA	CYMOSE	DEALER	DEPICT
COHUNE	CORBAN	CROAKY	CYPRES	DEARLY	DEPLOY
COILER	CORDER	CROCUC	CYPRUS	DEASIL	DEPOSE
COITUS	CORDON	CROUPE	CYSTIC	DEBARK	DEPUTY
COLEUS	CORING	CROZER		DEBASE	DERIDE
COLLAR	CORNEA	CRUDDY	D	DEBRIS	DERIVE
COLLET	CORNET	CRUISE		DEBTOR	DESALT
COLLOP	CORNUS	CRURAL	DABBER	DECADE	DESCRY
COLONI	CORONA	CRUTCH	DABBLE	DECANE	DESIRE
COLONY	CORPSE	CRYPTO	DACOIT	DECEIT	DESORB

DESPOT	DIRECT	DOURLY	E	EMEROD	ESCAPE
DETAIN	DIRHAM	DOVISH		EMETIC	ESCARP
DETENT	DISARM	DOWERY	EAGLET	EMEUTE	ESCORT
DETEST	DISCUS	DOWNER	EARFUL	EMODIN	ESPIES
DETOUR	DISMAL	DOWSER	EARING	EMPALE	ESPRIT
DEVEIN	DISMAY	DOYLEY	EARNER	EMPIRE	ESTEEM
DEVISE	DISPEL	DOZILY	EARTHY	ENABLE	ESTRAY
DEVOID	DISTAL	DOZING	EARWAX	ENAMEL	ESTRUS
DEVOIR	DISTIL	DRACHM	EASIER	ENCAGE	ETCHER
DEVOUR	DITHER	DRAFTY	EASILY	ENCASH	ETHANE
DEWILY	DIVERT	DRAGEE	EASTER	ENCORE	ETHNIC
DEWORM	DIVIDE	DRAGON	EATERY	ENCYST	ETHOXY
DEXTER	DIVING	DRAPER	EATING	ENDEAR	ETHYNE
DEXTRO	DOABLE	DRAWER	ECARTE	ENDIVE	ETOILE
DHARNA	DOBBIN	DRAWLY	ECHARD	ENDRIN	EUCHRE
DHOOTI	DOBIES	DREDGE	ECHOER	ENDURO	EULOGY
DHURNA	DOCILE	DREICH	ECHOEY	ENFACE	EUREKA
DIACID	DOCKET	DREIGH	ECLAIR	ENGAGE	EUTAXY
DIADEM	DOCTOR	DRIFTY	ECTYPE	ENGINE	EVADER
DIALER	DODDER	DRIVEL	EDGIER	ENGLUT	EVENER
DIALOG	DODGER	DROGUE	EDGING	ENGULF	EVENLY
DIAMIN	DOGDOM	DROLLY	EDIBLE	ENIGMA	EVILLY
DIAPER	DOGGER	DRONGO	EELIER	ENLACE	EVINCE
DIAPIR	DOGLEG	DROPSY	EFFACE	ENLIST	EVOLVE
DIAZIN	DOILED	DROSSY	EFFETE	ENMITY	EXACTA
DIBBER	DOITED	DROUTH	EFFLUX	ENNUYE	EXAMEN
DICAST	DOLING	DROWSE	EFFORT	ENRAGE	EXCEED
DICING	DOLLAR	DRUMLY	EGESTA	ENRICH	EXCEPT
DICKEY	DOLLOP	DUALLY	EGGNOG	ENROOT	EXCITE
DICTUM	DOLMEN	DUCKER	EGOISM	ENSILE	EXEDRA
DIDACT	DOMAIN	DUDEEN	EGRESS	ENTAIL	EXEMPT
DIDIES	DOMING	DUELLO	EIGHTH	ENTERA	EXHALE
DIESEL	DOMINO	DUENNA	EJECTA	ENTICE	EXHUME
DIESIS	DONATE	DUFFER	ELAPID	ENTITY	EXILIC
DIETER	DONNEE	DUIKER	ELAPSE	ENTOIL	EXODOS
DIFFER	DOOLIE	DULCET	ELATER	ENTREE	EXOGEN
DIGAMY	DOOZER	DUNKER	ELEGIT	ENVIED	EXOTIC
DIKTAT	DOPANT	DUNNER	ELEVEN	ENWRAP	EXPEND
DILATE	DOPIER	DUOLOG	ELFISH	ENZYME	EXPIRY
DILUTE	DORADO	DUPING	ELIXIR	EPARCH	EXPORT
DIMITY	DORMER	DURBAR	ELOIGN	EPHEBE	EXTANT
DIMOUT	DORMIN	DURESS	ELOPER	EPIGON	EXTERN
DIMPLE	DORPER	DURING	ELUATE	EPIMER	EXTORT
DINDLE	DORSUM	DURION	ELUENT	EPONYM	EYEFUL
DINERO	DOSAGE	DUSTUP	ELVISH	EQUATE	EYELET
DINING	DOSSAL	DYABLE	EMBARK	EQUINE	
DIOBOL	DOSSER	DYADIC	EMBLEM	ERASER	F
DIOXID	DOTIER	DYEING	EMBOLI	ERENOW	
DIPOLE	DOUBLE	DYNAMO	EMBOSK	ERGATE	FABLER
DIPSAS	DOUBLY	DYNODE	EMBRUE	ERMINE	FACADE
DIQUAT	DOUCHE		EMBRYO	ERRATA	FACETE

FACIAL	FELINE	FLAMEN	FORMOL	FURROW	GARVEY
FACILE	FELLAH	FLANGE	FORNIX	FUSAIN	GASKIN
FACING	FELLOW	FLAPPY	FORRIT	FUSING	GASSES
FACTOR	FELONY	FLATUS	FORTIS	FUSION	GATING
FACULA	FEMALE	FLAUNT	FOSTER	FUSTIC	GAUCHE
FADING	FENDER	FLAVIN	FOUGHT	FUTILE	GAUCHO
FAECES	FENNEC	FLAXEN	FOULLY	FUZING	GAVAGE
FAILLE	FERBAM	FLECHE	FOURTH		GAVIAL
FAIRLY	FERITY	FLEDGE	FOWLER	G	GAWKER
FAKEER	FEBLIE	FLEECE	FOXING		GAYETY
FAKERY	FERREL	FLENCH	FRACAS	GABBED	GAZEBO
FAKING	FERRIC	FLETCH	FRAISE	GABBLE	GAZING
FALCON	FERULA	FLEURY	FRAMER	GABION	GEISHA
FALLACY	FERVID	FLIMSY	FRAPPE	GADDER	GELADA
FALLER	FESCUE	FLINTY	FRATER	GADFLY	GELATE
FALLOW	FESTER	FLOCKY	FREEST	GADGET	GELDER
FALTER	FETIAL	FLOOEY	FRENCH	GAFFER	GELLED
FAMILY	FETISH	FLORAL	FRENUM	GAGGER	GEMOTE
FAMINE	FETTER	FLORET	FRESCO	GAGGLE	GENERA
FAMING	FEUDAL	FLOSSY	FRIARY	GAGING	GENIAL
FAMISH	FIANCE	FLOURY	FRIDGE	GAIETY	GENIUS
FAMOUS	FIASCO	FLUENT	FRIEZE	GAINER	GENTIL
FANEGA	FIBRIL	FLUKEY	FRIGID	GAINLY	GENTRY
FANJET	FIBULA	FLURRY	FRILLY	GAITER	GEODIC
FANNER	FICKLE	FLYMAN	FRINGE	GALAGO	GERBIL
FANTOD	FIDGET	FOAMER	FRISKY	GALAXY	GERMAN
FANTOM	FIERCE	FODDER	FRIVOL	GALENA	GERUND
FARCER	FIESTA	FOETAL	FROGGY	GALIOT	GEYSER
FARDEL	FILIAL	FOETOR	FROLIC	GALLEY	GHARRY
FARFEL	FILING	FOETUS	FROSTY	GALLON	GHERAO
FARING	FILLET	FOGGER	FROUZY	GALLOP	GHETTO
FARMER	FILMIC	FOISON	FROWSY	GALOOT	GHOSTY
FARROW	FILTER	FOLATE	FRUGAL	GALYAC	GIAOUR
FASCIA	FIMBLE	FOLIAR	FRUSTA	GAMBIA	GIBBON
FASTEN	FINALE	FOLIUM	FUCOID	GAMBLE	GIGGLY
FATHOM	FINELY	FOLLOW	FUDDLE	GAMBOL	GIGOLO
FATTEN	FINEST	FOMENT	FUELER	GAMETE	GILDER
FAUCAL	FINIAL	FONDLE	FUGGED	GAMINE	GILLER
FAUCET	FINITE	FOOTLE	FULFIL	GAMING	GIMBAL
FAULTY	FIRING	FOOZLE	FULMAR	GAMMON	GIMLET
FAVOUR	FIRMLY	FORAGE	FUMIER	GANGLY	GIMMAL
FAWNER	FISCAL	FORBID	FUMING	GANOID	GINGER
FEARER	FISTIC	FORCER	FUNDUS	GANTRY	GINNER
FEATLY	FITCHY	FOREBY	FUNGAL	GAPPED	GIPPER
FECIAL	FIXATE	FOREDO	FUNGIC	GARAGE	GIRDER
FECULE	FIXITY	FOREST	FUNKIA	GARBLE	GINING
FECUND	FIZGIG	FORGAT	FUNNEL	GARGET	GLACIS
FEDORA	FIZZLE	FORINT	FURANE	GARGLE	GLADLY
FEEDER	FLACON	FORKER	FURIES	GARNER	GLAIRE
FEELER	FLAGGY	FORMAL	FURLER	GARRET	GLAIVE
FEISTY	FLAKER	FORMEE	FURRED	GARTER	GLANCE

GLAZER	GRAZER	HADRON	HEARER	HIPPED	HOSTEL
GLEAMY	GREASY	HAEMIC	HEARSE	HIRPLE	HOSTLY
GLEETY	GREEDY	HAEMIN	HEARTH	HIRSLE	HOTBED
GLIDER	GREIGE	HAFFIT	HEATHY	HISPID	HOTBOX
GLIOMA	GRIEVE	HAFTER	HEAUME	HITHER	HOTDOG
GLITCH	GRIFFE	HAGDON	HEAVEN	HOAGIE	HOTROD
GLOBAL	GRIPER	HAGGED	HEAVER	HOARSE	HOTTED
GLOSSY	GRIPPE	HAGGLE	HECKLE	HOAXER	HOTTER
GLOVER	GRIPPY	HAILER	HECTIC	HOBBLE	HOURLY
GLUING	GRISLY	HAIRED	HECTOR	HOBNOB	HOUSER
GLYCAN	GRIVET	HAKEEM	HEDDLE	HOCKEY	HOWDAH
GLYCIN	GROCER	HALEST	HEDGER	HODDIN	HOWLET
GLYCYL	GROOVE	HALIDE	HEEDER	HOGGED	HOYDEN
GNARLY	GROPER	HALITE	HEELER	HOGGER	HUBRIS
GNATTY	GROUCH	HALLOT	HEFTER	HOGTIE	MUDDLE
GNEISS	GROUSE	HALTER	HEGIRA	HOLDER	HUGGED
GNOSIS	GROVEL	HAMAUL	HEIFER	HOLDUP	HUGGER
GOALIE	GROWER	HAMLET	HEINIE	HOLIES	HULLER
GOATEE	GROYNE	HAMMED	HELIAC	HOLILY	HUMANE
GOBBED	GRUTCH	HAMMER	HELIUM	HOLISM	HUMATE
GOBBET	GUAIAC	HANDLE	HELLER	HOLLER	HUMBLE
GOBIES	GUANIN	HANGAR	HELPER	HOLPEN	HUMMED
GOBLET	GUENON	HANSEL	HEMMED	HOMBRE	HUMMER
GOGGLE	GÜGGLE	HANTLE	HEMMER	HOMELY	HUMOUR
GOGLET	GUIDER	HAPTEN	HEMOID	HOMIER	HUNGER
GOITER	GUILTY	HARASS	HENBIT	HOMILY	HUNKER
GOLOSH	GÜIMPE	HARDEN	HEPTAD	HOMINY	HUNTER
GOODLY	GUINEA	HARDLY	HERALD	HONEST	HURDLE
GOOIER	GUITAR	HARING	HERBAL	HONIED	HURLER
GOORAL	GULLET	HARLOT	HERDIC	HONKER	HURLEY
GOOSEY	GULPER	HARMIN	HEREBY	HONOUR	HURRAY
GOPHER	GUNNEL	HARPER	HERESY	HOODIE	HURTER
GORGET	GUNSEL	HARROW	HEROIT	HOOFER	HURTLE
GORGON	GURGLE	HASLET	HERMIT	HOOKED	HUSKER
GORIER	GURNET	HASTEN	HEROIN	HOOKER	HUSSAR
GOSPEL	GUSHER	HATBOX	HERPES	HOOLIE	HUSTLE
GOSSIP	GUSSET	HATING	HETMAN	HOOPLA	HUTTED
GOTHIC	GUZZLE	HATRED	HEXADE	HOOPOE	HUZZAH
GOUGAR	GWEDUC	HATTER	HEXANE	HOOPOO	HYBRID
GOURDE	GYPPER	HAULER	HEXONE	HOORAH	HYDRIA
GOVERN	GYRATE	HAULMY	HEYDAY	HOOVES	HYETAL
GRADER	GYRING	HAVIOR	HIATUS	HOPING	HYMNAL
GRADUS	GYROSE	HAWKEY	HIDDEN	HOPPED	HYPHEN
GRAHAM		HAWSER	HIDING	HOPPER	HYPNIC
GRAINY	H	HAYING	HIGGLE	HORNET	
GRAMME		HAZARD	HIGHLY	HORRID	I
GRASSY	HABILE	HAZILY	HIGHTH	HORROR	
GRATER	HACKEE	HAZING	HILLER	HORSEY	IAMBIC
GRATIN	HACKIE	HEADER	HILLOA	HORSTE	IBIDEM
GRAVEN	HACKLE	HEALER	HINDER	HOSIER	ICEBOX
GRAVID	HACKLY	HEALTH	HINGER	HOSING	ICECAP

ICEMAN	INDOOR	INVOKE	JASPER	JURANT	KIDNAP
ICICLE	INDUCE	INWIND	JASSID	JURIST	KIDNEY
ICIEST	INDUCT	IODATE	JAUNTY	JUSTER	KILTER
IDEATE	INDULT	IODINE	JAZZER	JUSTLY	KILTIE
IDIOCY	INFANT	IODISM	JEJUNE		KINASE
IDLEST	INFARE	IODIZE	JEREED	K	KINDLE
IGNIFY	INFECT	IODOUS	JERKER		KINDLY
IGNITE	INFEST	IONISE	JERKIN	KABAKA	KINGLY
IGNORE	INFIRM	IONIZE	JESTER	KABAYA	KIRTLE
IGUANA	INFLOW	IPECAC	JESUIT	KABUKI	KISHKA
ILLITE	INFORM	IREFUL	JETSAM	KAINIT	KISHKE
ILLUME	INFUSE	IRENIC	JETSOM	KAISER	KISMET
IMARET	INGEST	IRIDES	JETTED	KALIAN	KITING
IMBARK	INGULE	IRIDIC	JETTON	KALIPH	KITTLE
IMBIBE	INHAUL	IRITIS	JEWELS	KALMIA	KNAWEL
IMBODY	INHERE	IRONIC	JIBBER	KALPAK	KNIFER
IMMANE	INJECT	IRREAL	JIGGLE	KAMSIN	KNIGHT
IMMIES	INJURE	IRRUPT	JIGGLY	KANTAR	KNIVES
IMMUNE	INKIER	ISATIN	JIMMY	KAPUTT	KNOTTY
IMMURE	INLACE	ISLINE	JINGAL	KARROO	KOBOLD
IMPACT	INLAND	ISOMER	JINGLE	KATION	KOLHOZ
IMPAIR	INMATE	ISOPOD	JINGLY	KAVASS	KOODOO
IMPALA	INNATE	ISSUER	JINKER	KEBBIE	KOPPIE
IMPALE	INNING	ISTHMI	JITNEY	KECKLE	KOSHER
IMPARK	INPOUR	ITALIC	JITTER	KEENER	KOUMIS
IMPART	INSANE	ITERUM	JOBBER	KEENLY	KOUMYS
IMPAWN	INSEAM	ITSELF	JOCKEY	KEEPER	KRATER
IMPEDE	INSECT	IXODID	JOCOSE	KEGLER	KRONOR
IMPEND	INSIDE		JOGGER	KELPIE	KUCHEN
IMPHEE	INSIST	J	JOGGLE	KELSON	KULTUR
IMPING	INSOLE		JOINER	KELTER	KUMISS
IMPISH	INSOUL	JABBER	JOKING	KELVIN	KUMMEL
IMPONE	INSPAN	JABIRU	JOLTER	KENNEL	KVETCH
IMPOSE	INSTAR	JACANA	JOSTLE	KEPPED	
IMPURE	INSTIL	JACKAL	JOUNCE	KERMES	L
IMPUTE	INSULT	JACKER	JOVIAL	KERMIS	
INARCH	INSURE	JAGGED	JOYFUL	KERRIA	LACUNA
INBORN	INTACT	JAGGER	JUBHAH	KERSEY	LADDIE
INCAGE	INTAKE	JAGUAR	JUBILE	KETENE	LADLER
INCEPT	INTEND	JALOPY	JUDGER	KETOSE	LAGEND
INCEST	INTENT	JAMMED	JUGFUL	KETTLE	LAGGER
INCISE	INTIMA	JAMMER	JUGGED	KEYSET	LAGOON
INCITE	INTIME	JANGLE	JUGULA	KEYWAY	LAGUNA
INCLIP	INTONE	JAPERY	JUICER	KHALIF	LAGUNE
INCONY	INTORT	JAPING	JUMBLE	KHEDAH	LAKING
INCULT	INTUIT	JARFUL	JUMPER	KIBBLE	LALLAN
INDEED	INULIN	JARGON	JUNGLE	KIBOSH	LAMBDA
INDENT	INVADE	JARINA	JUNGLY	KICKER	LAMBER
INDICT	INVERT	JARRAH	JUNIOR	KICKUP	LAMBIE
INDIGO	INVEST	JARRED	JUNKER	KIDDER	LAMEDH
INOITE	INVITE	JARVEY	JUNKET	KIDDIE	LAMINA

LAMING	LEAVES	LOCKUP		MANTIC	MAZILY
LAMMED	LECHER	LOCUST	M	MANTIS	MEAGER
LAMPAS	LECTOR	LOFTER		MANTLE	MEANER
LANATE	LEDGER	LOGGED	MACACO	MANTRA	MEANIE
LANCER	LEEWAY	LOGGIA	MACING	MANTUA	MEANLY
LANCET	LEGACY	LOGIER	MACRON	MANUAL	MEASLY
LANDER	LEGATO	LOGILY	MACULE	MAPPED	MEATAL
LANGUE	LEGGED	LOMENT	MADAME	MAQUIS	MEATUS
LANNER	LEGION	LONGAN	MADCAP	MARACA	MEDDLE
LANOSE	LEGUME	LONGER	MADDEN	MARAUD	MEDIAD
LAPDOG	LENGTH	LONGLY	MADDER	MARBLE	MEDIAN
LAPFUL	LENITY	LOOKER	MADMAN	MARBLY	MEDICO
LAPSUS	LENTIC	LOOSEN	MAENAD	MARGAY	MEDIUM
LARDER	LEPTON	LOOSER	MAFFIA	MARINA	MEDDLE
LARDON	LESION	LOPPED	MAGGOT	MARINE	MEDIAD
LARINE	LETHAL	LOQUAT	MAGILP	MARISH	MEDIAN
LARKER	LETTER	LORDLY	MAHOUT	MARKUP	MEDICK
LARRUP	LEUCIN	LOREAL	MAHZOR	MARMOT	MEDIUM
LARYNX	LEUKON	LORICA	MAIGRE	MAROON	MEDLAR
LASHER	LEVANT	LOSING	MAIHEM	MARQUE	MEDUSA
LASTLY	LEVIES	LOTION	MAILER	MARRAM	METTER
LATEEN	LIABLE	LOUDEN	MAIMER	MARRON	MEETLY
LATENT	LIAISE	LOUDLY	MAINLY	MARROW	MEGASS
LATEST	LIBBER	LOUNGE	MAKEUP	MARTEN	MEGILP
LATHER	LICHEE	LOUVER	MAKING	MARVEL	MEINIE
LATIGO	LICKER	LOVAGE	MALADY	MASCON	MELLOW
LATISH	LICTOR	LOVELY	MALATE	MASCOT	MELODY
LATTEN	LIENAL	LOVING	MALFED	MASHIE	MELOID
LATTIN	LIFTER	LOWBOY	MALGRE	MASJID	MELTER
LAUNCE	LIGASE	LOWERY	MALIGN	MASQUE	MELTON
LAUNCH	LIGULA	LOWISH	MALINE	MASSIF	MEMOIR
LAUREL	LIKEST	LUCERN	MALKIN	MASTER	MEMORY
LAVAGE	LIKING	LUCKIE	MALTED	MASTIC	MENACE
LAVEER	LIKUTA	LUGGER	MALTOL	MASTIX	MENDER
LAVING	LUMBER	LUGGIE	MAMMAL	MATING	MENHIR
LAWFUL	LIMBUS	LUMBER	MAMMER	MATRES	MENIAL
LAWMAN	LIQUOR	LUMPER	MAMMEY	MATTED	MENSAL
LAXITY	LISPER	LUNATE	MAMMON	MATTIN	MENTOR
LAYOFF	LISSOM	LUNGAN	MANAGE	MATURE	MERCER
LAYOUT	LITCHI	LUNULE	MANANA	MATZOH	MERGER
LAZIED	LITMUS	LURDAN	MANCHE	MATZOT	MERINO
LAZING	LITTER	LURKER	MANEGE	MAULER	MERLON
LEACHY	LITTLE	LUSTER	MANGEL	MAUMET	MESCAL
LEADER	LIVELY	LUSTRA	MANGEY	MAXIMA	MESSAN
LEAGUE	LIVIER	LUSTRE	MANGLE	MAXIXE	MESTEE
LEAKER	LIVING	LUTEIN	MANIAC	MAYEST	METAGE
LEAPER	LOBBED	LUTIST	MANITO	MAYFLY	METEOR
LEARNT	LOBULE	LYCEUM	MANITU	MAYING	METHOD
LEASER	LOCALE	LYRISM	MANNED	MAYPOP	METHYL
LEAVED	LOCATE	LYSATE	MANNER	MAYVIN	METOPE
LEAVER	LOCKET	LYSINE	MANTEL	MAZARD	METUMP

MEZCAL	MOBBER	MUCOSE	NAPKIN	NODOUS	OCTANE
MEZUZA	MOBILE	MUCOUS	NARROW	NOETIC	OCTANT
MICELL	MOCKER	MUDCAP	NARWAL	NONCOM	OCTIVE
MICRON	MOCKUP	MUDDER	NASION	NONFAT	OCTAVO
MIDAIR	MODERN	MUDDLE	NATION	NONMAN	OCTROI
MIDDAY	MODEST	MUFFIN	NATIVE	NOMPAR	OCULAR
MIDDLE	MODIFY	MUFFLE	NATRON	NONTAX	ODDITY
MIDGET	MODISH	MUGGAR	NATURE	NONUSE	ODIOUS
MIDRIB	MODULO	MUGGER	NAUSEA	NOODLE	OEDEMA
MIDWAY	MOIETY	MULETA	NAUTCH	NOOSER	OEUVRE
MIGNON	MOILER	MULISH	NAVAID	NORITE	OFFICE
MIKADO	MOLDER	MULLEN	NAVIES	NORMED	OFFING
MIKVEJ	MOLEST	MULLET	NEARBY	NOSHER	OFFISH
MILAGE	MOLINE	MULLEY	NEATLY	NOSTOC	OGRISH
MILDEW	MOLLIE	MUMBLE	NEBULA	NOTARY	OGRISM
MILLER	MOLTER	MUREIN	NEBULY	NOTICE	OILCAN
MILLET	MOMISM	MURING	NECTAR	NOTING	OILIER
MILORD	MONGER	MURPHY	NEEDER	NOUGHT	OILILY
MIMBAR	MONGST	MURREY	NEEDLE	NOVENA	OILMAN
MIMOSA	MONISH	MURRHA	NEGATE	NOWAYS	OILWAY
MINCER	MONIST	MUSCLY	NELSON	NOWISE	OLEATE
MINGLE	MONKEY	MUSHER	NEPHEW	NUBBLE	OMELET
MINIFY	MONODY	MUSKIE	NEREID	NUBILE	ONAGER
MINIMA	MOOLEY	MUSKIT	NEREIS	NUCLEI	ONWARD
MINING	MOOTER	MUSTEE	NEROLI	NUDEST	OOCYTE
MINIUM	MOOPED	MUTANT	NESTER	NUDISM	OODLES
MINUET	MOPPER	MUTATE	NESTOR	NUDIST	OOMIAC
MIOTIC	MOPPET	MUTEST	NETTED	NUDITY	OPAQUE
MIRING	MORALS	MUTING	NETTER	NUMBER	OPENER
MIRROR	MORASS	MUTISM	NETTLE	NUMINA	OPENLY
MISACT	MORBID	MUTTON	NEURON	NUNCIO	OPERON
MISCUE	MORGEN	MUTUEL	NEUTER	NUNCLE	OPIATE
MISCUT	MOROSE	MUZHIK	NEWISH	NUTANT	OPPOSE
MISEAT	MORSEL	MYASIS	NEWTON	NUTLET	OPPUGN
MISERY	MORTAL	MYELIN	NICKER	NUTMEG	OPTICAL
MISHAP	MORULA	MYOSIS	NIDGET	NUTTED	OPTION
MISLAY	MOSQUE	MYOTIC	NIDIFY	NYMPHA	ORACLE
MISLIE	MOSTLY	MYRIAD	NIFFER		ORALLY
MISPEN	MOTHER	MYRICA	NIGGLE	O	ORATOR
MISSAL	MOTILE	MYTHIC	NIGHTY		ORBITAL
MISSEL	MOTION		NIMMED	OBJECT	ORCHID
MISSIS	MOTIVE	N	NIMROD	OBOLUS	ORDAIN
MISSUS	MOTLEY		NIPPER	OBSESS	ORDEAL
MISTER	MOTMOT	NAEVUS	NITRID	OBTAIN	ORDURE
MISUSE	MOULIN	NAGGER	NITRIL	OBTECT	ORGANA
MITHER	MOUSER	NAILER	NITWIT	OBTUSE	ORGASM
MITIER	MOUSEY	NAMELY	NOBBLE	OBVERT	ORIENT
MITRAL	MOUSEE	NAMING	NOBLER	OCCULT	ORIOLE
MITTEN	MOUTON	NANISM	NOCENT	OCCUPY	OROIDE
MIZZLE	MUCKER	NANKIN	NODDED	OCHERY	ORPHAN
MIZZLY	MUCKLE	NAPERY	NODDLE	OCHONE	ORRICE

OSCULA	PANFUL	PEDLER	PIECER	PLAYER	POTSIE
OSCULE	PANTRY	PEEPER	PIEING	PLEASE	POTTED
OSMIUM	PAPAIN	PEERIE	PIGEON	PLEDGE	POTTER
OSPREY	PAPERY	PEGBOX	PIGGED	PLEIAD	POUNCE
OSSIFY	PAPIST	PELITE	PIGGIN	PLENTY	POUTER
OSTEAL	PAPULA	PELLET	PIGLET	PLEURA	POWWOW
OSTIUM	PARAGE	PELOTA	PIGSTY	PLIANT	PRIASE
OSTOMY	PARAMO	PELTER	PILAFF	PLOIDY	PRANCE
OUTBID	PARENT	PELVIS	PILEUP	PLOWER	PRATER
OUTBOX	PARGET	PENCEL	PILFER	PLUMMY	PRAXIS
OUTEAT	PARITY	PENNED	PILLAR	PLUNGE	PREACH
OUTFIT	PARLAY	PENNER	PILLOW	PLURAL	PREAMP
OUTFOX	PARODY	PENNON	PILOUS	PLUSHY	PREARM
OUTING	PAROUS	PENTYL	PINANG	PLUTON	PREFER
OUTLAW	PARREL	PENULT	PINATA	POGIES	PREFIX
OUTLAY	PARROT	PEPLOS	PINCER	POGRAO	PREMED
OUTMAN	PARSON	PEPLUM	PINDER	POINTE	PREMIX
OUTPUT	PARTLY	PEPTID	PINERY	POINTY	PREPAY
OUTSET	PARTON	PERDIE	PINING	POISON	PRETOR
OUTSIT	PARVIS	PERMIT	PINION	POKIER	PREVUE
OUTWIT	PASSEL	PERUSE	PINKIE	POKIES	PRICEY
OVALLY	PASSER	PESADE	PINNAE	POLDER	PRICKY
OWLISH	PASTEL	PESTER	PINNED	POLICE	PRIEST
OXCART	PASTON	PETARD	PINNER	POLICY	PRIMLY
OXTAIL	PASTRY	PETITE	PINTLE	POLISH	PRINCE
OXYGEN	PATACA	PETTED	PINYON	POLITE	PRIORY
OYSTER	PATHOS	PETTER	PIOLET	POLLEE	PRISSY
	PATROL	PETTLE	PIPIER	POLLER	PRIVET
P	PATRON	PEWTER	PIQUET	POMADE	PROBER
	PATTED	PHALLI	PIRANA	POMELO	PROBIT
PACIFY	PATTEN	PHAROS	PISTIL	POMMEL	PROFIT
PACING	PATTIE	PHASIS	PISTON	POMPOM	PROJET
PACKER	PAULIN	PHENIX	PITCHY	PONDER	PROLAN
PAGODA	PAUNCH	PHENOL	PITTIED	PONTON	PROMPT
PAINCH	PAUPER	PHENYL	PITTIER	POODLE	PROPEL
PAINTY	PAUSER	PHOEBE	PITIES	POPGUN	PROPER
PAJAMA	PAVIOR	PHONEY	PITMAN	POPLAR	PROPYL
PALACE	PAWNEE	PHONIC	PITSAW	POPPER	PROTON
PALATE	PAWPAW	PHONON	PLACER	PORKER	PROVER
PALELY	PAYDAY	PHOTIC	PLACET	POROSE	PRUNER
PALING	PEACHY	PHRASE	PLACID	PORTAL	PSYCHE
PALISH	PEAHEN	PHYLAE	PLAGAL	PORTER	PUCKER
PALLID	PEANUT	PHYSIS	PLAGUE	PORTLY	PUDDLE
PALMAR	PEARLY	PHYTIN	PLAGUY	POSSET	PUGGED
PALMER	PEBBLE	PIAFFE	PLAINT	POSSUM	PURELY
PALPAL	PEBBLY	PIAZZA	PLANAR	POSTAL	PURISM
PALTER	PECHAN	PICKER	PLANCH	POSTER	PURLIN
PAMPER	PECTIN	PICKET	PLANET	POSTIN	PURPLE
PANADA	PEDANT	PICKLE	PLASMA	POTENT	PURRED
PANAMA	PEDDLE	PICNIC	PLATAN	POTHER	PURVEY
PANDIT	PEDLAR	PICRIC	PLATEN	POTION	PUSHER

PUTLOG	RAMJET	REFACE	RIPPLY	SAILER	SECOND
PUTRID	RAMMED	REFINE	RIPSAW	SAILOR	SECRET
PUTTER	RAMOSE	REFLEX	RITUAL	SALAMI	SECURE
PUZZLE	RAMOUS	REFUGE	RIVAGE	SALARY	SEDATE
PYRENE	RAMSON	REGALE	RIVING	SALIFY	SEDUCE
PYRITE	RANCHO	REGINA	ROAMER	SALIVA	SEEDER
PYRONE	RANCID	REGION	ROBBED	SALLOW	SEEKER
PYURIA	RANGER	REGIUS	ROBBER	SALMON	SEEMER
	RANKER	REGLET	ROCKET	SALOON	SEETHE
Q	RANSOM	REGRET	RODENT	SALTER	SEGGAR
	RAPIER	RELENT	RODMAN	SALUTE	SELDOM
QINDAR	RAPING	RELIED	ROLLER	SALVER	SELECT
QUAGGA	RAPIST	RELISH	ROMPER	SALVIA	SELVES
QUAGGY	RAPPEN	RELUME	ROOFER	SALVOR	SEMPLE
QUAICH	RAREFY	REMARK	ROOMER	SAMPLE	SENARY
QUALMY	RAREST	REMISS	ROOTER	SANDAL	SENATE
QUARTZ	RARIFY	REMOTE	ROPERY	SANDER	SENDAL
QUASAR	RASHER	RENDER	ROPING	SANITY	SENORA
QUATRE	RASING	RENNIN	ROSERY	SAVANT	SEPTIC
QUEAZY	RASSLE	RENTER	ROSINY	SAVOUR	SEQUEL
QUINCE	RATANY	REPAIR	ROSTER	SAWYER	SEQUIN
QUININ	RATHER	REPAND	ROTCHE	SAXONY	SERENE
QUINSY	RATLIN	REPENT	ROTTEN	SCABBY	SERIAL
QUIRKY	RATTAN	REPINE	ROUGHE	SCALAR	SESAME
QUIVER	RAVAGE	REPOSE	ROUPET	SCALER	SETOFF
	RAVINI	RESIDE	ROUSER	SCAMPI	SETOUT
R	RAWISH	RESIGN	ROVING	SCANTY	SETTER
	REAGIN	RESILE	ROWING	SCATTY	SETTLE
RABBET	REALLY	RESORT	RUBIES	SCHEME	SEVERE
RABBLE	REALTY	RESTER	RUBRIC	SCHISM	SEWING
RABIES	REAPER	RETAIL	RUFFLE	SCHLEP	SEXIER
RACHET	REASON	RETAIN	RUMBLE	SCHOOL	SEXUAL
RACIAL	REAVER	RETAKE	RUMBLY	SCILLA	SHAKER
RACISM	REBORN	RETARD	RUMMER	SCLERA	SHAMMY
RACKET	RECALL	RETENE	RUMPLE	SCONCE	SHANTI
RACKLE	RECESS	RETIAL	RUNDLE	SCORIA	SHAPER
RACOON	RECITE	RETIRE	RUNOFF	SCOUSE	SHARPY
RADISH	RECOIL	REVEAL	RUNOUT	SCRAOE	SHAVER
RADIUM	RECORD	REVERE	RURBAN	SCREAK	SHEATH
RADIUS	RECTOR	REVERT	RUSTIC	SCRIBE	SHEAVE
RAFFLE	RECTUM	REVISE	RUSTLE	SCROLL	SHEEVE
RAGBAG	RECUSE	REVOLT		SCUMMY	SHELLY
RAGMAN	REDACT	RHUMBA	S	SEABAG	SHERIF
RAGTAG	REDBUG	RHYTHM		SEADOG	SHERRY
RAIDER	REDBUG	RIBBON	SABBED	SEALER	SHEWER
RAILER	REDDEN	RIBOSE	SACBUT	SEAMAN	SHIFTY
RAISIN	REDEAR	RICHEN	SACRAL	SEARCH	SHIMMY
RAKING	REDEYE	RICHES	SACRED	SEARER	SHINNY
RAKISH	REDTOP	RICING	SADDEN	SEASON	SHIVER
RALLYE	REDUCE	RIPPER	SAFETY	SEAWAY	SHOGUN
RAMIFY	REEFER	RIPPLE	SAGGAR	SECEDE	SHOPPE

SHOVEL	SMARTY	SPLEEN	STUBBY	TANNIC	TINGLE
SHOWER	SMELLY	SPLICE	STUDIO	TARIFF	TINKLE
SHREWD	SMOGGY	SPLINT	STUMPY	TARMAC	TINSEL
SHRIMP	SMOKER	SPOOKY	STUPID	TARPAN	TINTER
SHRINK	SMOOCH	SPOUSE	STURDY	TARRED	TIPPED
SICKEN	SMOOTH	SPRAIN	SUBDUE	TARSAL	TIPPLE
SICKLE	SMUDGE	SPREAD	SUBLET	TARTAN	TIPTOE
SIDING	SMUDGY	SPRING	SUBMIT	TARTAR	TIPTOP
SIFTER	SMUGLY	SPRINT	SUBURB	TARTLY	TIRING
SIGHER	SMUTTY	SPRITE	SUBWAY	TARZAN	TISSUE
SIGNAL	SNAGGY	SPRUCE	SUCKER	TASSIE	TITBIT
SIGNET	SNAPPY	SQUALL	SUCKLE	TASTER	TOASTY
SILENT	SNALRY	SQUARE	SUFFIX	TATTED	TOGATE
SILKEN	SNATCH	SQUEAK	SUGARY	TATTER	TOGGLE
SILVER	SNIPER	SQUEAL	SUITOR	TATTLE	TOILET
SIMPLE	SNIPPY	SQUINT	SULFUR	TATTOO	TOLING
SIMPLY	SNOBBY	SQUIRM	SULLEN	TAUGHT	TOLLER
SINFUL	SNOOPY	SQUIRT	SULTAN	TAXMAN	TOMBOY
SINGLE	SNOOTY	STABLE	SUNDAE	TEAPOT	TONGUE
SINKER	SNOOZY	STAGER	SUNDER	TEMPER	TONING
SINNER	SNUFFY	STALKY	SUNTAN	TENSOR	TONSIL
SIPHON	SOAKER	STANCE	SUPPLE	TETTER	TOOLER
SISTER	SOBBER	STAPLE	SUPPLY	THALER	TOPFUL
SITTEN	SOCCER	STARCH	SURELY	THATCH	TOPING
SIZING	SOCIAL	STARVE	SURFER	THEORY	TOPPED
SKATER	SOCKET	STATIC	SURREY	THINLY	TOPPLE
SKEWER	SODDEN	STATUE	SURVEY	THIRST	TORRID
SKIBOB	SOFTER	STEADY	SWAMPY	THORAX	TOTTER
SKIDDY	SOFTIE	STEAMY	SWAYER	THORNY	TOWARD
SKINNY	SOLACE	STICKY	SWEATY	THOUGH	TRADER
SKYCAP	SOLEMN	STIFLE	SYMBOL	THRALL	TRASHY
SKYMAN	SOLUTE	STIGMA	SYSTEM	THRASH	TRAVEL
SKYWAY	SOMBER	STINKY		THREAD	TRICKY
SLAKER	SONDER	STITCH	T	THREAT	TRIFLE
SLATER	SONNET	STOCKY		THRIFT	TRIMER
SLAVER	SORBIC	STONEY	TABBED	THRIVE	TRIPOD
SLEAVE	SORELY	STOPER	TABLET	THRONE	TRIVET
SLEAZY	SORROW	STOUND	TACKER	THWART	TRIVIA
SLEEKY	SORTER	STRAIN	TACKET	THYMIC	TROLLY
SLEEVE	SOURCE	STRAKE	TACKLE	TICKLE	TROPHY
SLEUTH	SPACER	STRAND	TACTIC	TICTAC	TROPIC
SLICER	SPADER	STREAK	TALCUM	TICTOC	TRUFFE
SLIDER	SPARKY	STRICT	TALKIE	TIDBIT	TRUSTY
SLIGHT	SPARSE	STRIDE	TALLOW	TIDIES	TUBBER
SLIMLY	SPECIE	STRIKE	TAMALE	TIGHTS	TUBING
SLIVER	SPEECH	STRING	TAMELY	TILTER	TUCKET
SLOGAN	SPEEDY	STRIPE	TAMPER	TIMBER	TUFFET
SLOPER	SPEWER	STRIVE	TANDEM	TIMELY	TUFTER
SLOPPY	SPHERE	STRODE	TANGLE	TIMING	TUGGER
SLOUCH	SPHINX	STROKE	TANKER	TINDER	TUMBLE
SLUSHY	SPLASH	STRONG	TANNER	TINFUL	TUNING

TURBAN	UPRISE		WHINNY	YONDER
TURBID	UPROSE	WADDER	WHIRLY	YOWLER
TURBIT	UPSTEP	WADDLE	WHOLLY	
TURKEY	UPWIND	WADIES	WICKED	Z
TURNIP	URGENT	WADING	WICKER	
TURTLE	URINAL	WAFERY	WICKET	ZADDIC
TUSSLE	USABLE	WAFFLE	WIGGLY	ZAFFER
TWANGY		WAFTER	WIGWAM	FANANA
TWEAKY	V	WAGGED	WILDER	ZANDER
TWIGGY		WAGGER	WILDLY	ZANIES
TWIRLY	VACATE	WAGGLE	WINDLE	ZAREBA
TWOFER	VADOSE	WAGGLY	WINDOW	ZEATIN
TYMBAL	VAGINA	WAILER	WINDUP	ZECHIN
TYPHON	VALLEY	WAIVER	WINKER	ZENITH
TYPHUS	VALOUR	WAKIKI	WIRING	ZIGZAG
TYPING	VALVAR	WALIES	WISDOM	ZIZZLE
TYPIST	VAMOSE	WALKER	WISHER	ZODIAC
	VANDAL	WALLIE	WITHER	ZOMBIE
U	VANITY	WALLOP	WITHIN	ZONING
	VASSAL	WALLOW	WIZARD	ZOYSIA
UBIQUE	VAULTY	WALRUS	WONDER	ZYGOTE
UGLIER	VECTOR	WAMPUM	WOODEN	
UGLIFY	VELOUR	WAMPUS	WOODSY	
UGSOME	VELVET	WANDLE	WOOFER	
ULTIMA	VENDER	WANTON	WOOLLY	
UMPIRE	VENEER	WARDEN	WORKER	
UNBEND	VERBAL	WARIER	WORKUP	
UNBIND	VERIFY	WARMLY	WRIGHT	
UNBOLT	VERTEX	WARMUP	WRITER	
UNCAGE	VESPER	WARPER		
UNCAKE	VICTIM	WARREN	X	
UNCASE	VIEWER	WARSAW		
UNCOIL	VIKING	WASHER	XYLENE	
UNCURL	VILIFY	WATERY	XYLOID	
UNDOCK	VINERY	WAVERY	XYLOSE	
UNISEX	VIOLET	WEAKEN	XYSTER	
UNLEAD	VIOLIN	WEAKLY	XYSTUS	
UNLOAD	VIRTUE	WEAPON		
UNLOCK	VISION	WEARER	Y	
UNMOLD	VITALS	WEASEL		
UNREST	VIVARY	WEDDER	YABBER	
UNROLL	VOICER	WEDGIE	YAMMER	
UNSNAP	VOIDER	WEEDER	YAPPER	
UNTIDY	VOLLEY	WEEKLY	YASMAK	
UPBEAT	VOLUME	WEEPER	YAWPER	
UPDATE	VORTEX	WEEVIL	YEARLY	
UPGAZE	VOTIVE	WEINER	YELLER	
UPHELD	VOYAGE	WELDER	YELPER	
UPHOLD	VULGAR	WELTER	YESTER	
UPKEEP		WHEEZY	YOGURT	
UPMOST	W	WHIMSY	YOKING	

MOUNTAINS NAMES	LOCATION	HEIGHT IN FEET
McKinley	Alaska	20,320
St. Elias	Alaska-Canada	18,008
Foraker	Alaska	17,400
Bona	Alaska	16,550
Blackburn	Alaska	16,390
Kennedy	Alaska	16,286
Sanford	Alaska	16,237
South Buttress	Alaska	15,885
Vancouver	Alaska-Canada	15,700
Churchill	Alaska	15,638
Fairweather	Alaska-Canada	15,300
Hubbard	Alaska-Canada	15,015
Bear	Alaska	14,831
East Buttress	Alaska	14,730
Hunter	Alaska	14,573
Alverstone	Alaska-Canada	14,565
Browne Tower	Alaska	14,530
Whitney	California	14,494
Elbert	Colorado	14,433
Massive	Colorado	14,421
Harvard	Colorado	14,420
Rainer	Washington	14,410
Williamson	California	14,375
Blanca Peak	Colorado	14,345
La Plata	Colorado	14,336
Uncompahgre	Colorado	14,309
Crestone	Colorado	14,294
Lincoln	Colorado	14,286
Grays Peak	Colorado	14,270
Antero	Colorado	14,269
Torreys	Colorado	14,267
Castle	Colorado	14,265
Quandary	Colorado	14,265
Evans	Colorado	14,264
Longs Peak	Colorado	14,256
Wilson	Colorado	14,246
White	California	14,246
North Palisade	California	14,242
Shavano	Colorado	14,229
Belford	Colorado	14,197
Princeton	Colorado	14,197
Crestone Needle	Colorado	14,197
Yale	Colorado	14,196
Bross	Colorado	14,172
Kit Carson	Colorado	14,165
Wrangell	Alaska	14,163
Shasta	California	14,162

RIVERS	FLOWS INTO	LENGTH IN MILES
Alabama	Mobile River	729
Albany	James Bay	610
Arkansas	Mississippi River, Ar.	1,459
Brazos	Gulf of Mexico	923
Canadian	Arkansas River, Ok.	906
Cimarron	Arkansas River, Ok.	600
Colorado (Ariz.)	Gulf of Mexico	1,450
Colorado (Texas)	Matagorda Bay	862
Cumberland	Ohio River	720
Fraser	Strait of Georgia	850
Gila	Colorado River, Az.	649
Green (Ut.- Wyo.)	Colorado River, Ut.	730
Illinois	Mississippi River	420
James (N.D.- S.D.)	Missouri River, S.D.	710
Koyukuk	Yukon River	470
Kuskokwim	Kuskokwim River	724
Liard	Mackenzie River	693
Little Missouri	Missouri River	560
Mississippi	Mouth of Southwest Pass	2,348
Mississippi, Upper	Mouth of Missouri River	1,171
Missouri	Mississippi River	2,315
Missouri-Red Rock	Mississippi River	2,540
Mobile-Alabama-Coosa	Mobile Bay	774
Neosho	Arkansas River, Ok.	460
Niobrara	Missouri River, Ne.	431
North Canadian	Canadian River, Ok.	800
North Platte	Platte River, Ne.	618
Ohio	Mississippi River, Il.-Ky.	1,310
Ohio-Allegheny	Mississippi River	1,306
Osage	Missouri River, Mo.	500
Ouachita	Red River, La.	605
Pearl	Gulf of Mexico, Ms.-La.	411
Pecos	Rio Grande, Tx.	926
Pee Dee-Yadkin	Winyah Bay, S.C.	435
Pend Oreille	Columbia River	490
Porcupine	Yukon River, Ak.	569
Red(Okla.-Tex.-La.)	Mississippi River	1,290
Republican	Kansas River, Ka.	445
Rio Grande	Gulf of Mexico	1,760
St. Francis	Mississippi River, Ar.	425
Salmon	Snake River, Id.	420
Smoky Hill	Kansas River, Ka.	540
Snake	Columbia River, Wa.	1,038
South Platte	Platte River, Ne.	424
Susquehanna	Chesapeake Bay, Md.	444
Tanana	Yukon River, Ak.	659
Tennessee	Ohio River, Ky.	652
Wabash	Ohio River, Il.-In.	529